THE REVOLT OF
OWAIN
GLYN DŴR

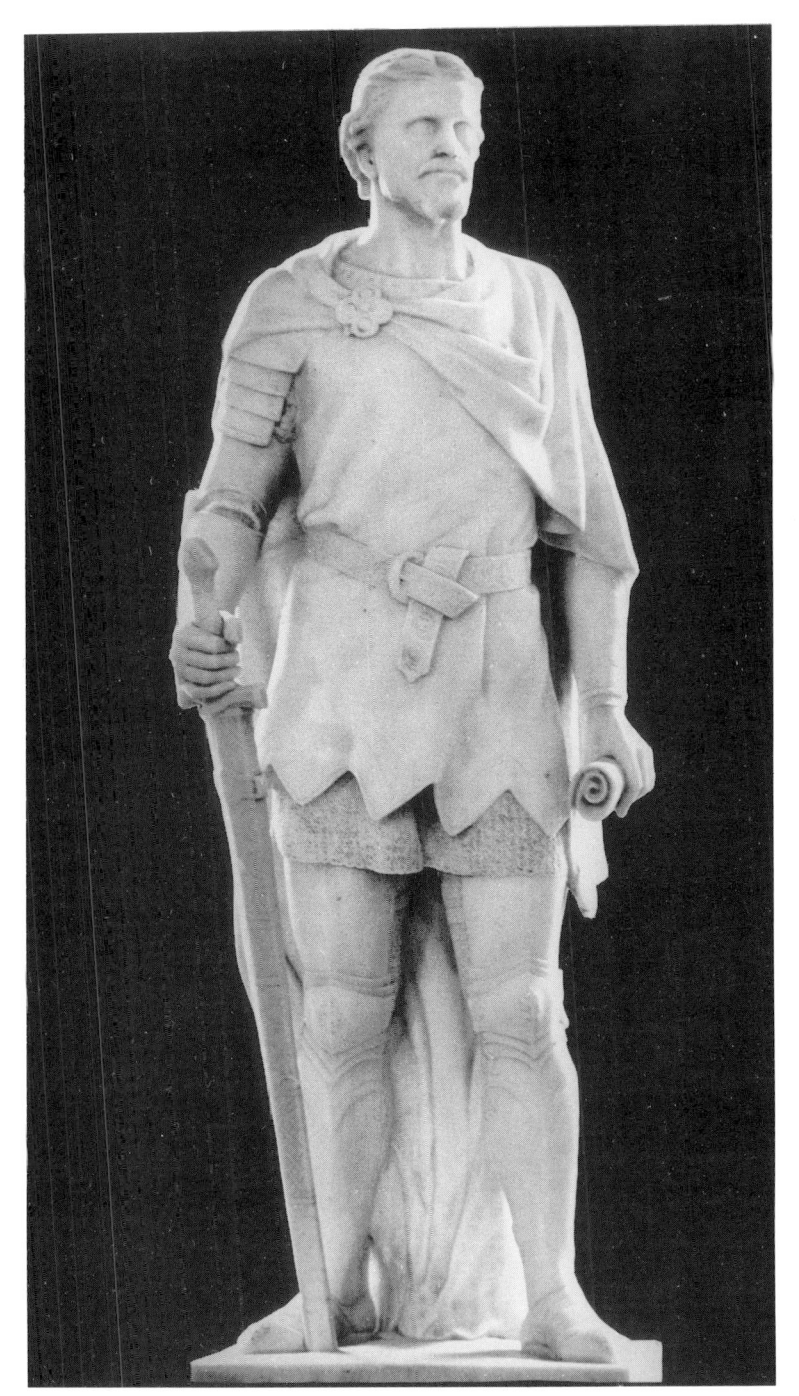

The statue of Owain Glyn Dŵr at Cardiff City Hall unveiled by David Lloyd George, 27 October 1916. The citations on the occasion referred to Glyn Dŵr as 'the soldier-statesman . . . who fought with splendid courage for the independence of Wales and the advancement of the people'.

THE REVOLT OF
OWAIN
GLYN DŴR

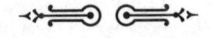

R. R. Davies

Oxford · New York

OXFORD UNIVERSITY PRESS

1995

Oxford University Press, Walton Street, Oxford OX2 6DP

Oxford New York
Athens Auckland Bangkok Bombay
Calcutta Cape Town Dar es Salaam Delhi
Florence Hong Kong Istanbul Karachi
Kuala Lumpur Madras Madrid Melbourne
Mexico City Nairobi Paris Singapore
Taipei Tokyo Toronto
and associated companies in
Berlin Ibadan

Oxford is a trade mark of Oxford University Press

Published in the United States
by Oxford University Press Inc., New York

British Library Cataloguing in Publication Data
Data available

Library of Congress Cataloging in Publication Data
Davies, R. R.
The revolt of Owain Glyn Dŵr / R. R. Davies.
p. cm.
Includes bibliographical references (p.   ).
1. Glendower Owen, 1359?–1416?   2. Revolutionaries—Wales—Biography.
3. Nationalism—Wales—History
4. Princes—Wales—Biography.   5. Wales—History—1284–1536.   I. Title.
DA716.G5D5   1995
942.904'.092—dc20   95–10826
ISBN 0–19–820508–2

1 3 5 7 9 10 8 6 4 2

Typeset by Pure Tech India Ltd., Pondicherry
Printed in Great Britain
on acid-free paper by
Bookcraft Ltd., Midsomer-Norton, Avon

PREFACE

On 27 October 1916 David Lloyd George, then Secretary of State for War but within a few weeks to be Prime Minister, unveiled eleven statues of distinguished figures from the Welsh past which had been commissioned to be placed in the City Hall at Cardiff, itself a building opened ten years earlier. One of his Welshmen—for with the anomalous exception of Boudicca they were all men—now immortalized in the finest statuary marble in the headquarters of the putative capital of twentieth-century Wales was Owain Glyn Dŵr. His statue was the work of Alfred Turner, who had already designed statues of Queen Victoria at Sheffield, North Shields, and Delhi and of King Edward VII at Lyallpur, India. It was a nice irony that the chisel which once had etched three statues of the Empress of India should now do similar service for that 'most profligate rebel', as Owain Glyn Dŵr was called in the sixteenth century. But the commemorative unveiling of October 1916 had a further significance: it brought together the two most famous Welshmen, arguably, in the history of Wales—Owain Glyn Dŵr and David Lloyd George. Both have suffered from a surfeit of books about them; so the appearance of yet another—albeit an account of the revolt of Glyn Dŵr rather than a biography of the man—calls for some justification.

Personal piety is one reason. I was brought up in Glyn Dŵr country. My home lay only a few miles from Glyndyfrdwy, the village from which he took his cognomen; my father in his youth walked over the Berwyn mountains to Llansilin, much as Glyn Dŵr and his entourage centuries earlier traversed the same mountains as they travelled from Glyndyfrdwy to his other manor of Sycharth, likewise in the parish of Llansilin; my mother told me tales of caves and tunnels associated with Glyn Dŵr in our locality and was impatient with my scepticism about their authenticity. This book may not, in Thomas Carlyle's words, have 'come out hot from my own soul'; but it would be idle to deny that local affection, for the neighbourhood and its people, have in part prompted me to write it. Indeed, unfashionable as are such sentiments in the austere world of academic historiography, I proudly affirm that this is so.

But I had my academic reasons for writing this book also. First, I was anxious to place Owain Glyn Dŵr and his revolt firmly in the context of contemporary society in Wales and indeed beyond, for it is this context alone which makes his revolt and the remarkable degree of support it enjoyed comprehensible. Secondly, I wanted to bring the detailed scholarly work of historians who have written about Owain and his revolt since the appearance of J. E. Lloyd's classic

biography, *Owen Glendower* (1931), to the attention of a wider public. Most of that work—especially a very impressive array of articles by Tony Carr, Ralph Griffiths, Rhidian Griffiths, Beverley Smith, and Llinos Smith—is tucked away in scholarly journals; I hope a general book about the revolt will give it the wider recognition it deserves. Thirdly, I have scoured the archives for every fragment of information to try to re-create as best as I could the world of Owain Glyn Dŵr and of his revolt. Like J. E. Lloyd himself, I readily concede that 'there are no startling departures from the traditional portrait' of Glyn Dŵr in the book; but I fondly hope that I may have added a little in texture and historical depth to our understanding of the last great revolt of the Welsh people.

While this is, I hope, a respectably scholarly book, I have tried to write it in a way which will also make it approachable to the general reader. That has entailed some departures from the conventions and conveniences of the academic monograph. In particular the references to sources for statements in the text have been consolidated into a single note at the end of each paragraph, and the end-notes have in turn been exiled to the back of the book. The references have been kept deliberately brief and assume that those who consult them will also use the Bibliography.

This book has been written in fits and starts among other academic and scholarly preoccupations. That I have been able to complete it at all owes a great deal to the generosity of three institutions: the President and Fellows of Magdalen College Oxford, who elected me to be a Visiting Fellow in Hilary and Trinity terms 1992 and allowed me thereby to recharge my sadly depleted academic batteries; the Leverhulme Foundation, which once again financed my extended visits to the archives in London; and the Wolfson Foundation, which provided the where-withal for the British Academy to appoint me to a Research Professorship from April 1993. In rather grim days for humanities in British universities, I count myself singularly fortunate to have received such munificent support.

I have received support from other directions also. Gill Parry spent her evenings converting my untidy manuscript into beautiful pages of typescript. David Robinson and his colleagues at CADW: Welsh Historic Monuments; Mark Redknap and his colleagues at the National Museum of Wales; and Jack Spurgeon and Chris Musson at the Royal Commission on Ancient Monuments in Wales were kindness itself in helping with illustrations. Tony Morris, Anna Illingworth, and their colleagues at OUP were, as usual, helpful and encouraging. My wife and children made no direct contribution to this book, though Prys Davies gave invaluable help with the index; but they have put up with me, and Owain Glyn Dŵr, over many years; at least they won't have to put up with Owain any more. *Diolch calon, eto.*

R. R. DAVIES

August 1994

CONTENTS

LIST OF PLATES

The statue of Owain Glyn Dŵr at Cardiff City Hall   *Frontispiece*

(between pp. 180 and 181)

Acknowledgements and thanks for permission to reproduce the photographs are due and gratefully given to the following: the British Library for plates 1 (BL Royal Ms.14 E 4 fo.1. 23), 5 (BL Harley 1319 fo.14v), 6 (BL Harley 1319 fo.37v), and 7 (BL Cotton Julius E. IV. art (6) fo.3v); Cadw, Welsh Historic Monuments, for plates 3, 8, 9, and for Map 6b; Clwyd-Powys Archaeological Trust for plate 10; the National Museum of Wales for plates 2 and 4; and Cardiff City Council for frontispiece.

MAPS

FIGURES

GENEALOGICAL TABLES

ABBREVIATIONS

ANLP	*Anglo-Norman Letters and Petitions from All Souls Ms. 182*, ed. M. D. Legge (Anglo-Norman Text Society, 1941)
Annales H. IV	*Annales Ricardi Secundi et Henrici Quarti*, ed. H. T. Riley (Rolls Series, 1866)
Arch. Camb.	*Archaeologia Cambrensis*
BBCS	*Bulletin of the Board of Celtic Studies*
BL	British Library, London
Cal. Anc. Corr.	*Calendar of Ancient Correspondence concerning Wales*, ed. J. G. Edwards (Cardiff, 1935)
Cal. Anc. Pets.	*Calendar of Ancient Petitions Relating to Wales*, ed. W. Rees (Cardiff, 1975)
CCR	*Calendar of Close Rolls* (1892–)
CCh.R	*Calendar of Charter Rolls* (1903–)
CFR	*Calendar of Fine Rolls* (1891–)
CIPM	*Calendar of Inquisitions Post Mortem* (1904–)
CPL	*Calendar of Papal Registers, Letters* (1894–)
CPR	*Calendar of Patent Rolls* (1891–)
CSL	*Calendar of Signet Letters of Henry IV and Henry V* (1978)
Cat. Mss. Wales in BM	*A Catalogue of the Manuscripts relating to Wales in the British Museum*, ed. E. Owen, 4 vols., Cymmrodorion Record Series, no. 4 (1900–22)
DKR	*Annual Report of the Deputy Keeper of the Public Records*, esp. *Thirty Sixth Report* (1875) Appendix II: 'Recognizance Rolls of the Palatinate of Chester'
DNB	*Dictionary of National Biography* (1885–1900)
Ellis, *Letters*	*Original Letters illustrative of English History*, ed. H. Ellis, 2nd series, vol. i (1827)
Emden, *Biog. Reg.*	A. B. Emden, *A Biographical Register of the University of Oxford to 1500*, 3 vols. (1955–9).
F.	French
GDG	*Gwaith Dafydd ap Gwilym*, ed. T. Parry, 2nd edn. (Cardiff, 1963)
GEC	*The Complete Peerage of England, Scotland, Ireland, Great Britain and the United Kingdom*, ed. G. E. C.[okayne], new edn., ed. V. Gibbs (1910–59)

GIG   *Gwaith Iolo Goch*, ed. D. R. Johnston (Cardiff, 1988)

Giles's Chronicle *Incerti Scriptoris Chronicon Anglie*, ed. J. A. Giles (1848)

Glam. CH   *Glamorgan County History*, III, *The Middle Ages*, ed. T. B. Pugh (Cardiff, 1971)

Griffiths, *Principality* R. A. Griffiths, *The Principality of Wales in the Later Middle Ages. The Structure and Personnel of Government. I, South Wales 1277–1536* (Cardiff, 1972)

Historia R. II *Historia Vitae et Regni Ricardi Secundi*, ed. G. B. Stow jnr. (Pennsylvania, 1977)

IGE   *Cywyddau Iolo Goch ac Eraill*, ed. H. Lewis, T. Roberts, and I. Williams, 2nd edn. (Cardiff, 1937)

L.   Latin

Matthews, *Records* *Welsh Records in Paris*, ed. T. Matthews (Carmarthen, 1910)

NLW   National Library of Wales, Aberystwyth

NLWJ   *National Library of Wales Journal*

OG   J. E. Lloyd, *Owen Glendower/Owen Glyn Dŵr* (Oxford, 1931)

PPC   *Proceedings and Ordinances of the Privy Council*, ed. N. H. Nicolas, 7 vols. (1834–7)

RLH IV   *Royal and Historical Letters during the Reign of Henry IV*, ed. F. C. Hingeston, 2 vols. (Rolls Series, 1860–1965)

RO   Record Office

Rot. Parl.   *Rotuli Parliamentorum*, 7 vols. (Record Commission, 1783–1832)

TCS   *Transactions of the Honourable Society of Cymmrodorion*

UCNW   University College of North Wales

Usk, *Chronicle* Adam of Usk, *Chronicon*, ed. E. Maunde Thompson, 2nd edn. (1904)

W.   Welsh

WHR   *Welsh History Review*

NOTE ON WELSH PLACE-NAMES AND ASSOCIATED MATTERS

The spelling of Welsh place-names in this volume generally follows the forms suggested in *A Gazetteer of Welsh Place-Names*, ed. Elwyn Davies (Cardiff, 1957), or Melville Richards, *Welsh Administrative and Territorial Units* (Cardiff, 1969). In a book written in English I have naturally used English forms where these are in common use, for example Brecon, Cardiff, Carmarthen, River Dee, and so on. Where the name of a town or castle derives from an older Welsh district name I have used the Anglicized form for the former while reserving the Welsh form for the latter, for example the town or castle of Kidwelly (which figure prominently in the book) in the commote or lordship of Cydweli. North and South Wales (with capital N and S respectively) refer to the post-1284 northern (that is, Anglesey, Caernarfonshire and Merionethshire) and southern (that is, Cardiganshire and Carmarthenshire) restricted Principality of Wales of the years 1284–1536; north and south Wales (without capitals) are simple geographical descriptions.

Translations from medieval Welsh, Latin, and French are my own, unless otherwise indicated. Quotations from sources written in English have normally been modernized in the text.

On Thursday 16 September 1400 a motley group of Welshmen from north-east Wales assembled at Glyndyfrdwy, a small vill located in the valley of the River Dee between Corwen and Llangollen, just within the borders of the county of Merionethshire. Their venue was well chosen for their purpose. The lord of Glyndyfrdwy, and the focus of the assembly, was Owain ap Gruffudd, better known to his contemporaries and posterity as Owain Glyn Dŵr, Owain of Glyndyfrdwy. The venue and the man were, therefore, matched. But there was a further significance to the choice of location for the meeting. Glyndyfrdwy, and the nearby districts of Edeirnion and Dinmael, lay beyond the normal ambit of any English lord or official. They were an enclave of native Welsh rule which, through sufferance or oversight, had not been enveloped into the English governmental and judicial framework which had been so firmly wrapped around most of north Wales after Edward I's conquest of the area between 1277 and 1283. They were an area where time, as it were, had stood still, an anomalous memorial of an earlier age. Where better to foster memories of former glories? Where better to plot a revolt?[1]

Wales has never been short of dreamers, but dreamers and plotters are unlikely to get far without support. Owain Glyn Dŵr's supporters on that momentous day in September 1400 were a collection of his kinsmen, in-laws, neighbours, and friends. Among them were his son and his brother, two of his wife's brothers, and his sister's husband; they were abetted by some of his companions among the Welsh squires of the north-east, notably from the lordships of Chirkland and Bromfield and Yale and from Ellesmere in Shropshire; the dean of St Asaph, an elderly gentleman of good stock, was there to give ecclesiastical respectability to the occasion; so also was Owain's personal soothsayer, who fifteen years earlier had accompanied him on the royal campaign to Scotland. They were a companionable group of men who had known each other for the better part of a generation or more, the sort of gathering one might expect at a Welsh wedding feast (W. *neithior*) or a wake. But their purpose was much more serious, ridiculously so: they proclaimed Owain prince of Wales. Two days later, having assembled a gang of a few hundred men from among their tenants and neighbours, they set out to attack Ruthin and other English towns in north-east Wales. So began the revolt of Owain Glyn Dŵr.[2]

Some ten miles or so from Glyndyfrdwy lay the small market town of Bala close to where the River Dee flows out of Llyn Tegid or Bala Lake. There, on

Saturday 10 March 1414, the earl of Arundel, Sir Edward Charlton, and David Holbache held a judicial session in the name of Henry V. Six hundred men kneeled on the ground before them and took a corporal oath on Holy Scripture that they and their heirs would henceforth be loyal lieges of the king of England and would never again rise in rebellion. They conceded that they merited death for their rebellion; it was little wonder, therefore, that (according to the record) they gave praise to God on bended knee for giving them such a merciful king. In return for this graphic act of public contrition, they were duly pardoned; and on payment of a collective fine of £100 they were allowed to recover their lands (which were technically forfeit) and to continue to hold them by Welsh law. Similar ceremonies of public submission, accompanied by formal pardons and communal fines, were staged in different parts of Wales in 1414. But the one at Bala was particularly welcome and significant: Bala was not far from the spot where the flame of revolt was first kindled, and the county of Merioneth proved to be one of the last refuges of the rebels. The embers of revolt were indeed not formally extinguished in 1414; it was not to be until April 1421 that Owain Glyn Dŵr's son finally received a pardon for all his offences. But the revolt which had erupted so suddenly to life in September 1400 was dead as a general movement by March 1414; indeed in most parts of Wales it had been dead for several years. It is this revolt which is the subject of this book.[3]

The revolt struck Wales like a bolt from the blue in September 1400; indeed some Englishmen came to wonder whether the king was not taking it altogether too seriously. Might it not be just a flash in the pan, a bout of post-harvest madness, yet another example of the light-headedness (*L. levitas cervicosa*) and impetuosity for which the Welsh were notorious in the Middle Ages? Yet a movement which spread, albeit briefly, through much of north Wales within weeks and which was followed a few months later by the equally sudden and even more spectacular capture of Conway Castle was clearly rather more than the personal aberration of a disaffected Welsh squire and his close companions; it quickly tapped an undercurrent of frustration, resentment, and aspiration in Welsh society. It soon became a truly national revolt. To try to understand the revolt, therefore, requires us to portray the society in which Owain Glyn Dŵr grew to manhood and with whose support alone his private vision might be converted into a national movement.[4]

PART I

⊷⊙⊶

Portrait of a Society
Wales in the 1390s

1

THE COUNTRY
A TALE OF TWO TRAVELLERS

W ales in Owain Glyn Dŵr's day was, to most outsiders, a largely unknown, inaccessible, and uninviting country. The character of its terrain—notably its 'horrid and frightful' mountains, rocks, and precipices—was one of the major reasons for its reputation, and remained so for centuries. Roads were poor and inadequate. At the very borders of Wales—whether in the forests of Ewloe in the north-east, the steep-sided valley of the Wye north of Chepstow in the south-east, or the daunting tracts of moorland and mountain that fell on the traveller's eye at Leominster or Shrewsbury—the prospect for the traveller seemed to be grim indeed. But the greatest deterrent of all to the traveller was the image which had been created in his mind of the Welsh themselves—hardy and brave certainly, even generous, hospitable, and devout; but also totally unreliable, 'wild', back-ward, and, in the words of a contemporary English abbot, 'fierce and fickle'. The England that he left behind was, by modern-day standards, hardly a haven of peace; but it did provide him with the institutional framework of legal process and redress. This was, or seemed to be, patently lacking in Wales: the king's writ could not be served in most parts of the country; nor did royal justices or English sheriffs have any authority there; there was no legal process available for the recovery of goods stolen from English merchants travelling through the country; and the Welsh seemed to take a delight in capturing and ransoming travellers, whether to recover debts owed to them by others or for the sheer devilry and profit of it. Anyone visiting the border towns of Shrewsbury, Hereford, and Gloucester in the 1380s would have been told horrifying stories of what had happened to merchants in Wales and how the Welsh were infiltrating these border towns. It would need considerable determination—and quite possibly a small military escort and a guide—to enter such a country.[1]

Yet travel into Wales men did; indeed it was imperative for them to do so if their images of the country and its inhabitants were to be matched against the test of reality. They came as merchants, by land and sea, from the English border towns from Chester in the north to Bristol in the south; they came regularly as

royal and seigncrial officials to audit accounts, review the state of castles, super-
vise local bailiffs, and to escort heavily laden treasure carts of money back to
England; they came as craftsmen and labourers hired to repair and redesign
castles and churches; they came in the household of English magnates conducting a very occasional progress through their Welsh estates (as did the earl of
March in 1393 and the duke of Hereford in 1397); they came on pilgrimage to the
shrine of St David; and they came in armies *en route* across south Wales to
Haverford and Milford prior to sailing to Ireland, as did Richard II in September
1394 and May 1399. None of these men—and their overall total was not inconsiderable—kept an account of his journey and of his observations of the country
and its people which we can set beside those of Gerald of Wales two centuries
earlier or of John Leland and other travellers and topographers in the sixteenth and seventeenth centuries. But they did occasionally leave a detailed account of their expenses, which at least allows us to reconstruct the main
stages of their travels. Armed with such accounts we can reconstruct a rapid
tour of Wales which an English visitor, most probably a royal or seignorial
official, might have undertaken in the mid-1390s, in the age of Owain Glyn Dŵr
(Map 1).

Journeys into Wales from England often began at the border town of
Oswestry. It was a small but bustling market town, enclosed by walls and entered
through one of its four gates. Formerly a frontier outpost dominated by its castle,
it now wore a much less military aspect. Its life-blood was its trade, especially in
cloth and cattle. It was already, as it was to remain for centuries to come, the focal
point not only for the rich lowland districts to the east but also for the produce of
the uplands of the west, of the valleys and foothills of the rivers Dee, Tanat, and
Ceiriog. It was proudly proclaimed by the poets to be 'the London of Wales'. Any
visitor to Oswestry in the 1390s would already be struck by the fact that many of
its burgesses bore Welsh names, and that Welsh jostled with English as the
language of trade and business. He would also certainly have been told that the
greatest power in the land was none other than Richard Fitzalan, earl of Arundel,
whose vast block of border estates extended from the gates of Chester to the
uplands of Clun. The earl rarely came to Oswestry; but resident or not, he was
directly involved in the economic well-being of the area, having a large flock of
sheep and a stud of fine horses there. Had our traveller enquired, in the fashion
of later topographic authors, as to the gentry houses in the district, his attention
would doubtless have been drawn to the newly refurbished moated house at
Sycharth, owned by one Owain Glyn Dŵr and standing some seven miles east of
Oswestry.[2]

From Oswestry the preferred route lay northwards past Chirk, another formidable Arundel castle but one whose glass windows (now becoming a familiar

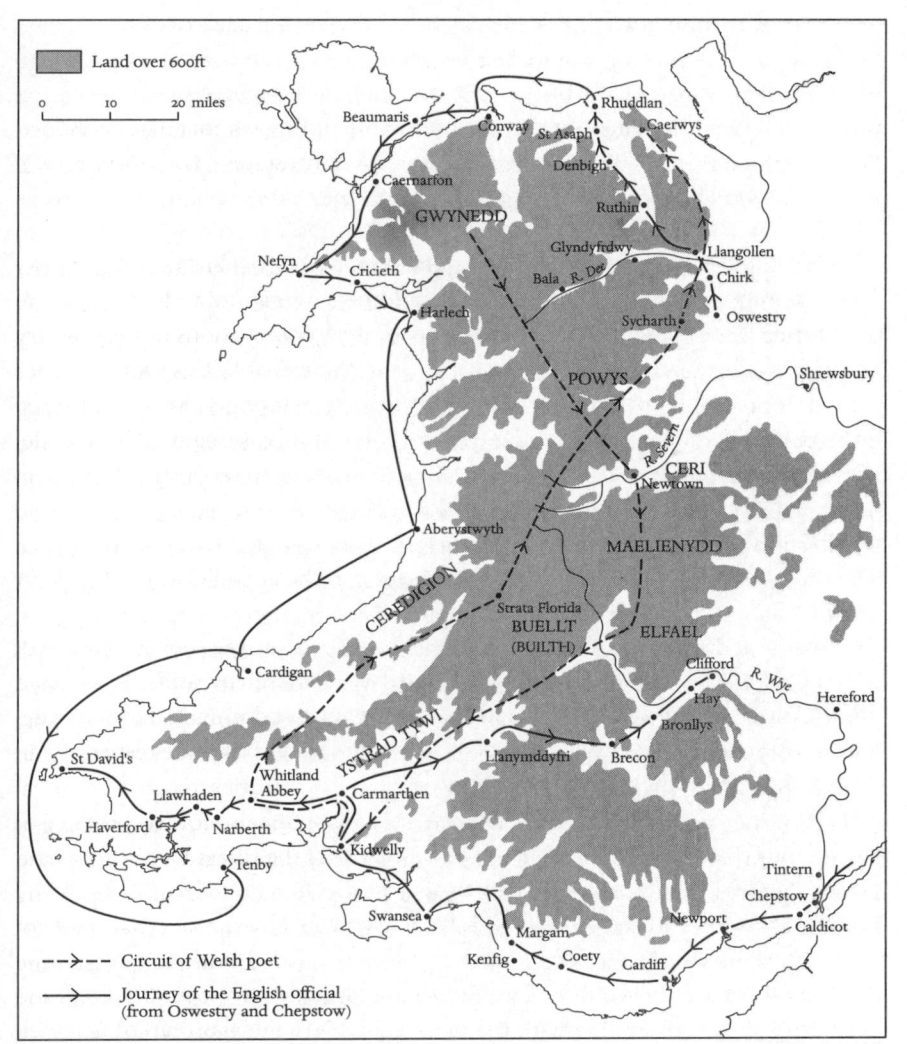

MAP I. The Wales of the two travellers

feature of Welsh castles) betokened that its military role was now secondary to
its functions as an occasional residence (especially for hunting in its fine park)
and, more regularly, as the administrative and judicial centre of the lordship of
Chirkland. At Chirk one was well aware that one was leaving the plains to one's
rear and entering a very different country in terrain, language, and people. A
common stopping-place was Llangollen, so beloved of later generations of
'refined lovers of picturesque scenes, the sentimental and the romantic'. The
opinion of our traveller would have been uncomfortably different. Llangollen's

importance to him was that it provided—as it had for generations—a stone
bridge across the rushing waters and treacherous rocks of the Dee. The bridge
had been refurbished by the bishop of St Asaph in the mid-fourteenth century; it
was to be known by later generations as one of the Three Beauties of Wales.
What daunted the traveller was that directly above Llangollen lay those 'horrid'
mountains which he could no longer avoid if he wanted to penetrate into north
Wales.[3]

Before undertaking that adventure, and possibly in order to find a bed for the
night, he might be directed to the nearby Cistercian abbey of Valle Crucis, just
over a mile from Llangollen. It was a consoling sight compared to the mountains
all around—its majestic west front with its beautiful rose window and delicately
carved doorway, its eastern end overlooking a charming fish-pond, and work
quite possibly still in progress on some of its claustral buildings and its striking
rib-vaulted chapter-house. Valle Crucis, like so many monasteries, had unfortunately fallen on evil days and was burdened with debts; but among its glories was
a collection of funerary monuments such as were unequalled in north Wales.
The most striking of them lay directly in front of the high altar of the church. A
heraldic slab, it commemorated the burial place of Madog ap Gruffudd Fychan,
the great-grandson of the founder of the abbey and a member of the native Welsh
dynasty of Powys (plate 3). Madog's direct descendant, it might have been
pointed out, was a man called Owain ap Gruffudd, alias Owain Glyn Dŵr, who
had a very fine lodge some three or so miles up the nearby River Dee at
Glyndyfrdwy.[4]

The journey from Llangollen northwards lay across glowering mountains and
barren moorland, skirting Valle Crucis's grange at Hafod yr Abbad. It was with
great relief that the traveller after such an arduous journey saw opening before
him the altogether friendlier and fertile Vale of Clwyd; he might have shared the
rhapsodical view of Daniel Defoe, writing some 300 years later on approaching
the Vale from a different direction, of 'a most pleasant, fruitful, populous and
delicious vale . . . all smiling with the same kind of complexion; which made us
think ourselves in England again all on a sudden'. He and his escort would make
straight for Ruthin or, if the going had been good, might even consider reaching
Denbigh by nightfall. Ruthin and Denbigh were similar in many respects: both
were sited on hillocks rising out of the plain of the River Clwyd, though the rock
on which Denbigh was sited was much the more impressive; both were the seats
of castles founded in their present form after the Edwardian Conquest, that at
Denbigh being especially magnificent; at both places privileged boroughs with
their own charters and extensive commercial monopolies had developed, that at
Denbigh originally within the walls, though quickly overspilling them; at both
there were religious institutions—a collegiate church of St Peter served by seven

priests at Ruthin, a Carmelite friary at Denbigh; in both towns and in the immediate rural hinterland there had been deliberate and directed plantation of English settlers. Ruthin was the centre of the lordship of Dyffryn Clwyd. Its lord in the 1390s was Reginald Grey, who not infrequently visited the lordship (it was much the most substantial part of his inheritance) and issued ordinances in person in full court there. It would not have needed a particularly sharp ear to pick up gossip about some of his high-handed decrees or stories of how his father had been on such bad terms with some of the Welshmen of the area in the 1380s that he had taken the very unusual step of petitioning parliament about their 'malice'.[5]

Impressions would have been rather different in Denbigh. There the dashing young Mortimer earl had, at long last, been allowed to take possession of his lordship in 1393. Much was expected of him. He might be able to open doors of service, adventure, military exploits, and reward largely closed since his father's premature death in 1381. And he was, after all, a man who had the blood of the native Welsh dynasty of Gwynedd in his veins, albeit in proportions altogether much thinner than his Welsh flatterers—including one of his tenants in Denbigh and the leading Welsh poet of his day, Iolo Goch—cared to admit. There was certainly a sense of bustling activity at Denbigh in the 1390s and a sense of being caught up in large enterprises: officials and servants from other Mortimer estates—Usk, Ludlow, Wigmore, Montgomery—passed through with messages and supplies *en route* to the earl in Ireland; important functionaries, such as the treasurer of the earl's household, Thomas Walwayn, or one of his most trusted stewards, Philip ap Morgan, called by; troops were being collected for service in Ireland; prospectors were sent to look for lead in the lordship; and the castle was being prepared to receive the earl on his return from Ireland. Denbigh had not been as lively for many a long year.[6]

From Denbigh, road and river led naturally to St Asaph. To anyone used to the splendour and opulence of English cathedrals, it must have come as a shock to see what passed for a diocesan church at St Asaph. Its bishop had just pleaded to hold his former rectory of Meifod *in commendam* (that is, jointly with another ecclesiastical living) because of the desperate state of his diocese's income; he had also initiated a major programme of repairs on the cathedral. The new and enterprising bishop, consecrated on 17 April 1395, was unique in the Welsh Church of his day: he was a Welshman. John Trefor had been nominated to the see unsuccessfully in 1389; but, after a period in papal service, his second nomination was successful. It was an event which must have brought great comfort to his countrymen and kinsmen: too long had the attempt to secure a Welshman as bishop been thwarted; too often had Welsh sees been held by absentee royal nominees. Once more the bishop's household was in his see: the poet was

extravagant in his praise for its splendour—its exotic foods, its rich hangings, and—not least for an invalid—the comfort of its feather bed. With a new lord of Welsh descent at Denbigh and a Welsh bishop at last at St Asaph, things were looking better. Whether that would be the view at Rhuddlan was a different matter. There, just inside the county of Flint, the great castle, still in a fine state of repair, was a reminder that this was a once-conquered country. In these very years of 1395–7 a vast sum was being spent on the bridge that crossed the Clwyd at Rhuddlan. It was to the quay just below the castle that ships carrying wool from north Wales plied, and the wool was weighed at the staple there; from there the traveller took a boat heading for Caernarfon, rather than face the hazardous journey by land—across the estuary of the River Conwy and around the treacherous promontory at Penmaenmawr.[7]

The boat from Rhuddlan is likely to have called on its voyage at both Conway and Beaumaris. There had been hardly any work on either castle since the 1330s (at the obviously uncompleted Beaumaris) or the 1340s (at Conway). There was, inevitably, some dilapidation; but they were still magnificently imposing fortresses. As the boat passed Beaumaris stories of foreign, probably Scottish, ships seen in the neighbourhood would be related; more recent was the news that thirteen Lollards had been imprisoned there in 1396. Leaving Beaumaris, the boat would pass near Bangor before heading down the Menai Straits for Caernarfon.[8] Even to the weary and the well travelled, the castle at Caernarfon must have been breathtakingly majestic—with its assemblage of polygonal towers, its unique banding of differently coloured stones, the unparalleled magnificence of its Eagle Tower, the staggering massiveness of the King's Gate with its statue of Edward II in a niche above the portal. In the 1390s major repairs were in progress, especially on the Eagle Tower; ships were anchored at the quay carrying stones from Cheshire and timber from the forests of Delamere and Shotwick for the purpose; and a master mason travelled several times from Chester to keep an eye on the work. Remote Caernarfon might be, but its inhabitants could at least look forward to the prospect of some good wine, such as the white Spanish wine which arrived there in a Bristol ship in May 1392. Caernarfon was also a governmental centre: the justiciar and chamberlain of north Wales had their quarters in the town; officials from all parts of the northern Principality reported there to hand over their revenues and submit their accounts; in the treasury were kept the key documents of government, including a newly made transcript of the great survey of Caernarfonshire and Anglesey of 1352. Men still recalled the daring escapade in which thieves—using counterfeit keys, so it was thought—broke into the king's exchequer in the town in August 1392 and stole a bag containing £14 13s. 4d. Had our traveller arrived at the castle in March 1395 he would have witnessed a very large assembly of Welshmen from the surrounding countryside

reluctantly granting a large subsidy of over £400, through their proctors, to the king in the presence of Hugh Huls, the justiciar of North Wales. He might have noted the mutters of dissent, accompanied by caustic comments that it was less than a year since the country had been asked to raise a contingent of troops to accompany the king to Ireland. He might have even overheard the names of the three war-hardened Anglesey brothers who had captained these men—Rhys, Gwilym, and Maredudd ap Tudur. They were names to remember.

It was difficult to escape a sense of tension in Caernarfon. The tiny town was encompassed by strong walls; its burgesses bore English names and took pride in them; they complained bitterly at the way the Welsh inhabitants of the hinterland were ignoring the town's commercial privileges. There was none of the relaxed atmosphere here that there had been at Oswestry; indeed, paradoxically there was probably more English spoken at Caernarfon than at Oswestry. And then there was the lonely figure of Roger Sparrow keeping a nightly watch on the town walls 'because of certain rumours of the king's enemies' (L. *ob certos rumores de inimicis dicti Regis*), and the five English burgesses who were posted at the gates of the town. It was difficult not to feel on edge there, even though men of an older generation might recall that nothing had ever come of the recurrent 'rumours', and that the Welsh, though they were certainly fickle, had accepted their lot.[9]

Caernarfon was the end of the road for most travellers to north Wales. Apart from adventurous merchants from Bristol carrying casks of wine to the tiny boroughs of north Wales, or traders from Chester, Flint, and Beaumaris who had local connections in the area and saw a chance to make a penny on exporting the coarse wool of the district, or the small teams of craftsmen sent from time to time to undertake some emergency repair work on the North Wales castles, visitors to Caernarfon were largely confined to messengers, auditors, or officials on an unwelcome leg of their tour of duty. To travel further west or south than Caernarfon was to show considerable courage bordering on folly. Here lay what even Gerald had no hesitation in calling 'the wildest and most terrifying region in all Wales' (and he was bolstered by the ecclesiastical security of his mission). Should anyone be tempted to go by horseback he would probably be well advised to follow the general steps of Gerald's itinerary—south-westwards from Caernarfon towards Nefyn (anything was preferable to the mountain passes of Snowdonia), across the neck of the Llŷn peninsula to the picturesque castle of Cricieth, memorably if extravagantly memorialized a few years earlier in a poem to its Welsh constable, Sir Hywel y Fwyall (Sir Hywel of the Axe), one of the heroes of the Anglo-French wars; and hence painfully and slowly southwards across the three great tidal estuaries of north-west Wales—Traeth Mawr and Traeth Bach, Mawddach, and Dyfi—before heading eventually to the relative safety of the

castellated borough of Aberystwyth. Had our traveller indeed undertaken that hazardous journey he could doubtless have felt, like Gerald and Archbishop Baldwin two centuries earlier, that a pilgrimage to Jerusalem now held few terrors for him. If he were not in training for such an enterprise, discretion might well have persuaded him to take one of the Bristol boats that called at Caernarfon and sail in it as it hugged the Welsh coastline, calling in at the majestic but desperately isolated castle of Harlech, stopping again possibly at similar outposts at Aberystwyth and Cardigan, but feeling no sense of relief until he reached the bustle and comforts of the port of Tenby, where the companionship of other Bristol merchants, the sight of ships unloading wine from Bordeaux and other goods from France, and the welcoming accents of the English language made him feel more at home. The great majority of travellers would even have willingly forgone the prospect of such a sea journey and packed their bags to return to Oswestry or even to Chester. If one really wished to see south Wales, Caernarfon was not the natural point of departure for one's journey.[10]

Gloucester or Hereford would be a more obvious choice. The journey through south Wales was altogether a far less daunting experience than that in the north. Roads and routes were generally very well known; the landscape was friendly and obvious resting-places frequent, be it as castles, abbeys, or towns; English was a familiar, if not necessarily the primary, language of many of the people in the coastal lowlands; provisions and goods were generally of good quality and not very different from those one might find in most of southern England; and there were other travellers a-plenty on the roads—workmen, merchants, soldiers, ecclesiastics, pilgrims, and agents of lords. So one could set out briskly and confidently. The journey might begin at Bristol; if so, the quickest route would be to take the ferry from Aust to Beechley and thence to make quickly for Chepstow. Alternatively one might start from Gloucester, riding easily and comfortably along the widening Severn estuary through villages such as Minsterworth (famous for its salmon) and Newnham until Chepstow was reached. One could not avoid Chepstow, for it was the only feasible crossing-point on the lower Wye south of Monmouth. Attractive as it might have been to call in at the Cistercian abbey of Tintern—to see its magnificent church and to be wined, dined, and accommodated at the recently constructed lodgings of its abbot—that would have required a journey up-river through the narrow, wooded gorge of the Wye. Chepstow itself was a busy little town, with quite a few ships deliberately choosing to unload their cargoes at its quay in order to avoid paying customs at Bristol. The town was overawed by its huge castle, the oldest in Wales. Its living quarters had been greatly and grandly improved by the last of its Bigod earls in the early fourteenth century; but there was now a cavernous silence about the massive pile. Chepstow had been ruled since 1372 by

Margaret Marshall, countess (and soon to be titled in her own right duchess) of Norfolk. Having outlived two husbands and her son-in-law, and now herself well in her seventies, she ruled Chepstow in her absence.[11]

In those circumstances, there might be little comfort at the castle; it might be well to break one's journey elsewhere. Five miles away, and much more comfortable, was Caldicot Castle. An old Bohun estate, it had passed into the hands of the king's uncle, Thomas of Woodstock, now duke of Gloucester, in 1380. During the next few years he spent lavishly on reshaping and refurbishing it, building a new tower, constructing crests, battlements, and a new stone bridge, and installing a chamber for himself appropriately called 'the Dressinghouse'. This was truly a labour of love: Duke Thomas had had stone blocks with his own name and that of Eleanor, his wife and daughter of the last Bohun earl of Hereford, inserted into the masonry of the new tower. From Caldicot the journey would be resumed westwards through Caerleon (where no doubt the Roman remains were as impressive and intriguing as they had been to Gerald of Wales), across the tidal estuary of the Usk to Newport. There was much that was new at Newport: the town's first charter granted as recently as 1385; a house of Austin friars, the first religious house to be founded (1377) in Wales for almost a century and, as it proved, the last before the Dissolution; and the unfinished towers and walls of a castle. But the shadow of death also lay over Newport: its lords were the recently ennobled earls of Stafford, three of whom had died in rapid succession between 1386 and 1395. Their heir was the 17-year-old Edmund Stafford who was to take as wife his brother's widow, Anne, daughter (and as it proved heiress) of Thomas, duke of Gloucester and lord of Caldicot.[12]

The prospects at Cardiff, the next stopping-place, were altogether brighter. Cardiff was a walled town with four main gates, and was already one of the most important towns in south Wales. The lord of the area was Thomas Despenser, scion of an ancient family which had experienced more than its share of the ups and downs of political fortune. For the last two generations the family had been distinguished for its martial prowess in many of the theatres of war—in Scotland and France, Ireland and Italy. But the young Thomas Despenser who was installed in his lordship of Glamorgan in March 1394 had the opportunity to make a name, and a fortune, for himself in the heady atmosphere of Richard II's court in the 1390s. He was soon to experience a truism which his genetic inheritance should already have transmitted to him: that the fortunes of medieval politics could take one to dizzy heights in a very short time, but could cast one down even more precipitately.[13]

From Cardiff the Portway, along the pathway of the old Roman road, took one through the rich Vale of Glamorgan. This was a region where the Welsh poet and the English traveller vied with each other in paying it compliments: the former

greeted it as 'the countess, the lady of countries', lavishing his praises on its opulence, whitewashed halls, and well-stocked orchards; the latter would readily echo the words of a later observer, that it was 'a pleasant and agreeable place and is very populous'. It was a land of rich farmland, nucleated villages, manor houses, and well-constructed parish churches; it faced southwards across the Bristol Channel rather than northwards towards the grim uplands, *Blaenau*, so that the poet's description of it as 'a corner opposite Cornwall' (W. *cornel ar gyfair Cernyw*) had a particular appositeness; its gentry—they were already referred to as *gentiles homines* in 1340—moved easily in English county society, often indeed (as was the case with families such as the Somerys, Stradlings, Turbervilles, and Umfravilles) owning estates in England as well as Glamorgan. Here, if anywhere, was a society where the Welsh and the English, at least at the higher echelons of society, were increasingly at ease with one another.[14]

There was a choice of places to break one's journey. Two in particular seemed attractive. The one was Coety Castle, at which Richard II's entourage called in September 1394. It involved a diversion from the main route, but it was well worth it. Compared with most of the castles of Wales, Coety had been largely remodelled and rebuilt in the fourteenth century. It had the modern conveniences which one would expect for a resident lord who had extensive lands in Glamorgan and wide social contacts in England—new domestic quarters, service rooms, and a new latrine tower. Its childless lord, Sir Lawrence Berkerolles, would extend visitors a warm welcome. Impressive as the castle was and comfortable as were its facilities, one might well wonder whether it was sufficiently well constructed, standing far inland and isolated as it was, to withstand a long siege. Such idle thoughts could be dismissed as bad dreams. Glamorgan had been at peace for over eighty years and there was no hint in 1395 that such a peace would ever again be broken.[15]

The alternative to Coety Castle was Margam Abbey, where Richard II chose to stay on his travels through Wales, *en route* to Ireland in May 1399. As he moved towards Margam the traveller's attention would doubtless have been drawn to the view towards Kenfig and Merthyr Mawr, where billowing sand dunes were already threatening to engulf whole settlements. At Margam itself it was the best of times and the worst of times. The monastic buildings—most notably, the extraordinarily striking polygonal chapter-house—were still hugely impressive and bespoke the certainties, vision, and healthy recruitment of former days. But the talk in the monastery was all of decline and hardship, of the sharp fall in the number of monks, the disappearance of *conversi* (lay brothers), the leasing of estates, debt, expensive lawsuits, unrepaired buildings, murrain, pestilence, inundation of the sea, and—rather pointedly—the demands of hospitality. The monks would proudly show the papal bull of 1394 which they had just received, fulmi-

nating against those who maliciously detained or concealed the house's possess-
ions. Whether sonorous Latin cadences could solve Margam's deep-seated problems was another matter, especially as other threats were just around the
corner.[16]

From Margam to Swansea the journey was short but involved negotiating two
estuaries, those of the rivers Nedd and Tawe. Just short of Swansea our traveller's
attention might have been drawn to the flourishing coal industry at Llansamlet.
Despite heavy overhead costs, especially in labour and candles, production and
profits were high. Swansea itself was an attractive walled town, largely English in
population, a centre for active sea-borne trade with Bristol, Somerset, and south-
west England, and the administrative and judicial centre for the lordship of
Gower. Notable buildings included the hospital of St David's and the castle. The
latter's distinctive arcaded parapet would certainly catch the visitor's eye; it
would be well for him to retain that memory as he travelled westward. More
disturbing might be the rumours that he might already have picked up about a
possible challenge to the title of the lordship. For the last forty years the Beauchamp earls of Warwick had been lords of Gower and Swansea; but the cross-cur-
rents of politics and royal favour were soon to initiate a process which led to a
dramatic change of fortune for the family and its title to the lordship. Such shifts
of political fortunes were not private matters for two English aristocratic families
(Beauchamp and Mowbray); they also threatened the confidence and ties of
service and reward of local society.[17]

Swansea might well have been a lunch-stop; by evening our traveller might
have made it—as Richard II's retinue did in 1394 and 1399—to John of Gaunt's
castle at Kidwelly (plate 8). Even by the standards of earlier castles which he had
seen, Kidwelly was truly impressive, as befitted the most westerly castle of the
vast Lancastrian inheritance of the richest aristocrat in England. Most impressive
of all was the massive gatehouse where extensive work was still under way in the
1390s. Compared with the forbidding castle, the little town in its shadow was
paltry; indeed only six years later, in 1401, a report proclaimed the town within
the walls to be 'ruinous, waste, and desolate'. Paradoxically that may have been
so because the burgesses felt sufficiently safe and confident to move into the
suburbs outside the cramped walls of the old town. Here, under the shadow of
the tall stone tower of the Benedictine priory church (a daughter-house of
Sherborne abbey), they would pursue their crafts and trades, hold their fairs and
markets, and be within easy reach of the four water-mills and the fulling mill
which served the needs of a rich agricultural hinterland. There was no reason for
them to feel insecure. Much of the area around the town—the foreignry or
Englishry as it was known—was settled by old English families. More reassuring-
ly still, much the richest merchant at Kidwelly bore a Welsh name, John Owen;

while the most recent and current stewards of the lordship for John of Gaunt were two of the most prominent and powerful Welshmen of the district, Henry Don and William Gwyn ap Rhys. There was no cause for nervousness here; and had there been, one might easily believe that the castle was well-nigh impregnable, even if the little town was vulnerable.[18]

From Kidwelly one turned north to Carmarthen. Though only a short journey from Kidwelly it was well to tarry at Carmarthen before beginning the last leg of the journey westwards. The town was entered across a bridge, long famous as a crossing point over the River Tywi. Only a year earlier, in 1394, major repairs had been undertaken on the bridge so that the king, his army, and his baggage train could cross it safely; indeed King Richard himself had contributed £20 towards the work. Carmarthen was a cut above the towns, probably even Cardiff included, through which the traveller had so far passed. It was larger and busier than any of them; ships plied there not only from Cardiff, Tenby, and Bristol, but from much farther afield—from Ireland, Gascony, and Spain; it was the staple port for south-west Wales, and as such considerable quantities of wool and hides were stacked on its quays ready to be weighed on the new balance recently bought in London. It had two churches—St Peter's on the site of a very old Welsh *clas* and St Mary's built near the commercial hub of the town—and two religious houses—a priory of Austin canons at one end and a Franciscan friary at the other. Indeed, Carmarthen itself could claim that it was two towns in one—the 'old town' built on the site of a Roman settlement and under the control of the priory, and a smaller, compact, walled 'new town' directly opposite the bridge and beneath the castle. Carmarthen could pride itself on other advantages: it was the administrative, financial, and judicial capital of South Wales (even if that term in this period referred only to the two counties of Cardiganshire and Carmarthenshire and some annexed lordships); it was the gateway to the east and thence to England, whether one chose to follow the coastal route or to head inland for Brecon and Hereford; and for the historically curious it had the rich appeal of its links, real or imagined, with a Roman past and—thanks to Geoffrey of Monmouth in particular—with Merlin. This was a place to loiter at; the only worrying elements were the way in which the River Tywi was silting up and the somewhat tense relations between the local English and Welsh.[19]

An easy day's riding westwards from Carmarthen took one past another Cistercian abbey at Whitland and so on either to Narberth or to Llawhaden. One might stay at the former if one had connections with the Mortimer family. It was the most westerly possession of that powerful family in Wales, so far indeed from the rest of the Mortimer lands that two years later, in 1397, the earl of March was to grant it in fee to his brother, Edmund. These seemed to be sunny days for the Mortimer family. Even so it was worrying to be told that relations between the

Welsh and English in the Narberth area were also strained; indeed so fraught were they that they had been placed on the agenda of the Mortimer council. An alternative to Narberth as an overnight stop was Llawhaden, where Richard II had chosen to stay in 1394. Llawhaden had the appearance of a castle, but it would be more appropriately described as a palace. Remodelled in the late thirteenth century by the bishops of St Davids to be the administrative centre of their estates, it also had a splendid hall which could readily be used for grand social occasions. What was particularly acceptable to the visitor, however, were the four sets of residential apartments, possibly installed or updated by Bishop Adam de Houghton (1362–89). Each apartment consisted of a large room and an adjoining bedchamber (with latrine). This was *en suite* accommodation of the highest order.[20]

The traveller was now on the last leg of his journey. A short morning's ride would bring him to Haverford, Richard II's destination in 1394 and 1399. From its steep main street, dominated by yet another castle, one looked southwards towards the complex web of inlets which made this corner of Wales both one of the most sheltered and one of the most vulnerable entrances to shipping. The lordship of Haverford was in royal hands and had been used as a reward for a succession of the king's close companions. Its present acting lord was Sir Thomas Percy, currently holding the key post of steward of the royal household and in the future to be raised to the earldom of Worcester and to give distinguished service as royal lieutenant in south Wales. If one was intent on crossing to Ireland, one could wait at Haverford until word came that the ship—and the wind—was ready for one to embark at Milford. But the temptation was great to slip in a hurried pilgrimage to the shrine of St David. William I was the first English king to have done so in 1081; Richard II followed his example in 1394. After all, the bishopric was now held by his former treasurer, John Gilbert.[21]

St David's must have been as great a revelation then as it is now, possibly more so. Here in the farthest, bare, treeless, rocky promontory of west Wales lay a cathedral tucked away out of sight in a dell on the banks of a rivulet. Entering by the gateway known as Porth y Tŵr, one's eye took in the complex of buildings enclosed by the cathedral's expansive walls and four gateways. This was truly an episcopal city. Work within the last two or three generations had helped to transform and beautify the original cathedral. Such work included the magnificent stone *pulpitum* which divided the nave from the choir, the chapel of St Thomas, and, to the north, the College of St Mary founded in 1365 by Bishop Adam de Houghton as a home for a master and seven fellows to serve the needs of the cathedral. The name of Houghton would certainly be on the lips of anyone who visited St David's; he was undoubtedly one of its most innovative benefactors. He was only outdone by one of his predecessors, Henry de Gower, bishop

from 1328 to 1347. Gower's presence was overwhelming in the magnificent bishop's palace which lay across the little River Alun from the cathedral. Its two magnificent halls, its majestic staircase and porch, and the striking wheel window in the great hall bespoke an air of opulence and grandeur quite out of proportion to the remoteness and poverty of the area. Most immediately eye-catching were the distinctive arcaded parapets of the southern and eastern ranges; they immediately triggered memories of the castle at Swansea. Obeisance at the shrine of St David, behind the high altar, and at the tomb of Bishop Gower in the *pulpitum* of the cathedral might appropriately complete a visit which was also a pilgrimage.[22]

Returning eastwards towards England the traveller, on reaching Carmarthen, might decide to follow the overland road up the Tywi valley instead of retracing his steps along the southern coastal route. In that case he might have taken lunch at Llanymddyfri, the headquarters of a thoroughly Welsh lordship now under the control of the widowed Elizabeth, Lady Audley. She was also lady of the distant Welsh lordship of Cemaes (bordering with the bishop of St David's estate) and it was to Llanymddyfri that its officials brought their revenues for onward dispatch to her ladyship on her English estates. The journey eastwards from Llanymddyfri might well remind one of some of the terrors of the landscape of north Wales— mountain passes, the little deserted township of Llywel, and to the south the forbidding expanses of Fforest Fach and Fforest Fawr. It was with a sense of considerable relief that one arrived at Brecon, passing the elegant Dominican friary church on one's right before crossing the River Usk into the town. Brecon was a typical small market town, largely, though by no means entirely, English in population (one of its most successful burgesses was one Thomas ap David), claiming a monopoly of trade throughout the large lordship which bore its name, a centre to which the well-esteemed wool of the Epynt flocks as well as the produce of the rich farms of its eastern hinterland were brought, and also the focus of pilgrims attracted by its famous rood-screen. (W. *y grog yn Aberhonddu*). Out of town and across the River Honddu stood its two most imposing buildings, mementoes of its original role in an age of conquest, military and ecclesiastical. The one was its castle, of recent years more an administrative centre than a military or residential base, though the installation of a new drawbridge might have prompted some to wonder whether its days as a frontier fortress were indeed over; the other was the Benedictine priory of St John's, the second-richest Benedictine priory in Wales, sharing its large and imposing parish church with the men and women of the town. The lords of Brecon for generations had been the Bohun earls of Hereford but they had failed in the male line in 1373. The new lord was none other than Henry Bolingbroke, son of John of Gaunt, a major figure in English politics and a noted crusader (to Prussia) and international pilgrim (to the Holy Sepulchre). He had not yet visited his Welsh lordships, much

the most important part of his estates; his coming—he eventually made a pro-gress to the lordship in autumn 1397—was anticipated with a mixture of delight and trepidation—delight because the arrival of a world-renowned lord and heir to the great Lancastrian inheritance might open, or reopen, avenues of service and reward; but trepidation because the first coming of a lord was almost always used as a pretext for raising a vast 'gift of recognition' to salute him.[23]

From Brecon the traveller would spend most of the rest of his journey in Wales traversing Bolingbroke's estates. Proceeding north-eastwards through fertile farming country he would reach the castle of Bronllys, the headquarters of the sub-lordship of Cantrefselyf and the site of an unusually elegant round keep. It was a good time to arrive there because a long dispute between Bolingbroke and his uncle, Thomas, duke of Gloucester, had at last been settled on 20 June 1395, confirming the former's title to Bronllys in return for concessions elsewhere. Soon the traveller would be in the Wye valley. Cutting through the small Mortimer lordship of Glasbury he made his way thence to the walled town of Hay, gateway to England. He left Wales behind as he headed for Hereford.[24]

The journeys he had undertaken in north and south Wales would certainly have given our traveller a clear impression of the country, its geography and peoples, its weather and its varying landscapes. But it would have been a partial and largely external view—partial, because he had not seen large tracts of the country, notably its great interior network of river valleys, moorland, and moun-tain ranges; external, because he had leap-frogged from one castle, walled town, or abbey to another, tarrying as little as he could in between these oases of security and comfort. He would, of course, have picked up gossip and formed impressions a-plenty; but, like all travellers, he would have processed them through his own filter of assumptions, experiences, and expectations. It would be as well to supplement his impressions from those of a very different kind of traveller.

The obvious candidate would be a professional native Welsh poet. Such a poet would have good reason to know the country well: its historical lore, its place-names, and the genealogies of its ancient families formed much of the fabric from which he wove the learned references with which his poetry was studded; the calls of patronage and the prospects of employment likewise required him to treat Wales, or much of Wales, as his parish. A circuit of the country, *cylch Cymru*—whether actual or imaginary—might well have formed part of his ap-prenticeship and the subject of some of his earliest literary conceits. After all, the greatest Welsh poet of all time, Dafydd ap Gwilym (d. *c*.1350), had encompassed the whole of Wales in the ambit of his muse—from his native Cardiganshire in the west across to Maelor in the north-east, from farthest Anglesey in the north-west to Basaleg near Newport in the south-east. He had been frustrated in

his romantic pursuits by the waves on the River Dyfi, but equally he had considered it an appropriate penance on an uncooperative nun in Anglesey to dispatch her on a pilgrimage to St David's.[25]

Dafydd's greatest successor was Iolo Goch, a skilled poet who probably died in the closing years of the fourteenth century. It is from one of his poems that we can best grasp the character of a poetic circuit, albeit dressed up in the form of a dialogue between the soul and the body. The journey moves rapidly across the face of Wales—Gwynedd in the north-west, Powys in the east, Ceri and New-town in mid-Wales, Maelienydd and Elfael in the unwelcoming uplands between the rivers Severn and Wye, across the land of Builth to the vale of Tywi, thence to Kidwelly and the Cistercian abbey of Whitland, meandering slowly through Ceredigion (Cardiganshire), not least at the abbey of Strata Florida, and returning to north-east Wales to complete his circuit at the house of a leading Welsh ecclesiastic near Caerwys in Flintshire.

The poet's circuit presents a notable contrast with that of our official traveller. It is notable for what it excludes—south-east Wales and the whole of the south-ern lowlands. This was a circuit that seemed to exult in the challenge of the interior and uplands of the country, rather than in shunning them. Equally striking are the features of Wales it highlights. For the poet Wales was not a land of castles and walled boroughs, but of familiar regions (W. *gwladoedd*)—Maelie-nydd, Elfael, Buellt, Ystrad Tywi, Ceredigion, and so forth. Its stopping-places included two of the premier Cistercian abbeys of Welsh Wales—Whitland and Strata Florida—and the home of an archdeacon of St Asaph, famous both for his patronage of Welsh littérateurs and for the way his election to the see of Bangor had been quashed. The other heroes of Iolo Goch's poem were not dukes, earls, and bishops but Welsh esquires—the sons of Philip Dorddu in Maelienydd, Rhydderch ab Ieuan Llwyd and the grandsons of Gruffudd ab Einion Fychan in Ceredigion—noted for their support for, and expertise in, the traditional learning of Wales. Best of all was it to return to Sycharth, the seat of Owain Glyn Dŵr.

The poet's circuit and the official's itinerary had only overlapped at two points—in the vale of Tywi and at Kidwelly; even there what they chose to see, savour, and experience were worlds apart. Iolo Goch, it is true, could by proxy and poetic licence enter the world of the English; he addressed two of his odes to Edward III and Roger Mortimer, earl of March. But his Wales and that of our official traveller were still largely, though not entirely, foreign countries to each other. This was indeed a tale of two countries; and so long as Wales was two countries it could never truly be at ease with itself. Such was the Wales of Owain Glyn Dŵr.[26]

The quality of a journey is not measured by the number of miles travelled but by the windows that it opens into the country and society through which the

traveller journeys. Our English official and Welsh poet chose very different routes and commenced their voyages of discovery with very different mental maps and social and cultural norms. For the one Wales was an intimidating and alien country, a land where it might not seem incredible to locate tales of Gog and Magog and other such terrifying wonders, a country into which women or careless men might be kidnapped, to be released only on payment of a ransom. For the other Wales was a familiar country, a collection of regions whose names tripped easily off the tongue and which were bound together, and to him, by a nexus of tales, learned lore, topographic legends, genealogies, friendships, net-works of kinsmen and affines, and deeply rooted customs of hospitality. Between them the impressions of the two travellers—in their contrasts as well as in the measure to which they complemented each other—might help us, vicariously as it were, to compose a mental image of the Wales of Owain Glyn Dŵr.[27]

To the first-time traveller two features immediately stood out about the physical aspect of the Welsh countryside. The first was, of course, its mountains. It had ever been so. When English observers first began to commit their impress-ions—or, more frequently, their assumptions and prejudices—about Wales to parchment in the twelfth century this was inevitably their first observation. John of Salisbury, the much-travelled and self-assured humanist, may speak for them all: 'the king of England' he remarked rather preciously in one of his letters 'has set out on his journey to conquer the Welsh in their Alps and sub-Alps.' Daniel Defoe, centuries later, would from direct experience echo his sentiments: 'for a whole week's travel we seemed to be conversing with the upper regions.' It was the mountains—whether the endless expanse of the high moorlands of central and eastern Wales or the jumbled-together peaks of the north west—which above all made Wales 'horrid and frightful'. That revulsion was compounded by its forests. No traveller in England was, of course, unfamiliar with forest; and indeed anyone who stopped to consider the role of the forests in the society and economy of Wales would quickly have concluded that they were vital both to the profit and pleasure of the lord and to the well-being and, indeed, survival of the peasant. For the lord they provided good hunting, especially on the eastern borderlands, and a stock of falcons and sparrowhawks for which Wales was famous. They also yielded him handsome profits from the sale of timber, the charcoal-burning industry (especially in south-east Wales), the large sums paid for pannage, and the substantial annual revenue of forest administration and forest courts (the lease of the Great Forest of Brecon, for example, more than doubling to £110 between 1340 and 1400). For the peasant the forest, of course, was an essential supplement to his other pastoral and arable resources; indeed for many communities, such as that of Hopedale, it could truly be said that 'the greater part of their sustenance is derived from the woods'. All that could not be

gainsaid; but it was the impenetrability and terror of the forests which impressed the traveller. Wherever he tried to enter Wales he was confronted by forests— whether the great forests of Wentwood and Strigoil in the south-east or Ewloe in the north-east or the Great Forest of Brecon in central Wales.[28]

Mountains and forests were facts of nature, but to the Welshman they were familiar and not necessarily unfriendly facts. For him the ridgeways which often ran across moorlands and meandered their way along the sides of hills—*cefnffyrdd* as they were often known in Welsh—made living in a mountainous country manageable. Iolo Goch's imaginary journey had taken him undaunted through the upland interiors of Wales; Owain Glyn Dŵr might have negotiated the passage from his estates at Sycharth to those in the Dee valley—a journey which would have broken the spirits of a lowland traveller even contemplating it—by taking one of the trackways over the mountains. It was these very trackways which allowed Glyn Dŵr's troops in later years to criss-cross Wales so rapidly and to surprise their foes at the most outlandish venues. For the Welshman indeed, rivers, especially their estuaries, rather than mountains were the hazard: when Dafydd ap Gwilym dispatched a nun unresponsive to his advances on a pilgrimage of penance across western Wales he warned her in advance of the obstacles of channels and estuaries, not mountains, that she would have to face—the Menai Straits, Traeth Mawr and Traeth Bychan (near modern Porth- madog), the rivers Artro, Dysynni, Dyfi, Ystwyth, Aeron, and Teifi. As to forests, the Welsh were more likely to see their positive side rather than to cower in fear at their impenetrability: their economic importance was fully recognized in the vast sums that local communities were willing to pay for licensed or unlicensed exploitation of their resources; for the lovelorn poet they were, of course, the ideal trysting place; more daringly, they are frequently portrayed as a welcome refuge for the outlaw and the bandit (W. *herwr*). Native affection for the forest and the Englishman's fear of it met in the poem addressed to 'The Forest of the Grey Rock' (*I Goed y Graig Lwyd*), where the forest was lovingly greeted not least as providing an opportunity to unhorse and plunder an Englishman; but they met also in life, for the most remarkable correspondence of the closing years of Glyn Dŵr's revolt was the letters of defiance which a Welsh outlaw deep in the forest of Bryncyffo dispatched to Reginald Grey, lord of Ruthin. In nature, as in life, there seemed to be more than one Wales.[29]

On the question of weather, there might be a closer coincidence of views. Wales was wet, windy, and cold; on that, all could surely agree. 'When it is summer elsewhere,' noted Peter Langtoft sourly, 'it is winter in Wales.' And when it was winter, it was deep winter: that is why the Black Prince's councillors were given a special allowance of warm clothing when they were dispatched to Wales on a winter tour of duty. The Welsh could hardly dissent from such

observations. Even Dafydd ap Gwilym, the poet of the sunniest disposition in the whole history of Welsh verse, wrote feelingly of swirling mists and roaring winds, lived in dread of the winter months with their wind, hail, rain, and rushing streams, and spoke with deeply felt regret of the brevity of the summer (*Gwae ni . . . fyrred yr haf*). Welsh weather was cruel: it was the grimness and harshness of the winter of 1407–8 which eventually broke the spirit of many of Owain Glyn Dŵr's most devoted supporters. The facts of climate did not admit of argument; but even these facts are assimilated into a web of other expectations and assumptions. For the English Wales's weather only compounded the unattractiveness of the country and their suspicion of its people: when Henry IV's expedition into Wales in September 1402 was overwhelmed by a rainstorm and the king's life put in danger, it was not only nature which was blamed but the Welsh themselves who seemed indeed able not only to cope with, but also to command, such weather. Be that as it may, it is certainly true that for the poet the nature and the weather of Wales, however frustrating they might be on occasion, were ultimately a source of exultation and delight. Familiarity with them had bred acceptance at worst, admiration and enjoyment at best.[30]

Even a view of the character of the country would quickly reveal differences in emphasis of a very significant kind. To the Englishman Wales was remote, inaccessible, and unknown. Jibes on that issue reverberate down the centuries— from the contemptuous observation of Archbishop Pecham in the 1280s that the Welsh lived 'in their little corner in the far end of the world . . . The rest of humanity scarcely know that you are a people', to the equally unflattering comment of a later dramatist that Wales 'is a country in the world's back-side'. Remoteness was compounded by fragmentation. England, it might be retorted, was a collection of regional and local societies; but such variety was overlaid by a profound culture of unity: a single ruler, a unitary common law, a common coinage and taxation, a single political community in parliament, to name but the most obvious institutional features of such unity. It was meaningful to talk of England and of the governance of England. Wales, on the other hand, could hardly be said to be more than a geographical expression. In governmental terms it was an amalgam of lordships and shires; it enjoyed no administrative, jurisdictional, or legal unity; it had no common focus, no common assembly, no common tax or law. It was no more than the sum of its parts. Some of its most characteristic governmental instruments—mutual-extradition conventions (W. *cydfodau*), letters of March, love-days at lordship boundaries, regional statutes, local collections of laws—bespoke a world of profound fragmentation. Wales, it might be concluded, was (as it has been aptly said of Gaelic Ireland in the same period) no more than a state of mind, and a profoundly disturbed state of mind at that.[31]

The Welsh riposte to such a comment might be to say that incomprehension itself is a state of mind. Had not Jean Froissart observed shrewdly about an English governor in Ireland that 'he never succeeded in learning the lie of the country or in understanding the mentality of the Irish'? One man's disordered fragmentation was another man's rich diversity. The poets certainly exulted in the plurality of Wales; to them, as we have already seen in Iolo Goch's ode, Wales was a federation of countries. Each country (W. *gwlad*) had its own character, ethos, traditions, lore, shrines, and saints: Gruffudd Llwyd could sing a paean of praise to Morgannwg (Glamorgan) and Sion Cent to Brycheiniog (Brecon). It was only to the uniformist mind or the nervous traveller that the governmental fragmentation of Wales posed problems. Poets such as Dafydd ap Gwilym or Iolo Goch had no problem in traversing the whole of Wales in pursuit of patrons and experiences, and could clearly feel as much at ease in Anglesey in the north-west as in Basaleg in the south-east. Nor were these merely flights of poetic fancy: Philip ap Morgan, whom we shall meet later, moved easily from his base at Usk across mid-Wales to his lord's lordship of Denbigh. As to inaccessibility and the difficulty of travel, these were clichés, it might be concluded, which told one more of English apprehension and prejudices than of the true state of affairs. In Owain Glyn Dŵr's own lifetime parliamentary legislation specifically allowed Welsh labourers to travel unimpeded to England to help in the harvest. And that is what they did: in 1396, for example, the bailiff of the abbot of Hailes was said to have hired over a hundred Welsh reapers for the harvest in Gloucestershire. They had also, of course, travelled by their thousands across the generations to serve as archers and foot-soldiers in the armies of English kings and lords in Scotland, France, and elsewhere. By the 1380s and 1390s the opportunities for military service, and the numbers who responded to those opportunities, were far fewer than before; but they had by no means disappeared altogether. Thus, almost 400 men were assembled in north Wales in the early autumn of 1386 to march to south-east England to defend the coast against an anticipated French invasion; in 1394 another substantial force (some of them veterans of the 1386 journey) set off from north Wales for Ireland in Richard II's army. The Welsh were the Gurkhas of the English armies of the Middle Ages; and, like the Gurkhas, they had often seen more of the world, through the necessity of service, than had many of their allegedly worldly wise neighbours. Some of them had indeed travelled even further afield on pilgrimage, quite possibly never to return. Such were the three Welshmen who bade farewell to their friends in the church at Welshpool before setting off for Compostella, or the steady trickle of very ordinary peasants who are recorded as leaving the security of Dyffryn Clwyd for the perilous journey to the Holy Land. In short, inaccessible and remote much of Wales most certainly was, and highly localized the lives of many of its people; but

the rhythms of pastoral husbandry, the poverty of an overpopulated countryside, and the inducements of adventure and pay may well have meant that the horizons of Welshmen of Glyn Dŵr's day—whether directly or through the experience of neighbours and kinsmen—were often wider than was, and has been, assumed. It is not without significance that contemporaries recognized that the rising of Owain Glyn Dŵr was more than a flash in the pan when reports came in that Welsh scholars and labourers were fleeing back from England to Wales.[32]

The Wales that our two travellers saw and experienced differed in one other crucial respect: the English official moved hurriedly and nervously from one castellated borough to another; the Welsh poet travelled at his own pace from the home of one Welsh patron or from one Welsh abbey to another; the English official's evening company would have been that of constables, local officers, merchants, and burgesses; that of the Welsh poet a Welsh squire, his family, friends, and followers and such other Welshmen as he met on his travels. The worlds of the two travellers certainly touched each other and overlapped; yet they remained worlds apart and need to be introduced as such. It is to the world of castles and boroughs that we first turn.

By the fourteenth century there were some eighty to ninety small towns in Wales, very unevenly distributed across the country. Our English traveller had visited a good dozen of them on his journeys. At two of them—Caernarfon in the north and Carmarthen in the south—he had made extended stays. This might have prompted him to compare the two boroughs with each other and with towns and cities in England with which he was familiar. What would have immediately struck him was how tiny and anaemic were many of these boroughs: Caernarfon is unlikely to have had a population of more than 500; even Carmarthen, which was possibly the largest borough in Wales, had probably less than 1,500 inhabitants. Many towns, like Ruthin, were little more than a huddle of houses aligned along four streets, and dominated by a local church or friary. The tubs of water at each street corner were a reminder of the ever-present fear that the whole little settlement might be wiped out by fire. These towns had inevitably a rural and agricultural aspect to them, as of course did many English boroughs: the burgesses of Caernarfon had been given an endowment of almost 1,500 acres of land around their borough in order to entice them to settle there; at Carmarthen the cattle and horses of the burgesses grazed on the meadows along the Tywi just outside the town; while at Ruthin the prohibition on leaving mounds of manure outside the houses was an eloquent comment on the importance of agriculture in the life of its burgesses.[33]

Yet for all their puny size and rural aspect, these little boroughs stood apart from the countryside, self-consciously and defiantly so. They had communal

buildings and areas in which to manifest their burghal identity: a market-place and cross, court-house, shops, a pound, and perhaps above all a toll-house or toll-booth, the symbol of burghal privilege and seignorial profiteering. The town also had its own pattern of governance and governors which it jealousy defended—occasionally a mayor, always its own hierarchy of officials, its town court, court of fairs, and piepowder court (to deal with minor commercial cases). Its privileges were itemized in its carefully preserved charters and their solemn confirmations. It was a momentous day for Carmarthen, for example, in July 1386 when it was conceded that its burgesses had the right to elect a mayor, two bailiffs, and a coroner annually on the first Monday after Michaelmas. Most important of all, ultimately, was the fact that these little towns were, for all their dung-heaps, privileged centres of trade and crafts. Their weekly markets and two or three annual fairs were the engines of commercial life and commodity distribution for their wide hinterlands. Most of the townsmen were small-scale craftsmen and traders; but the modesty of their production, markets, and turn-over should not lead us to underestimate their importance. Their activities helped to accelerate the circulation of goods; and, however much tension there might be between them and the country-dwellers, they helped to familiarize the Welsh with the practices, *mores*, food, and clothes of the English and perhaps, above all, with the use of money (even the florins to which Dafydd ap Gwilym referred). Some of them indeed gave a glimpse of accumulated, non-territorial wealth and of reserves of capital which opened a window onto a world very different from that of subsistence production, small-scale exchange in kind, rural markets, gift-giving, and largess to which most Welshmen in the countryside were habituated. At Caernarfon our traveller would surely have been told about Robert Parys, who owned two taverns, six burgages, and 200 acres of land, or of Richard Golding, who held twenty-nine burgages and 300 acres of land in Beau-maris, had property in other boroughs along the north Wales coastline, and was eminent enough to serve as sheriff of Anglesey 1385–7. Even Parys and Golding were small beer compared with some of the burgesses whom our traveller would have met in south Wales. Their trading contacts and capital assets put them in a league quite apart from even the richer townsmen of north Wales. John Owen of Kidwelly, for example, was not merely a local entrepreneur but also an international wool merchant, while the fact that two of the townsmen of Carmarthen could lend £400 between them for the defence of their town was an indication of the liquid assets they commanded.[34]

Our traveller would surely have been struck by the contrasts between Caernarfon and Carmarthen—in size and age, but above all in the scale of their trading activity and in the network of their commercial links. He would also have sensed the rather tense, defensive, lone-outpost atmosphere in Caernarfon in contrast

with the confident expansiveness of Carmarthen. But experience of both towns and the other towns he visited in Wales would also have drawn to his attention certain marked contrasts between them and towns of similar size he knew in England. First, they still clearly bore the marks of their military origin: even at Carmarthen the castle still physically overshadowed the town, while at Caernarfon the little borough was little more than an annex of the massive castle, cowering beneath its protective skirt. At both places town walls—at Caernarfon built simultaneously with the castle, in eleven hectic months—reinforced the impression. Town walls were, of course, not unknown in England; but in Wales, unlike England, they were a feature of the vast majority of towns and, as at Caernarfon, might still be actively manned. Furthermore, in Wales, unlike any-where in England, guard duty in defence of town and castle was an obligation due from all burgesses, and many of them were soon to discover that it was no merely theoretical obligation.[35]

Then again, while many of the smaller market towns of England had an important role in the governance of their respective hinterlands, none of them could compete in this respect with their often much smaller Welsh counterparts. Every one of the towns on our traveller's route was the administrative and judicial capital for a large lordship of several hundred square miles; Caernarfon and Carmarthen had even a greater importance for they were respectively the regional capitals of the Principality lands of North and South Wales. They had evolved from military outposts into governmental headquarters: indeed Caernarfon fulfilled both roles *ab initio*. All the major offices of governance—including the chancery, exchequer, and justiciar's office—were located there; all the major courts and judicial eyres were held there. Government meant business and customers: that is why, for example, the burgesses of Cardigan claimed that they used to live by the goods they sold to suitors who attended the county court in their town. And governmental responsibilities brought opportunities for numerate and literate burgesses, many of whom also had a useful smattering of legal knowledge.[36]

An English visitor would also have been very struck by the extensive commer-cial privileges enjoyed by these minuscule Welsh boroughs. Medieval towns were, of course, notorious for the economic monopolies, and exemptions, they claimed; but few could match the claims made by the Welsh boroughs. The town of Brecon, for example, claimed that its burgesses had exclusive trading rights throughout the vast lordship of Brecon. Caernarfon claimed a more modest exclusive trading zone of an eight-mile radius from its walls, Carmarthen one of fifteen miles (a common one for Welsh towns). And in the 1390s, as town court rolls show, the burgesses were still vigorously defending their rights and seeking to snuff out, or at least penalize, any trade, even in victuals or ale, outside their bounds. They were stoking up trouble for the future.[37]

But perhaps what would have most struck the visitor in many of the towns he had visited in Wales was that they were oases of Englishness. Many of the burgesses were English by descent and name; the street names were also English. It is true that in several towns, such as Aberystwyth, Ruthin, and even Carmarthen, there were a substantial number of Welshmen, sometimes even a majority; and this figure would no doubt be higher were servants, maids, and apprentices to be included. But Englishness was a matter of perceptions and attitudes as well as of descent and language; and the current orthodoxy still spoke of 'the English burgesses of the English boroughs' in Wales. That orthodoxy was, understandably, proclaimed most raucously in those towns which still felt they were threatened border outposts. Such certainly was Caernarfon; so also, more surprisingly, was the border borough of Hope (co. Flints.) whose burgesses bemoaned the precariousness of their 'exiled status' in the 1390s. Deeply worrying were the indications, from different parts of Wales, that the mentality of English exclusiveness was, if anything, becoming more deeply entrenched institutionally as the century drew to its close, rather than being softened by the passage of time. Thus at Laugharne in 1386 and St Clears in 1393 a clause was included in the town charter promising that no burgess would be 'convicted or adjudged by any Welshman . . . but only by English burgesses and true Englishmen'. This was hardly an auspicious basis on which to build bridges between the two worlds that were Wales.[38]

A series of visits to the castellated, walled boroughs of Wales would certainly have been a valuable introduction to one of those worlds. The towns of Wales were certainly important, far more important than their puny size suggested; but even on their own terms they were not as important as their burgesses thought, or wanted, them to be. On the one hand, much of the most lucrative trade to and from Wales was in the hands of English merchants—notably those of Chester and Shrewsbury in the north, of Bristol and Hereford in the south. Even some Italian, German, and Flemish merchants and their agents had long since spotted the potential of exports of Welsh wool and hides. On the other hand, a picture built too exclusively around the old boroughs would have missed out much that was most vibrant in Wales. It would have overlooked growth-points such as Wrexham in the north-east, flourishing in spite of the absence of a castle and walls, and the welcoming arms it extended to Welsh craftsmen; it would ignore a host of tiny Welsh settlements—such as Llanrwst, Llanfyllin, Llangollen, Caerwys, or Machynlleth—which serviced the needs of inland Wales without relying on the prop of a garrison economy; it would fail to recognize the importance of rural markets and fairs or the role of the travelling craftsmen and salesmen, such as the salt-carrier (W. *halenwr*) mentioned in court rolls and poetry alike. Above all, of course, was the fact that Wales was overwhelmingly a rural country.[39]

*

No traveller could ignore that; but what he saw was again shaped by his expectations, experiences, and perspective. Our traveller, long habituated to the champion (that is, open-field) countryside and cereal-dominated agriculture of midland and southern England, would note a great deal that was familiar to him in Wales, or at least in parts of Wales. On his southern journey in particular he would have encountered landscape and a society which differed little from the one he knew—a countryside of nucleated villages and hamlets, moated manor houses, and seignorial parklands, open fields subdivided into stripes or quillets (W. *lleiniau*) and billowing crops of cereals, and a labour force composed in part of unfree tenants (sometimes, it is true, making their journey down from Welsh upland settlements) and in part of hired *famuli* or servants. Such was the image that he might have formed in Wrinstone or Bonvilston in Glamorgan, Castlemartin in Pembrokeshire, or, as he neared his journey's end, in Bronllys. He would have been told that at Bronllys and many other places seignorial demesne agriculture, that is, direct agricultural exploitation by the landlord, had been abandoned within the last generation or so (at Bronllys in 1373); but that would hardly have occasioned surprise since much the same policy was being pursued in many parts of England. Indeed it was reassuring to know that not far from Bronllys the earl of Warwick was still, in 1395, maintaining large flocks of sheep in his lordship of Elfael.[40]

Even beyond the southern coastlands and the eastern river valleys a shrewd observer with an open mind might soon have concluded that the Wales he toured hardly corresponded with the images of the wild, wooded and pastoral society on which he had been reared. As he passed quickly down the Vale of Clwyd or crossed hurriedly through Eifionydd in far western Caernarfonshire, or glimpsed Anglesey from across the Menai Straits, he would have noticed an agricultural landscape which, though different in its scale and its pattern, was not so very dissimilar from that of England. It was also a landscape of quilleted, open fields and of joint cultivation, a countryside in which the plough-team of oxen was king, where cereal growing was central to the economy, and in which the water-mill was often the dominant building in the neighbourhood. Acquaintance with Welsh poetry would quickly have confirmed such an impression: it was from the world of arable agriculture that the poets regularly borrowed their images of excellence, for high-born and low-born alike. That is why the best compliment of all to the sons of Tudur ap Goronwy—two of whom were to be so dramatically involved in the early days of the Glyn Dŵr revolt—was to call them *eithefigion*, the most reliable oxen in the plough team.[41]

Such similarities were reassuring; but there was of course no escaping the fact that much of Wales was an upland country, and that upland regions—in England as much as in Wales—developed patterns of agriculture, rhythms of economic

activity, and forms of social relationships which were, at the very least, unfamiliar to the men of the lowlands. Arable cultivation was certainly important; but both the soil and the weather of Wales determined that oats was far and away the most popular crop in much of the country. Over large tracts of Wales, of course, not even oats could be grown; there pastoral agriculture prevailed. Compared with much of England, Wales was pre-eminently a land of cattle and, to a lesser extent, sheep. Drovers already plied their trade, taking herds from Powys to the fairs of Oswestry or 400 head of cattle from north Wales to meet the needs of the king's household in 1382. Amercements (fines or penalties) in Wales were still calculated in cattle, the basic Welsh amercement being that of three cows; while at Brecon our traveller would have been surprised to learn that the biennial tribute—the only render given to the lord by most of the Welshmen of the lordship—was payable in 136 cows and their calves. The economy of the hoof had a very different rhythm and made different demands from its practitioners from a cereal economy. It encouraged mobility (even if not on the scale of that of the shepherds of Montaillou); it allowed the prospect of summer work elsewhere, not least in the harvest in England; it was often accompanied by transhumance as peasants and their herds betook themselves to their upland shiels (W. *hafodau*, summer houses), only returning to the more solid lowland house (W. *hendrefi*) in the winter. Most of inland Wales was a land of mixed rather than of exclusively pastoral agriculture; but the proportions of that mixture were very different from those still familiar in much of lowland England. The unfamiliar for the English traveller was a source of pride for the Welsh poet: when Gruffudd Llwyd saluted one of his patrons he noted proudly how his lands in western Wales rose from sea shore to mountain and how his wealth was expressed both in water-mills and in upland herds.[42]

But perhaps what would have struck the external observer most forcefully was how sparsely populated was much of Wales and how dispersed was its settlement pattern. Wales, like England and the rest of Europe, had a far smaller population in 1395 than it had fifty years earlier. Recurrent visitations of plague—the Great Death, *Y Farwolaeth Fawr*, as it was known in Welsh—had taken a huge toll of the population of the country from end to end; it was little wonder that a poet, commenting in macabre fashion on the plague buboes or boils, should observe that 'an inch can be the death of man' (W. *modfedd a bair marw dyn*). More striking still to an English observer was that Wales was, for the most part, not a land of villages. Small hamlets, often huddled around a church or the demesne centre (W. *llys*) of former Welsh princelings, there were; but much of the population seemed to live in single farmsteads. For travellers in Wales, from at least the twelfth to the sixteenth century, this was one of the most striking features of its society. Archbishop Pecham may speak for all such travellers: 'they' he remarked of the Welsh 'do not live together,

but far from each other.' From at least the tenth century the nucleation of population in villages had been one of the distinctive features of much of north-western Europe; the failure of Wales, other than peripherally and to a limited degree, to follow suit in this respect was one of the features which set it apart.[43]

So also did its relative poverty, the very limited monetization of its economy, and the absence of any substantial differentiation in the distribution of its rural wealth. Regional and local variations in all of these respects, of course, there were; but it is difficult not to believe that an external, casual observer would not have been struck by the poverty and backwardness of what he saw—in housing and clothes, in the absence of money (it was not so long ago that the Welsh of west Wales had commented plaintively that 'they were never accustomed to have money in the Welshry'), and in the apparent absence of a truly rich knightly and gentry class, let alone a resident aristocracy whose levels of consumption and broader horizons could have served to transform the character and tempo of economic activity in the countryside. Observers had long since commented on the frugality and hardiness of the Welsh, noting that they often lived more abstemiously than monks. There was certainly a tinge of admiration in such comments, but they also reflected the self-satisfied surprise of a society of plenty when confronted with a society whose expectations and levels of consumption were so much lower. Different conclusions could be, and had already been frequently, drawn from such observation: such a hardy, frugal, and mobile society could show a resilience and a resourcefulness in the face of adversity far greater than more settled, more affluent, and more tightly regimented societies; but equally such a society might eventually be starved into submission, both by economic blockade and by the destruction of its narrow economic survival base. Gerald of Wales and Edward I had in different ways recognized as much; Henry IV would have to re-learn the lesson slowly and painfully.[44]

Poverty and backwardness are, of course, relative concepts. The view of Wales that Iolo Goch, the poet, and his comrades conveyed was a very different one. Theirs was a Wales which could scarcely have been suspected from the boroughs and the castles. It was a Wales of bardic patrons, noted for their munificence, geniality, and luxurious living, a Wales of the courts (W. *llysoedd*) of squires and squireens—Bathafarn, Basaleg, Penmynydd, Chwilog, Ystum Cegid, Sycharth. Here, if we take the poets at their word, were to be found feather beds and chimneyed fireplaces, sumptuous foods worthy of the best in London and wines from Gascony and Spain. This was a world as conventionally idealized as that in any miniature in a book of hours and a world repeatedly described in the language of exaggeration. Yet we should not dismiss it. The poets made no pretence of describing the whole of Welsh society. Theirs was a deliberately élitist and idealized view of the freeborn leaders of native society, the *uchelwyr* or

'high men' as they were appropriately called. The poets could on occasion, as we shall see, sing the praises of the humble husbandman; but their more normal social orientation was reflected in their contemptuous reference to 'the wretched serf's house' (W. *tŷ taeog blwng*) or to the 'turf-roofed house of the peasant' (W. *tŷ taeog do tyweirch*).[45]

The poet's view of the world was, therefore, highly selective and socially limited. But it is an invaluable view for at least two reasons. It opens the window on to a world of power and a network of relationships in rural Wales which was scarcely known to the men of castles and boroughs, and which therefore lies beyond the normal documentation of the historian. It also helps us, with the aid of other sources, to re-create some of the values, assumptions, and practices of this other Wales.

It was a society in which status was still largely determined by birth and lineage and in which the ties of kinship and affinity were of premier importance. In such a society legitimacy of descent (W. *bonedd*) was the most prized of all assets: the bards declared as much by assuming that the best way to honour a leader, such as Owain Glyn Dŵr, was to recite his genealogy; but the ordinary peasants of north-east Wales likewise shared the same view when they decreed that loss of land could not deny a freeman's son of his status as a freeman. Status and legitimacy were to be central to Owain's propaganda. But the bonds of common lineage and kinship were matters of practical power as well as of propaganda. It was in respect of lineage that Welshmen claimed land, and paid their dues; it was with their co-parceners, those of the same descent as them, that they shared the title to 'tribal' mills and the advowson of churches; it was on their kinsmen that they still frequently relied for many of the processes of law-keeping; and in pursuit of their quarrels, it was on men of their own 'affinity and kinship' (L. *de consanguinitate et affinitate*) that they frequently depended. These bonds of blood and marriage constituted a formidable network of relationships, influence, and common action, alongside and often far more powerful than obligations of obedience to royal or seignorial command and governance. They were to prove remarkably powerful and effective during the Glyn Dŵr revolt.[46]

Welsh society—or more accurately native Welsh society—was not characterized by the vast disparities of wealth which were so characteristic of contemporary English society; but that, of course, did not mean that it was a society of equals. Far from it. Wales had a much narrower series of bands of wealth than did contemporary England; but the chasm in wealth between a rich *uchelwr*, of whom Owain Glyn Dŵr was an obvious example in the north-east, and the ordinary peasant was very clear and very real. Differences in wealth were compounded by those of status and lineage. Wales was by tradition a hierarchical society ruled by warrior freemen. By the late fourteenth century such traditions

were wearing very thin, diluted and enfeebled both by a century of relative peace and by the impoverishing, corrosive impact of partible succession practices. Nevertheless, the sense of superiority and ancient birth of the 'noble free tenants' (as they occasionally called themselves) was very real. Indeed, as in other societies, the uncomfortable disjunction between perceived status and expectations on the one hand, and the chill economic realities of a hard-nosed and fast-changing world on the other, was not the least of the factors which made for disillusion and hurt pride in the Wales of Owain Glyn Dŵr. Such sentiments might be expected to be particularly fostered in the ranks of the élite group of free tenants who claimed descent from Welsh dynasties, called themselves barons (W. *barwniaid*), and held their small estates by the distinctive, and terminologically inflated, tenure of 'chieftainship' (W. *pennaethium*). Owain Glyn Dŵr was 'the king of such barons', *brenin ar y barwniaid*.[47]

Such men had a range of expectations and obligations which made them the natural leaders of native society. The network of local office and the power-structures emanating from castle and borough might temporarily conceal the leadership of such men; but in truth the castle-establishments had little choice other than at best to harness the power of such men into the framework of their own authority, at worst to accept that they formed an alternative, and ultimately more effective, source of authority in the localities. We know little about the mechanisms of deference, control, and pressure exercised by such men, but we can guess—especially by combining the judicial and the poetic evidence—that tenancy, neighbourhood, kinship, marriage, sustenance, clientship, unofficial subsidies or *commorthau* ('commonly gathered by gentlemen . . . more for fear than love', as it was later declared), and service in a retinue (W. *plaid*) or on campaign were among the essential ingredients. The practice of fosterage was another vital force in binding together this society, and it was a practice which was all the more significant in that it was common for freemen to foster their children with bond families. In spite, therefore, of its divisions and inequalities Welsh society was intimately bound together at local and regional level under the leadership of the *uchelwyr*, by a combination of fear and favour, deference and obligation, intimacy and self-interest. The bonds of social cohesion in peace might also prove to be powerful and fundamental in rebellion.[48]

Such a society lay, almost by definition, beyond the ken of our casual English visitor, and even beyond the scrutiny of the local English administrative cadre. The latter would have recognized that the local Welsh community was often largely self-governing: it assessed and raised its own subsidies, shared out its own communal dues (often in the local church) among itself, appointed its own proctors to negotiate with the lord, secured its own charter of liberties, and declared and administered its own Welsh law in its own courts. So much might

indeed have been well enough known to the castle administration; but beyond these points of contact with English lordship, royal and seignorial, lay a 'private' world with its own customs, conventions, and personnel. This was a world of arbitrators and extra-curial settlements, quasi-professional experts in Welsh legal lore (W. *ynaid*), local wise men, elders, scholars (W. *ysgolheigion*), and medical men (W. *meddygon*). It was also a world where professional poets, minstrels, and prophets (W. *brudwyr*) were apprenticed in ancient lore and kept it vigorously alive, and where their work was supplemented (often to the disgust of their own professional standards) by more popular versifiers (W. *y glêr*). The castle establishment would have known that these 'rhymers and wasters', as Henry IV's legislation was to refer to them contemptuously, were frequently purveyors of sedition and idle day-dreams as well as of entertainment and flattery. More worryingly, they might have known that though the lord's proclamations were regularly announced in fairs, courts, and parish churches, there were alternative assemblies—commonly known in Welsh as *cymanfaoedd* or *dadleuoedd*—where the Welsh gathered, often on hilltops, to vent a mythology which was in its essence a challenge to all that English authority and governance stood for. There, so a report of almost two centuries later records,

their harpers and crowthers singe them songes of the doeings of theire auncesters, namelie, of theire wars againste the kings of this realme and the English nation, and then do they ripp upp theire petigres at length howe eche of them is discended from those theire ould princes. Here alsoe doe they spende theire time in hearinge some parts of the lives of Thalaassyn [Taliesin], Marlin Beno Prybbye [Myrddin pen beirdd], Jerue [? Iorwerth], and suche other the intended prophets and saints of that cuntrie.

It was a report which doubtless could have likewise been made in Owain Glyn Dŵr's day, for it referred to a mythology and aspirations which were apparently timeless in their appeal on Welsh society. This was part of the Wales which the English official traveller would barely have skirted on his tours or in his consciousness; it was a secret Wales which was yet at the very heart of the experience and vision of the poets and their patrons. Owain Glyn Dŵr and his like straddled these two worlds to a considerable degree. So long as they could do so, so long as there was a prospect that the two worlds might in some measure overlap, and preferably increasingly so, the tensions within Wales could be sustained. But the existence of two worlds, two peoples, and two sets of aspirations within one small community also had the potential for explosion.[49]

PEOPLES AND POWER

Wales in Owain Glyn Dŵr's day was a small and sparsely populated country; its total population, after the ravages of successive outbreaks of plague, is unlikely to have exceeded a quarter of a million, and it may have been even less. Yet, for all its smallness, it was a varied and complex society. If we are to understand the nature of the revolt which overwhelmed the country after 1400 and also the measure of resistance it met, we must make the effort to understand that society in all its complexity. Contemporary social and legal classifications may help us to do so. Two in particular stand out. The one was the almost universal distinction in medieval society between the free and the unfree. It was as prominent in Wales as elsewhere: it was fundamental to the great cadastral surveys of the period, recording in detail as they did the status and obligations of tenants; it permeated the language and assumptions of law and administration, and it was taken for granted—if only in the contempt that was normally shown towards the unfree—in the vernacular literature of the age. But it was also a distinction which, in Wales as in England, was appearing increasingly anachronistic, even irrelevant and indefensible. The same could be said to be true, but arguably less so, of a second fundamental legal classification that was particular to Wales, that between the English and the Welsh. It was a distinction which, to a greater or lesser degree, prevailed throughout much of Wales. In some places indeed it was formalized into a clear administrative division between two areas, the Englishry and the Welshry, as well as between two peoples.[1]

These twin contemporary socio-legal distinctions were certainly still important in Glyn Dŵr's Wales. Both had loud historical resonances in a custom-based society; both were bolstered by intense administrative and legal conservatism and by the conveniences of privilege; both reveal much of those perceptions and assumptions which are so important in the construction of social reality; and both were arguably a greater source of social tension now that they were so patently outdated. As such we will need to return to them in our portrait of Welsh society on the eve of the Glyn Dŵr revolt. But in composing such a portrait, and in particular in emphasizing the diversity of Welsh society, it may be more immediately rewarding to adopt an older and more flexible medieval

social classification, that between *potentes* and *pauperes*, between those who exercised power and lordship within society in varying degrees, and those who were, in equally varying measure, dependent on them and whose prime concern was the struggle for subsistence and survival. These were the men and women who composed the Wales of Owain Glyn Dŵr's day; it is through individual sketches of the lives of some of them that we can perhaps best reconstruct the complexity and diversity of their world.

Wales in the fourteenth century, much more so than most of contemporary England, was a land of large, compact territorial lordships (map 2). Their lords were the great lords of Wales. The greatest of them all was the king of England. In 1395 Richard II, as prince of Wales and earl of Chester, was direct lord of a good third of Wales—the five shires of the north and west (Anglesey, Caernarfonshire, Merioneth, Cardiganshire, and Carmarthenshire), which constituted the Principality of Wales strictly speaking, and the county of Flintshire which was administratively and judicially attached to the county of Chester. He had also secured control in 1390 of the two strategically important lordships of Pembroke and Haverford. This assemblage of lands was far and away the single largest consolidated bloc on the map of territorial power in the British Isles. Its potential was highly significant in terms both of Richard II's power and of the opportunities for local Welsh society. It looked in the 1390s as if that potential might be realized. Richard II was the first ruling king to visit Wales willingly, indeed to do so twice, since Edward I, albeit on both occasions (1394 and 1399) *en route* to Ireland. Furthermore, from 1397, through massive confiscation and the accidents of minorities, he secured control, direct or indirect, of much of the rest of Wales, amalgamated the Marcher lordships of the north-east into a new principality of Chester, and gave credence to rumours that he was restructuring his power-base to rule his kingdom from the west, notably from the twin principalities of Wales and Chester. Such a reordering could have profound repercussions for Welsh society as well as for Richard's power: it opened up the prospect of service and reward, and a measure of political significance, for the leaders of Welsh society such as they had not enjoyed since the days of Edward II. There are indeed signs that this was happening; it is little wonder that the poet referred, almost wistfully, to 'the days of Richard' (W. *dyddiau Rhisiart*) when his patrons had 'a proper job' and 'due standing' as defenders of society (W. *iawn waith, cyfion wart*). These were exciting days in Wales.[2]

The king shared the lordship of Wales with some of the greatest English aristocratic families of the day. Beyond the king's lands, the rest of Wales was divided into some forty Marcher lordships, four of which (Glamorgan, Brecon, Powys, and Denbigh) were each not much smaller than a small English county

and all of which were compact, large, and very powerful territorial units by contemporary English standards. In 1395 two English dukes (Gloucester and Lancaster) and seven earls (Arundel, Derby, March, Norfolk, Salisbury, Stafford, and Warwick) between them controlled most of those lordships, in number, wealth, and area. Two of them in particular stand out, because between them they held some nineteen Marcher lordships and drew an annual income in excess of £5,000 from Wales—at a time when £666 13s. 4d. was considered a sufficient minimum income level for an earl.

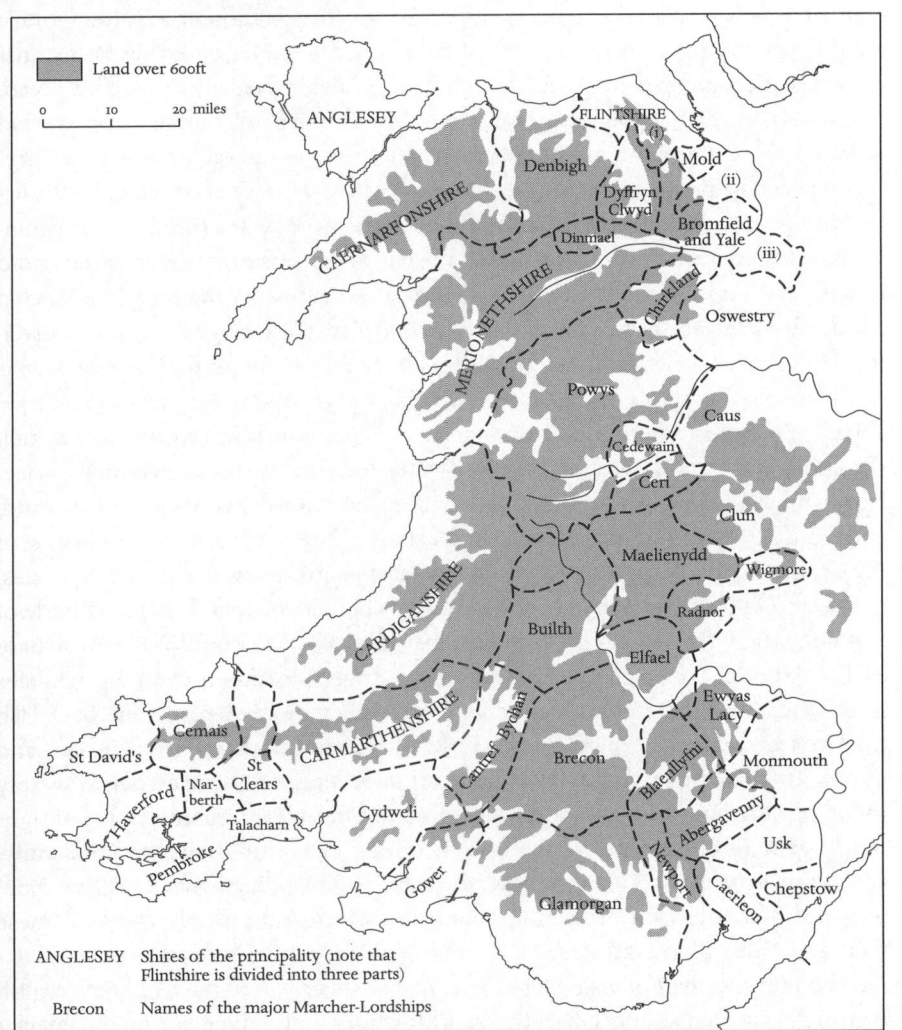

MAP 2. A fragmented country: the major administrative and lordship divisions of Wales *c.*1400

The first was Roger Mortimer, earl of March. His title was a singularly appropriate one; he stood head and shoulders above his fellow earls in the extent of his lands in Wales and the borders and in the proportion of his income he drew from them. His estates extended in fact right across the country—from Denbigh in the north to Usk in the south, from Ludlow and Wigmore in the eastern borderlands to Narberth in the far west. He secured possession of his inheritance, after a twelve-year minority, in 1393 and inaugurated his rule with a forty-day progress through his lands in Wales and the March. Expectations of him were high and he seemed to be well placed to meet them, for he was by all accounts a 'parfitt gentil knight', a doughty warrior, a lover of tournaments, and a noted dispenser of largess. Expectations were particularly high in Wales, especially among his own numerous tenantry. Here was a man who could be the focus of their service and worship, all the more so since he was lineally descended—albeit in the female line and at several generations' remove—from the native dynasty of Gwynedd. A lord in whose veins the blood of both Llywelyn Fawr and Edward III mingled might work wonders for Welsh morale. It comes as no surprise that he was the first English earl for whom a Welsh praise poem was written, by the poet Iolo Goch about 1395. We need not dismiss as mere poetic platitudes the greeting addressed to Earl Roger as 'chief lord' (W. *penarglwydd*), or the comment that he was 'very dearly beloved by the people' (W. *annwyl iawn wyd yn y wlad*). Nor was Mortimer apparently insensitive to such plaudits: genealogies which traced the history of the family back to Cadwaladr and so to Brutus were cultivated at Wigmore, and Roger himself was to show in Ireland that he was ready to adopt Irish customs and clothing. Here was a man who might channel the service, loyalty, and even the dreams of the Welsh. So it may well have appeared in 1395.[3]

Owain Glyn Dŵr might not have known the earl of March personally; he certainly knew the second greatest Marcher lord of the 1390s. Richard Fitzalan, earl of Arundel, was a generation older than Roger Mortimer, even though he took Mortimer's sister as his second wife. His military experiences went back to the late 1360s and were matched from 1380 by a tumultuous and bruising career in politics. His territorial interests were not as predominantly Marcher as were those of Mortimer; nor did he quite command the affection and expectations which gathered round the young earl of March. Yet throughout the 1380s and early 1390s he was, second to the king, the most commanding figure in Wales. He was lord of a huge bloc of lordships in north-eastern and central Wales (Bromfield and Yale, Chirkland, Oswestry, and Clun) which yielded him an annual income in themselves of well over £2,000; he was chairman of the highly effective consortium which administered the vast Mortimer inheritance during the years of custody, 1384–93; and he also held a third of the lordship of Abergavenny after the death of its lord in 1389. If to that are added the enormous cash assets inherited

by him from his father and the family's reputation for vigorous estate management and entrepreneurship, it is not difficult to see why he was such a towering, even menacing, figure in the England and Wales of his day. The status that Wales and its borderlands occupied in the earl of Arundel's affections and ambitions in those years was reflected in the attention he lavished on two of his castles there, Shrawardine in Shropshire and Holt, the headquarters of the lordship of Bromfield and Yale. He repaired the former, refurbished it lavishly, visited it frequently, and renamed it Castle Philippa in the 1390s in honour of his young new bride; the latter was his premier castle treasury in Wales and stood as a defiant symbol of his power in the area. Such a great lord had the means and the power to stamp his authority over a considerable part of Wales and to attract some of the local leaders of Welsh and border society, at least periodically, into his service. Owain Glyn Dŵr was one of them. What, however, must have been worrying for such men as the 1390s progressed was that the earl of Arundel's growing alienation from the royal court and its favours might not only blight their own careers but also endanger established power-structures and affiliations in the area generally.[4]

The personality, individual style, and policies of each of the great lords of Wales—of whom the king and the earls of Arundel and March were but the greatest—left their particular imprints on each of the individual lordships and shires of which Wales was composed. Lordship, it always needs to be remembered, was personal and individual. But over and above the personal and the individual, aristocratic lordship and local society, in Wales as elsewhere, also interacted in a variety of general ways. One was through the processes of exploitation and control. Lordship meant power over men, land, and resources; its effectiveness and its reputation, for good or ill, depended considerably on how that power was exercised.

Personality and power came together, interestingly, when the lord paid a personal visit to his estates—as did the earls of March and Derby to their Welsh lands in 1393 and 1397 respectively. Such a progress was an occasion for a visual display of both the genial and the authoritative faces of lordship, as the tenants, individually or communally, swore fealty to their new lord on his first entry to his lands; but profit came close on the heels of display, since the tenantry was expected to give a mise or gift (L. *donum*) of recognition to the lord on the same occasion. Seignorial progresses were, mercifully, rare in Wales; but seignorial control and power were recurrent facts of life for the peoples of Wales. Lordship was no less exacting for being an absentee lordship. The pre-eminent reminder of its power was the castle, now the seat of governance and control and only secondarily and very occasionally of military power. As the earl of Arundel's surveyor put it eloquently in describing Holt Castle in 1391, it was 'the common focus for the whole lordship, for it is to this castle that the whole lordship is

dependent, intendent and annexed as its principal seat'. The castle was the seat of the exchequer where local officials paid over the receipts from their bailiwicks and submitted their accounts twice yearly for scrutiny. Such accounts—with their array of respites and atterminations (instalment arrangements), their auditorial comments and warrants, and their punctilious lists of the transfer of moneys from local officials to the receiver and thence to the lord's central treasury—are the most eloquent comment on the persistent regularity of the lord's financial exploitation of his lands. When the auditors of the prince of Wales came to examine the accounts of his officials in Cheshire and Wales in 1400, it took them almost three months to complete their work; lordship was certainly thorough, even at a distance.[5]

The castle was also the seat of justice and discipline. At or near it—in the case of Holt, in front of the castle gate—were held the three-weekly courts and the six-monthly great courts at which the lord's officials brought the judicial and disciplinary powers of lordship down to bear on almost every aspect of the lives of the men and women of the lord's estates. Such minute and profitable control was periodically reinforced by judicial sessions held by the lord's justices in eyre, by a tourn or investigating commissions conducted by his chief steward, or by an inquisitorial visit by members of the lord's council. And at least once a lifetime the dues and obligations of every tenant were recorded in a detailed survey or extent of the lordship. The earl of Arundel had commissioned such surveys for each of his north-east Wales Marcher lordships in 1391–3. The minuteness with which these surveys—especially the great survey of Bromfield and Yale—list the obligations of tenants and assemble the seignorial decrees and court decisions which constituted important ground-rules for life in the lordship shows graphically how far the power of the lord penetrated into, and shaped, the lives of his tenants, or subjects as they might be more appropriately called. Lords were distant; lordship was not. The peace and equilibrium of society depended very considerably—and arguably more so in Wales than in England, because of the exclusive power of the great lords—on how sensitive such lordship was to the tolerable limits of exploitation, especially in a period of rapid social and economic change.[6]

Lordship had to be sensitive to its obligations as well as to its opportunities and power. Great lords, the king included, were the nodal points of power in the regionalized societies of Wales; but they were also expected to be, in person or by deputy, the focus of worship and service, reward and protection. Local leaders gravitated, and expected to gravitate, naturally into the orbit of such a great lord, to mediate his power in the locality, to partake of his patronage and support, and to find new avenues of reward and new opportunities through his service. Such lordship could also defuse, and arbitrate in, local disputes; it could prevent local

tyrannies and extortions from getting out of control. So it was, for example, that in the mid-1390s the earl of Arundel used his influence to support one of his Chirkland tenants, who was also dean of St Asaph, from being victimized by an over-powerful sheriff of Flintshire. That was good lordship in action, or so at least the dean of St Asaph would have seen it. Good lordship of this kind was crucial to the dynamics of local society, Welsh society included; that is why contempor-ary Welshmen were thrilled by the prospect of a powerful and open-handed young earl of March in the 1390s. Where such good lordship was lacking or deficient—be it through minority or a long widowhood or through a truculent and exploitative lord—then a dangerous vacuum of leadership and worship was created which other alternative forces might fill.[7]

Such a danger was particularly obvious in Wales where aristocratic lordship was too often foreign, absent, and, in every sense of the word, distant. A few of the smaller Marcher aristocratic families—the Greys of Ruthin, the Brians of Laugharne (who failed in the male line in 1390), or the Audleys of Cemaes and Llanymddyfri (who likewise failed in the male line in 1391)—may have visited their Welsh estates periodically; other individual magnates might have been attached to a particular residence in the eastern borderlands, as the duke of Gloucester was to Caldicot in the 1380s. But the earl of March, as was appropriate, was the only premier aristocrat who could be expected to spend a good propor-tion of his time in Wales and the English border counties. Earl Roger himself and his sister Elizabeth had been born in Usk, their brother and sister, Edmund and Philippa, at Ludlow, while it was at Denbigh that their father made his will in 1380. Even the Mortimers were increasingly less of a Marcher family than their forebears had been: Earl Edmund's (d. 1381) marriage had brought him exten-sive lands in England, especially in East Anglia, and it was in Ireland that he and his son were to spend much of their few active adult years. As for the king and the English aristocracy in general, their Welsh estates, though large and hugely profitable, were distant annexes of their English inheritances and peri-pheral to their main interest and to the web of their patronage, influence, and travels.

That need not, and by and large did not, cause problems in the governance of the lordships of Wales, at least in administrative terms. The estates of the great magnates were widely dispersed even within England, and many of those estates, likewise, were only infrequently visited by the lord in person. But a system of tight control and supervision, regular answerability by local officials, equally regular visits by auditors, central officials, and the lord's council, and the frequent dispatch of messengers, letters, and petitions all meant that estate policy was closely co-ordinated and directed. The Welsh lordships were part of this system. Its hub lay, ultimately, in the king's or the lord's council; its agents in, and to, the

locality were the lord's professional or quasi-professional officers. Formally at least, the governance of Wales lay very considerably in their hands.

Four such men—two clerics and two laymen—may be briefly introduced as representative of the effective governing class in Wales in the 1390s. It was to the clerics, as the literate élite, that the key financial offices—notably those of auditor, chamberlain, or receiver—fell; it was on their shoulders that much of the routine business of governance and supervision was placed, especially when the senior administrative post (justiciar or steward) was treated as a virtual sinecure; their reward often took the form of an ecclesiastical living in their lord's gift. Robert Eggerley was such a clerk. Born—or so at least his name suggests—on one of the earl of Arundel's manors in Shropshire, his talents commended themselves to the earl whom he served from at least the late 1380s, becoming his receiver for the lordships of Oswestry and, briefly, Chirk. Robert Eggerley's greatest service probably to the earl, and certainly to the historian, are the three surveys (especially the magnificent survey of Bromfield and Yale, extending to almost 180 beautifully written folios) of Arundel's north-eastern Marcher lordships for which he was primarily responsible during 1391–3. His reward was a series of ecclesiastical livings, including the Arundel benefice of West Felton, and a reputation as a financial manager which enabled him to pick up posts elsewhere after the execution of his first master in 1397. Eggerley operated essentially on a local stage, though on that stage his efficiency and conscientiousness were essential to the effective functioning of the earl of Arundel's lordship. Walter Brugge—whose path Robert Eggerley would almost certainly have crossed on several occasions—operated at a more exalted level. He was the receiver-general (that is, the chief financial officer) of the Mortimer estates, both while they were in custody in the 1380s and after Earl Roger assumed control of them in 1393. He knew, and was trusted by, some of the leading magnates of the day—including the duke of Clarence (whom he had served as receiver of Ulster), and the earls of Arundel, Gloucester, and March. We know more of his activities in minute detail than most seignorial officials in the fourteenth century, for his detailed and crabbed expense-accounts survive in considerable number. What they show above all is how he exhausted himself in the service of his masters, travelling from Ireland to East Anglia, from Denbigh to Canterbury ceaselessly. Much of his time was spent on the central affairs of the large Mortimer inheritance, but what is equally impressive is the detailed personal attention he gave to the accounts and affairs of every local lordship, those in Wales included. We can follow him and Thomas Hildeburgh, the auditor, for example, as they rode with a small escort of six men from Usk to Caerleon and thence, via Wigmore and Ludlow, to Montgomery and thereafter to farthest Denbigh in the closing

months of 1386. This was lordship by deputy; but even so it was a remorselessly thorough lordship. Walter Brugge was a man to be respected and feared wherever the earl of March had estates. He was also a man to be rewarded—with a glowing testimonial from Roger Mortimer, a prebend in St David's, and the archdeaconry of Meath in Ireland.[8]

Clerks were crucial in ensuring that lordship worked effectively and thoroughly at local level; but if an absentee royal and aristocratic lordship was to command respect it needed also to operate through powerful laymen. In Wales many such men, serving as justiciars or stewards (that is, the head of the local administration), were drawn from the ranks of the gentry of the English border counties. Such a one was John Skidmore (or Scudamore). By the 1390s he could certainly regard himself as one of the up-and-coming generation which was exercising power by proxy on behalf of great English magnate families in Wales. He was, successively, if not concurrently, deputy-steward of Ewyas and constable of Clifford for the Mortimers, steward of William Beauchamp in the lordship of Abergavenny, and constable and custodian of the Talbot lands at Castle Goodrich. Most significantly for the future, he had become Henry Bolingbroke's deputy-steward for his most important estate, the great lordship of Brecon, by 1393; and Bolingbroke's accounts make it clear that Skidmore was highly regarded by him. Most of Skidmore's important, and sometimes controversial, career lay in the future; but by any measurement of the realities of power he was already a towering figure in south-east Wales in the 1390s. It is, therefore, all the more intriguing that later tradition suggests—and there is no reason to doubt it—that he may already have taken to wife none other than Alice, the daughter of Owain Glyn Dŵr.[9]

Though Englishmen, especially from the border counties, held most of the top posts in the governance of Wales in the later fourteenth century, Welshmen were not totally excluded from holding office at that level. One such Welshman was Philip ap Morgan, whose career and connections straddle the two societies of which Wales was composed. Born into a native family in south-east Wales, and quite possibly a younger son, he chose a career in the service of his local lords, the Mortimers, becoming successively steward of the lordships of Usk, Clifford, and Denbigh and a very busy member of the earl of March's council in the 1390s. Here was a career which showed what doors of service could be opened to a talented Welshman by aristocratic lordship and how such service encompassed the whole of Wales (and frequent visits to Ireland and to various places in England) in its ambit. But there was another side to Philip ap Morgan's character. He was descended from the native Welsh dynasty of south-east Wales; his uncle was none other than Ifor ap Llywelyn, alias Ifor Hael, the munificent patron of the greatest Welsh poet of all time, Dafydd ap Gwilym. In terms of his

age and the geographical range of his activities in Wales, Philip's career, indeed, straddles the generation that separates Dafydd ap Gwilym from his greatest successor as poet, Iolo Goch. It may not be fanciful to suggest that Philip, who had been reared near Basaleg, one of the great literary centres of fourteenth-century Wales, and rose to be steward of Denbigh in distant north Wales, may have commissioned Iolo Goch, himself a Denbigh man, to compose the ode of praise to Roger Mortimer, earl of March and lord of both Philip and Iolo. Be that as it may, it is difficult to think of anyone in Wales in the 1390s whose career, in civilian terms at least, illustrates better the opportunities to which Owain Glyn Dŵr might have aspired; few men indeed could have provided a better insight into the Wales—indeed the several societies that were Wales—of those years.[10]

Philip ap Morgan, John Skidmore, Walter Brugge, Robert Eggerley, and their like exercised authority officially, and no doubt often officiously, on behalf of great English aristocratic lords. Theirs was power by temporary delegation and in respect of their official position; but it was real power for all that. Absentee lordship depended on the efficiency, honesty, and sensitivity of such men. The effectiveness of absentee lordship was more seriously threatened, and its working relationship with local society undermined, from two other directions. One was the habit of treating lordships, along with their offices and profits, as pawns on the board of political patronage and reward. Wales lent itself particularly well to such habits: the pawns of power there were large and profitable and the sinecure character of office in such a distant country readily conceded. So it was, for example, that the top post of justiciar of North Wales, with an annual fee of a hundred marks, was granted successively to the duke of Gloucester and the earl of Nottingham in the 1390s, with little prospect that either would serve in person. Many more local offices were likewise granted to royal and seignorial favourites and servants as rewards, and the income of estates was mortgaged for years to annuitants who did little more than send an attorney to collect the revenue due to them. In terms of the general reward system of medieval lordship, such practices are readily comprehensible: the prime purpose of any component part of a great inheritance was to provide its lord with the means to sustain himself and to promote his policies, of which the due reward of his followers was a major consideration. Nevertheless, such a patronage system, especially if it grew lop-sided, was in danger of diluting the bond between lord and local society; to do so could endanger the status of lordship itself.

The status of lordship was subject to a second danger—that of the erosion of its effective power by its own local, and locally entrenched, officialdom. Here, as with patronage, the difficulty was to strike a balance between necessity on the one hand and ultimate control on the other. Regular effective power in medieval society was largely local power; local power meant relying very considerably on

local men, almost always on local men who already enjoyed a standing in their own society. Particularly was this so in Wales. An essentially alien and absentee royal and aristocratic lordship depended for the weekly and monthly exercise of its powers of governance, justice, and revenue-raising on the services and co-operation of the leaders of the local Welsh communities. The price was the surrender of a proportion not only of the profits but also of the effective power of lordship into their hands. Periodic purges and fines could contain the process; but it was singularly difficult to strike a balance between alienating the leaders of the localities by denying them the authority and the profits which they regarded as their due on the one hand, and alienating the communities themselves by allowing them to fall under control of local officials who too often behaved as local tyrants on the other. The English lords themselves certainly recognized that the attitude of the local officials was crucial to the tranquillity, or otherwise, of Welsh society. One of their first acts on hearing the first murmur of discontent or rebellion was to bind over these officials as leaders of their communities in large sums for the good behaviour of their localities. Later Reginald Grey, lord of Ruthin and Dyffryn Clwyd, similarly acknowledged that the key to bringing the Welsh rebels to heel was the efforts and loyalty of local officers. It was a recognition that, powerful as was royal and aristocratic lordship in Wales, with its imposing superstructure of control, accountability, and audit and its un-doubted ability to extort large sums of money from the country, it was dependent for its authority and effectiveness on local power-brokers and power structures, over which its control was limited.[11]

Wales was a land of powerful royal and aristocratic lordship, all the more impressive and powerful because it operated within large and exclusive territorial blocs. Yet kings and nobles did not enjoy a monopoly of power over local society; they shared it with others. Indeed in much of English-settled Wales the pattern of the distribution of lordship and power was not very dissimilar to that to be found in contemporary England. Such a pattern may be more difficult to detect in Wales because the documentation is much more unforthcoming than in England; but that such a pattern prevailed in the lowlands of Gwent, Glamorgan, southern Gower, and southern Pembroke and in some of the eastern valleys of Wales, notably those of the rivers Usk, Wye, Monnow, and Severn, hardly admits of doubt. Here, as we have already seen, was a world and a society which a traveller from midland and southern England would not have found unfamiliar.

His problem, as it is ours, was by what term he should identify these lesser lords. In the contemporary documentation he would have found that feudal terminology—'barons', 'knights', 'mesne lords'—still survived, and appropriate-ly so in the March of Wales where feudal institutions had a longer life and

meaningfulness than they had in England. But feudal terminology was restricting and inappropriate. So it was that more generalized terms—'major tenants' and 'gentlemen'—were beginning to come into use. The latter term, gentlemen (L. *gentiles homines*, Fr. *gentils*), especially as its usage is associated with changes in official status-designations, comes close to the generic term which recent historians of late-medieval England have chosen to adopt for this group of lesser lords, the gentry. Lesser lords they certainly were, in wealth and status, compared with great noblemen such as the earls of Arundel and Mortimer; yet within their own ranks there were vast disparities in power, wealth, and social importance. So it is that English historians have been driven to classify the gentry or lesser lords into two broad categories—greater and lesser gentry or, alternatively, county and parish gentry.[12]

Such a distinction would certainly be likewise applicable to the English-settled lowlands of Wales. On his journey our traveller had called at Coety Castle, the home of Sir Lawrence Berkerolles. The size and opulence of the castle would of themselves have indicated that Sir Lawrence belonged to the higher gentry, at the very least. This could have been confirmed by the fact that his lordship was titled a barony, was held with 'royal liberty', and brought him in an annual income of at least £90. There was a world of difference between Sir Lawrence and the owner of the single manor of Bryndu (Brecon), whose wealth extended no further than a well-endowed home-farm, manorial buildings, and a rent roll of 30s. per annum. A further distinction between greater and lesser gentry was important in Wales. The latter's base and importance was limited and local; the former often had estates, often more-lucrative estates, in England or even (especially in the case of leading Pembrokeshire families) in Ireland. This meant that the social and marital orbit and connections, and often the prime residence, of many of the greater English gentry of Wales lay in England. In terms of power and leadership, and the interaction of both with local society, this was of no small significance: the greater gentry as well as the great Marcher lords were often distant—geographically, culturally, and in social orientation—from the societies in which they exercised lordship. Thus the Devereux and Waldeboef families regarded their lands in Brecon as outliers of their Herefordshire estates; the Carews, Roches, and Wogans had wide-ranging connections in Ireland; while many of the families of the rich Vale of Glamorgan and Gower, such as Sully and Umfraville, forged marriages and built estates across the Bristol Channel in the west country.[13]

Two of the representatives of these greater English gentry families of south Wales in the 1390s were the Stradlings and the St Johns, both of them to figure among the dominant families of the Vale of Glamorgan for generations to come. The Stradlings were to weave a web of great and bogus antiquity around the

origins of their family; in fact they had arrived in England only in the late thirteenth century in the train of one of Edward I's Savoyard companions. From the very first generation of their arrival in Britain, their territorial fortunes and residential habits, like that of so many Glamorgan families, straddled the Bristol Channel, from St Donat's in Glamorgan to Combe Hawey in Somerset. The head of the family in the last decade of the fourteenth century, Sir Edward Stradling, greatly enhanced its territorial power in Glamorgan by marriage to Sir Lawrence Berkerolles's sister and co-heiress; but it is the careers of two of his grandsons which perhaps best exemplify on what a broad stage the English greater gentry in Wales conducted their lives. The eldest, John, married into and inherited the estates of the Dauntsey family in Wiltshire, which henceforth became his home; the next son, Edward, kept his estates and interests in Glamorgan, and held key offices in the Principality and March, but his horizons and ambitions reached much further, for he served, for example, as sheriff of Dorset and Somerset, and took to wife Joan, the natural daughter of the immensely powerful Henry Beaufort, bishop of Winchester. The Stradlings must frequently have rubbed shoulders with their neighbour, Sir John St John of Fonmon. The St Johns were an old eastern Glamorgan family and Sir John certainly took his duties in the governance of his home district seriously. By the late 1390s he was sheriff of Glamorgan and steward of Gower; later he was to become steward of the Mortimer lordship of Usk. In resisting the Welsh rebels and in effecting the pacification of the country, Sir John, like many of his class, was to play a vital role in south Wales, from Chepstow to Gower. But Wales and its affairs only consumed part, and a diminishing part, of his time and interest; his ambitions and horizons were much broader. He had gained unwelcome attention at an early age by killing the young earl of Pembroke in a tournament in 1389; he was a confidant and leading counsellor of the Mowbrays; and he was to seek to promote his career by becoming a knight of Richard II's household. His marriage likewise reinforced his links with this wider English world: his wife was a Northamptonshire widow, and in respect of her estates he entered into Northamptonshire society serving as the county's member of parliament on four occasions after 1410 and giving distinguished service for years as mayor of Bordeaux.[14]

There were many families like the Stradlings and the St Johns in southern and eastern Wales. A few were richer; many more were poorer; all shared the view that they were lords (a title which they frequently gave themselves) and part of an *immigré* gentry class. Some of them could plausibly trace their ancestry back to the camp-followers of the earliest Norman lords of Wales; many others had arrived from England much more recently, through the routes of marriage or royal or seignorial service. In their castles and moated manor houses they lived a

life which was socially and culturally very little different from their peers in England; they moved easily and comfortably in the social and political circles of English county and court society; the doors of service and reward to kings and great magnates were open to them. They intermarried with other settler familes in Wales and with their social peers in England. A few of them had certainly married into Welsh famlies; but the days when this became a common pattern and when the English gentry families in Wales—the Stradlings of St Donat's and the St Johns of Fonmon among them—patronized Welsh bards and cultivated Welsh antiquities largely lay in the future. As yet they were still proudly immigrant families or, as later genealogists were to call them, *advenae*. In wealth, life-style, social and cultural assumptions, and even political aspiration theirs was a very different world from that of most of Wales, even from the world of the majority of the native Welsh 'gentry'. Yet in any balanced portrait of Wales's society in Glyn Dŵr's day, we must assuredly not overlook them.

The group that came closest to the greater and lesser gentry of English Wales in the range of their connections and in their outlook, though not in their social and economic status, were the richer merchants of the Welsh boroughs. The towns of Wales were for the most part too small and the range of their activities too limited for a substantial urban élite to emerge in them. It is true that in most towns there was an identifiable superior group of burgesses, holding houses and land by burgage tenure and often investing in the agricultural exploitation of the town's hinterland. Robert Parys of Caernarfon and Richard Golding of Beaumaris—both of whom were to be deeply involved in the defence of their respective towns during the Glyn Dŵr revolt—belonged to the higher echelons of this group. But it is only in a few of the older, richer, and more populous towns of south Wales that we can find a mercantile élite, whose members' capital assets and geographical range of activities might be said to give them substantial power in Welsh society. Such men were Thomas Rede of Carmarthen and John Owen of Kidwelly. Thomas Rede's career illustrates vividly how much the world of the English communities of southern lowland Wales was one and how easily that world, as in the case of the greater gentry, merged economically, socially, and administratively with a wider English world. Born almost certainly to a marriage which bonded together two English settler families in Roche in furthest Pembrokshire and Kidwelly, his own career and business interests stretched from Carmarthen to Bristol. It was in Bristol, appropriately enough, that he made his will, but in the church of St Peter's at Carmarthen that he decreed that he should be buried. He had almost certainly received at least a smattering of legal education, for he was appointed to several posts which required legal expertise. His administrative skills were clearly considerable and were widely appreciated: he was by turn steward of lordships from Pembroke to Usk and deputy-justiciar of

the southern Principality for varying periods between 1381 and 1400. In these offices he would have been in touch with many of the key men in south Wales in these years. Among them would have been Sir David Hanmer, himself justiciar of South Wales in 1381, a future justice of the King's Bench and father-in-law of Owain Glyn Dŵr. Thomas Rede may have made much of his money out of law and administration; but with his base at Carmarthen he was probably also an active trader. That he was rich is certainly not in doubt; he was able to lend 100 marks to Henry IV on one of his expeditions in Wales and later he raised, with a Welshman, £400 for the defence of his home town of Carmarthen. Rede would have certainly been well acquainted with John Owen of Kidwelly, whose credentials as a long-distance merchant are beyond doubt. John Owen towered over his fellow burgesses in the little town of Kidwelly. He had cornered some of the most lucrative leases in the area—such as those of the local mills and pasturelands—for himself. But what gives his career a more than local significance was his role as a major exporter of wool in south Wales. In the 1390s he was exporting as much as fifty sacks annually (worth some £450) through the Carmarthen staple. By any definition he was a man of power in the local economy and society. When Glyn Dŵr whipped the Welsh into revolt it was to men such as Sir Edward Stradling and Sir John St John, and to well-heeled burgesses and merchants such as Thomas Rede and John Owen, that the English government would turn for assistance to quell the rebellion.[15]

John Owen and Thomas Rede, Sir Edward Stradling and Sir John St John were undoubtedly men of power and wealth. Indeed in terms of the control of rich agricultural land, flourishing regional and national trade, and liquid assets they and their like accounted for a very large, and quite disproportionate, share of the wealth and power of Wales. Disproportionate, because in geographical terms their power extended over a fairly small—albeit exceptionally fertile and economically developed—part of the country, notably southern Wales. In the rest of Wales local power resided in the hands of native Welsh gentry, the *uchelwyr*. There were, of course, continuities and overlaps between these two worlds of local power and there was much that was common to the exercise and manifestation of domination and authority in both worlds. It was to be at the gentry level that social and cultural ties between the peoples of the two worlds were to be forged earliest; but for most purposes the world of the Welsh *uchelwyr* was still a private, ingrown world, of which we get only an occasional, if distorted, glimpse through the corpus of vernacular poetry and some caches of family deeds.

Social observers, both English and Welsh, frequently noted that the Welsh rated lineal descent more highly than wealth. There was considerable truth in this observation. Descent and gentility (W. *ach, bonedd, gwaedoliaeth dda*) were of

the essence of nobility in Welsh society; they were, in the famous words of an Elizabethan antiquary, 'a great heartsease', not least of course to impoverished families. In an intensely conservative and past-oriented society, the power of genealogy and the legitimist claims which accompanied it should never be under-rated. The poets, themselves skilled and professional genealogists, saw to it that they were not. In fact almost all the *uchelwyr* families of Wales in Owain Glyn Dŵr's day could spin a genealogical descent which made their English immigrant peers appear as latter-day *arriviste* families. Yet images, whether self-created or externally promoted, cannot keep reality at bay indefinitely. Impeccable noble descent was a necessary, but not of itself a sufficient, guarantee of power even in native Welsh society; were it to be so, power would be so widely shared and fragmented that it would forfeit its potency. Power came, or came additionally and necessarily, from elsewhere.

It came considerably, and inevitably in a landed society, from land and control of men and women who lived on the land. Native Wales was certainly an impoverished society compared with contemporary England; in terms of the distribution of landed or of taxable wealth it did not have the wide range and gradations which characterized English society or even lowland Anglicized society in Wales; its practice of partibility of inheritances between male heirs, its extremely restrictive practices in terms of the sale or alienation of land *inter vivos*, and the absence (in legal theory, if not always in actual practice throughout Wales) of the possibility of the transfer of land by or through women (and in particular through marriage) closed the avenues for estate — and capital — accumulation which were so central to the establishment and augmentation of the wealth and power of the nobility and gentry in medieval England. Yet in spite of its undoubted comparative poverty and the relatively narrow band of its distribution of territorial wealth, native Welsh society was far from being a society of equals; it was in fact, as is often the case with traditional societies, a strongly hierarchic and deferential society. Families and individuals stood out in wealth and eminence; they thereby exercised power and leadership over local society.

Two such individuals in north Wales in the 1390s, certainly known to Owain Glyn Dŵr though both senior to him in years, were Hywel ap Tudur and Gruffudd ap Gwilym. Hywel ap Tudur conformed well with the paradigm of a Welsh *uchelwr*. He could trace his genealogy back effortlessly to the tenth-century king, Hywel Dda (the Good), and from there of course it was a small matter to traverse the centuries and millennia to Adam; he belonged to a large brood, whose male members pushed and shoved their way into the limelight of power in north-east Wales in the fourteenth century. By the 1390s Hywel ap Tudur stood out as undoubted leader in this society in at least three respects. First, in territorial wealth: Hywel's father had been a land-purchaser on a large

scale, often buying out impoverished kinsmen and neighbours; Hywel's own estates were to be valued at £30, which made him the wealthiest landowner in Flintshire by far and would rank him as an English gentleman of sound, if not spectacular, means. Secondly, he had held important offices in his shire—coroner of Engelfield and even sheriff of Flintshire in 1390–1. Finally, he was a man not afraid of throwing his weight around—attacking his neighbours with a large retinue, staging a dramatic scene when the justice of Chester held his sessions in Flintshire in 1394, and being dispatched to the Tower of London in May 1396, along with eleven others, to cool off his heels. Hywel ap Tudur was a name on everyone's lips in north-east Wales in the 1390s; no one could be in any doubt that he was, for good or ill, one of the most powerful men in the area. Gruffudd ap Gwilym (ap Gruffudd ap Heilin) does not appear to have shared Hywel ap Tudur's buccaneering spirit; but his territorial power was broader-based than that of Hywel. His ancestral family lands, like those of Hywel, were in Flintshire, but he had acquired lands also in Dyffryn Clwyd, Caernarfonshire, and Anglesey. In short, his estates lay astride the whole of north Wales. Even more significant for the future was the way those estates had been assembled: some by direct male inheritance, but most by routes which had until recently been denied to Welshmen—through his mother and his wife, both of whom were substantial heiresses. His landed wealth can be gauged by the fact that his son's estates in Anglesey and Caernarfonshire alone yielded rents of £112 annually, making him the richest Welshman in north Wales and putting him in income terms in the same rank as the greater gentry of English county society. His son, already during his father's lifetime, was sheriff of Anglesey in 1396: that was no more than an official acknowledgement of the power that he and his father wielded in local society.[16]

What is clear from the careers of Hywel ap Tudur and Gruffudd ap Gwilym and their companions was that in the Wales of Owain Glyn Dŵr territorial wealth brought power in native society and, more significantly, that for two or three generations some families had been consolidating their position, and thereby their opportunity to dominate local society, through practices which would eventually transform the distribution of territorial wealth in Welsh society. Kinsmen were quit-claiming their lands (doubtless in return for a consideration) to a single individual: it was two such quit-claims in 1311 and 1377 which ensured that the lands which Gruffudd ap Gwilym held *en bloc* were not fragmented between his relatives. The prohibition on any permanent alienation of Welsh land was being regularly circumvented, for a price, by the device known as Welsh mortgage (W. *prid*): it was extensive use of this device which had enabled Hywel ap Tudur's father to assemble his estate, which in its turn allowed his son to strut so domineeringly on the stage of Flintshire society. Finally, the acceptance that land could descend to and through females introduced the concepts of the

dowager and the heiress to Welsh society and were ultimately to be among the most potent solvents of its traditional territorial order. Gruffudd ap Gwilym's wealth and status—based very considerably on the landed fortunes of his mother and his wife—bore eloquent testimony to that fact.[17]

Power came from land; but it also came from, and was expressed in, military leadership. The two were, indeed, often twinned, as they were in English society. Welsh free and noble society had a strong militarist tradition; its leaders clung to that tradition in the age of Owain Glyn Dŵr. The effigies of Owain's contemporaries—some of them to be his future companions in rebellion—were overwhelmingly military; next to the purity of their lineage, it was their military prowess which earned the plaudits of the poets. Wales had produced its fair share of military heroes during the wars of Edward III—Sir Rhys ap Gruffudd, Sir Hywel y Fwyall ('of the Axe'), and Sir Gregory Sais among them; it was important that it should continue to do so. In a militarist society success in war and public acknowledgement of that success (in rewards, pensions, titles) was vital to its self-esteem; without them warriors grew restless. In north Wales in the 1390s the onus for sustaining this military self-esteem fell very considerably on the shoulders of Rhys and Gwilym ap Tudur, cousins of Owain Glyn Dŵr through their mother (Table 3 p. 209). Their genealogical credentials for leadership were impeccable: they were lineal descendants of Ednyfed Fychan, the steward of Llywelyn the Great, prince of Gwynedd (d. 1240), and could be regarded as the senior members of the greatest extended noble clan in fourteenth-century Wales. Their territorial and official position in north-west Wales, especially in Anglesey, was also impressive. But what was most distinctive about them was their exceptional record of military service and leadership. They first appear at the muster of the large retinue that the Black Prince assembled at Northampton in September 1369 for service in Gascony; they led the force of 120 archers from Caernarfon to guard the southern English coast from anticipated French attack in 1386; they accompanied Richard II with an even larger force of Welsh archers to Ireland in 1394; and so sterling were their military qualities that they were both retained for life with the king in 1398 and rewarded with an annuity of £10 apiece. Their next appearance was to be the sensational capture of Conway Castle by them on 1 April 1401.[18]

In the analysis of social power and the ties of loyalty, the significance of military leadership should not be underestimated. It reinforced the standing and power of men who already regarded themselves as leaders in the locality (the obstreperous Hywel ap Tudur ab Ithel led the Flintshire contingent to defend the English coasts in 1386); it bound leaders and followers together in a sense of shared camaraderie, which could do good service at home as well as on expedition; it hugely broadened the horizons and experience of a society which was

otherwise ingrown and inward-looking; and it provided an outlet for men whose opportunities for adventure, promotion, and profit at home were very limited. In these respects military service and leadership were proportionately more important to the well-being of Welsh than they were to contemporary English society, other, significantly, than to the men of Cheshire. The opportunities were still there in the 1380s and 1390s—on garrison duty in Berwick, on expeditions to Scotland and Ireland, on the defence of the English coast, and even on periodic forays in the Channel or on the Continent. But war, especially after the truce with France in June 1389, was not what it had been, nor were war profits and honours to be compared with those of former days. That was bad news for a military-oriented society.

Men who were important in lineage, land, and war leadership almost inevitably cornered the important posts in the governance, be it in the name of the king or of a great English aristocrat, of their local societies. To note only briefly the offices held by some of the men mentioned in the last few paragraphs immediately confirms this truism: Rhys ap Tudur was on occasion sheriff and escheator of Anglesey, Gruffudd ap Gwilym's son was likewise sheriff of the same county, while the rumbustious Hywel ap Tudur rose to be sheriff of Flintshire before his hot temper brought his official career to a temporary close. Lists of appointments to offices are, in fact, one of the few barometers the historian has for gauging the importance of these local men; but such lists are tantalizing and even misleading. Offices conferred some power, and certainly respectability, on those who held them; but in local society they more often than not confirmed power which these men already exercised, and simply added to it the veneer of official responsibilities. Their official accounts will inform us of the discharge of their official duties; but rarely will they reveal the extent and mechanics of their actual power in society. That can only be very spasmodically glimpsed through the charges, exaggerated as they are, which were periodically brought against them. Local office in Wales, as in England, was overwhelmingly in the hands of local men, often indeed held at farm (that is, on a lease for a number of years) so that the official had an added reason for wielding his authority to maximum effect, for he would be the beneficiary of his own efforts. But in one respect Wales was different from England: the highest posts—the justiciarship and chamberlainship in the Principality, the posts of steward and receiver in the Marcher lordships, and very often the shrievalties and constableships of castles in both—were very rarely filled by Welshmen. That was a fact of life; but a local-governmental system in which the key posts are out of bounds to the actual leaders of local society is a system which invites criticism and resentment. It is a system which can cultivate the mentality of the excluded, the *exclus*.

Such a mentality is all the more likely to develop where there is a disjunction between the cultural world and norms of the privileged and those of the ex-

cluded. Such in a measure was true of Wales. The ingredients of local power mentioned so far—lineage, land, military leadership, local office—were the very stuff of power in local English society likewise; but in terms of their cultural orientation the leaders of local Welsh society still dwelt in a largely different world. By no means all the Welsh *uchelwyr* were patrons of the poets or discriminating collectors of Welsh manuscripts or devotees of Welsh law; but they lived in a society where such attributes were considered to be virtues in the well-bred noble freeman. The Welsh *uchelwyr* readily and successfully made all sorts of compromises with the world of their English kings and lords and often exulted in the opportunities it offered them; but they also lived in a world whose mythology and literary and legal traditions made a very different set of claims on their affections and aspirations. Treading a *via media* between these two worlds, and choosing the appropriate priorities between them, could not always have been easy.

One who trod it with apparent success was Rhydderch ab Ieuan Llwyd, an elder contemporary of Owain Glyn Dŵr and almost certainly known to him, if only because both had lands in Cardiganshire and both were patrons of the poet Iolo Goch. A man of princely descent (the Lord Rhys of Deheubarth was his forebear) and of military experience, Rhydderch conformed with the paradigm of the Welsh *uchelwr*. But it is two other features of his career which particularly merit attention here. First, he rose to eminence in the governance of his county, serving as deputy justiciar and holding the county courts and the sessions in the 1380s—clearly a man who was trusted. Secondly, he came of a family which was quite exceptional for its patronage of, and expertise in, Welsh literary and legal lore; Rhydderch made his own distinctive contribution to this tradition and also transmitted it to the next generation. He was known to be exceptionally knowledgeable in Welsh law and was professionally employed by the Crown for his expertise therein; he continued the family tradition of commissioning collections of Welsh literary antiquities, and was almost certainly the man for whom *Llyfr Gwyn Rhydderch* (the White Book of Rhydderch)—one of the cardinal collections of medieval Welsh religious and secular prose—was written; and he was the most renowned, munificent, and catholic patron of poets in west Wales in the fourteenth century. Here was a man whose family library contained a veritable golden treasury of Welsh prose tales, poetry, devotional works, and native law and whose discriminating connoisseurship of these works was fully acknowledged by his contemporaries. Rhydderch's library put him fully in touch with a remarkably resilient and conservative native lore; but he also lived successfully in the present. His death in 1398/9 meant that he escaped the dilemma of having to make a choice between the two worlds which he appears to have straddled so effortlessly.[13]

Hopcyn ap Tomas ab Einion of Ynys Forgan in the lordship of Gower did not enjoy the luxury of such an escape route, and in any case appears to have been altogether a more troubled soul than Rhydderch. The two men shared much in common in respect of their love and cultivation of the arts: both were outstanding patrons of the poets; both were recognized as being exceptionally widely read and, as was said of Hopcyn, 'father(s) of the great good art of poetry': both were great collectors of a wide variety of vernacular manuscripts; and both may between them have commissioned the compiling of the two fundamental collections of Welsh medieval literary texts—*Llyfr Gwyn Rhydderch* and the even more remarkable and comprehensive *Llyfr Coch Hergest* (the Red Book of Hergest), written quite probably in the closing years of the fourteenth century at Hopcyn's request. But in spite of these similarities it is Hopcyn's literary tastes which are arguably the more significant, if only because they open a window on to a world where the cultivation of a literary and historical past intersected with present and future political aspirations and programmes. Hopcyn was a conservative who drew his inspiration from the past: it was the treachery of men of a distant and mythological past, such as Vortigern and Medrawd, which exercised his mind, and it was in the conservative, even archaic, format of the *awdl* that the poets addressed him. But his eyes were also on the future: he owned copies of Welsh prophetic tracts (W. *daroganau*) and it was as a 'master of brut', an acknowledged expert in the interpretation of the prophecies, that he was to be consulted by Owain Glyn Dŵr in 1403. Hopcyn ap Tomas was at ease with the past and the future; it was with the present that he was out of sorts, and it was his scribe who in a justly famous passage bemoaned 'the pain and deprivation and the exile' which the Welsh suffered in their own land. It is a reminder that the greatest chasm between the worlds of the Welsh *uchelwyr* and the English gentry of Wales lay, or could lie, in their interpretations of the past and the future. It is in men's minds and hearts that worlds are created and re-created.[20]

The *uchelwyr* dominated the local and regional societies of much of Wales; on that score the opinions of external observers and the native poets coincide. To the former they were 'the great ones of the country', 'those who are men of position', 'the great men of north Wales', 'so powerful that no man dared indict them'; to the latter they were the men who exercised 'lordship' (W. *arglwyddiaeth*) and were the natural 'governors of their districts' (W. *llywiawdwr ardal*). By contemporary English standards many of them were backwoods and impoverished squireens; but in their own eyes and those of their neighbours they were men of enviable means and status. Their 'whitewashed halls' (W. *neuaddau calchaidd*) and individual chambers stood in stark contrast to the miserable dwellings of the peasantry; so did their wealth in worldly goods—such as the two silver cups, twelve silver spoons, a chalice, a vestment, a book, and a chessboard

complete with a set of chessmen which were mentioned in an inventory of the goods of a Flintshire gentleman. This superiority was also expressed in an obligatory munificence: the poet's compliment to Rhys ap Tudur and his brothers as 'giants of wine' (W. *cewri'r gwin*) was matched more prosaically by Adam of Usk's characterization of one of Owain Glyn Dŵr's early supporters, Llywelyn ap Gruffudd Fychan of Caio, as 'a man of gentle birth and bountiful, who yearly consumed sixteen tuns of wine in his household'. Divided as they often were by bitter and violent quarrels, they yet shared a common set of values and aspirations. Furthermore, their sense of self-importance and of exclusiveness was fostered by a network of marriage links which encompassed a good part of Wales within their ambit: Goronwy ap Tudur of Anglesey, for example, had chosen a wife from the border lordship of Chirkland, while Owain Glyn Dŵr's mother came from southern Cardiganshire. The *uchelwyr* could with some justice claim that most of Wales was their parish and that they were its ruling class, whatever the administrative records might proclaim. Nor did their superiority end with life, for their effigies—such as that constructed at Llanuwchllyn (Merionethshire) in the 1390s, in memory of Ieuan ap Gruffudd ap Madog—were calculated to memorialize their apartness and superiority in death.[21]

In life that superiority was manifested in a variety of ways, both menacing and genial. In its genial aspect it included the support and protection of their tenants and dependants: Tudur ap Goronwy and his sons were fulsomely greeted as 'providers of two hundred households' (W. *cynheiliaid deucan aelwyd*) and as men who ensured that the title of the humble to their land was not unjustly challenged or the poor outlawed. Such claims need not be cynically dismissed: in a patriarchal and deferential society the protection of the powerful was the best bulwark against more-menacing local tyrannies. So it was that affiliations—what would have been known in contemporary Ireland as lineages—gathered around these local leaders; they were composed, as one poet put it, of 'kinsmen and friends' (W. *ceraint, carwyr*), supplemented no doubt, more or less willingly, by tenants and neighbours. And, as in England, affections and dependence were fortified by the distribution of liveries to these followers. The poetry recorded the genial and cosy aspects of such domination; the judicial records show how easily it could be abused—for the maintenance of quarrels and the perversion of justice, for the promotion of private vendettas, and above all for the extortion of illegal aids (W. *commorthau*) in money, corn, or wool from tenants and dependants. This was a stratum of power which was overlaid by that of royal and aristocratic lordship; but to the Welsh peasantry it was the more immediate and direct source of power and obligations as it was also the source of loyalty and leadership. The men who exercised such power were indeed 'the great ones of the country'. Owain Glyn Dŵr was certainly one such man, and if his protest was to bear any fruit it had to

operate along the power channels already familiar to, and well cultivated by, his fellow *uchelwyr*.[22]

The lay lords of Wales—king, great English magnates, greater and lesser gentry, English and Welsh—shared their power over society with the Church. The power of the Church, like that of lay society, was vested in a wide range of institutions, offices, and individual appointments—bishoprics, cathedral chapters, collegiate churches, archdeaconries, parish churches, monasteries, and friaries, to name but the most obvious categories. As in lay society, so again in the Church, land was one major source of power. By the standards of the contemporary English Church, the Welsh Church was poorly endowed: three of the four Welsh bishoprics were 'worth together only about as much as the poorest English bishopric; the total income of all the Welsh abbeys was less than that of the single house of Glastonbury; and three-quarters of the beneficed clergy received less than £10 a year'. But standards of poverty and wealth are, of course, relative; in terms of the general standards of income and wealth in Wales the Church was certainly not poor. The bishopric of St David's, admittedly far and away the richest Welsh see, had a landed annual income of almost £500 and large and valuable estates throughout its extensive diocese; even the modest territorial income of the bishopric of St Asaph enabled its lord bishop to maintain a household and a living standard which prompted the poet, Iolo Goch (more familiar with the more modest standards of his lay patrons), into paeans of ecstasy. Of monastic houses, those of the Cistercians certainly figured in the premier league of wealth in Wales: several of them had an income well above that of most of the Welsh bishops, while the nine southern Cistercian houses alone controlled well in excess of 40,000 acres of land (exclusive of rough mountain pasture or waste). The Church's power in Welsh society came also from other sources, notably from its spiritualities, particularly its very substantial income from tithes and appropriated churches. Thus the income of the bishopric of St Asaph from its spiritual revenues in 1389 was estimated at £280 per annum.[23]

The Church's power came in good measure from its wealth and in the control over men and resources that came in the wake of such wealth. But its power came also, and arguably more importantly, from other, much less measurable, sources. Two in particular may be briefly mentioned. First, it provided in its personnel, from bishop to parish priest, the literate and articulate élite within contemporary society. This élite commanded the sacramental and disciplinary powers of a universal Church; its leaders had the training and outlook to bring the values and norms of a wider world to bear on the local concerns and power-structures of Wales. Secondly, the centrality of the Church at a local level in the

social relationships and moral disciplines of society gave it a focal role in the life of the community. It was in or near the local church that contracts were made, proclamations declaimed, community-dues divided, official letters read, games played, and oaths sworn; it was the Church's ministers who often composed quarrels, drew up contracts, baptized children, solemnized marriages, and in general proclaimed and enforced a code of personal and social morality by which the community was expected to live. In any analysis of power in contemporary society the Church's role—ultimately founded as it was on a theology of judgement and salvation—should in no way be underestimated, least of all for not being measurable. In any challenge to the existing pattern of authority, the lead and the leadership of the Church would be crucial. It was not fortuitous that Owain Glyn Dŵr had taken the dean of St Asaph along with him to the meeting at which he was to be proclaimed prince of Wales.

But the Church in Wales could not be expected to speak with a single voice, since, like the rest of Welsh society, it belonged to a greater or lesser degree to two different worlds. One world turned primarily in the orbit of the king of England, the archbishop of Canterbury, and the English magnates and gentry who controlled so much of lowland Wales. Of the sixteen bishops appointed to sees in Wales between 1372 and 1400 only one was a Welshman; the rest were men who had distinguished themselves in the service of the king or, occasionally, the pope and for whom a see in Wales was patently a reward for service rendered, or to be rendered, elsewhere. Thus the bishop of St Asaph 1390–5 was a former royal confessor (Alexander Bache) and his colleague in Llandaff 1393–5 the king's medical adviser (Tideman of Winchcombe); while the premier see of St David's was occupied 1389–97 by the long-serving John Gilbert, treasurer of England and a highly experienced diplomat. Even more demoralizing for the career prospects of native Welsh clerics was the way in which many of the senior positions in the Church, especially those which could be held in plurality—notably canonries in cathedrals, prebends in collegiate churches, and the rectories of some of the more profitable churches—were reserved for royal or aristocratic clerks. An occasional explosion of anger showed how much such promotions were resented in native society. In 1390, during a vacancy in the see of St Asaph, the archbishop of Canterbury was unwise enough to foist an English clerk, one William Brown, on the church of Llanrwst; the local Welsh leaders were outraged and peremptorily expelled him and seized his goods. Two of those involved in the attack were Rhys Gethin and his brother, Hywel Coetmor; the tomb of the latter (in which he is styled as *armiger*, esquire) still reclines in Llanrwst church, proclaiming to all his sense of status and proprietorship. Even more significantly, Rhys and Hywel were to be distinguished supporters of Owain Glyn Dŵr. Of such resentments are the ingredients of revolt assembled.[24]

Rhys and Hywel belonged to a native society which felt, rightly or wrongly, that its claim to a share of ecclesiastical power was being deliberately snubbed or overlooked. The sentiment was, in fact, only partially true and was not particularly more true of Wales than of any other part of the western Church. But sentiments and perceptions are immune to such considerations. As in the lay governance of Wales, so in the higher echelons of the Church, the greater native families of Wales felt themselves excluded. The exception only served to prove the general rule. That exception was John, or Ieuan, Trefor promoted to the see of St Asaph and consecrated bishop at Rome in 1395. His career was a glittering demonstration of what opportunities should have been open to a talented Welsh cleric: a doctor of canon and civil law from the university of Oxford, he came to hold canonries in five English and Welsh bishoprics, gained experience at the Roman curia, and was entrusted with major diplomatic missions by the English court. But he did not sever his connections with his Welsh background: he was drawn, as was true of almost all the higher native-born Welsh clergy, from a prominent family of north-east Wales; the two odes addressed to him by Iolo Goch show how much the success and munificence of a native-born bishop could restore heart to Welsh society. John Trefor was certainly known to Owain Glyn Dŵr; they came from the same district and the same background. Bishop John's career showed that it was indeed possible to bridge the gap between the two worlds of which the Church in Wales seemed to be composed; it would be a test of Owain's leadership and credibility whether he would be able to persuade such a distinguished churchman to join his ranks.[25]

Master Hywel Cyffin needed no such persuasion; he was the dean of St Asaph who was present at Owain's inauguration ceremony as prince of Wales on 16 September 1400. Master Hywel may serve as a representative of the higher Welsh clergy of the day. Most of them were prominent members of leading Welsh noble families: Master Hywel was certainly such and was accompanied on his high-risk mission in 1400 by two of his nephews. As such they were men of considerable territorial standing in their own right, apart from any lands which came with their office; again that was certainly true of Master Hywel. Some of them had the advantage of university education: Master Hywel could certainly look back on a career at Oxford. Between them they cornered many of the choicer plums in the Welsh Church that had not already been picked for royal or aristocratic servants: thus three of the uncles of Hywel ap Tudur ab Ithel secured three of the most desirable livings in Flintshire; another Flintshire man, John ap Rhys ap Robert, son of an eminent *uchelwr* and brother of a romantic Welsh mercenary captain (Ieuan Wyn, *Le Poursuivant d'Amour*), became archdeacon of Merioneth; while Master Hywel Cyffin, as we have seen, was promoted dean of St Asaph in 1386. Such men had reason enough to be thankful for what they had

received; but it must have rankled with several of them that the highest accolade which their Church could offer was denied to them. They would recall sourly the career of one of their own, Ithel ap Robert: canon of Bangor and St Asaph and dean of St Asaph, his election as bishop of Bangor had been quashed in 1357. Ithel's career summed up the frustrations of the Welsh higher clergy; the great crowds at his funeral in 1382—commemorated in one of Iolo Goch's more memorable odes—were a measure of the affection in which he was held. Men such as Ithel ap Robert and Hywel Cyffin were regarded by the Welsh as their natural ecclesiastical leaders; the day might arrive when they would seek to align practice closely with aspiration.[26]

Beneath the ranks of the higher clergy Wales, like other countries at the time, had a considerable clerical population, beneficed and unbeneficed, at the parish level. The only comprehensive figures that survive are those for the poll-tax returns for the diocese of St Asaph 1377–81. They reveal a total of 247 clerics, of whom 132 were beneficed and 115 unbeneficed. The proportions are unlikely to have been very different in the rest of Wales; indeed the St Asaph figures may well have underestimated the number of unbeneficed clerks or *offeiriaid* as they were called in contemporary parlance. These ordinary parish clergymen were, alongside the *uchelwyr*, often the natural leaders of their communities and the spokesmen of their hopes and frustrations. In the detailed lists of Owain Glyn Dŵr's first band of supporters in 1400 four unbeneficed priests (L. *capellanus*, W. *offeiriad*) and one scholar (W. *ysgolhaig*) make their appearance; and of the 2,000 or so people who contributed to Anglesey's submission fine in 1406, at least thirty-four were described as clergy, while a further ten clerics were excluded by name from the pardon.[27]

Among those ten were six friars from the Franciscan house at Llanfaes. That should serve as a reminder that in a map of ecclesiastical power and influence in Wales we must not lose sight of the religious houses. There were just under fifty of them in 1395—including thirteen Cistercian houses and two Cistercian nunneries and some ten houses of friars. Most of them by that date were but sad shadows of their former selves: at Strata Marcella, for example, the number of monks had allegedly fallen from sixty to eight; numbers were down to single figures in several other Cistercian houses; while many of the anaemic Benedictine houses were in an even more parlous state. Yet the religious houses remained influential institutions: Margam Abbey, for example, still supported a hundred people in the 1380s; the abbots of the greater houses were certainly men of status and influence; and the variety of roles that the monasteries played in society as owners of extensive estates, employers of skilled and unskilled labour, centres of building projects, and the greatest repositories of books and manuscripts, meant that their importance could never be overlooked. Religiously and

culturally, they bolstered the social order and the fabric of power in the areas in which they were located. All the Benedictine monasteries of south Wales were Anglo-Norman or English foundations; by the 1390s they were mementoes to an earlier age of conquest and colonization. Many of the great Cistercian houses of the south and east likewise looked towards English settler families for their recruits and patronage: nothing registers this fact more vividly than the tiles at Neath Abbey bearing the arms of its benefactors—the Clare earls and the English families of the Vale such as Berkerolles, Norreys, and Turberville. There were pockets of Welsh monastic affiliation in south Wales (as in the Cistercian house of Llantarnam) and Welsh monks were certainly recruited to southern monasteries such as Margam. But it was in west and north Wales that one entered a world where the monasteries, like all other institutions, were absorbed into a world whose cultural and political values were still overwhelmingly Welsh. In his imaginary journey around Wales Iolo Goch had broken his journey at Whitland and Strata Florida; he could, had he wished, have done so likewise at Cwm Hir, Strata Marcella, Valle Crucis, and Aberconwy. At Strata Florida he would have met its abbot, Llywelyn Fychan ap Llywelyn, the earliest of the Welsh Cistercian abbots who is known for certain to have patronized the bards. It was from some of these Welsh Cistercian monasteries that Owain Glyn Dŵr was to draw some of his most committed supporters.[28]

That is no surprise; for in the winning of hearts the support of the ecclesiastical establishment in Wales, or a proportion of it, was crucial. Clergymen and monks were often the natural leaders of their communities: when the poet memorialized Ithel ap Robert, the dean of St Asaph, as 'the soul of Gwynedd' (*enaid Gwynedd*) and 'the darling of his country' (*câr ei wlad*) he was only registering poetically what others must have felt. Monasteries likewise were centres where native traditions and prophecies were often preserved and cultivated; they could easily become headquarters for preaching sedition. It was a monk of Strata Marcella who, earlier in the fourteenth century, had been accused of arranging unlawful assemblies 'to excite contentions and hatred between the English and the Welsh', and it was a brother monk from Aberconwy who was alleged to have forwarded letters to Owain Lawgoch, the Welsh pretender, from sympathizers in Wales in the 1370s. The higher clergy, both secular and monastic, wielded an influence out of all proportion to their numbers. Drawn as they almost invariably were from the leading Welsh families, they were alive to the frustrations and aspirations of their lay kinsfolk. They had the talents to clothe those aspirations in fine language, to draw up a reasoned programme of action, and to seize the opportunity to locate a protest movement in a more general, even international, context. In short, they were the natural ideologues and strategists; therein lay their power. When a widespread conspiracy had been engineered in north Wales

in 1345 it had been masterminded by Master Hywel ap Goronwy, aided and abetted by the deans of St Asaph and Llŷn, the archdeacon of Bangor, and the abbot of Aberconwy. It was to men such as these, on the one hand, and to his fellow Welsh *uchelwyr* on the other that Owain Glyn Dŵr would have to appeal successfully if his movement was not to be still-born.[29]

Power in medieval Wales—the capacity to dominate, control, and exploit society, be it local, regional or national—was, as always, concentrated in few hands. Even if we cast the net of our definition very widely it is difficult to believe that those who wielded such power would encompass more than 5 per cent of the population; and that is a generous estimate. The rest of the population were, in terms of the medieval formula, *pauperes*, not necessarily economically poor (though many of them were certainly that also) but rather lacking power (L. *potencia*). Many of them were dependants of those who enjoyed power—be it as servants, retainers, serfs, or tenants; others, while not formally or territorially dependent on a lord, acknowledged his protection and became his advowry men, that is, men who paid a small fee (normally fourpence a year) to acknowledge a link with a lord and to enjoy his protection. Not all the men and women of Wales were necessarily formally enmeshed in the web of lordship; but so comprehensive and ubiquitous were the powers of lordship, especially its disciplinary and exploitative powers, that few were immune from their ambit. Furthermore, power flowed through several channels—through royal and magnate lordship, through the Church and its courts, and through the powers exercised by greater and lesser gentry and *uchelwyr*. The demands and constraints of plural lordship helped to shape the lives and fortunes of most of the population of Wales.

Welsh society in Owain Glyn Dŵr's day was still predominantly a peasant society; most of its members lived on family holdings and spent their lives producing food for the subsistence needs of their own households or providing the services that such households required. A peasant society is not a society of equals, nor was Welsh peasant society so. There was a basic distinction between those with and those without a direct stake in the land and in the means to exploit it: the latter helped to swell the ranks of the craftsmen, servants, migrant labourers, vagrants, and the truly destitute who make but an occasional appearance in the documentation of the period. Even among those with land there were disparities, occasionally formally recognized, in wealth—notably between those with or without subtenants of their own and those who owned a plough-beast and those who did not. Nor was the distinction between free and unfree tenants one to be overlooked: it had, admittedly, been profoundly challenged by the collapse of the population in the wake of the recurrent visitations of plague in the later fourteenth century; but it was still vigorously exploited and sustained by

lords, great and small, for reasons of control and profit. Yet in spite of such divisions and distinctions, there seems, from the little evidence that survives, to have been a greater equality of wealth, or rather poverty, in contemporary Wales than in England, and within Wales in the north and west than in the more fertile and more prosperous south. Such a socially and economically undifferentiated society is one more likely to be dominated by its lords.

It was in the heartland of such a society that Owain Glyn Dŵr launched his revolt in September 1400. As a Welsh *uchelwr* of impeccable lineage, as the owner of serfs and lord of manors, and as a man who took his power over his dependants for granted, he is unlikely to have given much thought to the attitude or aspirations of the ordinary peoples of north-east Wales nor to the impact of his rebellion on their lives. His was the duty and the prerogative of lordship; theirs was the obligation to follow. Yet in several respects their response was, and would be, critical; the powerless after all were not without power. Medieval social theory readily recognized that without the toil and sweat of the labourers (L. *laboratores*) the lords would not have the means to survive and to play their self-designated part as the leaders and protectors of society. Nowhere was that social theory more eloquently or effectively expressed in the whole medieval epoch than in the remarkable ode that Iolo Goch (the poet who was, to all intents and purposes, Glyn Dŵr's household bard) addressed to the labourer or the ploughman. The poet's paean of praise to his lowly hero contains an explicit critique of the values and ambitions of aristocratic society: the ploughman is no 'plundering Arthur' (W. *Arthur anrheithiwr*); unlike such men, he does not make war or oppress others for their goods; he is not overbearing nor does he pursue wrongful claims. But the ploughman's virtues are not merely negative; his is truly a fundamental role in society: 'without him no pope or emperor can live, no king . . . no living man.' Iolo's immortal compliment—'there is no life, no world without him' (*Nid bywyd, nid byd heb ef*)—was a truism which all men of power, in peace and especially in war, would ultimately ignore only at their peril.[30]

Particularly was it important to keep that message in mind, at a time of rapid economic and social change such as the closing decades of the fourteenth century were. In Wales, as in England, the population collapse after 1349 inaugurated seismic changes in the social fabric and in the pattern of authority. Land was abandoned; tenants were scarce; enticements had to be offered to sons to succeed fathers and to persuade aliens (L. *extranei*) to take vacant tenements on favourable terms; labourers demanded higher wages; and in many directions seignorial authority was openly challenged and flouted. Most symptomatic of the malaise of the time was the collapse of villeinage and the challenge to its very rationale. In one area of Dyffryn Clwyd, for example—a lordship which bordered with

Owain Glyn Dŵr's own lands—the number of villein tenants had fallen by over three-quarters in the decades before 1381, and the lord fought a desperate, but ultimately unsuccessful, struggle to sustain his authority over those that remained. One incident epitomizes the challenge to lordship that was involved in those changes: in May 1401 the villeins of Abergavenny rose against their lord, killed his steward, and released three criminals under sentence of death. Defiance was in the air. The ties of leadership and power were being loosened, largely under the pressure of changed economic circumstances. Such social dislocation was a propitious background for launching a revolt, for transferring loyalty from one focus of authority to another.[31]

Discontent and disillusion among the populace may have provided favourable conditions in which dreamers, prophets, and ambitious leaders could set to work. But if a revolt was to be more than a temporary outburst of protest, it would need to harness and retain the loyalty of people who had hitherto moved in very different orbits of authority and obedience. It was one thing to whip up support from 280 or so local men in Edeirnion and Dinmael to accompany Owain Glyn Dŵr on his initial foray in September 1400; it would require a much more fundamental challenge to the power-structures of medieval Wales, or at least to those represented by English rule, to convert such a movement into a sustained national revolt. Such a challenge could only be undertaken with the support, be it willingly given or an automatic response, of the populace of Wales, or a goodly proportion of it. Their willingness to mount such a challenge, or at least actively or passively to support it, implied that they had ceased to accept the power-structures and framework of authority under which Wales had been ruled for generations. It also implied that they supported, or at least accepted, the validity and appeal of the claims of Owain Glyn Dŵr to authority, leadership, and power. Revolts, especially sustained national revolts, involve ultimately the redrawing of the mental contours of authority and legitimacy. By that token the protest movement led by Owain Glyn Dŵr was, or perhaps more correctly became, undoubtedly a national revolt. At its heart lay a frontal challenge to the structures of lay and ecclesiastical power in Wales.

TENSIONS AND ASPIRATIONS

R evolts are born of, and feed upon, unresolved tensions and unfulfilled aspirations within society. So it was in Wales in 1400. The rebellion of Owain Glyn Dŵr owed a great deal to the personal vision and grievances of Owain himself, while the unexpected success that attended it is likewise, no doubt, to be very considerably explained by the preoccupations, and incompetence, of the English government. Yet the wide degree of support that the revolt came to enjoy and the programme that its leaders eventually came to espouse can ultimately only be explained in terms of the tensions and aspirations of Welsh society itself. It is no easy matter, of course, to penetrate the tensions and aspirations of any medieval society; in Wales the difficulties are compounded by the fact that, with the exception of the native poetry and some individual and communal petitions, the surviving historical evidence is overwhelmingly that of the English kings, lords, and governors of Wales. Even this evidence, however, may allow us to characterize some of those frustrations and grievances which were simmering within Welsh society on the eve of the Glyn Dŵr revolt.

None was more fundamental than the tension which arose from the fact that Wales was, formally as well as actually, a land of two peoples, English and Welsh. It was a situation which had been centuries in the making, but one which had acquired a much greater measure of definitiveness from the mid-thirteenth century. From the days of the Normans—and indeed in some areas well before then—waves of English conquerors and colonists had taken control of, and settled in, various parts of the country we know as Wales. The final military conquest of the country by Edward I in 1277–84 coincided broadly with the last such major wave of English colonization of Wales in the Middle Ages. Over a period of 200 years or so this tide of conquest and colonization had transformed the character of society in Wales profoundly, but very unevenly. An ethnic map of Wales in 1400—even were one to disregard the large numbers of mixed and overlapping communities and to ignore the major shifts that were taking place within the ethnic map in each generation—would be a highly complex mosaic. There were areas of the southern coastland and river valleys where an English or Anglicized population was in the overwhelming majority; equally over most of

north and west Wales, and indeed over much of southern Wales likewise, such English settlements as existed were tiny islands in a vast sea of indigenous Welsh settlement. In between these two extremes lay much more complex localized patterns where Welsh and English lived cheek by jowl with each other in the same region, in neighbouring settlements, and not infrequently in the same vill.[1]

Such a rich and complex ethnic situation must have been common in many parts of medieval Europe in the wake of the waves of migration, conquest, and colonization which had swept the continent from the eleventh century. What was distinctive, though by no means unique, about Wales was that this ethnic duality had been formally institutionalized into the governance, law, and administration of the country, especially from the thirteenth century, and had been fossilized thereafter. Much of the country, especially the south, was divided administratively into Welshries and Englishries or, as in Gower, into Welsh and English counties; even in many of the areas where such a formal administrative division did not exist, patterns of governance and law were informed by the assumption of separate practices for the English and Welsh populations. This duality pervaded almost every aspect of social life and governance. At law there would be separate courts for English and Welsh, separate (or at best mixed) juries, and major differences in procedures and substantive law. Administratively the two peoples would be ruled by different hierarchies of officials, and their rights *vis-à-vis* their lord might well be defined by separate charters of liberties. Rents and dues from the two peoples were often entirely different in character, assessment, and collection, and when the lord chose to collect a tax or subsidy it likewise might be levied separately from the Welsh and English tenants of his lordship. In an overwhelmingly landed and rural society nothing proclaimed the contrast between the two peoples more loudly than the fundamental difference in their inheritance-practices and methods of alienating land. Separate lists of English and Welsh tenants were compiled; even the labour services owed by them and the pannage dues (that is, the payment for permissions for swine to feed in the lord's forest) might be separately itemized.

Formally, therefore, the distinction between English and Welsh was fundamental in the ordering and governance of society in many parts of Wales in the fourteenth century. It was a distinction which could be readily explained and defended. At one level, after all, it was no more than an honest, even enlightened, recognition of the profound differences between the Welsh and the English in customs, law, and social organization and of the need to be sensitive to those differences and to show respect for them. More defensively, it could hardly be denied that most of the English settlers had entered Wales in the wake of military conquest and that it was imperative to defend the interests and even to sustain the purity of this minority group. Wales was still a security-risk for the English

government, be it from external attack or internal revolt; in those circumstances the English in Wales, especially in the more isolated areas of Wales, provided and were meant to provide a first line of defence in an emergency. That is why they unctuously proclaimed their loyalty to the king and were exempt from contributing to expeditionary forces raised in Wales for service in France or Scotland. It was not difficult, therefore, to explain and defend the institutionalized duality between Welsh and English in Glyn Dŵr's Wales. Furthermore, the duality in practice was much less impressive and effective than legal and administrative theory proclaimed it to be. The division into Englishries and Welshries coincided only very loosely with the actual ethnic distribution of the population, while the complexities of migration, marriage, and the land market made nonsense of the neat theorems of administrators. Particularly was this so in the later fourteenth century as Welshmen moved in ever-greater numbers into the self-styled 'English towns' of Wales, as other Welshmen bought charters of English liberty and ensured that their lands descended to their heirs by English law, and as English settlers for their part began to be less on the defensive and used the opportunities of a lively land market to move into Welsh neighbourhoods. The passage of time—as so often in similar circumstances—seemed to be undermining the rationale and usefulness of the duality between Welsh and English.

Yet it is precisely in such circumstances, when social and legal categories have become increasingly threadbare and indefensible, that they are often most vigorously upheld and even more vigorously resented. It was not the categorization as such which was necessarily resented so much as the blatant discrimination which was so often part of it, and perhaps above all its arbitrary character. No one could doubt that the panoply of restrictions on the activities of Welshmen was often invoked for purely profiteering reasons. So it was, for example, that the Black Prince's officers in Flintshire instituted inquiries in the 1350s and 1360s into English lands which had been acquired by Welshmen without licence, 'contrary to the proclamation made at the conquest of Wales'. That some of these lands had been purchased over forty years ago and that their illegal purchasers were now to be given preference if they offered as good a price as the highest bidder made it transparent that ethnic discrimination was being kept alive as a source of seignorial profit. In much the same fashion, English king and Marcher lord alike insisted on sustaining antiquated Welsh customs such as *amobr* (virginity fine) and *prid* (four-year renewable mortgages of land) because of the handsome income they yielded, just as the royal administration in South Wales used Welsh law and hired professional Welsh jurists to overturn legal decisions for the simple reason that it might reap as much as £44 from each fine for a wrongful decision overturned.[2]

Self-interest likewise dictated why other groups were anxious to keep the policy of ethnic discrimination in good heart and to insist that it be flaunted publicly on occasion. No group was more vociferous in its protestations of Englishness and in the need to keep Welshmen at arm's length than the burgesses of the small towns of Wales, especially north Wales. Genuine fear of the consequences of infiltration may have been a motive for their stance, but the jealous protection of commercial privileges was, equally assuredly, another. The burgesses of the castellated boroughs of north Wales felt impelled in the 1360s and 1370s to mount a campaign to secure the reissuing of the ordinance of Edward I instructing Welshmen to trade in the English boroughs. But it is the charter which was issued to the English burgesses of Hope (co. Flint) in February 1399 which perhaps best reveals how ethnic discrimination was still being vigorously promoted on the eve of the revolt: no burgess was henceforth to be convicted by a Welshman; no Welshman was to hold a market or to brew ale within three leagues of the town; all the Welshmen of Hopedale were to bring their victuals to Hope for sale; and Welshmen were prohibited from holding assemblies. Discrimination against the Welsh and the maintenance of commercial privileges were clearly still close bedfellows in the 1390s.[3]

The anaemic little towns of Wales might be expected to be natural homes for paranoia and monopolies; but the discrimination against Welshmen surfaced periodically in other areas of life and was all the more disconcerting for being spasmodic and apparently arbitrary. Most of the top jobs in the governance of Wales—notably the justiciarships in the Principality, the stewardships of Marcher lordships, and the constableships of key castles in both—were normally beyond the reach of Welshmen; but other posts—such as deputy-justiciarships, shrievalties, and some constableships—had been gradually opened to some of them, at least periodically. Yet such appointments could never be secure, least of all from a whispering campaign that they contravened ordinances laid down at the time of the conquest of Wales. So it was, for example, that an order was issued for the dismissal of a Welshman appointed to be a deputy-steward in Cardiganshire because his appointment was 'in contravention of the ordinance of Edward I at the conquest of Wales'; just as later two prominent Welshmen appointed to be sheriff and constable of Flint were required to nominate 'a loyal and sufficient Englishman' as under-constable, 'because we will that the same castle be kept by none other than an Englishman'. Nor was such occasional harassment confined to security-sensitive posts. Welshmen who had lived peacefully for years in English towns might suddenly be challenged to produce their title for doing so and might only recover their status as burgesses on payment of a large fine. Even where burghal privileges were not involved, officious stewards and profiteering lords continued to exploit the antiquated divisions between

Welsh and English tenants to weave a whole web of delays, prohibitions, and extortions, notably on issues such as legal procedures and land transactions. Their spirit of petty and profiteering restriction is captured in an example from Dyffryn Clwyd in 1367: in letting a vacant tenement the lord specifically refused to grant English status (L. *libertas anglicana*) to the new tenant, 'in case the lord's claims upon him in respect of his Welsh status should thereby be annulled elsewhere'.[4]

There is little doubt that Welsh society adjusted to and largely learnt to bypass this institutionalized ethnic duality; there is equally little doubt that its continuing, and often arbitrary and whimsical, enforcement was at best a source of irritation, at worst of deep resentment to the native Welsh. It was a reminder to them that they were the descendants of a conquered people and that the mentality of conquest was still being cultivated and exploited by the victors. At Hope in 1401 the noses of Welshmen were rubbed in the memory of 'the statutes, provisions and ordinances decreed for burgesses and English towns at Caernarfon at the time of the Conquest and thereafter observed through the whole of North Wales'. It is little wonder that Welshmen felt demeaned and the victims of discrimination. Hopcyn ap Tomas's scribe, we have already noticed, bewailed 'the pain and deprivation and exile' which his fellow Welshmen suffered in their own land; the poet who addressed an ode of praise to Rhys Gethin, one of Owain Glyn Dŵr's supporters, was even more blunt: 'where once there were Britons, we now have Englishmen; Welshmen suffer daily thereby'. The truth was that ethnic suspicion and contempt were never far below the surface in fourteenth-century Wales. English lords and communities in Wales referred recurrently to 'the malevolence and enmity of the Welsh' and to 'the malice of the Welsh'; and the Welsh no doubt returned the compliment in kind, for, as the burgesses of Conway put it, 'if anything was taken from the Welsh, they held it for extortion and the greatest wrong that ever had been put on them'.[5]

One might have expected such ethnic tension to diminish with the passage of time, as the two peoples adjusted to each other and as the formal distinctions between them became increasingly archaic and unreal. In fact it is precisely in those circumstances that the unacceptability of such distinctions becomes more evident and that, equally, artificial attempts are made to sustain and enforce them. So it was in various parts of Wales in the twenty years or so before the outbreak of Glyn Dŵr's revolt. In 1380, for example, a petition laid before parliament rehearsed in full the orthodoxy that no Welshman or Welsh woman should be allowed to live or to purchase lands in the towns of Wales or in neighbouring English counties, and spoke hysterically of the scale and consequences of such illicit infiltration. The towns of south Wales likewise periodically ventilated their anti-Welsh sentiments: the burgesses of Cardigan, Dryslwyn, and

Llanbadarn secured confirmation of their privilege to be tried only before their fellow-Englishmen; their companions in Carmarthen in 1386 inveighed against the malice and oppression of the Welsh and asked to be convicted only by 'true Englishmen'; and the residents of Laugharne secured precisely the same concession in their charter in December 1389. In north Wales there could hardly be a more discriminatory charter than the one already quoted which was granted to Hope in 1399. The mechanics of ethnic separation and discrimination were still in place and were readily activated: thus, in Dyffryn Clwyd in 1396 six Welshmen were charged with having exercised English liberties for ten years 'to the no small prejudice of the lord', while in Cydweli practices such as drawing up separate lists of English and Welsh tenants and corresponding separate juries were still very much alive. In these circumstances it is little wonder that episodes of ethnic tension were reported from different parts of Wales: in Flintshire the men of Englefield were so outraged by the commercial monopolies claimed by the English towns that they raised a communal subsidy among themselves to try to secure the abrogation of such monopolies; in Narberth in south-west Wales the earl of March's council was warned around 1390 that an imaginative appointment to the post of steward was essential if the tensions between the English and the Welsh in the district were to be resolved. This was precisely the kind of atmosphere in which a rebellion could quickly take hold.[6]

In England in 1381 antiquated and resented status-distinctions had been at the root of the Great Revolt; so also had been the unacceptably high level and novelty of royal taxation. In Wales in Owain Glyn Dŵr's day likewise the extortionate financial demands of English lordship, especially at a time of acute economic difficulties, prepared a fertile ground in which the seeds of revolt could readily germinate. Adam of Usk, in a remarkable aside in his chronicle, remarked that the English extracted £60,000 annually from Wales before the revolt. His estimate was certainly exaggerated; it probably more than doubled the revenue that flowed from Wales every year. But he had made a shrewd point which deserves to be borne in mind in the study both of the English aristocracy and of Welsh society. English kings and magnates certainly waxed rich on the income they derived from Wales: the king of England could expect to collect over £5,600 from the Principality lands in North and South Wales and the county of Flint; the earl of March's Welsh estates yielded close on £3,000 gross in the 1390s; those of the earl of Arundel in Wales and the border counties, over £2,000; John of Gaunt, who was in a league of his own among the magnates in terms of landed wealth, collected 15 per cent of his income from his Welsh estates; while a single great Marcher lordship such as Brecon could yield over £1,500 annually to its lord. We can put these figures into some sort of contemporary perspective when we recall

that £666 13s. 4d. was regarded as the territorial competence for an earl; that many a comital family in England had to be content with a landed income of some £2,000; and that even the king of England's ordinary net annual revenue (that is, exclusive of any forms of taxation) was not much in excess of £12,000 per annum. Seen in this perspective, Wales was certainly an important source of revenue for the king of England and many of his aristocracy; it is little wonder that the Black Prince's council had referred gleefully to the 'fair lordship' he had in Wales.[7]

But there was a price to pay for this handsome financial return, and it was paid by the inhabitants of Wales. It may be open to question whether the financial pressure upon them was much greater than that on the peasants and taxpayers of England; but it is beyond doubt that the nature of the financial extractions made on them was different from that experienced in contemporary England, and was at the very least as demanding. In the lowland manors and lordships of south Wales, rents and farms accounted for a large proportion of the revenue raised; in the more thoroughly Welsh districts of the north and the west old native renders and tributes figured prominently. But it was two features in particular which gave distinctiveness to the revenue-patterns of Welsh lordships; both of them had the potential to be exploited when other sources of income faltered and both of them spread the burden of financial pressure across the whole community. The first was judicial income, both the issues of courts and fines. In some cases such income accounted for a quarter of the lord's revenue; in a few districts for as much as 80 per cent of it; in all parts of Wales it was a much more important source of income than it was correspondingly in England, if only because the lord's judicial powers were much more extensive in Wales. The second distinctive source of revenue was even more important. This was composed of the communal subsidies, aids, and fines which were regularly collected by kings and lords from every part of Wales. Wales was exempt from the heavy and regular parliamentary taxation which became such a notable feature of the fiscal life in England in the fourteenth century, and which was such a heavy burden on its peasantry; but the benefits of such exemption were more than cancelled by the recurrent pattern of extraordinary grants levied by the kings and lords of England from their lands in Wales. The pretexts were multifarious—communal fines, aids on the entry of a new lord, subsidies towards military expeditions or other seignorial needs, fines to buy off the prospect of a judicial eyre (that is, a judicial sessions held periodically by the lord's officers), to name but the most obvious of the pretexts mentioned; but whatever the pretext the consequence was the same—a major addition, at the very least comparable to English parliamentary taxation in its severity and incidence, to the financial burdens on the peoples of Wales, sometimes (as in the subsidy of £1,670 levies on the counties of Anglesey,

Caernarfon, and Merioneth in 1394) specifically on its Welsh inhabitants. To give but two examples from the years immediately before the outbreak of the revolt: on his first visit to his great lordship of Brecon in 1397 Henry Bolingbroke was granted a subsidy of £1,333 to be collected over three years, thereby adding at least 35 per cent to the financial demands on his tenants there during that period; when he succeeded his father as duke of Lancaster his demands from his tenants of Cydweli lordship—for a charter of pardon, a confirmation of their charter of liberties, and an aid to recognize him as their new lord—were even more extortionate at £1,575, almost two and half times the annual yield of the lordship. It is little wonder that the men of Brecon and Cydweli welcomed Owain Glyn Dŵr with open arms.[8]

They had the more reason to do so, since the financial pressure on Wales had been intensified of late. Wales, in common with the rest of western Europe, had suffered a major economic setback in the wake of the recurrent visitations of plague in the second half of the fourteenth century; but the English lords of Wales made very few concessions to changed economic conditions in their determination to maximize the profits from their estates. New rentals were prepared; lists of outstanding arrears were compiled in order to ensure that they were not overlooked; special commissioners were dispatched to reinforce the efforts of local officials. In the closing years of the fourteenth century individual and communal fines were as crushingly heavy as they had ever been: the earl of Arundel as justiciar of South Wales imposed massive fines of 1,000 marks (£666 13s. 4d.) and £200 on two of the leading men of Cardiganshire, and so severe were his methods that news of them even reached Westminster; the same earl imposed communal fines of over £500 on his tenants of Chirkland in 1390 for failing to perform their customary duty of carrying timber to his castle at Chirk; while in Denbigh in the late 1390s the earl of March extorted large individual fines from many of his tenants.[9] Likewise the exaction of large communal subsidies, which had become such a distinctive feature of the finances of lordship in Wales, continued unabated in spite of adverse economic circumstances: Richard II imposed subsidies on his Principality lands in South Wales in 1392 and in North Wales in 1394 and used them to finance his Irish expedition; John of Gaunt used the occasion of a judicial visitation by his chief steward in 1395 to raise communal fines from his Welsh lands; while the first entry of the earls of March and Derby to their Welsh estates respectively in 1393 and 1397 were the occasions for requesting obligatory gifts (exceptionally large for the earl of Derby) from their tenants. Kingship and lordship in Wales in the 1390s were still remarkably extortionate and avaricious.[10]

They were also remarkably successful. Almost all the detailed figures on seignorial revenue from Wales show a marked upward trend during the

fourteenth century, scarcely faltering even as the century drew to its close. Revenue from the great lordship of Brecon rose by 40 per cent across the middle years of the century and had scaled even greater heights by the 1390s; and the same story is repeated, though rather less dramatically, on the estates of John of Gaunt and the earls of Arundel. There are, it is true, some indications from the 1380s of growing difficulties in collecting the full amounts due; but such difficulties can be easily exaggerated, and it is the determination and resilience of the lords which are most striking. Even when they made concessions, it was still within a general context of asserting their rights and maximizing their income. When Roger Mortimer agreed to the desperate pleas of his Denbigh tenants regarding their fines in 1397, he did indeed remit a proportion of them but only in return for prompt payment of the remainder; likewise when the young prince of Wales conceded in 1400 that half of the debts owed from South Wales should be cancelled and the remainder paid in instalments, the price of his act of generosity was a further payment of 1,000 marks! In the closing decade of the fourteenth century the lords of Wales could congratulate themselves that their income from the country was as buoyant as it had ever been. In 1393 the various Mortimer receivers in Wales transferred £2,775 to the young earl of March to spend on his pleasures and policies; at the same period Richard Fitzalan, earl of Arundel, was accumulating at least £1,500 a year net from his group of Marcher lordships in north-east Wales to add to the massive sums which his father had hoarded in Holt Castle; while in 1400 the receiver of Brecon was able to hand over to his lord, now king of England, close on £1,600 raised from the tenants of the lordship in one year.[11]

Wales was a joy for indigent, or greedy, English kings or lords. Nor did they sense any real danger, or see any need to change their policies, once a wayward Welsh squire went on the rampage in September 1400. On the contrary, rarely did the hand of English financial extortion lie more heavily on Wales than in the years 1399–1402. And that hand was pre-eminently the hand of one man and his son—King Henry IV and his son Henry, created prince of Wales on 15 October 1399. Between them they controlled well over half of the surface area of Wales, more than any previous royal dynasty had ever controlled (see Map 3*b*). Henry IV was lord of Brecon, the richest of all the Marcher lordships, in his first wife's right; he had also inherited the lordships of Cydweli, Ogmore, Monmouth, and Threecastles on his father's death in 1399. His accession to the throne in that year gave him, and through him his son, all the Crown lands in Wales. Communal aids, subsidies, and fines totalling at least £5,000 were imposed on these royal estates in 1400–1 alone. It was very much a case of pouring petrol on a fire which had already taken hold.[12]

For it is difficult to believe that these punishing and recurrent financial demands, falling as they did on the whole community, were not deeply resented.

The visit of a subsidy-raising delegation—such as that, later recorded, of two officials, accompanied by an entourage of thirty men and horses—must have been intimidating and deeply objectionable to the local communities. Such a delegation arrived in south Wales in 1376–7; the report of its visit is one of the very few insights we have into the cajolery and threats which must often have accompanied negotiations for subsidies. The local tenants and their leaders were assembled; when the request for a subsidy was put to them they pleaded their poverty, especially as a result of plague and murrain; it was only after consider-able persuasion that they eventually agreed to grant an aid to be collected in instalments over four years. Such reluctance must have been common; reluct-ance could quickly turn to resentment and thence into outright non-co-oper-ation. Even a contemporary English chronicler noted that there was 'great unrest among the Welsh' after the earl of Arundel's judicial sessions in the late 1380s. But it was a Welsh poet who perhaps best epitomized native resentment in the comment that 'it is avarice to demand taxes' (W. *trythyll yw cymell trethoedd*). That was the sort of observation that the English rulers of Wales would have been very well advised to heed as the fourteenth century drew to its close.[13]

Financial pressure was all the more explosive in its possible social consequences because it was being exerted on a society and economy which were undergoing a period of profound transformation. The shadow of recurrent visitations of the plague lay heavily across the face of Wales, as it did across that of virtually every other European society in the second half of the fourteenth century. From such scattered evidence as can be assembled, it would appear that Wales suffered at least as heavily as England from the impact of plague. Population levels tumbled, unequally it is true but often by a third or more; tenements went out of cultiva-tion and lay vacant or had to be leased at low rents; good arable land reverted to pasture; vills were left half-empty or, in a few cases, abandoned altogether. Such seems to be the story from almost every part of Wales. Estate officials and poets alike bewailed the impact of the 'Great Death' (W. *Y Farwolaeth Fawr*) and yearned desperately for the return of better days. The impact of such calamities, it is true, is by no means always obvious in the account rolls which form the staple diet of the historian's evidence for Wales for these years. On the contrary, seignorial income was frequently back to its pre-plague levels by the 1360s and 1370s, and sometimes indeed exceeded them; while during the 1380s and 1390s, as we have seen, seignorial pressure, especially in its demands for aids and subsidies, was as unremitting as ever.[14]

But financial buoyancy could not conceal social and economic reality indefin-itely; indeed the discrepancy between seignorial demands on the one hand and the capacity of society to meet those demands on the other may well have

compounded the tension within Owain Glyn Dŵr's Wales. As in England, so in Wales, one social group in particular felt increasing resentment at the inequity and anachronism of the demands made of it. These were the villeins. Their numbers had fallen catastrophically in many parts of Wales, partly through death and partly through flight; in one of the bond vills of Dyffryn Clwyd it was claimed in 1379 that there were now only fourteen villeins left where there formerly had been a hundred, that sixty-six villein tenements were now in the hands of the lord or his freemen, but that the communal villein dues had not been reduced at all. Exaggerated the claim may be, but that the future of villeinage and the lord's attitude towards it were now in the forefront of the seignorial agenda in Wales hardly admits of doubt. Lords could, and did, pursue contradictory policies on the issue. Conciliation and concession was one such policy: rent and services might be reduced, dues commuted, and customary lands leased to villeins on free terms; an amnesty might be offered (as in Dyffryn Clwyd) for those under sentence of outlawry, in a desperate attempt to coax fleeing tenants back; charters of enfranchisement might even be offered. But the stick as well as the carrot was used and was as evident in the 1390s as in the 1360s: in Dyffryn Clwyd (the source of our best information by far on seignorial policy in action in the whole of Wales) lists of villeins who were to be compelled to take up vacant bond tenements were compiled and each of the villein communities of the lordship were fined for not performing their labour services and mill works. The lords were certainly tenacious and even optimistic that the *status quo* could some day be fully restored. But in truth they were deluding themselves, and on occasion their delusions were dramatically shattered, as at Abergavenny in 1401. It would not be difficult to harness their resentment in support of other and less localized causes.[15]

Nor were they the only group that was likely to be disaffected. During periods of rapid economic change old social distinctions and established dues rapidly forfeit any rationale they once enjoyed and are soon openly challenged. Lords in Wales had sustained the distinction between English and Welsh, and especially between English and Welsh tenure, for reasons of profit and control rather than because of any commitment to ethnic separation. But the collapse in the population, the rapid acceleration of the land market, and the increasing mobility of the surviving population in the second half of the fourteenth century were serving to highlight the inequities and anachronism of the distinction. Concessions were certainly made: in Dyffryn Clwyd, for example, the number of new tenants, often indeed newcomers to the lordship, who were allowed to hold their lands by English tenure and laws of descent increased in the closing decades of the century, as did the number of those who were allowed to buy charters of English liberties. But in such circumstances concessions frequently only serve to fuel the

demand for even more radical change. When the lord tried to flaunt his authority by prosecuting six Welshmen who had not paid their Welsh services for ten years and had instead used English liberties 'to the no small prejudice of the lord', his bluff was called. Indeed the community was now openly defiant: in 1394, for example, the community of one commote 'rebelliously' refused to assemble to divide responsibility for a Welsh due, declaring that 'they had no intention of paying it' although their liability for doing so had been solemnly affirmed by the lord's council in the lord's own personal presence. The road from such a communal defiance to a much broader-based opposition might be a short one.[16]

The truth seems to be that in Wales as in England the authority of lords—for all, and indeed because of, their bluster and extortions—was being increasingly challenged in the last quarter of the fourteenth century. Desperate attempts were made to control the labour market and to contain wages; but the fact that in one year alone in one lordship over 200 men were fined for charging excessive wages suggests that the determination of the work-force was more than a match for the zeal of the lord. More subversive still of the lord's authority was the large number of tenants who left the lordship; even individual sureties of £20 were not enough to prevent them going. The cumulative effect of such developments, added as they were to increasing restlessness among villeins and open defiance among some free communities, was to corrode, if not to undermine, the authority of landlords. Some of them tried to rise to the challenge imaginatively, by drawing up new rentals in which some of the old status distinctions, notably that between the free and the unfree, were abandoned; but the majority, of whom Reginald Grey of Ruthin and William Beauchamp of Abergavenny were but two examples, strove to prop up the *status quo*. It is, of course, impossible to measure the degree of resentment in a medieval society or to know when, and if, the line had been crossed from chronic disaffection to a much more dangerous and defiant rebelliousness. What seems to be difficult to deny is that in Wales, as in so many parts of later fourteenth-century Europe, the pace of economic change was posing a challenge to accepted patterns and norms of authority on the one hand and producing a profound sense of social disorientation on the other. The comments of the Welsh poets that this was a gloomy and a comfortless world (W. *byd dudrist, byd gogaled, byd ergryd oergrai*) and a world in which the social values of a deeply conservative and hierarchic native society were being ignored and overturned were no doubt commonplace platitudes; but even platitudes in the appropriate circumstances can acquire the ringing force of truth.[17]

The sense of social and economic malaise and disorientation was compounded by the undoubted fact that the closing years of the fourteenth century were years of profound political turmoil. The source of the turmoil lay above all in the

activities and policies of the court of the king of England; but its reverberations reached deep into the heart of Welsh society. The coming of peace was part of that turmoil. In 1389, after twenty years of conflict, England and France concluded a truce and began an almost desperate search for a definitive peace. Peace is rarely an attractive prospect for a militarized society habituated to war and to the profits and opportunities that come with war. The men of Chester were to reveal as much in their 'rising' in 1393–4, and their frustration was echoed by those of a hawkish disposition among England's magnates. Many of the leaders of native Welsh society are likely to have shared the same view. War after all provided them with one of the few opportunities for adventure, glory, fame, and even modest fortune beyond the confines of their small, poor, and suffocating local worlds. Were not the few Welshmen who had achieved the accolade of knighthood in the fourteenth century and who had become folk-heroes in Wales in their own lifetimes military men almost without exception—Sir Gruffudd Llwyd, Sir Hywel y Pedolau ('of the horseshoes'), Sir Hywel y Fwyall ('of the axe'), Sir Rhys ap Gruffudd, Sir Gregory Sais? For such a society peace not only raised the spectre of unemployment; it also closed one of the few avenues of promotion and glory available to Welshmen. Richard II's Irish expeditions of 1394 and 1399 might provide an alternative sphere for their prowess: three of the leading Welsh *uchelwyr* of the day (Henry Don in south Wales, Rhys and Gwilym ap Tudur in the north) and their retinues responded to the challenge in 1394. But the prospects for regular and profitable service certainly declined in the 1390s; military men had time, too much time, to wallow in the memories of former days of glory and to kick their heels in frustration at the lack of opportunities and openings in the present. One of them might well have been Owain Glyn Dŵr, veteran of service in Scotland and of an exciting sea-battle in the English Channel in the 1380s and, in the words of the poet, a man who saw himself as primarily a military leader (W. *cannwyll brwydr*).[18]

The excitement offered by war was certainly on the wane; it was replaced by the excitement of political confrontation. Not since the 1320s had England been so convulsed by political drama as in the 1390s, and it was striking how much of this took place in, or had a profound impact on, Wales. In normal times Wales and the Welsh were peripheral to the world of English politics, nor did this situation change in the 1390s. Yet Wales found itself deeply involved in the political convulsions of that turbulent decade. The central character in the drama was, of course, Richard II. Whether he had any conscious intention of reshaping the basis of his power by concentrating it in the west—in Chester, Wales, and even Ireland—may be doubtful; but that these areas came to occupy a higher profile in his policies is less open to question. The county palatine of Chester was, of course, the apple of his eye; but his attention could also stray to Wales, if only

because it was contiguous to Chester. No reigning English king since the Edwardian conquest visited Wales as frequently. Richard's earliest experience of the country, if the chroniclers are to be believed, came during his 'gyration' in 1387 when he sought solace from his political emasculation by touring his kingdom; twice, in 1394–5 and 1399, he led his household and armies through south Wales *en route* to Ireland (being the first king to have visited that country since King John); during his hour of political triumph in January 1398 it was in Shrewsbury that he was to hold his parliament, and more than one of his journeys that year took him to Holt and thence to Chester. It was at Oswestry, no more than a good five miles from Owain Glyn Dŵr's home at Sycharth, that the dukes of Hereford and Norfolk appeared before King Richard II on 23 February 1398 to pursue their mutual challenge of treasonable activity. Richard's visits to Wales were short and little more than passages to more important destinations, but even so it is not difficult to believe that they raised the level of political awareness and excitement in Wales.[19]

Such excitement reached fever pitch during the summer months of 1399, for it was in Wales that the final episodes of the political drama of that year were staged. On his hurried return from Ireland, Richard by 29 July was back in or near Whitland Abbey in south-west Wales, trying to devise a strategy to counter the threat posed by Henry of Bolingbroke's victorious march through his kingdom. He had already sent Thomas Despenser, recently created earl of Gloucester, to the lordship of Glamorgan in an attempt to raise support from the Welshmen of that area, and John Montagu, earl of Salisbury, on an even more crucial mission to undertake a similar task in north Wales (plate 6a). Both, as it proved, failed in their enterprises. Richard himself headed for north Wales in late July–early August, travelling according to some accounts via the castles of Harlech, Caernarfon, Beaumaris, and even possibly Flint. By the 8/9 August he was at Conway Castle. By the same date Henry Bolingbroke had entered the city of Chester, the 'inner citadel' of Richard II's power. He had travelled to Chester from Bristol along the Welsh border, via Leominster, Ludlow, and Shrewsbury. From Chester he sent a delegation headed by the earl of Northumberland to interview Richard at Conway, probably on 11/12 August (plate 6b). Whether duped or not, Richard eventually agreed to accompany Northumberland to meet Bolingbroke: setting out from Conway probably on 14 August he and his escort reached Flint, via Rhuddlan, by nightfall. Thence, after a fateful meeting with Bolingbroke and Archbishop Arundel, he was taken to captivity at Chester and thereafter to the Tower of London. Deposition lay only a matter of weeks away.[20]

What was, perhaps, the greatest political drama of the fourteenth century had thereby reached its climax in Wales. The *dramatis personae* were, of course, the leading figures on the English political stage; but the communities of Wales, and

especially their leaders, were caught up in the confrontation. Richard II had been building up support in the Principality: Welshmen were beginning to appear among the lists of his esquires and the yeomen of the livery of the Crown, and two of the doughtiest esquires of north Wales, Rhys and Gwilym ap Tudur, had been retained to stay with the king for life on an annual pension of £10. It is not difficult to believe that the events of the summer of 1399 were distressing for such men; they left them leaderless and deprived of opportunities. Other communities in Wales were caught up in the maelstrom: the men of Glamorgan refused to respond to the summons of their lord in August 1399 and were to be left lordless in the following January when he was executed; those of Usk just managed to escape Henry Bolingbroke's wrath as he moved westwards from Bristol, if we are to accept Adam of Usk's versions of events and of his own personal role in it. At Brecon the story was a different one, for Henry Bolingbroke was lord of Brecon and had come to claim his inheritance. His tenants rode out to Gloucester to meet him and reinforce his army; the castles of Brecon and Hay were hurriedly defended 'against the malice of King Richard and the lord's enemies coming from Ireland'; spies were dispatched to find out Richard's movements; and the receiver of Brecon rode at speed to arrange for the defence of the castles of Kidwelly and Carreg Cennen (now part of the rightful inheritance of Bolingbroke after the death of his father in February 1399). The Lancaster castles in the east—Monmouth, Whitecastle, Grosmont, and Skenfrith—were likewise repaired and guards placed in them. As Bolingbroke's army moved north, ripples of excitement and terror must have spread throughout the Welsh communities of the north-east. Even in Dyffryn Clwyd, well away from the direct route of the various armies, the *frisson* of excitement was sufficient for the commote court at Coelion to be adjourned on 7 August 'because of the coming of Henry, duke of Lancaster, with a great army into Cheshire'. Normal life was suspended as news spread of an imminent confrontation.[21]

  There had not been such excitement in Wales since Edward II's day, and many of the country's local communities were, directly or otherwise, involved in it. It is of course impossible to gauge exactly the impact of such dramatic events so close at home on the atmosphere in Wales; but it is difficult to believe that they did not lead to raising the level of political awareness and engagement. As news of the short-lived and abortive Cheshire rising of 1400 reached Wales the heightened tensions and nervousness were again inflamed, barely after they had subsided. In no part of Wales was the atmosphere likely to be more fraught than in the north-east corner of the country. There, within the space of two short years, the map of power and authority had been dramatically transformed and redrawn yet again; the two premier lords of the area, the earl of Arundel and Richard II, had each in turn been ousted and eliminated; the major castles of the district—

Flint, Holt, and Chirk in Wales, Shrewsbury and Chester across the border in England—had been deeply involved in the unfolding of traumatic events. It was in such a hothouse political atmosphere that Owain Glyn Dŵr, formerly a squire of the earl of Arundel and subsequently a tenant of Richard II as prince of Chester, contemplated his options for the future.[22]

He and his fellow squires in Wales had witnessed, especially after 1396, a more fundamental redrawing of the map of English power in Wales than anyone could recall (Maps 3a and 3b). Death, as usual, had played a prominent part. The young earl of Pembroke had died in 1389, leaving three of the Marcher lordships of Wales—Pembroke, Abergavenny, and Cilgerran—without a lord or even an heir. Thomas, earl of Stafford and lord of Newport and Caus, died in 1392, to be followed to the grave within less than three years by his brother William, leaving the lordships in custody during the minority of a third brother, Edmund. Most devastating and unexpected of all was the death in Ireland in July 1398 of Roger Mortimer, earl of March and lord of sixteen Welsh lordships. The vacuum of authority he left was matched by the desolation of the individuals and com-munities, especially in Wales, who had built their expectations around him. Finally, in February 1399 John of Gaunt—lord of Monmouth, Threecastles, and Cydweli—died in the fullness of years; within a month the exile of his son, Henry Bolingbroke (himself already lord of Brecon in his wife's right), was converted into permanent banishment and his estates confiscated. Death, aided and abetted by royal high-handedness, had wrought mighty havoc in the March of Wales; more than half its lordships were either in royal hands or formed the jointure or dower rights of widows.

Nor was that all by a long shot. Between 1396 and 1399 Richard II eliminated what death by natural causes had not already culled. The first menacing indica-tion of Richard's intentions came in 1396 when he arranged for the earl of Warwick to be deprived of the lordship of Gower in favour of the earl of Nottingham, and compounded the loss by imposing a fine of £5,333 on Warwick for illegal possession of the lordship by the Beauchamp family since 1383. This was indeed, as the earl of Warwick's clerk called it, 'the year of tribulation of my lord'; but worse was to follow, for Warwick and others. The earl of Nottingham, or duke of Norfolk as he now was, did not enjoy Gower long. In September 1398 he was banished from England for life and Gower was taken into royal custody. His grandmother, the long-lived duchess of Norfolk, died in March 1399 and her estates (including Chepstow) were appropriated by the Crown. Meanwhile, in autumn 1397 the earl of March's title to his greatest Marcher lordship, that of Denbigh, was challenged by another of the king's favourites, the earl of Salisbury; and though the challenge was not successful it placed a question-mark not only over Mortimer's title to Denbigh but over his whole political future in the bizarre

world being created by Richard II. The single greatest act in the creation of that world was the coup that Richard staged against his opponents, the earls of Arundel, Gloucester, and Warwick, in July 1397; the impact of the confiscations that followed on the map of English power in Wales was little short of devastating. The three great Arundel lordships in the north-east—Bromfield and Yale, Chirkland, and Oswestry—were retained in the king's own hand; the other Arundel lordship in the area, Clun, was bestowed for life on the duke of Aumale. The elimination of the duke of Gloucester brought the lordship of Huntington, the castle and manor of Caldicot, and a share of Brecon into the king's control, while the forfeiture of the earl of Warwick, already deprived of Gower, likewise brought the lordship of Elfael into the king's control.[23]

Never, not even in Edward II's turbulent reign, had there been such a dramatic redrawing of the map of English royal and aristocratic power in Wales as in the three hectic years 1396–9, and the mastermind behind the exercise was Richard II. In the north-east he created a new principality for himself, annexing the three Arundel lordships into his enlarged and newly titled principality of Chester. Elsewhere he placed his trusted friends in control of lands seized from his enemies or falling into royal custody: Thomas Percy, earl of Worcester, at Haverford, the duke of Aumale at Clun, and the duke of Exeter at Huntington, Cydweli, Monmouth, and in control of the Mortimer estates in south Wales. But it was the favours showered on William Lescrope, newly created earl of Wiltshire, which showed how Richard prized Wales as an area in which he could reward his friends and consolidate his power: between 1396 and 1399 Lescrope secured a life-grant of the county of Anglesey, custody of the Mortimer estates (including Denbigh) in north Wales, and the forfeited Beauchamp lordship of Elfael; he was appointed justice of north Wales, Chester, Flint, and the Arundel lordships; he was keeper of the strategic castle of Pembroke; and he was appointed constable of Beaumaris, Caernarfon, Conway, and Holt for life.[24]

Nowhere, in short, was the impact of Richard II's political revenge so complete and dramatic as in Wales. Nowhere, by the same token, was his downfall in August–September 1399 to have more far-reaching repercussions on the territorial order. Some of the earlier confiscations were now reversed, notably as the great bloc of Arundel estates was restored to its heir. But the territorial map could not be restored to its shape in 1396: death had removed Mortimer, Gloucester, and Mowbray. Indeed the story of forfeiture continued after 1399, as Glamorgan fell into royal custody on the execution of its lord, Thomas Despenser, for his part in a plot against the new king in January 1400. Ironically, Richard II's deposition allowed Henry IV to enjoy a territorial pre-eminence in Wales such as none of his predecessors as kings of England had enjoyed: even if we ignore the extensive estates in temporary royal custody, he held the Principality lands in North and

South Wales and Flintshire as king, the lordships of Monmouth, Threecastles, Cydweli, and Ogmore as duke of Lancaster, and the very rich lordships of Brecon and Hay as the husband of the late Mary Bohun. The map of Wales would never be the same after the *bouleversements* of the last four years.

But were these great upheavals more than the working out of the tensions and quarrels of English politics on the atlas of territorial power in Wales? It is difficult to believe that they left the communities of Wales, and especially its leaders, unmoved and unaffected. In a society where ties of lordship were elemental, men found themselves disoriented by the rapidity of change. Where, for example, was a man like John ap Harry to place himself? A man of noble Welsh lineage, he was also active across the border in Herefordshire politics and administration. It was no surprise that he should have found service with Henry Bolingbroke, acting as his deputy steward of Brecon by 1396 and taking Elizabeth, the daughter of Sir Hugh Waterton (Bolingbroke's chamberlain), to wife. For such a man Boling-broke's exile in September 1398, converted into permanent banishment in March 1399, must have come as a hammer blow. But he learnt to adjust to the new dispensation, for he appears in July 1399 as steward of Elfael for William Lescrope. Barely had he adjusted to his new post than the arrival of Bolingbroke's army at Bristol recalled him to his old loyalties, and it was to be in Bolingbroke's service as King Henry IV that John ap Harry's career was to flourish. John ap Harry could certainly not have been indifferent to the political upheavals of these years: it was he who was given the task of carrying Richard II's goods and jewels, deposited hurriedly in Pembroke as he dashed back from Ireland in July 1399, to London, and it was his erstwhile master, William Lescrope, who was one of the earliest victims of Bolingbroke's arrival in England. Many others must have been caught in the same kind of cross-winds of loyalty. Which way should John Skidmore, for example, jump, for his career before 1399 (steward of William Beauchamp's lordship of Abergavenny, Bolingbroke's deputy steward in Brecon but also a royal esquire of Richard II and a member of the council of the duke of Exeter) pulled him in several directions? And who would now be the focus of service for men such as Rhys and Gwilym ap Tudur of Anglesey who had hitched their wagon so firmly to Richard II's star? And what of Owain Glyn Dŵr, whose family had moved in the orbit of the powerful earls of Arundel, lords of Chirkland, before the trauma of 1397?[25]

It is in this respect primarily that the English political earthquakes of the years 1397–1400 had an impact on native Welsh society and its mood. Territorial counters might be moved blithely at the whim of a high-handed king; but loyalties could not be so easily broken and reforged. Richard II's new, augmented principality of Chester was too recently assembled to submerge memories of the rule of the Arundels, and in any case he seems to have made little effort to

cultivate the support and affection of the men of Welsh lordships or to reward them with office. Elsewhere his favourites—Aumale, Exeter, Lescrope—had immense power in theory; but in practice they were *parvenus* who did not have the time to exercise the delicate arts of good lordship which were the best guarantee of a community's support in a crisis. So it was that when the crisis arrived in July–August 1399 the Welsh sat on their hands. The men of Glamorgan refused to respond to Despenser's rallying call and those of north Wales to the desperate pleas of the earl of Salisbury. The duke of Aumale, according to Creton, believed that the Welsh pitied Richard II's plight; but their pity was not a sufficiently potent emotion to prompt them to fight for him once Bolingbroke had seized the initiative. Whether through lack of commitment or want of leadership, the Welsh contented themselves with being passive bystanders at the momentous events happening in their country. Such passivity was an eloquent comment. They were at sea in a world where they had been asked to make frequent somersaults with their loyalties. Men so disoriented were dangerous men. Detached from old loyalties, they could now enjoy the disturbing experience of being free to forge new ones, indeed to redraw entirely the map of their priorities and affections. Such, at least for some, was the world of Wales in 1400.[26]

Such a dislocation of loyalties was, arguably, more potentially dangerous in Wales than in England since it allowed atavistic mythologies and suppressed national ambitions to emerge once more. Wales, so it appeared, had been thoroughly and irreversibly conquered. More important, the fact that there had been no major revolt since 1294–5 suggested that the Welsh had come to terms with the facts of conquest. Yet a lingering suspicion remained. 'Welshmen', as two royal officers had observed in the wake of the conquest, 'are Welshmen, and you need to understand them properly.' That still remained true a century later; Welshmen were still different, suspiciously so. They were still not part of the English state governmentally, judicially, legally, fiscally, or politically; their customs, language, and culture still kept them apart from their English neighbours; and their political volatility and general unreliability were notorious. They may have lived down much of their reputation during a century of peace; but a few isolated incidents and ample rumours (especially from English settlers in Wales) still kept old suspicions and distrust of the Welsh alive. 'Beware of Wales', the warning of an English political pamphlet of the 1430s, could well have been the watchword of the English governors of Wales throughout the fourteenth century.[27]

Even if one trusted the Welsh, the vulnerability of the country to invasion from the sea was a fact of life in the late fourteenth century. The threat came from two directions. In the south, the Franco-Castilian fleets which were such a

menace to the southern English coastline in the 1370s and 1380s posed an equally obvious threat to Wales, all the more so if their ambitions could exploit native Welsh discontent. In the north, rapidly deteriorating relations between England and Scotland in the 1380s allowed Scottish ships to use the western sea-route to embarrass the English. For example, when a small Scottish landing party made a

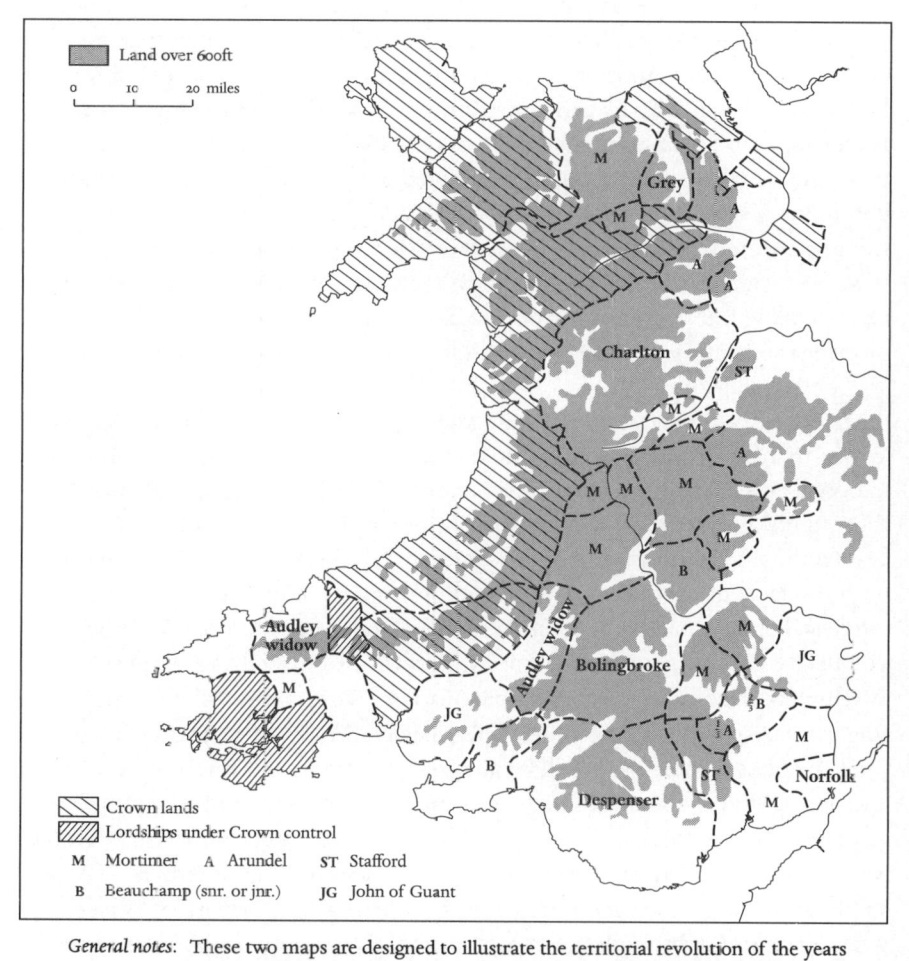

General notes: These two maps are designed to illustrate the territorial revolution of the years
1396–9 in Wales in broad terms. They do not attempt to represent all the details
of wardships, dower-and jointure–rights, etc. In some cases there is uncertainty
as to the titles, especially the short–lived titles, to certain lordships.

MAP 3. (*a*) The distribution of territorial power in Wales *c*.1395 (to illustrate the power of the Crown and of the Mortimer, Arundel, and other English aristocratic families)

surprise attack on Anglesey in 1381 and damaged a few houses in Beaumaris, the alarm was no doubt completely disproportionate to the seriousness of the incident. For twenty years after 1369—in other words from the recommencement of England's war with France to the conclusion of a long-term truce between the two countries—periodic reviews were undertaken of Welsh castles; repairs were ordered; the chamberlain and an armed escort toured the countryside; and

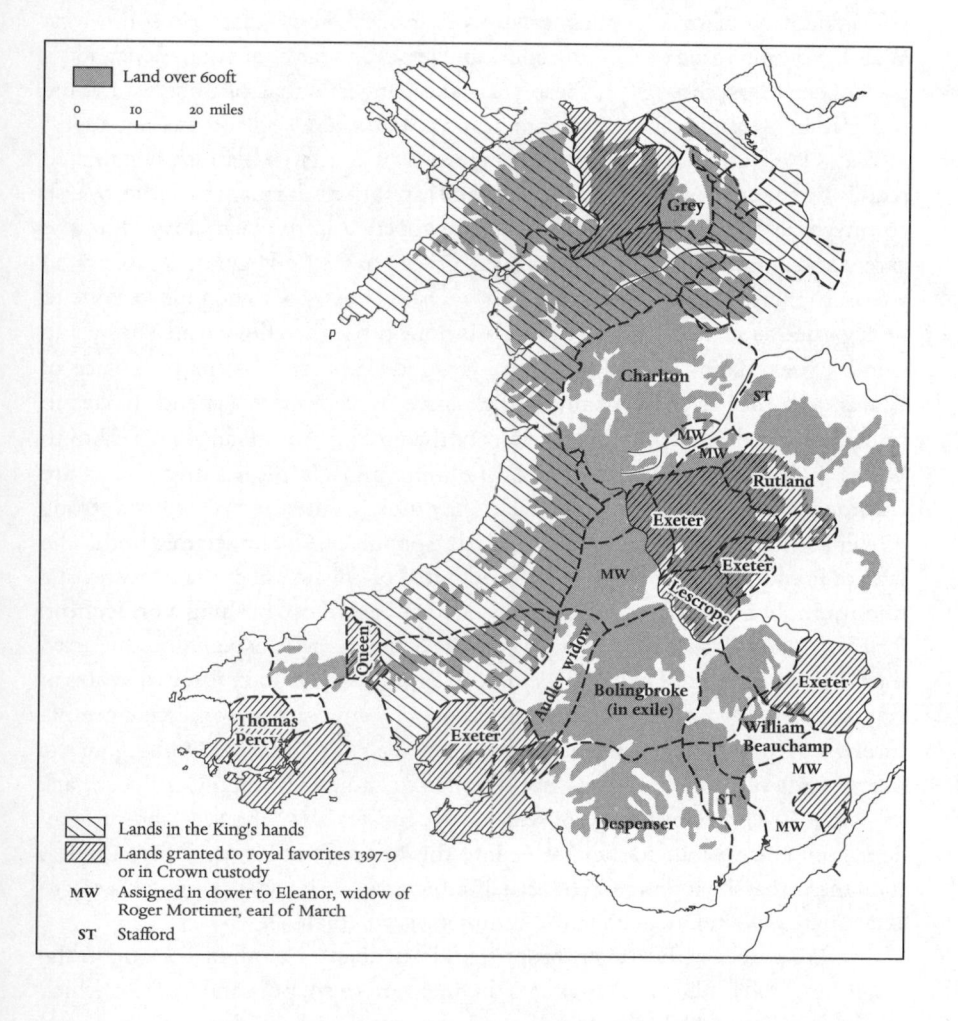

(b) The distribution of territorial power in Wales, May 1399 (to illustrate the transformation, especially in the Crown's power either directly or through its favourites, as a result of the deaths and confiscations of 1396–9)

garrisons were located in several castles, notably Beaumaris, Caernarfon, cricieth, Carmarthen, and Pembroke. Many of these garrisons were small and temporary, but others were substantial by contemporary standards—140 men at Pembroke in 1377; twenty-four archers in Carmarthen during the summer of 1385; or the twenty men placed in Beaumaris Castle in 1389 on the chamberlain's order, 'because of enemies at sea'. The atmosphere of suspicion and rumour was fed by extraordinary incidents such as the report in 1387–8 that two respectable burgesses of Llansteffan had taken a Castilian spy on a tour of the king's castles in south-west Wales. Nothing came of these rumours and invasion scares, but in understanding the collective psychology of these years the danger is that of underestimating rather than of exaggerating their significance. Wales, like England, was on edge.[28]

Wales's edginess was the more dangerous of the two, because it could so readily be twinned with the disaffection and aspirations dormant in native Welsh communities. That is precisely what had happened in the years 1369–78 in the career and ambitions of Owain Lawgoch (Owain of the Red Hand), the man who was in so many respects the forerunner of Owain Glyn Dŵr and indeed came to be regarded as such. Owain Lawgoch was none other than Owain ap Thomas ap Rhodri, great-nephew of Llywelyn ap Gruffudd, first and last native prince of Wales, and the last descendant of the native dynasty of Gwynedd. It was in respect of this exalted and unique descent that, in 1372, he advanced his claim to Wales, 'which country is and should be mine by right'. Legitimist claims are common; but to acquire any credibility they must secure the backing of a strong power and a measure of acceptance from the populace. Owain secured both. The king of France quickly recognized the potential of Owain's claim as a means, at a minimum, of embarrassing the English, and at best of establishing a bridgehead for French power in Wales. So it was that he actively and substantially supported the two attempts that Owain made to lead a naval and military force to Wales in 1370 and 1372. Owain returned the compliment by concluding, somewhat prematurely, a perpetual treaty of alliance between Wales and France. Nothing, in the event, came of either enterprise nor of a plan to launch a Franco-Castilian attack on Wales in 1376–7; but they showed clearly how Wales, like Scotland or Flanders, could be exploited as an entrée into the kingdom of England. The English took the threat, be it potential or actual, sufficiently seriously to dispatch a spy to assassinate Owain Lawgoch in the summer of 1378 (plate 1).

Owain's career is, however, more significant than as a minor episode in the Anglo-French conflict after 1369; it is the measure of support and interest which his claim elicited which is striking. Owain was the captain of a force of Welshmen drawn from various parts of Wales which played a not-undistinguished part in the French king's highly successful campaigns against the English in the 1370s, and also betook itself into the service of others when the opportunity arose.

Many of these soldiers were indeed to serve in France for twenty years or more. Such free companies of military adventurers were, of course, not unusual; but it is still striking that Owain ap Thomas ap Rhodri was able to assemble and retain the services of such a group of Welshmen. What is even more striking is the evidence that has been convincingly assembled of late to demonstrate that Owain's company and, even more significantly, his claim to be true prince of Wales received support from various Welshmen, including powerful and influential ones, from Flintshire to Anglesey. Messages passed to and fro, and so did money.

There is a strong tinge of the romantic and the quixotic about Owain's career; but there is also a considerable significance to it. It opens a small window on to a world which we have largely otherwise to imagine. It was a world in which legitimist claims were taken seriously, where the arms and the blood of the house of Gwynedd were still remembered and regarded. It was a world in which men hedged their bets, as Sir Gruffudd Llwyd and others had done so in the days of Edward II, co-operating fully and effectively with the English powers-that-be without altogether forfeiting their memory of, and loyalty to, a vision of an independent Wales. It was a world in which men had travelled abroad in military service and had at least noticed what role even humble Wales might play in an Anglo-French conflict which had spilt over the borders of many other European countries. What men made of this world was as yet largely a matter for their private conversation and for their consciences. But they cannot have been oblivious to it. Rhys and Gwilym ap Tudur in Anglesey must have been well aware of it, for their household poet addressed an *awdl* full of encouragement and expectation to Owain Lawgoch; and one of Owain's staunchest supporters was a distant relative of theirs. Owain Glyn Dŵr likewise cannot have been indifferent as a young man to the stories about Owain Lawgoch's bravado and, quite possibly, to the secret support he was receiving in Flintshire. In the fullness of time he was to remind the king of France that Owain Lawgoch, whose mantle had now fallen on Glyn Dŵr's shoulders, had died in the service of Charles V. These were years in which lessons were being learnt.[29]

The years between Owain Lawgoch's assassination in 1378 and the Glyn Gŵr revolt in 1400 are not a period in which one can say, without the benefit of hindsight, that tension within Wales palpably increased (at least as far as the fragmentary evidence allows us to assess the mood of public opinion). But equally, tension does not appear to have subsided greatly. In May 1381 the government established a commission—one of whose members was Owain Glyn Dŵr's father-in-law—to review 'the condition of Wales and its people', to hold discussions with key persons, and to make arrangements for the general peace. Clearly there was some unease in government circles; but within the

month much more dramatic events in south-east England diverted attention elsewhere. There was sufficient concern about Wales's security for small garrisons to be posted at various Welsh castles in the 1380s, for very considerable sums (over £400) to be spent on repairs at Caernarfon Castle in 1383–97, and for a man to be posted on the walls there in 1394 and 1397 'because of certain rumours'. In south Wales two events in 1385 and 1389 raised the temperature of fear and resentment considerably: the first was the murder of John Lawrence, deputy justiciar of South Wales and a prominent burgess of Carmarthen town, by a leading Welshman; the other was a judicial inquiry held by the earl of Arundel at Carmarthen when 'a prominent Welshman of gentle birth' died in custody and 'there was great consequent unrest among the Welsh'. In the 1390s a spectacular incident took place in the county court at Flint in June 1394 when some of the leading Welshmen of the county disrupted the court, insulted the steward, and trampled the court rolls under foot. Several of the ringleaders were subsequently sent to the Tower of London to cool their heels; even more significant is that thirteen of them were later to be prominent supporters of Owain Glyn Dŵr. The volatility of this particular region of Wales was given ample opportunity for expression once again during the dramatic events of 1397–9, so it comes as no surprise that in the summer of 1398 fifty of the leading men of Flintshire (headed by Hywel ap Tudur ab Ithel) were bound over to be of good behaviour towards the king.[30]

It is difficult to know what significance, if any, is to be assigned to isolated incidents such as these (and no doubt others like them). Many of them were born out of local feuds and were of little import beyond their immediate localities; others blew up quickly and died away with equal speed. What is, however, clear is that old tensions and suspicions were still in good heart and being well cultivated—be they the vocal resentment of the Welshmen of Narberth in south-west Wales or of the Welsh burgesses of Caerwys in the north-east towards their English neighbours, or equally the paranoid anti-Welsh opinions of the English border shires and the English plantation boroughs in Wales. The two communities were still not fully at ease with each other, and the fear—or expectation—of raids from across the seas only served to compound the mutual suspicion. Yet neither the tensions nor the nervousness were new; they were no more than a mildly chronic condition. No one could have anticipated the thunderbolt which struck Wales in 1400.[31]

No one could have anticipated the thunderbolt; and yet no one should have been surprised by it. An early fourteenth-century observer would certainly not have been caught off his guard, for he had commented perceptively, if wearily: 'The Welsh habit of revolt against the English is an old-standing madness . . . From

the sayings of the prophet Merlin they still hope to recover England. Hence it is that the Welsh frequently rebel, hoping to give effect to the prophecy.' Whether the equation between prophetic expectation and revolt was quite so direct may be open to question, but that an understanding of contemporary Welsh political ideology is central to an analysis of the mentality of revolt is not in doubt. Rebellions, especially rebellions which are sustained for years against the odds, can only ultimately be explained in terms of men's convictions and aspirations.[32]

In Wales those convictions were both profoundly old and utterly contemporary; it was their antiquity and agelessness which gave them their potency and relevance. They were indestructible until the day arrived when they would be realized. Features of Welsh political mythology are recorded as early as the ninth century in the *Historia Brittonum* later attributed to Nennius, and even then they are said to be based on 'the tradition of our ancestors'. Its prophetic aspects are even more clearly delineated in the tenth-century Welsh poem *Armes Prydein Vawr*. Thereafter across almost five centuries until the days of Owain Glyn Dŵr this mythology was solemnly transmitted from one generation to the next, each generation doubtlessly adding its own interpretations and encrustations to what was now a canon of history, mythology, and prophecy. The most serious challenge to this essentially native Welsh oral mythology came with the appearance of Geoffrey of Monmouth's remarkable *History of the Kings of Britain c.*1136; but so indebted was Geoffrey to many of the native Welsh traditions and so resilient and unimpeachable was Welsh mythology that its response to Geoffrey's book was to absorb it, on its own terms, as essential confirmation of the truthfulness of its claims. Such was the mythology on which Owain Glyn Dŵr and the Welshmen of his day were reared; such was the mythology in which his revolt was rooted. But it was a mythology which long survived his revolt. In Wales in Elizabeth's day it seemed as green as ever, and the prophecies of Myrddin (Merlin) and Taliesin as meaningfully pregnant as they had ever been. When Daniel Defoe remarked on his visit to Wales in the 1720s that 'the stories of Vortigern and Roger Mortimer are in every mouth here', he was recording the resilience of a mythology which was by then at least a thousand years old and in which unrelated episodes from the past were yoked together to make them serviceable for the present and the future. It was a mythology in which the heroes and villains of the Welsh past—Macsen (Magnus Maximus), Hengist, Vortigern, Arthur, and Llywelyn, to name but a few—stood shoulder to shoulder with each other across the centuries in the service of a common reading of past and future. In time, the name of Owain Glyn Dŵr would be added to this pantheon.[33]

One prominent feature of the mythology was the conviction of the Welsh that they were the descendants of the original inhabitants of the Island of Britain and that they would one day reclaim it in its entirety, reinstate its ancient name,

Britain, delete the hated name 'England', and see their rightful prince crowned in London and exercising the 'sovereignty of Britain'. As an archbishop of Canterbury had put it: 'The Welsh, being sprung by unbroken succession from the original stock of Britons, boast of all Britain as theirs by right.' It was a reassuring and uplifting vision and one which was as intoxicating in the fourteenth century, as the letters of Sir Gruffudd Llwyd and Owain Glyn Dŵr showed, as ever. Such an escape into the world of fantasy could, of course, only be sustained by casting the bread of hope utterly on the waters of prophecy. And that is what the Welsh had done throughout the Middle Ages and beyond. They based their case on the unimpeachable prophecies of the twin ancient soothsayers, Myrddin and Taliesin; it was their vaticinations which 'the masters of Brut' reinterpreted for each expectant generation. It was in the light of this vaticinatory lore, as we shall see, that Glyn Dŵr was to launch one of the most remarkably audacious of his political programmes. It was likewise in the light of the same lore that he could cast himself as the deliverer, ̦y *mab darogan*. For one of the central axioms of Welsh mythology—in common with so much prophetic writing and popular belief throughout medieval Europe—was that a Messiah would arrive who would fulfil the Merlinic prophecies, expel the English, and restore the Welsh to their old name (that is, 'Britons') and to the control of the Island of Britain. Cynan and Cadwaladr, both of them historical personages securely cocooned in a web of traditions, were early contenders for this role, while Arthur likewise quickly acquired a similar reputation. The name of Owain had also now been added to the short-list; it was an addition which some of Glyn Dŵr's supporters were unlikely to overlook, even if he himself had not drawn attention to it.[34]

Hope and deliverance were, therefore, two of the cardinal motifs of contemporary mythology in Wales; hatred and revenge were the others. Hatred was directed in particular at two groups—first at those men, of whom Vortigern and Medrawd were the prime exemplars, whose personal ambitions had brought about the downfall of the Britons and whose treachery alone could explain the losses and oppressions (W. *gormesoedd*) of such a proud people; secondly at the Saxons—variously identified through their leaders such as Hengist, Horsa, or Edwin or collectively as the children of Rhonwen (Hengist's daughter betrothed to the arch-betrayer, Vortigern)—whose expulsion from their illegal control of the island was the necessary precondition for the recovery of British sovereignty. To this age-old sense of treachery and defeat were added more recent memories of disinheritance at the hands of Normans and English in the last few generations. A Glamorgan Welshman, for example, could recall almost three centuries later how his ancestor had been dispossessed by Robert fitz Hamon; even more recent was the resentment of the men of Dyffryn Clwyd, who recalled in 1379 how their forebears had been wrongfully expelled more than a century earlier by Reginald

de Grey. The pent-up resentments of disinheritance and defeat, of suffering exile in their own land, as Hopcyn ap Tomas's scribe put it vividly, weighed heavily on the Welsh; it fuelled a crude anti-Englishness which lay but barely below the surface of fourteenth-century Welsh society. 'Rout the English' (W. *rhuthro Eingl*) was the war-cry of the poet; it would soon be matched by Owain Glyn Dŵr's venom against 'the madness of the Saxon barbarians who have usurped the land of Wales'.[35]

It was upon mythologies, prophecies, and ideologies such as these that his revolt was nourished and sustained. There is little doubt that they circulated widely in the Wales of Owain Glyn Dŵr as they had for generations, the hopelessness of the situation making it, if anything, all the more necessary that they be believed. They were rehearsed and elaborated at those open-air, hilltop assemblies (W. *cymanfaoedd*) of which later observers tell us, or at 'nightly gatherings of Welshmen called Dadelowes [debates]' recorded in an early four-teenth-century source. When on the morrow of the revolt a report referred to 'divers congregations and meetings privily . . . whereby young people are the more wild in governance', it takes us perhaps closest to the world in which the ideology of discontent was being ventilated and promoted.[36]

Two groups in particular might be regarded as the fomenters and propagators of such an ideology. The first was composed of monks, friars, and other church-men. Cistercian monasteries might be especially singled out as potential centres of disaffection in that they were among the premier repositories of Welsh literary and historical traditions and because of the close links they enjoyed with neigh-bouring Welsh *uchelwyr* families. Already in the earlier fourteenth century it was claimed that 'unlawful assemblies' were held at Strata Marcella Abbey 'to excite contentions between the English and the Welsh'. Whitland Abbey connived at these activities and continued to do so, for more than a century later one of its monks was charged with wandering through Wales, holding riotous assemblies, propagating Welsh chronicles and prophecies, and inciting the people to rebel-lion. It is little wonder that Owain Glyn Dŵr found some of his doughtiest supporters in the ranks of the Cistercians, nor equally that Henry IV should visit his spleen on the monastery of Strata Florida, the Cistercian house with an unparalleled commitment to collecting and promoting the historical and literary antiquities of Wales. The second group which was, not without good reason, suspected of being professional purveyors of sedition were the bards, rhymers, and minstrels. Their professions were suspect because they were itinerant and lived by levying subsidies (W. *commorthau*) from local communities. Some of them might be quasi-professional court poets of high status, such as was Iolo Goch who sang the praises of Owain Glyn Dŵr most fulsomely; the majority, one suspects, moved in far less exalted circles and practised an art which was far

less refined and archaic but at the same time more approachable and popular. These were the poets patronizingly dismissed by the true craftsmen as jongleurs, y glêr, hawking their ballads around the rural fairs and communal assemblies of Wales (W. *pastynwyr ffair*). Almost none of their poems has survived, but contemporaries were convinced in England that at the very least they 'excited the populace to evil through scandals and lies', and at worst that 'their prophecies, falsities [*messonges*] and incitements' could be, and indeed were, the cause of 'insurrection and rebellion' in Wales.[37]

The ingredients of insurrection and rebellion, and the ideology to justify them, were in place in Wales in the fourteenth century. Yet, in so far as the evidence permits us to see and in so far as we can divest ourselves of the historian's besetting sin of hindsight, there was no specific indication that revolt was imminent in the 1390s. What we do seem to register from some of the native poetry is a society out of sorts with itself, one in which long-standing tensions, resentments, and frustrations were now even more raw in a world turned upside down, in social values as well as in economic fortunes, by recurrent visitations of plague. Such was also the world of many parts of Europe, and there (as contemporaries observed) social dislocation and disillusion had relieved itself in 'the plague of rebellion', especially in the years 1378–82. At much the same time the Welsh poet Gruffudd Llwyd penned an ode which best expressed the morose sense of bitterness of a world of 'black sorrow' and 'evil' (W. *dudrist, drygfyd*). It was a world where social values and hierarchies were inverted, crops failed, and Welshmen staggered 'like drunken crows' under the yoke of 'oppression' (W. *brain brwysg . . . camrwysg*). From such a dire world there could in his view be only two escape-routes. The one led either to a distant past peopled by men such as Arthur and the roll-call of kings who had ruled the Island of Britain from their court in London, or to the glories of more recent days when a Welsh knight, Syr Hywel 'of the Axe', had served the Black Prince in France. The other route led to the only Welshman who could nowadays don the mantle of such heroes. He was, said the poet, none other than Owain Glyn Dŵr, a man who would not tolerate wrong and who would sit with earls.[38]

These were heady words, but heady words must normally attend on circumstances and personality if they are to be more than words. If any set of circumstances could be said to provide an ideal seed-bed for revolt, it was the political earthquake which overwhelmed Wales in the years 1396–1400, upending old loyalties and certainties and casting men adrift from established allegiances. As to personality, the poets were not amiss to devote such an amount of cloying attention to Owain Glyn Dŵr. His career epitomized the unresolved contradictions of native Welsh society—deference and defiance, acceptance of the

prospects of service to English lords balanced by memories of Welsh glory and prophecy, a training in English law and its opportunities, but accompanied by a bitter resentment of the exploitation of Wales and of the exclusion of Welshmen. Owain shared many of these qualities with other fellow Welshmen; but he also held a unique position and responsibility: he was, and was regarded as, the sole legitimate claimant to the dynastic pretensions to be the true native prince of Wales. It would be he alone who would have to decide whether and when that claim was to be activated.

PART II

⊷≖◦≖⊶

Revolt

⟶ INTRODUCTION ⟵

*I*n 1931 John Edward Lloyd published his classic study entitled *Owen Glendower Owen Glyn Dŵr*, based on lectures he had given in Oxford eleven years earlier. There was a distinct tone of disappointment in the prefatory note he wrote to the book: 'I have waited, perhaps unduly, for fresh evidence to come to light . . . In the picture I now present of Glyn Dŵr . . . there are no startling departures from the traditional portrait.' Lloyd's almost apologetic comment was at once both too modest and not modest enough. It was too modest because, with his usual meticulous care and shrewd judgement, Lloyd had securely established most of what can be known about the career of Owain Glyn Dŵr, cleared away (in his own words) 'a good deal of the undergrowth of legend and error which had gathered around' him, and reconstructed carefully the chronology of the revolt. In the sixty and more years which have elapsed since the publication of Lloyd's book, it is inevitable that some of the details of his narrative and an occasional dating of documents should stand in need of correction or amplification. Local studies of the character and impact of the revolt in different parts of Wales—such as Flintshire, Cydweli, and Cardiganshire—have added considerably to our understanding of the movement and the measure of support it commanded. Some new sources can now certainly be tapped for the study of the revolt: an important sheaf of letters about the revolt saw the light of day when M. Dominica Legge published her *Anglo-Norman Letters and Petitions from All Souls Ms. 182* (1941), while it is only since Lloyd's day that many of the unpublished English government records dealing with the period of the revolt—notably those of the Exchequer, the King's Bench, the Duchy of Lancaster, and the palatinate of Chester—have begun to be systematically explored. Yet in its account of the revolt Lloyd's book still remains the unchallenged and fundamental account; to borrow his own phrases, 'the fresh evidence' unearthed since his day has amplified and qualified his account without in any way providing 'startling departures' from it. As with so much of Lloyd's other work, there is an enduring solidity about his account of Owain Glyn Dŵr and his revolt.[1]

Yet in a way his self-effacing preface was not modest enough. His book announces itself as a biography and he himself presents it as 'a portrait'. It is

neither. His account of Owain before 1400 extends over no more than ten generously printed pages of text. What follows thereafter is a carefully crafted account of the revolt that overwhelmed much of Wales for the next few years; Owain appears in it regularly as an actor and a leader, but such appearances hardly constitute what can by normal standards be called a biography. The fault, of course, was not Lloyd's. The materials for a satisfactory biography of Owain Glyn Dŵr do not exist. He is ultimately a far more shadowy figure than his great Welsh predecessor, Llywelyn ap Gruffudd, Llywelyn 'the Last'. We should not mistake an account of the revolt for a 'portrait' of the man, however closely he and his revolt have become identified. A portrait is, by definition, an intimate and precise delineation of the character of an individual; for Owain Glyn Dŵr such a portrait is not historically possible. In such circumstances an alternative approach is to portray the society and the movement whose leader is such a historically elusive figure, to make good, in other words, the deficiencies of an intimate portrait by locating the individual on a much broader, panoramic canvas.[2]

Lloyd's approach to the problem was essentially different; he was true to the title of his book. The core of his short volume consists of a chronological account of the story-line of the revolt associated with Glyn Dŵr's name and led by him. Only one chapter, that on the Church during the revolt, is allowed to interrupt this rather austere story-line. Narrative was supreme; analytical comments or general observations on a society in revolt were made, if at all, *en passant*. Such an approach accorded well with Lloyd's talents as a meticulous scholar and fine narrator. It also identified the prime historiographical need of his day with regard to Glyn Dŵr, that of establishing as secure and well documented a chronological account of the revolt as possible. No one could do that better than J. E. Lloyd; no one, as has already been indicated, need undertake the task again.

Lloyd's account is taken for granted in the following chapters; their aim is essentially supplementary to his. Their primary purpose is to try to depict how the society which was portrayed in Part I of this book responded to the experience of a prolonged revolt. In other words it seeks to anatomize the nature of a rebellion which held most parts of Wales in its grip, to a greater or lesser degree, for at least three to six years, or longer. What did the experience of revolt mean to those who lived and fought in Wales across these turbulent years? What can be learnt about the nature of Welsh guerrilla warfare during the revolt and of the response of conventional English military strategy and thinking to the challenge it posed? What measure of support and opposition did the revolt enjoy within Wales and how was it deployed? Can the nature of the charismatic leadership of Owain Glyn Dŵr himself, and his liaison with local leaders, be brought into clearer focus? What does the revolt reveal about the dreams and aspirations of Welshmen in what was to prove to be their last major revolt? These are the kinds

of questions which the following chapters will try to address, in order, as it were, to get beyond the story-line of rebellion to recover the experience of revolt.

But it is with the story-line that we must begin. The next chapter attempts to provide a brisk chronological account of the revolt from its outbreak in autumn 1400 to the fall of Harlech Castle to English forces early in 1409. In essence it is a summary of the narrative story as established by Lloyd in 1931, following as he was in the footsteps of two earlier Welsh antiquaries, Robert Vaughan of Hengwrt (d. 1667) and, especially, Thomas Pennant (d. 1798); but it also supplements and amends Lloyd's account in several directions in the light of work undertaken since his day and of unpublished documents. These amendments in themselves are rarely of great significance; but they do serve to draw attention to certain major considerations which need to be borne in mind in considering the revolt and in constructing what may often prove to be much too firm a story-line for it. It is as well to approach the following chapters with these 'health warnings' firmly in mind.

The first relates to the often highly localized and fragmented nature of the revolt. This may, of course, be in part a factor of the very uneven nature of the surviving documentation: we are far better informed, for example, about events in certain parts of Wales—in Flintshire or around the town of Kidwelly, or in the Tywi valley for a week or so in July 1403—than we are about what happened in the rest of the country. But there is more to this localism than documentary accident. The more closely the revolt is studied the more obvious is it that, like so much guerrilla warfare, it often has its own local chronologies. Occasional battles and sieges of regional and even national significance there certainly were during the revolt; but much of the rebel activity took the form of local ambushes and skirmishes. It is only by chance, for example, that we learn of an attack by Owain on the lordship of Dyffryn Clwyd in September 1402. More significantly, the records of Flintshire report three skirmishes on 19 July 1404, 13 April 1405, and 6 March 1406 in which several prominent Welshmen in the area were killed. None of the skirmishes seems to have altered the military balance in Wales as a whole; in none of them, apparently, were more than six Welshmen rebels killed. Yet in the story of the revolt in Flintshire itself these local skirmishes may not have been without significance: in the second attack Maredudd ap Llywelyn Ddu, a prominent landowner and official in Maelor Saesneg, a close acquaintance of Owain Glyn Dŵr and uncle to his wife, was killed; while the third episode, in which the burgesses of Flint attacked and killed a local rebel leader in his hilltop hide-out, entered into local legend.[3]

The Welsh were certainly able to show a considerable degree of co-ordinated planning and action in their activities, often using the upland tracks of the country to move over great distances and to surprise their enemies. The initial

outbreak of the revolt, the capture of Conway Castle in April 1401, the great march down the Tywi valley in the summer of 1403, the summoning of parliaments, the co-ordination of plans with the French, and the dispatch of commands to local leaders such as Henry Don of Kidwelly or Rhys Ddu at Aberystwyth—to name but a few episodes—all of them indicate that we should not underestimate the measure of central direction and co-ordination on the Welsh side. But the very nature of the terrain and the character of guerrilla warfare must often have meant that for long periods the revolt was little more than the sum of its local episodes. Therein indeed lay part of the explanation for its resilience and longevity.

And since the episodes of the revolt were often localized, so also was the English response to them. We can construct our accounts of that response around the royal expeditions into Wales and the creation of regional and sometimes national commands to cope with the rebellion. Even at that level we are often dependent on the vagaries of documentation: thus, were it not for the survival of one damaged account we would have virtually no record of the substantial force of over 450 men urgently dispatched to raise the siege of the town and castle of Cardiff in December 1404 and of the desperate collection of supplies in Bristol and Monmouth to meet its needs. In fact the grand military expeditions had no more than a limited success. The defeat of Owain Glyn Dŵr was to be achieved through a slow process of attrition and local defections and victories. In that story it is the unspectacular services of garrison troops and local forays and punitive expeditions which were often most crucial. In short, a single story-line may well over-simplify the nature of the revolt and suggest a single chronology where a multiple one might be more appropriate.[4]

Secondly, such a military story-line may also serve to simplify our image of the revolt itself. As is so often the case with revolts, it is difficult for a narrative account to do justice to the complexity of the situation and to the shifting character of loyalties. In the early years of the Glyn Dŵr revolt in particular the situation changed rapidly from month to month and place to place; revolts flared up suddenly and unpredictably, but submissions and pardons show that such outbreaks were often extremely short-lived. In late winter 1401, for example, Owain and his forces were laying siege to Harlech and threatening the town and castle of Caernarfon, but in the same month the men of Cardiganshire and Carmarthenshire were submitting to the king and judicial sessions were being proclaimed. Likewise, in January 1402 Owain Glyn Dŵr was attacking the Grey lordship of Dyffryn Clwyd; but the courts of the lordship were scarcely disrupted and during the same month the prince of Wales's auditors were hearing accounts in north Wales. What episodes such as these illustrate is that the situation in Wales in these years was much more fluid than an *ex post facto* narrative might

suggest, and that generalized conclusions as to the state of the country should not necessarily be drawn from what are often localized incidents. What we can therefore best hope to do is no more than to highlight some of the key episodes in the military history of the revolt from 1400 to 1409, to register some of the most significant shifts in the balance of military power during those years, and to communicate something of the confused and confusing state of a country swept by revolt for so many years.

REVOLT IN WALES 1400–1409

Owain Glyn Dŵr was proclaimed prince of Wales at his own manor of Glyndyfrdwy on 16 September 1400. The immediate trigger for this extraordinary, indeed bizarre, act of defiance was almost certainly a quarrel with his near neighbour, Reginald, Lord Grey of Ruthin, be it over a deliberately delayed summons for Glyn Dŵr to accompany the king on his expedition to Scotland or over a local boundary dispute. The immediate pretext for the revolt is, in fact, of little importance, for the very nature of the proclamation made it clear that this was a premeditated act based on long-festering grievances and an attachment to an ideology of an independent Wales governed by its own native, legitimate ruler. Such dreams are not suddenly manufactured in a moment of pique. It is also clear that the movement of 1400 was carefully planned and co-ordinated among the disaffected leaders of Welsh society in north Wales. For five days, 18–23 September, Owain's supporters attacked English towns in north-east Wales: Ruthin, Denbigh, Rhuddlan, Flint (where they attacked an English relieving force under Robert Mascy), Holt, Oswestry (where they caused so much destruction that the earl of Arundel was prompted to grant a new charter to his English burgesses there), and Welshpool. Equally striking, though frequently overlooked, was the outbreak of rebellion in north-west Wales, including Anglesey, at much the same time. The whole of north Wales was to some degree involved in the rising: that is confirmed by the general pardon issued in March 1401.[1]

The outbreak was deemed sufficiently serious to galvanize the English authorities into action. Henry IV diverted his army on its journey home from Scotland, arrived at Shrewsbury on 26 September, and led a lightning campaign into north Wales, returning to Shrewsbury by 15 October. It is a measure of how much he saw the danger as being concentrated as much, if not more, in north-west Wales as in Glyn Dŵr's home base in the north-east that he left a garrison of twenty men-at-arms and eighty archers to defend the castles at Caernarfon, Cricieth, and Harlech, and smaller forces at Conway, Denbigh, and Beaumaris. In Dyffryn Clwyd itself, the very first target of the rebels, the authorities showed that they were firmly back in control by ordering the execution on 28 September

of eight of those involved in the attack of Ruthin, while the dispatch of the four quarters of the body of Gronw ap Tudur to four border towns was calculated to put fear into the hearts of the rebels and resolve into those of nervous English burgesses.[2]

The English authorities could congratulate themselves that their rapid and firm response had nipped the revolt in the bud; it was almost literally a one-week, or at most a one-month, wonder. Already by 23 October 1400 the special relief forces assembled at Chester had been disbanded and the garrison at Flint Castle scaled down to a mere two men-at-arms and eight archers. Some of the leading rebels, including one of Glyn Dŵr's own sons, had already thrown in the towel, while the government for its part showed magnanimity by extending a pardon and its protection to all Welshmen who submitted. The outbreak had been confined to north Wales, and when defensive measures were taken elsewhere they were specifically directed against 'the rebels of north Wales'. By early 1401 perhaps only two factors could be said to be worrying. The first was that Owain and some of his key supporters were still at large and unreconciled. Spies were sent in various directions, into Merionethshire and Llŷn and Eifionydd, to try to track him down, while the confiscation of all his estates indicated that the government had very little intention of forgiving and forgetting him at least. Secondly, the short-lived revolt had rekindled the flames of anti-Welsh sentiments in the political classes in England. Such sentiments were given full vent in the Hilary parliament of 1401, and the king and his council acceded to the outcry by issuing the first batch of statutes and ordinances against the Welsh in March 1401. Such measures could be dismissed as no more than a sop to popular prejudice and a reminder to the Welsh to toe the line and show due deference; but in truth they were counter-productive. They convinced the Welsh that they were right to regard themselves as second-class citizens and they drove the remnant of unreconciled desperadoes of the September uprising into further desperation.[3]

It was two of those desperadoes who relaunched the rebellion in a dramatic fashion on 1 April 1401 by capturing the castle of Conway, one of the strongest in Wales, while the garrison was at prayer. To have captured such a fortress by a ruse on the holiest day of the Christian calendar—for 1 April 1401 was Good Friday—was to cause maximum embarrassment to the English. The captors were Rhys ap Tudur and his brother Gwilym, two of the most powerful men in north-west Wales, men of great and ancient lineage and long military service, former life pensioners of Richard II and relatives of Owain Glyn Dŵr. Their act of bravado appears to have been an isolated incident, calculated above all to enable them to secure the pardons denied to them for their support for the original act of rebellion in September 1400. Hotspur, as justiciar of North Wales,

seems to have been willing to accede to their terms; but the government in London, more concerned with its own bruised *amour propre* and furious at the ineptitude of the local military commander, was much more loath to make an agreement. It was not to be until late May or June that the castle was handed back to the English, and it was early July before Rhys and Gwilym secured their pardons, and then at the price of the surrender and execution of some of their co-conspirators.[4]

The capture of Conway Castle is the sort of daredevil act from which folk memories are quickly woven. Militarily it had no immediate significance beyond detaining an English force on a demeaning siege and prompting the dispatch of messengers to the constables of Cricieth and Harlech to warn them against the repetition of such an incident at their castles. Psychologically the episode no doubt caused glee among the Welsh; it also sowed some of the first seeds of dissension in the ranks of the English government, as the increasingly peevish correspondence between Hotspur and the king and his council reveals. In the short term, however, the government treated the capture of Conway as an isolated and self-contained incident. It in no way softened its stance or made concessions to local sensibilities. In late April–early May 1401—as the siege and negotiations at Conway proceeded—Hotspur held a judicial sessions at Caernarfon, where the communities of Caernarfonshire and Merionethshire gave subsidies of 1,000 marks each to the prince of Wales, payable over the next four years. Two months later the communities of Cheshire and Flintshire underwent the same experience, granting the prince a subsidy of 3,000 marks and £722 respectively. Some generosity was shown by reiterating pardons to the rebels of the north-eastern lordships of Wales; but this was more than counterbalanced by the hard-line ordinances which the prince's council issued at Chester on 14 June. The government had clearly decided that any incipient signs of discontent should be met with the toughest of tough responses, financial and judicial. Owain Glyn Dŵr, it is true, was still at large and spies were dispatched to look for him in the uplands of Nantconwy or on the distant shores of Traeth Mawr. But in general the government had good reason to be content: Hotspur had written on 3 May to report that the men of north-west Wales were in a most submissive mood.[5]

A month is a long time in a revolt. Hotspur's letter from Denbigh on 4 June was much gloomier, and it would have been gloomier still had he been apprised of the news from other parts of Wales. From May 1401 onwards a new chapter opened in the history of the rebellion: contemporaries referred to it as a 'new rebellion' and even in Norwich news had come through of 'these new diseases in Wales'. What was now truly alarming was that what had hitherto been a localized infection had now become a general contagion. Reports of robbers and malefactors in Brecon and of rebellious villeins in Abergavenny in May might not

be part of a national movement; but before the month was out reports of encounters with rebels in Powys, of more rebels assembling in the marches of Carmarthenshire, and of the need to install a garrison in Kidwelly Castle could leave no one in doubt that the situation was deteriorating rapidly. It continued to do so dramatically across the summer months. By the autumn the well-informed Adam of Usk could report that the whole of north Wales, Cardigan, and Powys had defected to Glyn Dŵr and were attacking the English and their towns in those parts. Record evidence makes it clear that he was underestimating, rather than exaggerating, the scale of the movement: defections to the rebel ranks were also reported in Carmarthenshire, Builth, and the middle March; the garrison at Kidwelly was doubled in size; even at Swansea a garrison was posted in the castle and a flurry of letters was sent to inform Sir Hugh Waterton (the king's receiver in the lordship) of the situation. What was happening could not be dismissed as the actions of a few disaffected hotheads: the prince of Wales reported ruefully that his tenants in south Wales were deliberately refusing to pay their dues and debts because they anticipated a new rebellion.[6]

If the situation had deteriorated so rapidly in central and south-west Wales across the summer months of 1401, we might anticipate that matters were even more serious in north Wales. And so indeed they were. Harlech Castle was being besieged by the Welsh and a force of over 500 men was organized at Chester and dispatched via Bala to relieve it in the autumn. At the same time Owain threatened the town and castle of Caernarfon, and a report reached the prince of a skirmish, known as the Battle of Tuthill, between the defenders and the besiegers, in early November. The government could be under no illusion that the situation in north and west Wales was now grave. The scale of its response was a measure of its concern. A royal expedition in early June in response to the growing alarm was aborted; but early in October Henry IV did lead his second royal expedition into Wales. The fact that this second expedition travelled down the Tywi valley and thence to Strata Florida indicated that the government recognized that the revolt had now taken a firm hold in south-west Wales. That was confirmed by the military dispositions that Henry made at the end of his short campaign: the earl of Worcester was appointed lieutenant in south Wales for three months; and garrisons were placed in an arc of castles from Aberystwyth and Cardigan in the west to Builth, Brecon, and Painscastle in the east. Strikingly, the largest garrisons by far were at Aberystwyth and Cardigan; but more significant was the recognition that short punitive expeditions achieved little and that only garrison forces and a long process of pacification could now bring the revolt to an end.[7]

The summer months of 1401 were certainly significant in the history of the revolt. It was clearly now more than a flash, or two flashes, in the pan. Its

geographical range now extended into southern and central as well as into north-western Wales. The Welsh had learnt how easy it was to isolate, if not to take, some of the remoter castles of the west and also how to nullify much of the impact of royal expeditions. Glyn Dŵr, one year after he had proclaimed himself prince of Wales, was still no more than a hunted guerrilla leader; but during that year he had shown that his cause could ignite the flame of defiance in many parts of Wales. Yet hindsight should not tempt us to exaggerate the achievement of the rebels as the year 1401 closed. On the contrary, in spite of some embarrassing reversals the initiative still lay firmly with the English governors of Wales. North-east Wales, and certainly Flintshire, was still unaffected by the revolt, and so were the rich lowlands of south Wales. Even in areas where the rebels made occasional appearances, the machine of government and law-enforcement was still apparently in good order. Thus, the justices itinerant of the Duchy of Lancaster held their sessions throughout the Duchy's southern Welsh estates (from Cydweli in the west to Monmouth in the east) in late September–early October 1401 and imposed huge communal fines on the tenants there; as part of their policy of trying to anticipate trouble they bound over seventeen of the leading men of the commote of Iscennen in a massive recognisance against the possibility of anyone from the commote joining the revolt. In the Principality lands of South Wales likewise the government's response to the challenge to its authority was to issue a commission of oyer and terminer and to announce that judicial sessions would commence on 9 January 1402. Nor were such acts necessarily a case of whistling in the dark to keep one's spirits up. Revolts frequently run out of steam after a few months of heady activity; so it appeared in Wales as the winter nights of 1401 lengthened. On 7 October two prominent Welshmen (one of whom was the leader of the attack on Conway Castle) formally surrendered themselves and their lands to the prince of Wales and some of his councillors at Chester; much more importantly, the men of Cardiganshire and Carmarthenshire apparently deserted Owain in November and accepted a pardon from the king. Indeed, there was more than an outside chance as the year closed that Owain himself might be persuaded to surrender on acceptable terms; he might well have done so had some of Henry IV's advisers shown more imagination. In December 1401 it was still finely in the balance whether the revolt had a future or not.[3]

That balance remained a fine one in the opening months of 1402. Two sets of events in January of that year indicate that, though some spectacular hit-and-run raids could be staged by the rebels, normal life and governance were far from being suspended. In late January Owain raided the area around Ruthin and carried off spoil, especially cattle, to replenish his depleted stocks in the

mountains. But in the same month the courts of Dyffryn Clwyd assembled as usual, and, even more striking, auditors visited North Wales to hear the accounts. It was with the advent of spring and summer that Owain delivered two dramatic blows which served notice that the government and its advisers should not underestimate his bravado or the range of his activities. In early-mid April he captured his arch-enemy, Reginald Grey of Ruthin, in an ambush (possibly stage-managed by Welshmen in Grey's household) and took him captive to the mountains to negotiate the terms of his surrender. Almost exactly a year after the dramatic seizure of Conway Castle, the English had been dealt a second embarrassing blow. It was an incident which must have given Glyn Dŵr and his followers a huge psychological boost; but militarily it was soon overshadowed by a much more significant episode. On 22 June on a hill, Bryn Glas, to the west of Pilleth—a small village south of Knighton, just to the west of Offa's Dyke, and as one contemporary observed only twelve leagues from Leominster—Welsh forces, led by Owain in person, overwhelmed a considerable county levy from Herefordshire, led by Edmund Mortimer, uncle of the heir of the earl of March. Mortimer and several of his companions were captured; some of the leading gentry leaders of western Herefordshire were slain; and the carnage on the battlefield was horrendous.[9]

There can be no doubt that the Battle of Bryn Glas or Pilleth was one of the most momentous of the revolt. This was no ambush or hit-and-run raid. On the contrary, an English county levy had set out in pursuit of the Welsh and had been demolished by them. The Welsh rebels could no longer be dismissed as 'barefooted rascals' 'of small reputation'. The bloodiness of the victory and the alleged mutilation of the bodies confirmed contemporary fears of the savagery of the Welsh and fed the anti-Welsh hysteria of the men of the border counties. The location of the battle was also ominous: it showed that Glyn Dŵr's forces could now raid easily into the southern central Marches and even threaten the English border settlements. News of the disaster was dispatched post-haste to the king at Berkhamsted and to Hotspur at Berwick. The seriousness of the setback was measured in the response it elicited: steps were immediately taken to safeguard border castles such as Clifford and Radnor; Brecon was placed in a state of defence; and even in far-away Swansea a garrison was installed for twenty-eight days in July–August.[10]

Such measures, however, could not wrest the initiative back from Glyn Dŵr. His tail was now up, and support flowed to him. Welshmen in border lordships such as Bishopscastle flocked to his cause, and there were the first stirrings of disaffection in Maelor Saesneg (the detached portion of Flintshire). He now began to invade areas hitherto untouched by revolt and far from his base. If Adam of Usk is to be trusted—and he is now a less reliable witness, since he had left

England in February—Owain now invaded Gwent and Glamorgan, threatening centres such as Usk, Newport, and Cardiff; such a report may well be premature, but it is certainly true that the districts around Brecon and Radnor were now well within the reach of his troops' marauding raids. Furthermore, it was during these months that Owain was taken seriously enough to be able to begin to exploit the fissures in English political life. The English government committed a double blunder when it dragged its feet over a proposal to negotiate a settlement with Glyn Dŵr and, even more unpardonably, over the ransom of Edmund Mortimer (in stark contrast with the anxiety it showed to secure the release of Reginald Grey). It paid a heavy price for its folly: on 30 November 1402 Edmund Mortimer was solemnly married to Glyn Dŵr's daughter. It was a diplomatic coup to parallel the military victory of Bryn Glas: a Mortimer had been won over to the Welsh cause and thereby an English political dimension had been added to Owain's revolt. His cause had also been enhanced in Wales: one of the first acts of Owain's new son-in-law was to inform his former associates on the borders of Wales of his defection to the Welsh cause and to assert his right to the Mortimer lordships in mid-Wales.[11]

The measure of the increasing threat which Glyn Dŵr's revolt posed over a considerable area of Wales during 1402 is reflected in the military measures that the English government and lords took in response to it. Co-ordinated military commands were created: in January the earl of Stafford and the bishop of St Asaph were commissioned to establish measures for the safe custody and good governance of north Wales; even more innovative was the decision at the end of March to appoint Hotspur as lieutenant in north Wales and his uncle, Thomas Percy, earl of Worcester, to a similar post in the south. This vested military command throughout Wales in the hands of the Percies and gave them an opportunity to co-ordinate their response to the revolt at the outset of spring. Repairs were put in hand at castles, such as Kidwelly and Monmouth, which were far away from any imminent danger. Garrisons were naturally maintained in all the castles of north Wales; more significantly, it was also decided to install garrisons from May in some of the more isolated castles of south Wales, such as the craggy outpost of Carreg Cennen (see cover). In May likewise a naval force of over seventy men left from Chester to provide relief for the castles of North Wales, while in June a force of Cheshire archers and esquires was rushed to Denbigh.[12]

Such local measures might normally have served at least to contain the revolt; but when news of the Battle of Bryn Glas reached the government, and its implications were realized, more drastic measures had to be considered. The threat that was now posed to the English border counties led to the creation on 26 July of two new military commands to attend to their security: the northern

one, from Holt to Wigmore, under the earl of Arundel and the southern, from Wigmore to Chepstow, under the earl of Stafford. The fear that the battle had caused was further reflected in the decision to protect Leominster with walls and ditches. New commands were also established in other parts of Wales to cope with a military threat which was now recognized to be too immediate and unpredictable to be dealt with by an overall strategy: Edward Charlton was posted to his own castle at Welshpool in order to stanch the power of rebellion in Powys, while Richard, Lord Grey of Codnor, who was to prove to be one of the most successful English commanders in Wales, was given a military command which extended from Cardiganshire, through Carmarthenshire, to Brecon. Static military commands might stabilize the situation in mid- and south Wales, but in the north the rebels were so rampant that a military expedition was called for, both to relieve the pressure on English castles there and to try to tempt the Welsh into battle in order to avenge the humiliation of Bryn Glas. So it was that the young prince of Wales was sent with a force to relieve the castles of Harlech and Caernarfon in late August; letters of comfort were dispatched by sea to put heart into the defenders of Beaumaris, and the earl of Arundel also led his retinue into Wales accompanied, among others, by Thomas, Lord Furnivall. Simultaneously Henry IV led a force from Shrewsbury into north Wales in early September: he destroyed the vill of Llanrwst on his march, but otherwise the expedition was an unmitigated disaster, overwhelmed by the most appalling weather and returning to its base utterly dishevelled and empty-handed. The king returned to England buoyed by reports of Percy's victory at Homildon Hill (14 September 1402), so painfully contrasting with the shambles of his own Welsh campaign. Any solution of the Welsh problem, whatever it might be, would have to be deferred. The government recognized as much when on 30 September it renewed Richard Grey of Codnor's appointment as king's lieutenant from Aberystwyth to Hay, agreed that he should have a total force of 750 men in his service for the next three months, and encouraged him to set up his headquarters at Brecon with forty men at arms and 200 English archers. It was a recognition, if any was required, that the suppression of the revolt was going to be a long haul and would now encompass much of Wales.[13]

The military situation had undoubtedly deteriorated in Wales in 1402; but we should be chary of concluding that English rule in the parts of the country touched by the revolt had altogether collapsed. Embarrassing military reverses and ambushes were not as yet incompatible with the maintenance of some, at least, of the façade of civilian control. In Dyffryn Clwyd, for example, the year had witnessed two major recorded raids, in January and September, and the traumatic blow of the capture and eventual ransom (in November) of its lord; yet the courts of the lord met almost uninterruptedly during the year. Even more

strikingly, the account of the chamberlain of North Wales shows that he was still able to collect dues, though admittedly on a reduced scale, from various parts of Caernarfonshire; and it was an indication of the government's determination to prop up its judicial and civilian administration that sessions were held in North Wales in May and South Wales in June. Such an impression is confirmed by the fact that the officials of Hotspur were still auditing his accounts in Anglesey as late as December 1402. Elsewhere in Wales the revolt had not in any way undermined the local administration or affected its determination to maximize its revenues. Thus in Flintshire on 11 July collectors were appointed to raise a massive subsidy of 1,000 marks from the tenantry. Even more striking of both the determination, and the insensitivity, of the government are the figures from the great complex of Duchy of Lancaster estates in Wales (Monmouth and Threecastles, Ogmore, Cydweli, and Brecon) for 1401–2: the net gross (potential) yield stood at the massive figure of £3,507, up by over 50 per cent on the yield of the previous year, largely as a result of the huge subsidies raised at the sessions in autumn 1401; almost £900 was sent to the Duchy's central treasury; and the officials' cocksureness and greed were vividly indicated in the demand that the inhabitants of Brecon should contribute a 'war loan' of £210 towards the expenses of Lord Grey and his troops before the ordinary income of the lordship was tapped for such purposes.[14]

Such confusing signals—of military setbacks on the one hand and of an apparently functioning civilian administration on the other—are not unexpected in a revolt. They indicate that English control in Wales, or many parts of Wales, had not yet collapsed; but they also indicate how reluctant governments and their accountants are to concede that they are losing their grip on a situation. That is certainly what was happening. Even the audited accounts of the Duchy of Lancaster could not conceal it: the gross expected yield of the Duchy estates in Wales might be £3,507; whether that sum was collectable was another matter; and what was beyond doubt was that not far short of half that sum (£1,684) was already committed to repairs of castles (£379) and payment of troops (£1,305). In North Wales the situation was, of course, much worse: none of the subsidy could be raised from Merionethshire 'because of various new insurrections of Owain Glyn Dŵr', and even in Caernarfonshire most of the instalment of the subsidy due to be collected after Christmas 1401 remained uncollected. The situation in Wales was certainly variable and confused; but the mood of the year was perhaps best caught by the well-placed monk of Evesham, whose chronicle, unfortunately, finished in that very year. 'From that day', he remarked, commenting on the news of the Battle of Bryn Glas, 'Owain's cause grew excessively, and our cause began to wane.' His comment on Henry IV's September expedition to Wales was no more encouraging: 'he returned home ingloriously', was his tart observation.

Owain had more than held his own in 1402; it remained to be seen whether he could build on his successes.[15]

The year 1403 proved in fact to be a turning-point in the history of the revolt; it was in that year that what had hitherto been a series of isolated, if dramatic, incidents was converted into what could be termed a truly national revolt. Owain Glyn Dŵr had up till now been a fugitive guerrilla leader who staged periodic hit-and-run raids; he now began to acquire some of the trappings and credentials of a truly national leader. One prerequisite for him was to establish an area of power, where his authority was generally unquestioned and which could serve as a base for much more wide-ranging ambitions. The upland districts of north-west Wales fulfilled these functions for Owain from 1403. The government's authority in this area was to remain for the next three years at best vestigial, at worst non-existent. The four castles of Beaumaris, Caernarfon, Harlech, and Aberystwyth were now isolated outposts of English authority: frequently besieged by the Welsh, they relied desperately for their survival henceforth on supplies delivered by sea and on a very occasional relief-expedition launched from Chester.

Another indication that the Glyn Dŵr revolt was now posing a much more serious and sustained threat lay in the fact that its momentum was not altogether lost in the winter months. In January 1403 at least two reports of the activities of the rebels should have occasioned considerable alarm in government circles: the one spoke of continuing pressure from Welsh rebels in the march of Shropshire; the other indicated that rebels from Llŷn and other distant parts of north Wales had recently infiltrated Flintshire and incited the people to insurrection. What was doubly worrying was the bravado of the rebels in launching raids deep in winter, and their deliberate targeting of areas in north-east Wales which had hitherto escaped the infection of revolt. The pressure continued during the next two months: the town of Hope, only a few miles from Chester, was burnt by rebels on 22 February; Owain Glyn Dŵr himself was said to be in the area in March; there were tales of men beginning to defect to the rebels again in Dyffryn Clwyd; and so ominous was the situation that a garrison of 120 men was posted at the frontier castle of Montgomery and another at Flint. If the rebels were so menacing in winter and early spring, there was clearly a very hot summer ahead for the English in Wales. So indeed it proved to be.[16]

May and June brought recurrent messages about the desperate plight of the besieged castles of Harlech and Aberystwyth and prompted equally desperate measures to bring relief to them. But what made the summer of 1403 truly memorable was the way the tide of revolt overwhelmed almost every part of Wales. By late June it was clear that Glyn Dŵr had returned to the southern

middle March where he had enjoyed such a remarkable success a year earlier: on 24 June the garrison at Radnor was more than tripled in size to seventy men and Welsh rebels were laying siege to Brecon. But it was to be July which really transformed the situation. Early in the month there was what contemporaries termed a general uprising in the Tywi valley, as the men of the area flocked to recognize Glyn Dŵr as prince of Wales. Owain himself led a great army down the valley in a triumphal progress reminiscent of the great marches of Llywelyn the Great almost two centuries earlier. Castles surrendered or were over-whelmed, Dryslwyn, Newcastle Emlyn, and Carmarthen apparently among them; and Owain's forces reached as far as St Clears and Laugharne, not far from the borders of Pembrokeshire. A contingent of Owain's army was heavily de-feated in an engagement to the north of Carmarthen on 11 July; but such a setback did little to dent the achievement of Glyn Dŵr in the south-west.[17]

His achievements there were more than matched by what was happening in north-east Wales. On 10 July Hotspur raised the standard of revolt at Chester. So began a movement which ended eleven days later with the defeat and death of Hotspur and his uncle, Thomas Percy, earl of Worcester—the two men who had borne much of the brunt of military leadership in Wales in 1401-2—at, or in the aftermath of, the Battle of Shrewsbury. It is difficult to believe that the campaigns of Glyn Dŵr in south Wales and of the Percies in the north were not co-ordinated. Glyn Dŵr's cause had now been formally locked into the tensions and turmoils of English politics: this was both an explanation of his success and a comment on the growing significance of his movement. As justice of Chester (including Flintshire) and custodian of the lordship of Denbigh, Hotspur was able to command the allegiance of many of the prominent Welshmen of north-east Wales; several of them fell fighting for his cause at Shrewsbury. But Hotspur's cause was also Glyn Dŵr's cause, and so it could outlive Hotspur's death. So indeed it did. Contemporary records are not in doubt that July 1403 marked the watershed of loyalties for the men of Flintshire: 'it was then that the men of the county of Flint became rebels', was one comment; 'then the men of the county of Flint became rebels to the lord and joined Owain Glyn Dŵr', was another. Their actions soon showed that a switch of loyalty was more than a matter of words. In early August the Welsh of Flintshire burnt various English towns in the county and in Shropshire and laid siege to the castles of Flint, Rhuddlan, and Hawarden; and during the next few weeks there were genuine fears that Welsh rebels would extend their raids into Shropshire, Cheshire, and Herefordshire.[18]

Flintshire and adjacent districts had clearly now thrown their support behind the revolt; but what made the high summer of 1403 so momentous was that virtually no part of Wales was now immune from the virus of rebellion. The Welsh of Cydweli and Carnwyllion launched a mass attack on the castle of

Kidwelly on 13 August, killing several Englishmen; later in the month the lord of Abergavenny reported that he was all but ruined by the revolt; Kidwelly was the object of a new attack in early October; the men of the border lordships of Monmouth and Gwent were now implicated in the revolt; and by the end of the month urgent messages were being dispatched to ship troops from Somerset to come to the relief of the besieged castle of Cardiff. What was striking was not only the unprecedented geographical range of the revolt, but also the fact that a punitive royal expedition seems in no way to have daunted the spirit of the rebels. Nor did the advent of winter do so either: the castles of Aberystwyth, Caernarfon, Beaumaris, and Cardiff are all known to have been besieged by the Welsh during November and December. Indeed, the growing confidence and ambition of the Welsh was demonstrated in the fact that in the sieges of Kidwelly and Caernarfon they were accompanied by French troops. The revolt was acquiring an international dimension; there could be no better measure of its success.[19]

The English government's response likewise indicated a realization that co-ordinated action was necessary if such a serious and widespread revolt was to be defeated. Attempts to arrive at a negotiated settlement were not altogether abandoned, but the government placed its main faith in a single unified military command for the whole of Wales and in the long-term deployment of a large force of troops. From 1 April 1403 the young Prince Hal, now in his sixteenth year, was created royal lieutenant throughout Wales and agreed to serve there for one year with a force of four barons, twenty knights, 500 men at arms, and 2,500 archers. His accounts show that though these figures were not in fact attained, the prince did in fact command a force of over 2,700 soldiers in or near Wales in the month before the Battle of Shrewsbury (21 June 1403), most of them in garrison forces in north and south Wales but a substantial number also forming a rapid deployment force around the prince himself. Such a force could be employed in whatever way the military opportunity or emergency of the day dictated—be it on a punitive foray against Glyn Dŵr's own manors at Sycharth and Glyndyfrdwy in early May or on a rescue mission to a besieged castle—such as the very large relief force of 1,300, mainly composed of Cheshire men, sent to the relief of Harlech in early June or the naval force likewise dispatched to Beaumaris in October.[20]

Such long-term arrangements might have worked well if the military situation in Wales had been fairly stable; but the trauma of the Battle of Shrewsbury—in which the young prince was himself injured and some of his crack forces (notably the contingent of the earl of Worcester) defected to the enemy—and the rampant successes of the Welsh rebels during the summer months meant that other methods had also to be pursued. One was the by now well-tested expedient of a royal campaign. So desperate were the pleas for help in late August and so humiliating was the temporary loss to the rebels of the castle of

Carmarthen that Henry IV agreed to undertake such a campaign yet again in mid-September. He marched via Brecon to Carmarthen, where he stayed for some five days, returning to Hereford in less than a fortnight. If he held out any expectations that such a short demonstration of royal power and presence could effect any long-term change in the military situation in Wales, then he would indeed have allowed hope to triumph over experience. Hope, as usual, emerged the loser. Recovery of effective control in Wales was clearly to be a very long haul. Henry IV acknowledged as much when, during October, he appointed his cousin Edward, duke of York, to be lieutenant in south Wales for a year, and Richard, earl of Warwick (who was to have such a bright military future ahead of him, see plate 7), and John, Lord Audley, to take control of the castle and lordship of Brecon for a similar period. It was a further acknowledgement that pacification was going to be a long-drawn-out affair that on leaving Carmarthen (now back in English control), Henry designated a large force of over 550 men to stay there for a month to secure the recovery of this key castle. Even such a modest move quickly ran into trouble: the new commanders found garrison duty in a distant Welsh fortress little to their liking, especially when their pay was not forthcoming, and warned the king that the troops would not stay there a day beyond the stipulated month. Even more striking was the fact that the government's substantive efforts were now largely confined to trying to contain the situation in lowland south Wales. Elsewhere—as at Radnor, Montgomery, and Builth—isolated garrisons kept the English flag flying; in at places as far apart as Beaumaris and Cardiff relief and supplies had to be brought in by sea; while the future of some of the northern and western castles was by now seriously in doubt.[21]

There could be no doubt that much of Wales had been overwhelmed by revolt during the summer months of 1403. The fact that much of the financial documentation (upon which—for all its stilted and even misleading character—the historian has to rely in order to try to reconstruct the state of the country) is lacking after Michaelmas 1402 is itself probably the most eloquent comment on the effective collapse of civilian rule in much of Wales during the course of the year 1403. Collapse, it is true, was not total: even around Kidwelly, whose castle was the subject of at least two assaults during the summer, officials never surrendered complete control over the commotes immediately next to the town, and the hundred court is known to have met on 12 December 1403; in Dyffryn Clwyd likewise the courts were regularly held and presentments made, though the revenue they yielded was strikingly low; while in Flintshire the revenue-gathering mechanisms seem to have been in tolerably good order until they collapsed in the wake of the events of July 1403. But in much of Wales—especially the north, west, and central areas—the pretence of ordinary civilian governance could no longer be sustained. No records were kept and no revenues were

forthcoming. Accounting officers may, of course, have occasionally exaggerated their plight; but in general the situation was too disturbed for officers to dare to go about their tasks, other than in the lordships of either the far south-west or the far south-east of Wales. In those circumstances the best that could be done—and it was a route that was followed, for example, in the lordships of Montgomery, Radnor, Cydweli, and Brecon—was to suspend the ordinary civilian administration and to vest all governmental, judicial, and financial powers in the hands of the local military commander, in the hope that he could raise some revenues locally towards his military costs. Even that for the most part was a forlorn hope. The revolt would have to subside considerably before revenue collection and ordinary governance could begin to be resumed. As 1403 closed there could be no doubt that Wales was truly a society in revolt.[22]

The same could be said to be true of the next two years, 1404–5. The Welsh, it is true, suffered some serious setbacks during that period and the balance of military superiority varied somewhat from region to region in Wales; but what is striking is that the dominance which the Welsh rebels had secured in 1403 should be sustained for another two years. The opening months of 1404 revealed that the military appetite of the Welsh and their stamina for winter campaigns were undiminished: the constable of Harlech Castle was captured and so was the deputy sheriff of Anglesey, while most of his escort was killed; the castles of Caernarfon and Harlech were said to be in dire straits: an attack on the former with the help of the French was expected at any moment, while it was rumoured that the latter was to be delivered by agreement to Glyn Dŵr 'at a certain day for a specified sum of gold', while the alarm at the activities of the Welsh even in deep midwinter was such that the garrison at Radnor was suddenly augmented on 24 January. As the year progressed, what became increasingly clear was that the Welsh were now so confident of their control of northern, western, and most of inland Wales that they could challenge English authority right up to the eastern borders of Wales and indeed beyond them into the English counties themselves. During the spring and summer reports poured in of attacks on Cheshire, Shropshire, Herefordshire, Archenfield, and Abergavenny. Nor were such reports mere scaremongering: accounts from the Arundel estates of Ruyton, Sandford, and Aston in western Shropshire reveal a trail of burnt villages and mills and of fleeing tenants only a few miles to the west of Shrewsbury, while by the autumn the situation in this area was so desperate that the government had no option but to allow the communities of Shropshire and Powys to conclude treaties with the Welsh. The concession was as eloquent a comment as any on the failure of the English government to contain the revolt, let alone to defeat it; all it did was to post substantial garrisons at the castles of Welshpool and

Bishopscastle in the hope that those castles could be held and serve in the fullness of time as bases from which counter-attacks might be launched.[23]

Nor was the situation any better in the rest of Wales. In the north and west, needless to say, matters were desperate, with lonely garrisons hanging on grimly in their isolated fortresses; indeed, they might not even have succeeded in doing that, since the key castles of Aberystwyth and Harlech almost certainly fell to the rebels during the course of the year. But it was the fact that the rebels still very much had the upper hand in the rich lowlands of south and south-east Wales which was the real measure of the superiority they had achieved. On 20 August 1404 the town of Kidwelly was captured and burnt by the Welsh of the region; in the far west Haverford was said to be 'situated among the Welsh rebels'; in the south-east Welsh forces chased the English to the very gates of Monmouth; even the authorities in London had to acknowledge that English power in Wales now survived by the thinnest of threads, for in November and December two very substantial expeditions had to be mounted to relieve the castles of Coety and Cardiff. As 1404 drew to a close effective English authority in almost the whole of Wales was vestigial: it was a situation which had hardly been paralleled since the arrival of the Normans in the country. The rebels may not have been in control; but they most certainly held the initiative.[24]

With so many military successes to his name, it is little wonder that Owain Glyn Dŵr's cause could now flourish in other directions. His revolt was now no nine days' wonder; the international world could, and did, take note of him. It was in May 1404 that he sent off a diplomatic mission to Paris, and within less than two months a solemn Franco-Welsh treaty had been concluded. During the course of the summer a major naval force was assembled in France with the intention of establishing a French bridgehead in Wales. The Franco-Welsh alliance was to be more than a paper tiger. Owain's stature as putative prince of Wales had now to be taken seriously. It was during the course of this year that he held his first parliament, thereby indicating that his authority was acquiring a civilian as well as a military dimension. Even more indicative of the solidity of Owain's success was the defection to his cause of Welshmen of status and experience who had hitherto either served the English king loyally or had at least hedged their bets. The most prominent was John Trefor, bishop of St Asaph since 1395; a distinguished ecclesiastic, diplomat, and administrator—he had been chamberlain (chief financial officer) of Chester since 1399—he brought an immense amount of experience and wide contacts to Glyn Dŵr's cause when he defected to it in 1404. So also did the newly nominated bishop of Bangor, Lewis ab Ieuan or Lewis Byford, likewise a well-educated and much-travelled clergyman. When men of the calibre of Trefor and Byford were defecting to the rebels, it was surely time to take Owain Glyn Dŵr's pretensions very seriously indeed.[25]

The year 1405 brought ample confirmation of the seriousness of those claims. There was continuing evidence in January–February of the pressure that the Welsh rebels were still bringing to bear on the border communities of Shropshire and Herefordshire. Even more significant was the fact that the castles of Aberystwyth (alias Llanbadarn) and Harlech had at last fallen into Welsh hands, probably in the closing months of 1404. The self-styled prince of Wales and his entourage could now hold their court at a venue which was worthy of their pretensions. Owain admittedly had rather mixed military fortunes in 1405, as we shall see; but it would take considerable foresight to predict that his fortunes were yet on the wane. Indeed, Glyn Dŵr was still fishing very effectively in the turbulent pond of English domestic politics. It was quite probably in February 1405 that he concluded the Tripartite Indenture (to be discussed below) in which England and Wales were to be carved three ways between the earl of Northumberland, Edmund Mortimer senior, and Owain. The remarkable claim to a much enlarged Wales which was part of the Indenture may suggest that Owain was losing touch with reality; but it may also indicate that he realized that the vulnerability of his allies was his opportunity to drive a very hard bargain. Owain may not have been a good judge of causes or men; but he was shrewd enough to realize that his ambitions had their best prospect of long-term success by exploiting the fissures of English domestic politics and England's foreign entanglements.

The latter came to Owain's rescue in 1405 just as a series of military setbacks in the spring and summer had dented his own military standing and revealed the vulnerability of his position. At long last in early August 1405 a substantial French expeditionary force landed at Milford Haven. The achievements of this force were to be more showy than permanent; but for the time being it must have put great heart into the Welsh, and equal terror into the hearts of the English, that a joint Franco-Welsh force could march right across southern Wales, capture several important castles *en route*, and allegedly reach to within eight miles of the city of Worcester. It was after all this kind of *chevauchée* which the English had used so successfully during the fourteenth century to undermine the king of France's authority in his own country. There were also plenty of other indications that the Welsh were able to maintain the pressure in different parts of Wales, with or without French aid: in July Rhuddlan Castle was being besieged and there were reports that the Welsh were assembling in the south-east; in early September yet another army had to be sent to relieve the besieged castle of Coety in Glamorgan; while in the far south-west the men of Pembrokeshire, barely recovered from the trauma of the French invasion, felt obliged to buy off further Welsh depredations with a substantial bribe of £200 to their enemies. Owain could still look to the future with confidence. In August 1405 he held his second parliament in the impressive setting of the captured castle of Harlech. Even more

significantly, he now spoke of negotiations, but on his own terms and to his own advantage: he was intending to broker a peace between the English and the French, part of which would involve the formal acknowledgement of the newly forged Welsh principality.[26]

Yet sceptical observers might also have concluded that the revolt had only lasted as long as it had largely because of the preoccupations and relative inertia of the English. Never was that more true than in 1404–5. For most of these two years the government seems to have been content, whether through choice or not, with a policy of containment. Garrisons were located in all the major royal castles in an arc from Aberystwyth (until its fall), through Cardigan and Carmarthen, across to the eastern fortresses of Brecon, Radnor, Abergavenny, and Hay; substantial forces also kept guard in the frontier castles of the central eastern border, notably Welshpool, Oswestry, and Bishopscastle. Some of these forces were very considerable even if they fall well short of the figures suggested by the council: Rustin de Villa Nova's force at Carmarthen during May–June 1404 comprised eighty-one men at arms and 240 archers, that of Edward Charlton at Welshpool in December 1404–January 1405 twenty men-at-arms and 100 archers. Forces on this scale clearly had more than a defensive role; they could be used for local forays and for beginning the process of reimposing some measure of control in the immediate neighbourhood of their respective bases. They stand in marked contrast with the much smaller garrisons—normally ranging from six to twenty-four archers—which were charged with the much more demanding, but limited, task of holding on to the castles of north Wales from Caernarfon to Flint. But whether the garrisons were large or small, they indicated an intent of containing, and responding to, the revolt in a localized and piecemeal fashion.[27]

Rather the same impression is conveyed by the policies of the young prince of Wales in 1404. The January parliament of 1404 had vested the command of military operations in Wales in his hands; but it was not until the summer that he took his household to the frontiers of Wales, where he spent most of his time at Hereford and Leominster. He had in fact disengaged from major military activity in Wales, contenting himself with the much more delimited exercises of guarding the Herefordshire district from attacks and dispatching occasional forays into Gwent, Glamorgan, and Brecon to harass the Welsh and to bring some relief to hard-pressed castles. It may have been that the prince and his advisers had decided that the Welsh terrain did not lend itself to effective counter-offensives and that the revolt would sooner or later burn itself out; it is even more likely that it was the chronic shortage of cash which imposed such a policy of military self-denial on the prince. The financial situation of the government began to ease from 1405, and it may be no coincidence that plans for a much more ambitious

policy against the Welsh rebels began to emerge in the spring and early summer of 1405. On 27 April the prince of Wales was appointed lieutenant in north Wales, to serve there with 500 men at arms and up to 3,000 archers—an indication that north Wales, which had been largely abandoned to its own devices, was once more to be brought within the ambit of royal strategy. Simultaneously garrisons totalling over 2,000 men were to be posted at seven key castles. Even more significantly, plans were put in place for a major twin-pronged expedition against the Welsh—the prince leading the offensive in the north, while his father (who had arrived at Hereford on 14 May 1405) was to take command in the south. In the event, news of Scrope's revolt in Yorkshire led to the expedition being aborted, as Henry IV and the prince hurried north; with this sudden change of plan the king's last opportunity, as it proved, to deal with the Welsh revolt by a major expedition disappeared.[28]

It was, perhaps, just as well that it was so, for none of Henry's expeditions into Wales had brought him any military credit nor had they served to stem the tide of revolt, other than very temporarily. Military success for the English began to come in 1405 in much less spectacular and much more humdrum and localized ways. The first task was to chip away at the extremities of the areas under Owain's military control and thereby to seize the military initiative from him. This happened in the far south-east of Wales with important victories over the Welsh at Grosmont in March and near Usk in May. Civilian consequences soon followed in the wake of military success: by August commissioners were dispatched to discuss with the men of Usk and Caerleon the terms on which they should surrender. These first signs of the crumbling of support for the revolt in the south-east were matched by similar signs in the north-east. None was more significant than the decision of Gwilym ap Gruffudd ap Gwilym, the most powerful man in Flintshire, his two brothers, Rhys and Robin, and four other Welshmen to surrender their bodies to prison in Chester during August 1405. It was an ominous vote of no confidence in Glyn Dŵr; others would soon be casting theirs. Another vulnerable area of his dominion was Anglesey, so easily attacked from the sea; and so it was in June by a naval force led by the deputy lieutenant of Ireland. Even inland in such places as Brecon, there were ominous signs by October that support for Owain was ebbing. Added to these losses were the personal blows that Owain had endured as 1405 progressed: his brother was killed and his son captured at the battle near Usk in May; his secretary was taken later in the month; in June John Hanmer, Owain's brother-in-law and close confidant, was likewise captured, the measure of his importance being gauged by the reward of £26 13s. 4d. given to his captor. The personal losses were arguably more important than the military setbacks; together they might have prompted contemporaries to ask, in the words of Owain's first biographer,

whether 'fortune now began to frown upon Glyndŵr', and when fortune frowns on one, it smiles on the other. K. B. McFarlane remarked that '1405 can be taken as the turning of [Henry IV's] reign'. It was also to be the turning-point of Owain Glyn Dŵr's revolt.[29]

Turning-points, however, are generally more striking in retrospect than they are at the time itself. As 1405 closed, Wales was still in turmoil. Devastation was clearly common. During the last two years most of the revenue-collecting and law-enforcing agencies had ground to a halt. The comment of a Chirk official doubtless spoke a general truth: no revenue could be levied 'because the tenants of the said lordship remain rebels and obey Owain of Glyndyfrdwy, traitor'. Even in the south-eastern border lordships of Monmouth and Threecastles no courts could be held because the tenants were rebels. Such was the picture throughout Wales. The despair of seignorial officials at the situation is best expressed in an undated letter addressed to the council of the earl of Arundel regarding his lordship of Bromfield and Yale. Many tenants had fled the lordship with their goods, so that the lordship is largely empty of tenants; but other tenants wished to return if they could be assured of a pardon. It is the ambivalence of the report which is its most intriguing feature; it is a reminder that, although seignorial administration may have temporarily collapsed well-nigh throughout Wales, ordinary civilian life doubtless continued. Rebellion was occasional and localized; life could return to normal with astonishing speed; today's rebels, or at least those who acquiesced in rebellion, could quickly become tomorrow's loyal tenants. Two episodes during these peak years of revolt may serve to remind us of that tension in miniature, as it were. The first took place in the mountainous districts of upland Brecon in February 1404: the men of the district promised that they would submit to the king if he should defeat the rebels in Glamorgan; if he failed to do so, then they could not be expected to submit. It was an utterly hard-headed and pragmatic assessment of the situation; it must have been repeated—privately or publicly, individually or communally—in every part of Wales at some stage during the revolt. The second episode took place at Kidwelly in September 1404, only a month after a devastating rebel attack on the town. A local Welshman (and former rebel) took a lease from St Mary's Abbey, Leicester, of the altarages of two churches in the heart of Cydweli, adding the proviso that he should be released from payment of rent if the district were destroyed by rebels. Men insisted on leading their lives as normally as possible, regarding rebellion as a contingency, no more. Such episodes are surely instructive. Wales was certainly a society in revolt in these years, but neither the absence of financial accounts nor the apparent suspension of civilian governance should lead us to forget that men and women for most of the time and in most places led lives which were as normal as they could be in such circumstances. Rebellion was certainly tantamount to a

defiance of the existing pattern of government, but a society in revolt can and does make its own arrangements for survival.[30]

If there had been any doubt that the tide had turned against Owain Glyn Dŵr as 1405 drew to a close, there could be no such doubts a year later. It was in a way paradoxical that it should be so, for it was in 1406 that Glyn Dŵr's ambitions reached their expansive apogee. On 12 January he solemnly ratified his alliance with the French king 'at our castle of Llanbadarn, in the year of our Lord 1405 (?1406) and in the sixth year of our principate'. There is a confident assurance and almost pompous expansiveness about the language. But so also was there about his policies, for at the end of March 1406 Owain took the dramatic step of transferring Wales's ecclesiastical allegiance from the Roman pope (supported by the English) to the Avignonese pope (supported by the French). In the document that effected the transfer he laid out his vision of an independent native Welsh Church and a separate Welsh ecclesiastical province and the proposal to found two Welsh universities. Owain's advisers were still dreaming grand dreams. Nor was his military position perhaps quite as desperate as hindsight might suggest. His forces were still capable of launching raids which showed the fragility of the English recovery: thus, on 18 November 1406 the court of the commote of Coelion in Dyffryn Clwyd had to be postponed because Owain's army was devastating the area, and indeed throughout the winter of 1406–7 his forces led effective hit-and-run raids into north-east Wales, striking fear wherever they went. It was not without good cause that large garrisons were still maintained in some of the border castles of the north-east: thus, throughout 1407 and into early 1408 a force of 120 soldiers was still posted at Montgomery Castle. It proved exceptionally difficult to dislodge Owain from the heartland of his power in north and west Wales, and from this base he and his followers were able to launch periodic devastating raids deep into other parts of Wales for years to come. It was certainly premature in 1406 or even 1407 to write off the revolt of Owain Glyn Dŵr.[31]

Nevertheless 1406 certainly marked the turning of the tide in Owain's fortunes. During the course of the year the hope that his revolt could be sustained by external help gradually evaporated. The remnant of the French troops, left in the country after the summer invasion of 1405, departed in the spring; there were hints of further French aid during the year and virtual apologies for the paltriness of what was offered; but the attempt to send a second naval expedition from France to Wales was attended with very little success. It could have been ex-pected that the French might have been anxious to exploit the Welsh bridgehead to embarrass the English at the very time that they were bringing pressure to bear on the latter both around Calais and Bordeaux. But during 1407 even this prospect receded, as major shifts in French domestic politics led to the conclusion of a

truce with England in the November of that year. Even before that date any hope of help from Wales's other obvious potential ally, Scotland, effectively disappeared when the heir to the Scottish throne was captured by the English in March 1406 and detained in England at the royal pleasure and as a guarantor of Scottish diplomatic caution. Nor could Owain expect any help from his former English allies after the crushing defeat of Archbishop Scrope's rebellion in June 1405. The earl of Northumberland and Lord Bardolf were now broken reeds who were forced to flee from England to Scotland and, subsequently, in 1406 to Wales for their own safety; they were henceforth more of a liability than an asset. By 1406, at long last, the English state had recovered its political poise and unity. Owain was in effect left to carry on his struggle virtually unaided; no Welsh pretender could do that indefinitely.[32]

Least of all could he do it once the English state decided to pursue a more vigorous policy towards the rebellion in Wales. This is precisely what seems to have happened in 1406. An early indication of the change of mood came on New Year's Day when it was announced that parliament was to meet at Gloucester on 15 February, since the king had appointed the prince of Wales to march shortly into Wales to make war on the rebels. In the event the parliament had to be prorogued to Westminster; but a note of urgency in addressing the Welsh problem had been struck. It was recurrently re-echoed over the next few months: on 1 February the prince was appointed lieutenant in north and south Wales and was to be given a very handsome army of almost 5,000 men to discharge his obligation. When he proved rather reluctant to take up his post, the commons in parliament showed increasing impatience in their demands that he should do so forthwith. He was given a new commission to act as lieutenant in Wales with a reduced force in September 1406, and, what is more, during the next few months he was given ample supplies of cash—which had been so obviously lacking during the last few years—to perform his task. In short, in 1406–7 both the rhetoric and the financial measures of the English government, and the clamour of the commons in parliament, showed a determination to address the Welsh problem urgently. It was an ominous threat for Glyn Dŵr.[33]

In fact the renewed English initiative in Wales did not have to wait on the prince's dilatoriness; already in the opening months of 1406 measures had been initiated to wrest the initiative from Glyn Dŵr in the very heartland of his powers in north-west Wales. On 1 February the garrison at Caernarfon was more than quadrupled to four men-at-arms and fifty archers, and a naval force was dispatched to destroy the ships of the rebels in the Menai Straits. This latter move was part of a deliberate policy to isolate the island of Anglesey and to reassert English authority there. That was without a doubt the prime objective of English military policy in north Wales in 1406 and the reasoning behind it is clear. Control

of Anglesey, as Edward I had appreciated, would in effect give English forces a floating fortress from which they could assault the mountain fastnesses of north Wales; even more crucially, the seizure of Anglesey would deny the rebels access to their most valuable source of supplies and food, and might thereby be the prelude to a submission by starvation. Chester was the headquarters for the assault which began in January 1406. An initial force of forty men-at-arms and 300 archers was dispatched to begin the process of bringing the island under control; it sailed from the Wirral under John Mainwaring, sheriff of Chester, and his brother Ralph in a ship called *Nicholas of Dublin*, and headed for Beaumaris. As spring turned into summer the process of pacification gathered pace: a new detachment of some 220 men was dispatched to guard the island, while a force of sixty soldiers was placed along the Menai Straits 'to prevent rebels from other parts of Wales coming to Anglesey to incite the people, who had already come to peace, to rebel'. Now that the English were gaining the upper hand militarily, the process of civilian pacification under Thomas Tickhill, the steward of the prince of Wales's lands, could begin. It reached its climax at Beaumaris on 9 November 1406 when the names of over 2,000 men from Anglesey were recorded in the submission and fine made on that day. By December the Anglesey county court was meeting again and normal life, including the collection of revenue, was being resumed. Early in 1407 John Mainwaring was appointed military commander in the island with a force of some hundred men. Anglesey had been finally lost to Glyn Dŵr's cause.[34]

Economically and strategically the loss of Anglesey was a body-blow; but it was only one of several that Glyn Dŵr suffered during 1406–7. During 1406 he and his allies sustained two serious military setbacks, the first when over 1,000 Welshmen (including one of Owain's remaining sons) were slain in a particularly bloody encounter on St George's Day; the second in June when Edward Charlton, lord of Powys, and a Shropshire force trounced the earl of Northumberland and Lord Bardolf, now exiles in Wales and seeking to support Owain's cause. Support for his cause was evaporating in many different parts of Wales. The collapse is particularly clear in Flintshire. In March 1406 one of Owain's fiercest supporters in the country, Hywel Gwynedd, and some of his accomplices were ambushed and killed in their hilltop redoubt. By mid–late summer the revolt was crumbling there: on 20 August seven leading men were given safe conducts to come to Chester to make their submissions in person; from early October official inquiries were being held at St Asaph, Rhuddlan, Holywell, and Caerwys to gather information on who had died in the rebellion and what was the extent of their lands; the civilian administration of the country was being reinstated and offices filled. The revolt in Flintshire could be said to have formally ended in late March–early April 1407 when over 1,000 men from different parts of the

county appeared before Gilbert Talbot, the justiciar, and his fellow justices at Flint and agreed to pay a large communal fine for their adherence to Glyn Dŵr.[35]

The same story was being repeated throughout Wales, though the record evidence is nowhere as good as it is for Anglesey and Flint. According to the Welsh annals, during 1406 Gower, Ystrad Tywi, and most of Ceredigion abandoned Owain's cause, as the men of Glamorgan had done the previous year. The men of the earl of Arundel's north-eastern lordships—Bromfield and Yale, Chirk, and Oswestry—had apparently submitted by July 1407, while by September men from each of the commotes of the great lordship of Denbigh had travelled to Chester to the prince's council to make their formal submissions on behalf of their communities. Maelor Saesneg, the detached portion of Flintshire which had been the first part of the county to rise with Glyn Dŵr and the last to surrender, did so finally in May 1407. By that date there were still doubtless many covert supporters of Glyn Dŵr in various parts of Wales; but the only areas in which he could be said to have any sustained hold were probably Caernarfonshire, Merionethshire, and northern Cardiganshire. Even there the English forces were now shaping to go in for the kill. In May 1407 the prince of Wales contracted to serve for six months in Wales with 600 men at arms and 1,800 archers, and on 1 June he was given a grant of almost £7,000 for the purpose. English forces were closing in both north and south. In the north Gilbert Talbot, the justiciar, was given a huge escort of 100 men at arms and 400 archers to accompany him for sixty days as he proceeded on tour to punish the rebels of Caernarfonshire and Merionethshire and to collect fines imposed at the sessions. At much the same time what was anticipated to be the last great military spectacle of the revolt was being prepared at Aberystwyth. A very distinguished cast—headed by the prince of Wales, the duke of York, and the earl of Warwick and accompanied by some of the hardened warriors of Welsh campaigns—travelled to west Wales to be present at the *coup de grâce*, which was also very much meant to be a *coup de théâtre*. Siege engines and cannons were put in position and supplies of arrows and large amounts of gunpowder conveyed by sea from Bristol and Haverford. It was to be a David versus Goliath contest and a spectacle to savour.[36]

But in the event the English were denied, at least for the time being, the taste of victory. The walls of the castle proved to be exceptionally well built and one of the English guns exploded spectacularly. After a siege which had lasted several months, the Welsh defenders eventually made an agreement to surrender the castle by 1 November if no help was forthcoming. But when, according to the Welsh annals, the proposal was put to Glyn Dŵr, he rose to the occasion, gathered his forces, threatened to execute the Welsh captain, and took possession

of the castle himself. It was a demonstration of the spirit of the Welsh, even as their cause was failing, which stood in marked contrast with the bickering and the lily-livered behaviour of some of the English besieging forces. The Welsh were certainly on the ropes; but even in what appeared to be the dying months of the rebellion they showed extraordinary resilience. Even as late as May 1408 two envoys were sent to Paris in a desperate appeal for help against the English, while a hard core of rebels ensconced themselves in the fastness of the upper Conwy valley and planned to ambush the chamberlain of North Wales as he travelled to Chester. For years to come, in fact, the prince's officials in North Wales could not travel except under heavy escort and often preferred to travel by sea rather than to run the gauntlet of rebel attacks.[37]

It would be many years before the last embers of revolt were finally extinguished in Wales. The government had to tread extremely warily and could only feel at all secure if large garrisons were stationed at strategic spots—such as the force of twenty men-at-arms and 100 archers posted at Caernarfon from late August to early November to guard the Menai Straits, or the even larger force of 480 men installed in the monastery of Strata Florida to underpin the pacification of north Cardiganshire. But by late 1407 and certainly by 1408 the revolt of Owain Glyn Dŵr was reverting to what it had been in its early months—a guerrilla war conducted from the fastnesses of north and west Wales, embarrassing and irritating to the English government, but no longer a serious military threat to its authority even within Wales. Civilian administration would take some years to recover its authority and certainly to reach the revenue levels of pre-revolt days. Financial accounts show that the process had begun in areas such as Ogmore and Usk by 1406, in Kidwelly, Flint, and Denbigh by 1407, in Brecon by 1408–9. Most striking of all, the chamberlain of North Wales submitted his account from February 1407 and by the following year was declaring that Arllechwedd, Nantconwy, and Eifionydd were the only areas of Caernarfonshire from which he was able to collect no revenue. By then any prospect that the rebels might be able to rekindle the flame of full-scale revolt with external aid had disappeared: the envoys sent to solicit aid from the French must soon have sensed that the changed political situation in Paris had put paid to such hopes, while the defeat and death of the earl of Northumberland and his allies at the Battle of Bramham Moor on 19 February 1408 extinguished the last hope, on which Glyn Dŵr had recurrently founded his ambitions, that disaffection with the new Lancastrian dynasty in England might prove to be the salvation of the Welsh. It was a mark of the military failure of the revolt that it had only captured and held two major castles for any length of time—Aberystwyth and Harlech; the fall of these two to the English, probably in autumn 1408–early 1409, was the final indication that the revolt had in effect failed. Rebel activity continued, as we shall see,

spasmodically for years in different parts of Wales; but by early 1409 Owain Glyn
Dŵr, self-proclaimed prince of Wales, was no more than a desperate and hunted
guerrilla leader. Wales was no longer a society in revolt.[38]

PART III

The Anatomy of Revolt

OWAIN GLYN DŴR

*T*he revolt which engulfed Wales in the years after 1400 was assuredly the revolt of Owain Glyn Dŵr. Other local leaders, it is true, are occasionally mentioned—Rhys and Gwilym ap Tudur in the north-west, John Kynaston in the borderlands of Shropshire, or Henry Don in Cydweli. And on occasion the rebellion was known as 'the revolt of the Welsh'. But contemporaries, and not least the English government, were not in doubt that this was Owain's revolt. He was its leader and it was his claim that gave it legitimacy. Thus, when the men of Flintshire decided to 'become rebels' in August 1403 they were 'sworn to Owain Glyn Dŵr', and when the tenants of Dyffryn Clwyd defected to the rebels they became 'the men of Owain'. Theirs was a revolt, as we shall see, built around a cause; but the cause was built in turn around a leader.[1]

What can we know of that leader? The answer is clear: desperately little. The information about him, especially in the years before 1400, is very scanty. That is why our approach to him must be, as it were, a lateral one. It is through his family, his friends, his locality, that we can perhaps best begin to grasp the sort of man that he was and the sort of circles in which he moved. It is with his lineage that we start. That, we can confidently assert, is where contemporaries, at least contemporary Welshmen, would have started. Owain was who he was because of his lineage; what he added in personal charisma to that lineage was merely a bonus; the lineage itself was indispensable. It was, literally, the validating charter of his identity and of his claim. Wales was, as all external observers remarked from at least the twelfth century, a genealogically obsessed country. Gerald of Wales had, as so often, expressed the point succinctly: 'the Welsh value distinguished birth and noble descent more than anything else in the world'. It therefore followed, as a late fourteenth century poet put it, that 'a baron who was not of ancient lineage was a man of no account'.[2]

The poet in question was Iolo Goch and the patron whom he was addressing when he made his comment was none other than Owain Glyn Dŵr. It was the very splendour and impeccability of Owain's lineage which made it such a joy to address an ode of genealogical praise to him. Gross exaggeration was the common coin of medieval Welsh praise poetry; but in the case of Owain's descent

there was no need for such exaggeration. He was, said the poet, 'of the stock of the Lord Rhys' (ruler of Deheubarth or south-west Wales, d. 1197) and 'of the stock of Bleddyn ap Cynfyn' (regarded as the founder of the ruling dynasty of Powys or north-east Wales, d. 1075); and so indeed he was, as the accompanying diagram shows. In other words, the blood of two of the most prestigious princely dynasties of native Wales ran in Owain's veins; indeed, the poet had little trouble in demonstrating that the blood of the third princely dynasty, that of Gwynedd, was also part, albeit a much smaller part, of Owain's genetic inheritance.[3]

There is much, of course, that is conventional in such exercises, especially given that Welsh poets were also professional genealogists and inveterate flatterers. But we would be gravely mistaken to dismiss such exercises as mere poetic conceits. They fed nostalgia and inflated egos; but they could also be charters for claims and, ultimately, the justification for action. Iolo Goch drew his own conclusions: at the start of his poem he pitched them quite modestly by claiming that Owain was entitled to be lord of the whole of Powys; by the end of his ode he had cast modesty to the wind, proclaiming Owain to be 'the sole head of Wales' (*un pen ar Gymru*). Genealogically, it was difficult to fault him: the dynasty of Gwynedd had failed in the male line when Owain Lawgoch (descendant of the brother of Llywelyn the Last) had been killed by an English assassin in France in 1378; and as to the dynasties of Deheubarth and Powys, it was difficult to deny

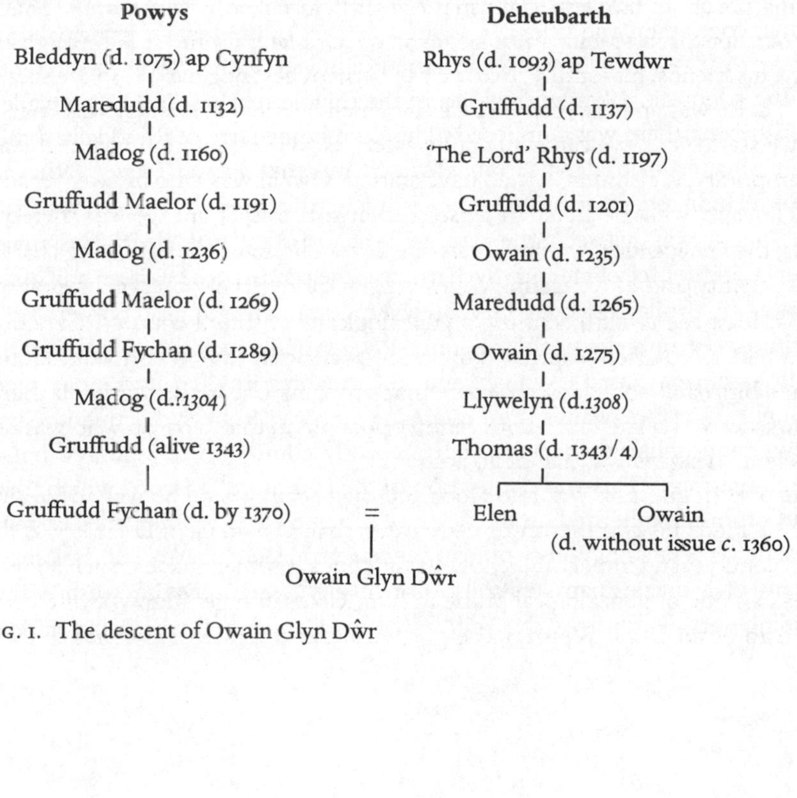

Powys	Deheubarth
Bleddyn (d. 1075) ap Cynfyn	Rhys (d. 1093) ap Tewdwr
Maredudd (d. 1132)	Gruffudd (d. 1137)
Madog (d. 1160)	'The Lord' Rhys (d. 1197)
Gruffudd Maelor (d. 1191)	Gruffudd (d. 1201)
Madog (d. 1236)	Owain (d. 1235)
Gruffudd Maelor (d. 1269)	Maredudd (d. 1265)
Gruffudd Fychan (d. 1289)	Owain (d. 1275)
Madog (d.?1304)	Llywelyn (d.1308)
Gruffudd (alive 1343)	Thomas (d. 1343/4)

Gruffudd Fychan (d. by 1370) = Elen   Owain
                                          (d. without issue *c.* 1360)

Owain Glyn Dŵr

FIG. I. The descent of Owain Glyn Dŵr

that Owain was—if a little irregularly, since his claim to Deheubarth came through the female line, contrary to Welsh custom—indeed the senior surviving representative of both. It was on this basis, of course, that he had himself proclaimed 'prince of Wales', nothing less, at Glyndyfrdwy on 16 September and that he adopted the four lions rampant of Gwynedd—the arms of the first, and last, formally acknowledged native prince of Wales, Llywelyn ap Gruffudd (1267–82) as the heraldic device on his great seal.[4]

Lineage was, therefore, fundamental to Owain Glyn Dŵr. But such lineage claims, however hard they might be peddled by the poets, lay dormant and of mere antiquarian interest until and unless they were activated by the individual claimant and by the force of circumstances. Neither seemed to be very likely in the late fourteenth century. Such at least must surely have been the conclusion that any detached observer would draw from the contrast between Owain's grandiose descent and the modesty of his fortunes and career. His forebears had apparently come to terms with their straitened circumstances: they pretended to no greater title than 'lord of Glyndyfrdwy and half (of the commote) of Cynllaith'. Owain also apparently shared their opinion, for in the one deed that survives in his name before 1400 he simply styles himself 'lord of Glyndyfrdwy'.[5]

Owain's modesty of title at that date was well in line with economic circumstances, for he was the owner of no more than three middle-sized estates in Wales (Map 4). The first lay around Glyndyfrdwy, the place which gave him his personal cognomen and title; it was the sole part of the former principality of northern Powys which Edward I had initially allowed Owain's forebears to retain after the conquest. Glyndyfrdwy lies in the middle reaches of the Dee valley; Owain's estate there was composed of his own home-farm of Rhuddallt, a mill, pasture, sheep-runs, and rents from vills further up the valley at Trewyn, Rhagad, Hendreforfudd, Bodorlais, and Corwen. Glyndyfrdwy may have given Owain his name; but it was his second estate, at Sycharth, that was clearly his major residence and source of income. Sycharth was the centre of the eastern half of the commote of Cynllaith. Today it is barely a mile from the English border; but it was almost certainly the site of the court (W. *llys*) of the native Welsh lord of the area in earlier days and its inhabitants and customs in Glyn Dŵr's day were thoroughly Welsh. Owain's third estate lay far away from Sycharth and Glyndyfrdwy, and unlike them it had only recently come into the family's hands through marriage. This was the portion of the commote of Iscoed which Elen, Owain's mother, inherited on the death of her uncle and brother, the last male representatives of the Welsh princely dynasty of Deheubarth still holding a remnant of a once-expansive Welsh principality. Iscoed was in west Wales, extending northwards from the Teifi valley and Cardigan. It was distant indeed

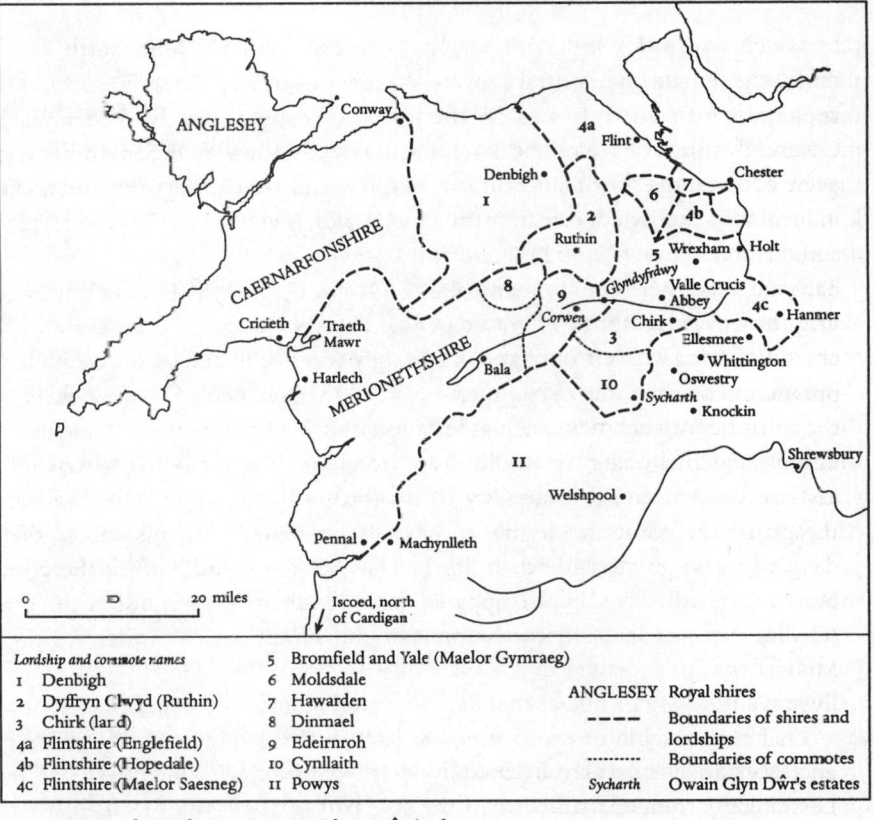

MAP. 4. North Wales in Owain Glyn Dŵr's day

from Owain's other lands; but it was a valuable acquisition which soon sported the name of Iscoed Glyndŵr.[6]

Owain's territorial inheritance was no match for his lineage; it was a paltry foundation from which to launch a campaign to be recognized as prince of Wales. It is impossible to gauge how much his estates would have yielded to him in annual revenue: a guess of £70 would probably be over-generous. Such an income would have put him comfortably into the echelons of the greater gentry of an English county and would certainly have qualified him technically in property terms for knighthood. It would not, however, have allowed him to cut a figure of great importance in English political society, even at the regional level: the fact that in the retinue of the earl of Arundel in 1387 he was listed among the esquires (all 127 of them) and below the four bannerets and thirty-two knights cut him painfully down to size.[7]

Painfully, and quite probably so for him, but also rather misleadingly. Wealth is relative, and by the standards of the noble-born freemen of Wales Owain was

certainly wealthy. A few Welshmen could certainly compete with him—Gruffudd ap Gwilym, whom we met earlier, was one of them—and others were
apparently learning to climb the ladder of economic success more adeptly than
Owain. But there are ample indications that he was comfortably, securely, and
even ostentatiously wealthy by the standards of his Welsh peers. One such
indication is the fact that the marriage of one of his forebears was considered a
sufficiently attractive prospect for a Lestrange of Knockin, a minor English
baronial family, to offer £50 for it. Owain's estates were sufficiently dispersed and
valuable to warrant his appointing a steward and a sergeant (*rhingyll*) to be in
charge of the Glyndyfrdwy group. And Owain's living standards certainly impressed contemporaries. In a famous ode Iolo Goch gave a vivid description of
the splendid moated manor house at Sycharth (plate 10), complete with the latest
innovations, including a tiled roof and a smoke-free chimney, and provided
idyllically with all that was necessary to sustain its household—demesne land,
meadow, orchard, stone dovecote, fishpond, heronry, mill, and deer-park. The
description is doubtless flattering and idealized, but when royal forces eventually
burnt Sycharth they likewise found 'a well-built house . . . which was his
(Owain's) principal residence' there and at Glyndyfrdwy 'a fine lodge in his park'.
Modest Owain's fortune may have been, but by Welsh standards he certainly
lived well.[8]

That he was able to do so was due in no small part to the foresight of his
ancestors. In 1328 his grandfather, doubtless at the prompting of his in-laws, the
Lestranges, arranged for Glyndyfrdwy and Cynllaith to be granted to himself and
his wife in tail. It was an arrangement which was becoming common among
landed families in England but it ran completely contrary to the principles of
Welsh law. In the first place it vested the wife with a title to the land during her
lifetime, in direct contradiction of Welsh practice. Secondly, and more crucially,
it converted the title to the estate in effect into one by English law, in which
descent would normally be by primogeniture as opposed to the Welsh custom of
partibility between male heirs. So it was that the integrity of the family's estates
was preserved intact for Owain, just at the time that the remnants of the other
few remaining Welsh families of native princely stock were being fractionalized
into ever smaller morsels. It is not the least of the ironies of Owain Glyn Dŵr's
career that it was the devices of English property law which allowed him, in
terms of wealth, to stand head and shoulders above most of his fellow
countrymen. In the light of this fact it is perhaps not surprising that the reinstate-
ment of native Welsh law nowhere seems to figure in his political programme.[9]

Owain's estates provided him with wealth; they also gave him status, that of a
Welsh baron. Owain belonged to a small, and diminishing, group of Welshmen
most of whom were descended from the pre-Conquest native dynasties who held

by the distinctive Welsh tenure of *pennaethium*, translated by English officials as 'Welsh barony'. They were a fossil of an earlier age. They held their lands directly of the king of England in chief and by services which would be regarded as minimal and honourable: homage, fealty, suit at the county court, and the obligation to accompany the king's army when duly warned. Occasionally an attempt was made to catalogue their privileges in terms which an English lawyer might understand; such attempts only served to show how ample were those rights: free gallows, view of frankpledge, cognisance of all pleas within the jurisdiction of a baronial court, and rights of chase on their lands. And what was true in theory was also true in fact; the districts held by this superannuated Welsh tenure were virtually exempt from the regular judicial, financial and governmental machinery of the English kings and lords of Wales. They were quasi-autonomous islets of native Welsh rule, caught as it were in a time-warp. Their rulers, notably in the two commotes of Dinmael and Edeirnion (of which Glyndyfrdwy was a part) still proudly called themselves barons (W. *barwniaid*); that is why it was particularly appropriate, and technically correct, for the poet Iolo Goch to refer to Glyn Dŵr's grandfather as 'the king of barons' (W. *brenin ar y barwniaid*). Such archaic hangovers in terminology and power were innocent in themselves; but they were also a recipe for frustration and illusion. The frustration arose in particular from the disjunction between grandiose titles and power on the one hand and puny economic means on the other; the illusion sprang from believing that 'a baron of Wales' was in some way on a par with a baron in England. No one could have been as profoundly frustrated and disillusioned as Owain Glyn Dŵr: by far the greatest of 'the barons of Wales', he could not even make it to the rank of a knight in England.[10]

Estates brought wealth and status; they also gave a nobleman a base from which he could control, or at least influence, a region, his 'country' in contemporary English parlance. Owain had three such 'countries', and it is worth looking at each briefly in order to grope towards the springs of his power. The first around Glyndyfrdwy was part of the remarkable enclave of native Welsh rule in the commotes of Edeirnion and Dinmael which, as we have seen, had survived fairly unchanged into the post-Conquest world. There was no castle or English borough in the area; no royal court or sheriff's tourn was held there; no extents or surveys itemized the dues and obligations of its peasantry. Here the petty lords who ruled the roost were the descendants of the Welsh dynasty of northern Powys, each ruling over tiny fractions of territory, their only route for escape into a modicum of prosperity being either through service to the king or by marriage to an English heiress. Edeirnion and Dinmael were governmentally and economically anomalous and anachronistic; but it was an area which had a deep appeal to Owain Glyn Dŵr. Here his forebears had ruled uninterruptedly

for centuries; nearby was the Cistercian monastery, Valle Crucis, which was his family's foundation and where the tomb of his great-grandfather lay under one of the finest sepulchral slabs in north Wales (see plate 3); nearby also lay the ruined remains of Castell Dinas Bran, the magnificently sited hilltop castle from which his ancestors had ruled northern Powys. Here the resonance of the past and the irritations of the present—not least in the form of border disputes with his neighbour, Reginald Grey, lord of Dyffryn Clwyd (Ruthin)—came together. It was here, not in Sycharth, that Owain was proclaimed prince of Wales in September 1400, and it was from this district that he drew the supporters who rampaged with him through the English boroughs of north-east Wales on his first foray.[11]

Glyndyfrdwy was a fine place to start a revolt; but if that revolt was to be sustained it would need support from other, and richer, districts of Wales. This is where the second locale of Glyn Dŵr's territorial power—the eastern half of the border commote of Cynllaith centred on his moated house at Sycharth—was significant. In a sense it was as thoroughly Welsh as Glyndyfrdwy and as anomalous in its governmental relationship (in this case with the Marcher lordship of Chirkland); but in other respects it was very different. Glyndyfrdwy looked introspectively backwards; Cynllaith opened out eastwards, towards England. Within an arc of some ten miles or so from Sycharth lay the Arundel castle of Chirk, the prosperous Marcher town of Oswestry, and the castles of Whittington and Knockin, the residences respectively of two of the older baronial families of the March, Fitzwarin and Lestrange. Rather longer journeys, but still manageable ones, took one to Chester and Shrewsbury; it was the beer of Shrewsbury which delighted Iolo Goch when he visted Sycharth. Sycharth lay in a comfortably prosperous and fertile part of Wales: the early thirteenth-century church with aisled nave at nearby Llansilin confirmed such an impression; so no doubt did the newly constructed home of Owain Glyn Dŵr himself or the nearby houses at Moeliwrch and Lloran. The area is notable for the quality of its early timber buildings. The proximity of market-towns doubtless quickened the pace of economic life and opportunity, and the ease of travel extended the orbit of social contacts. Such certainly had been the experience of Owain Glyn Dŵr. If he could draw the men of this area to his cause, its prospects of success would surely be much brighter.[12]

Of the final region of Owain's power—a share of the commote of Iscoed, lying north of the River Teifi between the castles of Cardigan and Newcastle Emlyn—we need only speak briefly. It was far away from his other estates and from what we know of the orbits of his movements and friendship. Like Glyndyfrdwy and Cynllaith it was a thoroughly Welsh district in population and custom; but unlike them it was within reach of a powerful English fort and governmental

headquarters, the castle of Cardigan. The importance of Iscoed in the configuration of Owain's lordship was doubtless that it gave him a range of links and loyalties which would come into their own once his revolt ceased to be more than a localized protest. It comes as no surprise, therefore, that the men of Iscoed were in the first group of Cardiganshire rebels to join him in November 1401.[13]

The significance of Owain's estates in providing him with a base of power and loyalties was therefore out of all proportion to their modest economic value and dispersed character. Yet in embarking on the extraordinary risk of staging a revolt it was to his family—both his immediate family and his extended kin—that he would initially turn. Who, then, were his family and how does knowledge of them help us to locate Owain in his milieu? We need not take the story back further than some two generations or so. By 1370 both Owain Glyn Dŵr's grandfather and his father were dead; but the careers which they had pursued doubtless provided a model which he was encouraged to imitate. His grandfather, Gruffudd ap Madog, had come of age in 1321; his standing in local society was manifest in the fact that, as lord of Glyndyfrdwy, his was the first layman's name to appear as a witness to the charter which Edmund, earl of Arundel, granted to his men of Chirkland in 1324. Even more significant as an indication of the orientation of the family was Gruffudd's marriage to Elizabeth, daughter of John Lestrange (V) of Knockin, a member of one of the premier English families of the Shropshire borderlands, and Gruffudd's guardian during his minority. The marriage may initially have been one of convenience, but soon Gruffudd was moving confidently in Lestrange family circles, acting as guardian of their lordship of Ellesmere and witnessing their deeds. The Welsh lord was still excluded from English political society, but he was in touch with it by marriage, for his brother-in-law (Ebulo Lestrange) and his wife's nephew (Roger Lestrange) were both accorded the honour of an individual summons to parliament. Gruffudd was also trusted in affairs governmental and military: he is probably to be identified with the steward of Maelor Saesneg (the detached portion of Flintshire) in 1331, and he was certainly one of the captains of the contingent of Welsh troops which served in Scotland in the 1330s. We know a great deal less about Owain's father, Gruffudd Fychan, than about his grandfather, but what we do know hardly modifies the image of the family's orientation presented by his grandfather's career. Gruffudd Fychan admittedly married a wife of Welsh princely descent and there seems to be no record of his military service. But he does appear in the highly influential post of steward (or chief governor) of the lordship of Oswestry for the earl of Arundel 1346–8, and it is a measure of the earl's trust in, and respect for, him that he was prepared to lend thirty marks from his vast fortune to his widow Elen.[14]

The family traditions which Owain Glyn Dŵr would have inherited are, therefore, clear: military service and leadership, important administrative posts in the north-east March, marriage alliances with either the minor baronial families of the English borderland or families of distinguished Welsh stock, the confidence and support of a premier English earl, and increasingly easy contacts with the leading families of western Shropshire and Cheshire. This was a comfortable and reassuring set of traditions; but it also set an agenda of social expectations. Such expectations seemed to be more than amply fulfilled when it came to Owain's own turn to marry. His wife Margaret not only had outstanding personal qualities—Iolo Goch went so far as to salute her as 'the best of all wives' (W. *gwraig orau o'r gwragedd*)—but she was also of knightly stock (W. *merch eglur llin marchoglyn*), the daughter of Sir David Hanmer.[15]

Owain's choice of a bride, and even more strikingly Sir David Hanmer's choice of Owain as son-in-law, are a telling comment on Owain's connections, standing, and orientation at this stage of his career. The Hanmers were a family which had settled in Maelor Saesneg in the Welsh borderlands in Edward I's reign, quickly assuming the name of one of their holdings, the village of Hanmer, as a family surname. During the course of the fourteenth century they adjusted comfortably to their Welsh habitat and doubtless became thoroughly bilingual. Sir David Hanmer's own wife was Angharad, daughter of Llywelyn Ddu, and so was drawn from one of the most prolific and powerful Welsh families of neighbouring Chirkland. Sir David himself was greeted in friendly and familiar fashion by the Welsh poets, clearly indicating that he was regarded as one of their patrons and a devotee of their art. It was significant that when the pope came to extend an ecclesiastical favour to Sir David's daughter, Owain's wife, he did so under her Welsh name, Marred ferch Dafydd.[16]

Important and significant as were these Welsh connections, however, they were by no means the most important dimensions of David Hanmer's career. It was the law which had opened the doors for David Hanmer into the higher echelons of English governmental and political life. He was a serjeant-at-law by 1375 at the latest, and by 1383 had risen to be one of the chief justices of the King's Bench. In respect of his legal expertise—to the Welsh poet he was the paragon of lawyers (W. *berffaith gyfreithiwr*)—he was appointed a member of the king's council and trier of petitions in parliament and served on scores of commissions in England. A man of such proven legal ability with strong Welsh connections was an obvious candidate for high office and delicate missions in Wales. The most important post he came to hold—and there was none which was more important in Wales—was that of joint justiciar or governor of South Wales in September 1381; but it might well be that some of the commissions he was given there were even more sensitive and top-secret. In 1376–7, for example—when

there was considerable jitteriness in government circles about a possible external attack on Wales—he was sent to north Wales along with other members of the king's council 'to expedite certain aspects of the king's business' there; in May 1381 he was one of a high-powered team of royal agents sent to 'survey the condition of Wales and its people' and to liaise with the leaders of the community there. Few men could have a better-informed view of the governance of Wales in the early 1380s than Sir David Hanmer.[17]

But Sir David services were not confined to the king. There were few men whose legal expertise was so widely sought in the later fourteenth century. It was no surprise that Marcher border families—the Charltons of Powys and the Lestranges of Knockin—should pay him an annual fee for his services. It was a more striking tribute to his status that John of Gaunt and the earl of Stafford likewise paid him an annual retaining fee as a legal adviser, and that the earls of March and Arundel had even gone a step further by appointing him a member of their councils. It may be doubted whether David Hanmer knew all his retaining employers well; but he clearly moved in exalted circles and knew the business affairs of two leading English earls intimately. He was a man who would have chosen his son-in-law carefully, and would surely have shared with him some of his wisdom in the ways of the world and his deep knowledge of the ways of English political and governmental society. Unfortunately for Owain, David Hanmer's career came to a close just as his own was beginning; it was in 1386, probably, that David Hanmer was made a knight; by midsummer 1387 he was dead. The man who was above all others best placed to open the doors of opportunity and promotion to his own son-in-law had been removed from the scene.[18]

Sir David Hanmer's death was a blow, but it in no way severed the links between Owain Glyn Dŵr and the Hanmers. Sir David's son, John, had accompanied Owain on Richard II's expedition to Scotland in 1385, and subsequently came to hold important posts in the government in Flintshire. His elder brother, Gruffudd, had followed in his father's legal footsteps: he was given a legal retaining fee from the lord of Whittington and throughout the 1380s and 1390s he was acting as a legal attorney in the principality of North Wales. It was a measure of the confidence that these brothers, and a third brother Philip, placed in their brother-in-law, Owain, that in the family settlement that was made immediately after Sir David Hanmer's death Owain was one of the two feoffees (or trustees) appointed to effect the settlement. Owain was clearly on good terms with his in-laws. They returned the compliment in September 1400: Gruffudd and Philip were to be among the band which proclaimed him prince of Wales, and John and Philip were to be among his staunchest and most important supporters.[19]

So far we have concentrated on a few individuals from Owain's immediate family—his grandfather, father, father- and brothers-in-law—but the ties and obligations of kinship, through males and females alike, were rarely more ample than they were in medieval Wales. Welsh free society indeed saw itself very considerably as a collection of great lineages descended from a few ancestral patriarchs and interlinked by bonds of marriage as well as of descent. The remarkable genealogical feats of memory achieved not only by the bards but also by free-born peasants illustrate the pride in, and compelling force of, these bonds of kinship and affinity. We need not, of course, assume that bonds of kinship and marriage led necessarily to an identity of attitudes and behaviour; but where we see kinsmen and in-laws acting together as witnesses and in other capacities we have reason to believe that the bonds between them were close and could be the basis for co-ordinated action.

Such indeed is what we find in the immediate kinship network of Owain Glyn Dŵr, as indicated in the accompanying simplified chart (Table 1).[20] His younger brother Tudur—some three years or so his junior—was a close companion; the brothers served together at Berwick and in Scotland in 1384–5 and again in the earl of Arundel's retinue in 1387. His wife's uncle, Maredudd ap Llywelyn Ddu, was also a close associate: they were the joint feoffees of the Hanmer estates in 1387. Maredudd's estates lay close to Hanmer itself and he was deputy-steward of Maelor Saesneg in 1397; he was a pillar of the local governing establishment of this border district. Owain's wife's other maternal uncle was John Kynaston, steward of Maelor Saesneg and of Moldsale in 1397 and of Ellesmere thereafter, and an equally important pillar of the establishment. The marriage of Owain's sisters brought him further links with important families of north-east Wales: one sister was married to Adda Moel ab Iorwerth Ddu, a member of one of the most prolific and powerful native Welsh families of Chirkland, while another sister had taken Robert Puleston, a member of an old English immigrant family, as her husband.[21]

One has to observe a self-denying ordinance in commenting on the family connections of a man such as Owain Glyn Dŵr; the tentacles of kinship and marriage were so all-encompassing in his world that it is easy to be overwhelmed by them. Even from the current very modest discussion of his family, however, it is possible to draw certain basic conclusions. The family setting was Owain's milieu, at least in peacetime; in getting to know his family we are getting closer to the man himself. It was a world in which old native Welsh families and more recently arrived English families were, at least at this social level, on excellent terms. The ease of their rapport in this area of north-east Wales was in marked contrast with the tension so noticeable elsewhere in the country, notably in the isolated English boroughs of the north and west. Here was a society in which families such as the Hanmers and Pulestons adopted Welsh names and married

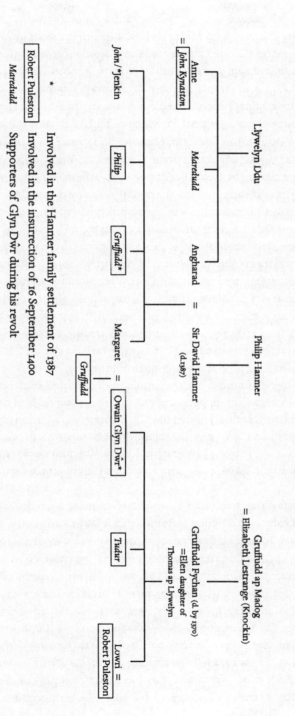

TABLE 1. The family network of Owain Glyn Dŵr (simplified)

* Involved in the Hanmer family settlement of 1387

Robert Puleston Involved in the insurrection of 16 September 1400

Maredudd Supporters of Glyn Dŵr during his revolt

Welsh brides, and in which Welshmen such as Glyn Dŵr readily returned the compliment. It was a world which was apparently at ease with itself. Glyn Dŵr's family connections also reveal that he turned in a circle well used to the exercise of local power, not perhaps (with the notable exception of Sir David Hanmer) to the highest offices, but to posts—stewardships, deputy-stewardships, escheator-ships, attorneyships—which were influential and profitable enough at local level. What might be worrying is that Owain Glyn Dŵr himself—unlike his father and grandfather—had not secured such a post. What was also worrying was that, as far as we can see, this family group was essentially localized in its orbit and influence in the 1390s. There had been a moment during the last ten years or so of Sir David Hanmer's life when it was, through him, at least in touch with a much wider and more powerful world, with all the excitement and opportunities such a world offered. By the 1390s Owain, the Hanmer brothers, Maredudd ap Llywelyn Ddu, and their kinsfolk seem to operate on a very local stage. That may be speculation; what is not in doubt is that this family group showed remarkable solidarity. Many of its members recur together as witnesses to deeds. The depth of their solidarity was demonstrated, and tested, when Owain broke into revolt in 1400. His may have been a private vision; but, then and later, he was able to carry much of his family with him. That tells us a great deal about both Owain and his family.

Family was obviously important in shaping Owain Glyn Dŵr and providing him with the initial support for his remarkable decision to proclaim himself prince of Wales. But a family conspiracy had to command the support of friends and acquaintances if it was to get further than a ridiculous act of self-promotion. Glyn Dŵr seems to have had two such circles of friends. One was centred on Glyn-dyfrdwy. The 'barons' of Edeirnion and Dinmael were linked to Glyn Dŵr by ties of descent (they were all ultimately of the stock of Bleddyn ap Cynfyn, the founding father of the dynasty of Powys), neighbourhood, and common tenure; to these were no doubt added ties of frustration and aspiration. Ten of these 'barons'—the petty squires of Rug, Hendwr, Crogen, Cilan, and such places—joined Owain on his initial foray in September 1400; and it was from the ranks of their tenants and those of Glyn Dŵr himself that the bulk of his initial marauding force was drawn. But in the royal indictments which are our key source for the launching of the revolt it is not these squireens but another circle of Glyn Dŵr's friends which figure as his key supporters. These were the squires of the eastern borderlands—of the county of Flint (more especially its detached portion of Maelor Saesneg), the Arundel Marcher lordships of Chirkland and Bromfield and Yale (Maelor Gymraeg), and of the contiguous manors of Shropshire such as Ellesmere. It was from this group that Owain had chosen his military

companions and marriage links; it was on their judgement and support that he would now pre-eminently have to rely.[22]

From this group four may be chosen to identify the kind of circles in which Owain turned. Hywel Cyffin, or Gethin was dean of St Asaph and came from a family which was among Glyn Dŵr's near neighbours in Cynllaith. He and his two nephews (both of them recent officials in the Arundel lordship of Chirkland) were to join him in his escapade. From the nearby lordship of Bromfield and Yale, and specifically from the lush lowlands bordering on Cheshire, came two more of Owain's friends and supporters. Neither cuts a very distinctive figure in the surviving records, but both came of distinguished Welsh families. Ieuan ap Hywel Pickhill figures prominently in the great Arundel survey of Bromfield of 1391 not only as a considerable landowner in his own right but also as one who was snapping up leases—of the lord's demesne and mill in Allington, 120 acres in Burton (both of them vills in the Dee plain), and vacant lands elsewhere in the area. He was a man on the make, seizing his opportunities with both hands; when he came to arrange for the descent of his estates he opted for the conveniences of English law—giving a life-title to his wife and a reversionary interest to his daughters, both of them devices precluded by Welsh law. But though he was aggressively on the make, Ieuan ap Hywel Pickhill chose to stand by his friend Owain Glyn Dŵr in 1400. So did his neighbour, Madog ab Ieuan ap Madog. The most important fact about Madog was his lineage. His grandfather, Madog ap Llywelyn, was memorably described on his death in 1331 as 'the best person who ever lived in Maelor Gymraeg' (Bromfield), and his effigy in full military dress still reclines in Gresford church. Madog junior seems to have inherited neither the talent nor the virtue of his grandfather—he was involved in a homicide in 1373—but he was still a man of means and importance whose support was worth cultivating. Owain must have known him well, for Madog's wife was the sister of Owain's own brother-in-law. Madog certainly obliged Owain, for he was with him at Glyndyfrdwy on 16 September 1400.[23]

Morgan Yonge was not there; but he certainly turned in Owain's circle of friends and acquaintances, albeit that he was of an older generation (for there is evidence that he was already married by 1364). Morgan's name is revealing of the ambivalence and compromises of border society. His surname sounds unmistakably English and so it was, because it had apparently been adopted by the family one generation earlier when it married into the western Cheshire family of Yonge. But in spite of this sleight of nomenclature, Morgan was according to Welsh genealogies of impeccable Welsh stock from Chirkland; and this is indeed confirmed by the fact that he often appears also under his Welsh name form as Morgan ab Iorwerth ap Morgan. But Yonge was a good name for a man who wanted to get on in the world and to rub shoulders with the knights and squires

of Cheshire and Shropshire. Morgan certainly did well for himself: his wife, Marred ferch Llywelyn Sais, was one of the richest heiresses in north-east Wales, with extensive lands in particular in Dyffryn Clwyd. He consolidated his position by securing favourable leases in the district and buying out the right of kinsmen. He also secured official positions to match his social and territorial standing: sheriff and *rhaglaw* of Flintshire in 1378 and under-sheriff in 1390. He was a pillar of the local establishment, and the English government was to lean heavily on him, even in his old age, to contain the Glyn Dŵr revolt in Flintshire. But Morgan Yonge was, like so many, to find his loyalty severely tested. After all, he knew Glyn Dŵr well: they had served together in Scotland in 1385 and had been closely involved together in making arrangements for Sir David Hanmer's estates in 1387; and the links between Morgan and the Hanmers were particularly close. One by one Morgan's family—his sons, Iorwerth Fychan and Jankyn, and subsequently his grandsons—defected to Glyn Dŵr, and so almost certainly did Morgan himself, at least briefly.[24] But his greatest contribution to Glyn Dŵr lay elsewhere: Master Gruffudd Yonge, the Oxford-trained clerk who rose to the key position of Glyn Dŵr's chancellor and quite likely the mastermind behind his more ambitious policies, was almost certainly Morgan Yonge's illegitimate son.[25]

But that is to anticipate. What we have been trying to do through these thumbnail sketches of family and friends is to get closer to Owain Glyn Dŵr by trying to locate him in his social context. It was the world of the middling and higher orders of Welsh and Marcher society in north-east Wales, more specifically in the frontierlands from Chester to Oswestry and so westwards into Bromfield and Yale and Chirkland. It was a world of deans and sheriffs, stewards and escheators. It included men (such as Morgan Yonge and Ieuan ap Hywel Pickhill) who were on the make economically and socially; but it includes others, notably the 'barons' of Edeirnion and Dinmael or Madog ab Ieuan ap Madog, who had little source of consolation other than their genealogical laurels. None of them was a man who would have cut a great figure in English regional society; they lived in a rather claustrophobic local society, cultivating their memories and their ambitions. They knew each other well, co-operated in public and private affairs, intermarried, shared a common culture of genealogical prowess and traditions, and had much the same view of the world (and shared that view whether their names were Welsh or English, or both). This was the world of Owain Glyn Dŵr.

But what of Owain himself? The little that we know of him before he proclaimed himself prince of Wales in September 1400 is based on three very different types of sources. First and most prolific are the odes (W. *cywyddau*) addressed to him by two of the premier Welsh poets of the period, Iolo Goch and Gruffudd Llwyd.

Their evidence is invaluable in many respects, not least in hinting at a range of aspirations, norms, and expectations which we could otherwise only guess at. They are, furthermore, virtually our only source (a few deeds excepted) from within Wales and Welsh society. But Welsh praise poetry was a highly stylized art-form governed by its own rules as to metre, format, subject, and content. In particular, its purpose was not to offer an individualized pen-portrait of its subject, but rather to extol the subject in terms of the conventionalized image of the perfect noble-born Welshman or *uchelwr*. Images are crucial to a society, and the fact that Owain apparently corresponded, or could be made to correspond, so closely to the image of the *uchelwr* is itself revealing of his character and of contemporary expectations of him. Image and character were in close alignment; therein lay part of Owain's strength and appeal. But images cannot tell us of the particularities of his character and career. We can be helped, albeit inadequately, with regard to his career by the two other sources. The first are the muster lists of English armies in the later fourteenth century; they can help us to fill out some, though by no means all, of the details of Owain's military career before 1400. The second—and less reliable—are the comments made by English chroniclers on his earlier career when the news of his revolt broke. It is from these three very different, but in some ways complementary, sources that we must try to piece together the little that can be known of Owain before his momentous decision in September 1400.

We can be fairly sure that he was born in the 1350s, though we cannot be exact about the year. What we can say with confidence is that his rebellion when it was launched was not that of a hot-headed, restless youth: he was certainly in his forties by 1400 and so were most of his prominent supporters whose ages we can determine. This was no revolt of the *juvenes*; it was the considered gamble of middle-aged men. By 1370 Owain's father was dead; but Owain was almost certainly too young to have succeeded to his estates. We do not know how he was reared during these formative years; but there is a strong possibility—though it has not hitherto been entertained by historians—that he and his estates were taken into the custody of Sir David Hanmer. The suggestion gains a measure of support from two directions: first, it would repeat exactly what had happened to his grandfather more than two generations earlier when he had been placed as a ward in the custody of another English border family, that of Lestrange of Knockin; secondly, it would explain how Owain came to be betrothed and married to Sir David's daughter, Margaret, exactly as Owain's grandfather had been married to his guardian's daughter in 1304. The suggestion is further supported by what appears to have been the next stage in Owain's career. The chronicler of St Albans comments that Owain spent a period of his youth as an apprentice at law at Westminster. The source is not a particularly reliable one;

but the episode is plausible on more than one count. We know that young English gentlemen, including some from the north-west, were sent at this period to serve as apprentices at the courts of Westminster and we have a good idea of the sort of legal education they might receive. Owain's career was so conventional in so many directions that such a spell as a lawyer's apprentice is perfectly plausible. It is, of course, all the more plausible given the Hanmer connection. A distinguished and successful lawyer such as Sir David Hanmer was more than likely to have insisted on a basic legal education for his ward and prospective son-in-law, all the more so when we know that Sir David's own son Gruffudd was embarked on precisely such a legal career. Indeed, it is quite likely that Sir David (as he was to become) sent his son and his ward together to the law courts at Westminster. The central role that Owain played in the arrangement of the Hanmer estates after Sir David's death in 1387 suggests that the family had complete confidence in his probity and legal competence.[26]

There may be a small element of speculation about Owain's legal education; there is none about aspects of his military career. We may wish to take with a large pinch of salt the sort of extravagant compliments which the Welsh poets paid to his military prowess: he was 'the candle of battle' (W. *cannwyll brwydr*); his sole delight was 'to ride war-horses' (W. *ni wnaeth ond marchogaeth meirch*). But contemporary English chronicles recognized that he was 'an exemplary warrior' (L. *armiger formosus*) and his own ambassadors to the French court declared that he exulted in the trappings of war, for he was above all else a soldier. This should not surprise us, for the heroes of fourteenth-century Welsh noble society were overwhelmingly military leaders, past and present. This had always been so in what was a strongly militarist society, but it had become more so of late when military prowess had become almost the sole route for Welshmen to find fame, fortune, and favour beyond their local and impoverished societies.[27]

It is in the service of one of these professional and successful military leaders, Sir Gregory Sais, that Owain makes his debut in the military records of the time. Sir Gregory's career might almost be a role-model for the one that Owain Glyn Dŵr had in mind for himself at this stage of his own career. Sir Gregory had spent most of the 1360s and 1370s on campaigns, skirmishes, and garrison duty in France and Spain; he had been present at some of the memorable military events of these years, such as the Black Prince's expedition into Castile in 1367 or the sack of Limoges in 1370; he had hob-nobbed with the famous, such as Sir Simon Burley, Sir Hugh Calveley, Sir David Hulgreve, and Sir Thomas Percy. War had brought him adventure and fame; but it had also brought him more material rewards. These included major military posts and commands in England, Wales, and France; two castles and their associated estates in Poitou (though both were to be lost as the French advanced during the 1370s); a rich Poitevin heiress as a wife; an

annual pension of £200 for life; the wherewithal to invest the profits of war, even in a period of rapid military decline for the English, in the purchase of land in his native Flintshire; and, by no means least, the accolade of knighthood. Sir Gregory's career must have been a source of inspiration for the young Owain Glyn Dŵr; the stories that he had to recount opened avenues of adventure and prospects of profit and promotion which were truly thrilling.[28]

Compared with such feats of arms, Owain's own initial military assignment was prosaic, verging on the dull. In March 1384 he was one of ninety-nine men-at-arms and 200 archers who took up garrison duty at Berwick-on-Tweed under the captaincy of Sir Gregory Sais. The posting came at a significant juncture in Anglo-Scottish relations: a long truce with Scotland was drawing to a close; the Scots were pressing hard to recover lands lost to the English; and the English now found themselves with no more than three fortresses under their control on the Scottish border—Roxburgh, Jedburgh, and Berwick itself. So a posting to Berwick at this stage was certainly no military holiday; indeed later in the year, after Glyn Dŵr had left, the castle was to be captured in a surprise attack (a remarkable foretaste for the Percies of the military humiliation and recriminations which they were to experience when Conway Castle was likewise captured from them in April 1401). For Glyn Dŵr himself the stint of garrison duty at Berwick was probably an important part of his military apprenticeship. His household bards back in Wales found themselves torn between exaggerated fears for their patron's safety in such outlandish parts and even more exaggerated praise of his military feats there. For Owain himself, what is likely to have been important is the insight he gained into garrison duty and border skirmishes; the camaraderie of serving with a host of fellow-Welshmen, including his own brother Tudur; the opportunity for making the acquaintance of hardened military warriors such as Sir John Mascy of Cheshire; the glow of serving a world-renowned commander, Sir Gregory Sais; and the chance of sharing garrison duty with two men who were to figure prominently in his future life, Henry Percy, earl of Northumberland, and his son Hotspur. His military appetite had been truly whetted.[29]

So much so that he joined the large army that Richard II assembled to invade Scotland in summer 1385. We have no details on this occasion to tell us in whose service Owain enlisted; but it may well be that he now first saw service in the retinue of the earl of Arundel who certainly contributed a force to the expedition. Alternatively he may have been part of the considerable Cheshire contingent which was raised for the occasion and which initiated the close link between Richard II and the military potential of the county palatine. What we do know is that some of Owain's closest relatives and associates joined him on the occasion: his brother Tudur was with him once again; so on this occasion was his brother-

in-law, John Hanmer, and his sister's husband, Robert Puleston; also present was one of Owain's closest associates, Morgan Yonge. The expedition itself was short-lived; it burnt and plundered its way to Edinburgh and then retired. But it had given Owain his first experience of a marauding expedition and had doubt-less deepened friendships already well established at home.[30]

In particular the 1385 expedition may well have seen him enlist for the first time under the military banner of the earl of Arundel. The link with the Arundels was, as we have seen, a family tradition: it seems to have been particularly strong in the time of Owain's father, as is witnessed by the latter serving as Arundel's steward of Oswestry and Arundel in turn lending his widow money. Given the fact that Sycharth lay next to the Arundel lordship of Chirkland, the connection is not at all surprising. But such connections have to be reaffirmed and rebuilt in each generation. Owain Glyn Dŵr was a young man who had to demonstrate his qualities and worth to a new earl, Richard Fitzalan (who had succeeded his father in 1376). One contemporary chronicle says that Glyn Dŵr was the squire of the earl of Arundel. In the sense that he had become a permanent member of the earl's retinue, tied to him for life in peace and war by a contract or indenture, there is no supporting evidence for such a claim; in the much more limited sense that Glyn Dŵr enlisted in the earl's retinue for a specific military occasion, the claim is undoubtedly true. The occasion was the expedition commanded by the earl of Arundel in his capacity as admiral of the West and North in the spring of 1387.[31]

The military and political context of the expedition can be very summarily outlined before we focus again on Owain Glyn Dŵr. Since 1385 England had been threatened annually by a major French invasion to be launched from Flanders. Troops from Wales were amongst those which had been rushed to south-east England to anticipate such an invasion. The best prospect of removing the threat however, lay in a pre-emptive strike, both to destroy or at least disable the Franco-Flemish navy and to ravage the area around Sluys from which such an invasion was most likely to be launched. It was to achieve these twin ambitions, at the very least, that on 10 December 1386 the earl of Arundel was retained to serve the king with 2,500 men for three months from the following 1 March. It is at this stage that the political context of the enterprise becomes important. Since 19 November 1386 Richard II had been effectively stripped of control of the country's government. One of those who now shaped policy and guided the country's affairs was Richard's bitter political critic, Richard Fitzalan, earl of Arundel.

When Owain Glyn Dŵr, therefore, enlisted in the personal retinue of the earl of Arundel during the early months of 1387 he was not only joining the military ranks of a neighbouring magnate and family patron, he was also hitching his

wagon to the star of a man who was politically and territorially in the ascendant. The earl of Arundel was in overall command of a force of 2,500 men; but this force was in turn composed of some twenty-seven retinues. It was in the personal retinue of the earl of Arundel himself—consisting of four bannerets, thirty-two knights, 127 esquires, and 217 archers—that Glyn Dŵr enlisted. It was an experience which was transforming his contacts and horizons. There were powerful neighbours there whom he would have known well by name or even personally. Two of the bannerets were powerful Shropshire neighbours: Fulk Fitzwarin of Whittington and Richard Talbot of Ellesmere, Blackmere, and (eventually) Goodrich Castle. Among the knights was a distant family relative also from Shropshire, Roger Lestrange of Knockin. Also in the ranks of the knights was Reginald Grey, heir to the lordship of Dyffryn Clwyd and Glyn Dŵr's future deadly foe. But there were also men who were total strangers to Glyn Dŵr: Sir Edward Dallingridge, the builder of Bodiam Castle, was a member of the retinue; so was Sir John Bohun of Midhurst, also in Sussex. As the forces were mustered at Sandwich in early March 1387 Glyn Dŵr must have felt a *frisson* of exhilaration: he was now moving in the best English military circles of the day under the command of one of the most powerful magnates of the kingdom.[32]

Such exhilaration must have turned to pure joy when Arundel's force routed the Franco-Flemish fleet on 24 March 1387, in one of the most notable naval victories of this period of warfare, and proceeded to raid the countryside around Sluys. Arundel and his force returned to England covered with glory and further enhanced their reputation by selling the vast quantities of wine they had captured at knock-down prices. It was the sort of military triumph with which any soldier would be delighted to be associated. Glyn Dŵr had chosen his military patron well. As the turbulent political events of late summer 1387–spring 1388 unfolded in England he had further reason to congratulate himself in his choice of patron. In the titanic power-struggle which was waged during these months between Richard II and his opponents, ending in the utter humiliation and defeat of the king, the earl of Arundel was very much a leading figure. We do not have evidence of Glyn Dŵr's relationships with the earl during these critical months, but at the very least Glyn Dŵr could hardly but have been aware of the crisis that was unfolding. By July 1387 he had returned to north-east Wales to settle the Hanmer family's affairs; at precisely the same time Richard II was touring the border and gathering support in Cheshire. Later in the year the earl of Arundel was putting his castles in the March of Wales in a state of defence and nailing a copy of the appeal against Robert de Vere, Richard II's favourite, on the door of St Peter's church at Chester. Whether Glyn Dŵr had any role in these events we shall never know; but given that they were happening within a few miles of his home, he could hardly have been indifferent to them. Nor could he have been

indifferent to the fact that the man whom he could in some respects regard as his natural patron had emerged triumphant from the power-struggle. That should surely have enhanced his own chances of making his way in the world, militarily and otherwise.[33]

The years 1387–8 could have made Glyn Dŵr. In the event it turned out to be otherwise. During 1387 itself two very different episodes might, especially in retrospect, have served to qualify his euphoria. The first was something that did not happen. On 24 March 1387 the earl of Arundel knighted some of his squires in celebration of his great naval victory that day; Owain Glyn Dŵr was not one of them. The second was the death during the early summer of 1387 of Glyn Dŵr's father-in-law, Sir David Hanmer. Owain returned home to make arrangements for the care of Hanmer's estates, and his increasing domestic preoccupations may well explain why, in spite of having initially enrolled to serve in Arundel's retinue again for an expedition to western France in May 1388, he did not in fact serve.[34]

Owain Glyn Dŵr's military career was, to the best of our knowledge, confined to the years 1384–7. Whether it was personally distinguished is impossible to tell; it is difficult to doubt, however, that it was formative for him. It had given him a range of experiences, friends, and acquaintances which had greatly extended his horizons and geographical knowledge. He was a man who had fought alongside some of the most experienced warriors of his day and he had been present at one of the few major English victories of the decade. We shall never know why his military career was so abruptly terminated and whether he ended it of his own choice. What we can, however, suggest fairly confidently is that the prospects for such a career, for repeating the exploits of Sir Gregory Sais, dimmed rapidly after 1389. During the course of that year Richard II resumed the reins of power and the earl of Arundel's political authority and military standing went into instant decline. He was still a power in the land, especially in his own estates; but he was increasingly politically marginalized, until eventually in July 1397 Richard II felt sufficiently sure of himself to proceed against the earl and secure his execution. Some of the earl's followers, including some of Glyn Dŵr's military comrades of the 1387 expedition, quickly read the signs of the times and switched their allegiance to the king, Sir Edward Dallingridge and Sir Roger Lestrange among them. There is no evidence that Owain Glyn Dŵr did so; but equally there is no evidence that he was a close associate of Arundel during these years. Unlike his father, he is never known to have become steward of one of Arundel's Marcher lordships. Nevertheless, even if relations between the two men were cool or strained, what is obviously true is that Glyn Dŵr's most natural aristocratic patron in English society and in whose retinue he had fought was now a spent political force, indeed a liability. Owain's other obvious patron in military matters, Sir Gregory Sais, died in 1390. Even had both lived the opportunity of carving

out a dazzling military career were no longer there: in June 1389 England and France concluded a truce which in the event was to last for the rest of the century. Owain would have to satisfy his aspirations in other directions.

After the events of 1387, both military and domestic, Owain virtually disappears from view of the historical evidence until he bursts into rebellion in September 1400. These may have been, as Sir John Edward Lloyd surmised, years of domestic contentment, of 'an Owain at ease, wealthy, generous, respected, happy in the life of his home', of a man who delighted in the patronage of poets (W. *mab yn adnabod canu clêr*) and who was making the appropriate arrangements for the well-being of his soul and that of his wife at death. Had he died in 1399 he would hardly have earned himself more than a passing mention in the annals of Welsh history. The poets would certainly have been extravagant in their elegies for such a munificent and caring patron; an appropriate sepulchral slab or monumental effigy might have been erected at the parish church at Llansilin or even possibly at Valle Crucis Abbey, very much in the style of the effigy of 1395 at Llanuwchllyn commemorating one of his military companions, Ieuan ap Gruffudd ap Madog. But there would be little else by which he could be remembered: his career had been utterly conventional and he had not even held any offices, which are often the sole measure of contemporary standing that registers in the historical evidence. All that may be true; but one wonders whether the picture of domestic quiescence adequately reflects the reality of Owain's life and state of mind in the 1390s. As we have seen already, the tempo of political change accelerated furiously after 1397 and much of that drama took place in, or impinged upon, Owain's home area and its environs; he could not have been indifferent to such tumultuous events. Domestic contentment, and inactivity, might also paradoxically have encouraged him, egged on by the bards to whom he was so indulgent, to turn his mind to past dreams and future visions to make amends for the *ennui* and disappointments of the present. For what is beyond doubt is that the man who burst into rebellion on 16 September 1400 had been nursing his dreams and frustrations for a long time; it is not after a morning's or a week's or even a month's pique that one decides to have oneself proclaimed prince of Wales and persuades a goodly number of friends and associates to support such an outrageous gamble.[35]

We have been on Owain Glyn Dŵr's trail through his ancestors, his family, his kinsmen, his friends, his localities, and his career. All are crucial to an understanding of the man; but they are not the man himself. It may be, as we have suggested, that Owain's lineage was in itself a passport to the loyalty of his followers; it may be also that his character and his virtues coincided closely with the idealized image of the Welsh *uchelwr*. Yet the capacity to command and

above all to retain loyalty in the way that Owain did surely suggests that part, possibly a very important part, of his appeal lay in his own character, in the charisma of his own personality. That is a topic on which our sources almost completely fail us, especially before 1400. One of Iolo Goch's poems, it is true, presents a formal rounded portrait of the man; but the virtues which it itemizes— such as noble descent, justice, even-handedness, courage, mercy—are derived from the contemporary stock of conventional compliments. We can extrapolate a few hints of his character from episodes of his behaviour during the revolt, and these probably take us as close as we can ever hope to get to the individuality of the man himself. He was a man who stood his ground with dignity and firmness: that is clear in the reports of the negotiations of the earl of Northumberland with him in 1401. As his confidence grew he knew how to drive a hard bargain with his opponents and not to yield when the tide was flowing strongly for him: so it was that when John Skidmore was in a desperate plight in Dryslwyn Castle in July 1403 and pleaded for a safe-conduct for the womenfolk in his entourage, he had to report that 'he (Owain) wolde none graunte me'. He was already a man who commanded loyalty to an extraordinary degree; that is evident from the outset of the revolt to the end. He was also a man who reciprocated that loyalty: one of the few attractive glimpses we catch of him is of his attending the funeral of two Welsh squires killed during one of the king's expeditions into Wales.[36]

His leadership of the revolt was never challenged, even though several of the local leaders were men of high spirits and ambition themselves. The poet's compliments to his grandfather could be more appropriately addressed to him: he was indeed 'the king of the barons', *brenin ar y barwniaid*. When important prisoners were captured during the revolt they were sent directly to Owain himself. In the death throes of the revolt, with the king's cannons and siege engines poised to capture the castle of Aberystwyth, the local Welsh commander, Rhys Ddu, did not dare make an agreement without consulting Glyn Dŵr. Owain's response, as reported in the Welsh chronicle, speaks volumes for the authority and spirit of the man even in defeat: 'Owain kept Rhys with him until he had gathered his power around him and then went with Rhys to Aberystwyth, where he threatened to cut off Rhys's head, unless he might have the castle; whereupon the castle was given to Owain.' This is the authentic response of one who was a consummate leader of men. Even in defeat he retained their loyalty: his cause might be lost, but he himself never formally surrendered and, even more significant, was never betrayed. He passed from the annals of history directly into legend.[37]

We may accept, therefore, that Owain was a charismatic leader; but even charismatic leaders can be no more than nine days' wonders unless the cause they espouse elicits a wide degree of sympathy and active support. Leadership and

programme must ultimately be matched if a temporary protest is to be converted into a sustained movement. Iolo Goch, in spite of the wooden and tired images of his poems, hinted at how that fusion might be effected in the person of Owain when he greeted him as 'the sole head of Wales', *un pen ar Gymru*. It is from the context, career, and character of the man to the programme and vision of the leader that we must now turn.[38]

THE PROGRAMME
NATIONAL SALVATION

Revolts are often triggered by a minor incident whose importance is soon overwhelmed by the deep and long-festering grievances which it releases. Such seems to have been the case with Owain Glyn Dŵr's revolt. Two stories were circulating in English monasteries as to why he was stung into his outrageous act of defiance. The first, reported by the well-placed Evesham Chronicle, presents Owain as a man deeply wronged by the duplicitous behaviour of his neighbour, Reginald Grey, lord of Ruthin and Dyffryn Clwyd. Grey had been charged by the king, so the story ran, with delivering to Owain a summons under the royal signet to accompany the proposed royal expedition to Scotland. Grey deliberately delayed delivering the letter to Glyn Dŵr until a mere three days before the expeditionary force was due to depart, leaving Owain with no option but to respond that he could not come at such short notice. Grey now compounded his duplicity by reporting back to the king that Owain had spurned the king's letters, insulted him and shown contempt for the orders. The story is perhaps more elaborate than accurate. Yet it may have an element of truth in it: Henry IV certainly led an expedition into Scotland in August 1400, and among his army of some 13,000 troops were Reginald Grey and some of his tenants from Dyffryn Clwyd. Given Glyn Dŵr's experience of war, not least on the Scottish frontier, he might well have been asked to serve on this occasion. The second story, as reported in Thomas Walsingham's Chronicle, explains Owain's outburst in less sinister and more familiar terms as arising from a dispute about land, again with Reginald Grey. The story has rather greater plausibility than the first: Glyn Dŵr's land certainly bordered with the Grey lordship of Dyffryn Clwyd; disputes between neighbouring lordships about boundaries and the extradition of wanted men were common and can indeed be documented from these two specific lordships; and the Greys are known to have been on particularly bad terms with their Welsh tenants and neighbours in the closing years of the fourteenth century. Whichever of these two stories we may care to believe—and there may well be an element of truth in both—they are at one in agreeing that it was a personal quarrel between Glyn Dŵr and Grey which was

the immediate trigger of the events of 16 September 1400. And it was, of course, the Grey town of Ruthin which was the initial target of Glyn Dŵr's first foray.[1]

A bitter personal quarrel may explain why Owain acted when he did, on 16 September 1400. It does not, of course, explain what he did. That, as the official judicial indictment and the chronicles (even the ones written without the hindsight of what happened after 1403) agree, was to have himself proclaimed prince of Wales. Such a breathtaking claim can surely only be explained in terms of long-cherished dreams and aspirations. From its outset Glyn Dŵr's rebellion was a national revolt; it was to be its national vision and ambition which sustained it.[2]

To claim as much is not to assert that Glyn Dŵr and his advisers had from the outset a blueprint for the new principality which was implicit in their act of proclaiming him prince of Wales, nor is it to claim a single-mindedness of purpose which hindsight so often imposes on historical events. On the contrary, the story of the early years of revolt bespeaks hesitation, compromise, and uncertainty. Indeed, it could be argued that Owain's claim to be rightful prince of Wales was either a by-product of a patriotic rush of blood to the head or a piece of bargaining bluster from which he might be willing to retreat. The latter suggestion gains a good measure of support from the fact that on several occasions before 1403 he seems to have been willing to contemplate submission, provided he could recover the share of his inheritance which had been wrongfully withheld from him. A petition from the burgesses of Holt of *c.*1430 indeed went so far as to identify that what he had in mind was the great Arundel lordship of Bromfield and Yale. Such a claim might have appeared ridiculous to the English authorities; but to Owain and his circle it was one which historically made very good sense, since it represented a large part of the principality of northern Powys of which his ancestors had been arbitrarily dispossessed in 1282. If that indeed was the limit of Owain's realistic ambitions in these initial years, it might help to explain why there survives no evidence prior to 1403 that Owain consistently claimed, let alone used, the title prince of Wales. Indeed in one letter—which admittedly can no longer be traced and whose authenticity can therefore not be verified—he apparently still styled himself 'lord of Glyndyfrdwy' as his ancestors had done. In none of the negotiations which the Percies held with him during the years 1401–3 was any reference apparently made to his claim to be prince of Wales. It might indeed have been quietly dropped had the English government been less intransigent.[3]

We may accept, therefore, that his very uneven military fortunes in 1401–2 and his rather desperate position as a hunted fugitive may have prompted Owain to make a more realistic assessment of his ambition than his initial act of bravado suggests. But by the same token, as the tide of military fortune turned in his

favour in 1402–3, and as he secured the support of Edmund Mortimer senior and the Percies, his old dreams were reactivated. There can be no doubt that Owain's remarkable successes during 1403 transformed his prospects and thereby his ambitions. What had hitherto been a patchwork of spasmodic hit-and-run raids, with admittedly some spectacular coups (notably the seizure of Conway Castle and the capture of Reginald Grey and Edmund Mortimer senior), now became a truly national revolt, embracing almost every part of Wales, including the north-east and the south-east, and spilling over into England. It was no longer a matter of guerrilla raids, though those continued, but of an awesome Welsh army marching from Brecon down the Tywi valley and sweeping all before it. Whole communities now defected *en masse* to the Welsh cause and, as in Flintshire and Cydweli, organized their own activities on Owain's behalf. Men who had hitherto kept their options open now saw no alternative but to throw in their lot with Glyn Dŵr.[4]

Two individual examples may be cited of the sort of men who now defected to the Welsh cause. William Gwyn ap Rhys Llwyd was a powerful landowner and steward of the Lancastrian lordship of Cydweli in the 1390s and again in 1400–1. In England he was the sort of man who would have been justice of the peace, sheriff, and quite possibly an MP. Until at least November 1402 he was certainly regarded as loyal by the government; indeed he was charged with transporting large sums of money to the leading English commander in the Brecon area, Richard, Lord Grey of Codnor. But during the course of the next few months he defected to Glyn Dŵr's cause and became one of the most prominent leaders of rebellion in south-west Wales. The depth of his commitment to the Welsh cause was to be shown by the fact that he was killed defending Glyn Dŵr's last outpost at Aberystwyth. He paid for his defection with his life; his family paid the price of being permanently disinherited. Much at the same time William Gwyn was crossing the Rubicon in his loyalties in the spring and summer of 1403, a man of similar background and standing was undergoing the same experience in north-east Wales. Maredudd ap Llywelyn Ddu, as we noted above, was an important land- and office-holder in Maelor Saesneg, the fertile detached portion of Flintshire bordering on Cheshire and Shropshire. Owain Glyn Dŵr's revolt must have posed a dilemma for Maredudd from early days, since he was an uncle of Owain's wife and had been a close associate of Owain's in making arrangements for the Hanmer estates. But the government had no reason to doubt Maredudd's loyalty and showed its confidence in him by placing him on commissions to deal with disorder in his home area as late as August 1402. But no government could have anticipated the strains placed on its supporters' loyalties in Wales by the events of 1403. During the course of that year Maredudd defected to Owain's cause and died a rebel in April 1405. But his descendants,

unlike those of William Gwyn ap Rhys Llwyd, were allowed to make amends for his lapse of loyalty: his son paid a fine of 10 marks (£6 13s. 4d.) in 1409 to recover his father's lands, while his grandchildren were to be among the patrons of Gutun Owain, the most prolific poet, historian, genealogist, and herald of later-fifteenth-century Wales.[5]

The careers of William Gwyn ap Rhys Llwyd and Maredudd ap Llywelyn Ddu serve to illustrate in miniature how critical were the closing months of 1402 and the spring and summer of 1403 to Owain Glyn Dŵr's cause. These were truly the make-or-break months, when he could either retreat into as dignified a submission as the Percies could arrange for him or give new heart and new prospects to his movement. It was the capture and then the defection of Edmund Mortimer senior (June–October 1402) and the growing disillusion of the Percies, eventually leading almost certainly to an informal agreement with Glyn Dŵr by June 1403, as well as his own military successes in Wales which tilted the balance towards the latter option. Nothing succeeds like success; as Owain's confidence grew, so did the wholesale defection of local communities and their leaders to him. On 14 June 1403 twelve of the leading Welshmen of the Flintshire commotes of Rhuddlan, Presta-tyn, and Coleshill were appointed by the government to appoint watches against the anticipated invasion of the county by Welsh rebels; all but one of the twelve subsequently defected to Hotspur and/or Owain Glyn Dŵr. A sea-change in calculations and loyalties was taking place. The heady dreams of September 1400 could now once more be entertained, and this time not as the private fantasies of a small group of disaffected conspirators in north-east Wales but as the pro-gramme of a rebellion which had the whole of Wales in its grip. From 1403 onwards the lineaments of Owain's ambitions come into clearer focus, even if several of them can be detected from the earliest days of the revolt.

The very first act of the rebels in September 1400 had in fact proclaimed what was to remain one of their central aims, the destruction of English power and authority in Wales. In their very first foray the rebels not only attacked Ruthin— as they might have been content to do had Owain's quarrel been essentially a personal one with Reginald Grey—but proceeded to launch similar raids on other English towns in north-east Wales—Denbigh, Rhuddlan, Flint, Hawarden, Holt, Oswestry, and Welshpool. The next major act of the rebellion was equally well directed, the capture of Conway Castle on 1 April 1401. Borough and castle were the twin symbols of English privilege and power in Wales. But Glyn Dŵr's supporters were not content with the destruction of the symbols of English authority; they were also intent on expelling its agents—burgesses, settlers, and officials. That was certainly the view of well-placed contemporaries: 'they in-tend', said one observer, 'to burn and destroy all English settlements (F. *toute la*

englissherie) in these parts', while the prince of Wales was convinced that if the rebellion was not crushed, 'no Englishman will henceforth be an officer in Wales'.[6]

For those familiar with the rhetoric and actions of the rebels such claims were perfectly plausible. Furthermore, they were sentiments which apparently commanded the support of the great majority of Welshmen. In the eyes of the chamberlain of Cheshire the revolt was quite simply 'the war between the English and the Welsh', while officials along the Welsh border had no doubt that the revolt had won the support of 'the whole Welsh nation'. For English settlers in Wales the revolt must have been truly frightening; it is little wonder that they and their supporters in England became increasingly hysterical and apocalyptic. Government propaganda and popular rumour were soon putting it about that the intention of the Welsh rebels was not only to discomfort the English in Wales but 'to destroy the whole English language [or nation]' and to effect 'the destruction of the kingdom and the English tongue'. Even contemporaries must have recognized that such claims were grotesquely exaggerated; but popular, and occasionally government-inspired, hysteria is not amenable to reason. Demonizing the enemy is a powerful and all-too-convenient weapon at a time of war; it is all the more powerful if accompanied by stories of atrocities, such as those alleged to have been perpetrated by Welsh women on the bodies and particularly the genitalia of the English killed at the Battle of Bryn Glas in June 1402. As early as February 1401 the tidal wave of feeling against the Welsh was so strong among the commons in parliament that the government had little option but to ride with the tide and issue virulently anti-Welsh legislation.[7]

Owain Glyn Dŵr himself claimed that the popular belief that he wished and intended to destroy the English people (F. *la lange Engloys*) was one of the major reasons why it was unsafe for him to come to the English border to negotiate. His protestations that the genocide of the English was no part of his intention are, of course, totally convincing; but within Wales and *vis-à-vis* English settlers in Wales his actions and his rhetoric were profoundly anti-English. In his earliest propaganda statement to survive—his letters to the king of Scotland and lords of Ireland of 1401–2—he made much play with the oppression and bondage that his people had suffered at the hands of 'your and our mortal enemies, the Saxons'. It was much the same language that he used within Wales to his supporters, declaring that it was his intention 'to liberate the Welsh people [L. *progeniem Wallicanam*] from the bondage of our English enemies'. Finally, in his most solemn international communiqué—his letter of March 1406 to the king of France—he declared how 'his nation for many a long year had been trodden underfoot by the madness of the English barbarians' (L. *per rabiem barbarum Saxonum*). There is doubtless much that is rhetorical about such language; but it drew its force and conviction, as we have

seen, from the deep sense of humiliation, discrimination, oppression, and deliberate belittlement which, to a greater or lesser degree, was experienced by all
Welshmen throughout Wales in the fourteenth century. When, over a century
later, Welsh peasants marched on the market cross at Denbigh and proclaimed
'that Welshmen were as free as Englishmen', they were tapping, albeit in a milder
form, the same sentiment of outrage which lay at the heart of Glyn Dŵr's revolt
and of the popular support for it.[8]

The profound resentment against the English was grounded in the experience
and discriminations of daily life in the present; but it drew its ideological force
from the deep wells of history, mythology, and prophecy of medieval Welsh
culture. Glyn Dŵr's letters to Scotland and Ireland in 1401–2 put us immediately
in touch with this ideology. It is not the bitterness of the present but the glories
of the past and the prospects of the future which take precedence. The letter to
the king of Scotland opens with a brisk history lesson:

Brutus, your most noble ancestor and mine, was the first crowned king who dwelt in this
realm of England which was formerly called Great Britain [F. *Brataygne graunt*]. Brutus
begat three sons, namely Albanactus, Locrinus, and Kamber. You are descended in a
direct line from Albanactus. The descendants of Kamber reigned as kings until Cadwaladr,
who was the last crowned king of my people [F. *de ma . . . nacioun*]. I, dear cousin, am
descended directly from Cadwaladr.

Had the letter reached its destination its historical exposition might have been
given a rather mixed reception in the Scottish court. It was good to know that the
Welsh gave priority to Albanactus and Locrinus, the alleged founder of English
kingship; and the Scots, as we shall see, were quite happy to exploit the historical
and contemporary possibilities of forging a common front with the Welsh
against the English. But they had had their fill of the Brutus legend: as late as
October 1401 an English delegation, headed ironically by Richard Young, bishop
of Bangor, had deployed the same legend to claim that the king of Scotland was
the vassal of the king of England, on the grounds that the latter was the descendant of Brutus's eldest son (Locrinus), to whom the descendants of the younger
son (Albanactus) were in duty bound to do homage. In fact had the Welsh been
rather more up to date with the development of Scottish historical propaganda,
they would have been wise not to have mentioned the Brutus legend at all. The
Scots had by now adopted a position which declared that Scotland had never
been part of Britain and had developed an origin story which traced the descent
of their kings to Scota, the daughter of Pharaoh.[9]

Owain's brief historical exposition might, therefore, be regarded as misplaced
and insensitive. But it indicated how firmly he grounded his own ideology and
claims in historical mythology. Prophecy was, of course, the other side of the

coin to history in the Middle Ages. And so it was with Owain. In his letter to the king of Scotland he followed his potted history lesson and invective against the English by declaring that 'the prophecy says that I will be delivered from the oppressions and bondages [of the English] by your aid'. He took exactly the same line in his letter to the Irish chiefs, once more invoking 'the prophecy' (L. *per propheciam*) as the basis of his appeal. Such references to prophecy and history are commonplace in much medieval propaganda and there is a danger that the modern reader may not take them seriously. As far as Wales is concerned it would be a mistake to ignore their importance. Wales was a country whose political and legal culture was dominated by age-old traditions and by a literary and legal élite which saw itself as the guardian and transmitter of those traditions. The very absence of indigenous native political institutions and of a ruling, governmental élite around whom a more practical and present-oriented political culture might develop, as in England and Scotland, endowed the mythological and prophetic ideology of the poets and their associates in Wales with arguably a much greater resilience than elsewhere. After all, it was the sole vernacular ideology in Wales. For a conquered people it had the twin advantages of pandering to a nostalgia for the glories of the past while feeding extravagant hopes and expectations for the future. It was about the realities of the transient present that it might appear to have little to say. Furthermore, it was an ideology which was not solely the preserve of a literate coterie and its aristocratic patrons; it is obvious that in a vulgar and often bowdlerized form it also dominated the popular, oral culture of Wales. The cultural fissure between the aristocratic and the popular—so marked in medieval England and increasingly a feature of Welsh life likewise from the sixteenth century onwards—was not, as yet, a feature of Welsh historical and political (the two were interchangeable) ideology. That is part of the reason why Owain Glyn Dŵr, the descendant of a princely dynasty, could be the leader of what was, or became, a truly popular revolt.

Glyn Dŵr subscribed fully to the historical and prophetic ideology of his own propaganda. At his inauguration ceremony as prince of Wales on 16 September 1400 one crucial supporter had been Crach Ffinnant, 'their prophet' (L. *eorum propheta*). He was no doubt a professionally trained poet and soothsayer, from Owain's home district. He may indeed have been loosely attached to Owain's service for some time—much as a modern politician might have a professional political adviser or agent—since he appears with him in Berwick in 1384. His encouragement and advice were regarded as crucial in 1400. But Owain was not averse to taking advice on the interpretation of 'the prophecy' from other sources. In a well-known and remarkable letter in which the burgesses of Caerleon—the very seat of Arthur's court—shared their latest news of the revolt in west Wales with their colleagues in Monmouth in June 1403, they reported how

Owain, on reaching Carmarthen, had sent for Hopcyn ap Tomas ab Einion of Ynys Forgan. Hopcyn, as was noted earlier, was the greatest Welsh bibliophile and literary patron of his day; but it was his expertise in interpreting the prophecy or *brut* which recommended him to Glyn Dŵr. 'And when Hopcyn came to Owain', so the letter reported, 'he prayed him, in as much as he held [i.e. deemed] him [to be] master of *brut*, that he should do him [Owain] to understand how and what manner it should befall him.' Owain was a leader who clearly took 'the prophecy' seriously. How seriously became again evident when he concluded the Tripartite Indenture in 1405. Central to that remarkable document was a crucial contingency clause: 'if it appears to the said lords [namely, the earl of Northumberland, Edmund Mortimer senior and Glyn Dŵr] as time unfolds that they are indeed the persons of whom the Prophet speaks between whom the governance of Greater Britain (L. *Britanniae Majoris*) should be divided'. Political decisions in Owain's mind had to wait upon, and be grounded in, the fulfilment of prophecy.[10]

Owain's thought-world was one of mythology and prophecy, of bitter tales of the oppressions of the Island of Britain, and of the fervent expectation of the deliverance of the Britons; of Cynan, Cadwaladr, Arthur, and other candidates for the post of the Promised One, the Son of Deliverance (W. *y mab darogan*). But Owain's revolt was also truly a national rebellion; he was the rightful prince of a people with its own identity and the right to be ruled by its own prince. There were two aspects to this claim. The first was essentially dynastic and legitimist. If the Welsh people were to have its own ruler drawn from its princely dynasties then Owain's claim to that position—drawn as he was from the stock of the princes of Powys and Deheubarth—was outstanding. There was only one major obstacle in his way: Llywelyn (d. 1282) ap Gruffudd, the last, the sole formally acknowledged native prince of Wales, was a member of the Gwynedd dynasty. It was only by an unacceptable sleight of hand—by claiming that Owain was descended from Gruffudd (d. 1137) ap Cynan of Gwynedd through Owain's great-grandmother, and even then in the female line—that Owain's lineage could be grafted onto that of the Gwynedd dynasty. But death served to clear the way for tender genealogical consciences. In 1378 the last direct male descendant of the main Gwynedd dynasty, Owain Lawgoch, died in France in the French king's service. Owain Glyn Dŵr proceeded to appropriate Owain Lawgoch's military reputation and genealogical claims for his own purposes. When Glyn Dŵr's ambassadors went to the French court in search of an alliance, they not only drew attention to Owain Lawgoch's services to the French but also emphasized that Glyn Dŵr was Lawgoch's rightful heir (L. *cui jure consanguineo successerat*). Such a claim was only true in a figurative and political, not in a precise genealogical, sense; but it served Owain's purposes well enough. He could now assert that he

was heir of Gwynedd as well as of Powys and Deheubarth; he showed it by appropriating the arms of Gwynedd in preference to his family's hereditary usage of the arms of Powys. This aggregation of the dynastic claims of the former princely families of Wales into his hands gave legitimacy to his title to be prince of Wales. No other local leader in Wales, however powerful his regional position, challenged Owain's claim to be prince of Wales. The unimpeachability of that claim provided a personal focus of devotion and legitimacy which was crucial to the success of his revolt. For example, when Welsh students began to become agitated in Oxford in 1402 they could not contain themselves from 'calling Owain Prince of Wales' and returning 'to the parts of Wales to Owain Glyn Dŵr, traitor'.[11]

Owain's dynastic claim gave crucial legitimacy to the revolt and linked it directly and genealogically with the political past of Wales. But a claim to dynastic legitimacy would remain a private fantasy until and unless it could be matched by and linked to the devotion of a people. This brings us to the second national dimension to the Glyn Dŵr revolt. Medieval men and women believed that human society was arranged into peoples (L. *gentes*) and/or nations (L. *naciones*). The individuality of each people was revealed in a variety of ways— in law, language, customs, genealogical descent, historical mythology, and so forth. Peoples, it was generally accepted, were at their happiest when they were ruled by men of their own race; if they formed a part of larger political agglomerations, it was important that their individuality, status, and dignity as a people be respected. The Welsh partook of these ideas. Indeed, in the final months of their political independence in the winter of 1282, their publicists had given one of the most eloquent definitions and defences of the right to be a people in medieval times. 'Even if their prince should transfer seisin of them to the king of England', so the people of Snowdonia are alleged to have asserted, 'they themselves would refuse to do homage to any foreigner, of whose language, customs and laws they were utterly ignorant.' It was this conviction that the Welsh were, and indeed remained, a separate people which Owain Glyn Dŵr had to foster and exploit if his legitimate dynastic aspirations were to be converted into a truly national movement. Prince and people had to be one.[12]

Owain and his advisers seem to have set out consciously to establish this relationship. Even before the outbreak of the revolt the poets had greeted him as 'the sole head of Wales or the Welsh' (W. *un pen ar Gymry*). During the revolt his official draftsmen referred frequently to 'our nation' or 'my nation', 'our homeland', 'the Welsh race', and 'our subjects'. They did everything in their power to promote and publicize Owain's claim to be prince of Wales and of the Welsh people. In his formal diplomatic documents—or rather in such of the original ones as survive from May 1404 onwards—he gives himself the most solemn and

challenging of titles, 'Owain, by the grace of God, prince of Wales'. His usage of the full title is certainly by no means consistent: he himself does not always use the phrase 'by the grace of God', nor is it, apparently, conceded to him in French diplomatic instruments. Nevertheless its adoption was undoubtedly significant. Owain had arrogated to himself a title, 'prince of Wales', which the kings of England had appropriated to themselves since the Edwardian conquest and had consistently conferred on their eldest sons as heirs to the throne, most recently on young Henry 'of Monmouth' (the future Henry V) on 15 October 1399. Owain was also claiming that his authority came directly from God, as did that of other rulers such as the kings of England and France. Native Welsh princes and their apologists in earlier periods had occasionally had recourse to the grace of God as a source of authority in their legal and political arguments, but Owain was the first native pretender who had added it to his official style. Such was the measure of his vision and ambition.[13]

He underlined his pretensions by dating his official documents in the year of his own reign and by commencing that reign with his self-proclamation as prince in September 1400. The practice of his clerks in this respect, as in others, was not always consistent. On one occasion they added no date, regnal or otherwise, to an important document to the king of France; in another the reference to the years of Owain's principate seems to be an afterthought; while on a third there seems some ambiguity about the date. Nevertheless they are consistent in not referring to the regnal years of Henry IV of England—whom they regarded as a usurper and referred to (in accordance with French practice) as Henry of Lancaster. And when their dating formula was fully shaped it was sonorous, majestic, and defiant: 'Dated in our castle of Llanbadarn, 12th January, in the year of our Lord 1405 and of our principate the sixth'; 'Dated at Pennal on the last day of March in the year 1406 from the birth of our Lord and the sixth of our principate'.[14]

Owain's seals were likewise an affirmation of the legitimacy of his claims and the scale of his ambitions (plate 2, 4). His great seal shows him enthroned, his sceptre in his right hand, his feet resting on two lions, with two angels holding a mantle adorned with lions behind him. The legend on the seal reads: 'Owain by the grace of God prince of Wales.' The reverse of the great seal shows Owain in full armour, on horseback, galloping; he wields a sword with his right arm and carries a shield with his coat of arms on it on his left arm; both his helmet and the horse's crest bear a winged two-legged dragon; the legend is the same as for the obverse. Owain's privy seal (plate 4) displays an upright shield bearing his arms; it bears the remains of the legend: 'the seal of Owain, prince of Wales.' The quality, sophistication, and pretensions of the seal are a far cry from the world of the backwater squireen or the hunted guerrilla. They show the amplitude of the

ambitions of Owain and his advisers in the years of the zenith of his powers, and their anxiety to impress others, especially on the international scene, with the seriousness of his claims. Their determination extended also to his coat of arms. It is probable (as was claimed by later writers on Welsh heraldry) that prior to the revolt Owain and his ancestors had borne a single lion rampant, the arms of the dynasty of northern Powys (plate 3). Now that he had had himself proclaimed prince of Wales, he adopted the arms of the house of Gwynedd, the sole Welsh dynasty to have assumed, and been officially accorded, the title prince of Wales. In heraldic language those arms were: Quarterly Or and Gules, four lions passant (plate 4, 5). Even here Owain's advisers showed how aware they were of every nuance of change which might enhance the legitimacy of his claims. During the fourteenth century the male descendants of the house of Gwynedd, the line which ended with Owain Lawgoch (d. 1378), had modified the heraldic position of the four quartered lions on their coat of arms from passant or passant gardant to rampant. It was this device of the four lions rampant which Owain adopted. He was anxious to present himself, as his ambassadors told the French king, as the rightful heir of Owain Lawgoch; his arms demonstrated visually the apostolic succession of his claims from the princes of Gwynedd, the rightful princes of Wales.[15]

Owain, during his few heady years of success, sought to clothe himself with some of the other emblems and offices of national rule. He had his own chancellor, Gruffudd Yonge, doctor in decrees. He also had a secretary, Owain ap Gruffudd ap Rhisiart; and he was able to say that discussion of his ransom of Reginald Grey would be determined by himself 'and his council'. Most intriguing of all are the references to two parliaments which Owain convoked. The first comes from the chronicle of Adam of Usk. Adam was a Welshman, a native of Usk and a protégé and supporter of the Mortimers, a man naturally not unsympathetic to Glyn Dŵr's cause (though he tried rather too hard to conceal any trace of such sympathy in his chronicle), and one who had conspired with the earl of Northumberland while the latter was in exile in Flanders in 1406–7. In short Adam was very well placed to be informed about affairs in Wales and about the various political conspiracies in England which were so crucial to Glyn Dŵr's cause. But he also had two distinct disadvantages as a reporter of events in Wales: from early 1402 until 1408 he was in self-imposed exile in Europe, for much of the time in Rome; and his chronicle, as we know it, was composed essentially after 1402 of undated and disjointed memoranda. It is in one of these memoranda that Adam records that 'Owain and his hill-men [L. *montani*], even in their misery, staged duels and usurped other trappings of regality. He also, though it only proved his undoing, held or faked or made a pretence of holding parliaments [L. *parliamenta*] at Machynlleth.' Adam was recording these events many years

later; but the context in which they appear clearly identifies the year as 1404. Nor is there any reason to doubt such a dating. The second reference to Owain summoning a parliament comes from a much more reliable source. On 30 July 1405 (the year is not given, but it is obvious), John Stanley, steward of the king's household, wrote a letter to Henry IV from the abbey of Vale Royal in Cheshire, passing on the latest information he had gathered about the revolt in Wales, especially from two extremely well-placed informants, David Whitmore and Ieuan ap Maredudd. David and Ieuan, two important Flintshire landowners, had in effect (to use the language of modern espionage) become English moles in the Welsh camp. They reported to Stanley that 'Owain Glyn Dŵr had summoned a parliament to be held at Harlech, which four of the more influential persons from each commote throughout Wales under Owain's control would attend'. David and Ieuan, who had themselves gone to attend the parliament and would then report back to Stanley, even knew in advance what was to be discussed at the session—a proposal, in the light of anticipated major support for the Welsh rebellion from France, to open negotiations with the king of England regarding a treaty.[16]

Such are the two reports on parliaments held by Owain; there is no reason to doubt their essential accuracy. All that we know of Owain and his advisers, especially in the years 1404–6, indicates that they went to great lengths to ape the trappings and institutions of regality—be it in the royal style, the use of coats of arms, the establishment of a post of chancellor, the making of a great and privy seal, the accreditation of ambassadors, and ceremonies and junketings (including duels). Convoking a parliament was but another exercise to the same end. Owain would have been familiar with parliaments and the role they played in the political process in England: his father-in-law, Sir David Hanmer, was an auditor of petitions in parliament in the 1380s, while several of Owain's military companions of the years 1384–7 and his acquaintances in Shropshire had sat in parliament. He would also surely have heard that there were parliaments in Scotland and Ireland. Some of the bishops whose support he was now winning—notably John Trefor, bishop of St Asaph—were equally well acquainted with parliament; while all the major ecclesiastics in his service were doubtless aware of the role of convocation in England and of the ferment of conciliar ideas in Europe. All in all there is no reason to be surprised that Owain convoked assemblies which contemporary English observers equated with their own parliaments, nor that he should proudly declare to the king of France that he had taken the decision to join the Clementist cause after 'gathering together, on the advice of our council, the nobles of our race [L. *proceres de prosapia nostra*] and the prelates of our principality'.[17]

Equally we should not be surprised by the reference to four men from each commote in the areas under his control being summoned to parliament. The commote, and to a lesser extent the *cantref*, had been the basic units of communal

and seignorial governance in most of Wales before the Edwardian Conquest; beneath the larger units of shire and lordship, the commote in particular retained that role after the Conquest. It was the unit for local jurisdiction, the assessment of renders, and the levying of troops. That it should be the unit for selecting men for the process of political consultation was a natural extension of its functions. In England, it is true, representatives to parliament came on behalf of shires and boroughs, not in the name of the smaller unit of the hundred which corresponds most closely to the commote. But the English formula could not have been applied to Wales. Only part of the country—the north and the west—had been shired, and there the shire was still a foreign-imposed unit of governance; and as to boroughs, they were overwhelmingly associated with English settlement and power. Historical traditions and the smallness of the scale of Wales under Owain's control made the commote the natural unit from which spokesmen might be chosen for any centralized process of consultation.[18]

Wales had almost no experience of parliamentary assemblies. Only on two occasions had representatives from Wales sat in an English parliament, in 1322 and 1327; and even on these occasions it was only the shires of the Principality that were invited to return MPs. In that sense Glyn Dŵr's initiative in summoning parliaments for those parts of Wales he controlled was certainly innovative. It was an initiative which identified all too clearly the lack of vision which the English government persistently showed in its dealings with the native peoples of Wales and Ireland in the Middle Ages. The novelty and imaginativeness of Owain's initiative is not to be gainsaid, however short-lived it was. Yet we need to put it into perspective. By concentrating so exclusively on parliament, English historians have arguably underestimated the other forms of, and opportunities for, community representation in medieval society. Such opportunities certainly existed in Wales and had been exploited there for generations. Leaders of the local community spoke frequently on its behalf in discussions of subsidies and aids (taxes), in the sharing of local dues, in compiling and organizing communal petitions, in levying troops, and in securing charters of liberties. Some of Owain's literary-minded supporters would no doubt be familiar with the texts of medieval Welsh law which declared how Hywel Dda (d. 950) had allegedly convoked six men from each of the commotes of Wales and all the leading churchmen of the country to Whitland to discuss a major overhaul of Wales's laws. Such legal antiquarianism may indeed have contributed towards Owain's idea of convoking a national assembly; but his initiative was also securely grounded in the current practices of community representation at local level—that of vill, commote, lordship, and shire—in the Wales of his own day. What Owain did was to see the opportunity for welding those practices into a single assembly which could forward his cause. In this, as in so many other respects, he clearly saw and seized

the opportunity to present himself within and without Wales as a true national leader, the prince of Wales and the prince of the Welsh.[19]

Exiguous as is the evidence it is sufficient to make it clear that Owain and his advisers, in the few hectic years that they were given, made every effort to promote and present him as the true prince of Wales. Drawing on Welsh historical mythology and prophecy on the one hand and frenziedly borrowing contemporary emblems of monarchical status and the habits of statehood on the other, they did their utmost to create a novel political construct—a native, independent principality of Wales. Two documents in particular help us to catch a glimpse of the sort of vision which they entertained in their most euphoric moments.

The first is the highly problematic document known as the Tripartite Indenture. It is problematic both in format and in content. It survives only in a copy inserted into a chronicle (known as Giles's Chronicle) which has not been highly regarded by historians for its reliability. The copy, though it appears to summarize the terms of the Indenture, does not reproduce the treaty verbatim but rather in *oratio obliqua*. The crucial initial clause or clauses of the Indenture are omitted and so are any dating and witnessing clauses that may have been appended to it. Owain Glyn Dŵr is not accorded a title nor is Edmund Mortimer given his social designation as a knight. The chronicle prefaces its summaries of the Indenture by referring to the date 28 February but without stipulating the year. Unsatisfactory as are these and other features of the copy of the Indenture, they are not sufficient to dismiss it as a fabrication. As to the dating of the Indenture, it is located in the text between an account of the election of Pope Innocent VII (October 1404) and the crushing of the revolt of the earl of Northumberland and Lord Bardolf in June–July 1405. The year and the month to which the Treaty is now generally ascribed—February 1405—are, therefore, plausible and accord with other events; whether the Indenture was concluded by proxy 'in the house of the archdeacon of Bangor' (as recorded in a sixteenth-century chronicle) is a secondary issue. Giles's Chronicle is certainly a rather erratic and occasionally fanciful compilation; but it is particularly well informed about events in the north of England and its summaries and citation of official documents for the reign of Henry IV are generally accurate and are one of its distinguishing features.[20]

It is the content of the Indenture, as much as the format in which it survives, which has led to the raising of historical eyebrows. It claims to be a tripartite alliance between Henry Percy, earl of Northumberland, Edmund Mortimer senior (the brother of Earl Roger (d. 1398) and since November 1402 Owain Glyn Dŵr's son-in-law), and Owain Glyn Dŵr. The three bind themselves in a com-

mon alliance, promise to help each other against their common and individual enemies and to give warning of any impending danger to one of themselves, and in the event of a quarrel or disagreement between two of them agree to accept the judgement of the third. So far there is nothing very surprising about the carefully drafted terms of such a three-way alliance. It is the rest of the Indenture which is extraordinary. 'If it appears to the three lords with the passage of time that they are indeed the persons of whom the Prophet speaks, between whom the governance of Greater Britain. [L. *regimen Britanniae Majoris*] ought to be divided and partitioned, then they will strive, communally and individually, to the best of their abilities to ensure that this is effected.' Not content with this conditional reference to the fulfilment of prophecy, the indenture proceeds to outline the terms of the prospective partition. Each share is to be held in full sovereignty and on equal terms; no one party to the agreement is to make a payment or acknowledgement to another which might be construed as a claim to superiority. The earl of Northumberland's share consists of twelve named counties stretching from the Scottish border deep into the midlands and East Anglia (but curiously excluding Cumberland and the county palatine of Durham); Edmund Mortimer is to have the whole of the rest of England. Both are to hold these portions to them and their heirs. The portion assigned to Glyn Dŵr is as follows:

the whole of Cambria or Wales divided from Leogria now commonly called England by the following borders, limits, and bounds: from the Severn estuary as the River Severn flows from the sea as far as the northern gate of the city of Worcester; from that gate directly to the ash trees known in the Cambrian or Welsh language as Onennau Meigion which grow on the high road leading from Bridgnorth to Kinver; then directly along the highway, popularly known as the old or ancient road, to the head or source of the River Trent; thence to the head or source of the river commonly known as the Mersey and so along that river to the sea.

To read such an apparently bizarre description is to invite the immediate conclusion either that the Indenture, or at least this part of it, is a fabrication or alternatively that the men who concluded it had taken leave of their political senses. Either conclusion might be correct. But equally it is possible to suggest that it is our historical hindsight on the one hand and a modern refusal to take the language of prophecy seriously on the other which prompt such a reaction. England was in a state of extraordinary political turmoil during the first half of Henry IV's reign, at least until 1406. Plots focusing on the possibility of the restoration of Richard II, the dynastic claims of the Mortimers, and the overweening ambitions of the Percies abounded and were interpreted and elaborated with the aid of prognostications, prophecies, and rumours. By 1405 these plots

had lost some of their potency after the disastrous defeat of the Percies at Shrewsbury in July 1403 and the subsequent abject submission of the earl of Northumberland. But as so often defeat only made the conspirators redouble their efforts and take even greater risks. The plots against Henry IV in the first half of 1405—Lady Despenser's attempt in February to abduct the Mortimer heirs to Wales, the preparations for a new coup being forged at much the same time by the earl of Northumberland and Lord Bardolf, and the insurrection in York organized by Archbishop Scrope and the earl Marshal in June—showed that the appetite for conspiracy had in no way been satisfied and that the future of the Lancastrian regime was by no means secure. Owain Glyn Dŵr would have been politically slow-witted, especially in the light of his newly forged alliance with the French, to have passed by such an opportunity.[21]

The apportionment of England and Wales in the Tripartite Indenture is certainly surprising, but it was not beyond the ken of political dreamers. The superiority of the Mortimer claim to the English throne to that of the house of Lancaster was a central feature of political dissent in Henry IV's England. It may be that the decision to promote this Mortimer claim in the name of Edmund Mortimer senior rather than in that of his young nephew (who was the legitimate pretender) was prompted by two reasons. First, after the abortive attempt to abduct the two nephews (news of it reached the king on 15 February 1405, nine days before the Indenture was concluded) it may have been felt that any realistic Mortimer claim had now to be vested in their uncle. Secondly, of course, Edmund Mortimer senior lived in Wales and was now Owain's son-in-law. As to the vast share of England claimed by the earl of Northumberland, it can be interpreted as the true measure of Percy ambition in these years, concealed beneath their public protestations of having been duped and unworthily misused by Henry IV. Owain's greed seems to have been scarcely less, for his portion added the whole of Cheshire and a goodly share of Shropshire, Herefordshire, and Worcestershire to the Welsh kingdom. He was, of course, bargaining from a position of great strength: with a French alliance to his name and French military support for his campaign in Wales imminently expected, and with Edmund Mortimer senior under his control, he could afford to drive a very hard bargain with the earl of Northumberland.

We need not, therefore, dismiss the proposed division of England and Wales in the Tripartite Indenture as being, at the level of a blueprint, totally beyond the bounds of political possibility; what it tells us about the world of illusions in which the three conspirators now dwelt is another matter. It is more difficult for the modern mind to engage seriously with the language of mythology and prophecy which is such a startling feature of much of the Indenture. Yet at one level it should not surprise us: Glyn Dŵr's bards had steeped their poems in the

allusions and teaching of Welsh mythological writings; and he himself, as we have seen, had consulted masters of prophecy as if they were political pundits and had larded his diplomatic correspondence with historical and prophetic lore. The enlarged Wales which was Owain's share in the three-way partition of the island was a reflection of his wildest ambitions and bargaining position; but it was also confirmed by, and confirmed, Welsh prophetic teaching. The Welsh Triads spoke about the Three Realms of Britain (W. *Teir Ynys Prydein*); here at last they were realized. The River Severn ran deep into England and had long been replaced by the Dee in the north and the Wye in the south as the riverine boundaries of Wales. But anyone versed in ancient geographical lore would have known that the Severn had once divided Leogria (England) from Cambria (Wales). As to the ash trees of Meigion which were to form one of the boundary markers of the new Wales, they were, according to Merlinic prophecies, the place where the Great Eagle would muster the Welsh warriors. The name Meigen had a further historical resonance since it was the name of one of the great battles in which the heroic British king, Cadwallon, had triumphed over the Saxons. Hard-headed observers might have found these references puzzling at best, bizarre at worst; but for some of Owain Glyn Dŵr's advisers they would have been part of the common coin of their literary discourse and a wonderfully reassuring indication that past, present, and future were at last to be brought into alignment. It is certainly striking that it is only in defining Glyn Dŵr's portion of the island that such mythological references are employed; the earl of Northumberland's portion is defined prosaically in terms of named English shires. The difference in the mode of definition is a measure of the difference in political cultures between England and Wales in 1400.[22]

However much we try to explain its content and language, the Tripartite Indenture remains a remarkable document. We may more readily accept its authenticity if we consider another document in which Glyn Dŵr and his advisers lay out some of their grandiose plans. In a long, formal letter, dated at Pennal (near Machynlleth) on 31 March 1406, Owain announced to the king of France his intention to transfer the ecclesiastical obedience of the new principality of Wales from the Roman pope, Innocent VII, to the Avignonese pope, Benedict VIII. The move was a calculated political act for both parties. The French king was anxious to bring all France's allies into the Avignonese fold, if only to prevent any conflict between diplomatic and ecclesiastical policies; Owain for his part was willing to switch his ecclesiastical allegiance in order to fortify the French alliance which, as he must have realized, was the lifeline to his future. The document survives in its original form, so none of the doubts about authenticity, which can be directed at the Tripartite Indenture, apply to it. What, then, does it tell us of Owain's policy and vision for his principality of Wales?[23]

Much the greater part of the document is concerned to rehearse at length the reasons for the schism in the Church and why the Avignonese cause was to be preferred to the Roman one. This section no doubt repeats verbatim the arguments rehearsed by the French in their diplomatic messages to Owain. It is the short sections of the document in which Owain expounds the conditions and expectations which are the price of, or more correctly the hoped-for return on, his transfer of ecclesiastical allegiance which constitute the real interest of the document. They reveal Owain and his advisers both as shrewd bargainers and as remarkable visionaries. While willing to have rehearsed for him at inordinate and *parti pris* length the French arguments for the righteousness of the Avignonese case, Owain made no bones about his own particular political and ecclesiastical reasons for being disenchanted with the Roman pope. The latter had consistently shown his favour to 'Henry of Lancaster' by nominating English prelates to Welsh benefices, by denying convenient dispensations for marriages within the prohibited degrees for Welshmen, and by other acts which indicated how much he was the cat's-paw of the king of England. On a more positive note, Owain's letter laid down a precise list of politico-ecclesiastical benefits which he expected from the Avignonese pope: the confirmation of existing ecclesiastical appointments, favours, and dispensations; security that future appointees to benefices in Wales will be of Owain's political persuasion (the king of France seems to have anticipated these two requests and used them as bait to entice Owain); absolution from any vows entered into during the time when he recognized the Roman pope; the lifting of any ecclesiastical censures imposed by the Avignonese pope; the proclamation of a crusade against 'Henry of Lancaster, intruder into the realm of England' (to counter the holy war which Archbishop Arundel had declared against the Welsh); and full remission of sins for all Owain's supporters, 'of whatsoever nation they be', in their war against Henry of Lancaster, his heirs, and subjects.

Such a list of demands was utterly unexceptional and could be readily conceded. It is the remainder of Owain's requests which reveal the amplitude of his vision and the bravado of his approach. He asked, first, that all papal appointments to ecclesiastical benefices in Wales should be made to those who knew the Welsh language. By the late fourteenth century all appointments to bishoprics in western Europe and many to the major and most profitable ecclesiastical posts (canonries, precentorships, and soon) were made formally by papal nomination (known as provision), though very considerably in the light of lists of petitions from interested parties. The system was clearly open to abuse and had frequently been criticized for granting major ecclesiastical posts to non-resident foreigners. Owain's request involved no criticism of the system *per se*; he was asking—as were all rulers throughout Europe—for the right to manipulate it for his own

purposes, and specifically to exclude the English-speaking clerks who were bat-
tening on the Welsh Church. Given the pattern of appointments to major
benefices in Wales in the last generation or so, it was a request which would have
met with the enthusiastic support of Welsh clerics, especially the more ambitious
of them. So would Owain's next request, that the appropriation (that is, the
effective transfer of the revenues) of the parish churches of the principality of
Wales to English monasteries and colleges should be cancelled and the rights of
presentation to these churches restored to their original patrons. Here again
Owain was raising an issue which was high on the agenda of ecclesiastical
criticism throughout Europe; what was distinctive about his version of it was
that, again, it was directed specifically against the English. Owain also asked that
his own chapel and that of his successors as princes of Wales should be of free
status (that is, should have jurisdictional immunity from the control of the
diocesan bishop) and enjoy such privileges, exemptions and immunities as 'it
enjoyed in the time of our predecessors the princes of Wales'. Royal chapels
enjoyed this privileged status in England; it was part of Owain's campaign to
appropriate the trappings of monarchy that his personal chapel should enjoy a
similar standing. His emphasis on his predecessors and successors as princes of
Wales showed his anxiety to emphasize his place in an apostolic succession of
native rulers of Wales.[24]

It is with two final requests in the letter that we reach the visionary and the
extraordinary in Owain's programme. The first asked for two universities to be
established, one in north and the other in south Wales at places to be nominated
by Owain's ambassadors. The founding of new universities was certainly in the
air: twenty-two had been founded across Europe in the century before 1400, a
further thirty-four (including three in Scotland, of which St Andrews (1413) was
the first) were established in the next century. Countries without their own
university felt increasingly at a disadvantage. That was why, for example, the
proposal to found an university at Dublin was fitfully pursued from 1311 onwards
and justified by reference to the absence of a university in Ireland, Scotland, Man,
and Norway. And if a new university were to be launched the initiative would
more likely than not come from a secular ruler such as Glyn Dŵr. By the fifteenth
century, as it has been observed, 'universities had lost their supranational character and were increasingly regarded as integral parts of political, territorial units,
designed to serve the needs of national institutions and to be of benefit to those
living in the realm'. If that were so, and given Glyn Dŵr's pretensions for his
principality, the establishment of a university made good sense. Furthermore,
several of Owain's leading advisers—notably John Trefor, Gruffudd Yonge, and
Hywel Kyffin—were university-trained clerks of considerable eminence and with
a wide experience of European travel and of the papal court. It was they who

doubtless pressed the current proposal on Owain. In the context of the period it was not totally unrealistic; but to establish one, let alone two universities, in a thinly populated and economically poor country like Wales was certainly extraordinarily ambitious.[25]

The second proposal was even more breath-taking. The bishopric of St David's should be restored to its original status as a metropolitan see. This claim was supported by compiling 'from the chronicles and ancient books of the church of St David's' the list of twenty-five archbishops of the see from David to Samson (of Dol). Such lists certainly existed, for Gerald of Wales had quoted them in his works. They may well have been initially compiled as part of the evidence assembled by Bishop Bernard (1115–48) in his attempt to claim metropolitan status for the see and to liberate it from dependence on Canterbury. They were certainly used, along with every other scrap of evidence, by Gerald of Wales in his prolonged but eventually futile struggle in the same cause during the years 1198–1203. After lying dormant for two centuries they were now called into service to bolster Glyn Dŵr's programme for an independent ecclesiastical province of Wales to coincide with his own principality of Wales. But it is the final clause of this proposal which has attracted the scorn of historians as an indication of the total unreality of Glyn Dŵr's plans. The new, or rather revived, archbishopric of St David's was to have metropolitan jurisdiction not only over the three other Welsh sees (Bangor, Llandaff, and St Asaph) but also over five English bishoprics in the west Midlands and south-west of England, namely Exeter, Bath, Hereford, Worcester, and Coventry and Lichfield (formerly Chester). Ecclesiastical Wales was to be even more extensive than the political Wales of the Tripartite Indenture. In practical terms the proposal was, it is true, fantastic, but that is to misunderstand its origin. The ecclesiastical mythology current at St David's in the medieval period claimed that these five English bishoprics had indeed been within the ambit of the archbishopric of St David's from the time of St David himself to that of his twenty-fifth successor, Samson of Dol. The claim to the five bishoprics was not, therefore, the hare-brained scheme of an irresponsible leader; rather was it a measure of the degree to which he grounded his ambitions in mythology and prophecy, ecclesiastical and secular. His ambition may still appear hare-brained, but at least we should appreciate how it had been shaped. Furthermore, a recognition of the source of the claim to the five English bishoprics in the letter of March 1406 helps to confirm the credibility of the Tripartite Indenture; the most puzzling features of both documents are woven from the same weft and bear the stamp of the same author.[26]

Owain Glyn Dŵr's appeal as leader of a Welsh rebellion did not rest initially on a fully worked-out programme or manifesto. Rather does it seem in its early days

to have drawn its strength from three sources. The first was a profound sense of anti- Englishness, directed in particular at the privileges of the boroughs in Wales, the exploitation of the anachronistic ethno- legal distinction between English and Welsh, and the sense of exclusion, alienation, and belittlement felt by a conquered people. The second was the conviction of many Welshmen that the rulership of Wales belonged of right to a prince of their own race and that Owain Glyn Dŵr's credentials for that position were, or could be shown to be, outstanding. Thirdly, both of these sentiments were deeply grounded in a mythology and prophecy whose potency was recurrently renewed and whose applicability to the present was capable of endless adaptation.

It was only as the revolt blossomed, particularly in the years 1403–6, that Glyn Dŵr and his advisers could afford to raise their sights from these almost visceral sentiments to a more sustained vision of where the revolt might lead. That vision drew heavily, as we have seen, on a corpus of lore and prophecy interpreted with a surprising literalness; but it also picked up the concepts, analogies, institutions, and practices of contemporary kingship and the Church and used them to try to create the vision and indeed, in some small respects, the practices of an independent principality of Wales. It is easy to dismiss the propaganda and pretensions of Glyn Dŵr's statements as grotesquely premature and totally unrealistic; but it is surely equally striking how far, in a few hectic years and under immense military pressure, those statements sketched the outlines of a prospective native principality of Wales. Owain Glyn Dŵr's Wales was certainly not short of dreamers. Whether those dreams would remain the fantasies of over-excitable clerics and the reveries of those who had drunk too deeply at the wells of Merlin's prophecies would depend largely on the support that Glyn Dŵr was able to command, at home and abroad.

ALLIES

*T*he revolt of Owain Glyn Dŵr was born out of resentment of English rule in Wales and from the conviction of Owain that he was the rightful prince of Wales. It quickly became, as it was called at the time, truly the revolt of the Welsh. It was as such that it commanded widespread support, and it was as such that it was to be eventually defeated. But from its first year it became entangled with the domestic politics and international problems of the kingdom of England. The revolt in Wales would surely not have lasted as long as it did had not Henry IV been recurrently preoccupied with the defence of his throne from internal and external enemies. Equally, it is very doubtful if the revolt could have achieved the measure of success that it did or Owain been allowed to entertain such grandiose schemes had he not learnt how to exploit, and allow himself to be exploited by, the opposition to the new Lancastrian monarchy. Owain, for all his dabbling in Merlinic prophecies, was no political innocent. Service in Berwick, on the Scottish expedition of 1385 and in the earl of Arundel's victorious retinue in the Channel in 1387 would have provided him with a basic grounding in England's foreign policy. Likewise his family's tradition of service to the Fitzalan earls of Arundel, his own close involvement with Sir David Hanmer and his family, his personal appearance to give testimony in one of the most famous heraldic disputes of the 1380s, the Scrope–Grosvenor trial, and his ringside observation of the dramatic political events in north-east Wales and Cheshire from July 1397 to January 1400 were all likely to have honed his political susceptibilities. We must not cast Owain too readily in the role of an out-of-touch backwoodsman. His own actions suggest otherwise. Thus, the speed with which he dispatched envoys to Scotland and Ireland in 1401–2 indicates an early awareness of the need to find international allies in his struggle with the English. Similarly his reported response to a peace initiative from the Percies is indicative of how he might exploit the volatility and embarrassments of English politics to his own end. He dare not come to England to discuss terms, so he commented, because he had heard that the commons of England had a reputation for lynching their great lords against the will of the king and without trial. It was a deliberately provocative comment from a man who knew how to exploit the acute instability and nervousness of English political life for his own ends.[1]

The political atmosphere in England in Henry IV's reign, and especially during the years 1399–1406, was certainly exceptionally fraught. Rumours of plots and conspiracies abounded and were deliberately fanned by disaffected clerics, monks, and friars and by loose-tongued braggarts and drunkards. It was a time when men could put it about—and be readily believed—that the realm would be turned upside down within two years 'just as a tally is turned over [L. *vertitur*] at the exchequer'. Many of the rumours were but a variation on the farrago of prophecies that were such a feature of medieval society; others—such as the tale of a plot to dispose of the king by oiling his saddle with a poisonous substance— pandered to the popular appetite for the sensational. As so often in such circum- stances, an insecure government compounded the situation by giving too ready credence to the most far-fetched of rumours, by demonizing its critics, and by striking savagely at any perceived or imagined challenge to its authority. Yet rumours only succeed ultimately when a society is on edge and profoundly uncertain of itself.[2]

That was certainly the case in England in the opening years of the fifteenth century. The psychological disarray of the country was compounded of many elements: deep doubts about the legitimacy of the dynastic revolution of 1399, recurrent noble conspiracies, resentment of high taxation, anticlericalism and heresy, invasion scares, bad harvests, and poor weather. The disintegration of English authority in Wales only served to confirm the impression that the world was deeply out of sorts. Events in Wales were soon sucked into the vortex of rumours in England. Stories circulated widely that large sums of money were being dispatched by abbots, priors, and laymen to subsidize Owain Glyn Dŵr's activities in Wales. More credibly, Welsh students in Oxford were accused of holding secret meetings in the public toilets and elsewhere to plot against the king, to spy out the street plan of the city, and to send reports back to Owain on the state of the king and kingdom. Even in Hertfordshire a trouble-maker was apparently bold enough to declare that Glyn Dŵr was indeed the legal prince of Wales and that the pope had dispatched a letter granting remission of all sins to those willing to help him. Some of the accusations are more fantastic than others; many of them were peddled by men desperate to save their own skins. Their importance lies not so much in the small grains of truth which they may possibly contain as in revealing the atmosphere of suspicion and jitteriness which pre- vailed in England. It was a tension which Glyn Dŵr's revolt both heightened and exploited for its own end.[3]

A mood of national self-doubt and nervousness may be debilitating; but it must find a political focus and the support of the politically powerful if it is to lead to political action. This was easily achieved in Henry IV's England. The restoration of the deposed Richard II was the first focus. Stories that King Richard had

survived and would return to claim his throne abounded; one such claimant was to be buried with royal honours in Stirling as late as 1419! Such stories found ready credibility in Wales where the late king had assembled a strong power-base for himself and had begun to weave a web of loyalty to his person. Some of Owain Glyn Dŵr's key early supporters—notably Rhys and Gwilym ap Tudur—had been beneficiaries of the deposed king's patronage and looked back wistfully to the golden age of his power; even Glyn Dŵr himself might well have hoped that the establishment of the short-lived principality of Chester on 25 September 1397, including as it did the Arundel lordships in Shropshire and north-east Wales, might open up avenues of service, promotion, and reward of which he had been so painfully deprived for a decade. Be that as it may, Owain's revolt quickly acquired an anti-Lancastrian aspect. It was reported that he was of the view that 'king Henry was duke of Lancaster and not king of England', and in December 1402 his allies were still proclaiming their intention to secure the restoration of Richard II, 'if he were alive'. If indeed Richard were alive, Wales was thought to be one of the likely places where he had taken refuge; hence the penance imposed by Franciscan friars that men should go looking for him there. But they would, of course, search in vain. A new pretender with a sound legitimate title was now required. He was easily identified, in England and Wales: Edmund Mortimer, the son and heir of Roger (d. 1398), fourth earl of March.[4]

The Mortimer claim of a superior title to the English throne was one which haunted the new Lancastrian dynasty. It was genealogically persuasive, if not overwhelming, as the accompanying table (Table 2) shows: young Edmund Mortimer was, through his grandmother, Philippa, the direct heir of Lionel of Clarence, second surviving son of Edward III. Since Richard II had begotten no heirs of his body, it could be argued that the Mortimer claim to the throne of England was superior to that of Henry IV as the son of Edward III's third surviving son. Even if the young Mortimer heir himself were kept under close royal surveillance (as indeed he was until 1413), and even if he and his advisers eventually decided that the path of loyal service was the safest route to survival in Lancastrian England, others had no such scruples about exploiting the Mortimer claim to promote their ambition to undermine, and even to topple, the Lancastrian regime. And where better to launch a Mortimer-centred bid for the throne than in Wales? Political observers would hardly need to be reminded that it was in Wales that the careers of the two deposed kings of fourteenth-century England had been terminated. More positively, it was in Wales and along its borders that the Mortimers had built their formidable power-base and the pool of support necessary to support their ambitions in the fourteenth century. It is little wonder, therefore, that it was for Wales that Constance, Lady Despenser, was heading after abducting young Edmund Mortimer and his brother in 1405;

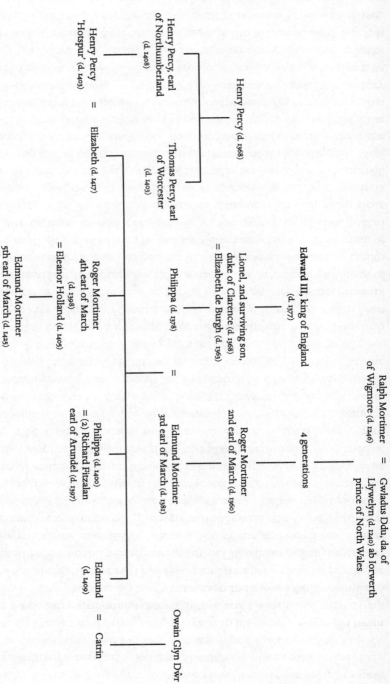

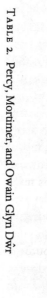

TABLE 2. Percy, Mortimer, and Owain Glyn Dŵr

ten years later it was in Wales again that the earl of Cambridge seems to have intended to launch his rising in the name of Mortimer; and when the government feared another Mortimer revolt in 1421 Wales was once more considered to be the most likely locale for it.[5]

But the significance of the Mortimer claim for the Welsh, and thereby for Owain Glyn Dŵr, was much greater than merely that of the geographical location of the Mortimer estates. The Mortimers had a powerful entrée into the loyalties and affections of the Welsh through the most hallowed of all routes, that of genealogy. Around 1230 Ralph Mortimer of Wigmore had taken to wife Gwladus, one of the daughters of Llywelyn ab Iorwerth, 'the Great', prince of Gwynedd. Distant and vestigial as the link might appear to be by 1400, it was in fact cherished and nurtured by both the Mortimers and the Welsh. How the link could be emphasized and its implications explored is evident in the pages of the chronicle of Adam of Usk, a Welsh cleric reared on a Mortimer estate and the beneficiary of Mortimer support in his educational career; it is even more evident in a Mortimer family chronicle, probably composed in the early fifteenth century. The chronicle asserted that Llywelyn ab Iorwerth had annexed south Wales to his principality of north Wales, thereby by implication making him prince of the whole of Wales. The next stage of the argument centred on Gwladus. She was, according to the chronicle, the sole daughter of Llywelyn, conveniently suppressing the fact that Llywelyn had at least three other daughters. When Llywelyn's male descendants failed to produce heirs, Gwladus's offspring by Ralph Mortimer became the lineal claimants to Llywelyn's principality of the whole of Wales. The claim is not put explicitly, but it is implicit in the way the genealogical evidence is presented and manipulated. Should English genealogical sensibilities be squeamish about such a descent through a Welsh woman, Gwladus's status as a matriarchial figure was underpinned by reminding the reader that her mother was none other than Joan, daughter—the fact that she was an illegitimate daughter was conveniently overlooked—of King John. Descended, therefore, from two English kings—John, through his daughter Joan, and Edward III, through his son Lionel of Clarence—and from a prince of Wales—Llywelyn 'the Great', through his daughter Gwladus—the Mortimer claim to be the heirs to the rulership of both England and Wales in the late fourteenth century was, for those who take these exercises seriously, a very impressive one.[6]

It was not the sort of case which it would be wise to shout from the political roof-tops in England. But Welsh poets were not inhibited by such reservations and they certainly took their genealogical exercises very seriously. Already in the 1390s Iolo Goch, the premier Welsh poet of his day, had addressed a fulsome ode to the young Roger Mortimer, fourth earl of March, in which Roger's genealogical descent was clearly expounded. We could dismiss the ode as a typical piece of

poetic flattery and extravagance; but we would surely be wrong to do so. It is, after all, a unique ode, the only one in the whole corpus of fourteenth-century Welsh poetry to be addressed to a premier English earl. Given the extent of Earl Roger's territorial power in Wales (he held about a third of the country under his sway), and given that he could be presented, if a little anomalously, as the true descendant of the house of Gwynedd through Gwladus—and by then the Gwynedd dynasty had certainly failed in the direct male line, with the murder of Owain Lawgoch in France in 1378—it is easy to understand how Welsh political expectations might come to focus on him. A century and more after the Edwardian conquest he might be the means whereby the Welsh might at last find a place in the English political sunlight. Such expectations were cruelly dashed when Earl Roger was cut down in Ireland at the age of 24 in July 1398; but at least he had sired a male heir who could carry forward the Mortimer claim into the next generation.[7]

Owain Glyn Dŵr must have been fully aware of the expectations that were building up around the Mortimers. Glyn Dŵr's own estate at Glyndyfrdwy lay close to the great Mortimer lordship of Denbigh, while Iolo Goch, who had been so fulsome in his praise of Earl Roger, was in effect if not in name Glyn Dŵr's household bard. Glyn Dŵr's attitude to the Mortimer claim was likely, however, to be rather ambivalent. On the one hand, his own claim to be prince of Wales was hardly compatible with the propaganda that was being peddled about the Mortimer descent from the house of Gwynedd. On the other hand, the opportunity of exploiting the Mortimer claim to the English throne as a bargaining pawn in Owain's own struggle was too good to be missed. The pawn fell conveniently into Owain's lap on 22 June 1402, when Edmund Mortimer—brother of Earl Roger IV and uncle of the young Mortimer heir, also called Edmund—was captured at the Battle of Bryn Glas. Edmund senior, who had been handsomely endowed by his father and brother in land and money, was the effective acting head of the Mortimer family in Herefordshire and the Welsh borderland during his nephew's minority. One would have expected Henry IV to make every effort to secure the release of such a powerful and politically sensitive person; instead he steadfastly refused to contribute towards his ransom, in marked contrast (as contemporaries observed) to his attitude towards the ransom of Reginald Grey, likewise captured by Glyn Dŵr earlier the same year. The king may have had doubts about Edmund's loyalty; there were even dark hints that Edmund had allowed himself to be captured at Bryn Glas. Henry IV might also have calculated that Edmund Mortimer posed less of a threat to his regime as a prisoner in Wales than as a natural focus for Mortimer loyalties and aspirations when he was at liberty in England. Be that as it may, before the end of October 1402 Edmund had defected to Glyn Dŵr's side, married his daughter Catherine

with great solemnity, and formally aligned Mortimer ambitions to the Welsh cause. Before the year was out he issued a manifesto to his followers in the Welsh borderlands proclaiming that his nephew was the rightful heir to the English throne should Richard II be shown to be dead, and asserting that Owain should have his right, left suitably vague and undefined, in Wales. Edmund Mortimer's defection was without a doubt a major coup for Owain. It diverted Mortimer loyalties in Wales to Owain's cause; even more powerfully, it twinned his revolt with the most plausible legitimate threat to the Lancastrian dynasty in England and the greatest source of its political insecurity.[8]

There was, furthermore, yet another dimension to Edmund Mortimer's defection; it helped to bring Owain and his cause closer into the orbit of the Percy family. The support of the Percies—Henry Percy, earl of Northumberland, his son Henry, called Hotspur, and the senior Henry's brother, Thomas Percy, earl of Worcester—had been decisive in Henry Bolingbroke's bid for the throne in 1399; their growing disillusion with the king in 1402–3 served to sour the political atmosphere in England and ultimately prompted the greatest threat to Henry IV's throne. The reasons for that disillusion were many and complex; but among them certainly lay Percy attitudes to the Mortimers and the Welsh revolt. The links between the Percies and the Mortimers seem to have been genuinely close and affectionate. Hotspur was married to Earl Roger Mortimer's sister, Elizabeth, and was favoured with a handsome annuity of 100 marks by Earl Roger himself. The Percies regarded themselves as among the natural protectors of the young Mortimer heir and his lands after Earl Roger's death, and Henry IV pandered to their wishes. The great lordship of Denbigh was handed to Hotspur on very advantageous terms, while he and his father headed a consortium which took over the custody of other Mortimer estates. Hotspur in particular, therefore, had a good opportunity of stepping into Mortimer shoes, at least temporarily and especially in north Wales. There was every reason why the Percies should have been prominent in lobbying the king to secure the release of Edmund Mortimer senior from Owain Glyn Dŵr's prison. Whether they were moved by genuine family affection or were exploiting the Mortimer cause for their own conspiratorial ends, there is no reason to doubt the contemporary view that Henry IV's failure to respond to, indeed curt dismissal of, their pleas on behalf of Edmund further stirred the pot of their disillusion with the new Lancastrian dynasty.[9]

Such disillusion was further compounded by the king's attitude towards the revolt in Wales and in particular the Percies' role in it. The Percies were, of course, pre-eminently by the later fourteenth century a powerful northern England landed family; they had no inherited lands in Wales. It was in the 1390s that they first came to hold land and offices there. Thomas Percy was one of the close

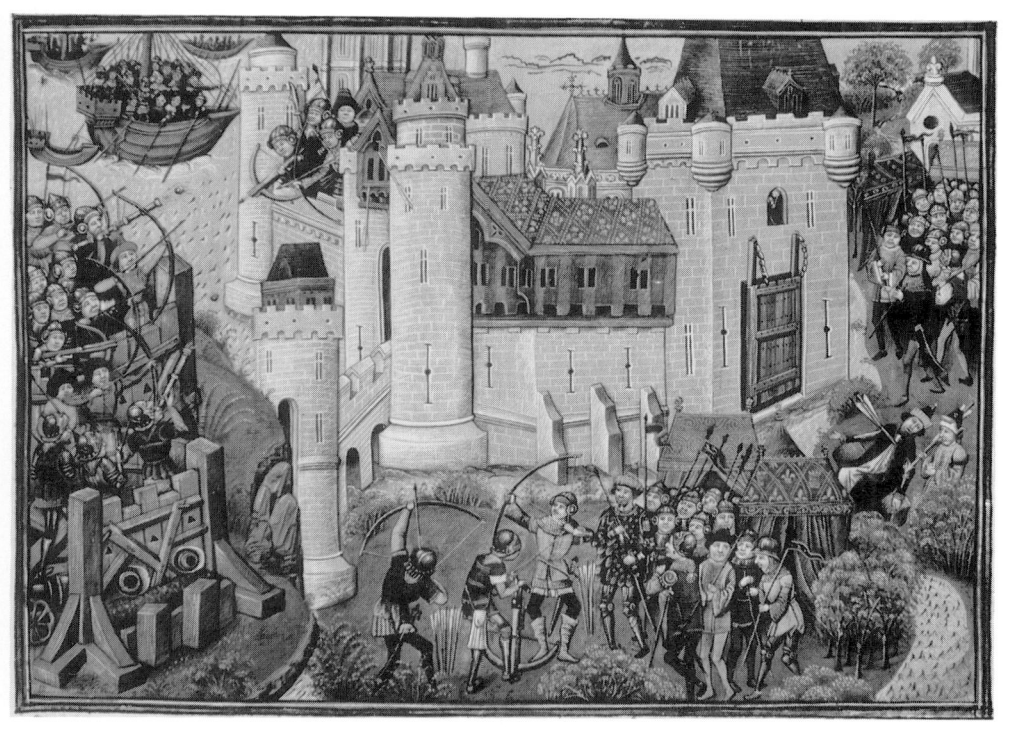

Plate 1. This miniature depicts the assassination of Owain of Wales (Owain Lawgoch) by an English agent at the siege of Mortagne-sur-mer in 1378. Owain Glyn Dŵr claimed to have inherited Owain of Wales's claim to be rightful Prince of Wales.

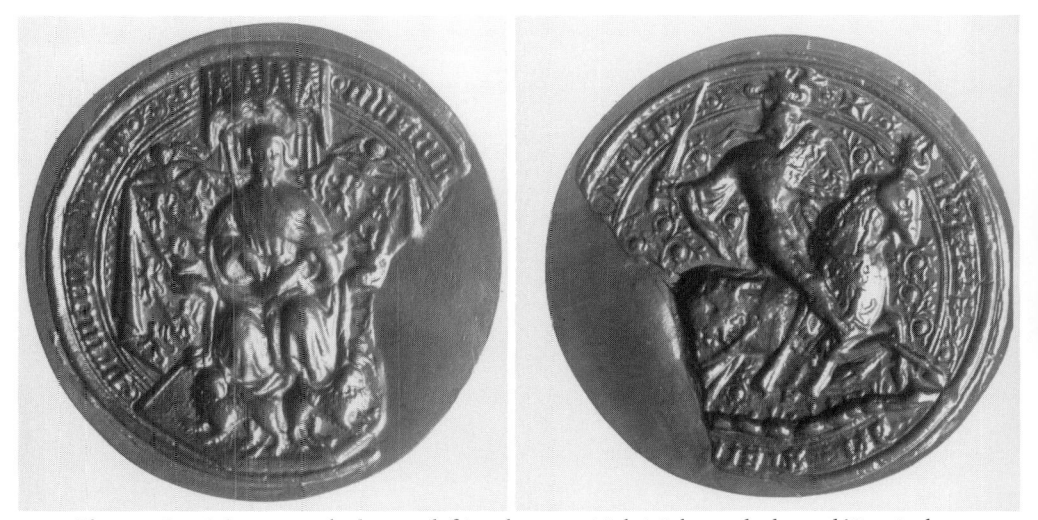

Plate 2. Owain's great seal, obverse (left) and reverse (right). It bears the legend 'Owain, by the grace of God, prince of Wales' and the arms of the Gwynedd dynasty—four lions rampant—which Owain had assumed. The original seal is in the Bibliothèque National in Paris.

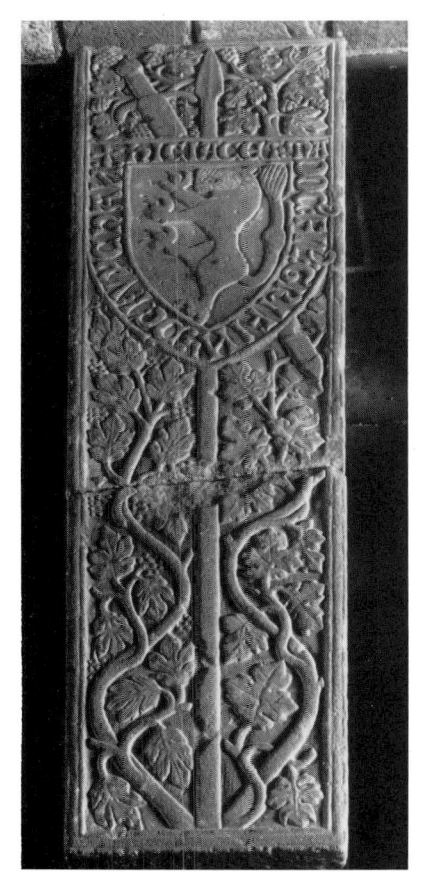

Plate 3. This fine heraldic slab of Owain Glyn Dŵr's great-grandfather was uncovered at the Cistercian abbey of Valle Crucis in 1956. It bears the single lion rampant of the dynasty of northern Powys. Height: 2.16 m, width: 0.69 m.

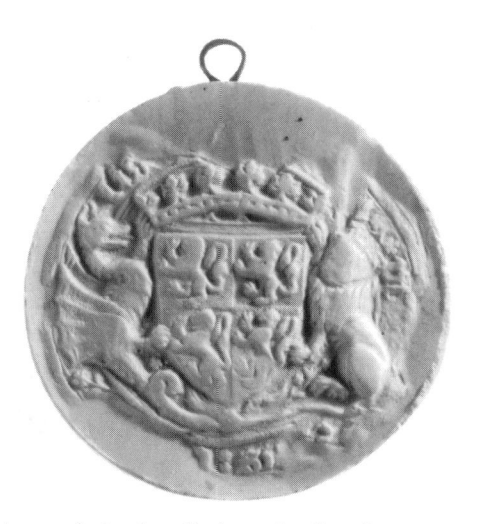

Plate 4. Owain's privy seal. It also displays the four lions rampant and bears the same legend as the great seal opposite. It was attached to Owain's commission to his ambassadors to the king of France.

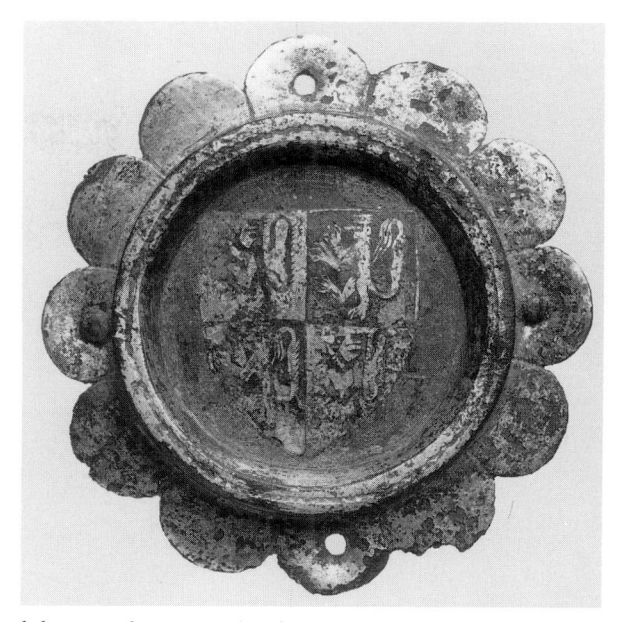

Plate 5. This gilt bronze object, possibly from a belt or harness mounting, bears the four lions rampant of Owain as prince of Wales. It was found at Harlech (the last castle held by Owain) in 1923. Actual size.

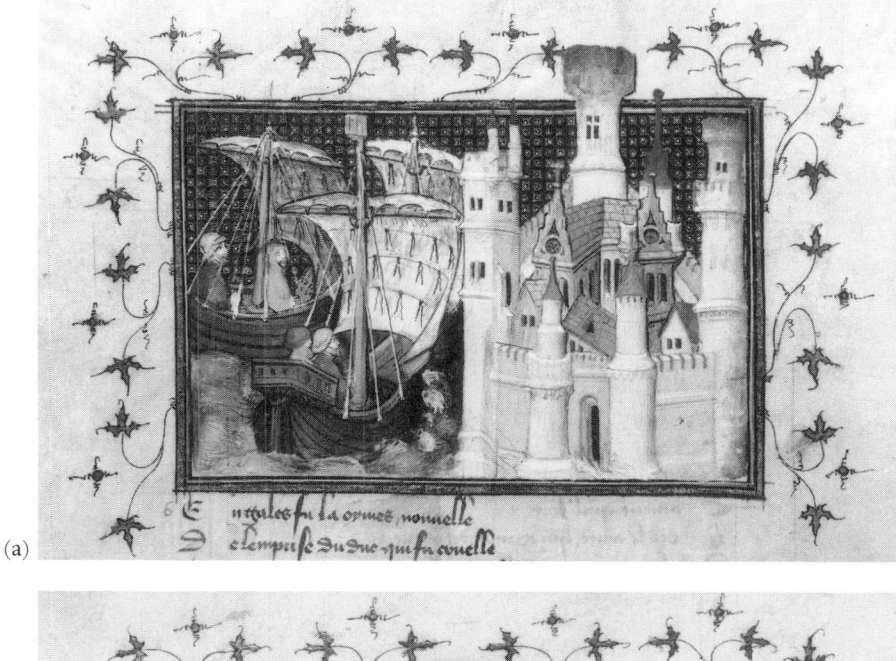

(a)

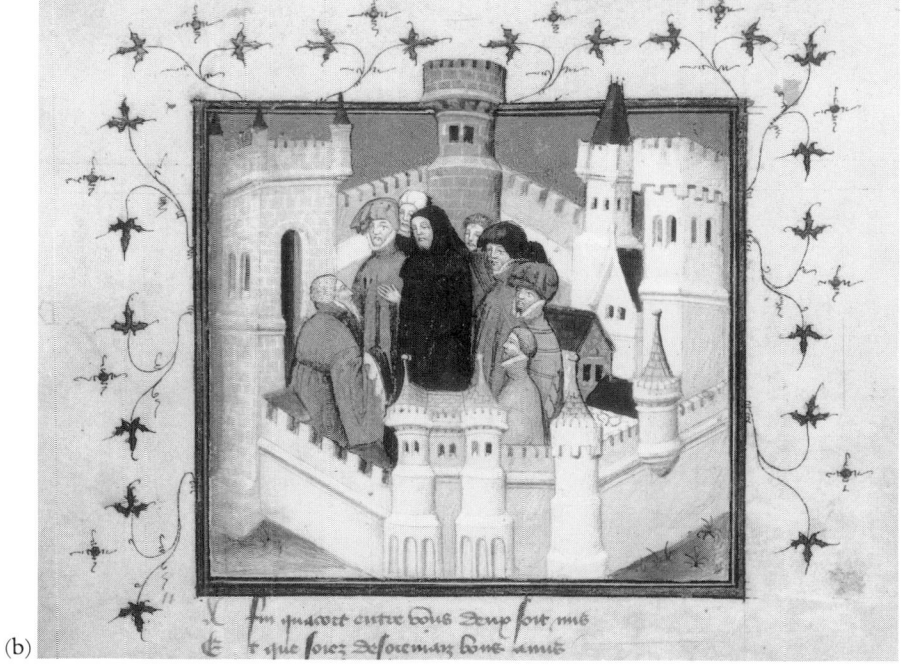

(b)

Plate 6. The downfall of Richard II was effected in north Wales. These two miniatures are taken from the *Chronique de la Traison et Mort, de Richart Deux Roy Dengleterre* by Jean Creton who accompanied the king on his fateful journey. Part (a) shows the earl of Salisbury arriving at Conway Castle. Part (b) illustrates the crucial meeting between Richard II and Henry Percy, earl of Northumberland, also at Conway Castle.

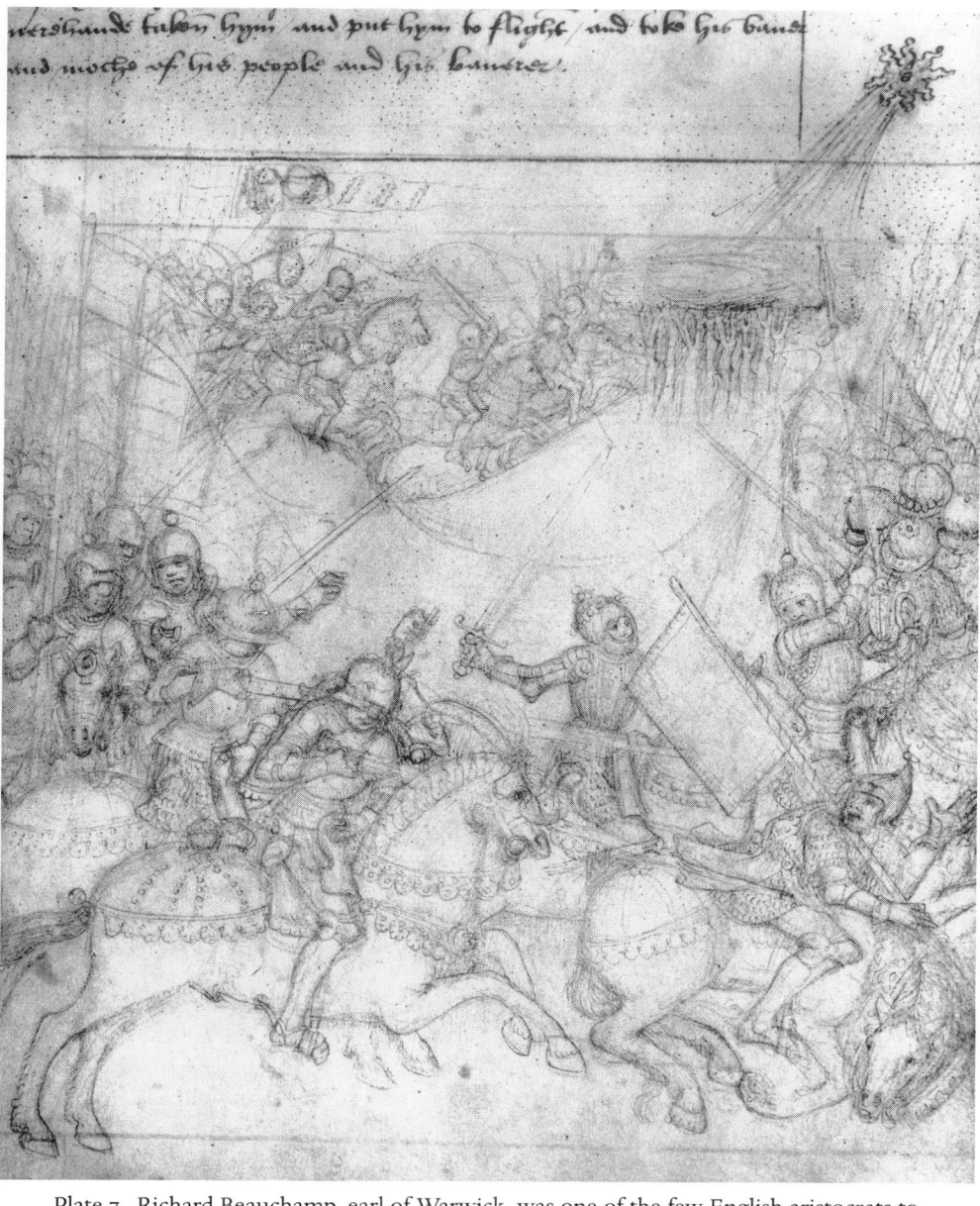

withstande takon hym and put hym to flight / and toke his banst
und mothe of his people and his banerez.

Plate 7. Richard Beauchamp, earl of Warwick, was one of the few English aristocrats to distinguish himself in the Welsh wars. This drawing of one of the earl's victories over the Welsh is taken from an illustrated life of the earl composed in the late fifteenth century.

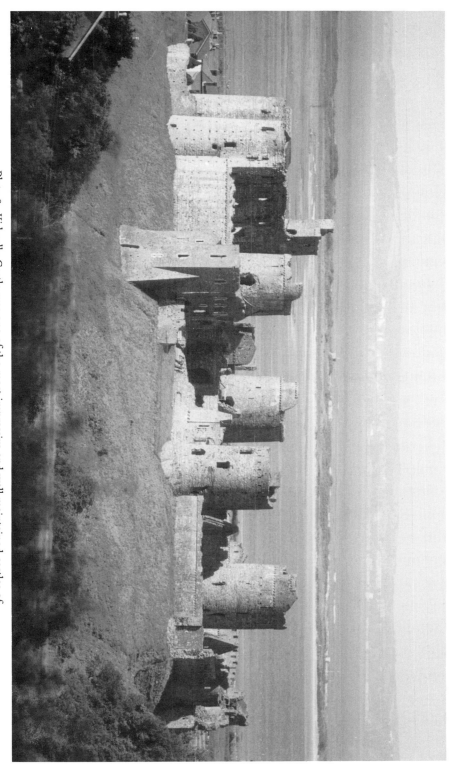

Plate 8. Kidwelly Castle was one of the most impressive and well-maintained castles of south-west Wales. It was owned by the earls and dukes of Lancaster. Work was still in progress on the great gatehouse in the 1390s.

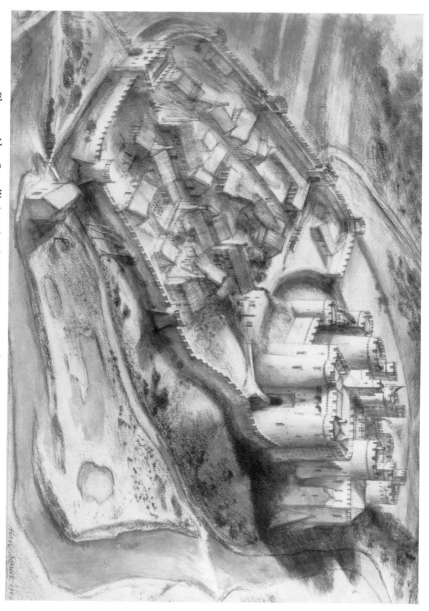

Plate 9. Alan Sorrell's imaginative reconstruction of Kidwelly Castle and town in the fifteenth century. Though the reconstruction, produced in 1963, requires some modification, it conveys well how the castle dominated the little borough and formed an integral unit with it.

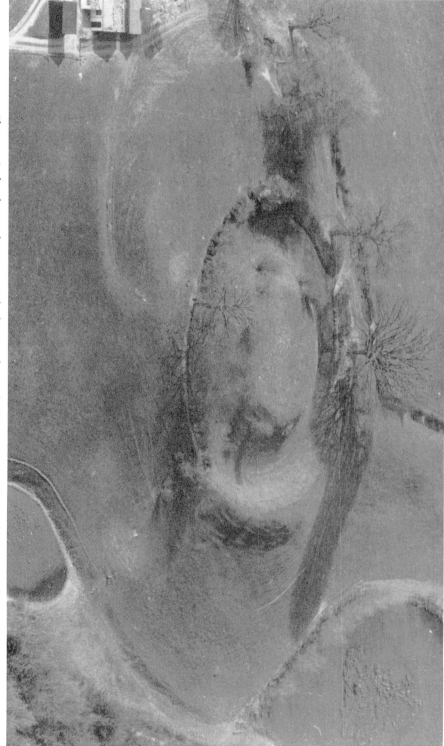

Plate 10. Sycharth was almost certainly the site of an early Norman motte. It was the main residence of Owain Glyn Dŵr; his court there is memorably, if extravagantly, described in a poem by Iolo Goch.

political followers of Richard II in the 1390s, and rewards were duly piled upon him—the justiciarship or governorship of South Wales for much of the period 1390–5, the constableships of key castles in south-west Wales, the custody of major lordships (notably Pembroke and Haverford) in the area, and the title of earl of Worcester. If revolt were to break out in south Wales, Thomas Percy would, in respect of his lands, offices, and military experience, be expected to play a prominent role in suppressing it. But it was in north Wales that the revolt initially broke out and it was in north Wales that the Percies were catapulted into a new political prominence after 1399. Here it was Hotspur who was the recipient of extraordinary favours dispensed by Henry IV in return for the support he had received from the Percies in his coup in summer 1399. In October Hotspur was appointed justiciar or chief governor of North Wales (the three counties of Anglesey, Caernarfon, and Merioneth) and likewise of Cheshire and Flintshire for life; he was given a life grant of the castles of Chester, Flint, Conway, and Caernarfon and of the shrievalty of Flintshire; to these official posts were added the even more valuable life grant of the county of Anglesey and its castle of Beaumaris and the custody of the great Mortimer lordship of Denbigh on excep-tionally favourable terms. It was a remarkable concentration of official power and landed resources in the hands of one man. There was every reason for Hotspur to take this cornucopia of responsibilities and opportunities seriously; after all, it gave him a handsome income and major offices while his father was still alive. He quickly appointed a long-standing Percy follower from Northum-berland, Sir William Swinburne of Capheaton, to be steward of Denbigh and constable of Beaumaris; he enlisted the support of one of the key men of Denbigh, William Lloyd, as his personal squire and deputy steward, and he himself was soon holding judicial sessions in North Wales.[10]

What Hotspur could not have anticipated was that his new posts and lands would bring him, one of the most renowned warriors of his day, fresh military challenges. But once the Glyn Dŵr revolt had broken out and had proved to be more than a nine days' wonder, it was inevitable that Hotspur and, later, his uncle Thomas Percy should be expected to play a prominent part in dealing with it. Responsibility for the fiasco of the capture of Conway Castle by the Welsh on 1 April 1401 fell upon Hotspur as its titular constable, and it was to him that the tricky task of recovering the castle, either by negotiation or by military effort, fell. During the spring and early summer of 1401 it was he in person who directed many of the forays against Glyn Dŵr and sent regular communiqués to the king on the progress of the revolt. As the situation deteriorated during 1401–2 Hot-spur's uncle, Thomas Percy, a man with a record of fine military service to his name, was brought in to stanch the rebellion in south Wales, and, following Henry IV's rather futile expedition in autumn 1401, he was appointed lieutenant

in south Wales and sent with a contingent of troops to Cardigan and Aberystwyth. The government's confidence in the role that the Percies could play in Wales reached its apogee in March 1402 when Thomas Percy was appointed lieutenant in south Wales (as well as governor of the young prince of Wales), while his nephew was given a parallel command in the north. Both were men with impeccable military credentials, while their experience of border warfare against the Scots was the best possible training for the rapid raids best suited to the Welsh terrain. Thomas Percy in particular showed more imagination and determination in dealing with the Welsh revolt than any other military commander during the early years, directing activities from Swansea to Denbigh and putting forward a plan for a co-ordinated three-pronged attack on the Welsh.[11]

But in the event the Percies' military experience in Wales contributed to the unravelling of any remaining bonds of respect between them and the new king. As the military disasters of 1402—including the capture of Reginald Grey and Edmund Mortimer—unfolded, it may be that the government's confidence in the Percies' military skills, at least in Wales, was dented. It was certainly the case that more localized commands were created during the summer and entrusted to new commanders. When a new integrated command for Wales was created on 1 April 1403 it was vested in the prince of Wales. Did the Percies feel snubbed? We shall never know; but that the power of military command which they had enjoyed in Wales until the middle of 1402 had been eclipsed is certain. They had other bones of contention to pick with the government—over the usual slowness in the payment of troops, the decision to resume Anglesey into the king's control so that it could be added to the prince's appanage in spite of the fact that it had been granted to Hotspur for life, the appointment of royal constables in Conway and Caernarfon in 1401 even though these posts had likewise been granted to Hotspur for life, the resumption of the custody of the Mortimer estates from the earl of Northumberland into the Crown's hands in November 1401, and above all over the king's stubborn refusal to make arrangements for the paying of the ransom of Hotspur's brother-in-law, Edmund Mortimer senior.[12]

This last issue touched on a more general difference of opinion between the Percies and Henry IV over the best policy to be adopted in Wales. From a fairly early date the Percies seem to have decided that the revolt in Wales could be more speedily and effectively brought to an end by negotiation and concessions than by outright military victory. The reasons for the position they adopted may be several. It could be that they had developed a healthy respect for the Welsh as hardy fighters: Thomas Percy could still doubtless recall with a shudder that it was a Welshman, one of Owain Lawgoch's followers, who had taken him prisoner in France more than thirty years ago, while Hotspur's military ego had been hugely bruised by his failure to recapture Conway Castle quickly in 1401

after it had been seized from him by a ruse. Long experience of border warfare with the Scots had taught them that grand military triumphs were not easily secured in guerrilla warfare. The opinion was certainly ascribed to Hotspur that the effort and hazards involved in fighting in the sterile, mountainous terrain of Wales were quite disproportionate to the returns in booty and ransoms. Why bother with Wales when glorious victories and massive ransoms could be gained from the Scots, as the Battle of Homildon Hill (14 September 1402) showed so triumphantly? Furthermore, the Percies seem to have been recurrently of the opinion that a workable accommodation could be reached with Glyn Dŵr were it not for the *amour propre* of the king and the short-sightedness of his councillors.

The earliest evidence of a serious disagreement between Henry IV and the Percies over policy in Wales came in the spring of 1401. Hotspur had been given authority to conclude an agreement with the rebels who had seized Conway Castle, but when the king learnt of the terms he disowned them as being too soft. It was the first but not the last rebuff that the Percies suffered. In the closing months of 1401 a major attempt seems to have been made to get Owain Glyn Dŵr to submit. Once again the initiative does not seem to have pleased the king and once again a Percy, almost certainly Thomas Percy, seems to have been the intermediary. Further negotiations were apparently undertaken in 1402 with the earl of Northumberland this time acting as a go-between. The final attempt of the Percies to bring the war in Wales to an end through a negotiated settlement is recorded in a chronicle. The episode is ascribed to 1403, the central actor is Hotspur, and the chronicler goes so far as to assert that it was the rebuff that he received on this occasion which finally drove Hotspur to revolt. We need not accept the details or the chronology of the chronicler's story; but it does surely carry its own kernel of authenticity. According to the chronicler's account Hotspur and Glyn Dŵr met face to face; Glyn Dŵr agreed to submit to the king on certain stipulated conditions, most specifically concerning his safety and his inheritance; Hotspur in turn agreed to suspend hostilities for three months while he tried to win the king's consent to the agreement. This, however, he singularly failed to achieve, especially in the face of hostility from courtier knights (L. *milites curiales*). Indeed, they suggested that Hotspur should have used the opportunity of the negotiations to seize Glyn Dŵr, a convicted traitor. Hotspur was outraged both at his reception in the king's court and at the suggestion that he should break his pledged oath, even to an enemy. He left the court in high dudgeon, without the king's permission.[13]

For all its dramatic embellishments the account communicates vividly the chasm in attitudes between hard-headed, realistic, and self-opinionated military leaders on the one hand and the king's court advisers on the other. 'You courtier knights', so Hotspur is alleged to have commented acidly, 'say great things and

promise to do even greater ones. In the ease and comfort of the court nothing seems difficult.' What must have galled Hotspur and Thomas Percy was that their military and diplomatic judgements of what was feasible in Wales were being recurrently challenged and rejected. For their part Henry IV and his advisers must have wondered whether there was more to the Percies' promotion of a peace policy in Wales than met the eye; their suspicions were doubtless nourished by rumours that in his raids for booty Owain Glyn Dŵr was deliberately sparing Denbigh and other Mortimer lordships in Percy custody.[14]

The significance of disputes about policies in Wales and the failure to effect the release of Edmund Mortimer should not, of course, be rated too highly in any explanation of the final breakdown between Henry IV and the Percies; there were other, more substantial issues dividing them. But for Owain Glyn Dŵr the disaffection of the Percies and their readiness to embrace him, albeit for reasons of self-interest, within their plans and propaganda were a huge boost. He had now aligned both the Mortimers and the Percies with his own cause and had thereby transformed his own prospects. Nor was Wales an unimportant sideshow in the Percies' own plans. The axis that now operated between their traditional power-base in the north of England and their new-found territorial and official position in Wales put them in a league on their own, however briefly, among the magnates of Lancastrian England. The regular passage of messengers, letters, and funds between north Wales and Berwick, Warkworth and Newcastle indicated how effectively this axis was being exploited. It was significant that it was in Chester that Hotspur raised the standard of his revolt on 9–10 July 1403. The men of Cheshire, still smarting from the calamities of 1399–1400, were to provide the backbone of his army; the prince of Wales's household at Shrewsbury was the initial target of that army. But the role of Wales in his plans should not be overlooked. Preparations were afoot in Denbigh to receive him in June 1403; he was there in early July, no doubt drumming up support; and provisions were sent thence to him and his associates in Flint. Meanwhile Thomas Barneby, his chief financial officer in Anglesey, was trying to whip up support for Percy on the island and, interestingly, promising that success in the rebellion would bring peace between England and Wales. It is impossible to know exactly whether Hotspur and Glyn Dŵr co-ordinated their activities as the former finalized his plans to raise the standard of revolt, but there are several indications which can be interpreted as pointing in that direction. Rebel activity in several parts of mid- and south Wales certainly intensified from mid-June onwards and reached a spectacular crescendo in Glyn Dŵr's march down the Tywi valley in the first week of July. News of Glyn Dŵr's initial successes is very likely to have reached Hotspur before he launched his revolt and indeed may have persuaded him that the time was ripe for him to show his hand. In the meantime there are indications

that Glyn Dŵr's agents, or Hotspur's, or both, were stirring up support in Flintshire, an area which had hitherto been almost immune from Welsh rebel activity. Either before, or very soon after, the Battle of Shrewsbury the men of Flintshire defected in droves to Glyn Dŵr. Contemporaries certainly suspected a direct link between Hotspur and Glyn Dŵr; they even went so far as to identify two named go-betweens in the affair: John Kynaston of Ellesmere (and a brother-in-law of Sir David Hanmer) and William Lloyd, Hotspur's squire in the lordship of Denbigh.[15]

Both the evidence and probability suggest, therefore, that Hotspur and Glyn Dŵr were acting collusively in midsummer 1403. While Hotspur was finalizing his support in Cheshire and north-east Wales, Glyn Dŵr's striking successes in the south were leading to frenzied appeals for a royal expedition. Henry IV's instinct that Hotspur's was much the more serious of the twin threats was amply justified. On 21 July 1403 he defeated the Percies comprehensively at Shrewsbury; Hotspur was killed in the battle and Thomas Percy executed two days later. The defeat of the Percies was undeniably a blow to Glyn Dŵr. His hopes of using Percy disaffection and the Mortimer claim to the throne as levers to further the success of his own movement had received a severe setback. But the momentum of his own rebellion was now sufficiently powerful to withstand the defeat of his ally. His link with the Percies in fact survived the Battle of Shrewsbury, but it was henceforth confined to the various conspiracies launched by or associated with the earl of Northumberland, the surviving member of the Percy trio. In that changed relationship Glyn Dŵr in many respects now had the stronger hand; it was the earl of Northumberland who relied on his support, rather than vice versa. The Tripartite Indenture, probably of February 1405, reflects the altered balance of power well: the hugely enlarged Welsh principality which it envisaged was a comment on the strength of Glyn Dŵr's bargaining position.

It was now clearer than ever that disaffection in England, especially northern England, and revolt in Wales were, for good and ill, yoked together. How closely they were linked became evident once more in 1405. In February of that year Constance, Lady Despenser (widow of Thomas Despenser, executed for treason in January 1400), managed to abduct the young Mortimer heirs from Windsor and set out for Wales, no doubt intent on linking with Edmund Mortimer senior (now Glyn Dŵr's ally and son-in-law) and of using the Mortimer claim as the basis of a challenge to the Lancastrian regime. Her plot collapsed when she and her wards were captured near Cheltenham; but the subsequent inquiries revealed the disturbing extent of the conspiracies against Henry IV and confirmed that the Mortimer–Glyn Dŵr axis was still in good heart. That of itself may have persuaded Henry IV that a further expedition against the Welsh was required, if only because there was little prospect of political tranquillity in England so long

as would-be plotters could make use of Welsh support for their own ends. So it was that in late April–early May 1405 Henry IV moved westwards towards Hereford and set in motion major plans for an invasion of Wales. Those plans had to be peremptorily shelved when news reached the king of renewed plots in the north, masterminded as ever by the earl of Northumberland, and of an incipient revolt in Yorkshire. The Welsh rebels had been let off the hook once more by political disaffection in England. But the involvement of the Welsh in the conspiracies of 1405 was more direct than that. When the earl of Northumberland fled to Scotland on the failure of his plot he was, significantly, accompanied by the bishops of Bangor and St Asaph, doubtless dispatched by Glyn Dŵr to co-ordinate policy with the Percy earl. It was not surprising that when Northumberland was in turn forced to flee from Scotland, it was in Wales that he initially sought refuge. Equally significant was the fact that in the manifesto published by Archbishop Scrope of York in May 1405 one of the promises made was to bring the Welsh to perpetual peace and to make them contented subjects of the king of England 'as they had been in the time of King Edward and King Richard'. Glyn Dŵr's revolt had at least intruded Wales on to the agenda of political opposition in Henry IV's England. But by 1405 such opposition was becoming steadily less effective. It was finally buried at Bramham Moor on 19 February 1408 when the earl of Northumberland was killed in a last, hopeless attempt to challenge the Lancastrian regime. It was an appropriate epitaph on the Percy–Welsh axis of the last few years that one of those taken prisoner at the battle was Lewis ab Ieuan, alias Lewis Byford, former bishop of Bangor and supporter of the Welsh cause.[16]

The Mortimer claim to the throne on the one hand, and the overweening ambition of the Percies on the other were certainly the twin major ingredients in the political instability of England in the years 1400–5. It was a measure of the qualities and insight of Owain Glyn Dŵr as a leader that he seems to have been quick to recognize how crucial it was for his prospects to exploit this instability for his own purposes; it was also a measure of the significance that was now attached to his revolt that both the proponents of the Mortimer claim and the Percies were willing and anxious to align his cause with theirs.

Owain's greatest opportunity certainly lay in exploiting domestic disaffection in England to his own ends; but he might also be served by hitching his cause to that of England's external enemies. This is what he assiduously did. Since the 1290s England and France had been periodically involved in protracted war, which increasingly sucked more and more of their satellites into it, be it as allies in the main confrontation or as occasions and pretexts for subsidiary hostilities. The way in which succession disputes in Brittany or Castile or long-standing alliances

such as those between France and Scotland or between England and the men of Ghent fed upon the war and contributed to it suggested that Wales could play a similar role in complicating the Anglo-French conflict. Wales, it is true, was very small fry compared with Castile or Flanders or even Brittany; but it had the considerable attraction for the French of providing what they had so badly needed as they went on the offensive in the war in the 1380s—a bridgehead in Britain from which they could embarrass the English more rapidly and effectively than through their other point of entry in Scotland. For the French, therefore, a revolt in Wales would present an attractive opportunity to diversify their means of striking at the English.

Owain Glyn Dŵr and his advisers were certainly acutely aware of the potential, and indeed the necessity, of integrating the Welsh revolt into the wider European arena of conflict. Their own military and professional careers had given many of them a basic understanding of the power struggles and alignments of the day. Some of them, Owain Glyn Dŵr himself included, had served in English raids in France or Flanders or in the expedition to Scotland in 1385; others had been in service in castle garrisons in Gascony or on the Scottish border, or in Ireland; while yet others had been among the contingents of troops rushed to defend the southern coasts of England against anticipated French invasions in 1385–6. Owain's ecclesiastical advisers included men who had served long in the papal court and who were well placed to explain to him the role of the papacy in international affairs and the true significance of the Great Schism which since 1378 had divided the Church, and with it the governments of Europe, into two opposing camps of ecclesiastical allegiance. Lewis Byford, who was briefly bishop of Bangor from 1404, was one such. Other ecclesiastics brought Owain even more valuable insight into the world of international relations: John Trefor, bishop of St Asaph, who eventually defected to Owain's cause in 1404, had served on diplomatic missions to Scotland and Spain as well as having acquired administrative and financial expertise as chamberlain of Chester. Such men would give Owain invaluable advice on the niceties of diplomatic negotiations and the format of diplomatic credentials and treaties. In short, Owain was not short of knowledge or advice, at least by the later years of his revolt, of how he might exploit the international situation in Europe to his own advantage.

This is indeed what he did. His messengers were busy promoting his cause in different directions: we hear, for example, of envoys being sent with messages in 1401–2 to Ireland and Scotland, of Gruffudd Yonge and John Hanmer being formally accredited in May 1404 as ambassadors to the king of France's court, of the Dominican Hugh Eddouyer and Maurice Kerry sent as envoys to the same king in 1405, of the same Hugh Eddouyer being dispatched on further missions to 'the king and lords of France, the lords of Scotland, the parts of Ireland and the

Outer Isles', and of John Trefor, bishop of St Asaph, venturing to France twice to try to muster military support for Owain. These are doubtless no more than the tip of the iceberg of such diplomatic contacts. Third parties were also working for Owain on the international stage: we hear, for example, of a Cardiganshire knight, Dafydd ab Ieuan Goch, who had spent twenty years of his career fighting the Moslems in the eastern Mediterranean, being sent as the envoy of the French king to the king of Scotland on behalf of Owain. The Welsh knew full well how to make a good case diplomatically: they pointed out to the Irish chieftains when making an appeal for armed support that so long as the Welsh revolt could be sustained the English would be in no position to prosecute their campaigns in Ireland. They were also well aware of the negotiating leverage which came from strong foreign alliances: it was reported in 1405 that once Owain had secured promises of substantial military aid from the French he would be in a sufficiently strong position to open negotiations with the English kings.[17]

Owain targeted his diplomatic initiative at three allies. The least important and the least hopeful of the three were the Irish. In some degree this was perhaps surprising. The Irish were, after all, geographically the closest allies to hand; they had occasionally in the past shown a common awareness of the oppression they and the Welsh had shared at the hands of the English; and in the early fourteenth century a proposal to mount an attack on the English from Ireland through Wales had been actively canvassed. Furthermore, by 1400 the position of the native Irish in Ireland was considerably stronger than it had ever been since the original English conquest; the decline in English control of the country was to accelerate markedly during Henry IV's reign. Knowledge of events in Ireland, though doubtless very patchy, was not inconsiderable in Wales. It was through Wales that Richard II marched with his army to Ireland in 1394 and 1399; among those who served him on the former expedition were some of Owain Glyn Dŵr's most talented lieutenants—notably Rhys and Gwilym ap Tudur of Anglesey and Henry Don of Cydweli. Others would have had experience of Ireland through service, military or administrative, to Roger Mortimer, earl of March on his Irish estates or in his position as royal lieutenant in Ireland. Philip ap Morgan of Usk, for example, crossed over to Ireland and back three times in 1396–7 in the service of Earl Roger. All in all, it is not surprising that Owain Glyn Dŵr should direct one of his earliest letters soliciting support to the lords of Ireland. The fact that the letter was addressed in the plural identified at once the major reason for the failure of the approach. The native Irish in the fourteenth century may have been resurgent; but they never managed, or even tried, to secure a measure of political unity which alone would have enabled them to co-ordinate their actions and to supply aid for the Welsh. Not only did Ireland provide no help for Owain—it was in fact a launching-pad for attacks upon him. In June 1405 Stephen Scrope, the

deputy governor of Ireland, led a highly successful raid on Anglesey, put the Welsh rebels to flight, recaptured Beaumaris Castle, and took one of the most valuable ecclesiastical relics of the island back as a trophy to Christ Church Cathedral in Dublin. It was the beginning of the end of the revolt in Anglesey.[18]

Owain's approach to the Irish had proved to be an unmitigated failure; he had good reason to expect to do far better in Scotland. Scotland was an unitary monarchy; and it was to its king that Owain confidently addressed his letter of appeal. It was a country which had shown remarkable resilience in its defiance of the English, and its record of military toughness was confirmed by the stunning victory which its army achieved over the English at Otterburn (August 1388). There were also historical, mythological, and practical reasons why Owain could expect his appeal to the Scots to be heeded. From the days of Edward I Wales had been a chilling reminder to the Scots of the fate of those who were unfortunate enough to fall under 'the yoke of the English' into 'a most wretched serfdom'. So dreadful was that prospect that on more than one occasion in the early fourteenth century the Bruce dynasty in Scotland and some of the leaders of native Welsh society in north Wales had come close to forging an alliance against the English. Such an alliance was grounded in the convenience of standing together against a common enemy; but it was also greatly reinforced, as so often in the Middle Ages, by the conviction that such collaboration was indeed the fulfilment of one of Merlin's prophecies. The language of the prophecy was certainly compelling and reassuring: 'The successors of Brutus [that is, the Britons or the Welsh], allied with the men of Scotland, will grind down the English kingdoms with warfare, suffering and slaughter . . . The Britons will flourish as friends of the people of Scotland . . . The Britons and the Scots will rule their ancestral kingdoms.'[19]

In the glow of such eloquence and heart-warming reassurances it should be easy to forge an alliance. Indeed, Walter Bower was to observe some decades later that 'the Welsh say that they can never recover their rights in full without the help of their ally from long ago, the people of Scotland'. But the proof of the prophecy would lie in the performance. Here again there was room for optimism. Scottish ships raided along the western sea-route, plundering sites in Man, Ulster, and Wales. In 1381 a group of Scots landed in Anglesey and caused considerable damage to houses there; for much of the 1380s a guard was posted on the walls of Caernarfon because of rumours of impending Scottish raids. The threat from such raids—many of them probably by privateers or by the ships of the Lords of the Isles—diminished in the 1390s as Scotland was drawn into the general truce between England and France. But with the accession of Henry IV tension between Scots and English again rose sharply and with it came the opportunity for the Welsh to forge a Scottish alliance. It was while Henry IV was on his way home from his futile expedition of 1400 against the Scots that news of

Owain's revolt reached him. At first the prospects for an effective liaison between Welsh and Scots seemed promising. Owain addressed King Robert III in effusive terms, and in June 1401 Hotspur reported briefly that Bardsey had been taken by the Scots and that a Scottish ship had been chased all the way to Milford.[20]

But here again Owain met with great disappointment. Nor are the reasons hard to find. In September 1402—just as Owain's credibility as a rebel leader in Wales was making great strides—the Scots were devastatingly defeated by the English at the Battle of Homildon Hill, a defeat which has been described as 'comparable to Flodden'. Over eighty leading Scottish earls and noblemen were killed or captured; the confidence of the Scots was shattered. They had no option but to conclude a truce which seems to have been extended until 1406; they were certainly in no position to give the Welsh any substantial help. Their cup of woe was filled to overflowing when James, the young heir to the ailing Robert III, was captured by an English vessel on his way to France in March 1406 and taken off to spend the next eighteen years in honourable captivity in England. One scene summed up graphically both the potential of the ties between Scotland and Wales in these fateful years and the way that potential was dashed. As James was marooned for a month on Bass Rock in the Firth of Forth in February 1406 waiting for the ship to take him to France, one of those who kept him company was a Welsh bishop. The Welsh certainly continued to live in hope that the Scots would come to their aid: two Welsh bishops apparently made their way to Scotland on Owain's behalf in 1406, and in 1407–8 the regent of Scotland was making claims for his expenses in entertaining envoys from Wales. The degree of interest that the Welsh revolt elicited in Scotland is reflected in the five interesting, if very wayward, chapters that Walter Bower devoted to it in his *Scotichronicon* written in the 1430s or 1440s. Yet Bower's reason for writing at such length about the Welsh said it all: for the moralistic Bower, the fate of the Welsh was only worthy of attention as illustrating to the Scots the dangers of excess, luxury, and inconstancy. Such moral crowing was hardly the best basis for an effective alliance. Ultimately the best that Scotland could provide for the Welsh was a refuge when life became impossible in Wales: it was as bishop of Ross in Scotland that Gruffudd Yonge, Owain Glyn Dŵr's chancellor, began a new career for himself in 1418 when it became clear that he would never be able to return to Wales.[21]

Owain could, perhaps, have accepted disappointment in his search for aid from the Irish and the king of Scotland were he to be successful in forging an alliance with France. It was France which had much the most to offer him in military, financial, and diplomatic aid; and it was to France that he in turn had the most to offer in military terms, by providing it with a bridgehead in Britain from which to attack England. Furthermore there was a body of past precedent and goodwill

on which a Franco-Welsh accord could be quickly built. Those who were devotees of the concept of an 'auld alliance' might even recall that ententes between the Welsh and the French had been forged in the twelfth and thirteenth centuries, specifically at the instigation of Owain Gwynedd in 1168 and Llywelyn ab Iorwerth in 1212. But there were much more recent and powerful precedents to be quoted. Dominating the negotiations between the French and the Welsh in 1404 was the ghost of Owain Lawgoch, the claimant to the principality of Gwynedd and Wales who had been powerfully backed by the French in the 1370s and who had been captain of a well-known detachment of Welsh troops in the service of the French. Here indeed was a debt of loyalty and service which could surely be exploited.[22] Nor had the French been resistant to such approaches. As the initiative in the Anglo-French war began to shift decisively in France's favour in the 1370s, the prospect of making a pre-emptive strike against the English on their own ground—rather than waiting to confront their armies in France—grew ever more attractive. In that event, it is true, Flanders would prove to be the ideal launching-pad and the southern coasts of England, from the Isle of Wight to the Thames estuary, the obvious target. But just as English raids on France proved more effective by having more than one entry and/or exit-point, notably Calais and Brittany, so French strategists were attracted by the possibility of an alternative route through which to attack the English. In such thinking Wales, particularly south-west Wales, had much to offer, the more so if French strategic thinking could be supplemented by Welsh disaffection. It was around Pembroke and Haverford in particular that the French had concentrated their attention— and the English their counter-measures—in the 1370s; that this area was seen as the most vulnerable was confirmed by the extraordinary stories of Castilian spies touring the castles of south-west Wales in 1387–8.[23]

Military plans must, however, wait on political and diplomatic conditions and opportunities; and those seemed to be distinctly lacking in the 1390s. In June 1389 the English and the French concluded a truce. Attempts to convert the truce into a final peace failed; but on 9 March 1396 the next best solution, namely a twenty-eight-year truce, was agreed between the parties in Paris. Henry IV's seizure of the English throne in September 1399, however, transformed the situation once more. The Anglo-French truce, it is true, was formally renewed in May 1400 and in June 1403; but there could be no concealing the fact that tension between the two countries had escalated sharply. The French regarded Henry IV as a usurper and refused to acknowledge him other than as Henry of Lancaster; there was much bitterness and haggling over the return to France of Isabella, the deposed Richard II's queen and daughter of the French king, and of her dowry; and the duke of Orleans, the head of one of the most powerful factions in the French court, went so far as to issue three formal challenges to the English king.

There was in effect a cold war between the two countries. By 1403 a series of incidents made the situation even more critical: French ships under the command of the admiral of Scotland (thereby not formally sanctioned by the French authorities) had long been involved in attacks on English shipping; in August 1403 Plymouth was sacked by Bretons; in December the count of St Pol, acting as a private individual but hardly without the tacit connivance of the French government, landed on the Isle of Wight; in April 1404 there was a raid on Dartmouth, and among French privateers taken prisoner on that occasion were a number of Welshmen. It was little wonder that contemporaries were convinced that the Anglo-French war had recommenced.[24]

This was too good an opportunity for Owain Glyn Dŵr to miss. It is difficult to believe, indeed, that he had not already sent messengers to the French court to solicit help. The French privateering raids of 1403 had certainly encompassed Wales in their ambit, and the opportunity to co-ordinate activity with the Welsh rebels had already been seized. In early October 1403 men from France and Brittany joined Henry Don, the local Welsh leader, in an attack on the castle and town of Kidwelly, and during the next month they were involved in a similar attack on Caernarfon. All that was now needed was to formalize the *de facto* Franco-Welsh alliance. That is what happened in 1404. Tension between England and France grew yet more acute in the early months of the year as both took a yet more aggressive stance. Then, on 27 April 1404, Philip the Bold, duke of Burgundy and the man who was above all responsible for keeping the flickering hopes of peace alive, died; the hawks in the French court, led by the duke of Orleans, now saw their opportunity. So did Owain Glyn Dŵr. On 10 May he despatched Gruffudd Yonge, his chancellor, and John Hanmer, his brother-in-law, to the court of the king of France to conclude a perpetual or temporary alliance with him.[25]

The outcome could not be in doubt. The ambassadors were warmly received; the king interrogated them about 'the condition, life and manners of the Welsh', and proceeded to give them valuable gifts to take back to Glyn Dŵr. Such treatment was suitably flattering; but what the ambassadors wanted above all was practical aid. That was also forthcoming. Already by mid-June the king had ordered the count de La Marche to assemble a force of 800 men-at-arms and 300 crossbowmen to go to Wales 'to make war on the English, our enemies, and to help our cousin and ally, the prince of Wales, against them'. The Welsh expedition was to be part of a co-ordinated strategy: measures were put in place simultaneously for attacks on the English positions in Gascony. In the meantime the formal negotiations continued and bore fruit in the solemn treaty concluded in the house of the French chancellor on 14 July 1404 in the presence of three bishops, a count, and two knights of the French king. Charles VI and the prince

of Wales bound themselves in a formal league of friendship against their common enemy, Henry of Lancaster. Much of the rest of the treaty was common form; but it was greatly reassuring to Owain to know that neither party was to conclude a truce or peace with the English without the other being given a full opportunity to be included in it if he so wished. The treaty of July 1404 was a high point in Owain's career. Less than four years after his initial act of rebellion he was now accepted as prince of Wales by the king of France and his struggle had been locked formally into the Anglo-French conflict. His ambassadors returned home in triumph.[26]

It was now a matter of waiting for action to follow where ceremonies and words had led. The Welsh ambassadors had led the way by handing over to the count of La Marche a detailed list—which the chronicler of St Denis claimed to have read—of the most famous harbours of Wales, the best routes for armies, and the districts in which they were likely to find the most abundant supplies. Expectations were high on the Welsh side and fears correspondingly so on the English side: from early August until the late autumn messages arrived warning that a French fleet was indeed about to set sail for Wales (or possibly eastern England) and that an army was simultaneously going to attack English positions in Gascony. The count of La Marche certainly did assemble a fleet of sixty or so ships at Harfleur and elsewhere. In the event, whether because of incompetence or indolence on the part of La Marche or because of stormy weather off the Breton coast, the fleet returned to port without having left the Channel. With winter weather settling in, Glyn Dŵr would have to wait until the next year to reap the fruits of his alliance with the French.[27]

Owain had good reason to be expectant and optimistic. In February 1405 a force of Frenchmen joined the Welsh of Caernarfonshire in ambushing the sheriff of Anglesey; in the same month a number of French ships laden with wine and spices arrived in the Llŷn peninsula. Owain could live well; but what he wanted was troops rather than gastronomic delights, all the more so as the military pendulum had begin to swing fairly decisively against him in various parts of Wales during the spring and summer of 1405. Political tensions in Paris may well have delayed the dispatch of the anticipated French force; but during July a force of some 2,500 or so men was assembled at Brest. It eventually left port on 22 July under the leadership of some distinguished French nobles—notably Jean de Hangest, lord of Hugueville, Jean de Rieux, marshal of France, and Renaut de Trie, admiral. Many of the horses perished during the journey for lack of fresh water; but in early August the force put to land in Milford Haven. Owain Glyn Dŵr's dream had at last come true.[28]

What exactly the French force, in alliance with Glyn Dŵr's own troops, achieved in Wales is by no means easy to determine. Only one English chron-

icler, Thomas Walsingham at St Albans, gave the episode any attention. Of French chroniclers the garrulous author known as the monk of St Denis gave the most detailed and credible account; far less reliable and much more fanciful is the narrative of the invasion provided by the later chronicler Enguerrand de Monstrelet. What is clear is that the combined Franco-Welsh force made some striking advances in south-west Wales but also suffered some notable setbacks. They burnt the town of Haverford, but quickly abandoned the siege of the castle there. They burnt their way through southern Pembrokeshire and laid siege to the walled town of Tenby; but showed no more tenacity there. Indeed, the sight of an English naval squadron drove them allegedly into a frenzy of fear; they burnt many of their own ships which they had beached and abandoned valuable siege engines as they left in panic. Proceeding via St Clears, where again they were unable to storm the castle, they headed for Carmarthen. This was clearly the prime target of the advance, for Carmarthen was the English headquarters in south-west Wales and the key to control of the area. Owain had captured it briefly in July 1403; for both military and mythological reasons—for Carmarthen was believed to be Merlin's town—it was imperative that he should do so again. This indeed he and his allies achieved, but more by negotiation than by military prowess. The townsmen were given permission to leave freely for England or English-controlled parts of Wales, and Owain and his allies proceeded to destroy the town walls.[29]

The achievement of the French expedition so far is fairly clear and, within limits, quite impressive. What is perhaps more open to doubt is the story that Monstrelet then recites—and which even that most cautious of historians, Sir John Edward Lloyd, accepted—that the Franco-Welsh force marched through south Wales and into Herefordshire and Worcestershire. There—and here Monstrelet's graphic account is elaborated by local tradition—at Woodbury Hill, eight miles from the city of Worcester, the Welsh and their allies glowered across the valley at an opposing English army under the king's command for eight days before both armies decided that the prospect of an engagement was too risky. It is a good story and derives some measure of indirect support from the fact that Henry IV was at Worcester for ten days in late August 1404 before proceeding to Hereford. But the story, uncorroborated as it is, savours of a flight of chivalric literary fancy. A marauding contingent of the Franco-Welsh army might possibly have penetrated so far; but it is difficult to believe that a major expedition deep into England would not have left a trace in contemporary record or chronicle sources.

The Franco-Welsh force's proven impact was confined to south-west Wales. It was its success in this area which doubtless persuaded the men of Pembrokeshire in November 1405 to pay £200 to secure a truce with the Welsh. The French had

established a bridgehead in Wales and Owain's position in this corner of the country had been substantially enhanced. But in the event that proved to be all that the Franco-Welsh alliance achieved and even that achievement proved to be short-lived. A small contingent of the French troops returned home in November 1405; the remainder overwintered in Wales. A fleet of twenty-eight ships sought to bring reinforcements from France in 1406, but eight of them fell into English hands. During the course of the year the remaining French troops seem to have withdrawn from Wales. Glyn Dŵr did all in his power to keep the alliance in good heart, notably by transferring his ecclesiastical allegiance to the Avignonese papacy in March 1406 at the request of the French. But as the French suffered major rebuffs in the autumn of 1406 on the other two fronts which they had opened against the English in Picardy and Gascony, there was little prospect that they would have the resources or the will to support their ally in Wales. The Welsh certainly did not give up trying—Welsh representatives were present, alongside ambassadors from Scotland, at a grand assembly convoked by Charles VI on 21 May 1408, and even as late as February 1415 Gruffudd Yonge and Philip Hanmer were forlornly pressing the Welsh cause in Paris. But in spite of the rhetoric and the promises the Franco-Welsh alliance which had been launched so promisingly in midsummer 1404 was effectively a spent force by 1407. And with its effective demise Owain Glyn Dŵr's cause went into rapid and terminal decline.[30]

In retrospect the wonder, surely, is that the alliance achieved as much as it did. In spite of the flattering talk at the French court, Wales could never have been high on France's diplomatic or military agenda. If warfare was a way of bringing the English to the negotiating table then attacks on the areas around the two English outposts of Calais and Bordeaux took priority over any succour to the Welsh rebels; and if the English were to experience the horrors of war in their back garden, the distant coastlands of south-west Wales were much too remote to serve the purpose. When it came to tactical considerations the French must have recalled the bitter frustrations and disappointments of trying to co-ordinate their tactics with the Scots back in 1385. Working with the Welsh proved no easier: the French chroniclers could hardly conceal their contempt for the Welsh and their cowardly ways, or their distaste for the country and its climate. At the end of the day there could be no question but that the French were using the Welsh, and that the value of the latter would ultimately be determined by the domestic and international politics of France. During 1407 two interrelated events sealed the fate of the Franco-Welsh alliance. On 23 November, after years of intense hostility, the duke of Orleans, the most hawkish of the French princes, was assassinated by the agents of the duke of Burgundy. On 7 December the French and the English concluded a truce to come into operation on 15 January

1408. That truce was to be renewed for short periods up to 1 May 1410. It sealed
the fate of the Franco-Welsh alliance; it also in effect sealed the fate of Owain
Glyn Dŵr.

Owain Glyn Dŵr had not in the end been well served by his allies. One by one
they had either failed or deserted him. The recurrent failures are a comment on
the immense problems of communication and co-ordination, of effective timing,
which confronted any medieval alliance; the will for joint activity was often
present but the means to make it work in practice was not. Nor could there be
any doubt that the Welsh were used as junior, and expendable, partners by their
allies: had the Percies dislodged Henry IV in 1403 or 1405 they would almost
certainly have reneged on any promises they had made to Glyn Dŵr; as to the
French, the solemn promise of July 1404 that the Welsh would be invited to join
any peace they made with the English counted for nothing when domestic and
international considerations dictated the need for an Anglo-French truce in
December 1407.

Yet brittle as were all the alliances, formal and informal, Glyn Dŵr had no
option but to conclude them; they were the best prospect for the long-term
success of his movement. Indeed, what is surely remarkable is the degree to
which Owain, especially in the years 1403–6, succeeded in integrating his revolt
fully into the domestic and international agenda of English and northern European politics. Alongside his ambitious plans for the new principality of Wales, it
surely bespeaks a largeness of vision which is quite astonishing. Had all the cards
fallen the right way; had the domestic and foreign enemies of the English Crown
not been riven by dissension and been able to co-ordinate their actions; had
Hotspur timed his revolt better in July 1403 and thought through more carefully
how to co-ordinate his support; had the abduction of the Mortimer heir, the
Scrope–Percy revolt, and the French invasion of Wales all been made to coincide
in early summer 1405 . . . Historians are warned not to entertain such might-
have-beens; but even to glimpse them is to recognize that not since Edward II's
or even Edward I's day had the chances for a successful Welsh revolt been more
propitious. Glyn Dŵr seized every one of those chances, and yet he failed. Such
success as his revolt enjoyed depended ultimately on the degree of support he
could command within Wales itself.

FRIENDS AND FOES

*T*he revolt of Owain Glyn Dŵr began as the conspiracy and vision of a group, or possibly two groups, of men in north Wales in autumn 1400; by midsummer 1403 it had become a movement which took the whole of Wales for its stage and drew its support from all corners of the country. The success of the revolt, first in surviving beyond its first, very uncertain, year and then in transforming itself into what may be truly termed a national revolt, owed not a little to the incompetence and distractions of the royal government and of the English lords in Wales as well as to the difficulties of countering guerrilla warfare in mountainous terrain. Feeble and uncoordinated response by the powers that be is often the key to the success of a revolt, since it quickly leads to the collapse of the mechanisms of legal and social control on which obedience and deference depend. In other words the collapse of the *status quo* and the loss of its credibility leave a vacuum of power in which revolt can flourish and rebels seize the initiative. Men need not necessarily commit themselves enthusiastically or out of conviction to the rebel cause, though some most certainly do so; rather it is that the current regime forfeits its respect and authority, allowing new allegiances to be forged and new loyalties to be proclaimed. Such is what seems to have happened in Wales in 1402–3.

In this transfer of loyalties the crucial group were the leaders of local Welsh society. Native Wales did not have an aristocratic class of great magnates or barons, nor even a group which could stand comparison economically with the greater gentry of the English counties. Its relative economic poverty on the one hand and the practice of partibility of lands between male heirs on the other meant that it lacked the great disparities in wealth and in social status and designations characteristic of contemporary England. Yet it was also a profoundly conservative and, on its own terms, hierarchic society. The local leaders identified themselves, to themselves and others, by the superiority of their lineage, the nobility of their blood, their relative wealth in an impoverished society, their military experience, and their confident exercise of the legitimate and oppressive weapons of local power and influence. If Glyn Dŵr's revolt was to succeed it must come to command the connivance and, preferably, the active support of such men. It did so.

Contemporaries soon recognized that the revolt of Owain Glyn Dŵr was no peasant rebellion or *jacquerie*; it was launched by a man of the noblest Welsh birth and came to be sustained by men who had been the pillars of local society and governance. It was natural that Owain himself should refer flatteringly to 'the nobles of our race' (L. *proceres de prosapia nostra*) as assenting to his policy; but Adam of Usk also uses precisely the same term (L. *cum pluribus Wallie proceribus*) in referring to Owain's supporters. We may dismiss these phrases as examples of imprecise and laboured Latinity, but the same charge cannot be directed at the observation of the constable of Dinefwr that 'many gentlemen have joined Owain in person' (E. *moni gentils bun yn person wyth Oweyn*). The English government realized full well that its only hope of nipping the revolt in the bud was to secure the allegiance, through force and threat if need be, of these local leaders. In Iscennen in south-west Wales in October 1401 seventeen of the leading men of the area were summoned to appear personally before Sir Hugh Waterton and his fellow justices at Kidwelly and were bound over in a massive pledge of 10,000 marks (£6,666 13s. 4d.) that neither they nor any one else from the commote would come out in support of Glyn Dŵr. Such a policy was hardly a vote of confidence in the loyalty of these men, but it was a recognition that it was their attitude and decision which determined whether the tide of revolt could be contained in their locality. The same was true throughout Wales. As the situation deteriorated rapidly in Flintshire in the spring and summer of 1403, royal officials there likewise turned desperately to the leaders of the local community to hold the line, appointing groups of them in each commote to set up watches and to prepare for imminent rebel attacks. The measures taken in Iscennen and Flintshire were but individual examples of a policy which, so the commons in parliament believed, should be pursued throughout Wales. In the parliament of October 1402 they requested that 'the most important and powerful Welshmen' (Fr. *les pluis grandes et sufficiauntz persones Galois*) in each lordship should be appointed guardians of the peace and held responsible for any offences committed in the lordship. That, so they added sanctimoniously, would be to revive the policies pursued by King Edward at the time of the conquest. Be it an old policy or not, no one could doubt that the key to peace or otherwise in Wales lay in the hands of these local potentates. During 1402–3 more and more of them— whether out of conviction or because they felt that they had no other choice— opted for war. Glyn Dŵr won the battle of local loyalties among those who really counted.[1]

Owain's leadership and control of the revolt was never called in question; that was a measure of his stature and the respect in which he was held by his fellow Welsh squires. But in a society which was as geographically fragmented as was Wales and lacking any obvious central political focus, and in which power

structures and networks were inevitably local and localized, the status and commitment of local leaders were crucial to the success of the revolt. That was obvious within its first few months. It was Owain Glyn Dŵr who had staged the dramatic critical act of revolt in September 1400, but when that initial phase fizzled out in failure, submission, and execution, it was the largely independent action of a group of men led by Gwilym ap Tudur of Anglesey in seizing Conway Castle on 1 April 1401 which rekindled the flame of revolt. The survival of the list of those involved in this sensational act also makes it clear that several of them could claim to be among the leaders of local society. Gwilym ap Tudur could certainly do so in respect of his military experience, his royal pension, and his considerable estates in Anglesey and Caernarfonshire (including the lease of the manor of Aber, some nine miles from Conway); but so could some of his accomplices such as Dafydd ap Gruffudd Fantach, who owned the 'manor' of Dwygyfylchi, or Hywel Fychan ap Madog ap Hywel, a man of impeccable descent and landed means. These men were indeed, as they were to be described, 'sufficient persons' and 'men of note'.[2]

In each part of Wales such men took over the leadership of the revolt. In the north-east John Kynaston played a crucial role. His official position (as steward of the Lestrange lordship of Ellesmere, and the nearby districts of Maelor Saesneg and Mold) and his marriage links (he was brother-in-law of Sir David Hanmer) gave him an ideal base from which to operate. He was implicated in Glyn Dŵr's initial act of rebellion, nor did he deny the charge; he acted as a go-between in the links between Glyn Dŵr and Hotspur during the crucial summer months of 1403; and he was subsequently accused of having compelled the men of Ellesmere to march to Shrewsbury in Hotspur's cause in July 1403 and to have done so 'with dire threats and deception'. These are the characteristic acts of a local 'strong-man' and like so many strong men he was able to read the tide of changing political fortunes accurately and so not only saved his own skin but flourished into venerable old age in local office with most of his power extant. There were many like him: Rhys Gethin and Morgan Gethin who are several times identified in Gower as Glyn Dŵr's accomplices in revolt; Ieuan ap Jenkin Kemeys, a man of considerable means (his landed wealth was estimated at £40 per annum) and of even greater local standing (his father had been steward of Abergavenny and constable of Senghenydd, and he himself was the earl of Stafford's master forester in Machen) who emerged as a prominent supporter of Glyn Dŵr in south-east Wales; or Rhys Ddu, 'the Black', alias Rhys ap Gruffudd ap Llywelyn ab Ieuan, who graduated from the post of a zealous royal sheriff of Cardiganshire to that of Owain Glyn Dŵr's captain of the castle of Aberystwyth in the final siege of 1407–8, and who paid the ultimate price for his rebellion on the gallows at London.[3]

We can do no more in the case of most of these men than gather a few disjointed fragments of information about their careers and fortunes and catch a fleeting glimpse of the sort of power they must have exercised within their localities. But for one individual we can take the story rather further and thereby lay bare some of the springs and tactics of his power and the reasons why his support was so crucial to Glyn Dŵr. His name was Henry Don of Cydweli. Don's standing in his locality, like that of most of his fellow squires, was comprised of several elements. Lineage and high birth were one: he was of the stock of Llywelyn ap Gwrgan, one of the patriarchal founding fathers of the noble families of Wales. Territorial wealth was another. We have no rental of his estates, but the fact that they yielded £252 in 1388 (possibly from the profits of several years) and that Walter Morton, who had held them from 1407 to 1413, was recompensed with a grant of £100 when they were restored to Don in 1413 indicates that they were very substantial indeed. Henry Don also had the appropriate military credentials: his father had seen service as the leader of a force of 350 Welshmen in the retinue of Henry of Grosmont, earl of Lancaster, in the 1340s; Henry himself kept up the family tradition, serving under John of Gaunt in Picardy and Normandy in 1369 and under Richard II in Ireland in 1394–5. Power in his own locality could hardly be denied to such a man. Nor was it, since in 1388–9 Don became Gaunt's steward, or chief officer, of the lordship of Cydweli. And what power was not conferred officially on Don he himself grabbed unceremoniously and outrageously. He evicted tenants, collected his own personal subsidies, and seized lands; recurrent large fines, threats, and recognizances (that is, legal undertakings underwritten by threats of large penalties) seem to have done little to curb his high-handed methods. He ruled the roost in the Cydweli area and ruled it in his own unappealing and buccaneering fashion.[4]

If Owain Glyn Dŵr's cause was to have any hope of success in this area of Wales it must come to terms with, and win over, Henry Don. By 1403, at the latest, it had done so, and Henry Don donned the mantle of leadership in revolt as naturally and unquestioningly as he had done so in peace. In early June and again on 13 August 1403 Henry Don—now a man well advanced in late middle age—and his son led 'all the Welsh' of the commotes of Cydweli and Carnwyllion in an attack on Kidwelly Castle in which several of its defenders were killed; late in September another major attack on the castle was anticipated in which the local Welsh could be joined by French and Bretons and in which Henry Don was once again named as leader. Don had shown that he had lost none of his military appetite even if he was now directing his attacks against the English whom he had once served; nor had he lost his eye for the profits of war, for among his trophies was a ship he had captured from a Llansteffan merchant in the port at Carmarthen. Once he had opted for the Welsh cause, Henry Don remained remarkably

steadfast to it. Owain Glyn Dŵr counted him as a confidant and a most effective lieutenant, as is suggested by the letter that he sent him. Don in turn paid a heavy price for his commitment: his lands were formally forfeited in 1407 and the title to them was granted to Walter Morton, the English constable of Kidwelly; Henry Don himself spent spells in prison at Kidwelly and Gloucester, and was only eventually pardoned in May 1413 in return for a fine of £200, one of the very largest recorded for a former rebel.[5]

In fact the fine was never paid and was eventually cancelled in February 1445. Nor had Henry Don been in any way chastened by the events of the last few years. He was as defiant as ever, even sheltering a fugitive rebel in his household as late as 1413. He lorded it over the area as masterfully as he had done for the last forty years and allowed no sense of contrition for his role as a rebel to cramp his style or his activities. Perhaps nothing expressed more vividly the view that for him the Welsh rebellion was no more than a formal change of the regime under which *he* exercised *his* power in *his* 'country' than the outrageous fact, from the government's point of view, that he now exacted fines from over 200 local Welshmen who had failed to follow him in his revolt and had dared to occupy his lands during the uprising! The brazen audacity of such an act beggars belief, but it is a measure of the degree to which effective social power—before, during, and after the revolt—lay in the hands of local potentates. It was only death which could loosen the grip of those hands; it did so for Henry Don in November 1416.[6]

We are unusually well informed about Henry Don; but the nature of his power and the high-handed way in which he exercised it were doubtless replicated throughout Wales. It was upon men of his ilk that the success of Glyn Dŵr's revolt in the localities would substantially depend. By no means all of them came to support his cause, even when it seemed politic to do so; but sufficient of them seem to have done so to convert his rebellion into a truly national movement. Thus, of the twelve leading Welshmen who were charged with taking measures to protect Flintshire from rebel attacks in June 1403, all but one are known to have subsequently joined the forces of either Hotspur or Glyn Dŵr. What qualities did these men bring to the revolt?

They were by definition men of stature and wealth by the relative standards of their own societies; stature and wealth led them to command, and demand, respect and obedience, be it as representatives of the English king and lords or now as sworn supporters of Owain Glyn Dŵr. We met several of them earlier in our gallery of portraits of the men who ruled the roost in Wales in the 1390s: Hywel ap Tudur ab Ithel, the swaggering, violent sheriff of Flintshire and the richest man in his county; Rhys and Gwilym ap Tudur of Anglesey, two brothers inordinately proud of their ancient lineage and military experience and the natural leaders (as they saw it) of society in their corner of north Wales; and

Gruffudd ap Gwilym, whose estates straddled the whole of north Wales and who had strong claims to be the wealthiest Welshman of his day, certainly in north Wales. All four of them sooner or later defected to Owain Glyn Dŵr, be it out of conviction or out of convenience, and brought with them the support of a network of kinsmen, tenants, clients and dependants. There were scores like them throughout Wales. In Cardiganshire one of Glyn Dŵr's die-hard supporters and defender of the captured castle of Aberystwyth was Maredudd ab Owain: his subsequent career was to show that he was a member of the office-holding and warrior class of his county, but the fact that even before the revolt he was fined for raising illegal subsidies (W. *cymorthau*) from his dependants, that his forfeited lands were leased for £14 per annum, and that he could pledge himself in the enormous sum of £300 on behalf of the hostages of Aberystwyth during the negotiations of 1407 is a measure of his local standing and wealth. In Anglesey a figure of similar local standing was Maredudd ap Cynwrig, who was already strutting officiously on his small stage before the revolt. For an ambitious social climber like him the revolt presented a particularly painful dilemma and one which he was loath to resolve. It was the rebels who resolved it for him. Riding forth from Beaumaris Castle in his capacity as acting-sheriff of Anglesey, he was caught and captured in a Welsh ambush in 1404. The experience of imprisonment seems to have concentrated his mind wonderfully, for he now defected to the rebels. But he was ever the reluctant rebel. He soon made his peace with the authorities, paid one of the largest fines for a pardon that was levied on an Anglesey man, and his later official career and status as an alderman of Newborough (Niwbwrch) showed all the hallmarks of respectability and good citizenship. When he died in 1428 the poet Rhys Goch Eryri heaped the conventional encomia on him as 'a good chieftain' and 'the generosity of Anglesey' (W. *bendefig da, haelioni Môn*), and indicated that he had the good palate, as well as the sound lineage and official standing, of a gentleman, by addressing Maredudd's elegy, with a nice touch of poetic conceit, to a ship laden with Spanish wine bound on its way to replenish Maredudd's cellar.[7]

It was the bouquet of fine wine which the poet associated with Maredudd ap Cynwrig; the memories of those who had lived under his rule in Anglesey might have been rather different. He and his like were not shy of deploying their authority for their own ends. Maredudd ab Owain, as we have seen, extorted subsidies from his own tenants. He was certainly not alone in this; indeed, he was more the rule than the exception. Of the seventeen leaders who are sufficiently eminent to be named as accompanying Henry Don in his attack on Kidwelly Castle in August 1403, at least half were later to be convicted of collecting illegal subsidies from their neighbours, often in sheep and corn. What was not seized through social oppressions could be secured under the guise of official power.

Thus the willingness of the men of Cardiganshire to serve under Rhys Ddu (Rhys ap Gruffudd ap Llywelyn ab Ieuan) as Owain Glyn Dŵr's commander in Aberystwyth might be tempered by the memory of the way he had fleeced them as the king's sheriff of the county. In 1397 he had ingratiated himself further with the royal administration by promising to extract £100 for the king's coffers from the next great sessions and £10 annually thereafter for the next ten years. His protestation that he could do so without oppression or extortion rings utterly hollow; Rhys Ddu was serving himself well in serving the king; it was the men of Cardiganshire who were the victims. And they remained victims whether Rhys acted nominally on behalf of the king of England or in the name of Owain Glyn Dŵr.[8]

As should be all too obvious the one major way we possess of gauging the standing of these men is through the offices they held. Offices in medieval Wales may be classified into three very broad categories: first were the provincial posts, such as those of justiciar or chamberlain in North Wales or the stewardship or receivership of a major Marcher lordship such as Denbigh or Brecon; second were the intermediate posts such as that of sheriff of a county or constable of a castle; thirdly, were the local commotal officials such as the *rhingyll*, beadle or reeve. Welshmen were normally excluded from the first category of offices and sometimes from the second. Many of the top posts were filled by absentee, or at least often absent, Englishmen who were in turn obliged to appoint local Welshmen as their serving deputies. Some of the second-category posts and all the vast range of local commotal offices were invariably filled from the ranks of local and often locally powerful Welshmen. They were the backbone of the local administration, especially the revenue-gathering administration, of later medieval Wales. If this group was to defect or even to cease to co-operate on any substantial scale, then the effective governance of much of Wales, at least beyond the castles, the boroughs, and their immediate environs, would become well-nigh impossible. This is precisely what happened, especially in the years 1403–6, in much of the country.

Men of power in the locality—those who had been entrusted with the key second-category posts—defected one by one. Among the defectors we can count sheriffs from Flintshire, Caernarfonshire, and Anglesey, two sheriffs from Cardiganshire, three sheriffs from Carmarthenshire, the constable of Dinefwr Castle, the stewards of the lordships of Cydweli, Maelor Saesneg, and Mold, and the deputy steward of Cantref Mawr. And no doubt the list could be easily extended. At the most local level of all, arguably much the most important level in terms of commanding the obedience of the local population, the defections seem to have been equally massive. Precise figures are beyond our reach, but in three of the districts for which the evidence is unusually full—the lordship of Cydweli and the

counties of Flintshire and Anglesey—local officials defected in droves, especially after 1403. One of them may stand for the others: Gwilym ap Gruffudd ap Tudur Llwyd, known to genealogists as the Green Squire, *Ysgweier Gwyrdd*. He was of impeccable descent, being of the stock of Iarddur ap Cynddelw one of the patriarchs of the noble lineages of Anglesey. His forebears had served the native princes of Gwynedd with distinction, but their successors had made the transition to the service of the English kings and princes of Wales, albeit on a more local level. Gwilym himself continued that tradition: he was *rhingyll* or beadle of the commote of Talybolion 1383–5 and *rhaglaw* or bailiff there 1391–2. His personal fortunes also flourished: to his inherited lands he added considerably through his own efforts, notably by exploiting the opportunities provided by the legal device of *prid*, or Welsh mortgage, and he also collected rents from his tenants. In short, Gwilym was a man of considerable authority and wealth in north-east Anglesey. But when the tide of revolt swept across Anglesey Gwilym was swept along with it and met his death as a rebel when the castle of Beaumaris was relieved by English forces.[9]

When individuals of the local stature of Gwilym ap Gruffudd ap Tudur Llwyd crossed the Rubicon of loyalty, they are unlikely to have done so merely as individuals. The local official cadres which ruled medieval Wales were often composed of dynasties and networks; defection was often, therefore, group defection. Gwilym belonged to such a local ruling dynasty: his father, uncle, and cousin had all held office in north-east Anglesey and another cousin was canon of the collegiate church of Caergybi (Holyhead). Rather higher up the ladder of local governance we can see how marriage ties bound together the local élite in peace and in rebellion alike: the powerful sheriff of Cardiganshire in the 1390s was Rhys Ddu, 'the Black', of Morfa Bychan; one of his adjutants as tax-collector and trainee administrator was Maredudd ab Owain, his son-in-law; the bond between them carried both into the ranks of Owain Glyn Dŵr and, for Rhys Ddu, to death in his service. When men of the standing of Rhys Ddu and Gwilym ap Gruffudd defected and often brought with them their kinsmen, officers, and dependants, the future of English rule in Wales was extremely bleak. These were the men and the families who knew the ropes of local control and whose word had commanded respect, even terror, in their respective districts for generations. Shrewd English observers recognized that the battle for the loyalty of Wales turned substantially on who was able to win the hearts and minds of such men. In the aftermath of the revolt, but when its last embers were still aglow, Reginald Grey, lord of Ruthin, who had more direct and sobering experience of the Welsh revolt than most English lords, sized up the situation as follows in a letter to the future Henry V: 'there are many officers . . . that are related to the group that have recently risen in revolt. And until you put those officers in better governance, this

country of North Wales shall never have peace. And if you had those officers under your governance, they could ordain remedy . . .' The key, so Grey in effect concluded, was control of the officers; control of the country would then follow. The commons in parliament had come to the same conclusion as early as 1402 but their proposed solution was more hard-line, the exclusion of all Welshmen from any of the major posts of local governance in Wales, certainly all the first- and second-category posts by our earlier definition. That was the sort of knee-jerk reaction to an emergency which is common, and understandable, among the political classes. It could even be formally implemented with regard to the major posts; but at the more local level there was no alternative to dependence on those local Welshmen who had local power, and alone could exercise it effectively. Once these local officers defected, the lords of Wales had no alternative but to wait for the tide of revolt to recede, to install the local officials, however grudgingly, back in their posts, and to rebuild the same patterns of authority in the same hands as before. Both Rhys Ddu and Gwilym ap Gruffudd ap Tudur died in and for the revolt; but Gwilym's cousin resumed the family's tradition of office-holding in north-east Anglesey and Rhys Ddu's son-in-law, Maredudd ab Owain, was eventually appointed to the post that his father-in-law had once held, that of sheriff of Cardiganshire.[10]

Before taking up his post as sheriff, Maredudd ab Owain had shown his loyalty to the regime by serving in Henry V's expeditions to France. This reminds us that the qualities which these local leaders brought to Glyn Dŵr's cause were not only lineage, wealth, and official positions but also military experience and leadership. In what was still a society with a strong militarist ethos and in which military service was one of the few outlets for fortune and adventure in a poor and overpopulated country, these were very considerable assets. It was, as we have seen, as a military leader that Owain Glyn Dŵr had fancied himself; and the same was certainly true of many of his close associates: his brother Tudur, Henry Don in Cydweli, Hywel ap Tudur ab Ithel in Flintshire, Rhys and Gwilym ap Tudur in Anglesey. Some of them had particularly wide military experience: Bleddyn ap Dafydd ap Madog of Caerfallwch (Flintshire) had served both the king of England and the king of France during his career and ended his life, appropriately enough, fighting alongside Hotspsur at the Battle of Shrewsbury. All of these men would have savoured the compliment that the poet paid to one of their number, Hywel Coetmor of Nantconwy, as 'leader under the planet Mars' (W. *blaenor o dan blaned Mars*). Hywel's effigy still reclines in Llanrwst church, complete with basinet, hauberk, vambrace, and breastplate and an inscription which describes him as an esquire, *armiger*. Hywel was one of Owain's most committed supporters. The military background of Hywel and his fellow squires—for in contemporary English muster-lists as well as in the vernacular

poetry they are termed squires (L. *armigeri*, W. *ysgwieiriaid*)—contributed at least two essential ingredients to Owain's revolt. The first was military know-how and appetite. Different as were garrison duty on the Scottish border or *chevauchées* (cavalry campaigns) across the French countryside from guerrilla warfare in uplands Wales, the experience gained in earlier campaigns and the military egos pampered by such experience were invaluable assets in a revolt which called for stamina and commitment. Secondly, the squires had been the leaders of contingents of Welsh archers and foot-soldiers in the service of the English; such leadership had bred ties of obligation and common service which would prove as invaluable in providing cohesion and authority in the armies of the rebels as they had once done in the retinues of the English king and his war-captains. Wales's long military apprenticeship and that of its local leaders were to serve Owain Glyn Dŵr well.[11]

The squires of Wales brought to his cause one other substantial advantage—a network of relationships through lineage and marriage which bound gentle society together across Wales, or at least across large regions of Wales, to a remarkable degree and thereby helped to override both the natural geographical and governmental fragmentation of the country and the lack of an obvious political and social centre. This should not surprise us. Medieval Wales was a country obsessed, especially at the level of free and noble society, with blood-descent and kinship relationships, especially in the male line but also to some degree through mothers and wives. This is the image overwhelmingly refracted through the medieval poetry, our best guide to the values and priorities of this society; it is also an image amply confirmed by external observers for centuries before and after Owain Glyn Dŵr's day. At one level the social history of late medieval Wales seems to dissolve into a tangled forest of family trees.

Yet in no society, not even in a kin-based society such as medieval Wales, have family descent and relationships been the sole and certainly not the automatic determinant of social and political action. Fission can be quite as common as fusion within families and lineages, especially when face to face with the dilemmas posed by a civil war, as the ties of kin solidarity are prised open by the alternative claims of obligations to lords and calculations of survival and advantage. So it was not infrequently during Glyn Dŵr's revolt. Perhaps the most famous example is that quoted by Sir John Wynn, the Elizabethan antiquary, from the annals of his own family: Ieuan ap Maredudd of Cefn y Fan and Cesail Gyfarch in Eifionydd (Caernarfonshire) 'clave fast to the King', but his brother Robert (Sir John's own direct ancestor) 'taking a clear contrary course, was out with Owain Glyn Dŵr'. There must have been many such divided families across the whole of Wales. In Brecon, for example, the family associated with Dafydd Gam, whom we shall meet below, remained intensely loyal to the king and both

benefited from, and paid a price for, its loyalty; but another branch of the same family, with which it had closely co-operated in earlier times, followed Glyn Dŵr into revolt and its representative, Dafydd ap Hywel Fychan ap Hywel ap Dafydd, forfeited his estates, including those in the suburb of Brecon.[12]

Yet we may well believe that such family divisions were more the exception than the rule. It took great courage not to toe the family line: even the normally restrained royal chancery could hardly conceal its admiration for Maredudd ap Madoc of Maelienydd who had remained loyal to the Crown 'when his brethren and kinsmen became rebels'. In a society where title to land and even office was largely determined by lineage, where the opportunities for personal advancement were still largely restricted by the custom of partibility among male heirs and by strict prohibitions on the outright alienation of land, and where many of the mechanisms of peace-keeping, contracts, and dispute-settlement were firmly grounded in kinship ties, it was more than likely that family solidarity would be the norm and family links pre-eminent in determining social and political responses. Particularly so in times of rebellion. Owain Glyn Dŵr himself referred proudly to two of his closest confidants, John Hanmer and Gruffudd Yonge his chancellor, as 'our kinsmen'; but equally the government could identify the group basis of the rebels' organization by referring to 'the kinsmen and affines' of a rebel leader, as if they were automatically implicated in his rebellion. In such a kin-dominated society one of the more obvious ways of containing the revolt was by the arrest of, and taking security from, kinsmen. This was precisely the policy urged by the commons in parliament on the government as a way of dealing with Glyn Dŵr's rebellion. In 1402 they urged that 'the most powerful and nearest cousins of a malefactor's kin group' be arrested and imprisoned until he himself was arrested; in 1412 they likewise demanded that 'the nearest relatives and blood relations' of those in rebellion should be imprisoned because, so they claimed, the rebels persisted in their rebellion precisely because they were supported by their relatives and kinsmen. They further drove home their point by recalling that such a policy had been used of old in Wales to scotch incipient revolts. Indeed, back in 1345 it had been pointed out that in the days of 'good King Edward the Conqueror' a Welsh judge had proffered precisely the same advice, by suggesting that the best way of keeping the peace in Wales was to ensure 'that when a prominent Welshman had committed a felony all the great men nearest to him by blood should be attached and arrested until the felon was taken'. In short, the English government had recognized that in a kin-based society the best way to strike at an individual was through his kin-group.[13]

But the formula also worked in reverse: defection or rebellion within the family spread quickly along the branches of the family tree and then leapt, through marriage links, to neighbouring or even distant families. The role of the

kin-network as one of the major agencies through which rebellion spread in Owain Glyn Dŵr's Wales is rarely, if ever, specifically commented upon in such documentation as survives. But all that we know of the society of the time suggests that it was a, and probably the, key agency in the process. The survival of an exceptionally rich corpus of genealogical manuscripts from the late fifteenth century onwards (that is, within three or four generations of Glyn Dŵr's death in some cases) means that we know far more about the descent and marriages of the *uchelwyr* the free noble Welsh, than about any group of comparable socio-economic standing in contemporary England. According to the classificatory nomenclature that was becoming current in England in this period a few of them were esquires, but the vast majority were yeomen or less. (When the word *uchelwr* is translated it is often by the English word 'franklin', with its emphasis on freedom, *franc*, rather than on wealth.) In spite of their often modest economic standing, so proud were they of their descent that they were scrupulously careful about committing it to memory and eventually to parchment and paper. Furthermore, the rule of partibility among male heirs encouraged the genealogical record to extend laterally as well as vertically into a cascading luxury of detail. Where these genealogies can be checked against record—as is particularly possible from the rich deed collections for north-east Wales—they prove to be remarkably accurate (though not without some significant errors).

The two accompanying diagrams (Tables 3 and 4) represent greatly simplified examples from north Wales of the interlocking characters of Welsh society at this socio-economic level and of the known participation of members of the families in question in Glyn Dŵr's revolt. This is not to suggest, of course, that support for the rebellion was determined solely or necessarily by ties of lineage and marriage. Yet the survival of such a rich corpus of genealogical writings and the recurrent dwelling on lineage and marriage links in the classical poetry of the period provides us with an insight into the way this society viewed and valued itself. It perceived itself as an extended family or, perhaps more accurately, a collection of interrelated and overlapping dynasties of noble birth. It was an intensely proud and inward-looking society which, unlike its successors three or four generations hence, largely drew its marriage partners from within a restricted group of Welsh families, often in flagrant violation of canon-law teaching on the prohibited degrees in marriage. The network of marriage and kinship links provided it with a pattern or relationship and contacts which not infrequently straddled the whole, or at least a good part, of north or south Wales and indeed extended occasionally into both. Blood and marriage were in turn reinforced by shared values and a common mythology. The world of the *uchelwyr* of late medieval Wales was claustrophobic and ingrown, but it was an intimate and

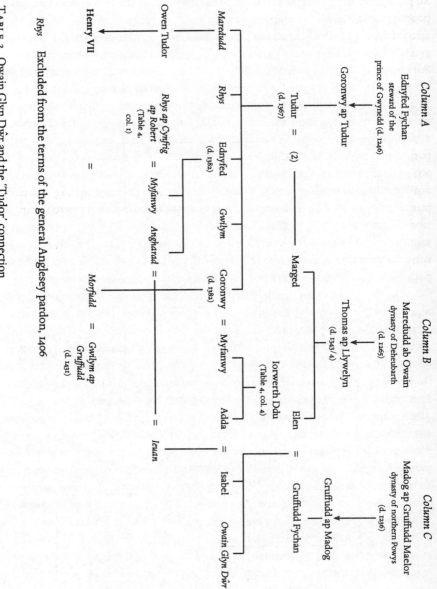

TABLE 3. Owain Glyn Dŵr and the 'Tudor' connection

Rhys Excluded from the terms of the general Anglesey pardon, 1406

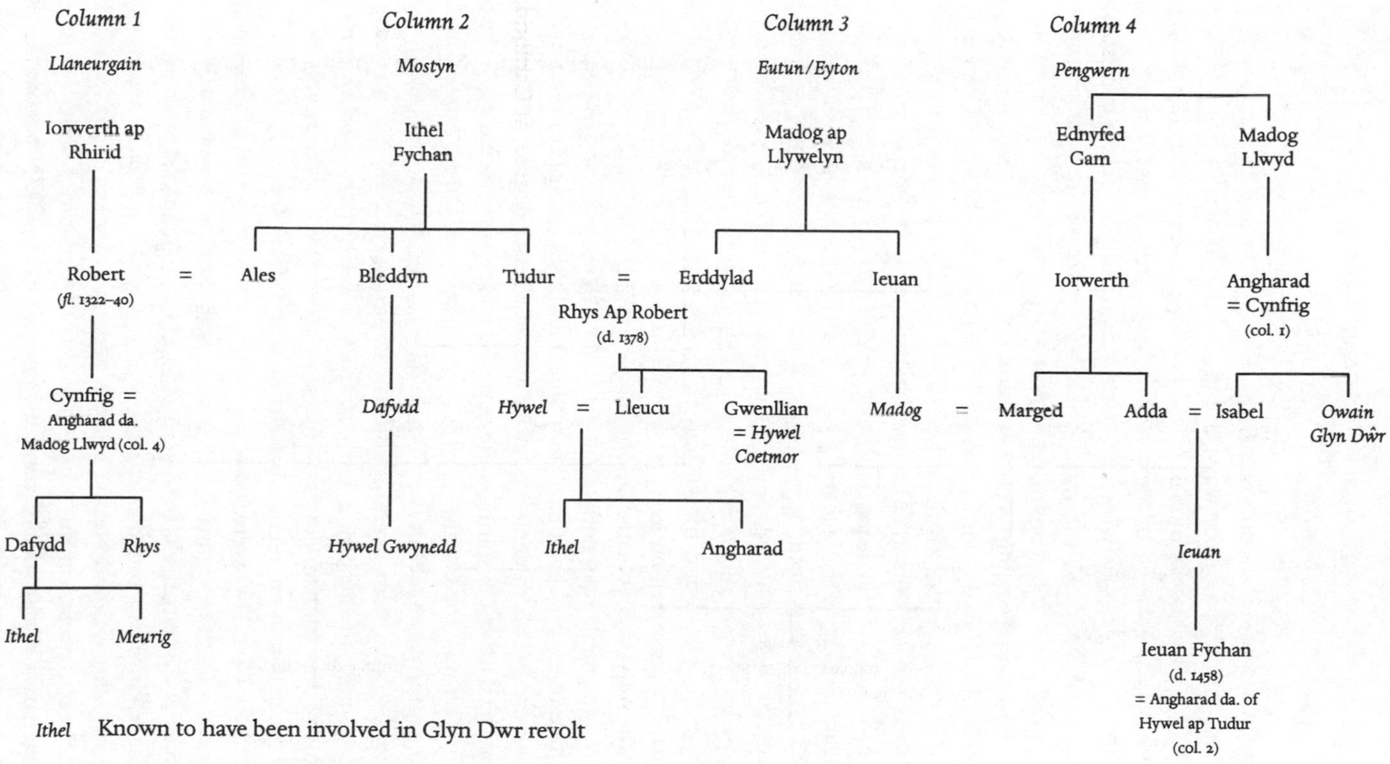
Column 1
Llaneurgain
Iorwerth ap Rhirid
Robert (fl. 1322–40) = Ales
Cynfrig = Angharad da. Madog Llwyd (col. 4)
Dafydd
Rhys
Ithel
Meurig
Column 2
Mostyn
Ithel Fychan
Bleddyn
Tudur = Erddylad
Dafydd
Hywel Gwynedd
Hywel = Lleucu
Ithel
Angharad
Column 3
Eutun/Eyton
Madog ap Llywelyn
Ieuan
Rhys Ap Robert (d. 1378)
Gwenllian = Hywel Coetmor
Madog = Marged
Column 4
Pengwern
Ednyfed Gam
Madog Llwyd
Iorwerth
Angharad = Cynfrig (col. 1)
Adda = Isabel
Owain Glyn Dŵr
Ieuan
Ieuan Fychan (d. 1458) = Angharad da. of Hywel ap Tudur (col. 2)

Ithel Known to have been involved in Glyn Dwr revolt

TABLE 4. Rebellion and family links in north-east Wales

remarkably cohesive world. That intimacy and cohesion served Owain Glyn Dŵr remarkably well.[14]

The other group whose support was essential if Glyn Dŵr's movement was to be more than a local conspiracy was composed of his local and regional secular clergy and members of the monastic and mendicant orders. They did not disappoint him; indeed, several of them turned out to be among his most zealous supporters. Some of those who held key regional positions in the ecclesiastical hierarchy—archdeacons, deans, prebendaries—were prominent in his support. They included the archdeacons of St Asaph and Bangor. They were drawn almost to a man from the leading Welsh native families; as such they were almost inevitably sucked into the vortex of revolt by their kinship links, and they in turn contributed no doubt not a little of their organizational experience to its promotion, as their predecessors in office had done to the earlier Welsh revolt *manqué* in 1345. Archdeacons and deans may have provided the organizational skills; but at this grass-roots level the leadership and the moral sanction of the local clergy, beneficed and unbeneficed, were even more important. When we find the rectors of Cilcain, Whitford, and Halkyn and three named chaplains named among the prominent rebels in Flintshire or note that four canons of Holyhead and sixteen beneficed and fifteen unbeneficed clerks were among those who craved pardon for rebellion in Anglesey, we are catching a glimpse of the wide support the movement elicited among the local clergy.[15]

But in terms of the fiery enthusiasm which so often makes revolts contagious, it was three other groups in particular who caught the eye of contemporaries. The first were Welsh students at Oxford and, to a lesser degree, at Cambridge: they were accused of conspiring, both in public and private (including in the city privies at Oxford), for Owain, of encouraging men to join his forces, and of purveying information about the state of affairs in England to him. Many of the accusations against them were doubtless wild and fabricated, but it is easy to understand both the suspicion they attracted and the starry-eyed enthusiasm with which many of them doubtless heard of the progress of the revolt. Within Wales a group which was recognized as providing a pool of ready and predictable supporters for Glyn Dŵr were the communities of Cistercian monks and Augustinian canons in those monasteries which were seen as essentially Welsh in orientation and sympathies. In Wales, as in Ireland, Cistercian monasteries in particular fell into two broad groups: on the one hand were those houses (such as Tintern, Margam, and Neath) in areas of secure English control and often monastic recruitment; on the other were those monasteries which were embedded in native Welsh society, recruited their monks and abbots from the local Welsh population, and were often zealous as upholders and preservers of Welsh

lore, literature, and mythology. These latter houses provided a ready and enthusiastic recruiting-ground of fervid supporters for Owain Glyn Dŵr; among
those known to have enlisted in his cause were the abbots of Conway, Strata
Florida, Whitland, and Llantarnam and the heads of the houses of Augustinian
canons at Beddgelert and Bardsey. The only one of them who emerged with
some individuality from the sources is John ap Hywel, abbot of the Cistercian
house of Llantarnam near Caerleon in south-east Wales: he was remembered as
a man of great wisdom and intense personal devotion, 'a Welsh Savonarola' as
Sir John Lloyd memorably described him; but it was his devotion to Owain's
cause and his readiness to die for it at the Battle of Pwll Melyn in 1405 which
ensured that his prowess entered into folk memory and so eventually reached the
ears of the Scottish historian Walter Bower. The third group which was widely
recognized as fomentors and supporters of rebellion were the mendicant friars.
The Franciscans in particular had a notorious record as plotters against Henry IV
and paid a horrific price for their conspiracies, alleged or real. Their brethren in
part of Wales followed suit: the Franciscans at Llan-faes in Anglesey joined the
initial revolt and paid dearly for it in the destruction of their house and the
dispersal of their goods; even as late as 1406 six of them were excluded by name
from the general pardon granted to the inhabitants of Anglesey, and when the
house was eventually re-established in 1414 it was specifically stated that only two
of the complement of eight friars were to be 'of the Welsh nation'. The Domini-
cans likewise provided Owain with some valued supporters: his roving ambassador, charged with key missions to Scotland, Ireland, and France, was one of
them, Hywel Edwere or Eddouyer.[16]

Owain seems to have enjoyed a fairly broad measure of grass-roots support
among the clergy, monks, and friars of Wales, or rather of Welsh-dominated
Wales. But the most striking manifestation of the success that came to attend his
movement was the eventual defection of ecclesiastics of national, even international, standing to his cause. During 1403–4, as the revolt reached its climacteric,
three prominent clergymen threw their support behind him. Lewis Byford could
look back on a career which had taken him to universities and a long spell of
service in the papal court at Rome before he was nominated by the pope to be
bishop of Bangor in August 1404. At that stage any effective control of his new
diocese involved acknowledging the reality of Glyn Dŵr's authority in the area;
Bishop Lewis seems to have done so with alacrity, for the profits of the parish
from which he took his name—Byford in Herefordshire—were declared forfeit
because he was 'in the company of Owain Glyn Dŵr' in April 1405. By that date
he shared that company with an even more ambitious and important defector.
Gruffudd Yonge had a brilliant academic career and a panoply of degrees to his
name; he had also collected a rich haul of ecclesiastical livings, canonries, and

prebends for which he could be truly grateful. He had little of which he could complain other, perhaps, than the fact that his illegitimacy might debar him from the highest ecclesiastical office. It may be that it was the prospect of achieving such an ambition in Owain Glyn Dŵr's service which persuaded him to defect in 1403–4; equally his relationship by blood to Glyn Dŵr—for both of them came from the tightly knit and intermarried dynasties of north-east Wales—may have been the determining factor. Be that as it may, once he had transferred his loyalty, his talent and ambition quickly gave him a pre-eminent place in Glyn Dŵr's affairs—as his chancellor, archdeacon of Merioneth, and from February 1407 bishop of Bangor. He may well have had ambitions for the new augmented archbishopric which Glyn Dŵr's programme envisaged for Wales; indeed, Gruffudd Yonge may have been the moving spirit behind the proposal.[17]

Another competitor for that post, and the most important ecclesiastical defector to Glyn Dŵr's cause, was John Trefor, bishop of St Asaph since 1395. In experience and background he was far and away the most impressive figure in the episcopate of Wales in his day: a university-trained doctor of civil and canon law and a papal chaplain and auditor, he had become from the 1390s a respected and experienced servant of the king of England at central and regional level. He served as an ambassador to Scotland, acted as a parliamentary spokesman and occasional member of council, and from 16 August 1399 (that is, the very day on which Henry Bolingbroke escorted King Richard II to Chester as his prisoner) he held the post of chamberlain or chief financial officer of the counties of Chester and Flintshire. His experience and credentials were similar to those of scores of 'civil servant' bishops of late medieval England, and his commitment to the new Lancastrian regime was obvious and well publicized. But as the turbulent events of 1403–4 in north-east Wales unfolded, his loyalty to his English employers was put to the test and ultimately found to be wanting. The first test came in the summer months of 1403 as Hotspur—the man who had been appointed justiciar or chief governor of Cheshire and Flintshire only two days before Trefor was chosen to fill the top financial post there—made his bid to oust Henry IV from the throne and launched that bid in Cheshire and north-east Wales. Trefor's loyalty seems to have survived that experience; but within the next year he seems to have defected to Glyn Dŵr: in his own account as chamberlain for 1403–4, his fee was cancelled with an explanatory note, 'because he is a rebel, so it is reported'. We cannot guess exactly how John Trefor wrestled with his conscience during these months; but it is not improper to guess that at least two considerations may have weighed with him. The first was immediate and geographical: in the summer of 1403 the Welsh of the county of Flint, and with it much of the diocese of St Asaph, defected *en masse* to Glyn Dŵr's (or Hotspur's) cause. As the year wore on and the tide of revolt flowed ever more strongly, it

may be that the bishop felt that he had no option but to follow where his flock had already led. The second consideration which is likely to have weighed with him was cultural and genealogical. As the sole native bishop in Wales, as an acknowledged and munificent patron of Welsh poetry and specifically of Iolo Goch (virtually Owain Glyn Dŵr's household bard), as one who had given ample warnings to the government of the need to deal sensitively and imaginatively with disaffection in Wales, Bishop John Trefor is likely to have found his position increasingly uncomfortable as the revolt gathered momentum. His discomfort was almost certainly compounded by genealogy. His descent is not known, but his name bespeaks an association with the area near Llangollen (in the lordship of Chirkland) and suggests that he came from the tangle of closely related and intermarried Welsh *uchelwr* families who ruled the roost in his corner of north-east Wales. He would almost certainly have been acquainted with his contemporary and neighbour, Owain Glyn Dŵr, squire of Sycharth; and once Owain's uprising became a truly national revolt, the strains on Bishop John's patriotic heart-strings were more than he could withstand.[18]

The support of men of the standing of Lewis Byford, Gruffudd Yonge, and John Trefor enhanced Owain's cause in several ways. It gave him the imprimatur of men of experience in the corridors of ecclesiastical and papal power. It also gave him the services of university-trained and worldly-wise clerics, who knew how to draft polished documents and formulate policies. It can be no accident that it was in 1405–6 that Glyn Dŵr's most imaginative and daring initiatives—the alliance with France, the Tripartite Indenture, and the transfer of ecclesiastical allegiance to the Avignonese pope—were put forward; they almost certainly came from the pens of his new-found ecclesiastical advisers. Such men—especially John Trefor, with his well-honed administrative and political skills—were particularly well placed to give an international dimension to Owain's revolt. It was Gruffudd Yonge who led the delegation which sealed the alliance with the king of France, and it was the bishops of Bangor and St Asaph who went on a mission to Scotland in 1406. They also brought one other quality which was crucial if the momentum of the revolt was to be sustained against the odds: steadfastness. Byford's fate is unknown; John Trefor possibly died in Paris in April 1410, appropriately enough on a mission to try to revive the Franco-Welsh alliance; Gruffudd Yonge was back in Paris in 1415 on a similar mission. Yonge never returned to Wales: he lived for at least another twenty years, having to content himself with the position, successively, of bishop of Ross in Scotland and of Hippo in North Africa to make up for the loss of his see at Bangor. His memoirs would have made for interesting reading.

In a hierarchic and deferential society, the support of the leaders of local society was crucial to the credibility and success of a revolt; but they in turn needed to

command, in whatever ways, the support or at least the acquiescence of a fair proportion of the local population. This indeed seems often to have happened in Wales during the peak years of Owain's revolt. On this score well-placed contemporary observers seem to have been agreed: 'in this autumn [1401]', commented Adam of Usk, 'all north Wales, Cardigan, and Powys sided with Owain'; 'the whole Welsh nation (Fr. *la natioun del Walsherie*) with few exceptions, are party to this evil scheme of rebellion, and are committed to it, as becomes ever more fully apparent from day to day by their support', was the opinion of John Fairford at Brecon in July 1403; the sheriff of Herefordshire and his colleagues took a similar view, that 'the whole Welsh nation was of the same mind as the rebels'; while the financial report for Flintshire in 1403 concluded despairingly that 'the whole community of the lordship of Maelor Saesneg became rebels before the feast of St Peter [1 August]'. Such comments are commonplace in the sources. One may, of course, discount them as exaggerated, since many of them were calculated to try to persuade the government to hasten its military plans or to explain the catastrophic fall in revenue from Wales. But that is no reason for dismissing them altogether. Such financial records as survive make it abundantly clear how total was the collapse of English administrative and financial control in Wales at the height of the rebellion. In Chirk in north-east Wales no current revenue was collected in 1403–4 'because the tenants of the lordship were rebels and obeyed Owain Glyn Dŵr, traitor'; at the same time it was reported that no courts could be held in Grosmont, Whitecastle, and Dingestow in the lordship of Monmouth in the south-east 'because the tenants were rebels'. The Duchy of Lancaster lordships in Wales are particularly well documented across the years of the revolt and reveal dramatically how the rebellion overwhelmed them from 1402 onwards. The lordships consisted of Cydweli (the three commotes of Cydweli, Carnwyllion, and Iscennen) in the south-west, the huge and profitable lordship of Brecon in eastern Wales, the sub-lordship of Ogmore on the Glamorgan coast, and the rich lordship of Monmouth and Threecastles in the south-east. In the three years 1399–1402 they yielded an average income of over £2,800 annually, equivalent to that of an average-sized English earldom. By 1403 no income was reported from Cydweli, Brecon, and Ogmore; by 1405 even Monmouth yielded no income; and as late as 1406–7 no revenue was apparently collected from any of the estates, 'because the lands and lordships had been devastated by the rebels'. Such comments, of course, are in part an indication of the havoc caused by the rebellion rather than a reflection of the measure of active support it commanded; but, so often are they accompanied by the phrase 'because the tenants are rebels', that we can also accept them as evidence of local acquiescence, if not necessarily active support, for Owain's cause. And the story is the same, especially during the years 1403–6, from every part of Wales. Pembroke in the far south-west figures in

the documentation of the revolt; so does Chepstow in the south-east; so likewise does Ellesmere on the border in Shropshire or Llangennith in Gower. Where there was evidence of the revolt, there we may also surmise there were sympathizers and supporters.[19]

It is, of course, quite another matter to gauge the depth and extent of such support; but an occasional figure adds credence to the supposition that the revolt did indeed win mass support. In three vills at Bishopscastle, on the north-east border of Wales, as early as 1402 seventy-seven Welshmen forfeited their lands because of their support for the rebellion. In Flintshire a series of inquisitions from October 1406 onwards identifies the names of almost 150 rebels: ninety-four of them had died during the rebellion, a further eleven are specifically said to have been killed at the Battle of Shrewsbury in 1403, ten had died after making their submissions but before they had made their fine for rebellion, twenty-nine were still regarded as rebels and two had fled to Scotland with the bishop of St Asaph. These figures from Flintshire are not, of course, an accurate guide to the numbers who actively supported the rebellion; they refer only to those who had died during or shortly after the rebellion and to the hard core who persisted in their rebellion even after Glyn Dŵr's cause had gone into decline. We are probably much nearer a realistic number in the 1,003 names which are listed in the communal fine imposed on the county (of Flint) at a session held before Gilbert Talbot in March 1407 'for divers rebellions, treasons, and other offences in adhering to Owain of Glyndyfrdwy'. In Anglesey over 2,000 names are included in the list of those who made their submissions in November 1406. It is likely that many of those included in such lists may not have been actively engaged in the revolt but rather were anxious to be included in a communal pardon in order to avoid any prospect of prosecution or challenge to their landed titles subsequently. Nevertheless the figures are very suggestive, especially in the light of a later account of 1408–9 which records the names of 159 landholders (thereby excluding wives, dependants, servants, labourers, craftsmen, and so on) in Anglesey who had either died in the revolt (102) or who had not yet submitted (forty-seven).[20]

All in all such record evidence as survives serves to endorse the opinion of contemporary observers that the revolt elicited a very wide measure of popular support in many parts of Wales. A considerable number of women figure in the list of rebels; so also do craftsmen, including smiths, clothworkers, and cobblers; while the registers of confiscated lands likewise confirm that men and women of very small means were committed to Glyn Dŵr's cause. Paradoxically, another barometer of the appeal of the revolt in its heyday was the number of Englishmen in Wales who came to support it. The revolt was, of course, essentially a Welsh revolt and was seen as such, 'the rebellion of the Welsh commons' (Fr. *rebellioun*

des comyns galeys) as one observer called it. Its programme was couched in virulent anti-English rhetoric; much of its fury was directed against the English establishment and English boroughs in Wales; and the striking successes of the rebels certainly inspired fears of an apocalypse among many English settlers in Wales. Yet the alignment of support for, and opposition to, the revolt did not coincide exactly with that of the ethnic divisions of Wales. Some men with convincingly English or Anglo-Norman names came to be acknowledged supporters of the revolt, either because they came to subscribe to its ambitions or because they had calculated that the tide in Wales had now turned irreversibly in Owain's favour and that they must come to terms with it. Defections were apparently few in the castellated and walled English towns of Wales; communal solidarity ensured that ranks were closed against the rebel in such places. Even in these boroughs a few English townsmen—such as John Sparrowhawk of Cardiff, Thomas le Ferrour of Rhuddlan, or David Perrot of Tenby—succumbed to the Welsh cause, as also, much less surprisingly, did Welsh burgesses such as Morgan ap Dafydd Fychan in Brecon or John Llwyd in Carmarthen. It was in the countryside, especially in eastern and southern Wales, that English defectors to the Welsh cause were particularly evident. The clerk who recorded that William Thorot, an Englishman (L. *Anglicus*) from Flintshire, had become a sworn supporter (L. *homo juratus*) of Owain Glyn Dŵr could hardly conceal his surprise at such an unnatural act. But his was a much less sensational case than that of Philip Skidmore of Troy near Monmouth: one-time master-sergeant of Monmouth Castle and subsequently captain of the garrison at Carreg Cennen Castle in the early days of the revolt, he defected to Glyn Dŵr and paid the ultimate price when he was executed at Shrewsbury in 1411. Among other Englishmen whose land was confiscated for their support of the Welsh cause were several who were moderately wealthy by Welsh standards: Thomas Huntley's lands in Monmouth and Abergavenny were valued at £20 as were those of William de la Mare of Llangennith in Gower, while the estates confiscated from John Merlawe, John Flemyng, and Isabel Lanfey in Glamorgan were estimated jointly to have a value of up to £40 per annum. Such examples may be no more than the tip of the iceberg of more widespread defections among English families which had been settled in Wales for generations. Even on their own terms they are an eloquent comment on Glyn Dŵr's revolt. An uprising which could attract such English supporters—and many other examples could be quoted—to its cause now enjoyed such a measure of success that it had the makings of a truly national revolt, a movement which was demanding the re-examination of allegiances in Wales right across the social and even ethnic spectrum and from one end of Wales to the other.[21]

Success breeds success; it also attracts to its cause those whose prime commitment is to the success itself, both to the opportunities it brings and the demands

it makes. As in all revolts commitment to the cause varied not only from individual to individual, but also from time to time within an individual's own response-pattern. On occasion the tide of enthusiasm was overwhelming. John Fairford's letter of 5 July 1403 recorded such an occasion: 'all Carmarthenshire, Cydweli, Carnwyllion and Iscennen were sworn to Owen yesterday.' He was reporting a massive act of defection and affirmation. It was one which was repeated in many parts of Wales across these months, publicly manifested, it would seem, in a formal swearing of allegiance to Glyn Dŵr—for the phrase 'sworn man of Owain' (L. *homo juratus*) recurs in different parts of Wales. Some who joined his cause were desperadoes and hot-heads: it was the Welsh chronicle which referred to them dismissively as 'youngsters and rascals' (W. *yfiengtid ar diriedwyr*). Others came to support him from compulsion, but once they had done so remained faithful to the cause. Such a one was Gruffudd ap Madog Crych of Hawarden. Captured on his way to market in Ruthin, he was forced to swear loyalty to Owain, but soon became more zealous than his captors in the service of his new lord. He was active in the attacks on the town and castle of Rhuddlan, was implicated in killing several of its burgesses, and extended the ambit of his activities to include assaults on other English towns in Hopedale and Shropshire, until he was eventually caught and hanged for his service to Glyn Dŵr. Many others followed his example, serving Owain far away from their homes and dying in his service: it was while he was defending Owain's control of Harlech Castle that Llywelyn ap Madog ap Llywelyn of distant Dyffryn Clwyd was killed, and likewise it was a cannon-ball at Aberystwyth which terminated the life of William Gwyn ap Rhys Llwyd, many scores of miles from his native Cydweli.[22]

Glyn Dŵr's revolt was founded on a vision and it drew more than its fair share of committed visionaries to its support. But as in all revolts many others joined because the tide of success was overwhelming. One man and one community may stand for them all. The revolt must have posed an acute dilemma for Gruffudd ap Gwilym. He had no reason to be disgruntled with the world as it was: possibly the richest Welshman in the north Wales of his day, he enjoyed two major territorial footholds in Flintshire and Anglesey; and the measure of his acceptability to the powers that be was the appointment of his son to be sheriff of Anglesey in 1396. The antics of his distant cousins, Rhys and Gwilym ap Tudor, in joining Glyn Dŵr's revolt from its beginning and then capturing Conway Castle must have been embarrassing for him, but not sufficiently so as to pose a challenge to his loyalty. But when the revolt swept across Flintshire in 1403 he and his brother and three sons were swept along by the tide. Gruffudd and his brother died—both were well on in years—before the tide turned and their lands were therefore technically forfeit; but his sons were able to extricate themselves by a timely surrender before further damage was done to the family fortunes. Indeed,

Gruffudd's son, Gwilym, was to be one of the most spectacular beneficiaries of the revolt. The family's flirtation with the revolt in 1403–5 was, one suspects, no more than a necessary and opportunistic convenience. So, no doubt, was that of many individuals and communities. The men of certain upland districts in Brecon were unusually honest in outlining their predicament. They struck a bargain with the king in February 1404 whereby they agreed to pay him 100 marks (£66 13s. 4d.) in ten weekly instalments. It is the conditions attached to the payment which are particularly revealing: the sum paid was to be deducted from their outstanding debts if they came to the king's peace, as they would indeed do as soon as the rebels of Glamorgan were punished; but if no action was taken against these rebels before next May, then they would not be able to come into the king's peace (Fr. *ne pourront venir al pees*) and the bargain would be void. It was a starkly candid assessment of the reasons why communities and individuals found it so difficult to withstand the rebels and how the absence of effective royal protection was tantamount to a surrender of power.[23]

The story was the same in many parts of Wales. Adam of Usk was perhaps the least convincing of these reluctant rebels when he claimed that he joined the Welsh rebels 'against his will and left them as quickly as he could'. It is easier to swallow the claim of the men of Whittington in Shropshire that 'they adhered to Owain Glyn Dŵr on account of the hard war he had made on them', or the protestations of the men of Flint that they 'were serving by compulsion in the ranks of the rebels . . . and wished to return home and dwell in peace'. Individuals likewise pleaded duress. Some of them were remarkably frank about the reasons for their temporary lapse of loyalty, such as the man from Denbigh who was 'in the company of Owain Glyn Dŵr until he had put his goods in safekeeping and afterwards he came to the castle of Ruthin'. It is easy to dismiss such claims as exercises in self-exculpation, but the English government and its local commanders made a similar point. Henry IV thought that coercion explained the support that Glyn Dŵr enjoyed; so in 1405 did John Stanley in Cheshire when he noted that it was the absence of an effective English presence which allowed the rebels to retain their grip over the local population. The keeper of Conway Castle was even more optimistic in his assessment. His comment (put into modern English) is worth quoting at some length, coming as it does from the heartland of the rebellion.

I would bet my life that if 200 men were placed in Conway and 200 in Caernarfon, stationed there from Candlemas (2 February) until the feast of Saints Philip and James (1 May), then the commons of Caernarvonshire would come to peace and pay their obligations to their lord as well as they have ever done; but if this proposal be delayed until the summer, that would not be achieved so easily, for then the rebels may lie low [lie withoute], but they cannot do so now. Also I have heard myself many of the gentlemen

and commons of Merionethshire and Caernarvonshire swear that all men of their shires, except four or five gentlemen and a few vagabonds, would wish to come to peace if Englishmen were left in the country to protect them from mischief-makers . . .

Such comments were in part designed to explain away the failures of the government and to galvanize the king and his advisers into decisive action; but they also surely rightly identify that, as in all revolts, the majority sat on the fence as long as it was possible to do so, and that the success of the rebellion owed as much to the absence of effective counter-measures as it did to the commitment of the zealots.[24]

In such circumstances it is no surprise that affiliations were often short-lived, as men calculated their advantages and sized up the situation. In particular it is not surprising that at the outset of the rebellion some of Owain's fellow-conspirators (including his own brother, Tudur, and the dean of St. Asaph) quickly decided that what had taken place was no more than a sudden and irresponsible rush of blood to the head. But the same was true later even in the heady days of the revolt: we know the names of at least three men who stood side by side with Henry Don in the attack on Kidwelly Castle in August 1403 but were within a very short time leasing land, holding office, and generally repairing the credentials of their loyalty. As in all revolts of a guerrilla nature, where the measure of success varied from region to region and month to month, it was very difficult for those of easy convictions, or none, to read the situation accurately. Under those circumstances some fled in order to avoid the dilemma: at least four men from Wrexham are recorded as opting to find refuge in Chester rather than be compelled to join Glyn Dŵr's cause in their own town. Others of a more malleable disposition cleverly sought to serve two masters while deceiving both: it is through the activities of two such men, David Whitmore and Ieuan ap Maredudd of Flintshire, that we know of Owain's parliament at Harlech. There must have been many like them throughout Wales.[25]

Paradoxically, such duplicities and haverings are a tribute to the success of the revolt. Whether they liked it or not—and most of them possibly liked it not at all—it put men on the spot. Its success was such that it demanded a response, even if that response turned out to be only temporary and calculated. By the end of 1403 it had encompassed virtually the whole of Wales in its ambit; it thereby demanded a response from every corner of the country. For the first time in its history Wales had been galvanized into a single political unit by the ambitions and pretensions of one man; its natural political fragmentation had been overcome in the vision that he presented and in the remarkable success and stamina which characterized his movement. Owain Glyn Dŵr's rebellion was the first, and last, truly national revolt that Wales has experienced.

*

National revolts rarely, if ever, command universal support; it is only subsequent historical mythology which occasionally casts such an aura around them. There could certainly be no prospect that Glyn Dŵr's revolt would command universal support or acquiescence, or anything like it. Wales in his day was formally an ethnically divided country; the English within it were the targets of Glyn Dŵr's spleen, and they were, therefore, naturally and inevitably his opponents. There were, as we have seen, some exceptions to this rule; but they were no more than exceptions; and the contemporary expectation that if one was English (L. *anglicus*) one was also an opponent of Glyn Dŵr was certainly generally true.

It was particularly true of the English boroughs in Wales. They were the prime targets of Glyn Dŵr's initial assault, and understandably so, since they were the obvious centres of Englishness, commercial privilege, and ethnic exclusion. By the same token they were both physically and psychologically the obvious centres from which resistance to the revolt was to be mounted. After all, the revolt was for them in a very real sense a matter of life or death. The burgesses certainly suffered the heaviest casualties of any group during the revolt: some fifty of the inhabitants of Carmarthen were killed in the assault on the town in 1403. Their houses were burnt to the ground, especially those in the extra-mural suburbs, as happened at Kidwelly again in 1403. The losses in goods, stock, and trade were immense even when we have made all due allowance for insurance claims being greatly exaggerated: nineteen English burgesses of Caernarfon estimated their losses at £1,275; John Collier, the leading townsman of Harlech, itemized his losses much more precisely—165 head of cattle, forty horses, 100 sheep, 100 goats, and goods to the value of £40; in Carmarthen, a much richer town, Thomas Dyer put a round figure of £1,000 on goods lost to the rebels.[26]

It is no wonder that such burgesses were in the forefront of the opposition to Glyn Dŵr. It was they who had to scramble together a scratch force to defend their towns when the first onslaught fell on them and to reinforce the professional garrisons when the revolt was at its height. It was no idle boast of the men of Denbigh to claim that they had kept watch and ward of the town for four years; the surviving local accounts—with the roll-call of local surnames such as Swynmore, Pigot, and Salisbury—bear them out. At Kidwelly likewise during the critical summer months of 1403 it was an amateur home-guard force of local townsmen—Balhedes, Castiels, Hicdons, Aylwards, and Jordans—who manned the castle walls as Henry Don and his allies launched their attacks. Similarly at Caernarfon it was appropriate that it was a man with a major stake in the town—Robert Parys, owner of two towers, six burgages, and 200 acres of land— who should have been in charge of the castle at the height of the revolt. The support of these local burgesses was crucial in other directions. It was from their

coffers that the moneys were found, sometimes supplemented by a royal subsidy, to make hurried repairs to the town walls and gates, as happened at Kidwelly, Monmouth, and Brecon. The richest merchants might be expected to dip even further into their purses to provide loans to tide over the recurrent cash-flow problem which overwhelmed Henry IV's government as it tried to quell the revolt: Thomas Rede of Carmarthen, whom we met earlier, loaned the king 100 marks on one of his campaigns into Wales and later, with Llywelyn Fychan ap Llywelyn Goch, raised £400 to help the young Prince Henry arrange for the defence of Thomas's home town of Carmarthen. It was these same burgesses who in the peak years of the revolt plied their ships to Bristol and Chester to provision the beleaguered little boroughs of Wales: Caernarfon was supplied by the public-spirited efforts of one of its burgesses, Thomas de Walton; while in south Wales one of the richest local merchants, John Sely of Llansteffan, sailed his ships (one of them was captured at Carmarthen by the rebel, Henry Don) to various ports in England and Ireland in search of victuals for the coastal towns and castles of Wales.[27]

The burgesses were the most identifiable group in their opposition to Glyn Dŵr and it is their activities which the essentially castle- and borough-oriented documentation highlights. But in lowland eastern and southern Wales and in the Englishries or 'foreignries' (as they were called) around the castellated boroughs of the north and west, the English rural settlers—many of whose families had been settled for generations, even centuries, in the area—were also no doubt in the forefront of local opposition. For example, Glyn Dŵr's great victorious march down the Tywi valley was stopped in its tracks west of Carmarthen on 11 July 1403 by a force led by Thomas, Lord Carew, and no doubt assembled from English tenants and neighbours in Pembrokeshire and the surrounding lordships. Around Hay on Wye on the English border the defence of the town and castle was organized by John Bedell and his son, members of a prominent local family with interests which straddled the town and its rich agricultural hinterland. A very similar role was played by the Harvards of Pontwilym in the defence of Brecon and by the Mortons in Kidwelly (one of whose number took over as constable of the castle in October 1403).[28]

It was altogether to be expected that those who were, or regarded themselves as, English should be prominent in the opposition to Glyn Dŵr within Wales; they had everything to lose by his success. But he was also opposed vigorously by a very considerable number of his fellow Welshmen; indeed, they often paid a heavier price for their opposition since it apparently cut so clean across the natural grain of their loyalties. They were an object of hatred to their fellow Welshmen and of deep suspicion to the English. Thus, the king had to issue special letters of protection to Maredudd ab Einion of Builth because, to quote the letters themselves, 'he has remained loyal throughout the Welsh rebellion . . .

during which time people not knowing him and supposing him a rebel have threatened to injure him'. Others had likewise to take special measures to counter the assumption that, being Welshmen, they were therefore by definition rebels. We hear, for example, of the parson of Hanmer in Maelor Saesneg (Flintshire) coming to Chester with eight of his parishioners to swear fealty to the king and prince of Wales and to proclaim publicly that 'they were never in the company of Owain Glyn Dŵr nor were they accomplices with him in the burning of towns and houses and the killing of Englishmen'. Others went further, indeed dangerously so, to show their loyalty, notably by spying on behalf of the English authorities. Bleddyn ap Madog Gryg was dispatched on various missions all over north Wales by the steward of the prince of Wales's household to spy on the movements of the Welsh rebels; Iorwerth ab Ithel ab Owen played an even more dangerous game by conducting a force from Rhuddlan to ambush the rebels at Caerwys. Iorwerth paid for his bravery with his life; and so did Maredudd Ieuan Gwyn, another Flintshire man. Maredudd's story as told by his daughter—even when we have made all allowances for the embellishments that such stories involve—lifts a welcome edge of the curtain on the perils of life for a Welshman loyal to the English government during the revolt. Maredudd was in fact an English mole in the Welsh camp. With the connivance of Sir Henry Conway, the constable of Rhuddlan, whose servant he was, Maredudd remained in his house throughout the rebellion, though the area was under rebel control, specifically in order to alert Sir Henry about rebel movements and intentions. When Glyn Dŵr's forces withdrew across the River Conwy, Maredudd felt able to show his true colours and fled with his family to Rhuddlan Castle. Once the rebels realized his treachery they returned and destroyed his goods, corn, and chattels. Nor was the family's tale of woe at an end. Maredudd died in Rhuddlan Castle, and his son—true to his father's example of loyalty to the English Crown—was killed by the Welsh rebels outside the castle while he was guarding the cattle of the burgesses.[29]

Maredudd's exploits may have been exceptional, especially in the eyes of his own family; but throughout Wales, in addition to the large numbers of Welshmen—quite probably the majority—who stood on the sidelines as long as they possibly could, there were many who openly resisted Glyn Dŵr. Their numbers are very likely to have been highest in eastern and southern Wales. There the traditions and mechanisms of co-operation and coexistence between Welsh and English were long-established and stood firm; and the revolt, though fierce enough while it lasted, tended to be short-lived and spasmodic in its impact. But even in north Wales, where English control collapsed most spectacularly and where the terror tactics of the Welsh rebels posed a very immediate threat, not a few Welshmen stood out defiantly against Owain Glyn Dŵr. Personal elements

no doubt entered into the decision. How otherwise can we explain how two brothers from Eifionydd commemorated in Sir John Wynn's *History of the Gwydir Family* went their different ways during the revolt—Ieuan ap Maredudd stubbornly defending Caernarfon Castle against the rebels and dying there (as the record shows), while 'Robert, his brother, taking a clear contrary course was out with Owain Glyn Dŵr'? We should certainly not discount sour family quarrels and personal vendettas as factors in the equation: perhaps the most famous opponent of Glyn Dŵr in popular legend was Hywel Sele ap Meurig of Nannau, and the story that was still current in the eighteenth century, and so was recorded by Thomas Pennant the antiquarian, was that he and Glyn Dŵr 'had long been at variance', though they were first cousins. Revolts could, as always, divide families; but they could also unite them, in opposition as well as in support. It may well be no accident that three of Owain's most prominent enemies in north Wales—Ieuan ap Maredudd of Cefn y Fan (above), Hywel Sele ap Meurig of Nannau (also above), and Einion ab Ithel of Penllyn—were all closely related by marriage. Networks of marriage and long-standing common interests, which we can no longer recover from our exiguous evidence, may well lie beneath the decisions that were made in these critical years.[30]

It may be a less speculative matter to identify two other features to explain why so many prominent Welshmen consciously decided not to follow Glyn Dŵr. One was the fact that many of them had now lived cheek by jowl, profitably and comfortably, with their English neighbours for generations and were not to be seduced by a revolt which was so tyrannous in its ethnic claims and such a threat to their livelihood. Most obviously was this true of the Welsh burgesses of the towns of Wales. Thomas ap David of Brecon was a conspicuous example. His Welsh name notwithstanding, he was bailiff of his home town throughout the emergency years of the revolt, and so public-spirited was he that, in the terms of a royal grant, he neglected his own affairs in order to throw all his ability and energy into the defence of Brecon. His own business was utterly destroyed; his reward was a clear conscience and a royal annuity of 20 marks (£13. 6s. 8d.). There were many others like him: his namesake in Skenfrith was one, Ieuan ap David ap Richard in Caernarfon another.[31]

But perhaps the single most important reason why many prominent Welshmen refused to transfer their loyalties to Glyn Dŵr and indeed actively opposed him was the network of ties which bound them, personally and often as families, to the service of the kings and lords of England. Many of them had climbed to fortune and positions of importance through such service. In the gamble which Owain's revolt certainly was, why should they sever the ties which had served them and their families so well in return for the transient thrill of supporting, or even acquiescing in, a revolt whose long-term chances were so slim and which in

any case threatened the very structures of power to which they were habituated? We might cite, for example, two of the men who served in the garrison of Montgomery Castle at the height of the revolt. Maredudd ab Adda Moel came of a family which had long served the Mortimers in this part of Wales; he was not to be blown off the course of his loyalty by the cross-winds of rebellion; and his calculation proved indeed to be well judged, for he benefited personally from the lands forfeited during the rebellion and rose to be steward (that is, chief official) of the lordship of Cydewain. One of his companions in the garrison in 1404–5 was Rhirid de Middleton, a man whose Welsh first name and English surname epitomized the compromises of border society. Rhirid had long been in the service of the Mortimers, accompanying Earl Edmund on his Breton expedition in 1375; thirty years later he had no doubt where his loyalty lay.[32]

There were men like them in every part of Wales: Einion ab Ithel of Penllyn in Merionethshire whose affections for the house of Lancaster were grounded in the annuity of 10 marks (£6 13s. 4d.) he had received from John of Gaunt in 1396; Hwlcyn Llwyd, the ancestor of the Glynnes of Glyn Llifon, who died while defending the castle of Caernarfon against the Welsh rebels; or Robert ap Rees, the deputy steward of the lordship of Ogmore in Glamorgan, who remained faithful to the royal cause whilst his English superior, John Fleming, defected to Glyn Dŵr's side. In Carmarthenshire Rhys ap Thomas ap Dafydd was of a similar persuasion. Nor is that surprising: he had been retained as an esquire of the royal household by Richard II, a very flattering honour for a Welshman, and he had accompanied the king's expedition to Ireland in 1394–5. He certainly stood out against Glyn Dŵr and paid the price as his lands were ravaged by the rebels. But his loyalty earned him long-term rewards: he was granted an annuity of 5 marks (£3 6s. 8d.) by the prince of Wales, was among the first to resume office once the revolt had subsided, and quickly became the linchpin of royal governance in the southern principality of Wales. He was appropriately enough among the first Welshmen to petition successfully to be exempted from the anti-Welsh penal legislation of Henry IV and to be made, along with his heirs, honorary English-men or, as the phrase had it, to be considered to be 'true English'. That was the ultimate compliment that could be paid to one who had shown such steadfast loyalty to the English Crown during the dark days of Glyn Dŵr's rebellion.[33]

It was a compliment which could also be paid to the most redoubtable and famous of Owain's opponents, Dafydd Gam. His story and that of his family is in many respects a reverse image to that of Owain Glyn Dŵr and his family. The contrast between them explains some of the profound paradoxes of loyalty and contradictions of conviction in the Wales of their day. Dafydd Gam, like Owain, could claim to be of princely descent: in his case the alleged founder of the family was an eleventh-century prince of Brycheiniog (Brecon), Bleddyn ap Maenyrch.

As might be expected of a family of the eastern borderlands it had come to terms at an early date with the English rulers of the area; it was appropriate that the head of the family in the thirteenth century bore the name Einion Sais, Einion the Englishman. The most striking feature of the family in the next century was its exemplary record of devoted service to the Bohuns, earls of Hereford and lords of Brecon, and its growing monopoly of important local offices in the lordship of Brecon. Successive members of the family stood by the Bohuns in the political crises of 1297 and 1322 and reaped the rewards of services in annuities, favours, leases, and gifts. They also cornered positions of local power—such as the posts of sheriff (virtually a family preserve), master-sergeant, and occasionally constable of Brecon. The family had good reason to be pleased with itself and with the way it had entrenched itself in local society and seignorial favour. Furthermore, 1399 brought with it prospects of dazzling new opportunities for the family. In that year Henry Bolingbroke, lord of Brecon since 1384 by marriage, seized the English throne; his Brecon followers could expect to do well from his coup. They indeed did so: Dafydd Gam, his son Morgan, and his brother Gwilym (or William) were all described as king's esquires early in the new reign and began to reap rewards in annuities and confiscated lands. Dafydd Gam himself was clearly marked out for particular favour, which suggested that he was already high in Bolingbroke's regard. He was given an unusually generous annuity, especially for a Welshman, of 40 marks (£33 6s. 8d.), and the fact that it was assigned on the issues of the city of London suggests that he was destined for service and a career on a national rather than on a local stage.[34]

But then the revolt of Owain Glyn Dŵr intervened. The family seems to have had no difficulty in deciding where its loyalties lay. Generations of services to, and rewards from, the English lords of Brecon, especially now that the lord of Brecon was also king of England, immunized them against the virus of rebellion. Dafydd Gam was soon being rewarded with confiscated rebel lands in Cardiganshire and in his native Brecon, specifically for his prowess in opposing the Welsh rebels. In May 1405 he was, according to one account, involved in one of the major victories of the war against the Welsh, the Battle of Pwll Melyn near Usk. He was also almost certainly involved in the military commands in the eastern March entrusted to his cousin, John ap Harry, a close confidant of Bolingbroke of long standing, now one of his major military commanders in the Welsh March and subsequently MP for Herefordshire. Legend has it that so intrepid a spirit was Dafydd Gam and so deep was his hatred for Glyn Dŵr that he infiltrated Glyn Dŵr's parliament at Machynlleth with the express purpose of assassinating the Welsh leader, but that he was foiled in his intent and only escaped with his life with great difficulty and in return for a promise to support the Welsh cause. The

legend, as we have it, is late and is implausible and inaccurate in its details; but its very survival, or manufacture, indicates that Dafydd Gam had acquired a legendary status as one of the most implacable and daredevil Welsh opponents of Owain Glyn Dŵr.[35]

There was a price to be paid for such opposition; Dafydd and his family were required to pay it. Already in February 1403 (or 1404) his father, Llywelyn ap Hywel, had been awarded an annuity of £20 both for his services and 'in consideration of the great damage, disinherison, and losses which he had suffered at the hands of our rebels of Wales'. Llywelyn's tale of woe did not end there, nor did the sharp decline of the revolt after 1406 bring him the prosperous and peaceful old age he might have expected. His detractors, many of them no doubt former rebels thirsting for revenge, pursued him through the courts and used every ruse to get him convicted under Welsh law. Old vendettas, generated by the revolt, were clearly still very much alive. How alive was revealed in 1412 when Dafydd Gam himself was captured by a remnant party of rebels and only released in return for a ransom.[36]

Dafydd Gam's services to the house of Lancaster were still not quite exhausted. In 1415 the lure of battle once more attracted him. He served at Agincourt with three men-at-arms, and was sufficiently distinguished to be retained individually rather than with the men of Brecon as a group. He was one of the few men of esquire's rank on the English side to be killed in battle, and for that reason alone his death was recorded in several contemporary chronicles. It was an appropriate end to a distinguished career. Like generations of his family before him he had lived and died in the service of the lords of Brecon; there could be no more fitting epitaph for him than that of a sixteenth-century Welsh antiquarian: 'a great stickler for the Duke of Lancaster.' It was an epitaph which identified correctly that in the test of convictions which all revolts eventually entail, Dafydd Gam, like many other prominent Welsh squires, decided that the ties of service to English lords were too important to be overridden by appeals to patriotism and mythology.[37]

Our evidence is much too sparse and one-dimensional to allow us to see why some men chose, or at least agreed, to fight for Glyn Dŵr while others, at equal cost to themselves and their families, chose otherwise; why Henry Don and his family were such enthusiastic and intrepid supporters of the Welsh leader while Dafydd Gam and his kinsmen, from not apparently very different backgrounds, were equally implacable in their opposition. At best we can only guess. But of two things we can be fairly sure. First, in Wales as in other societies which experience revolt, choice for the majority was only made reluctantly and when it could no longer be avoided. Secondly, the success of the revolt was such that sooner or later it demanded a response; it could not be ignored. Wales had been

set alight by Owain Glyn Dŵr's revolt. It failed to unite the country or its people; but in its demand for a response, right across the social and geographical spectrum of the country, it was truly a national revolt.

GUERRILLAS AND GARRISONS

*I*t is never easy to re-create the history of a revolt. The action is too spontaneous and fast-moving to be captured in the leaden prose of historical narrative. There is rarely a single stage on which the story unfolds neatly; rather are revolts often composed of fragmented and disconnected episodes and it is only with hindsight that patterns and connections can be imposed on them. As Thomas Carlyle put it memorably: 'Action is Solid, Narrative is Linear.' Even when the historian concedes, or accepts, that his circumscribed talents allow him to do no more than to piece together as convincing a linear narrative as he can muster rather than to evoke the pulsating, anarchic atmosphere of the revolt itself, he is further handicapped by the limitations of the evidence at his disposal. Revolts by their very nature lie largely, if by no means entirely, outside the established government's documentary record which constitutes, especially for the later Middle Ages, so much of the material from which the historian must try to reconstruct the past; while the rebels for their own part are normally too busy trying to turn the world upside down to have the time to commit an account of their actions to writing.

All these general problems are writ particular and writ very large for the historian of the Glyn Dŵr revolt. It was a revolt which erupted into unpredictable and apparently unplanned spontaneity in very different parts of Wales. Very occasionally, as during the summer months of 1403, there appears to be a measure of coherence and even centralized direction to the rebels' activities; but for the most part they seem to dissolve into a collection of episodic ambushes, raids and sieges. Nor is this a surprise given the geographical fragmentation of the country and the difficulty of creating and sustaining a network of command and communication across its broken terrain. Wales and the talents and resources of the Welsh lent themselves above all to guerrilla warfare, be it defensive or offensive; and guerrilla warfare—secretive, small-scale, spasmodic, and apparently uncoordinated—is the most difficult of all warfare to be imprisoned effectively in the historian's prose. It is also much the most elusive to document. The followers of Owain Glyn Dŵr have left no record of their activities as warriors; it is only his ecclesiastically trained advisers who have left a few footprints in the

documentary sand. Accordingly, in reconstructing the military character of the revolt we have to rely exclusively on the letters, reports, and documents of those whose task it was to withstand and suppress it. We see, therefore, through a glass very darkly; but we must make such virtue as we can of our necessity.

Glyn Dŵr and his allies revealed in their early attacks that it needed only small forces to challenge and embarrass the English regime in Wales. Owain himself was accompanied by a force of some 250 men when he attacked Ruthin and other towns in north Wales in September 1400, while the group which captured and held Conway Castle in the daredevil attack of April 1401 was composed of less than fifty men. Surprise rather than size was the essence of military strength on such occasions. This remained so throughout the revolt, even in the years of success. Small local groups—such as those led by Hywel Gwynedd in Flintshire or Rhys Gethin in the Builth area—led lightning raids from their mountain hide-outs against English settlements and castles in the lowlands, and disappeared as quickly as they had arrived. Guerrilla tactics of this kind needed only the services of the dedicated few to achieve some spectacular successes which would transform the rebels' morale: it was a well-placed ambush and his own ill-founded self-confidence which seems to have lured Reginald Grey of Ruthin into a trap in the spring of 1402, while it was a group of some 200 Welshmen and Frenchmen who overwhelmed the sheriff of Anglesey and his substantial escort in January 1405 as they left Beaumaris Castle. Most of the activity during Glyn Dŵr's revolt must have taken the form of such localized and small-scale ambushes, raids, and sieges. Their impact could be unnerving, disruptive, and sometimes spectacular; but they lacked the stamina, resources, and critical mass to be converted into sustained military campaigns. That is why, as we shall see, the small castle garrisons—often no more than two dozen men—were able to withstand their attacks so defiantly and effectively.[1]

Glyn Dŵr's revolt was, therefore, primarily a guerrilla war; but during the years of success he and his fellow leaders were able to muster much larger forces. Contemporary figures, often based on hysterical reports, need of course to be taken with a very large pinch of salt; but they do register clearly that by 1403, and at the height of the military season, Owain was able to command very substantial forces. Jankyn Harvard, the constable of Dinefwr, estimated that at the muster of Owain's forces on 2 July 1403 in the Tywi valley there were 8,240 men; in the same week another observer guessed that Owain had left 300 men to lay siege to the castle of Llanymddyfri while he pursued his own march towards Carmarthen; Richard Kingston, the highly excitable dean of Windsor, writing from Hereford 'in very great haste, at three o'clock in the afternoon, 3 September' [1403] estimated the rebel force which had entered the county of Hereford on a

harrying and foraging raid as 'more than four hundred'; while the prince of Wales, for the quite contrary reason of wanting to exaggerate the scale of his own victory at Grosmont in March 1405, boasted to his father that the force of Welsh rebels from south-east Wales which he confronted numbered 8,000 men, of whom up to 1,000 had been killed. Even if we divide these figures by ten, we are still left with the impression that during 1402–6 Owain Glyn Dŵr was indeed able to muster substantial armies, albeit for only a few weeks. Nor should this surprise us. Success bred enthusiasm and recruits: it was a Welsh observer who commented how an early victory brought Owain 'great fame, and a great number of youths and rascals from every region of Wales joined him, so that he had a great host'. Defections (such as, no doubt, many of the Mortimer tenants at the Battle of Bryn Glas in June 1402), the prospect of pillage and revenge, and the excitement of a call to arms all boosted the ranks of Owain's supporters so that, as the monk of Evesham observed despondently in 1402, 'his cause grew excessively'.[2]

Nor should we underestimate his military skill and resources. It was precisely such an underestimate which led to the most devastating and decisive English defeat in the field during the rebellion, the rout of the joint Mortimer and Herefordshire force at Bryn Glas on 22 June 1402. Most of the leaders of the revolt—Owain himself, Rhys and Gwilym ap Tudur, Henry Don, Hywel ap Tudur ab Ithel, Hywel Coetmor—were men of long military experience, having served English kings and lords on campaigns in France, Ireland, and Scotland. They were well versed in the arts of leading men; the men who had once been mustered under their command in the English cause now no doubt followed them, willingly or otherwise, in Glyn Dŵr's cause. They seem to have been able to mesh their forces fairly effectively with those of their allies, be it with the French in assaults on the castles of Caernarfon and Kidwelly or with the Scots in their attack on Beaumaris. Some of them in south-west Wales seem to have been alert to the possibilities of using sea-power to promote their cause: David Perrot of Tenby was certainly suspected of using his considerable naval experience in the service of the Welsh rebels, and the activities of the buccaneering Henry Don extended to the seizure of a ship at Carmarthen. But it was in the mountains rather than in the sea-ways of Wales that the rebels had the upper hand. The English armies trundled slowly and cumbersomely along the well-known valley routes while the Welsh moved swiftly and unpredictably along the highland ridgeways. It was high up in Pumlumon that in 1401 the rebels inflicted a crushing defeat on the forces of lowland south-west Wales; and it was along the upland spinal cord of mid-Wales that Owain's forces, no doubt drawn considerably from north-west Wales, moved with even more devastating effectiveness in June 1402 to within twelve miles of Leominster where they met and overwhelmed the English force. Both of these victories took place in midsummer. That, as

contemporaries observed, was the best of seasons for the rebels for then 'they may lie without': in other words, they needed little shelter and could readily find the exiguous provisions on which the Welsh, notoriously, could survive. The rigours of winter and early spring suited them less well; but even then they had the upper hand over the English. Rain and snow had always been the most powerful weapons in the armoury of the Welsh against the English; they served them well again during Glyn Dŵr's revolt. Indeed, English and Welsh alike had no doubt that the forces of nature connived at Owain's success: Thomas Walsingham, the waspish chronicler of St Albans, was driven to wonder whether Glyn Dŵr's control of the powers of magic helped to explain the series of meteorological disasters which overwhelmed Henry IV's campaign into Wales in September 1402 and almost cost the king his life; but the Welsh poet naturally took a very different view, celebrating the way the weather and the River Dee between them had foiled the English during one particular incident during the revolt.[3]

The Welsh needed the support of the weather and the terrain since they had so few other factors working in their favour. We know nothing of the recruitment, training, organization, or provisioning of their armies. Their leaders had experience aplenty of English armies and no doubt tried to bring their practices from that experience to operate in a Welsh context. We hear, for example, of their emblems and standards; Glyn Dŵr's own standard bore a golden dragon on a white field. In the ransoming of prisoners and the division of war spoils they are likewise likely to have followed the conventions known to them from English warfare: when Carmarthen was captured in July 1403 there seems to have been an agreement to divide the spoils between Owain Glyn Dŵr himself and Rhys Ddu, one of the local commanders. While Glyn Dŵr's authority as leader was never challenged and while his leadership could be highly effective and directive during a co-ordinated campaign such as that of the summer of 1403, much of the initiative must of necessity have lain with local commanders. The nature of the terrain and the character of guerrilla warfare dictated that it should be so. Rhys and Gwilym ap Tudur were among the local leaders in north-west Wales and the capture of Conway Castle in April 1401 seems to have been their personal escapade. Hywel Gwynedd terrorized the Flintshire lowlands from his hide-out on Halkyn mountain; John Kynaston clearly took matters into his own hands in Ellesmere and western Shropshire; Rhys Gethin operated as a much-feared free-lance rebel in south-eastern Wales; while in south-west Wales the local leadership was seized by Henry Don, Gruffudd his son, Rhys Ddu, and Gwilym ap Philip. Even when Glyn Dŵr was in overall charge of strategy, the realities of local power structures and the time-scale of military operations meant that effective command had often to be devolved into the hands of such men. For example, he delegated the task of besieging Llanymddyfri Castle to a group of 300

men and handed over the responsibility for securing the surrender of the castles and towns of Glamorgan, Gower, and Cydweli to the respective local communities. Such fragmentation of military effort and initiative had its dangers as well as its advantages. It meant that the revolt presented no single easy target for English military planners; its hydra-headed character required their response likewise to be plural and localized if it was to be effective. But there was also a heavy price to pay: co-ordination and communication between the various theatres of activity were exceedingly difficult, and the heavy military defeats that Glyn Dŵr's forces suffered at Grosmont and Pwll Melyn in March–May 1405 suggest that the rashness of local initiatives was endangering the revolt as a whole. After all, Glyn Dŵr's only real prospect lay in clinging to the principles of guerrilla warfare: sudden ambushes, tactical flights, avoidance of battle, and the gradual attrition of the enemy's morale and will to fight.[4]

For the most part, and possibly until ambition began to give him grandiose ideas beyond his military means from 1404 onwards, he appears to have stood by these principles. Adam of Usk gave, from close personal observation of the first years of the revolt, his assessment of the rebels' tactics: 'they lurk in the mountainous and wooded parts sometimes pillaging, sometimes slaying their foes who laid snares or attacked them. They harassed the parts of north and west Wales with no light hand.' The sudden, unexpected raid was one of their ploys: in August–early September 1403 they initiated a series of extensive raids into Flintshire and then retired, no doubt laden with booty and prisoners, to the safety of north Wales beyond the River Conwy; as late as November 1406 a similar raid led to the suspension of one of the courts of Dyffryn Clwyd. Well-planned ambushes, especially against key officials, were another favourite tactic: the constable of Harlech was caught in such an ambush when he was foolish enough to be lured outside the castle to parley with the rebels without taking the elementary precaution of demanding hostages from them first; a similar fate befell the deputy sheriff of Anglesey when he left Beaumaris Castle under what he thought was the safety of a large escort. Both men were doubtless ransomed. Kidnapping and ransoms, rather than killing or imprisonment, were high on the rebels' agenda and were deliberately and extensively employed as a means of raising that rarest of commodities in Welsh rural society, ready cash. High-status prisoners were, of course, particularly welcome both in propaganda and in profit terms. Reginald Grey, lord of Dyffryn Clwyd, was the most famous: his ransom, variously estimated at 6,000 (£4,000) or 10,000 (£6,666 13s. 4d.) marks was a magnificent windfall for Glyn Dŵr's coffers and caused Grey deep financial embarrassment. No other prisoner was in Grey's league in wealth or eminence; but the list of Glyn Dŵr's prisoners included men of considerable standing: Edmund Walsingham, captured near Brecon and freed for a ransom of £50; John

Horn, a London fishmonger, taken prisoner as he ferried victuals for the relief of Harlech Castle and ransomed for £20; Thomas Roche, a king's esquire, captured in 1405 and eventually released, after long intercessions by his wife, in exchange for four Welsh prisoners in Brecon and Huntington castles; and John Penres, the keeper of Llansteffan Castle. But Owain's men seem also to have indulged in a policy of systematically kidnapping ordinary men and women, taking them to their mountain fastnesses, and extorting ransoms from them: Ieuan Llyglyw of Dyffryn Clwyd, his Welsh name notwithstanding, found himself in such a predicament and agreed to pay 50s.; two Flintshire men paid 48s. 4d. and 63s. 4d. respectively. It is perhaps no surprise that, as the revolt faded and as the remnant of the rebels became more desperate for cash and supplies, the practice of kidnap and ransom was particularly prevalent.[5]

Kidnap and ransom were policies directed at individuals and were expected to yield profits; other rebel activities were communal in their targets and merely destructive in purpose. The revolt had begun with a great raiding foray on the English towns of north-east Wales; and throughout the revolt economic terrorism remained one of the prime weapons of the rebels. John Fairford, observing their behaviour at perilously close range in Brecon in July 1403, described their activities in these words: 'they have done such evil and destruction as they can in the neighbourhood of Brecon . . . and they intend to burn and destroy all the English district in these parts.' Mills and manorial buildings were a particular target for their attacks, but crops and cattle were also destroyed or plundered. The purpose of such destruction, as in all contemporary warfare, was in good measure psychological: the terrorizing of their opponents through the deliberate wasting of their resources. At Kidwelly, for example, the Welsh rebels under Henry Don's leadership, 'destroyed all the grain belonging to your poor lieges, on every side around your said castle and town'. It was an act of terror calculated not only at economic deprivation but also as a first step towards submission and surrender. But a further motive was also frequently involved, that of depriving the besieged defenders of the castles and towns and any relieving English force of the supplies to sustain themselves. That is certainly how the keeper of Conway interpreted the Welsh raids on Anglesey: 'all [the men of] Caernarfonshire propose to go to the island of Anglesey with all the speed they can in order to bring out all the men and the cattle there, and to bring them into the mountains, in case Englishmen should be sustained therewith.'[6]

Harrying, burning, and pillage can be interpreted as essentially destructive, or at best pre-emptive, acts; but to construe them solely in that light would be to underestimate their role in the strategy of rebellion. They were deliberate acts of economic warfare, and the only way to bring such warfare to an end was to buy peace. Such a peace might be no more than a temporary cease-fire during a

military campaign, such as the three-day remission of hostilities which the constable of Dinefwr Castle was able to secure in July 1403. But most of the treaties
(L. *treugae*, E. *tretys*) were bargains struck by local communities with the rebels to
avoid the prospect of further raids and harryings. The licence given to the abbot
of Dore Abbey (Co. Hereford) spells out their character bluntly: 'to treat with the
rebels of south Wales for the greater safety of the abbey, which is situated near
them and is in great peril of destruction and burning.' A parley would be
arranged, terms would be agreed, and the stipulated sum would be paid either in
instalments or in one lump sum. The men of Herefordshire and Shropshire,
more used to the ways of peace and more hysterical in their fears than the Welsh
communities, quickly concluded such truces with the Welsh. But the Welsh
themselves also saw the benefits of buying off the terrifying raids of the
Welsh marauders: we hear of treaties with the men of Powys, Denbigh, and
Dyffryn Clwyd and there were doubtless many other unauthorized treaties
which do not figure in the records. Much the best-recorded of these treaties was
the one confirmed in the county court of Pembroke in November 1405. It was to
last for six months to 1 May 1406 and was bought at a cost of £200 in silver to be
levied by a formal commission at the rate of 4s. per knight's fee. Such treaties
were still being concluded in the March in general and in the lordship of Moldsdale in particular as late as autumn 1409; the revolt might be over, but the
harrowing memories of what a Welsh raid might mean were still sufficiently
alive to persuade officers and communities alike to negotiate further treaties. The
king and his council frequently expressed their disapproval of such arrangements
(indeed it is that disapproval which is often the sole source of our knowledge of
the treaties); but such disapproval only showed how far out of touch they were
with the real situation in Wales. Part of the success of a guerrilla campaign lies in
its capacity to terrorize local communities into submission or acquiescence; by
that criterion Glyn Dŵr's revolt was a very considerable success.[7]

There was, of course, one other crucial purpose to the raids of the Welsh
rebels—to bolster their own utterly inadequate supplies of corn, cattle, and arms.
Contemporaries were very aware that this was the Achilles' heel of the rebel
cause, even in its heyday. It was 'want of victuals' which drove Glyn Dŵr from
his northern fastnesses towards Carmarthen and Pembroke in June 1403 'to seek
victuals and waste the country'. One of the most experienced of Marcher commanders, Edward Charlton, the lord of Powys, likewise had no doubt that the
purpose of the Welsh was to 'get their corn now for their supply and sustenance
for the future and to carry these supplies into the mountains'. Supplying their
own needs was quite as crucial a facet of Welsh raids as was the destruction of
their enemies' resources. We have already quoted the view of one contemporary
that the aim of the Welsh in stripping Anglesey of its resources was to prevent

the English from using them for their sustenance; but to another correspondent the purpose of the exercise was quite as much to feed the needs of the Welshmen of Caernarfonshire. Shortage of food and military equipment is the overwhelming fear of all guerrilla armies; it was a fear which haunted the Welsh, drove them into mounting raiding parties across Wales and deep into the border shires, and eventually was to contribute more than any single factor to the collapse of the movement. Equally it was a recognition on the part of the English authorities that starvation and shortage of arms and equipment would be the undoing of the Welsh, which explains why they did all in their power to mount an economic blockade of the country. A guerrilla campaign can be rarely defeated outright in military terms, but it can be slowly strangled.[8]

The Welsh achievement was in many respects remarkable. In a few areas their revolt lasted up to seven years or more; in many more areas it had taken effective control of much of the countryside for the better part of three to four years. Four royal campaigns did little to stem the tide of revolt, and several military commanders (including the young Prince Henry) found that Wales was not a country in which one made a reputation quickly, if at all. Some of the mightiest Welsh castles had fallen to the rebels—sometimes by a clever ruse as at Conway in 1401, sometimes by storm and surrender as at Carmarthen and Newcastle Emlyn in 1403, sometimes by bargain and attrition as seems to have happened at Aberystwyth and Harlech in 1404–5. Yet to mention the castles is also to recognize the limitations of the Welsh achievement: only two of the captured castles were held for any length of time; the others were recovered, and the great majority of castles, even those (in themselves a majority) that were lightly defended, were never taken by the Welsh. Truth to tell, the Welsh did not have the necessary equipment or the military stamina and resources to undertake the prolonged sieges of the castle which alone would have given them ultimate control of the country. The story of Welsh sieges of castles such as Caernarfon, Abergavenny, Kidwelly, Beaumaris, and Coety is overwhelmingly one of failure; indeed, it is striking that in the only siege of which we have a detailed account— that of Caernarfon in 1404, with 'engines and . . . ladders of great length'—the French took a prominent part. The fate of the castles sums up both the strength and ultimately the fatal weakness of the rebels' military power. They were capable of nullifying the effective machinery of governance and control throughout most of Wales for three years; they conducted devastating raids and terrorized communities into buying peace at a high price; and by their tactics they showed how embarrassingly ineffective was the English military response when confronted with a determined guerrilla campaign. As the revolt unfolded, the English authorities must have wondered whether English power in Wales was in danger of going the way of English lordship in contemporary Ireland, that

of becoming an attenuated Pale where the 'land of peace' formed small embat-
tled islands in a 'land of war'. Yet the vast disparities between the Welsh and
English forces—in resources, military equipment, and technology—and the singular failure of the Welsh to capture more than a handful of castles in a thickly
encastellated country—suggested that there were clear limits to Welsh success.
The passage of time, war-weariness, and shortage of food and equipment would
achieve what English military effort had patently not succeeded in achieving. It
was exhaustion and military frustration which eventually defeated Glyn Dŵr.[9]

Our view of the war effort of the Welsh has been shaped overwhelmingly from
English sources; to that extent we should be far better placed when we come to
consider the English military response. That is indeed true. There is an almost
embarrassing wealth of documentation for the English war effort in Wales in
Henry IV's reign, so much so that much of it has only recently begun to be
exploited thoroughly. But it is as well to recall that it is documentation of a
particular kind: some invaluable letters from commanders in the field and
keepers of castles survive; but the bulk of documentation consists of commissions or indentures of appointments, detailed lists of castle garrisons, and the
financial accounts of military commanders. Valuable as are all these sources,
what they provide overwhelmingly (other than the letters) is a static picture of
the English operations in Wales; what they fail to provide is an overall view of
the complex of local operations and expeditions of which the response to the
revolt was largely composed and of the various swings of the military pendulum
from one sphere of activity to another.[10]

Henry IV's initial response to receiving news of the initial outbreak of Glyn
Dŵr's rebellion in September 1400 was to launch an immediate expedition to
north Wales to deter the Welsh from their antics by an impressive demonstration
of force. News of the revolt reached him at Northampton on 19 September (three
days after Glyn Dŵr had been proclaimed prince of Wales) as he was *en route*
home from a punitive expedition to Scotland. By 26 September he was at
Shrewsbury. Thence he led his troops through north Wales as far as Caernarfon,
then struck south into Merionethshire and returned to Shrewsbury by 15 October. It was the first of four such expeditions that the king led into Wales over
the next three years. The second in October 1401 took him from Worcester to
Brecon, thence down the Tywi valley to Carmarthen before striking north into
Cardiganshire. Almost precisely a year later in September 1402 Henry IV
launched a more ambitious and co-ordinated three-pronged attack against the
Welsh, reminiscent of the approach adopted by Edward I. One army at Hereford
under the earls of Stafford and Warwick was to direct its efforts towards Brecon
and south Wales, a second under the king in person at Shrewsbury was clearly

intended to penetrate central Wales and to attack Glyn Dŵr's bases in the Berwyn mountains; the third at Chester under the young Prince Henry was intended in particular to relieve the hard-pressed castles of the northern coastline. The fourth and final major expedition was launched in September 1403, to counter the great upsurge in rebel violence across the summer months and the spectacular capture of castles (including Carmarthen) in the Tywi valley. The expedition followed the familiar route from Hereford to Brecon and thence to Carmarthen. Henry planned several other major expeditions against the Welsh but they had to be aborted because of other more pressing calls on his military attention (notably in May 1405 when news of Archbishop Scrope's rebellion diverted an army which had already been assembled at Hereford). He did lead a small force to relieve Coety Castle in Glamorgan in September 1405, but to all intents and purposes his own personal attempt to crush the Welsh rebellion was not resumed after 1403. It had been an episode in his military career which on the whole he would no doubt prefer to forget.[11]

The armies raised for these expeditions were, by contemporary standards, very sizeable, some 3,000–4,000 men. They were raised by commissions of array, notably from the counties nearest to Wales. Henry IV himself made clear the purpose and scale of the expeditions in a letter of July 1402: his intention was 'to pursue and destroy the rebels who were lurking in mountains, woods, and other places', and he estimated that fifteen days would be sufficient to ensure that they were utterly destroyed. Such confidence was, of course, a massive act of self-delusion. Yet we should not underestimate the impact nor misunderstand the purpose of these expeditions. Adam of Usk had no doubt that the 1401 expedition was a considerable success: Henry 'laid waste and ravaged with fire, famine and sword, leaving the area a desert . . . not even sparing the monastery of Strata Florida'. Had he been asked what tangible results, beyond destruction, the expedition had achieved he would doubtless refer to the public execution of one of the leading Welsh squires of Carmarthenshire and an early southern follower of Glyn Dŵr, Llywelyn ap Gruffudd Fychan of Caio, *pour encourager les autres*, and even more convincingly, the submission of the men of Cardiganshire. Adam even considered Henry's 1402 expedition a great success, even if other chroniclers dwelt on the miserable weather which overwhelmed it: 'he laid waste the land and returned victoriously, with a countless spoil of cattle.' Adam may have been easily impressed; but we need to bear in mind that the purpose of such expeditions was very different from that which Henry IV's rhetoric gave them, that of the 'utter destruction' of the rebels. Their aim, as with so many military campaigns of the Middle Ages (including Henry IV's own Scottish expedition of 1400) was not battle or outright victory, but a demonstration of military power both through the size of the army itself (compared with the puny Welsh forces) and

by the deliberate harrying of the countryside. In other words, their purpose was psychological. It was psychological also in the sense of putting heart into those who had to cope with the terrorism of rebel attacks from week to week. Richard Kingston at Hereford, for example, had no doubt that there was no substitute for an expedition led by the king in person: trust to no deputy, was his blunt message to Henry IV; come yourself in your own person; the Welsh are assuming that you will not do so and are deriving comfort from this hope.[12]

We should not, therefore, dismiss the expeditions out of hand; yet any military impact they had can only be deemed to have been short-lived. The opinion of a near-contemporary was dismissive: the Welsh, he commented, simply disappeared into the hills when the royal army approached, 'and there the king could do them no harm at all; but often they stole the king's transport ['carriage'] and every day destroyed his people'. Henry IV failed to realize—or perhaps, to be fair to him, because of his other multiple preoccupations and desperate shortage of cash did not have the opportunity to act on such realization—that in dealing with guerrilla warfare patience, stamina, and playing a long game are essential keys to success. Not one of his expeditions lasted a month; most of them were over in two to three weeks. Such flying visits were no more than showy flashes in the military pan; the attention they have received from contemporaries and historians alike is quite out of proportion to their military significance. Henry IV would have done well to verse himself in the military history of the reign of Edward I, the 'noble and wise King Edward the First' whose policies in Wales the commons in parliament pointedly drew to Henry's attention. Edward had planned his destruction of the principality of Llywelyn ap Gruffudd with meticulous care and with a very well-articulated overall strategy under his own direct command. The first campaign of 1277 had lasted almost exactly one year, from the proclamation of Llywelyn as a rebel to his submission; and the king himself did not set out from Chester to deliver the *coup de grâce* until he knew that the essential groundwork had been done for him in other parts of Wales. In 1282 Edward had to move with much greater speed since he was now responding to a rebellion rather than inaugurating a campaign at his own tempo. Even so, what is striking is the deliberateness and thoroughness with which he and his lieutenants moved: leaving Chester in June 1282 he was willing to face the rigours of a long Welsh winter and the discomfort of the Welsh mountains to ensure that his victory over the Welsh was utter and irreversible. Or well-nigh so, for again in 1294–5 he took six months at a particularly stressful time to crush the final Welsh rebellion of his reign, that of Madog ap Llywelyn. If any lesson was to be learnt from Edward's experience it was that stamina, perseverance, and a massive and sustained military presence were essential to bring the Welsh to heel. It was not a lesson which

Henry IV was willing, or had the time, to learn during his crowded and crisis-ridden early years.[13]

Once it became clear that a whirlwind royal expedition could not snuff out the revolt, it was necessary to devise a more permanent military plan and presence to deal with the situation in Wales. Already in the late autumn of 1400 after Henry IV's first expedition, young prince Henry was posted to Chester, with the intention, no doubt, that he and his advisers should keep an eye on the situation. There was, of course, initially no reason to believe that Owain's escapades would be anything more than a short-lived rush of blood to the patriotic head; no special measures were required other than to bolster the garrisons in a few key castles and to underline the military responsibilities of the justiciar, notably of Hotspur as justiciar (or chief governor) of North Wales and Cheshire (including Flintshire). But as the situation deteriorated rapidly in the summer of 1401 and the ambit of the revolt extended into central and south-east Wales, it became clear that more radical military measures would have to be taken and a new command structure inaugurated. The first step in this process was the appointment of Thomas Percy, earl of Worcester, as royal lieutenant in South Wales for three months from 21 October 1401 and, simultaneously, captain of Cardigan and Aberystwyth with a combined force of eighty men-at-arms and 200 archers.[14]

Percy's appointment was to be the first of an extraordinary number of confused and sometimes contradictory sequence of military commands which the government launched over the next few years to try to deal with the situation in Wales. In 1402, for example, as the situation deteriorated rapidly, the existing governmental and administrative framework was overlaid by a sequence of military lieutenancies. Initially there was a clear and unified line of command, with Hotspur deputed to be lieutenant in north Wales and his uncle, the earl of Worcester, in the south; but after the disaster at Bryn Glas (22 June 1402) a whole series of new military commands was inaugurated: the earl of Arundel was appointed royal lieutenant in the frontiers of north Wales from Holt to Wigmore and the earl of Stafford likewise in south Wales from Wigmore to Chepstow; Richard, Lord Grey of Codnor, was given a wide-ranging military commission in Brecon, Cardiganshire, Carmarthenshire, and Pembrokeshire and was subsequently, in September, appointed lieutenant of south-west Wales; while Edward Charlton was put in charge of the castle and lordship of Welshpool and operations against the rebels in that district. There is an air of panic about such a panoply of measures; it was to be an air which pervaded English military policy in Wales over the next few years.[15]

It is not difficult to explain why there was so much that was reactive and short-term in English policy during these years. The desperate shortage of cash and the almost equally desperate reluctance of English commanders and soldiers

to serve in Wales made it difficult to sustain a coherent military strategy over months, let alone years. When we have the earl of Somerset report to the king's council that his knights, squires, and other troops would not stay in Carmarthen at any price (*pour chose du monde*) for a single day beyond their contractual obligations, or read the pathetic terms, a combination of desperate French and cajoling English, in which the duke of York tried to persuade the government to provide the funds which alone would keep his troops at their post, we recognize the profound crisis of morale which the English authorities faced with their own men in Wales. Furthermore, English military traditions as they had developed in the fourteenth century, especially in the great *chevauchées* or systematic raids across France, were singularly ill-suited to deal with the demands of highly localized guerrilla warfare. What was the use of a grand strategy when there was no single enemy, no grand theatre of war, and no predictability other than that of bad weather and appalling terrain? Rarely was there a war where even the best-considered plans were so overwhelmed by unforeseen contingencies as the English war against Glyn Dŵr. The year 1403 provided a spectacular example. Grand plans for a unified command and coherent strategy were launched on 6 March with the appointment of the prince of Wales as his father's lieutenant in the whole of Wales from 1 April, with a force of over 3,000 men at his disposal and the promise that his wages would be paid by the royal exchequer. The next few months did indeed see some promising actions, both defensive (such as the dispatch of major contingents to relieve the hard-pressed castles of Aberystwyth and Harlech) and offensive (notably the prince's own raid on Glyn Dŵr's houses at Sycharth and Glyndyfrdwy). But the defections of the Percies early in July, the trauma of the Battle of Shrewsbury (21 July 1403), the wound that the prince suffered in the battle, and his effective marginalization from direct or sustained military involvement in Wales for the better part of eighteen months threw any new initiative into total disarray. All the government could do was to patch together a series of *ad hoc* responses. Some were localized: such were the appointments of Lord Burnell to defend Shrewsbury against the Welsh, or of Richard, earl of Warwick, and John, Lord Audley, to take charge of Brecon lordship for one year; others were defensive regional commissions such as that entrusted to the earl of Arundel, Hugh Burnell, and Edward Charlton 'to defend the Marches of England towards Wales against the invasion of the Welsh rebels'; yet others revived the general lieutenantships of earlier days, as when the earl of Somerset and subsequently the duke of York were appointed the king's lieutenant in south Wales. What was clear was that the prince of Wales's general lieutenantship had lapsed and had been replaced, formally and piecemeal, by a medley of uncoordinated appointments.[16]

It is easy to understand the quandary of the English government: it was responding to circumstances and to an unfamiliar kind of war rather than controlling events. Yet the confusing catalogue of general, regional, and local

commissions bespoke, as did the brief and ineffective royal expeditions, a lack of perseverance and overall strategy. Some contemporaries certainly viewed it in this light. The earl of Worcester, one of the most experienced of Henry IV's military lieutenants, seems to have grasped the need for a coherent strategy to deal with the Welsh revolt before it overwhelmed the country. He suggested that a substantial garrison be placed at Welshpool, that Sir Edmund Mortimer and his fellow Marchers organize the defence of the March, thereby providing one major route into north Wales, that the garrisons at Caernarfon and Harlech would provide another good base for attack, and that he (as lieutenant of south Wales) could bring his men in a co-ordinated pincer movement to drive home the assault. In life as well as in letters he appears to have recognized the need to have an overview of the military situation: it was he who saw to it that the as-yet unthreatened castle of Swansea was put in a state of readiness in 1401–2 and arranged for a naval relief force to be sent to Beaumaris and a garrison of twenty archers to be dispatched to reinforce the defences at Denbigh. The earl of Worcester was in effect asking for an overall offensive strategy rather than for a set of piecemeal responses. Another earl thought that a failure to translate words into action and to persist in that action over time lay at the heart of the miserable English military performance in Wales. The earl of Arundel was well placed to offer such a critique. He had very extensive estates in north-east Wales and along the Welsh borders; he had also seen long spells of service against the Welsh. Yet when he wrote from Oswestry to the king's council in February 1405 he was at his wits' end. He had served there, so he said, with a garrison of 180 men for eight weeks but he would not stay there any longer, partly because his force was inadequate and partly because well-laid plans to tackle the revolt effectively were regularly shelved. 'If', he told the council pointedly, 'the recent ordinance were quickly acted upon according to the express wish of the recent parliament, and then enforced for a whole year, then the rebels would either submit totally to the king's grace and mercy or they would be utterly conquered, harried, and destroyed.' There was a simplistic optimism to his statement, but he was surely right in identifying that what was required was persistence and consistency of purpose over time. Edward I would have heartily agreed.[7]

Henry IV might well have replied that persistent distractions, his own tenuous hold on his throne (especially up till 1405), and his chronic financial problems did not allow him the luxury—especially compared with Edward I—of giving his time, attention, and resources to the Welsh problem for more than a few weeks at a time, if that. He might also have added that several of his leading generals in Wales had hardly covered themselves with glory. Young Prince Hal might be at the top of that list. Admittedly only a boy of 13 (to the day) when Glyn Dŵr's

rebellion erupted, he was thrown at an early age on to an unpromising military stage where reputations were more readily sunk than made. He was certainly involved in sieges, relief of castles, and harrying raids over the next few years; but Wales and guerrilla warfare did not provide easy opportunities for a bravura military performance. The Battle of Shrewsbury, where the prince was wounded, provided a better stage. After Shrewsbury the prince's direct engagement with the suppression of the rebellion in Wales does not seem to have been great. He did not return to the borders until the summer of 1404, and even thereafter preferred the relative security of the sidelines at Leominster, Hereford, Shrewsbury, and Chester. His lieutenancy on behalf of the king in Wales was regularly renewed and its terms expanded after 1405; but although he took some part in the siege of Aberystwyth in 1407 and doubtless had hoped to bask in some of the glory had the castle been taken on that occasion, his own personal role in events in Wales seems to have been limited. This does not mean that these years were not important in his apprenticeship: it was during this period that his household and council were shaped, that he made some of the most formative friendships of his life, including those with the earls of Arundel and Warwick and a particularly influential and tightly knit group of Herefordshire knights, and that he learnt the value of close military discipline and a steady and reliable flow of cash as preconditions for any military enterprise. His experience may also have taught him that Wales was certainly not a country where great military victories were easily, if ever, secured. As king he quickly drew a line under the revolt and sought to channel the valour and appetite of the Welsh to his own military enterprises abroad.[18]

Others probably shared his view. His father's cousin Edward, duke of York, was a shifty political character for whom a spell of distinguished service in Wales might make amends for his tortuous political record. He was given his opportunity when Henry IV appointed him lieutenant of south Wales and keeper of the key fortress of Carmarthen in 1403; but if his letters are taken at face value he found garrison duty in that lonely outpost even more frightening than the high risks of the English political hothouse. He was to return to Wales, like so many others, to witness the grand finale of the siege of Aberystwyth; but it was at Agincourt that he was to find fame and death. Perhaps only two of the greater English aristocrats could look back on their period of service in Wales with some degree of satisfaction. Richard Beauchamp, earl of Warwick, began his distinguished military career there, participating in the Battle of Shrewsbury, taking charge of the key fortress of Brecon during the particularly dangerous winter of 1403–4, and inflicting a defeat on Glyn Dŵr near Abergavenny which entered into legend and so into his pictorial biography (plate 7). Richard Beauchamp had a personal reason for his involvement in Wales: he was owner of the Marcher

lordship of Elfael. The same consideration doubtless explains why Thomas Fitzalan, earl of Arundel and owner of extensive lordships in north-east Wales, played such a prominent and distinguished part in the defence of the northern March against Glyn Dŵr. It was a measure of Prince Henry's appreciation of the key role played by the earls of Warwick and Arundel and the profound bond of friendship that such service had created between them and the prince that both of them came to be retained for life by him and rewarded with a very handsome annuity of 250 marks (£166 13s. 4d.) each.[19]

But it was not among the higher echelons of the aristocracy that the English heroes of the Glyn Dŵr wars were to be found, but at the more modest levels of the regional commanders and the constables of castles. There were the men who sat out the rebellion month after month in their often lonely outposts and waited patiently and often very uncomfortably for it to blow itself out. Among the regional commanders two are immediately identified by contemporary commendations; they may serve to represent their comrades. In March 1406 parliament recommended that Richard, Lord Grey of Codnor, should be rewarded for his services against the Welsh rebels; it had chosen its man well. Grey was a man long in the military tooth; he had served in Ireland and Scotland and as one of the king's admirals. In Wales his postings included a spell as overall commander in south Wales in 1402–3 and a prolonged session as captain of Brecon. He was in Usk Castle when it was attacked by the Welsh and was also present when they were defeated at Pwll Melyn in May 1405. When the rebellion ended he was appointed, appropriately enough, justice of South Wales before assuming wider governmental and diplomatic responsibilities for Henry IV and Henry V. Few men had been more crucial to the English war effort in south Wales than Richard Grey. One who might compete with him was Gilbert Talbot of Castle Goodrich in Herefordshire. In 1406 Talbot was given a special reward of £100 by the king, nor would anyone begrudge it to him given his services past and future. He had led a retinue of 100 men in the prince's service since 1403, had taken a relief expedition to Beaumaris the same year, and was prominent in the defeat of the Welsh at Grosmont in March 1405. It was he, above all, who was responsible for bringing the siege of Harlech to a successful close in February 1409 and he was given the responsibility of guarding the borders with a force of 900 men in 1410. Nor were his duties over when the military action had ended, for it was he, as justiciar of both North Wales and Chester, who was entrusted with the task of holding judicial sessions throughout the region, where the communities submitted to the king, pleaded for pardons, and agreed to pay large communal fines. It was Gilbert Talbot appropriately enough who was also commissioned to hold discussions with the still-elusive Glyn Dŵr as late as July 1415, and subsequently with Glyn Dŵr's son, Maredudd. If there was a single English hero of the Glyn

Dŵr wars it was surely Gilbert Talbot; he was indeed a worthy elder brother of the great Sir John Talbot, later earl of Shrewsbury.[20]

Talbot and Grey operated on regional stages; but ultimately, as we shall see, effective resistance to Glyn Dŵr came to rest on individual castles and their keepers. Had these fallen—as it looked for a time in the summer of 1403 they might—then the Welsh forces would have made a clean military sweep of the country and the process of recovery would have been proportionately more difficult. So long, however, as their garrisons held out, the Welsh would be denied their triumph, and the castles would serve as bases from which the reconquest of the countryside would be achieved in the fullness of time. So the quality of the castellans, or constables of castles, was crucial to the English war effort. Some of them, like Robert Parys and his son at Caernarfon, were local men who had authority thrust upon them; some, such as Richard Arundel at Hay, were long-serving and experienced royal knights dispatched on a spell of service in Wales; others, such as Edward Charlton at Powys or Thomas Carew at Narberth, were local magnates with a vested interest in securing military control of their home areas; and yet others—such as Richard Massy at Harlech and Reynold Baildon at Conway—were drawn from the gentry of the English border shires, notably from Cheshire in the north and Herefordshire in the south. It is a member of this latter category, Sir John Greyndour of Abenhall (Co. Gloucs.), who may serve to illustrate how crucial were the services of these constables during the Welsh war. His own account shows that he was personally present in command of the garrison at Radnor Castle for a total of 422 days across the period August 1402–March 1404, including the critical summer and autumn months of 1403. He later took charge of the Duchy of Lancaster castles of Monmouth, Whitecastle, and Skenfrith and by 1404 was captain of Aberystwyth. Nor was his military service confined to garrison duty: he fought at Shrewsbury, led a retinue of 120 men in the service of the prince of Wales in June–July 1403, was mentioned in dispatches for his role in the victory over the Welsh at Grosmont in March 1405, and was among those at the siege of Aberystwyth in 1407. It was men such as Sir John Greyndour who had saved the English king's bacon in Wales during the Glyn Dŵr revolt.[21]

By the summer of 1401, and certainly by midsummer 1402, the English had lost the military initiative in Wales. Henceforth for the better part of four years they were on the defensive, rushing from place to place like an over-extended fire brigade to try to extinguish or at least douse the flames of revolt. Control of much of the countryside throughout Wales had effectively been lost by 1403, and much of the military effort in the short term had now to be concentrated on providing desperately needed relief for the hard-pressed and isolated castle garrisons, often

the sole surviving outposts of English authority in their districts. We can catch a vivid glimpse of what such enterprises might entail in the accounts of the frenetic efforts to bring relief to Harlech Castle in May–June 1403. Messengers were sent in advance to provide a fuller and more up-to-date account of the actual state of affairs; loans were raised; the steward and his fellow officials at Denbigh were asked to provide succour; twenty-six horses, escorted by a guard of six men, faced a perilous journey over five days to carry supplies from Chester to the castle (the round journey took some twelve days); an advance party from Cheshire, led by Sir John Stanley and Hugh Mortimer, began to raise the siege on 15 May; by early June a much larger force consisting of seven knights, ninety-nine esquires, and 1,200 archers had been assembled for the same purpose; while the prince of Wales himself added his presence to the venture, travelling from Chester to Harlech and thence to Aberystwyth before returning to Shrewsbury twelve days later. The relief-effort achieved its purpose, but at immense cost in money and resources. And it was an effort which had to be repeated scores of times across Wales in these years. Thus, within less than a month of the costly operation to relieve Harlech the sheriff of Hereford was reporting how he had led a force to raise the siege of Brecon, killing (so he claimed) 240 of its attackers in the process. Inland castles such as Brecon particularly needed to be relieved, since they could not be provisioned by sea. Coety Castle in Glamorgan proved particularly vulnerable: it had to be relieved twice, first in November 1404 by a force assembled by the prince of Wales and his brother, and secondly in September 1405 by Henry IV himself.[22]

The armies assembled by the English in these years spent their time not only in relieving hard-pressed castles but also in protecting the English border shires in so far as possible. From 1403 until 1405 the English seem, consciously or otherwise, to have pursued a policy of containment vis-à-vis the rebellion in Wales. They initiated no major expedition, but concentrated instead on defending their castles in Wales and on providing as much security as possible for the English border shires from Welsh raids. For much of 1404 the prince of Wales was stationed with a force of 600–700 soldiers at Hereford and Leominster, policing the frontier in that area and dispatching occasional detachments to serve in Welsh outposts such as Brecon. Substantial garrisons were likewise placed in major castles of the northern borderland, notably Oswestry, Montgomery, and Welshpool. The English border shires certainly paid a heavy price for the Welsh revolt, indeed doubly so. They were a natural target for Welsh raids (as the accounts for the Arundel manors in western Shropshire show vividly); it is little wonder that some of them were driven in despair to conclude temporary truces with the rebels. But they were also the natural recruiting grounds for the armies dispatched into Wales. It was on Cheshire in particular that the brunt of the effort

against the rebels in north Wales fell. Already in May 1402 the manorial court at Halton could only muster six jurors; the rest, so it was claimed, had been recruited to serve in Wales. And so the story continued for the next few years: in November 1403 an armed barge carrying twenty rowers, thirty archers, and ten men-at-arms sailed from Chester to inspect the Anglesey coast and re-view the state of Beaumaris Castle, and again in the spring of 1406 the pro-cess of the pacification of Anglesey was entrusted to the sheriff of Chester and a group of forty men-at-arms and 300 archers. It was little wonder that the good citizens of Shrewsbury observed with an air of jaundiced exhaustion in 1407 that they had served on every royal expedition to Wales 'without fee or reward'.[23]

The English may have been on the defensive in Wales for most of the period 1402–6, but every good commander knows that attack is the best form of defence. Counter-attack was not easy for English troops in the unfriendly Welsh terrain and against an elusive enemy, but it could be used to give the Welsh a dose of their own medicine. On 15 May 1403 the prince of Wales provided his father with an account of such an English raid. The date is significant. The prince had received a report that Glyn Dŵr was assembling a large force for a major offensive. It was a credible report: Hotspur may have already been preparing the plot that was to lead to the Battle of Shrewsbury and, even if he had not, Glyn Dŵr had certainly launched the summer offensive which was eventually to lead him on his great triumphant march through south Wales in early July. The prince must also have been aware that Harlech Castle was in a desperate crisis, for on the very day of his letter an initial force set out from Chester to relieve it. In these circumstances the prince's response was a pre-emptive raid which burnt Glyn Dŵr's home at Sycharth and the houses of several of his tenants, crossed the Berwyn mountains to Glyndyfrdwy where he likewise laid the district waste, proceeded to capture and execute some of Glyn Dŵr's supporters (though one of them had tried to buy his life with an offer of £500), and then harried the commote of Edeirnion. The account no doubt improved in the telling, but the letter shows that Welsh terror could be matched by English terror. There were many episodes like it, no doubt: the sheriff of Herefordshire in August 1404, for example, encouraged the prince to lead another pillaging raid into Gwent and Glamorgan to take the rebel pressure off Herefordshire and Gloucestershire, and the prince's own letter suggests that he indeed did so. And as always in war and rebellion, the cover of hostilities provided a golden opportunity for individ-uals and communities to pillage and profiteer, as did the men of Bristol when they invaded lowland Glamorgan or the men of Somerset and Devon who carried off whole boatloads of cattle, sheep, and goods from Glamorgan under the cover of rebellion.[24]

We may accept, therefore, that there was rather more to the English war effort in Wales than the sequence of pathetically brief and ineffective royal expeditions. Yet it cannot be denied that the overwhelming impression during the years 1402–6 is that of passivity verging on paralysis. It was in this situation that the castles of Wales were put to their severest test and were given an opportunity to show their true worth. It was appropriate that it should be so, for nowhere in the British Isles had the Norman and English conquerors invested so heavily in the castle as the guarantee of their continuing mastery as they had in Wales. It is very difficult to hazard a guess as to how many of these castles were in some sort of working order as defensive military fortresses in 1400; 100–120 might not be too wide of the mark. They varied widely in distribution and quality: the six shires in direct Crown possession (Anglesey, Caernarfonshire, Merionethshire, Flintshire, Cardiganshire, and Carmarthenshire) were protected by only about fourteen castles, but these included, of course, some of the most majestic and impregnable fortresses in medieval Europe. In Pembroke, Gower, and Glamorgan, on the other hand, there was a much higher density of castles, but many of these were now more in the nature of fortified private residences than military fortresses. Some of the Welsh castles—Caernarfon, Pembroke, and Kidwelly among them—seem to have been kept in a state of tolerable repair as defensible centres; a few others—Ruthin in the north and Caldicot in the south-east are examples— were still on the domestic circuit of their lords and had a modicum of comfort. But leaving aside the smaller castles and moated houses of the resident English squirearchy of the southern lowlands of Wales, the great majority of the castles of Wales in 1400 were in a sadly dilapidated state.

Nor is that surprising. They had become mementoes of a bygone military age. There had been no revolt or threat of revolt in most parts of Wales for over a century. Most castles now functioned only as administrative and financial centres and no more than a few chambers and stables were kept in repair to meet the needs of a small cadre of resident officers—often no more than three or four, with their servants—and visiting auditors and seignorial agents. Most of them had not been garrisoned for decades, other than during an occasional emergency or invasion scare as in 1369–70 or 1377, and even then the force stationed in them had been skeletal and short-term. Roofs leaked, lead was not replaced, timbers rotted: such is the recurrent theme of reports on the state of the castles. Stocks of armour and equipment, let alone food, were pathetic. A list of the contents of Harlech Castle in June 1403 helps to explain why it was so difficult for the garrison to mount an effective defence of it: there were only three shields, eight basinets, six lances (of which four lacked heads), ten pairs of useless gloves, four guns, and various stocks of iron and lead. The desperate measures that had to be taken once news of Glyn Dŵr's revolt broke were themselves a comment on the sad state of

decay of most castles: at Kidwelly, for example, frenetic repair works began in July 1401 and continued, especially on the Gatehouse Tower, throughout 1402; at Denbigh ditches were cleaned, 'barryers' were erected to defend the town, and carpenters and masons were hurriedly hired to repair the Westgate, Towngate, and town walls; even in Newport, in the relative safety of south-east Wales, the very considerable sum of £144 was spent on repairs to the castle in 1403–5.[25]

The castles were certainly in poor state of repairs; even so they were fundamental to the strategy of English survival and, eventually, recovery in Wales. *In extremis*, of course, they could provide safe havens into which the burgesses and English settlers of the surrounding countryside could retreat when the town itself was burnt. This is what happened at both Flint and Kidwelly in the torrid summer months of 1403. Their capacity to withstand extended sieges was enhanced by building mills within them, as happened at both Conway and Beaumaris during the revolt. Many of them were located on the sea or estuaries, which enabled them to be supplied even when control of their rural environs had been totally lost. Nor was their role merely negative. When it became apparent that the revolt was not to be intimidated into extinction by royal expeditions, the castles became the nodal points around which English military strategy in Wales was built, both as outposts which frustrated the Welsh rebels from securing total control of the country, and as bases from which punitive raids could be launched and, eventually, control of the countryside re-secured. The centrality of the castles is clear in some of the regional commands that were created: when Richard Grey of Codnor was appointed the king's lieutenant in south Wales in late September 1402 his command was defined not geographically but in terms of the six castles (Brecon, Aberystwyth, Cardigan, Carmarthen, Builth, and Hay) placed under his control. The same was true of Edward, duke of York, when he was appointed to a similar position a year later. Indeed, during the peak years of the revolt civilian governance and offices were suspended in most parts of Wales and the constables of castles were given full governmental, judicial, and financial powers (or such as they could manage to exercise) as well as military command over their lordships. It was an acknowledgement that the castle had become the residual English presence in Wales. How much this was so can also be illustrated cartographically by the accompanying map (map 5): it shows that at least eighty-two castles in Wales and its immediate borders were placed in a state of defence during the revolt; and the figure no doubt would be considerably higher were our records fuller and our search of them more assiduous.[26]

In fact the records of the castle garrisons are much the most prolific source for the military history of the revolt. They help to show that castles and their garrisons could be put to a variety of military uses. The vast majority of Welsh

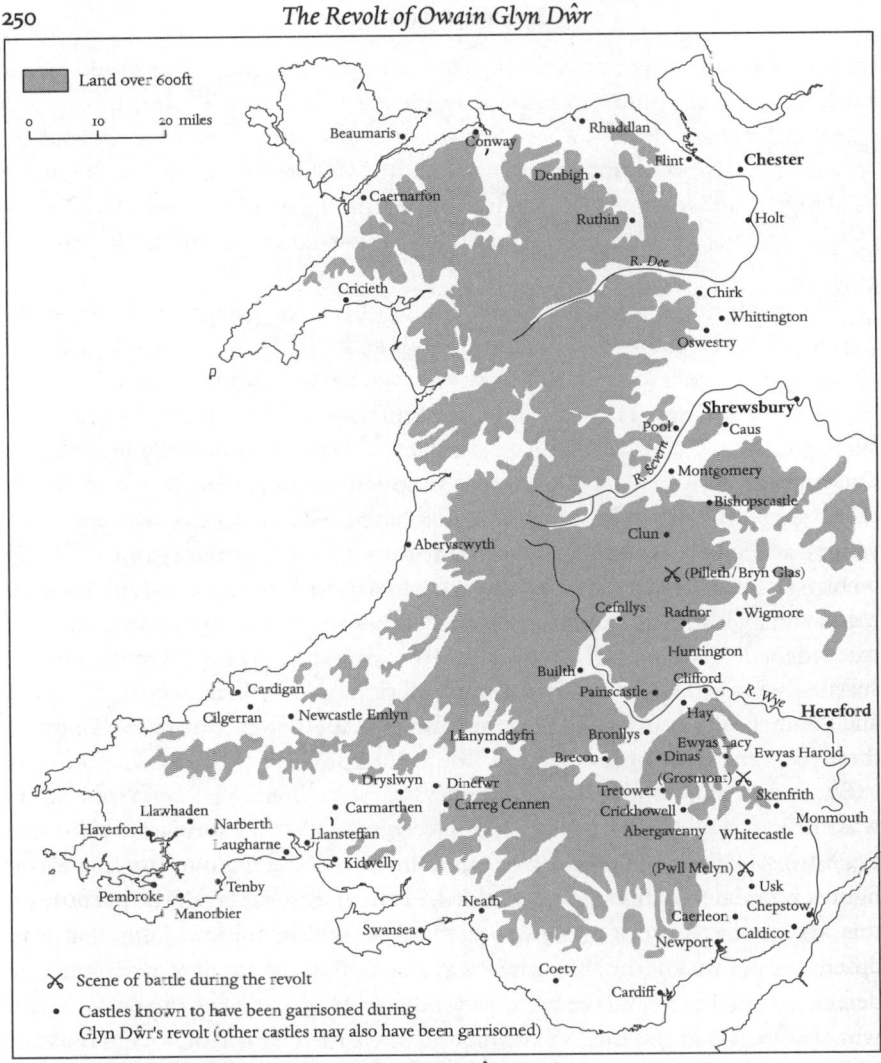

MAP 5. The castles of Wales during the Glyn Dŵr revolt

castles were defended by very modest garrisons, rarely more than thirty men, during the revolt, even in the most difficult periods. The purpose of these garrisons was no more than to keep the English flag flying by retaining control of often very isolated fortresses. Life must have been truly frightening in them at times. At Dinefwr in the Tywi valley on 7 July 1403 the constable, 'writing in haste and in dread', said that he would have no option if no relief was forthcoming but to abandon the castle by night and flee to Brecon. But it is from Caernarfon that the most vivid vignette of life in a besieged castle comes, for in that case a news report can be amplified by documentary evidence. The report of 16 January 1404

speaks for itself; it was brought to Chester by a woman, for no man dared act as a messenger:

The Welsh rebels of Owain Glyn Dŵr with the French and all his other forces are preparing to assault the town and castle of Caernarfon. They have begun to do so on the very day we write these letters with engines, siege equipment, and very long ladders. There are only twenty-eight fighting men in the town and castle and that is too small a force. Eleven of the more able men who were there during the last siege have died, some of them from wounds suffered at the time of the assault, and others of plague. The castle and town are in very great danger as the bearer of these letters will testify to you by word of mouth.

We have complete accounts of the garrisons of both the castle and the town of Caernarfon from June 1403 to May 1408, and they show that the report was not much exaggerated either for January 1404 or for the period as a whole. In January 1404 there were twelve archers defending the castle and twenty-seven defending the town (of whom two died shortly), and for most of the period as a whole this was the order of magnitude of the two garrisons at Caernarfon, some thirty-six men. The same was true for many of the castles of north and south Wales for which detailed accounts survive—such as Flint, Rhuddlan, Conway, Beaumaris, Kidwelly, Carreg Cennen, and Dinefwr. By and large the defence of the last outposts of English rule in Wales in these years rested on the shoulders of very few men.[27]

But this was not always so. In the very months that the defence of Caernarfon was run on a human shoe-string, the forces mustered at Montgomery on the English border was composed of twenty men-at-arms and 100 archers, and these figures were later increased to fifty men-at-arms and 150 archers. The purpose of this and similar large forces such as those at Welshpool and Oswestry was different from that of the tiny garrison at Caernarfon. It was in part certainly to defend Montgomery and the associated castles of Caus and Bishopscastle, but it was also to defend the English border districts from the raids of Welshmen and to do so by forays into north Wales as well as by stationary garrison duty. There were even larger garrisons in some of the major south Wales castles, and the contrast in purpose and size between them and the small garrisons of most castles is even more striking. At Brecon from October 1403 to February 1404—that is, at the very time that thirty men were expected to withstand the combined Franco-Welsh attack on Caernarfon—the earl of Warwick and Lord Audley were in charge of a force of 400 troops, while the duke of York, for all his pathetic whining, had 550 or so soldiers under his command at Carmarthen. Clearly garrisons of this order were performing a very different function from those of Caernarfon and Carreg Cennen. They were captained by men of great political eminence; they had been contracted to serve immediately after a royal

expedition had marched through Brecon to Carmarthen. Their purpose was to impress and terrify the rebels by their sheer size, and they were no doubt expected not only to defend the castles effectively (Brecon had been closely besieged in the summer of 1403 and Carmarthen briefly captured) but also to begin the process of pacification of the surrounding countryside.[28]

The English war effort in Wales, therefore, especially after 1402–3, was built around the castle. The cost was enormous. The budget for sustaining the garrison of Carmarthen alone for one year at the monthly level of expenditure of October 1403 would have been £5,160. The royal council came to the sobering conclusion, probably in 1404, that if sixteen of the castles in royal possession or custody in Wales were to be properly defended then the garrisons would total some 1,415 men at a daily cost of £42. But there was no alternative. Government military advisers had realized, after the fiasco of the four royal expeditions of 1400–3, that if the king's authority was to be restored in Wales forces based at some of the key castles would need to be integrated fully with any proposed expeditionary force. So when a blueprint was drawn up for a new attempt to loosen Owain Glyn Dŵr's grip in south Wales in 1405 the royal expeditionary force was to be only some 860 men, whereas 2,400 soldiers were to be posted in eight strategic castles from Radnor to Aberystwyth. In the event the proposed expedition had to be aborted (because of the news of Archbishop Scrope's rebellion in Yorkshire); but the plan was an acknowledgement that in the recovery of English control in Wales from 1405 onwards, as well as in the desperate defence of English power there 1402–5, the castle was central. Indeed, the Glyn Dŵr revolt had at last vindicated the huge investment in money and resources which had been put over the generations into the castles in Wales. Dilapidated as they might be, their walls were too strong to withstand the primitive military equipment at the command of the Welsh, and their supply lines proved remarkably effective. This was to be the last major war in Wales in which castles were to play a vital role; they came through the test with flying colours.[29]

The English had a priceless asset in the vast network of castles in Wales; but they had other advantages also which should serve them well, especially in the medium and long term. One was their control of the latest military technology and equipment. The list of military supplies ordered for Brecon in February 1404 illustrates the point: it included six cannon, twenty pounds of gunpowder, ten pounds of sulphur, and twenty pounds of saltpetre, as well as forty-two breastplates and twelve basinets. At Brecon the purpose of such an assemblage of arms was defensive, as it was for the guns that were taken to Harlech in 1402: the psychological impact of witnessing the latest military technology in action must have been disturbing for the poorly equipped Welsh besiegers. But it was in

attack rather than defence that such sophisticated armaments truly came into their own. The Welsh rebels had only captured and held on to two major castles during the revolt, Harlech and Aberystwyth; and the uprising was effectively brought to an end with great set-piece sieges of both of them in 1407–9. Guns were brought from as far away as Pontefract, transported to Bristol, and then taken by sea via Carmarthen to aid in the sieges. One massive canon deployed in the siege of Aberystwyth weighed almost 5,000 lb. and was called 'Messager', while another used at Harlech bore the affectionate name of 'the king's daughter'. The prospect of facing such fire-breathing monsters must have been daunting for the Welsh defenders of these outposts; one of them, William Gwyn ap Rhys Llwyd of Cydweli, is known to have died from wounds inflicted by a cannonball at Aberystwyth. The contest had become more than ever a confrontation of David and Goliath; but it was a tribute to the doggedness of the Welsh that the English had felt compelled to bring their heavy guns, literally, to crush the revolt.[30]

In the event one of those guns, the Messager, exploded when it was fired at Aberystwyth. This explosion has a twofold symbolic significance. On the one hand, it illustrates that superiority in equipment and technology, important as it certainly was, could not of itself deliver a quick victory in a guerrilla war; on the other hand it underlines the misfortunes and incompetence which attended the English war effort in Wales. Indeed, the sieges of Aberystwyth 1407–8 and Harlech 1408–9 ensured that the last two major acts of the revolt brought as little glory to the English as had the rest of their campaign in Wales. It had been planned otherwise. A distinguished cast, headed by the prince of Wales, the duke of York, and the earl of Warwick, assembled outside Aberystwyth in the summer of 1407 to witness what was expected to be a short siege. By early September even the terms of a formal surrender of the castle had been arranged by the mediation of none other than the chancellor of the university of Oxford. But in the event fiasco rather than success was the outcome of the siege: dissension and desertion sapped the determination of the English force, while Glyn Dŵr, by decisive military action, put new heart into the Welsh garrison. It was not to be until 1408 that Aberystwyth eventually capitulated to the English, and Harlech seems to have held out until early February 1409 after a prolonged siege by Gilbert Talbot. Both castles seem to have fallen eventually not to cannon-balls or exploding guns but to lack of supplies and a Welsh war effort exhausted by hard winters.[31]

Cannons and guns, therefore, may not have provided salvation for the English in Wales; ships certainly did. Land travel into Wales in the medieval period was always difficult, especially for the equipment, men, and provisions needed for invading armies and besieged garrisons; during the revolt such travel was

well-nigh impossible, other than in laboured and hugely expensive expeditions. It was then that the sea came into its own. In spite of some flurries of activity by French and Scottish ships and some buccaneering acts of piracy by the Welsh in south-west Wales, English command of the seas around Wales was unchallenged. It could be put to various purposes. One such purpose clearly was to provide military relief for the hard-pressed garrisons of the coastal castles, especially from 1403 onwards. It was, for example, from Bristol or Dunster that a force of seventy men-at-arms and 200 mounted men was to set out for the relief of Carmarthen in late 1403, and it was from the port of Uphill in Somerset that the men of Devon were commanded to go to the rescue of Cardiff Castle in the same period. Equally crucial, especially in the isolated castles of the north and west, was the part played by ships in providing vital supplies in the months and sometimes years when they were otherwise isolated. One episode can speak for scores of others recorded in the documentation: in April 1404 John Stevens of Bristol was commissioned to assemble five fully armed ships to take victuals to the castles of Cardigan, Aberystwyth, Harlech, and Caernarfon. Castles and ships between them alone permitted the English to cling on to the remnants of their power in Wales during the Glyn Dŵr revolt.[32]

The sea was equally crucial when the time was ripe to make a counter-attack against Welsh pretensions. Bristol and Chester were the key posts in this respect, as they were in the English war effort in general. It was from Chester, for example, that in October 1403 an armed barge, manned by sixty soldiers, set out to patrol the coastline of Anglesey and to provide succour to Beaumaris Castle. Such a patrol may have been essentially defensive but by July 1406 English naval power was crucial in what was to be the first, and highly successful, offensive against the rebels in north Wales for almost two years. Thomas Tickhill, the prince of Wales's steward, and John Mainwaring, sheriff of Cheshire, led a force by sea from Chester to begin the process of quelling the revolt in Anglesey. Simultaneously, Thomas Bolde, the constable of Beaumaris, was stationed with a detachment of sixty men on the Menai Straits to prevent 'rebels from other parts of Wales from crossing to the island of Anglesey to excite the people of the island to rebel'. Anglesey was crucial to the English strategy for the recovery of the upper hand in Wales; it was crucial because as an island it could be insulated from the rest of the country and could be subdued by the very means which the English had recognized as their strength, control of the sea. Indeed, already in 1405, if a later account is to be accepted, a massive raid led by Stephen Scrope, deputy lieutenant of Ireland, deep into Anglesey had shown how vulnerable the island was and how easily rebel control of it could be overwhelmed. Henry IV and his military advisers were beginning to learn another lesson that even a cursory reading of Edward I's strategy could have taught them: control of

Anglesey was the essential stepping-stone to the subjugation of north Wales, and control of Anglesey was readily achieved by sea.[33]

If castles and shipping were two of the keys to the survival and, subsequently, recovery of English power in Wales, the third was supplies. There were two aspects which worked to the advantage of the English in this respect. First, whatever the shortcomings of English military strategists, they were able to assemble and deliver the essential supplies of food and equipment for the garrisons, besieged populations, and military forces in Wales. Occasionally such garrisons might undertake raids into the surrounding countryside to replenish their depleted stocks, especially of cattle and sheep, as happened at Conway in 1404; but for much of the period 1403–6 they depended on provisions assembled in England. In general Chester was the provision centre for the castles of the north and west from Flint to Aberystwyth, Bristol for the castles of the south-west from Aberystwyth to Kidwelly. Along the border Hereford, Worcester, Gloucester, and Shrewsbury played similar roles for the inland castles of eastern Wales. Supplies were also shipped from Ireland and from across the Bristol Channel in Somerset and Devon. Leading merchants doubtless made considerable profits from such trade, but sometimes at considerable risk to themselves, as John Horn the London fishmonger found to his cost when he was captured taking provisions to English troops in Harlech and not only lost his boat but also had to pay a ransom for his release. Detailed accounts show the complex logistical problems which had to be confronted if lines of supply were to be kept open. Thus, when stocks ran low in the town of Carmarthen in the summer of 1404, wine, wheat, and salt were bought in considerable quantities at Bristol and Tewkesbury; a broker was instructed to search for a better bargain in wine; appropriate receptacles and packaging for the materials had to be arranged; the goods had to be transported to the ship at 'the Backs' at Bristol; and a pilot from Llansteffan was hired to guide the ship on its journey from Bristol to Carmarthen. The whole enterprise cost almost £79, but such arrangements were the very lifeline of survival for English rule in Wales in these years.[34]

But there was a second, equally important, and ultimately even more crucial, dimension to the English control of supplies, that of starving the Welsh of their supplies. Well-placed contemporary observers such as Sir Thomas Carew and the prince of Wales were not in doubt that shortage of food was the major reason for the wide-ranging raids of Glyn Dŵr's men. They were equally aware that an economic blockade, in respect both of food and arms, would eventually be one of the most effective ways of bringing the Welsh to heel. Here again their thoughts and actions had a long lineage in English policy towards Wales: already in the twelfth century William of Newburgh and Gerald of Wales had observed that Wales's economic dependence on England made it militarily and politically

vulnerable, and Edward I, with characteristic thoroughness, had used an economic embargo as one of his weapons against the Welsh. Henry IV and his advisers now followed suit. From 1401 onwards they and their local agents in the borders of Wales issued a whole barrage of prohibitions on the sale of food and arms to the Welsh. The merchants of Chester and Shrewsbury, long accustomed to good trading relationships with the Welsh, were a particular target for such prohibitions; but the ban was also extended to the counties of Cornwall, Devon, and Somerset and even, in respect of arms, to the city of London. But as so often in these matters rhetoric does not seem to have been matched by practical success, and a vigorous black market in trade with the rebels seems to have operated both within Wales (as the accusations against the double-dealing and corrupt chamberlain of north Wales, Thomas Barneby, suggest) and across the borders with England. Indeed, the government itself realized that a total ban would have harmed its own supporters in Wales and so it relaxed its own policy by issuing licences to named individuals to buy specified quotas of food for their own households. Yet in spite of evasions—of which the frequent reissue of prohibitions and the periodic confiscation of goods suspected of being destined for Welsh rebels are evidence enough—there is little doubt that the policy of an economic blockade and an arms embargo bit deep. It did so, no doubt, less because of government directives and more because of the suspension of normal trading relationships. But the end result was to starve the Welsh of the resources in food and arms which alone could enable them to sustain the revolt, and the situation was certainly compounded by the desperate winter conditions in 1407–8, one of the worst in living memory. Where English arms and armies had failed, deprivation and starvation eventually brought the Welsh to their knees.[35]

Suppressing a communal, guerrilla-style revolt is never easy, even where the advantages in technology, resources, and manpower are so transparently unequal. That has been a recurrent phenomenon across the centuries. So it was in Wales during Owain Glyn Dŵr's revolt. Over and above the reasons we have given so far there are at least two others which contemporaries recognized as helping to explain why the English authorities took so long to quell the revolt. One arose out of the structure of governmental authority in Wales. Wales had never known governmental or administrative unity; it lacked a governmental or political centre; it was no more than an assemblage of virtually autonomous units. The most coherent blocs of power in the country were composed of the six shires under direct royal control, but even these were effectively governed from three governmental headquarters—Carmarthen, Caernarfon, and Chester (for Flintshire). The rest of Wales was composed of some forty or so lordships, which were governmentally and judicially independent of each other and into none of

which did English administrative and legal control normally extend. Such utter fragmentation was a nightmare for anyone attempting to construct a coherent military command; only the force and ruthlessness of Edward I's personality had briefly overcome the problem in the 1270s and 1280s. It was now the turn of Henry IV and his commanders to be exasperated by the fragmentation that was Wales. Sometimes it took the form of petty bureaucratic obstructiveness: Richard Grey of Codnor was infuriated, as the king's commander in south Wales in 1402–3, to find that the officials of the lordship of Monmouth (a part of the Duchy of Lancaster and thereby of Henry IV's private inheritance) would not hand over the money assigned to him by the king himself on the grounds that it was Duchy rather than royal income. Even more seriously, Grey found that local communities took such a parochial view of their responsibilities that, like the men of Pembrokeshire, they refused to co-operate in military operations with him even though 'they were so close to the areas of rebellion'. The frustration of commanders also spilt over into angry letters when they realized that they had no authority to chase rebel forces into neighbouring lordships or even into royal lands without first securing a licence to do so. As the revolt intensified and civilian governance effectively disintegrated in most parts of Wales, some measures were indeed taken to address the problems raised by governmental fragmentation. Regional and even national military commands were created which ignored the existing framework of authority, and likewise an attempt was made to co-ordinate royal expenditure in Wales by channelling all royal funds directly to the prince of Wales and giving him authority to distribute them. These were measures in the right direction but they were only undertaken belatedly and executed half-heartedly. They did nothing to blunt the criticism of military commanders or of the political classes in England, especially the commons in parliament, that the governmental shambles that was Wales was a disgrace and that the great Marcher lords should be ordered—like the absentee English lords in Ireland—to return to their estates in Wales, fortify their castles, and be held personally responsible for quelling the revolt in their own areas from their own resources. In the event, and in spite of much righteous indignation, no major measures for the civilian or military reorganization of the country was under-taken. Nevertheless it was a tribute to the national character and impact of Glyn Dŵr's revolt that it had put the question of the future governmental and legal structure of Wales on the agenda of thinking political men.[36]

The other contemporary explanation for the inadequacy of the English gov-ernment's response to the Welsh revolt was not peculiar to Wales but rather was a general feature which bedevilled Henry IV's rule, especially in the first half of his reign—a desperate shortage of cash. Henry IV, it has been appropriately commented, was 'chronically indebted'. His financial crisis was at its worst in the

summer of 1402, when his income from customs revenues crashed dramatically and when his cash receipts reached the lowest levels of the reign. For the next four years or so Henry lurched from one financial crisis to another, desperately seeking loans to tide him over the latest emergency, pledging his jewels as security for such loans, defaulting or at least postponing many of the cash payments or assignments he owed, and generally living from hand to mouth in the most desperate and demeaning of fashions. The consequences of this pro-longed financial crisis were profound. Consistent policy, let alone long-term planning, was hardly possible, and the very credibility of the regime was likely to be called in question when, to quote but one example, the wages of the key English garrisons at Calais were two years in arrears. Above all, perhaps, such acute financial debility undermined the king's political authority, already deeply flawed by the highly questionable way he had seized the throne in 1399. During 1404–6 in particular he was forced to make a whole series of deeply humiliating political concessions and surrenders in order to persuade his highly critical parliaments to give him the minimum taxes which would just about keep him financially afloat.[37]

    This, then was the background—that of an acute and prolonged financial crisis and of a deeply damaged political regime—against which the revolt in Wales and the English attempts to deal with it, especially in the years 1403–6, need to be seen. The Welsh revolt compounded both the financial predicament and the political embarrassment of the English government. Wales had been a major source of revenue for the kings and lords of England throughout the fourteenth century. Henry IV had every reason to expect that this situation would continue after 1399; indeed, his family could expect to draw more revenue from Wales than any previous royal household. The estimated gross annual income of the six royal shires in Wales in 1400 was almost £6,000; the actual gross income of the Duchy of Lancaster in Wales (including the share of the Bohun inheritance acquired by Henry IV through his first wife) was £2,580 in 1400. If to these sums are added the revenue collected from estates forfeited by the Crown (such as the great lordship of Glamorgan forfeited from Thomas Despenser in 1400 and worth well over £1,000 per annum) and those lands temporarily in the king's custody (such as the vast Mortimer inheritance in Wales worth £2,400 per annum), then one might estimate that Henry IV could, at least potentially, expect to draw £12,000–£14,000 per annum from Wales. We can put this figure into some sort of perspective by recalling that Henry IV's net personal revenue in England was possibly of the order of £6,200 and 'his revenue [as king of England] in a good year rose to something over £90,000 . . . and never fell below £75,000'. Even if we treat such figures with caution, it is obvious that Henry IV had every reason to cherish Wales. Indeed, he would cherish it the more because the income he derived from

it was regarded as his personal fortune, outside the range of the backbiting criticism of his parliaments and detractors. He could use it for his personal needs or to grant a working appanage to his eldest son and heir or as a major source of reward for his political friends and servants.[38]

Any loss of revenue from Wales would, therefore, be a blow to this hard-pressed king. This was reason enough why Henry IV was initially unwilling to concede that the suppression of the revolt should be a drain on his general finances. So it was that the young prince of Wales was firmly told that the cost of recapturing Conway Castle in 1401 was formally a charge on his revenue, not on his royal exchequer. Towns were likewise told to find moneys to repair their walls themselves and even to meet the costs of garrisons stationed in them by raising their own war subsidies. It was in the same spirit that major judicial sessions were held in the royal and Duchy of Lancaster estates in Wales in 1401—to raise more money in order to quell the revolt. The result was, of course, quite the opposite. Throughout the revolt the political classes in England tried to wash their hands of any responsibility for the financing of the Welsh wars. As the speaker of the House of Commons put it in November 1407, 'they are in no way required or obliged to sustain the wars in Wales'. Their solution was quite simple and had been reiterated from the earliest days of the revolt: all Crown lands in Wales granted as gifts should be resumed into royal control and the income from them, from escheated estates and lands in custody, and from the fines and confiscated lands of rebels should be used directly for the subjugation of the country. Likewise the Marcher lords should be told in no uncertain terms to return to their Welsh estates and be held responsible for quelling the revolt from their own revenues.[39]

Solutions looked simple in Westminster; but from 1403 such solutions were pipe-dreams and ritual political rhetoric. From 1403 to 1407, and sometimes later, most of the estates of the English king and lords in Wales were financially a dead loss; they yielded virtually no revenue. Adam of Usk had grasped the consequences of this financial loss fully: the English, he remarked, 'were pressed to hold their own in war against France, Scotland, Ireland, Wales, and Flanders, and owing to war they had lost £60,000 which Wales was accustomed to pay'. Adam's estimate of the revenues normally derived from Wales may have been an exaggeration, but in another respect he may be said to have underestimated the impact of the Welsh war on the king's finances. For the impact of war was, of course, not to be measured solely in the loss of revenue but equally in the massive expenditure it entailed. Already, right at the outset of the revolt in late 1400, the king and his council were given a frightening insight into the scale the war expenditure might be: a plan to put substantial garrisons into eight castles across north Wales alone was estimated to cost £5,651 annually, that is, equivalent to

almost the gross estimated income (£5,996) of all the six royal shires in Wales. Expenditure at that level could clearly not long be sustained from local revenues. Nor was it. The revenue of the county of Chester, including exceptionally heavy taxes and fines imposed on the shire in 1401-3, was increasingly diverted to pay for the war in north Wales—by 1403 to the tune of £2,284, and thereafter about £1,300 per annum. But this, of course, fell far short of the sharply escalating costs of war in Wales. There was no alternative but to draw on large subventions from the royal exchequer. It has been calculated that the prince of Wales received over £72,000 between 1401 and 1413 towards the cost of troops and armies in Wales. While this global figure may represent a considerable share of the total expenditure on Wales especially after 1406, it gets nowhere near the total cost of the war to the English exchequer, let alone to other contributory sources. It does not include much of the costs of the royal expeditions of 1400-3, the disbursements made directly to regional and local commanders, the expenditure on provisions and equipment, and the high costs of garrisoning non-royal castles in Crown custody (the cost of garrisoning Radnor Castle, to give one example, from late July 1402 to January 1405 was almost £900). If to these sums we add the large sums that were disbursed by local lords on the defence of their individual lordships and the repair and garrisoning of their castles, we begin to recognize the scale of the financial demands that the war in Wales put on the revenues of the king of England and the Marcher lords in Wales.[40]

It is impossible to hazard a guess of the total or annual sums spent on the war in Wales or even on the royal contribution (though the latter is much nearer our reach). It has been estimated that Edward I's first Welsh campaign of 1276-7 cost the king some £23,000, the second great campaign of 1282-3 and the cost of the massive castle-building programme up to 1284, £120,000. None of Henry IV's campaigns in Wales was, of course, at all on the scale of those of Edward I, and his programme of castle repairs was paltry in comparison with Edward's castle-building enterprise. But Edward I's campaigns were short, sharp, and devastatingly effective, whereas Henry IV—preoccupied as he was with problems domestic and foreign—found himself confronted with a revolt which festered for seven to eight years and which consumed most of the country for two to three years. The haemorrhaging impact of the costs of Glyn Dŵr's war—especially when we add to them the large loss of anticipated royal revenue from Wales 1400-9—was no small contributory factor to Henry IV's financial embarrassment.[41]

Nor is there much doubt that Henry's chronic indebtedness helped to prolong the Welsh revolt. Commanders recurrently expressed their despair at the impossible situation in which they were placed by the government's failure to provide the necessary funds. A letter which the young prince of Wales wrote

from Shrewsbury on 30 May 1403 to the king's council echoes the tone of many other similar letters. He pleaded and threatened alternately: if the instalment payment of his funds were not forthcoming his troops threatened to leave; he had already pawned his own jewellery to keep his troops in service; the castles at Harlech and Aberystwyth were desperately in need of relief; the Welsh rebels were waiting to see if he would be paid or not and would mount another raid as soon as his troops withdraw for lack of wages; if the money were forthcoming, the prospects were indeed good, but if it were not, he would have no alternative but to withdraw to England to his abiding shame. There is, of course, a great deal of special pleading and deliberate wringing of hands in such pleas, but they are too frequently repeated, and indeed echoed by the king himself, to be dismissed. Lack of prompt payment led to regular defections and to equally regular reports of low morale among English troops in Wales. It was to be no coincidence that as the king's financial problems began to ease from 1406 onwards so did the revolt in Wales begin to wane and English military policy there begin to be characterized by decisiveness and a clear strategy for eventual victory. As has been so rightly observed, perhaps the most valuable lesson which the future Henry V learnt from his experiences in the Welsh campaign was that 'money is vital to the successful pursuit of war'.[42]

Shortage of cash, and more urgent priorities elsewhere, may well explain why English policy in Wales from 1403 to 1406 seems deliberately to have been one of containment. By then it was clear that the policy of royal expeditions of 1400–3 had not served to terrorize the hardened core of Welsh rebels into submission and surrender, while the traumatic experience of the revolt of the Percies in midsummer 1403 had shown vividly that the very future of the Lancastrian dynasty was in mortal danger. In those circumstances the government seems to have acquired a sense of proportion about the importance of the Welsh revolt and the time-scale and strategy for dealing with it. Three policies in particular seem to have been adopted in the light of this reappraisal of strategy. The first was to abandon for the time being the policy of punitive royal expeditions and to concentrate instead on locating garrisons, large and small, in the castles of Wales as a guarantee of a continued but very much attenuated English presence. The second, adopted after the collapse of the strategy of overall military command bestowed on the prince of Wales (1 April 1403) following his injury at the Battle of Shrewsbury, was to invest responsibility, at least for the time being, in the hands of local commanders such as the duke of York at Carmarthen, John Greyndour at Radnor, and Edward Charlton at Welshpool. The war effort was in effect being privatized: when Richard Grey of Codnor was given custody of Radnor Castle in January 1405 he was also given the profits of the surrounding lordships and all fines, ransoms, and perquisites of war. Wales was effectively

being handed over to a series of local military commanders, to do as well as they could to sustain an English presence, quell the rebellion, and line their own pockets. Thirdly, much of English governmental effort in these years concentrated on the defence of the English border counties; that is why the prince of Wales spent so much of his time moving up and down the border from Leominster and Hereford to Shrewsbury and Chester.[43]

This was tantamount to, even if it was not consciously, a policy of containment. After the failure of the Percy revolt there was less likelihood that the Welsh revolt would be a major factor in English politics. Even if the French were to exploit the Welsh for their own purposes, a French invasion of Wales was arguably much less of a direct threat to the English polity than the invasions and invasion scares along the southern English coast in the 1370s and 1380s. In other words, the revolt of Owain Glyn Dŵr could again be regarded as what it had been initially, a Welsh problem; embarrassing and awkward certainly, but not life-threatening to the English polity. As such the wisest policy—not least given all the other pressing problems of Henry IV—was to contain and marginalize it. In time it might blow itself out. In time conditions might change and the English could once more go on the offensive.

10

SURVIVAL AND RECRIMINATION

*H*indsight is the besetting sin of the historian. Nowhere is it, perhaps, more pernicious in its impact than when discussing a war or a revolt. Chaos is turned into order at the stroke of the historian's pen; isolated and unrelated episodes are arranged into neat causal patterns; lines of development and crucial turning-points are perceived with a clarity and confidence denied to contemporaries. The revolt of Owain Glyn Dŵr is no exception. Therefore, it behoves us to try to reconstruct as best we can the way contemporaries responded to the revolt and likewise to re-create what the experience of the revolt meant for them.

The English authorities had no reason to believe, in September 1400, that the outbreak of disorder in north-east Wales was anything more than a temporary outburst by a people who were notorious, in English perceptions, for their inveterate light-headedness (L. *levitas cervicosa*). Indeed, the council was critical of the king for paying too much attention to 'a people of such mean reputation' (Fr. *gens . . . de petit reputacion*); a deputy could undertake such a minor task. Yet it could be argued that the English government's initial response to the troubles in Wales was sharp, measured, and effective and that it would, in the words of a later memorandum, yield 'a good result and do so quickly'. There were, essentially, two aspects to the response. The first was punitive: leading major, if short, expeditions deep into Wales (October 1400 and October 1401) to demonstrate the power of the English military machine and to cow the rebels into submission, executing a few prominent rebels with full publicity *pour encourager les autres*, and placing local communities under the threat of large penalties, or recognizances as they were known, as a guarantee of their future behaviour. The second aspect of the response was conciliation: offers of pardon were generous and reassuring in their terms, particularly the one issued by the prince of Wales at Chester on 20 December 1400; such offers were renewed to whole communities down to the end of 1401. Negotiations with Glyn Dŵr were initiated on several occasions and seem to have come close to success more than once, while generous grants of confiscated lands to some leading Welshmen indicated that the government recognized that the support of such men was crucial to any strategy of recovering and sustaining its authority in Wales. It seemed, indeed, to be succeeding in

precisely this task in late 1400–early 1401; and it may well be that, as Adam of Usk argued, it was only the government's failure to extend its clemency to Rhys and Gwilyn ap Tudur of Anglesey which gave Owain Glyn Dŵr's movement a longer lease of life than that of an eight-day rampage.[1]

There was certainly no indication in 1400–1 that the English were facing a national revolt in Wales nor did the government behave as if this were so. On the contrary, the wheels of governance ground on as steadily and oppressively as ever: great judicial sessions were held in the Principality lands of north and west Wales and in the Duchy of Lancaster estates in south Wales in 1401–2; revenue levels were as high in most parts of the country as they had been for years and auditors were travelling to examine the accounts, with not a suggestion that much was amiss. The Welsh were even said, in May 1401, to be 'in a most submissive mood', and in August the justiciar of South Wales was dismissed from office precisely because 'the men of the country had not been governed and sessions cannot be held'. In other words, normality was the expectation and any failure in that direction was to be explained in terms of the negligence of officials rather than Welsh disaffection. As the events of 1402 unfolded such a stiff-upper-lip attitude might be criticized as self-delusion, but it was easy enough to understand why the government was deluded. Much of Wales was as yet barely touched by the revolt, other perhaps than by rumours or by a very occasional raid. Such was the case, for example, in Flintshire where there was barely a hint of disaffection before 1403. Such also was the case in much of the Duchy of Lancaster estates in Wales, extending from Kidwelly in the west to Monmouth in the east. In 1401–2 the anticipated gross revenue from these estates stood at the exceptionally high level of over £3,500. But it did not need profound auditorial insight to realize that such a healthy figure concealed a major retreat from normality: £1,800 of the income was earmarked for local defence expenditure.[2]

It should come as no great surprise that it took some time for the government to realize that it had much more on its hands in Wales than a set of isolated and limited incidents. Poor communications were certainly one reason. The gathering and transmission of news were never easy in medieval society, but it was particularly difficult in Wales because of the ruggedness of the terrain, the poor quality of the road network, and the absence of an effective and well-established pattern of information-gathering and news-reporting such as had developed in England in the liaison between the localities and Westminster. The problem was further compounded in Wales by the fragmentary character of the country's governance and the absence of any co-ordinated command or reporting structure. The normal pattern of visits by auditors and other central officials and the occasional dispatch of letters, petitions, and commands may have sufficed in a period of peace, but it was quickly put under intolerable strain by the fast-moving

and unpredictable tumble of events during a revolt. The circulation of letters became frenzied but not always well directed. The prince of Wales, for example, was bombarded with letters at London, Barnet, St Albans, and Shrewsbury in July–September 1401 reporting on the situation as it was seen in Caernarfon. The survival of a dossier of such letters from Brecon and the Tywi valley in midsummer 1403—often written at great haste in the deep of night—shows how frenetic such correspondence could be, but also how difficult it was to have a coherent and up-to-date picture of a situation which was changing rapidly from day to day. Nor was all this correspondence centrally co-ordinated, for much of it was directed to the lords and officers of the individual lordships of Wales. During the crucial year 1402, as one disaster followed another, messengers were despatched in all directions with a flurry of letters from Denbigh but very few of them indeed went directly to the government. Some were dispatched to local men, such as the sheriff of Flint or the constable of Conway, but the most important were taken by messenger to Berwick, Northumbria, or London to Hotspur (currently the custodian of Denbigh) in person.[3]

Assembling a coherent and relatively accurate picture from such disparate and uncoordinated correspondence cannot have been easy; but it was made much more difficult by the nature of the revolt itself. One of the letters dispatched from Denbigh expresses the problem crisply: the deputy steward sent a letter to the bishop of St Asaph 'to inquire where Owain Glyn Dŵr was'. It was a recurrent query, for Owain had some of the characteristics of the Scarlet Pimpernel and so did his supporters. The accounts bear this out often enough: thus, in August 1401 two men were dispatched from Caernarfon to Merioneth to try to find out Owain's movements and plans. The story was the same across the whole of Wales: in Gower in 1402 spies were sent to nearby lordships to try to discover news of the rebels, and in Carmarthen likewise several agents—called variously 'espies' and 'scrutatores'—were well rewarded 'for discovering news about the rebels of Wales and for making known what their intentions and plans were'. All in all, the elusiveness of Glyn Dŵr and his plans and the somewhat disorganized nature of the news-gathering and news-reporting facilities in Wales made it difficult to gather accurate information about the revolt and to assemble a coherent picture of its overall progress.[4]

Perhaps 'coherent' is an ill-chosen word in this context. Much of the strength of Glyn Dŵr's revolt, as so often in guerrilla movements, lay in its unpredictability. Surprise was its trump card. Between April 1401 and June 1402 it was transformed from a dormant local conspiracy into a national rebellion by three bolts from the blue: the capture of Conway Castle (1 April 1401), the seizure of Reginald Grey (spring 1402), and the massacre at Bryn Glas (22 June 1402). It was as unpredictable in its geographical range as it was mercurial in its actions: what

showed its rich potential as a guerrilla movement in 1401–2 was the way it broke out from its base in the mountain fastnesses of Snowdonia to erupt into dashing victories at Hyddgen in the Pumlumon range in mid-Wales (summer 1401) and, even more dramatically, at Pilleth not far from the English border (June 1402). It was to be part of its strength throughout its course that the revolt was not tied down to any particular area; it was its very fluidity which served it in good stead. That is why it is difficult, even misleading, to try to express its success cartographically. There came to be, it is true, areas which were regarded as rebel redoubts and virtually no-go areas for the government: north-west Wales beyond the River Conwy, and more specifically Snowdonia and the uplands of the commote of Nantconwy around Dolwyddelan, were regularly identified by contemporaries as such districts. But while virtually no area of Wales was exempt from rebel activities and raids after 1403, anything like systematic and sustained control of the country by the rebels is another matter. It may come as no surprise that the earl Marshal and his wife had no qualms about retiring to Chepstow in the far south-east of Wales from London in autumn 1403 and again in May 1404. Other lordships may have escaped the worst of the revolt through deliberate policy: Adam of Usk suggested that Glyn Dŵr deliberately spared Denbigh and other Mortimer lordships in 1402, doubtless because of his anxiety to curry favour with the Mortimers and the Percies. By 1403, it is true, almost the whole of Wales was ablaze with revolt; for the next three years or more almost no revenue was collected from the whole country. Even in these peak years of rebellion, however, it is well to ask what the experience of revolt meant to local communities.[5]

In only one area of Wales can we hope to approach that question with a minimum degree of historical confidence. The lordship of Dyffryn Clwyd, or Ruthin, has the advantage that it witnessed some of the most dramatic episodes of the revolt. It lay cheek by jowl with Owain's own lands at Glyndyfrdwy; his revolt began with a spectacular raid on Ruthin town on 18 September 1400; the capture of Reginald Grey, lord of Dyffryn Clwyd, in an ambush laid by Glyn Dŵr's men in spring 1402 proved to be one of the turning-points of the revolt; while a valuable shaft of light on the dying days of the rebellion is cast by the remarkably defiant letters which one Gruffudd ap Dafydd wrote to Reginald Grey from his hide-out in the park of Bryncyffo in Dyffryn Clwyd in 1411. All in all there is every reason to expect that the impact of the revolt on Dyffryn Clwyd would be very considerable and would manifest itself in the evidence. It is the character of this evidence that in fact singles out the area for our attention. Dyffryn Clwyd has a unique run of court rolls, that is, the record of judicial proceedings in the courts of the lordship, starting in 1294 and extending into the seventeenth century. It is far and away the best collection of such records for medieval Wales, comparable indeed with the finest series of English court rolls. Two sets of these survive for

the period of the revolt: the one relates to the town of Ruthin, the other to one of the three commotes of the lordship, that of Coelion in the western part of the lordship. It is difficult to gauge the significance of the absence of the rolls for the other two commotes of Llannerch and Dogfeilyn for the period 1399–1406; it may be that they were never compiled because of the turbulence caused by the revolt, but it is more likely that, as with some other earlier and later rolls, they have been lost or destroyed.[6]

What conclusions can we draw from these unique records of life in the town and countryside of Dyffryn Clwyd during the revolt? The revolt's impact certainly registers itself in the records. They provide us indeed with the names of over 280 persons, many of them from districts other than Dyffryn Clwyd, who were involved in the initial raid on Ruthin in September 1400; they show that as a result of that raid and subsequent ones several burgages in the town were permanently destroyed and their occupants had fled to England; they reveal that on at least two occasions, in September 1402 and November 1406, and possibly occasionally in 1405, courts had to be suspended because of rebel activity in the district; and the occasional note against a litigant's name that he was 'Owain's man' or 'sworn to Owain' (L. *homo Oweyni, juratus Oweyno*) indicates the impact of the rebellion on men's allegiance. This kind of evidence is certainly no more than we could have expected; but, along with later references to the burning of mills and the difficulties of leasing land, it is about all that the court rolls tell us directly of the impact of the rebellion in Dyffryn Clwyd.

It is surely a misleadingly, self-reassuring record. Court rolls, it should be remembered, are official documents drawn up primarily to record the names of litigants, the actions in which they were involved, and above all the fines and amercements which they owed to the lord. No more. Such light as they may shed on events beyond their immediate concerns is purely fortuitous. Like all official documents, especially those cast in a formulaic mould, they give the impression of an unchanging world and an unruffled officialdom. Just as it has been observed that one would hardly register from the official chancery documents that a political revolution had taken place in England in 1326–7, so the great Welsh revolt leaves no more than a few ripples on the surface of the court rolls of Dyffryn Clwyd. Paradoxically it was in the years after the revolt, as life was returning to normal, that the memory of the revolt registers most persistently in the records. Thus, when the manor, park, and demesne of Maesmynan were leased in September 1407 a clause was added giving a rebate on the lease-rent, if the lessee could not occupy the manor 'on account of war and rebellion'. Even more significant is the defence regularly deployed by litigants over the next few years, and quite unashamedly so, that at the time of the offence they were rebels or 'with Owain'. Clearly, the silence of the court rolls notwithstanding, the

rebellion had been a major and unavoidable fact of life in Dyffryn Clwyd from 1400 to 1406.[7]

To that extent we may approach the evidence of the court rolls with a large pinch of salt. But we should not dismiss it altogether. The holding of courts was regarded by contemporaries as an indication that civilian rule continued, or had been resumed, and that civilian officers therefore deserved their wages. By that token civilian rule was only disrupted very briefly and infrequently in Dyffryn Clwyd across the peak years of revolt. Court profits, it is true, were often very small, and there was little indication of the transfer of land by death or by sale which often figures prominently in earlier courts. But in Ruthin town and in the rich lowlands around it much of the normal routine of a small market town and its hinterland seems to have continued uninterrupted: lands and mills were leased; the burgesses' pigs were pasturing in the lord's park, while other animals were trampling his corn; wood was illegally taken from the park; officials were appointed, and in April 1403 a jury of Welshmen could be assembled to indict a local man of joining the rebels. There was no hint as yet that Welshmen were in any way being ostracized from the town, in spite of the traumatic experience of the raid of September 1400. When the town was leased in May 1401 four out of the five lessees (or farmers) were Welsh; in February 1404 the work of the Welsh judge was recognized by the court; and, most significant of all, in June 1405 a Welshman was allowed to pay £6 so that he and his heirs could be acknowledged as full burgesses of Ruthin.[8]

Some measure of normal life clearly continued in Ruthin and its environs during these fraught years. The same was doubtless true elsewhere. In Cydweli, for example, mills were leased in December 1402; and in September 1404—only a month after an attack on the town—the income from two local churches was leased on condition that if the district was destroyed by rebels the rent should be reduced. In parts of north-west Wales in particular, the control exercised by Glyn Dŵr and his followers may have been so complete and secure that an alternative power-structure may have been established or, perhaps more correctly, the existing regime may have answered to a new master. So much is suggested by Adam of Usk's pregnant phrase that Caernarfonshire and Merionethshire were 'at his beck in respect both of governance and of war.' It is also supported by the reports that Owain held two parliaments in 1404–5 and by evidence that the wheels of ecclesiastical administration were turning quite effectively in areas under Owain's control. But in much of Wales the kind of contradictory signals that the evidence from Dyffryn Clwyd and Cydweli yield probably best reflect the situation in the peak years of the revolt. Courts may have been held, a little revenue collected, and men and women got on with the routines of their lives as best they could in an atmosphere full of rumours and suspicions and interrupted

by occasional ambushes and raids. The structure of local governance may just about have survived; but the reality of local governmental power—in jurisdiction, discipline, and revenue-collection—was largely lacking. Burgesses in towns such as Ruthin and Kidwelly, or such as had not escaped to England, huddled behind the safety of their walls and in the shadow of their castles. Local truces, many of them unofficial and therefore unrecorded, were concluded and handsome sums paid to buy off rebel attacks. It was a case less of the rebels having secured control—their raids were too intermittent and their presence too spasmodic for that; rather, that their actions had undermined the credibility and effectiveness of the *status quo*. Into this power vacuum the local bully-boys entered, be they rebel leaders such as Henry Don, who strutted imperiously and ruthlessly on his little stage in Cydweli, or corrupt English officials such as Thomas Barneby, the treacherous chamberlain of north Wales, who duped rebels and the English government alike in his search for personal fortune and power. The month-by-month and season-by-season struggle for survival and subsistence that was life in medieval rural Wales probably continued much as before; any relief that came in the wake of the suspension of the financial and judicial extortions of English lords and officials was more or less cancelled by the disruption caused by rebel raids, harassment, and blackmail and by the desperate shortage of food and supplies caused by the effective economic blockade of the country. The years of revolt may have been years of euphoria and liberation for many Welshmen; but they are also likely to have been years of desperation, oppression, and misery.[9]

Life was desperate in the countryside during the revolt; but it was hardly rosier in the besieged little towns of Wales. There is, however, one difference. In the countryside we can do little more than guess what life was like during the revolt; in towns such as Caernarfon and Ruthin we have rather more straw from which to build the bricks of our speculation. Particularly is this so for the little town of Kidwelly; as part of the great Duchy of Lancaster, since 1399 in the hands of the king of England, it is quite exceptionally well served by surviving documents. We may therefore take its history during these years as a mirror image of that of many of the castellated towns of Wales.[10]

Kidwelly was indeed—as the reconstruction by Alan Sorrell suggests (plate 9)—a classic castellated town. It was dominated, indeed overwhelmed, by its massive castle, for the castle was its original *raison d'être* and would now prove to be its salvation. There had been a castle at Kidwelly since the early years of the twelfth century, and the care with which its original founders had chosen the site would serve it well three centuries later. It stood on a shale ridge on the western bank of the River Gwendraeth Fechan, at the upper limits of the tidal waters of

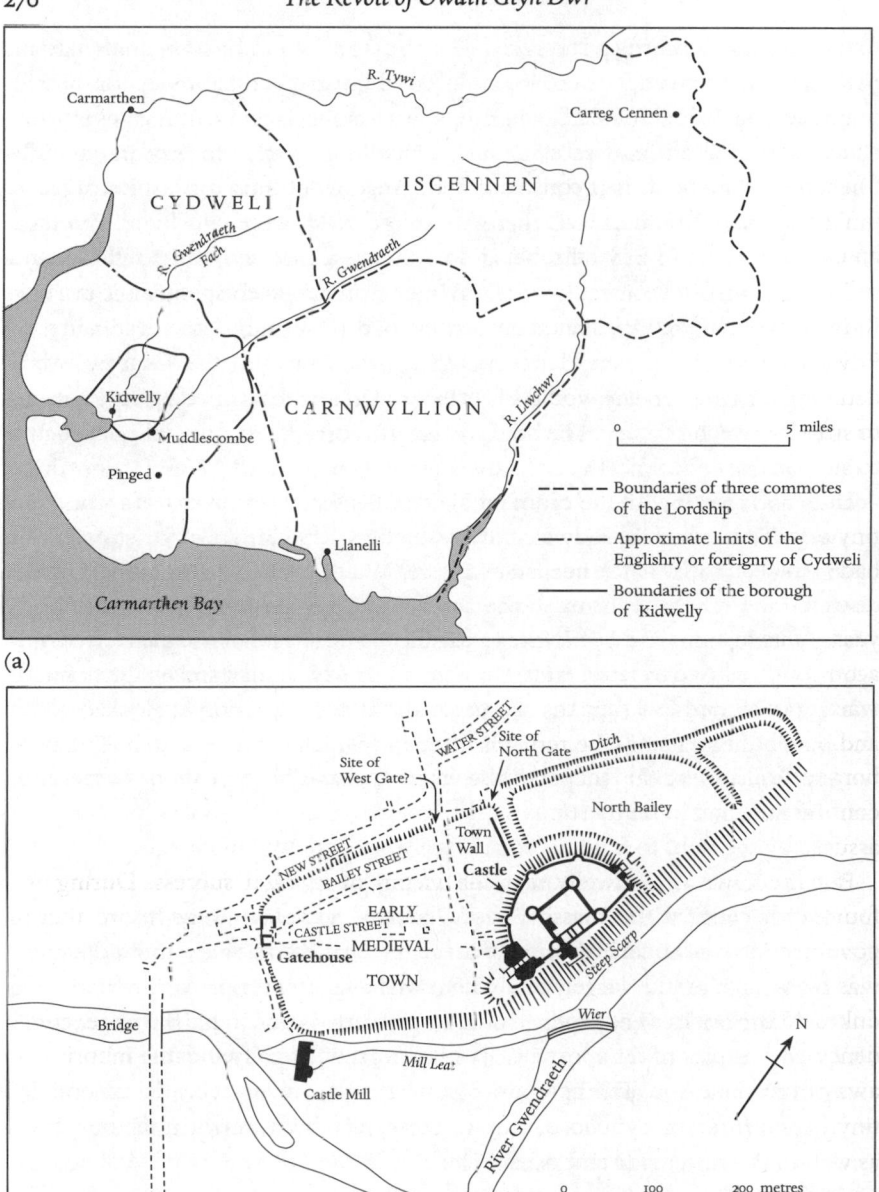

(a)

(b)

MAP 6. (*a*). The lordship of Cydweli. (*b*) A plan of the town of Kidwelly

that river. The estuarine waters provided a defence for the castle from the east, a means whereby it could be provisioned during a siege, and the water for the leat which served the castle mill. The castle as it stood in 1400, and as its magnificent ruins still stand today, was essentially a building of the late thirteenth–early fourteenth century. It was constructed on classic concentric principles, with an inner and outer circuit of walls and·towers, and its defences were completed by an exceptionally powerful three-storeyed gatehouse set in the outer circuit and still in process of construction in 1400 (over £100 had been spent on it in 1391). Kidwelly could, and can, stand comparison with some of the grandest castles of Edwardian Wales, such as Harlech and Caerffili. Its majestic walls presented a daunting challenge to any would-be rebel and had served as an effective deterrent to such for over a century. The hour had now arrived when it would be expected to show its true worth.[11]

Under the shadow of the castle and within its own *enceinte* of walls stood the tiny original borough of Kidwelly. It was more or less coeval with the castle and had grown up to serve the needs of its garrisons and of the English settlers of the district. Like the castle, its existence had been rather precarious for the first 150 years of its history; and like so many castellated boroughs throughout Wales, it acquired a new confidence from the second half of the thirteenth century on-wards. It was probably then that the town's defences were reconstructed in stone and possibly two gates (the remains of one of which survive) added. The little borough's institutional independence was recognized in its first charter in 1308, confirmed in 1357, and its status as the commercial centre of the lordship was assured by the right to hold two markets a week and one annual fair.

But the town of Kidwelly was the victim of its own success. During the fourteenth century the massive castle became increasingly no more than a governmental and financial centre for the lordship; its role as a military centre was now, apparently, largely redundant and its absentee lords, the earls and dukes of Lancaster, very rarely visited it. The town grew rapidly in size, confidence, and commercial importance; but it also grew, literally and metaphorically, away from the castle. The new town lay across the medieval bridge around the tiny Benedictine priory whose fine church answered the needs of the burgesses as well as serving as a distant outpost for Sherborne Abbey. No one worried too much about this suburban development until the outbreak of Glyn Dŵr's revolt served as a reminder that castle and borough had been constructed originally as a single defensible unit and that in the hour of need they would stand or fall together. When the Duchy of Lancaster council visited Kidwelly in October 1401, with uncomfortable rumours of the activity of Owain Glyn Dŵr's rebels ringing in their ears, they were appalled by what they saw. The 'old town' within the walls—'an ancient burgh of the lord king and his predecessors' as they piously

called it—was 'ruinous, waste, and desolate'. On 6 October they issued ordinances, which still survive, which tried rather desperately to breathe new life into it,
requiring that its houses be repaired, its burgesses be resident (or, if not, 'other
suitable and faithful English' be chosen to replace them), ale and bread be sold
only within its walls, and that no market should henceforth be held outside its
walls but that all victuals for sale should be brought to its public market-place for
sale every Wednesday and Saturday. It was a desperate attempt to turn the clock
back.[12]

But the truth was that Kidwelly had long outgrown the corset of its walls. It
was no longer a small garrison town but a thriving commercial centre, some of
whose leading merchants—notably the Aylwards, Dyers, and Owens—were
involved in the international trade in wool and hides through the staple port at
Carmarthen. Around Kidwelly lay some very rich arable land, much of it laid out
in strips in open fields; while the salt-marshes had long been recognized as some
of the best wool-growing pastures in Wales. The area immediately around the
town had been settled by Flemish and English families for generations. It was
known, appropriately, as the Englishry or foreignry of Kidwelly, and had been
detached from the Welsh administrative districts of the rest of the lordship and
placed under its own three officers—the reeve of the town, the reeve of the
castle, and the reaper. Here were to be found small estates such as the manor (so
called) of Muddlescombe which could readily be compared with similar small-
gentry manors in England; here the names of the mills, weirs, fields, paths, and
even the natural features of the landscape were mainly English; and here rich
farmers—such as Moris Nicol of Pinged with his flock of 360 sheep—were fully
alive to the commercial opportunities of a national and even international market. Yet within three or four miles of this island of Englishness one arrived at a
very different world. The rest of the commote of Cydweli, along with the two
neighbouring commotes of Carnwyllion and Iscennen (which between them
formed the lordship of Cydweli), were thoroughly Welsh by any measure one
would wish to apply—law, administrative divisions and office, inheritance practices, customs and language, and the rents and renders of the tenants. The two
worlds were very different, but for a century or so they seem to have coexisted
amicably, partly no doubt by influencing each other (though the town of Kidwelly was too far and, in every sense, too marginal to have more than an indirect
impact on many parts of the lordship), and partly by going their separate ways.
This was the society which now confronted the experience of a Welsh national
revolt; the test would be a particularly severe one for the castle, town, and
Englishry of Kidwelly.[13]

News of the revolt in north Wales arrived in Kidwelly within a few weeks or
even days of the initial outbreak; but for the better part of two years the threat

was no more than a distant and spasmodic one and the response was suitably low-key. The alert was first sounded in October 1400 and a small force of soldiers was placed in the castle. But the alarm was very short-lived, and was not to be revived until May 1401. Even then only six men were placed on garrison duty in the castle and only for one week. The fact that Henry IV's second expedition into Wales in October 1401 had moved from Brecon down the Tywi valley and across into Cardiganshire showed that the tide of revolt was flowing uncomfortably close to Kidwelly. The first sign that the atmosphere was changing and becoming less tolerant came during 1401 when the two Welshmen who had headed the administration of the lordship—William Gwyn ap Rhys Llwyd, the steward, and Gwilym ap Philip, the receiver—were removed from office. Both, significantly, were to emerge within less than two years as prominent supporters of the revolt. Precautionary measures were certainly being taken: twelve men were stationed in the castle for twenty-eight days in August–September 1401, and in February 1402 an order was given to repair the Gatehouse Tower and to cover it with lead. But these were no more than sensible insurance measures; there was every indication in the autumn of 1401, and even throughout 1402 (as the news in other parts of Wales became increasingly alarming), that Cydweli was still free of the infection of revolt and still firmly under the rule of the house of Lancaster. Indeed, this latter fact was massively, even insensitively, demonstrated in October 1401 when leading Duchy officials held a sessions at Kidwelly and expected to collect £1,790 (more than four times the normal gross yield of the lordship) from their visit, £1,575 of it by way of communal gifts and fines. Other signs of normality during 1402 were the sums of money handed over by the local receiver (including £200 as late as November 1402) and the renewal of mill leases in December 1402. There was certainly some nervousness about the castle of Carreg Cennen (cover), the lonely outpost in the far north-east of the lordship, during 1402: extensive repairs were put in hand, and the small garrison under John Skidmore was increased substantially—to one man-at-arms, a chaplain, and twenty-four archers—from 9 November onwards. Nevertheless, across the winter months of 1402–3 the burgesses of Kidwelly and the well-heeled farmers of the Englishry could sleep fairly securely in their beds.

It was Easter 1403 that the burgesses came to regard in retrospect as the watershed in their lives and fortunes during the revolt. Soon after this the revolt crashed in on their lives and inaugurated years of trauma for the town. The emergency started on 24 June. This was the same day that the garrison was tripled at Radnor and the Welsh were laying siege to Brecon. News had arrived that a great summer offensive was being launched by the Welsh in south Wales, doubtless to coincide with the Percy conspiracy in the north-east. A scratch force of seven archers and fourteen burgesses was assembled to defend Kidwelly

Castle; some of them were to find themselves at their post for over fifteen months. They had taken up their positions not a day too early. Alarming news was reaching Kidwelly, just as it was reaching the king. On Monday, 2 July, a force of rebels led by Henry Don (former steward of Cydweli), his son, and Gwilym ap Philip (receiver of Cydweli until 1401) was besieging Dinefwr Castle on the boundaries of the lordship; on Tuesday Owain Glyn Dŵr himself arrived in the area; by Wednesday Dryslwyn Castle had been surrendered to him; on Friday the castle and town of Carmarthen, the bastions of English authority in the area for centuries, were handed over to him. That same Friday, 5 July, John Skidmore wrote in near despair from his lonely outpost at Carreg Cennen to report how the whole area had been overwhelmed by rebellion. Not only were castles falling one by one, but the population was defecting *en masse* to the rebel cause. 'All Carmarthenshire, Cydweli, Carnwyllion and Iscennen', reported Skidmore, 'have pledged themselves to Owain yesterday . . . he is confident that all the castles and towns of Cydweli, Gower, and Glamorgan [will be his], for those same districts have undertaken to besiege them until they have been won.'[14]

It was a chilling message for the burgesses of Kidwelly. One can imagine the panic in the town. The 'foreign English', that is, the English who lived outside the town, set about repairing the town walls, no doubt bitterly regretting that they had not taken earlier notice of the ordinances issued by the Duchy councillors on 6 October 1401. Local burgesses, such as John Don, were enticed to serve in the defence of the castle and to find an archer each to help them, and to do so without pay. Survival may have been a sufficient enticement but it was enhanced by the prospect of securing, in due course, the escheated or forfeited estates of rebel Welshmen, such as William Gwyn ap Rhys Llwyd, until recently steward of the lordship. John Don and his colleagues certainly had their work cut out for them for the next few months. If we are to believe a later indictment, the assault on Kidwelly Castle began on Monday, 13 August 1403. It was led by Henry Don accompanied by some of the leading Welshmen of the area and supported 'by all the Welsh commons of the commotes of Cydweli and Carnwyllion'. Several burgesses, including Jenkin Don and Michael Don, were killed. It was the beginning of what contemporaries came to remember as a long siege. The outlook was grim and led to desperate pleas for help: three local men went by boat to Bristol and then two of them overland to London and elsewhere to apprise the government of the desperate state of affairs. The siege seems to have continued into the autumn and the assault on the castle was renewed in the early days of October. A letter from the constable on 3 October gives us an invaluable glimpse of the defenders almost in despair about their future during these fraught weeks:

Henry Don and all the rebels of south Wales, aided by the men of France and Brittanny, are advancing on the castle with all their power. They have destroyed all the corn of your subjects in the countryside all around the castle. Many of the townsmen of Kidwelly have fled to England with their wives and children; the rest have retreated into the castle and are in great fear of their lives.[15]

This is perhaps the most vivid cameo that survives from contemporary evidence of what life was like in the isolated and besieged little towns of Wales during the peak months of the revolt. There was nothing to be done but to hang on grimly and to take such counter-measures as were feasible. Much of the old town, including the court-house known as the Shirehall, seems to have been destroyed in the initial assault; the vast castle was now the sole outpost of English authority. Rich burgesses such as John Ailward and John Owen brought their stocks of victuals into the castle to feed its much-enlarged population. Hurried repairs were made to the castle to make it more comfortable and better placed to withstand the siege: a new ditch was cut outside the gate to make the approach to it more difficult; timber was transported from the destroyed Shirehall to be put to emergency use in the castle; and re-roofing work was carried out on the hall and various other buildings within the castle. No royal relief expedition was forthcoming; but late in the year a considerable supply of arms—including two cannons, 40lb. of gunpowder, forty bows, twelve lances, six pole-axes, and six basinets—were dispatched from London via Bristol to Kidwelly. The arrival of this stock of arms must have been welcome news to the besieged community; but even better was the news that the Welsh had raised their siege as the winter set in. We have no direct evidence of this, but the fact that the town court was held on 17 December indicates that a semblance of normality was returning.[16]

Kidwelly had survived the crisis of the summer and autumn of 1403, if only by the skin of its teeth or, perhaps, the walls of its castle. But the crisis was by no means over. For the next three years the burgesses remained on tenterhooks, and with good reason. On 20 August 1404—exactly one year and a week after the initial assault—William Gwyn ap Rhys Llwyd attacked the town and burnt it again, just as it was beginning to recover from the previous assault. The burgesses of Kidwelly must have come to believe that August was an ill-fated month; the events of 1405 and 1406 showed that their belief was no superstition. In 1405 the French force which had landed in Milford Haven moved on to Carmarthen and secured its surrender; it requires little imagination to picture the panic in Kidwelly just a few miles to the south. By 1406 the French had long since left; but it was 1 August which Henry Don chose as the date for showing that he was still not a spent force, by raising the Welshmen to the north and south of Kidwelly into rebellion once more. But this proved to be the last major act of defiance.

Across these years a small force—often no more than nine men, but rising sharply to twenty-one in the aftermath of the French invasion in autumn 1405—kept permanent guard on the castle, and was no doubt swollen by servants and by nervous townsmen passing in and out of the castle gate to keep an eye on the goods they had stored there. Travel was easier than it had been; but it was still safer to rely on ships from Tenby and Llansteffan to bring supplies to the castle and the town.[17]

Kidwelly was not a place for the faint-hearted in the years 1403–6. The rumble of rebellion was always present in the background, and sometimes—at least once every year in August—the alarm was sounded as the rebels launched, or were believed to be about to launch, a direct attack on the town and castle. The spasmodic nature of these raids meant that in between times a measure of normal life could resume and even some of the machinery of governance could operate, at least in western Cydweli and in areas within reach of the town and castle. Across the three years from October 1404 to September 1407 the receiver of the lordship admitted that he had collected £354 in revenue—that is, at a time when the area lived very much under the threat of rebel raids. Strikingly, almost two-thirds of that sum (£217) was accounted for by the three administrative regions which constituted the Englishry of Cydweli and which lay in an arc around the town.

In the rest of the township only token amounts of revenue were collected. No courts were held in the commotes of Carnwyllion and Iscennen after 1403, nor was any revenue forthcoming until 1406–7. Even elsewhere, in the Welsh districts of the commote of Cydweli the flow of revenue was but a trickle until 1406–7: the total revenue collected for the three years 1404–7 was considerably less than the anticipated income for a single year before the revolt. Nor is that all. The damage inflicted by the rebels, especially on the rich agricultural hinterland around Kidwelly itself, was very considerable. The bailiff of the town commented in November 1404 that it had been so ransacked and destroyed by Welsh rebels that no rents or tolls could be collected, and eventually in 1407 rents amounting to £30 over the last four years were cancelled. The mills outside the town had likewise been destroyed and therefore yielded no income, while areas in the Englishry such as St Ishmael could trade on the damage they had suffered at the hands of the rebels as late as 1411 to secure the cancellation of a fine of £105. In almost every respect what happened in the town and countryside of Cydweli was a mirror image of the impact of revolt up and down Wales in the years 1403–6. Destruction was extensive, especially in and around the English settlements; the collection of revenue and the holding of courts were suspended in most areas for several years; but castles held out, even when only garrisoned by modest forces; Welsh raids were intermittent and often not sustained; and in the immediate environs of the castle and borough the administration recovered its authority speedily.[18]

The story of Cydweli is a mirror image of what happened in Wales generally in another respect; the rebellion there was clearly running out of steam by 1406–7. By the summer of 1407 the garrison was reduced to five men (one of whom, Geoffrey Boton, had been on the castle walls during the summer of 1403), and the constable felt sufficiently secure to accompany the prince of Wales, who had called in at Kidwelly, to the siege of Aberystwyth. Civilian governance was beginning to stutter back into life—after a hiatus of almost four years in the commotes of Carnwyllion and Iscennen; for the first time since 1403 the steward was given his fee in respect of his responsibilities there. Bills still outstanding for provisions supplied to the castle at the height of the siege in 1403 were now at last being settled, and a programme of repairing destroyed or damaged walls had begun. Perhaps the surest sign of all of the return of confidence among the local officials was the fact that parchment and an accounting cloth were brought for compiling and examining the accounts, and that the Duchy auditor could resume his journey, coming via Brecon under armed escort, to distant Kidwelly to hear the accounts.[19]

Life was assuredly returning to normal, but slowly. It would be many years yet before the leading rebels of the district, who had caused such terror to the good burgesses of Kidwelly in the years 1403–6, were at last brought to book, and the Welsh community required to pay a heavy price for its enthusiastic support of the rebellion. It would be much longer, indeed many generations into the future, before the scars which the revolt had left on the collective psyche of the English burgesses and settlers of Kidwelly and its environs began to heal. Their paranoia was understandable and so was the institutionalized discrimination which now followed. When the first extra troops were put into the castle in May 1403 it was specifically laid down that they should have been 'born beyond Severn and not at all in Wales'. But it was to be in December 1443, when the town's charter was confirmed and substantially extended (including the right hereafter to have its own mayor), that the memory of Glyn Dŵr's impact on Kidwelly (some forty years after the siege of 1403) manifested itself formally most loudly in a public document. With the characteristic exaggeration of the preambles of such charters it referred to the 'large losses and the burning of houses and the various oppressions which the Welsh, out of malice, had inflicted frequently on the town in the past . . . so much so that the town was now largely waste and desolate'. The rhetoric of such sentiments was soon lost in the practical privileges which were now conferred on the town; but that it was more than rhetoric was made plain in the clause that no burgess of Kidwelly was henceforth to be tried or convicted by Welshmen but only by entire Englishmen (L. *per meros anglicos*). It was not so much the walls and houses of Kidwelly which had been irreparably damaged by Glyn Dŵr's revolt, but the trust between English and Welsh in the area. The same was true in many parts of Wales.[20]

Trust was important, certainly; but we should not underestimate the physical destruction caused by the revolt. Contemporaries certainly did not do so, and in the mythology about the revolt which developed in the sixteenth and seventeenth centuries this destructiveness occupied a very prominent role. John Leland's comments, based no doubt on reports made to him, are an early illustration: 'Montgomery, deflowered by Owen Glyn Dŵr'; 'Radnor, partly destroyed by Glyn Dŵr'; 'the town of Hay within the walls is wonderfully decayed. The ruin is ascribed to Owain Glyn Dŵr'. Such typical comments show how Glyn Dŵr had become the *diabolus ex machina*, wheeled out with regularity to explain the ruinous state of the towns, and sometimes the religious houses, of Tudor Wales. Welsh antiquaries, such as Sir John Wynn of Gwydir or George Owen of Henllys in Elizabeth's day, quickly picked up the idiom but at least explained Glyn Dŵr's actions as deliberate policy rather than sheer vandalism. It was Sir John Wynn who provided the most memorable vignette of the damage wrought:

Owain Glyn Dŵr's wars, beginning in Anno 1400, continued fifteen years, which brought such a desolation that green grass grew on the market-place in Llanrwst called Bryn-y-boten and the deer fed in the churchyard of Llanrwst, as it is reported, for it was Glyn Dŵr's policy to bring all things to waste, that the English should find not strength nor resting-place in the country.

The Glyn Dŵr revolt had established itself in the official memory of Tudor and Stuart society as a turning-point in the history of Wales and more particularly as an explanation of the social, economic, and political malaise which gripped the country for generations to come. When government surveyors, not men normally given to flights of historical fancy, sought to explain conditions in northeast Wales in 1620 they had no hesitation in identifying the two fundamental causes of decline: 'the great mortality and plagues which in former times had been in the reign of Edward the Third and also the Rebellion of Owain Glyn Dŵr that thereupon ensued'.[21]

Did Glyn Dŵr's revolt deserve this reputation? There is indeed ample contemporary evidence that the revolt was very destructive, but before considering this evidence briefly it is as well to utter two very important caveats about its trustworthiness. The first is the perhaps obvious point that all those who have suffered loss and damage are instinctively likely to exaggerate the scale of such losses, be it to win sympathy, to secure larger compensation, or to be granted a pardon for outstanding debts and obligations. Secondly there is an obvious danger, especially given the prominence of financial records among the archives of the revolt, that the collapse of royal and seignorial revenue from Wales be interpreted as evidence of profound economic dislocation and destruction. It

may be so; but it is more directly and securely evidence of the collapse of the revenue-collecting machinery of king and lords in the localities and the slowness with which that machinery recovered its authority.

These caveats are important; but they do not, of course, negate the evidence of the destructiveness of the revolt. There were certain obvious targets for the Welsh rebels. Towns were one such category from the earliest days of the revolt. The list of those that were damaged or destroyed was a long one: it included, for example, Beaumaris, Conway, Cardiff, Denbigh, Hay, Montgomery, Kidwelly, Radnor, Ruthin, Rhuddlan, Swansea, Usk, Welshpool, and many others. At Carmarthen, the premier town of Wales, about fifty persons were killed in the attack of 1403 and so extensive was the devastation that all rents were pardoned by the prince of Wales in 1408. The revolt did not reach Flintshire until 1403 but by August the towns of Rhuddlan, Flint, Hope, and Overton were all but destroyed, and at Flint (as doubtless in many other towns) the burgesses had no option but to withdraw into the relative safety of the castle. Interestingly enough, the upland Welsh town of Caerwys escaped damage, but that was small comfort to the government, since the townsmen had become rebels and paid no dues. Mills were another obvious target for the rebels, since they were symbols of seignorial authority and profiteering; the accounts for the post-revolt period show how much they suffered throughout Wales, both through direct attack and as a result of neglect of upkeep. Ecclesiastical buildings seem to have been the targets for English forces rather than Welsh rebels, more often than not as a direct punishment for the support that the clerics had given to the rebel cause. It comes as no surprise, for example, that Henry IV visited his spleen on the friary at Llan-faes (co. Anglesey), for the Franciscans in general were notorious for their opposition to his regime, while the friars at Llan-faes proved to be some of Glyn Dŵr's doughtiest supporters. For the same reason the Cistercian abbey of Strata Florida (co. Cardigan) was occupied by his troops in 1401 and a major force of soldiers was stationed there in 1410. It was little wonder that the monks were reduced to penury. At the cathedral of St Asaph the destruction was attributed to the Welsh rebels; but after the defection of Bishop John Trefor in 1403–4 it would hardly be surprising if the English likewise did not take their revenge on his episcopal see.[22]

It is natural that the evidence should concentrate on major buildings such as mills, friaries, abbeys, churches, and towns; it is also natural, of course, that we should learn far more about the victims of the rebels' spoliation than about the miseries of ordinary Welshmen in time of rebellion. But we cannot doubt that this misery was great, whether it was inflicted by English or Welsh forces. The timetable of the arable year was disrupted, and stocks of food and animals became depleted. Even in south-east Wales, in areas such as Monmouth and

Skenfrith, tenants claimed that they had been unable to sow their lands for three years, that they had been forced to take refuge in the castle, and that their houses had to be totally rebuilt. For the majority of Welshmen the revolt no doubt only made more desperate the already tough battle for survival. Flight was often the only solution: it was a pardonable exaggeration for the officials of the lordship of Bromfield and Yale to report to the council of the earl of Arundel that the area was 'empty of tenants for the most part'. Nor should we overlook the massive disruption to economic life and particularly to trade which the rebellion caused: Thomas Dyer of Carmarthen doubtless spoke for many of his fellow-merchants when he claimed that the Welsh rebels had despoiled him of goods to the value of £1,000.[23]

Most of the complaints that survive, like that of Thomas Dyer, speak of destruction caused by rebels; but English forces in Wales also pursued a policy of the deliberate destruction of the economic resources of Wales as a means of securing surrender. 'Our lord the king', so one correspondent wrote agitatedly, 'has proclaimed "havoc" throughout Wales'; it was, as he recognized, a licence, indeed an invitation, to plunder. The prince of Wales himself had given a clear demonstration of this policy of economic terror in a famous letter describing how he burnt Owain Glyn Dŵr's residences at Sycharth and Glyndyfrdwy and then proceeded to Edeirnion and 'laid waste a fine and populous country'. Even the destruction of Llanrwst, which has become, since the days of Sir John Wynn of Gwydir's famous passage (quoted above p. 278) about it, the *locus classicus* of the devastating impact of Glyn Dŵr's rebellion, was almost certainly the responsibility of the king's army as it passed through the district in 1402.[24]

The evidence of the destruction wreaked during the revolt can be amassed; but it can never be adequately assessed. Two conclusions, however, seem to be irrefutable. First, the destruction was great and the recovery slow. Many statistics, of greater or lesser reliability, can be culled from the records to drive home this point; but one contemporary estimate may serve for all the others. The share of the great lordship of Glamorgan held by the dowager Lady Despenser had been assessed as worth at least £340 in 1375; when it was let on a ten-year lease in February 1408 the lessor was to pay a rent of £100 in the first year, £200 per annum over the next two years, and £266 13s. 4d. for the remaining seven years. Recovery, in other words, was still slow in 1408–11, and even thereafter there seemed to be little hope of attaining the pre-revolt levels of revenue. Secondly, the impact of Glyn Dŵr's revolt was well-nigh universal throughout Wales and, indeed, into the border counties. Of course the scale of devastation varied from place to place, and overall the impact, both short- and long-term, on the towns may have been greater than on the countryside. But from Walwyn's Castle and Cemais in far south-west Wales to Newport and Tintern in the south-east, from

Gower in the south to Flintshire or Conway in the north, virtually no part of the country seems to have escaped. As to the border counties, there is a wide range of evidence from the western halves of Cheshire, Shropshire, and Herefordshire of the great damage inflicted by the rebellion. The men of Shrewsbury could claim that the revolt had come to the very gates of their town and brought it close to ruin; while the loss of trade that Chester had incurred as a result of the revolt had led to its farm (or annual lease) being reduced by 50 per cent. It might well be argued that the revolt, especially in the years 1403–6, was the most devastating experience of destruction that Wales has suffered as a country. It is little wonder that the name of Owain Glyn Dŵr became so deeply embedded in the social memory of so many parts of Wales.[25]

Extensive as was the physical damage caused by the rebellion, it was ultimately less profound in its impact than the collective psychological trauma which Wales had suffered. The trust and the practices of coexistence which had been built between the Welsh and the English in Wales over the generations had, at least temporarily, been shattered. Furthermore, the two peoples were now formally and legally separated from one another, to the disadvantage of the Welsh, in a way which had not been so before, at least legislatively and on a country-wide basis. To Tudor commentators in Wales this was the overwhelming shadow which the rebellion had cast over the history of their country. They had little time for Glyn Dŵr himself and condemned him as a contumacious rebel against his true sovereign lord; but the penal laws which Henry IV issued against the Welsh in the wake of the rebellion were criticized even more harshly by them. They were, said David Powel, 'more heathen than Christian'; to George Owen of Henllys, the Elizabethan antiquary, they had been devised 'not only for the punishment (of Welshmen) but to deprive them of good education and make them uncivil and brutish'. The charges are greatly exaggerated, deliberately so. The statutes were one of the few pieces of legislative evidence about the state of Wales that Tudor writers could find, and they greatly inflated their importance and significance in order to highlight the benefits of Tudor rule in Wales. Yet when we have made due allowance for the undoubted exaggeration of the comments, the statutes and other supporting evidence provide valuable insight into one important dimension of the English reaction to the rebellion in Wales.[26]

Not only was the reaction understandable, it had a much longer lineage than the outrage of Tudor observers was willing to concede. The anti-Welsh legislation of Henry IV only codified and generalized practices and prohibitions which had been in the making for generations. As the lineaments of the nation states of northern Europe began to take firmer shape from the thirteenth century onwards, so did the categorization of peoples, the disapproval of what were seen as

the deviant customs of subject peoples, the need to protect and privilege the status of a settler minority, and equally the need to take precautionary and discriminatory measures against the subject population become more common. This is what had happened in Wales. The commons in parliament came to believe that it had happened precisely at the conquest of the country under the guidance of 'the noble and wise King Edward I'. In this they were mistaken. There is nothing in the great Statute of Wales which Edward I issued for the governance of his newly conquered lands there in 1284 which can be construed as discriminating against the Welsh. Some of their legal and social practices, it is true, were outlawed; but many others were specifically endorsed; and the general tenor of the Statute was that of extending to the Welsh the benefits of the most recent legal and administrative practices of the English kingdom. It was, interestingly enough, in 1295 in the wake of the last great revolt of the Welsh against Edward I—and, as it turned out, the last major revolt in Wales before that of Owain Glyn Dŵr—that the first clearly discriminatory and general ordinance against the Welsh was apparently issued. They were not to reside in the English boroughs of Wales, or to bear arms in them, or to conduct trade outside them.[27]

The ordinance of 1295 identified the particular locale whose interests and privileges it was devised to protect, the English boroughs in Wales, more specifically those founded in north and west Wales in the wake of the conquest and in the shadow of the new Edwardian castles. It was to be the burgesses of these boroughs who were to be the most devoted, indeed paranoid, defenders of English exclusiveness in Wales throughout the fourteenth century. The 1295 ordinances also identified three of the preoccupying features of this mentality of English exclusiveness which were still in good heart, at least in some quarters, a century later: the emphasis on the ethnic purity of the boroughs as islands of Englishness, the fear of the Welsh (hence the clause prohibiting them from bearing arms in towns), and commercial privilege.

During the fourteenth century the division between English and Welsh was taken for granted in a whole host of ways in the life of Wales, as we saw earlier. Such a division was not of itself discriminatory; it was simply an acceptance of the facts of social and governmental life; it was frequently accompanied by cordial relationships and links between the two peoples. But the psychology and practices of discrimination and exclusiveness had not altogether gone underground; occasionally they broke through to the surface disturbingly, threateningly, and embarrassingly. The issues of tension were much the same as they had been identified in the 1295 ordinance, but other prohibitions and exclusions were periodically added to them: that Welshmen should not acquire English land in Wales without licences; that they should not be allowed to live or purchase land in English towns in Wales or the English border counties; that they should be

prohibited from holding assemblies; that they should be excluded from all the major posts of civil and military power in Wales; and that English burgesses should only be tried and convicted in Wales by fellow Englishmen. The legislation of Henry IV's parliaments had a list of anti-Welsh issues to hand when they set to work; they did not have to construct one *de novo*.[28]

What is more, it is during the fourteenth century, and notably during its second half, not at the time of the Edwardian conquest, that many of these discriminatory measures were incorporated in borough charters and used as a pretext for profiteering exercises at the expense, and to the embarrassment, of the Welsh. Few borough charters are so vitriolic in their anti-Welsh clauses as that issued at Hope (co. Flints.) in February 1399, little more than a year and a half before Glyn Dŵr's revolt erupted. It is from Hope also that we get a striking glimpse of how such clauses could be used to excite ethnic tension. In September 1401 Roger ab Iorwerth Felinydd (E. 'the miller'), a Welshman so described, lost fifty acres of land he had purchased, 'because it was English land and had been measured as such at the time of the conquest of Wales'. He had acquired it 'without licence of the lord Prince and contrary to the statutes, provisions and ordinances issued at Caernarfon at the time of the conquest for the burgesses and English boroughs (of Wales) and observed thereafter throughout north Wales. No Welshman can or ought to acquire to himself or his heirs . . . any English land . . . for any price, so long as an English burgess is willing to buy and hold it.' It was in an atmosphere already well attuned to such anti-Welsh sentiments that Henry IV's legislation was to be issued.[29]

Indeed, the sentiment should not be seen as specifically or exclusively anti-Welsh in its essence. Rather was it part of a more general process in which the British Isles had been caught for several generations, a process which involved, on the one hand, the articulation of a concept of Englishness and, on the other, the demarcation of the distance and the differences between the English and the other peoples, notably the Irish and the Welsh, who lived under the rule of the king of England. Some historians would argue that the psychological roots of this process are as old as the early twelfth century; but it is in the thirteenth and fourteenth centuries that it began to take legal and institutional forms. It was then that English identity—on such issues as law, institutions, customs, historical mythology, and language—began to be ever more stridently asserted and that the development of state institutions allowed it to find increasing expression in ordinances and legislation. It was then, likewise, that the problems of the governance of native peoples in Ireland and Wales and the urgent need to protect the status of the English settlers in both countries prompted administrators and legislators to address the issue of the relationship between the English and the native peoples in these two countries. It is surely no coincidence that the earliest

discriminatory ordinances against the Welsh of 1295 appeared only two years before the earliest legislation in Ireland directed against the slide into what was known as 'degeneracy', that is, the danger that the English settlers there would adopt the customs of the native Irish and thereby undermine the distinction between the two peoples. In Wales attempts to preserve this distinction, with all that was implied in it, were largely confined to the charters and petitions of the English boroughs and to the very occasional activities of zealous and profiteering English officials. In Ireland, where English control became increasingly uncertain as the fourteenth century progressed, the distinction was formally and authoritatively embedded in the Statutes of Kilkenny in 1366. English control was certainly far more secure in Wales than it was in Ireland; but in both countries the distinction between two (or, possibly in Ireland, three) peoples, and a very unequal distinction at that, remained part of the official governmental ideology. This was an essential part of the background to Owain Glyn Dŵr's revolt, and to the statutes that were issued in response to that revolt.[30]

An ideology of a duality of peoples and of discrimination between them has a further relevance for our understanding of the anti-Welsh legislation of Henry IV's reign. It implied that the Welsh (like the native Irish) could not be part of the political nation of England. They were excluded from the political, governmental, judicial, legal, and fiscal orbit of the English kingdom and polity. Their status was that of political outsiders *vis-à-vis* the English kingdom and that of second-class citizens within their own country, at least theoretically. All that Henry IV's legislation did was to codify and fortify these discriminations and exclusions. It highlighted, and further ensconced, the anomalous position of Welshmen: they were regarded as subjects of the English kings, but they did not share in the privileges and responsibilities of his kingdom; rather did they occupy a twilight world between that of being denizens and that of being aliens.[31]

The anti-Welsh statutes of Henry IV need, therefore, to be located in a broader and longer context than that of a knee-jerk response to the experience of a Welsh revolt. Viewed in such a context they surrender much of the novelty and Draconian character that Tudor antiquarians bestowed upon them. Nevertheless, there is no denying that they represented a most unpleasant threat to the *modus vivendi* which, in most parts of Wales, had come to characterize the relationships between English and Welsh in Wales, municipal charters and occasional episodes of heightened ethnic tension notwithstanding. The chronicler Adam of Usk had been a beneficiary of such a *modus vivendi*: a native Welshman (as his epitaph makes clear), his early academic career in Oxford had been promoted by the earl of March (as lord of Usk) and thereafter he seems to have made his way easily up the academic, legal, and ecclesiastical ladders in England and Wales. For a man at ease with the world in which he lived the anti-Welsh sentiments which now

suddenly burst to the surface presented a most unwelcome threat to the ordered progress of his career. He made his alarm abundantly clear: 'I heard discussed some very harsh measures to be ordained against the Welsh—such as they should not marry with the English, nor acquire land or live in England, and many other objectionable ideas.' For Adam the episode was a bad dream, but it was a dream which was about to come true.[32]

Adam's comment was prompted by the debates and discussions which he had witnessed at the parliament which met from 20 January to 10 March 1401. It was in response to petitions presented at this parliament that the first anti-Welsh statutes of Henry's IV's reign (2 Henry IV *c*. 12, *c*. 16–20) were issued. A week or so after the dissolution of parliament the king issued a set of even more discriminatory ordinances against the Welsh which were confirmed under the great seal on 22 March 1401. The tide of anti-Welsh sentiment was now in full flood, and the prince of Wales made his contribution with yet tougher ordinances issued at Chester on 14 June 1401. One might have thought that the thirst for penal measures had now been quenched; but when parliament reassembled in October–November 1402 it did so against a background of repeated disasters in Wales. The response was perhaps inevitable—a further batch of anti-Welsh measures (4 Henry IV *c*. 26–34), many of them putting on a statutory basis measures which had already been issued as ordinances in 1401. An occasional blast against the Welsh would be issued in subsequent parliaments, especially in 1404 and 1410, but in essence the legislative measures against them belong to the years 1401–2.[33]

The character of those measures can be quickly indicated. Many of them were security measures directed against a people which had been shown to be unreliable at best, treacherous and rebellious at worst. The Welsh were henceforth not to hold assemblies other than with official permission and in the presence of officers; their minstrels and rhymers, who were regarded, probably correctly, as the chief fomenters of sedition, were to be starved into silence by prohibiting them from collecting subsidies among the population. No Welshman was to possess a castle, fortress, or defensive house other than such as existed in the time of Edward I. In the same spirit no Welshman or man of mixed parentage was to serve in the garrisons of the English castles in Wales; that was henceforth to be the prerogative of 'Englishmen and strangers to the district'. Every effort was to be made to prevent arms and victuals from reaching the Welsh rebels, and an incentive for policing this prohibition was provided by stipulating that local constables along the Welsh borders would keep for themselves a sixth of the goods impounded. Finally, it comes as no surprise that no Welshman was to be allowed to carry arms in towns, markets, churches, or on the highways. The prince of Wales's Chester ordinances, indeed, required that any Welshman

visiting a town should surrender his arms to the guardians of the town before he was allowed entry. There is little that is surprising in these measures: they treated all Welshmen, in effect, as potential rebels and sought to deny them the opportunities and means to stage a rebellion or to threaten the English settlements in Wales.

It was the second set of proposals which could be regarded as vindictive and discriminatory. Their purpose was to re-erect the ethnic barriers between English and Welsh, especially in the towns of Wales and the English borders, and to prevent any further infiltration of Welsh people into these towns. The first of the statutes reaffirmed a position which had long since been advocated in those towns: it prohibited Welshmen from buying land in England or in English towns in Wales and from becoming burgesses in these towns. A further statute specified the eight border towns to which this prohibition was to apply and put stringent restraints on those Welshmen already living in these towns. Prince Henry's ordinances of 14 June 1401 went even further by stipulating that even a person half-Welsh by blood (Fr. *de demy sanc del partie galois*) was not to be received into a town. In theory at least, a *cordon sanitaire* had been erected around the towns of Wales and the English borders to prevent them from being infected with the Welsh virus.

Such a ruling could, in fairness, be regarded as no more than reiterating a long-established, if long-since practically abandoned, orthodoxy. Other measures were more novel. Most of the top posts in the government of Wales had not in fact been open to Welshmen, at least in the Principality, for generations; but it was only from 1401 that this exclusion was placed on a statutory basis. The list of prohibited offices extended from that of justice (or chief governor) to that of chief forester; it could not, for obvious reasons, be extended to the cadre of very local appointments. Initially the exclusion order applied to north Wales only, but by the 1402 statutes it was extended to apply to all Welshmen (other than those exempted by the king) and even to an English person married to a Welsh man or woman who was a supporter of Owain's cause, or indeed to any English man who had been foolish enough to marry a Welsh woman since the outbreak of the revolt, or did so in future.

It was this last clause which was arguably the most sinister since it was part and parcel of a campaign to establish a statutory ethnic divide between English and Welsh, very much reminiscent of the ideology incorporated in the Statutes of Kilkenny in Ireland in 1366. It was the prince of Wales's ordinances of 14 June 1401 which promoted the ideology in its crudest forms. No English man or woman, so they proclaimed, should henceforth marry or in any way align him or her self with a Welsh man or woman in marriage under pain of forfeiture of all that could be forfeited. This doctrine of ethnic purity was reinforced by an ordinance which

forbade the English from sending their children to be fostered among the Welsh; if this practice of fosterage (of which the English government so much disapproved, in Ireland as in Wales) was to continue, English children should be sent to England to be fostered. No parliamentary statute was as crudely racist as these ordinances; but Henry IV's first set of statutes after the revolt made it clear that the position of the English within Wales was to be a judicially privileged one. No entire Englishman—that is, English through both parents—was to be convicted at the suit of any Welshman within Wales; rather could he be convicted only by English justices or by a jury composed of 'entire' English burgesses. Initially this privilege was limited to a period of three years; but when the statute was reissued in 1402 such a time-limitation was removed. One people's privilege was, of course, another people's discrimination. In terms of freedom of movement, access to major public posts, and legal status *vis-à-vis* their English neighbours the Welsh were now statutorily disadvantaged in their own country. It was a situation very reminiscent of that which had developed in late-medieval Ireland and it was the price that the Welsh had to pay for the Glyn Dŵr revolt.

The moving spirit behind these statutes and ordinances may not have been the government itself, so much as English public opinion as expressed by the commons in parliament. This suggestion seems amply confirmed by the royal response to many of the petitions presented in parliament. Some were accepted, but only after they had been hedged about with important qualifications by the king. Thus, in 1401 the request that Englishmen in Wales should only be convicted by fellow Englishmen met with royal approval on condition that the privilege was to be enjoyed only for three years. In 1402 the king excluded from the ban on Welshmen from carrying arms in public places those 'who were loyal lieges of the king'; likewise he insisted that the prohibition on Welshmen holding high office in Wales should not extend to bishops and others whom he had found to be loyal; and in the same spirit he allowed bishops and other temporal lords in Wales the right to have their castles or places of defence in spite of the general veto on Welshmen from possessing defensible buildings. In other instances royal resistance went further, most often by the formal device of referring a petition to the Council, thereby in effect killing it off. So it was that the commons' request that all trade in Wales should take place in the English market towns was quietly shelved, as was the petition that English law should be used in all Crown pleas in Wales. The king and his advisers may have felt that such requests were impractical. For the same reason they side-stepped demands that Welshmen be held responsible for breaches of peace caused by their kinsmen, and they turned a deaf ear to most of the recurrent requests for an overhaul of some of the discredited features of peace-keeping in the March of Wales.[34]

The king tried to moderate the anti-Welsh hysteria which became rampant in 1401–2, but he could not will it away. The Welsh had often been thought of as volatile, as suffering from what was called light-headedness (L. *levitas cervicosa*), but for generations they had not been taken too seriously by the powers that be. That is why they could be patronizingly dismissed as 'bare-footed rascals' or as 'a people of little reputation'. Now that they had mounted a real rebellion and one which was not easily quelled, the sense of outrage at their treachery was proportionately the greater. This was nothing less than 'the war between the English and the Welsh'. In such a simplified view of the world it was inevitable that all Welshmen should be equated with rebels and all Englishmen as their automatic enemies. It was equally inevitable that stories should be put about that if the revolt were successful no Englishman would be left as an officer in Wales, and that indeed the Welsh intended nothing less than the destruction of the English language or people. It was this popular hysteria which was the context for Henry IV's anti-Welsh statutes.[35]

The Welsh were the most obvious target for such hysteria. But the commons in parliament directed their brickbats also at two other targets. One of them was the government itself. The commons had a simple response to the embarrassing failure of English policy in Wales: the restoration in full of the measures of the 'noble and wise King Edward I'. It is a theme which runs as a refrain through their petitions: 'as used to be done at the conquest of Wales in the time of King Edward', 'as was ordained at the conquest of Wales by King Edward'. Edward I, at least in his relations with the Welsh, had clearly become a mythic figure for the English political classes; he had also become a stick with which to beat the current government and an excuse for freezing Anglo-Welsh relations in the time-warp of an age of conquest. The other group which was the target of the commons' venom were the Marcher lords. Here again they based their argument on an appeal to history, or rather on their own interpretation of the past. The English lords in Wales, so they claimed, had been given their castles and lordships there by the king's ancestors on condition that they kept the land in firm obedience and subjection. They should be commanded, therefore, to dwell in person on their Welsh estates and be held personally responsible for their security. The English commons were in no way obliged to sustain the war in Wales financially; that was transparently the responsibility of the English lords in Wales. These were arguments about the duties of absentee English lords long since familiar in the political rhetoric of Ireland; rebellion had now prompted them to be transferred into Wales.[36]

The commons had some practical suggestions in support of their historical exposition. The first, to which the king agreed in the 1401 parliament, was that the Marcher lords should put ample supplies into their castles. Secondly, they asked

that the Marcher lords should be commanded by the king to act against the rebels in their lordships and to do so without resorting to fines and pardons, since this only encouraged the rebels. This suggestion assumed a degree of royal direction and co-ordination which cut across the grain of Marcher custom; it is not surprising that the king gave a temporizing reply. He did likewise when confronted with a third suggestion, that all lands in Wales which came to the king by forfeiture and custody should in effect be retained in the king's hands and their resources used for the suppression of the rebellion. These suggestions all indicate that the commons were impatient with the anomalous constitutional position in Wales and had become aware of the need to override such anomalies if the rebellion were to be suppressed swiftly, and at minimum cost to the English taxpayer.

One legal anomaly above all offended them; they returned to it time and again with a view to bringing it to an end. This was the practice of disclaimer. The Marcher lordships of Wales were in theory autonomous legal and judicial units; there was no common supervisory authority or appellate procedure whereby an offender in one lordship could be prosecuted and convicted in another lordship. On the contrary, he could claim that he was not judicially under the authority of the lord of the lordship in which he had been arrested (disclaimer); equally, if he wished to seek judicial asylum in another lordship he could technically do so by placing himself under the protection of the lord of such a lordship for an annual sum of fourpence (a practice known as avowry). These practices, along with the custom still common in the March whereby a convicted criminal could escape execution by the payment of a substantial fine, outraged English legal sensibilities. They saw the March as a criminals' paradise, a land lacking hierarchic and uniform judicial order, and a land whose practices were a standing affront to the basic concepts and procedures of English criminal law. The outrage was certainly exaggerated and even ill-informed, because the lords of the March had developed mutual extradition procedures—notably 'days' and 'courts of the March' and a virtual passport system called 'letters of March'—to deal with some of the consequences of the judicial fragmentation of the area. But in no generation has political outrage been unduly inhibited by close attention to the facts; and there is no doubt that the alleged practices of the Welsh March—rather like those of great judicial immunities such as the county palatine of Cheshire—were deeply puzzling and offensive to minds habituated to the apparently tidy and uniform practices of English criminal law. Furthermore, they had long been a source of complaint for the communities, especially the merchants, of the English border shires with Wales who felt that they could get no redress from criminals and debtors who fled to Wales. These practices now became a further convenient stick with which to beat the Marcher lords. Henry IV side-stepped several of the

complaints about practices in the March when they were first presented to him in 1401–2; but when a dossier of them was represented to him in the parliament of 1407 he agreed to act on most of them. Whether any practical consequences flowed from his agreement is very doubtful; rather was the king choosing to ride with the tide of complaint and criticism. Nevertheless, the Glyn Dŵr revolt had served to highlight in the minds of the English political classes how anomalous were the position and practices of the Welsh March. It was an issue which would have to be properly addressed one day.[37]

Much of the anti-Welsh legislation of Henry IV, it can be argued, was a case of letting off steam against the treacherous Welsh in the excitable atmosphere at Westminster. Such indeed might be the truth, but not the whole truth. The ordinances of March 1401 were certainly sent to north Wales to be acted upon, rather to Hotspur's embarrassment for, as he pointed out, some Welshmen had been faithful to him during the early stages of the revolt. The injunction that garrisons should be composed of Englishmen was certainly on occasion over-looked, as happened at Montgomery; but elsewhere, as at Grosmont, Brecon, and Kidwelly, the archers selected for service were specifically to be 'English, born beyond Severn and in no part of Wales'. Even more indicative of the way that the ethnic shutters had been pulled down firmly in the wake of the revolt are the measures taken in the towns. The major towns along the English border felt particularly vulnerable, since Welshmen had lived and traded in them for gener-ations. Oswestry was the first to register its response. It had been burnt in Glyn Dŵr's first raid in September 1400, and when the earl of Arundel granted it a new charter on 11 February 1401 the distrust of the Welsh was understandable. The charter was specifically granted to the *English* burgesses and limited the right to make new burgesses to the English. Hitherto, so the charter explained, the Welsh of the district around Oswestry had had the duty of guarding the four gates of the towns for three days and nights after the two annual fairs. But since they had taken part in the recent attack of the town they were now discharged from the responsibility and were required instead to raise money for English guards to be appointed. Even ahead of the parliamentary statute of March 1401, the charter decreed that the burgesses of Oswestry should only be tried in English courts by Englishmen, not, specifically, by Welshmen; while any hint of disobedience or disorder by a Welshman was to be immediately punished with a large fine.[38]

The ethnic temperature was clearly rising in Oswestry in February 1401; by September 1403—in the wake of the Battle of Shrewsbury and the large-scale defection of the men of north-east Wales to Glyn Dŵr's cause during the summer—it had reached boiling-point. At no stage during the revolt were more drastic measures issued against the Welsh than those proclaimed by Prince

Henry with respect to Chester in that month. Some of them echoed the statutes and ordinances issued since 1401: no Welsh person entering the city during the day was to carry any arms other than a knife for his meal; all Welshmen were to surrender their arms at the city gate; no Welshmen was to keep a tavern or to sell ale or wine; three or more Welshmen assembling within the walls were to be immediately imprisoned on the assumption that they were planning an insurrection. The good men of Chester were clearly desperately nervous; but it was the first two clauses which truly showed how paranoid the authorities were. All Welshmen and women were to be peremptorily expelled from the city; and any Welsh person staying within the city walls henceforth after sunset and before sunrise was liable to be executed. It was a policy very close to that of ethnic cleansing.[39]

The hysteria against the Welsh may have reached its highest pitch in Chester, but practical measures, often echoing the general statutes and ordinances, were also issued within Wales itself. The charter issued by Lord Charlton to the burgesses of Welshpool in June 1407 breathes the atmosphere of suspicion and intolerance which now prevailed in Wales. It sang the praises of the burgesses for their faithfulness during the recent revolt, and stipulated that the only Welshmen who were to be admitted to the liberty of the borough were those who had proved their loyalty during the revolt. All other Welshmen were to be treated with suspicion: none was to be allowed to stay overnight in the town and all were to surrender their arms on entering the town. As an indicator that language was becoming a measure of ethnic solidarity, it was decreed that French and English were to be the only languages used in the borough court. Much the same spirit informs the ordinances issued for other towns: at Kidwelly it was specifically decreed in May 1407 that 'no Welshman hereafter shall be an officer or governor of the town'; at Brecon ordinances proclaimed in November 1408 forbade the bailiffs from receiving any Welshman to be a burgess and decreed that any Welshman carrying any kind of arms into the town would be fined £20; and in the lordship of Denbigh it was assumed that, in accordance with the 1402 statute, all major officers hereafter would be English. There was doubtless much temporary vindictiveness and short-term rhetoric in such statements, but they were now clauses in municipal charters or statutes of the realm. As such they could be invoked to cause embarrassment at least, public humiliation at worst. So it was that, when Gruffudd ap Llywelyn forgot to divest himself of a short dagger when he visited Brecon in 1410, it was only an official pardon which released him from the £20 fine which such an offence involved for a Welshman.[40]

The ultimate significance of the anti-Welsh measures of Henry IV's reign—be they in statutes, ordinances, borough charters, municipal decrees, or seignorial directives—lies less in whether they were specifically applied, and much more in

their formal reaffirmation of a mentality of separation, discrimination, and mistrust. In the lives of individual Welshmen and Englishmen in Wales and in the world of some of the English boroughs of Wales the wounds caused by the rebellion and the legislation would be repaired, sometimes indeed quickly repaired; but official rhetoric and policies had returned, as it were, to the days of the cold war and they remained there for generations to come. The commons in the 1430s could still stir the ethnic pot by referring to the fact that 'the Welsh bear ancient malice and enmity towards the English' and insisting on the chasm in sentiments and attitudes between those who were 'English by nature and condition' and those who were 'in fact true Welshmen at heart and of lineage'. It was a world in which men could be hounded from office for being Welsh or being married to a Welsh woman; it was also a world where Welshmen who wanted a secure future had to secure formal letters of denizenship for themselves and their heirs, declaring them in effect to be of English condition.[41]

It is, paradoxically, a tribute to the far-reaching impact of Glyn Dŵr's revolt that it had held back the process of social reconciliation in Wales, at the institutional and legal level, for several generations. It had opened, or reopened, the two fundamental questions about the legal and constitutional character of the country—that of the status of, and relationship between, Welsh and English in the eyes of the law and that of the anomalous constitutional and political relationship between Wales and the kingdom of England. Given the hysteria that the revolt naturally evoked, there was little hope of addressing either issue rationally for some time in the future. Just as it has sometimes been argued that in religious matters the activities of John Wyclif and his successors delayed, rather than hastened, the reformation of the English Church, so it can be suggested that Glyn Dŵr's revolt delayed the birth of modern Wales, if only by giving the past and its categories a new and vindictive lease of life.

SUBMISSION AND AFTERMATH

*T*he revolt of Owain Glyn Dŵr was an unconscionably long time a-dying. In 1406–7 it looked as if it would be brought to an end quickly and systematically. Submissions and surrenders were reported from different parts of Wales and great public acts of capitulation were enacted. In November 1406 the major prize of the surrender of the island of Anglesey was formally secured and over 2,000 islanders were pardoned for their revolt in return for a large communal fine. Equally gratifying were the mass surrenders of the communities of northeast Wales to Sir Gilbert Talbot at the sessions held in Denbigh, Flint, and elsewhere in spring 1407. More or less simultaneously, arrangements for similar submissions were being made in south Wales, even in south-west Wales. The revolt appeared to have collapsed. So in most respects it had, but extinguishing it finally proved to be a stubbornly slow business. Two major castles—Aberystwyth and Harlech—were still in rebel hands, and any crowing about final victory was certainly premature until they were recaptured. Their significance was fully recognized by both parties: the English commented that once Aberystwyth had been retaken 'the whole rebellion of the Welsh is like to finish'; but the fall of Aberystwyth was delayed for the better part of twelve months due to the misplaced confidence of the English and the gritty resilience and determination of Owain Glyn Dŵr and his deputies. Harlech proved an even tougher nut to crack: this remote, majestic outpost required the besieging skills of 300 men-at-arms and 600 archers and some of the most advanced technology of the day before it eventually capitulated in the early spring of 1409. The revolt, it could now be believed, could be proclaimed officially dead. In most respects and by most criteria that was certainly true; but, rather like a peat fire, a series of incidents and alarums over the next few years showed that its embers had not been finally extinguished. Should the winds of fortune turn direction yet again, in England as much as in Wales, those embers might still flare up into full flame. It was not until 8 April 1421 that the final act of the rebellion was enacted. On that day—some twenty years and six months after his father had had himself proclaimed prince of Wales—Maredudd ab Owain, Owain Glyn Dŵr's surviving son, finally accepted a pardon from the king of England.[1]

The long-drawn-out demise of the Glyn Dŵr revolt should not occasion great surprise. Though the revolt had begun with a formal defiant act at Glyndyfrdwy in September 1400 followed by an even more public foray across north-east Wales, the rebellion was in most parts of Wales a guerrilla campaign, marked by the withdrawal of obedience and the collapse of royal and seignorial control, and punctuated by very occasional raids. In other words, the revolt was often less the replacement of one structure of authority by another, nor even necessarily the pledging of support to the rebel cause (though that certainly did occur), more the effective collapse of the existing pattern and mechanisms of authority. Wales had slipped out of its old pattern of obedience. By the same token, the return to obedience was often a hesitant and gradual process.

There are two major ways in which its progress can be outlined; neither is without its problems. The first is through the pardons, individual and communal, which the king issued to former rebels. Even in the March of Wales, where the lords had almost exclusive judicial powers over their tenants or subjects, treason was an offence against the king. Therefore the act of pardon was the king's; so, technically, were the lands forfeited for rebellion and the fines and ransoms paid by former rebels. It was only by formal delegation that these powers could, at least in theory, be handed to others. This means that royal records are much more comprehensive than usual as a source for the formal processes of the surrender and pardon of the rebels. Even so the pardons may be misleading. They may be premature, especially in the assumption that a general fine betokened the surrender of the whole community. Lord Charlton of Powys conceded as much when he secured a charter of pardon from the king for his tenants of Powys in November 1407; they had, he commented, 'for the most part surrendered to the king's grace', and only those who had done so were to be the beneficiaries of the pardon. Equally, a pardon might long post-date the actual act of surrender. Three of the prominent Welshmen of Flintshire are known to have submitted to the authorities in August 1405 but it was not until two years later, on 1 August 1407, that they received their official pardons. So we should treat our pardons with some suspicion. The second source that enables us to fill out the story of the decline of the revolt are the annual financial accounts of the shires and lordships of Wales. The holding of courts, the collection of revenue, and the auditing of accounts are among the surest signs that life, or at least the governors' control of society, was returning to normal. The accounts are, in fact, often more revealing than the official pardons: they show that recovery of control was patchy and hesitant, sometimes even within a single lordship, and that normal life could not be resumed at a stroke. Even with the accounts it is worth remembering that even when all is apparently well at the audit all may not be well in life generally.[2]

What, then, do these two major sources tell us of the final phase of the revolt? It is clear that the first signs that the tide of revolt might be ebbing were beginning to register in different parts of Wales from as early as summer 1405. It comes as no surprise that some of the earliest negotiations for surrender were held with the men of Usk and Caerleon in the far south-east and with those of some Welsh districts bordering with England rather further north. But there were already indications that the government believed that support for the revolt was also beginning to crumble in north-east Wales: only such an assumption explains its confidence in appointing to offices and letting land in Denbigh that year. But it was during the years 1406–7 that the revolt began to crumble around all the peripheries of Wales. It is rare that a precise date can be given, though in the commote of Carnwyllion (near Kidwelly in south-west Wales) 23 April 1406 came to be regarded as the terminus for the rebellion. During these two years communities in the four corners of Wales began to return into obedience: Anglesey in November 1406; Flint, Denbigh, and Dyffryn Clwyd by March 1407; the Arundel lordships of the northern and eastern borderlands (Bromfield and Yale, Chirkland, and Clun) earlier; and many of the major districts of south-east Wales, including the lordships of Abergavenny and Glamorgan, at much the same time. By 1408–9 the only major districts which had not returned into some measure of obedience were probably northern Cardiganshire, Merionethshire, and parts of Caernarfonshire. The revolt was contracting back into its north-western heartland, into the very area in which it had survived after the initial major setbacks of 1400–1.[3]

The broad picture is, therefore, clear enough; but the local cameos of which it was composed were doubtless rather more complex. Thus, on the English border at Monmouth life was already beginning to return to normal in 1406 after almost three years of upheaval, but within a few miles of Monmouth, in the districts controlled from the castles of Grosmont and Skenfrith, recovery was much more hesitant and did not register at all a few miles further west at Whitecastle. The contrasts were likewise clear on a regional scale: revenue was already being collected in Anglesey in 1407, but virtually none was gathered from much of Caernarfonshire in 1408 or even in 1409. Likewise in the lordship of Newport in south-east Wales income was certainly being gathered by 1406, but so paltry was the sum that it was not adequate to pay for the costs of the castle, let alone to meet the cost of the garrison. The revolt may have effectively come to an end, at least as a mass movement, in much of Wales by 1407–8; but the process of recovery, for society as well as lord, was often a painfully slow one.[4]

The process of submission must also have been psychologically painful. Our evidence is sufficiently full to enable us to reconstruct some of its main features. As with so many guerrilla movements, the end of the revolt was ushered in not

by a crushing military defeat but rather by an ebbing of confidence and support. During 1405–6 the rebels in effect lost the initiative. A series of telling defeats in south-east Wales, the capture of some of Owain's closest family and of his key supporters, and the realization that effective French military support was a broken reed between them served to puncture the euphoria which had built up across the years 1403–5. Once this euphoria and confidence were gone, the English could at last seize the military initiative. This is what they did early in 1406. Even they must have been surprised by the speed with which support for the rebels evaporated. There was no need for major military confrontation; the revolt simply petered out in one area after another. Pacification rather than suppression was to be the keynote of the next months and years; and pacification was essentially a combination of military safety-measures and an awesome demonstration of power. We get a vivid glimpse of its character in the measures taken in north-west Wales in the summer of 1407. By that date the English military commanders were so confident that the revolt had been extinguished in Anglesey that the garrison at Beaumaris was cut by half in August to a mere one man-at-arms and ten archers. Elsewhere caution was still necessary: from 23 August a force of twenty men-at-arms and 100 archers was posted at Caernarfon to guard the Menai Straits and to prevent the raids on Anglesey in which the desperate men of the mainland tried to replenish their depleted stocks. But caution had to be supplemented by a visible demonstration of power: so it was that Gilbert Talbot, chief justice of North Wales, set out with an intimidating escort of 500 soldiers during the summer to pacify the counties of Caernarfon and Merioneth. An exhausted, frightened, and demoralized populace was being cowed into final submission, and it was a submission made with scarcely a fight.[5]

The dispatch of a military force may have been essential to break the spirit of the men of north-west Wales, but elsewhere individual rebels and whole communities read the signs of the time early and took the initiative in making their submissions. The story is particularly well recorded in north-east Wales. From 1405 onwards the good citizens of Chester, whose trade had allegedly suffered so badly during the revolt, witnessed a steady stream of Welshmen travelling, with bowed heads, and a few servants, through their streets *en route* to the exchequer in the castle to make their submissions to the justiciar. Gwilym ap Gruffudd ap Gwilym (one of the richest men of north Wales), his two brothers, and four companions were among the first to surrender, as early as August 1405; with the consummate skill of political turncoats, they had judged that a short spell of custody in Chester Prison could wipe out the memory of their rebellion and launch them on new careers as prosperous loyalists. Others soon followed suit: on 23 March 1406 eleven Welshmen swore fealty before the justiciar, and during the summer a succession of Welshmen were given licence to come 'to communi-

cate with the council of the lord Prince', a euphemistic phrase reminiscent of the modern injunction 'to help the police with their inquiries'. By the summer the flow had become a flood, and individuals now came as spokesmen on behalf of communities. By September the prince of Wales could report that some of the leading men of the lordship of Denbigh had submitted 'humbly and unconditionally' to him at Chester, and had asked for his grace and pardon to be extended to the men of the lordship as a whole. So it was that the officials of Denbigh were given full power to admit all the rebels of Denbigh, who duly submitted, into the king's grace.[6]

What happened in Chester must have been repeated in different parts of Wales, as former rebels now realized that discretion was certainly the better part of valour. Some, however, came in more reluctantly than others; and behind the bland formulae of the official documents it is easy to imagine that a great deal of cajolery, persuasion, and negotiation is concealed. In Flintshire, for example, one of the surrenders which was most eagerly awaited was that of Hywel ap Tudur ab Ithel. Hywel, as we saw earlier, was one of the most powerful and outrageously lawless men in the country; he was also the head of an extended kin which had been prominently and sometimes murderously involved in the revolt. Hard-headed man that he was, he must have realized that the game was up; but it was not until September 1407 that he and his servant and two horses were given a safe-conduct to come to Chester 'to communicate and discuss there with our [the prince's] council'. It was rather a gentlemanly way of dealing with a wanted man. But he was not alone; others could delay their formal submissions until the justiciar next came into the area so long as they promised to be of good behaviour in the meantime and found the requisite guarantors for their eventual submission. Such arrangements betoken an official attitude that accepted that conciliation and cajolery were essential to bring about the process of pacification.[7]

Much the same message—and one which was not altogether acceptable to the government—came from other sources. As late as November 1409 the government expressed its grave disquiet to four of the leading Marcher lords of northeast Wales (including the earl of Arundel and Reginald Grey of Ruthin) that their local officials were concluding truces and armistices with Owain Glyn Dŵr and other rebels. There is no reason to doubt that the rumours which reached the king were well founded. An extraordinary exchange of letters between Reginald Grey and Gruffudd ap Dafydd ap Gruffudd, a Welsh bandit and doubtless erstwhile rebel, lifts the veil on the sort of bargains and cajoleries which lay behind the ending of the revolt. The letters almost certainly belong to 1411. Gruffudd was willing to submit but clearly not on any terms: he wanted a royal charter of pardon, an important local office, and arrangements to go on military service overseas. Such demands may sound outrageous, but it is clear that lords and their

officials were driven into demeaning bargains in order to secure the final extinction of the revolt. Thus, a Welshman was accused of having opened negotiations with Owain Glyn Dŵr in September 1409 and agreeing to pay a ransom to him on behalf of the lordship of Moldsdale. Welshmen might be expected to behave in this fashion, but the steward of Oswestry was later also to be accused of entering into negotiations with the Welsh rebels around 1409. These examples come from north-east Wales where the evidence is most abundant; but there is no reason to doubt that shady bargains and secret concessions characterized the end of the revolt in other parts of Wales. Thus, when the curtain is lifted briefly in 1413 on life in Cydweli we find Henry Don—local strong-man, former leading rebel, and a man imprisoned and heavily fined for his rebellion—as active as ever in throwing his weight around in local society. Rebellion and submission had not broken the pretensions of such men; pacification had to be bought at the price of acknowledging their power and even conceding their demands.[8]

We may readily concede, therefore, that the ending of the revolt, especially for powerful individuals, involved far more than the abject and unilateral submissions suggested by the official documentation. Nevertheless the revolt had undoubtedly collapsed. Its formal termination and the reinauguration of English authority were solemnly signalled by the holding of grand judicial sessions. It requires no great leap of the historical imagination to recognize how awesome such sessions must have been for a defeated populace. In May 1407 Gilbert Talbot, justiciar of Chester and North Wales, held such sessions in north-east Wales. The profits of the occasion were enormous—at least £1,765 in communal and individual fines from the county of Flintshire, the lordships of Denbigh, Dyffryn Clwyd, and Moldsdale, and the commote of Creuddyn. But it was the terror of the occasion which doubtless left its mark on the memories of men. Almost eighty men came to make their individual fines for their lives as erstwhile rebels, while the escort of 400 soldiers who escorted the justice was specifically charged with the duty of ensuring that the large fines imposed were collected with maximum speed. The inhabitants of north-east Wales could be under no illusion: English rule had been forcefully reimposed and at a heavy price. The same was doubtless true in other parts of Wales: Edward, duke of York, held a similar great sessions at Carmarthen, probably in 1407–8, while on the Duchy of Lancaster estates in Wales (Cydweli, Brecon, Ogmore, and Monmouth) similar sessions were held in April–May 1410.[9]

Formal pardons, judicial sessions, and communal fines were the collective symbols of the reaffirmation of English power after the years of rebellion. Authority had now been formally and visually restored in most parts of Wales, and in its wake the machinery of day-to-day governance could begin to function again. We can see it cranking back into action in Denbigh: a new court-house (L.

aula placitorum) was constructed to replace the one burnt during the revolt; two large chests were bought for the tolls collected from tenants now once again required to bring their corn to be ground at the lord's mill; mills were rebuilt and new millstones purchased in Anglesey and carried by sea to Rhuddlan before being transported by land to Denbigh. Such was the story in different parts of Wales. Auditors had resumed their visits, though they did so under heavy escort just as officials in north Wales preferred to travel to Chester in the relative safety of a ship rather than confront 'the malice of Welsh rebels' on land. Indeed, in some respects officials had learnt nothing and forgotten nothing as a result of the traumatic experiences of the last four years: in Brecon they set about to recover the large communal fines still outstanding since 1401, and collected £552 from them in 1410. By that year royal and seignorial government had been restored in every part of Wales other than in the far west and north. In that respect the revolt could truly be said to be at an end.[10]

Yet no one could be under any illusion that life had really returned to normal in Wales. For those who measured normality by the levels of seignorial income much of the evidence was disturbing. Income from the great lordship of Brecon immediately before the rebellion had been well in excess of £1,000 gross per annum; in 1409 it was a mere £364. Much the same was true in the northern lordships: in Chirkland contemporary valuations reckoned a yield of about £400 a year, but these expectations stood at a modest £130 in 1409, while in Denbigh the rosy picture presented by an anticipated revenue of £815 was soon shattered by the realization that £513 of it was classified as being 'decayed or respited' income, that is, virtually uncollectable. Such falls in revenue were no more than was to be expected, and they might well be repaired in years to come. More disturbing was the evidence that the country was in a sullen and resentful mood. Submission had been forced upon it, but the resentment smouldered just beneath the surface and could so easily be ignited into open revolt once more.[11]

It was not difficult to guess where such a renewed revolt might break out. Two areas in particular proved to be particularly recalcitrant. One was northern Cardiganshire, the district north of Aberystwyth. No contributions were collected there towards the great communal fines on the country in 1409–11, and as late as 1413 most of the rents from the district could not be realized. Beyond Cardiganshire lay the most recalcitrant of all Welsh counties, Merionethshire. This was truly the last redoubt of Glyn Dŵr's cause. It was thither that hardened rebels from Cardiganshire fled after the fall of Aberystwyth. As late as May 1417 a memorandum submitted to the king's council saw the control of Merioneth as the key to the whole security situation in north Wales: 'if that county is well and adequately guarded, the whole of north Wales will be at peace.' Negotiations

were still being conducted with the rebels there in 1415 and officers refused to discharge their revenue-raising duties there for fear of the Welsh. Merioneth still had many of the characteristics of a no-go area. Even the government had to recognize as much as late as July 1420 when it empowered the sheriff of Caernarfonshire and Merioneth to receive any Welsh rebels submitting to the king.[12]

It was a serious matter that the revolt had not been fully extinguished in the far west; but the threat within Wales was not confined to this remote and mountainous corner of the country. Harlech Castle may finally have fallen early in 1409, but barely a year passed over the next seven to eight years when troops were not deployed in Wales to guard against an anticipated crisis. In May 1409 almost hysterical warnings were issued of an imminent attack by the Welsh, quite possibly in association with the French and the Scots. The atmosphere was hardly calmer in 1410. In March there were fears for the safety of Anglesey; a naval detachment was sent from Chester to cruise in the seas between Wales and Ireland to forestall any rebel assaults. In June the king's council agreed to send a force of 900 soldiers to Wales for 135 days, and considered the situation so delicate that it authorized a detachment of 300 of them to be sent in advance. Though the revolt had officially terminated in Wales three to four years earlier, the government clearly thought that the situation was still very volatile. In summer 1411 there was renewed trouble in Cardiganshire: the garrison at Aberystwyth was increased and a force of almost forty men was stationed at Cardigan, well outside the normal danger zone, 'against the latest disturbance'. In 1412 an effort was made to quell the last signs of disobedience in Merionethshire by posting 180 men at Cymer and Bala, but by then nervousness had become chronic and doubtless explains the inquiry into unlawful congregations in Wales of November 1412. The accession of a new king brought no cure for the condition: information about the conduct and plans of Owain Glyn Dŵr was still very much on the government's agenda. Indeed, the condition was now complicated by the fear that Welsh disaffection might be exploited by the internal and external enemies of the English Crown, as had happened so signally in the years 1403–6. In particular, the revolt of Sir John Oldcastle, the Lollard leader, in January 1414 made the authorities nervous about Wales. And not without good reason: Oldcastle came from Herefordshire and knew Wales well from his distinguished service there in Prince Henry's company. Oldcastle was thought to have been in communication with Glyn Dŵr's son, and it was not without significance that it was to be in Powys that he was eventually tracked down. Nervousness about an Oldcastle–Welsh alliance was, therefore, understandable. A special guard was placed on Cardigan Castle from 19 February 1414, and messengers were dispatched post-haste to Carmarthen, Kidwelly, and Aberystwyth to put the constables on their guard. Oldcastle escaped through Henry V's net at this juncture;

but as the king prepared for his French expeditions of summer 1415 his jitteriness about Wales returned, prompting him to station a force of sixty men for sixty days in south Wales as his preparations for his voyage reached their climax. Nor could Henry V altogether banish from his mind the fear that the Scots might once more try to stir the Welsh pot and effect a landing in Wales, all the more so as they were also implicated with Oldcastle.[13]

All in all there was hardly a year between 1409 and 1417 when the prospect of disturbance or conspiracies in Wales did not cause some anxiety to the English Crown. The anxiety was no doubt minor in proportion to other anxieties, concerns, and ambitions. Yet it was galling that some ten years after the Welsh had submitted, their loyalty could still not be taken for granted nor could they be altogether forgotten in England's strategic thinking. The mood of uncertainty was induced not only by stock images of the proverbial fecklessness of the Welsh but also by a flow of stories which illustrated their continued defiance and sullenness. Forays, battles, and sieges may now have become things of the past, but ambushes, kidnappings, and ransoms indicated that the spirit of the Welsh was by no means completely broken. The evidence from north-east Wales is once again particularly abundant and illuminating. The communities of this area had formally submitted to the justiciar in March 1407 and had agreed to pay large fines to secure a collective pardon; but over the next three to four years a campaign of spasmodic harassment showed that total pacification was far from being achieved. Burgesses (such as John Hende of Denbigh) were murdered on their travels; well-known rebels were given shelter and sustenance; supplies were stolen and carried off to rebel hideouts in Snowdonia; men were kidnapped and ransomed, often for substantial sums such as the 40 marks (£26 13s. 4d.) demanded for the release of a man from Kelsterton (co. Flints.); rebels came openly and defiantly to the fair at Flint; and officials even conducted negotiations with Glyn Dŵr himself to see what price had to be paid to buy off future attacks. All these acts were committed in a community which had formally returned to the king's allegiance several years earlier. Some of them were no doubt the work of outlaws and bandits: such a gang was to be caught near Carmarthen in 1411 and its members promptly hanged. But the evidence makes it clear that it was in the name of rebellion and as a succour to the remnant rebel bands that many of the activities were undertaken. Men and women were still loyal to the cause of Glyn Dŵr many years after his revolt had effectively failed: in October 1412 a tenant of Dyffryn Clwyd was required to swear an oath and to find pledges that he would not support Owain; in February 1414 the same oath was exacted from a woman in the same district.[14]

Memories were long and bitter, and so was the taste for revenge. We might expect this to be particularly so in north Wales where the revolt had taken such

deep root; but it is, interestingly enough, from south Wales that the most striking piece of evidence comes. The family of Dafydd Gam of Brecon had been one of the most consistently loyal Welsh families during the revolt. Dafydd himself had been prominent in the fighting in south-east Wales. The family had doubtless suffered for its loyalty to the English Crown, but it could now expect to reap the rewards for its loyalty. And so indeed it did: it was given timber with which to repair its ruined houses; it was pardoned its outstanding debts; and Dafydd himself was promoted in August 1410 to be master sergeant of the lordship. He and his kinsmen could look to a secure and profitable future. But during the next two years they were hounded by their enemies in Brecon. Dafydd's father, Llywelyn ap Hywel—now a man of very advanced years—was the first target. He had already received an annuity of £20 from the king as a reward for his loyalty and in consideration of the losses he had suffered at the hands of the Welsh rebels. He had emerged on the winning side; but his enemies in Brecon, former rebels no doubt, were not to be denied their revenge and they plotted to indict him under the processes of Welsh law. It was only a comprehensive royal pardon issued on 25 May 1411 which thwarted their purpose; the fact that it had to be issued made it clear that old vendettas were still alive and that former rebels were still brazen enough to pursue their old enemies.[15]

Old age and a royal pardon may have come to Llywelyn ap Hywel's rescue, but there was no such easy escape route for his son, Dafydd Gam. In early 1412 he was captured in an ambush and taken to Owain Glyn Dŵr. The incident even created a stir in distant St Albans and prompted Thomas Walsingham to renew his vituperative comments on the Welsh leader. He had been released by August 1412, but not before he had agreed to pay a ransom variously estimated at 200 (£133 6s. 8d.) and 700 (£366 13s. 4d.) marks. Whichever the sum was, it was a punishing demand for a man whose estates and fortunes had already suffered heavily at the hands of the rebels; in an attempt to compensate him in his hour of need the king gave him permission to levy a private subsidy (W. *commortha*) from the tenants of the Duchy of Lancaster estates in Wales. Stories about Dafydd Gam became part of the legends which encrusted around Owain Glyn Dŵr, but the significance of the 1411–12 episodes lies elsewhere for us. They hint at the bitter and vindictive atmosphere which prevailed in Wales in the years which followed the official termination of the revolt. They also show that, though the Welsh rebels had had to concede defeat in the revolt, they were still sufficiently audacious and resourceful to hound their former enemies. Nor were the episodes peculiar to Brecon or to a particular family. So serious was the situation that in his first parliament in 1413 Henry V felt it necessary to issue a statute (1 Henry V c. 6) specifically directed against those Welshmen, be they former rebels or their kinsmen, who hounded those who had fought against them during the rebellion

and tried to extort large sums of money from them as compensation. In particular, the statute condemned the way that the Welsh law practice of demanding a massive compurgation (W. *rhaith*) of the oaths of 300 men to clear the names of those accused was being exploited to embarrass and humiliate those whose offence had been to fight for the king's cause during a revolt! It had come to a pretty pass when the brazen vindictiveness of former rebels could, as late as 1413, only be scotched by a parliamentary statute. What that statute and the other evidence reveal is how poisonous and unreconciled was the atmosphere in Wales six years or more after the end of the rebellion and how truculent former rebels and their families still were.[16]

All in all the atmosphere in Wales when Henry V ascended his throne in March 1413 was still distinctly uneasy, in terms both of the community's processes of reconciliation and of the government's sense of security. It is a clause in a Flintshire private deed of some ten years later which perhaps best catches the mood of nervousness: it makes allowance for rent to be remitted 'in the event of war between England and Wales or rebellion'. There could be no return to the slumbering days of the later fourteenth century. Garrisons were posted at many castles and detachments of troops were periodically sent to Wales, as we have seen. Even as late as 1416–18 small garrisons were retained at many Welsh castles: thirteen men each at Caernarfon and Harlech, sixteen at Conway, fourteen at Brecon, six at Hay are some of the examples. Above all, perhaps, the revolt had shown how indispensable castles were to the English regime in Wales, especially in a crisis. So the negligence and dilapidation of the fourteenth century were now replaced by major investment and some frenetic activity. In 1409–10 the not-inconsiderable sum of £423 was spent on three of the castles of the Principality of South Wales, £282 of it on Carmarthen alone. At Monmouth an order was issued in 1411 that a new gateway and two towers were to be built, and later up to £100 was earmarked for such purposes. The money was certainly spent, for the accounts show that in 1412–13 almost £650 was expended on repairs in the lordship of Monmouth, that is more than 50 per cent of the average annual value of the lordship. Figures from Kidwelly show that the process of repair was now an annual charge on local revenue: in the eleven out of thirteen years between 1409 and 1421 for which accounts survive a total of £442 was spent on this great castle. But most staggering of all are the figures for the castle of Carreg Cennen (cover). Perched dramatically on a remote cliff in the foothills of the Carmarthenshire Black Mountains, the castle's role had always been essentially military and psychological. There was no bustling town at its foot; rather was its purpose quite simply and literally to dominate the surrounding countryside and its population. It was an immensely imposing but vulnerable castle, not least because there was no direct access to it by water. During the great Welsh campaign of

1403 it had been isolated by the Welsh and taken. If English rule was to be successfully and unquestioningly reimposed in this part of Wales, money would have to be spent in making Carreg Cennen well-nigh impregnable. So it was: between 1414 and 1421 nearly £700 was spent in repairing its walls, gates, bridges, and chambers. The repair of castles such as Carreg Cennen was an essential aspect of the pacification of Wales; it was part of the price that had to be paid for the acute nervousness felt with regard to Wales and the Welsh. That price was still being paid when Henry V went to his early grave.[17]

It could be argued that the English authorities were themselves partly responsible for the long time it took to heal the wounds of revolt in Wales. They cannot be charged with vindictiveness; on the contrary, they were remarkably magnanimous towards former rebels. But they were financially greedy to an extraordinary degree; they failed to realize that the resentment of their financial avarice, which had been such a contributory feature to the support given to the revolt, would be fanned anew by the demands they now made. They readily granted charters of pardon, but the price they exacted was enormous. There were, broadly speaking, two sets of pardons which each community and often each individual were now required to obtain, either from the king directly or from the local lord or commander to whom he had delegated such powers. First was the personal pardon for treason, which technically bought off the death penalty (L. *pro vita habenda*). Such pardons could be granted to individuals and were carefully kept in family archives: such was the one granted to Dafydd ap Cadwaladr Ddu of Uwchaled in the lordship of Denbigh to cover the period of his support for Owain Glyn Dŵr from 17 August 1400 (the early date is striking) until Easter 1407. They were granted in return for a very substantial fine: Dafydd Fychan ap Dafydd Llwyd, a prominent Flintshire man, paid 20 marks (£13 6s. 8d.) for his. Similar pardons were granted to whole communities; such was the pardon granted to the men of Dyffryn Clwyd in 1407 for 'divers treasons, rebellions, felonies, transgressions, and other misprisions' in return for a fine of £120. The second category of pardons related to the lands and goods which were technically forfeit as a result of the rebellion and which could only be recovered by a formal pardon and an accompanying fine. Such pardons were likewise issued both communally and individually. Contemporary officials, such as the receiver of the Fitzalan lordship of Bromfield and Yale, fully recognized that there was no alternative but to grant such pardons; otherwise land would be left empty and tenants would not return. Nevertheless the fines that were the condition attached to the grant of such pardons were punitive. The men of Carmarthenshire were expected to pay £928 for such pardons, while it was not unusual to demand a fine of up to £20 from sons who wanted to succeed to the land of their father who had died a rebel.

Furthermore the authorities could interpret the terms of such pardons stringent-
ly: the lands of rebels who had submitted but who had died before they had paid
their fines were deemed to be forfeit.[18]

The impact of such a double set of fines on an impoverished and war-wracked
society must have been devastating. Some individuals incurred massive fines
which were probably more exemplary than practical. The single greatest fine
imposed was that of 500 marks (£333 6s. 8d.) on Owain Glyn Dŵr's brother-in-law,
John Hanmer, who had been captured in June 1405. By 1411 he was pleading
poverty, having already apparently paid £227 of the fine, but the sole concession
he won was the right to pay the remainder in instalments over eight years. Our
old friend Henry Don once more proved himself to be a shrewd operator: he
agreed a fine of 300 marks (£200) to recover his lands in 1413, but studied
procrastination and a timely death (in 1416) ensured that he paid nothing, and
eventually in 1444 his grandsons secured the cancellation of the debt. But Henry
Don was an exceptionally artful dodger; few others shared his skill or luck. Those
who had bound themselves over in large sums as hostages for the surrender of
Aberystwyth Castle in 1408 (the total amounted to £1,720) continued to pay hefty
instalments until they were finally pardoned in 1416.[19]

Fines on this scale must have spelt ruin or near ruin for the former rebels, but
what made the experience so devastating, albeit on a smaller scale, was that it was
extended to virtually every community in Wales. Society as a whole was paying
heavily for the price of its support, or more often probably its neutrality, during
the revolt. Our evidence is by no means complete, but such as exists is sufficient
to illustrate the punitive scale of the demands made. Three examples from
different parts of Wales may be cited. The royal county of Carmarthen provided
the first. In a good year in the late fourteenth century it could probably be
expected to yield a gross revenue of £750–£1,000 to the royal exchequer. Such is
the figure to bear in mind as we consider the series of fines imposed on the county
in 1407–12: a first general fine of £1,000 on two-thirds of the county (Cantref Mawr
and Cantref Bychan) in 1407; a second general fine of £1,666 13s. 4d. on an enlarged
county and its appendages at a sessions held by the duke of York in 1409; almost
£1,000 as collective fines for escheated and forfeited lands; and, to cap it all, a free
gift of £400 to the prince of Wales in 1412. In all about £4,000 was exacted from
the county over five years at a rate equivalent to the ordinary annual anticipated
revenue. And by 1412 a considerable proportion of these extortionate levies had
been collected. This was a level of recurrent annual taxation which even a rich
English county might well have resented.[20]

The other two examples come from north Wales. The first community in the
area to make its submission to the king was the county of Anglesey. It did so at
Beaumaris in November 1406 before three commissioners deputed by the prince

of Wales. A fine of some £500 was imposed as the price to be paid for the acceptance of this act of collective contrition. Two grand juries and six individual juries for each commote then assessed the distribution of the fine on over 2,000 inhabitants of the island in sums ranging from 2s. to a maximum of £6 13s. 4d. There is no need to accept that all those whose names were now listed were necessarily active supporters of the rebellion, but equally it is clear that much of the adult community was now having to pay the price for the island's defection to Glyn Dŵr's cause. On 31 March 1407 it was the turn of the community of the county of Flint to undergo the same experience. The justiciar, Gilbert Talbot, imposed a fine of 1,000 marks (£666 13s. 4d.) on the county for its adherence to Owain Glyn Dŵr, and the sum was immediately attributed to over 1,000 individuals. Here again the scale of the fine can perhaps best be indicated by recalling that the gross annual yield of the county of Flint earlier in the reign had been assessed as less than £450. Nor should it be forgotten that in addition to their contribution to such communal fines, individuals were also often expected to find money for individual pardons and fines for the recovery of their lands.[21]

Figures comparable to those for Carmarthenshire, Anglesey, and Flintshire could be cited from other parts of Wales. They leave one in no doubt that the years from 1407 onwards were ones of extreme financial hardship for an exhausted and traumatized society. It is little wonder that some men were broken by the experience: John Llwyd (or Lloyd) was a prominent Carmarthen merchant who was fined £200 for his support for Glyn Dŵr and when neither he nor his pledger had the means to pay the fine he was imprisoned in Carmarthen Prison for two years. In a world where men were on their knees bully-boys flourished and made life even more miserable. One of the charges against Thomas Barneby, the shamelessly corrupt chamberlain of North Wales, was that he had lined his own pockets from the goods of those who had submitted to the king. Nor does it need a lively imagination to guess what his neighbours thought of Owain ap Jankyn, who was given a special reward for his efforts in raising outstanding fines from former rebels in Cardiganshire. But neighbourly disapproval or not, Owain and his like were eminently successful. The records show clearly enough that the large fines were collected with remarkable promptness: in Flintshire and the lordship of Denbigh over £2,000 had been garnered as individual and communal fines by Michaelmas 1408, that is, within eighteen months of the official end of the revolt in those districts; in Carmarthenshire at least £1,620 of the communal fines of £2,000 imposed in 1409 had reached the king's exchequer by 1410. Officials and the government could rub their hands with glee as they now so quickly recouped some of the revenue they had lost and the vast sums they had spent during the peak years of the revolt. But the price of

official glee must have been intense misery and festering resentment among the populace of Wales.[22]

By March 1413, when Henry IV died, it could well be considered that the peoples of Wales had made sufficient financial penance over the last six years or so for their misguided support for Glyn Dŵr. Many of the steps taken by the young Henry V were indeed promising and indicated that he wished to draw a line under the memory of the revolt in Wales. Two days after his accession he authorized the earl of Arundel to head a commission to admit rebels in north and south Wales into the king's peace and to offer them a pardon. The policy of conciliation was apparently extended in April when Wales was mentioned in the general pardon issued by the king. Even the most hardened rebels were now embraced in the royal mercy: Henry Don of Cydweli, than whom there had been no more zealous supporter of Glyn Dŵr's cause, was formally pardoned in May 1413, and in June all his extensive lands were restored to him and so were all the debts due to him before the rebellion. Such calculated magnanimity was matched by the new king's determination to show that he was even-handed in his justice. So it was that in July he established commissions to investigate any offences committed by any officers in North and South Wales and the March. They were to yield a rich haul. The process of formal reconciliation was completed in November 1413 when Henry V issued a comprehensive pardon to the counties of North Wales not only in respect of all treasons and other felonies but also with regard to all debts and arrears still outstanding on 5 November 1411. It looked as if the slate of the past was being wiped clean. Indeed, the king was willing to be yet more positive: as the year drew to a close he ordered the chamberlain (or chief financial officer) of North Wales to spend £200 on the purchase of cows and sheep to help the tenants of Caernarfonshire and Merionethshire to restock their holdings.[23]

There is no denying that in the first nine months of his reign Henry V had taken a series of bold and decisive steps to turn over a new page in Wales and to put his own and the country's memory of the revolt behind him. He had good reasons to do so: the revolt had filled too many years of his youth, and none too happily so; and now that he was king his sights were set on more ambitious targets. But Wales would have to pay heavily for its new future to a king who took an exalted view of his responsibilities as upholder of law and justice and who never meant to be financially embarrassed in the way his father had been. The price that had to be paid for deleting the past was clearly indicated in various commissions issued from June 1413 onwards. One such commission was concerned with the great Duchy of Lancaster lordships in south Wales (Cydweli, Brecon, Ogmore, and Monmouth). Not only were the commissioners empowered to admit Welsh rebels into the king's grace, they were also, ominously,

instructed to stipulate ransoms for offences committed, to seize the lands and goods of former rebels and sell them, and to hand over the profits of their activities. Similar commissions were issued for North and South Wales. Mercy came to Wales with large price-tags attached to it.[24]

The justices toured the Duchy lordships in Wales in September 1413, with Sir Walter Hungerford heading the commission. The embers of the revolt were scrupulously raked over, especially in Cydweli, and the embarrassments of the past were exploited as a source of profit for the present. The men of the lordships of Cydweli and Brecon soon found that their joy at welcoming a new and merciful king could be counted in the coins that they now were required to find to fill his exchequer: £1,000 from Cydweli, £1,200 from Brecon, partly for confirmation of charters, partly as a welcoming gift (or mise) to a new lord, and partly to secure pardons for past offences, including rebellion. Other parts of Wales were soon to share the same experience. In November 1413 the four royal counties in north Wales (Anglesey, Caernarfonshire, Merioneth, and Flintshire) agreed to pay an enormous collective fine of £1,400 (2,100 marks) over the next six to eight years to secure communal pardons for their offences, including treason, against Henry IV and for the cancellation of their debts still outstanding in November 1411. Barely had they recovered from the shock of the imposition of a virtual annual taxation than they were struck by a second blow. In March 1414 a group of royal justices headed by the earl of Arundel held their solemn sessions at Bala (co. Merioneth), Caernarfon, and Beaumaris (co. Anglesey). At each venue huge numbers of local men appeared before the justices to make the most abject submission, to crave pardon, and in particular to secure the title to their lands (technically forfeit as a result of the rebellion), right of hereditary descent according to Welsh law, and protection of the rights of widows. Their pleas were successful, but again at a price—a further £833 6s. 8d. (1,250 marks) from the three counties of the north-west.[25]

The new government of Henry V may have pursued a policy of conciliation, but financially it was milking the sense of guilt associated with the rebellion for all it was worth. Nor was the process quite at an end. In November–December 1415 the communities of the counties of Cardigan and Carmarthen agreed to pay £1,000 each in order to recover land which had been forfeited to the king, contrary to the practices of Welsh law. Such forfeitures were likely to have arisen in the wake of the rebellion, and the government was using this pretext once again to extort yet more money from the people of Wales. By 1415 the English monarchy had virtually exhausted its opportunities for exploiting complicity in the rebellion as a pretext for its financial extortions in Wales. But as one avenue closed others were opened. In April 1417—while they were still in the process of collecting the moneys towards the large fines of 1413–14—the communities of the

three shires of north-west Wales were required to contribute a further subsidy of £733 6s. 8d. (1,100 marks) towards the king's war expenses, while even larger subsidies were contributed by the counties of Carmarthen and Cardigan.[26]

What are we to make of this unremitting financial pressure? It has to be conceded that it is very little different from the financial policies that Henry V pursued in England. There likewise the sale of pardons was used shamelessly as a way of raising money; in England also every expedient and every right was remorselessly exploited to raise vast sums of money to keep the king's war machine in good heart; there likewise was 'an even heavier incidence of taxation than in the years 1377–81'. Henry V's great war successes cost his country very dearly indeed. But Wales had a particular cause for complaint. It was not represented in parliament, nor did it assent or contribute to parliamentary taxes. But it was in fact as heavily mulcted financially as any part of the king's dominions and that under a host of more or less specious pretexts. Figures for the country as a whole cannot be calculated, and in any case many of the Marcher lordships lay outside the reach of the king's financial arm. But some figures may serve to indicate the scale of the demands made on the country. Almost a third of the revenue accounted for by the chamberlain (or treasurer) of North Wales in 1418 (£439 out of £1,373) came from collective fines and subsidies. In the two great lordships of Brecon and Cydweli over £5,700 was collected from similar sources in the seven years 1413–20 (excluding 1419). Furthermore, such sums were gathered with great promptness and thoroughness: on the Lancaster estates in Wales it can be shown that almost every penny was collected. Henry V was an exceptionally harsh financial taskmaster. In the closing words of his chronicle the Welshman, Adam of Usk, referred plaintively to the 'unbearable and grievous taxation of the people' which Henry V's continental ambitions entailed, and he went on to refer to 'the murmurs and smothered curses' with which the burden was borne by the people. Nowhere did his words ring more true than in his native Wales. Nowhere, arguably, were the dangers of such a level of taxation more obvious. Financial extortion on this scale, much of it under the pretext of deleting the consequences of revolt, only served to keep alive its memory and the communal resentment of financial hardship which that revolt had successfully exploited. It was little wonder that a final peace was so slow in arriving in Wales.[27]

But by 1415 peace could be said to have arrived. No further great communal pardons for involvement in the revolt were issued after that date. In that year Owain Glyn Dŵr finally disappears from the records, probably because he had quietly sidled out of life; in the same year Henry V set out on the expedition which took him to the kind of military glory which had so singularly evaded him in Wales. Among those who fought with him on St Crispin's Day at Agincourt

were Dafydd Gam, the squire from Brecon who had fought so doughtily and suffered so heavily for him in Wales, and Gruffudd Don who had accompanied his grandfather Henry Don at the siege of Kidwelly in the summer of 1403. The fact that Dafydd Gam and Gruffudd Don now fought together under the banner of Henry V may serve as a symbol that the revolt of Owain Glyn Dŵr was dead and buried and that the Welsh, loyalists and rebels alike, now had to concentrate on rebuilding a future rather than on raking over the recent past. It may also prompt some reflections on what legacy the years of revolt had left to Wales.

In a fashion it could be claimed that the shadow of Glyn Dŵr's revolt cast itself over the history of the fifteenth century as a whole in Wales. But time does not stand still; other shadows would soon become more dominant. It was in April 1421 that Maredudd, Owain's sole surviving son, finally accepted the offer of a pardon; it is as good a point as any, and probably more meaningful than most, to assess how the world had changed in the twenty or more years since his father had embarked on his remarkable adventure. It can be confidently asserted that virtually no parish in Wales and hardly a single family had escaped unscathed from the experience of the revolt, be it directly or indirectly. The cost in physical destruction, in ruined lives and livelihoods, as we have seen, was enormous; pillage and starvation and financial extortion had impoverished an already poor country.

The death-rate caused by the revolt can never be calculated; but the fifty burgesses allegedly killed at Carmarthen in 1403 or the 102 tenants who had been killed in Anglesey during the rebellion can be no more than the tips of an iceberg. The slaughter inflicted by the Welsh at the Battle of Bryn Glas and the alleged mutilation of corpses on the field of battle struck terror into the heart of the English and convinced them of the barbarity of the Welsh. But the English also used execution as an instrument of terror, especially at the beginning and end of the revolt. It was in that spirit that Henry IV had caused a wealthy Carmarthenshire Welshman, Llywelyn ap Gruffudd Fychan of Caio, to be executed in his presence at Llanymddyfri on 9 October 1401. For the same reason Prince Henry refused to spare the lives of prominent Welshmen he captured on his raids into Glyn Dŵr's home territory in May 1403, in spite of the large offers made to him. There was remarkably little spirit of revenge on the English side after the revolt had clearly failed; even so, some prominent men paid the ultimate penalty. Two sources confirm between them that around 1409 three of the most prominent rebels were executed: Rhys ap Tudur of Anglesey, who had led the surprise attack on Conway Castle in April 1401; Philip Scudamore of Troy (near Monmouth), who had treacherously defected from important military command for Henry IV into the service of Glyn Dŵr, at Shrewsbury; and Rhys Ddu, a prominent Cardiganshire man and Glyn Dŵr's captain in the defence of Aberystwyth,

at London. Many others, of course, died on active service: one of Anglesey's most powerful landowners, Gwilym ap Gruffudd ap Tudur Llwyd, was killed in front of Beaumaris Castle, while William Gwyn ap Rhys Llwyd of Cydweli was killed by a cannonball on the defence of Aberystwyth Castle for Owain. Some rebels were lucky enough to escape with a spell of imprisonment. The incorrigible Henry Don spent some time in prison both at Kidwelly and Gloucester reflecting on his stormy life before he was eventually released and pardoned. Others were dispatched to more distant prisons: David ap Cadwgan, captured near Welshpool, spent a year in the Marshalsea, while it required an escort of eight men and horses to take another batch of Welsh prisoners from Hereford to London. There they would join more famous prisoners: Owain's eldest son and heir, Gruffudd, was imprisoned in the Tower from May 1405, and after the fall of Harlech in 1409 he was joined by his mother, two of his sisters, and his three young nieces.[28]

Death, be it in battle or by execution, and imprisonment were certainly part of the price that had to be paid for rebellion. But it was not paid by the majority. Some, it is true, fled the country never to return. One such was Henry Gwyn, heir to the lordship of Llansteffan and former ardent supporter of Glyn Dŵr, who appropriately enough was killed fighting on the French side at Agincourt. But the vast majority of rebels remained in Wales seeking to reconstruct their lives out of the debris of the revolt. Many of them were hampered in their efforts by the crippling individual and communal fines with which they were now saddled, none more so than John Hanmer, Owain Glyn Dŵr's brother-in-law, who claimed that he was so reduced to indigence and poverty by 1411 that he could not pay the rest of his huge fine. There is no doubt that for some leading Welsh families, and doubtless scores of poorer ones also, the revolt proved to be a disaster from which they never fully recovered. The most spectacular example was that of the family of Rhys and Gwilym ap Tudur of Anglesey. The family had lorded it over north-west Wales during the fourteenth century and was of old and impeccable noble stock. But the three surviving brothers of the family threw in their lot, sooner or later, with Owain Glyn Dŵr, and either were not allowed, or refused, to be reconciled to the crown when the movement failed. The conse-quences were certainly disastrous for the family: most of its lands were forfeited and seized by men of easier conscience; its rump sank to the level of a minor squireen family at Penmynydd in Anglesey; and it was only the initiative, dash, and charm of a young adventurer from the family, Owain, son of Maredudd ap Tudur, which took him into the inner chambers of English royal court and assured for the dynasty of ap Tudur a renown and a future on a very different stage from that which its ancestors had enjoyed when they stormed Conway Castle on 1 April 1401.[29]

There were doubtless many other families like that of Rhys and Gwilym ap Tudur for whom the Glyn Dŵr revolt was, more or less, an unmitigated disaster. We can guess the names of some of them: Rhys ap Gruffudd ap Llywelyn Foethus, formerly royal constable of Dryslwyn Castle in Carmarthenshire, or Rhys ap Madog Fychan ap Madog Gloddaith whose family seemed to be coming up fast in the fourteenth century. Both seemed to be stopped short in their progress in the early fifteenth century, and their support for Glyn Dŵr (which can be established in both cases) may well have been the crucial factor. It is difficult to trace such families for the simple reason that historical archives often record success but rarely document failure. Success there certainly was in plenty for former rebels. Indeed the most striking feature of the social landscape and pattern of governance in Wales by 1421 was the degree to which it was dominated by men who had once been prominent supporters of Glyn Dŵr and his lieutenants in their respective localities. It is not a fact which should perhaps cause us surprise. The government of Henry V was in no mood to be vindictive; it could in any case satisfy any thirst for revenge in the practical and profitable form of heavy communal fines for pardons. Furthermore, the sullen resentment and occasional flare-up or revenge attacks in Wales from 1407 to 1413 must surely have convinced sensitive observers that what was wanted was constructive pacification and the channelling of the military enterprise of the Welsh into the king's service. Finally, and most crucially, it must have been painfully obvious that local governance could only be restored in Wales by vesting it once more in the hands of those who had exercised it before the revolt and who had temporarily defected in droves to Glyn Dŵr's cause when it was in the ascendant.[30]

This is indeed what happened. And it happened in every part of Wales. One of those who bought his peace from the king in Anglesey in November 1406 at a high price was Maredudd ap Cynwrig ap Maredudd. By 1409 he was back in high office as deputy sheriff; by 1417 he was the king's sergeant-at-arms in the county, and he ended life in the odour of burghal respectability as alderman of Newborough. At the other end of Wales Ieuan ap Jenkin Kemeys had temporarily endangered his own and his family's fortunes by his support for Glyn Dŵr in 1403, but by 1415 his two sons were already high in local favour within the lordship of Newport. The same story is repeated time and again: John Kynaston had been an arch trouble-maker in north-east Wales in 1400–3 but by 1408 had resumed his earlier office as steward of Maelor Saesneg (co. Flints.); while in Cardiganshire Maredudd ab Owain graduated from a massive fine of £300 as a pledge for the hostages taken to ensure the surrender of Aberystwyth (suggesting close complicity in the revolt) to local office and service to Henry V in Normandy. An observer returning to Wales in 1421 after an absence of twenty years might have

concluded that, at this level of society and governance, there had indeed been very little substantive change, but rather just a temporary hiccup of loyalty.[31]

Two examples in particular would have confirmed him in this view. By 1421 Henry Don had been dead some five years, but stories of his activities and of the remarkable recovery in the fortunes of the family were surely circulating widely. Here was a man who, with his son and grandson, had laid siege to Kidwelly Castle more than once, seized ships, and generally behaved as the most incorrigible of rebels. He had paid a penalty for his activities: his lands (variously estimated as worth £60 or £100, which is a clear indication of his wealth and standing) had been forfeited and granted to the English constable of Kidwelly, Walter Morton; he himself was imprisoned at Kidwelly and Gloucester and only eventually pardoned in 1413 for a fine of £200. But Henry Don was in no way chastened nor did he alter his behaviour one whit. A series of charges brought against him before the justices in their sessions at Kidwelly in September 1413 show that he was as contemptuous as ever of any authority other than his own. He sheltered a fugitive rebel in his household, seized the land of poor tenants, exacted fines from more than 200 Welshmen who had failed to follow him in his revolt and who had occupied his lands, and rode around the district with his retinue, bullying his opponents and even allegedly plotting the murder of the lordship's steward. Even this judicial dressing down (for he was found guilty on almost all the charges) did not break his defiance; he did not pay a penny of his fine, and it was only death, sometime during 1416, which exacted an eventual surrender from Henry Don.[32]

By that date his family was already clambering its way back to favour and power. Gruffudd, Henry Don's grandson and co-heir, had taken part in the attack on Kidwelly Castle in 1403, but he made amends for his youthful folly by accompanying Henry V on the Agincourt expedition and by his military prowess in France. By 1421 he had so salvaged his reputation for loyalty that he was exempted from the statute prohibiting Welshmen from purchasing land in England. Soon after he was appointed constable of Kidwelly, the very castle he had once attacked, and was even promoted to be sheriff of Carmarthenshire 'for his service to Henry V and Henry VI'. He had no scruples about taking up leases on the lands of his former colleagues as rebels in Cydweli, and completed his rehabilitation by taking an English wife, none other than Joan, daughter of the very Sir John Skidmore who had so often been the target of his grandfather's raids and plots. Gruffudd's brother, Owain, was a rather more rumbustious character; but he likewise now came to hold local office and to throw his weight around in Cydweli and far beyond. Gruffudd and Owain were pillars of local society: the one described himself as lord of Penallt, the other as lord of Muddlescombe. Revolt had in no way blighted their careers.[33]

Spectacular as was the recovery of the Don brood, it could not compare in its speed or its scale with that of the leading north Welsh squire of the day, Gwilym (d. 1431) ap Gruffudd ap Gwilym. We have already met Gwilym's father briefly: he had, through good fortune, assembled a considerable estate across north Wales but all was endangered by his involvement, and that of his brothers, in Glyn Dŵr's revolt. Gwilym himself seems to have been more circumspect: while he had little alternative but to be associated with the revolt during its climacteric in 1403–4, he was one of the first to desert Glyn Dŵr. He had certainly made his submission by August 1405, but his official pardon was not issued until 1407. No Welshman had a better eye for the change in the political climate than Gwilym; none seized the opportunity to turn the misfortune of revolt into a triumphant personal and family success as did he. Already in 1407 he had secured the forfeited lands of twenty-seven former rebels in Anglesey, and even more crucially, he was soon appropriating the estates of Gwilym ap Tudur, one of the leading squires on the island and Glyn Dŵr's close ally. Our Gwilym was not in the least squeamish about family affections when it came to the business of making himself rich and powerful: Gwilym ap Tudur (the captor of Conway Castle in 1401), whose estates he now gobbled up, was none other than his wife's uncle. He was soon the richest man in north Wales: his rent income in 1410 stood already at £110 per annum and he had many years ahead in which to add to it; he bought out small proprietors and re-let their lands to them as tenants; he loaned money and dealt in wine, corn, and other commodities. Gwilym may not be the first native Welsh agricultural capitalist, but he was the first whose network of business links and ventures can be reconstructed.

Wealth was, as ever, a powerful entrée into the brave new world of the post-Glyn Dŵr era; but there was also need to reconstruct Gwilym's identity if he were to fit comfortably into this new world. The death of his first wife proved to be a singularly happy blow in accelerating this process. Morfudd ferch (daughter of) Goronwy was of outstandingly good lineage, indeed distantly of the same stock as that of Gwilym himself (see Table 3). Furthermore the early death of her brother brought her, and through her Gwilym, the title to the family home at Penmynydd in Anglesey. To that extent Gwilym was certainly blessed in his first marriage; but the blessing turned to embarrassment when Morfudd's uncles became Glyn Dŵr's premier supporters in north Wales and the premier victims of the failure of his cause. Morfudd's death gave him the opportunity to delete the memory of such embarrassment and he did so with the shameless ruthlessness of the man on the make. About 1413 he took as his second wife Joan, daughter of Sir William Stanley of Hooton in Cheshire and widow of Robert Parys, formerly chamberlain of Chester and constable of Caernarfon. The marriage was a clear indication of his changing orientation and affiliations; but even

more striking were the landed settlements he made at the time of the marriage. He arranged that most of his estates in Caernarfonshire and Anglesey were now legally vested in him, his new English wife, and in the male heir of their marriage; he thereby disinherited his children, including a son, from his first, Welsh, marriage. Few men in Wales could have unhitched themselves from their past so brazenly as had Gwilym ap Gruffudd.

The process would be completed by acquiring the trappings of respectability. The most visible physical sign of Gwilym's good fortune was the new home that he had constructed for himself at Penrhyn in Caernarfonshire. It is memorably, if extravagantly, described in a poem by Rhys Goch Eryri. The poet contrasts the grim grey masonry of Caernarfon Castle with the sparkling brightness of the whitewashed walls—'of the same colour as the swan'—of Gwilym's oak-constructed home. The contrast, he adds, is not only one of colour and style, but also of purpose and ethos: the castle was built to lay siege to the population and to bend their necks and hearts in subjugation; Gwilym's new hall, on the contrary, was the home of happiness, munificence, bountiful gifts, food and wine aplenty, and a warm welcome for bards and minstrels. Poetic licence was at work; but so was poetic insight. Caernarfon Castle represented the English military domination of the past; the hall at Penrhyn the new habits of the social and economic domination of the future. Past and future met symbolically when Gwilym's son applied in 1438 for a licence to have a battlemented tower at Penrhyn. The new lords of Wales wanted to bedeck themselves in the architectural trappings of the old world.

Only one feature was missing to complete Gwilym's triumph. He was the richest and most powerful man in north-west Wales. Rhys Goch in another poem went so far as to claim that the justiciar, or chief governor, of North Wales did everything at his bidding. There lay the rub. Gruffudd might be the power behind the justiciar, but the post of justiciar itself was not within his reach. Nor was any major office. He had to rest content with local offices; he could not aspire even to be sheriff of Anglesey, as he had been before the revolt. He was Welsh. And as a Welshman he was legally debarred by Henry IV's penal statutes from high offices and indeed other privileges in Wales. So it was that he petitioned that he, his children, and their heirs be exempted from the consequences of the legislation and treated as Englishmen. For a man who had played so fast and loose with his past in pursuit of his future, it was not extravagantly misleading to claim that he 'and his children, as well as at all times after, have been and yet are faithful and loyal subjects to the king and his progenitors'. It required brazenness of an extraordinary degree, however, to end his petition with a thumping lie that he was 'born, engendered, and descended for the most part wholly from the English race'. His son was to continue his father's campaign to be regarded as an

English denizen, for that was the passport to ultimate acceptability in the new post-Glyn Dŵr world.

Gwilym ap Gruffudd behaved near death as he had lived in life. When he made his will in February 1430 he gave no role, nor even a word of mention, to his children by his first wife. It was only his second wife and his children by her who figured in the will. It was they, more especially Joan Stanley and his son, Gwilym, who were granted not only the lands he had purchased, especially after the revolt, but also the estates which had come to him through his first wife. Gwilym faced death as defiantly shameless as ever, and he faced it in the company of those who were now of his circle—Roland Stanley, Henry Hoton, and others. If Gwilym showed no twinge of conscience, his obituarist, the poet Rhys Goch Eryri, could not conceal the unease which many must have felt. For a profession given to massive exaggeration, Rhys's elegy for Gwilym is startling for its studied and deliberate restraint (as Welsh scholars have observed). Conventional compliments are heaped on Gwilym, especially on his wise judicial recommendations; but it is the reservations which stand out. Rhys asks the indulgence of his fellow bards for composing the elegy at all; he is doing it, he adds, because he is paid to do so. He makes his own viewpoint obvious by extolling the virtues of the kinsmen of Gwilym's first wife, the men who had been so prominent in Glyn Dŵr's cause and whose forfeited lands had been gobbled up into Gwilym's estate. There is not a word about Gwilym's second wife or his son and heir by her. The contrast between Gwilym's own confident last will and the studied ambivalence of his obituarist's elegy is surely symptomatic of the deep psychological rift that characterized so much of Wales in the generation or so after the formal end of Glyn Dŵr's revolt.[34]

Men such as Henry Don and Gwilym ap Gruffudd have the knack, in every generation and predicament, of turning misfortune to their own advantage. There were doubtless many like them, if rarely quite as outrageously successful as they were, in different parts of Wales. Small, disconnected fragments of their biographies can be assembled from such historical evidence as survives. Yet at the end of the day one might wonder whether the assembled biographies of the greater *uchelwyr* and gentry of Wales—be they cast down by, or ultimate beneficiaries of, the revolt—can ever be a secure guide to what the impact of the rebellion of Owain Glyn Dŵr was for Welsh society as a whole. Indeed, the impact itself cannot be disentangled from long-term changes which were already well afoot before the outbreak of the revolt and which no doubt contributed to the tensions upon which it fed.

Nevertheless we can hazard some broad suggestions as to how the world and society portrayed in Part I of this book, that of Wales in the 1390s, had been

transformed by the experience of revolt. Death and destruction, as we have seen, had been considerable in town and countryside: their scars were still evident in 1421 and in many places did not heal for generations. Yet there was no great vindictiveness and no massive expropriation. A cowed and sullen population was allowed to pick up the pieces of its former life, albeit at a price. Families even managed to recover forfeited lands which had been handed out as rewards: in 1408–11 Edward Charlton, lord of Powys, restored the lands of two of the leading Welshmen of Llannerch Hudol who had joined Glyn Dŵr and whose forfeited estates had earlier been granted to others. In proportion to its seriousness and extent, the revolt of Glyn Dŵr left patterns of inheritance, at least at one level, in Wales substantially unaltered.[35]

Yet a traveller revisiting Wales in 1421 could not doubt that massive changes had taken, or were taking, place. One visit might have taken him to the lowlands of Glamorgan, an area once remarkable for its prosperity and growing assimilation to southern English society. The scene which now confronted him was clinically but graphically recorded in the detailed survey of the lordship of Ogmore compiled for the Duchy of Lancaster council in 1428. The castle had been damaged and one of its chambers destroyed; the charred ruins of the corn-mills, fulling-mills, and home farms were chilling reminders of what revolt had meant in this locality. But it was the emptiness of the countryside which might have struck him above all. Some of the small hamlets which he had known in his youth, such as Sutton and Northdown, were now totally or virtually deserted; more than half of the land classified as customary or cottager tenements (a total of sixty-three cottages and over 623 acres) lay vacant. In those circumstances land was cheap, and our returning visitor might well have noticed how some of the families he had once known as modest peasant farmers were now leasing empty farms at knock-down prices and turning themselves into entrepreneurs. Here was a world which was changing rapidly, certainly by the standards of rural society, and there was no doubt that the traumatic experience and consequences of revolt were amongst the major catalysts of change.[36]

The survey of 1428 helps us to grasp the dimensions of change in one locality in Wales as they appeared a generation after the revolt had come to an end. But earlier snapshots and a closer focus might reveal even more graphically the scale of the seismic shock which Welsh society had recently experienced. The king's officers certainly had the evidence to hand, were they minded to use it; it still survives in the archives today. One such piece of evidence was a document containing extracts from the court rolls of the commote of Carnwyllion (the area including and to the north of Llanelli) in the lordship of Cydweli for the years 1408–12. It was doubtless compiled for financial purposes, but it had other striking messages for those who cared to receive them. In the two years 1411–12 alone the

land of at least thirty-six tenants who had died as rebels technically came into the lord's hands as escheats, or confiscated land, in all probably some 500 acres or so. In only eleven cases can the new tenant be clearly identified as a direct relative of his predecessor. In this rather remote and utterly rural corner of Wales the world might not have been turned upside-down by the experience of revolt but its foundations had certainly been severely shaken and quite possibly fatally undermined.[37]

Other similar examples of the shaking of the territorial foundations of society could be quoted from different parts of Wales, but one example is particularly significant since it provides us with a glimpse of who was seizing the opportunity to build a new territorial order out of the rubble of the old. Records from Flintshire indicate that at least 115 individuals forfeited their estates for rebellion in the years 1407–12. (The figure is certainly an underestimate, for it only refers to recent and large-scale forfeitures.) Eighty-seven men and women stepped into the territorial vacancies so created. Thirty-seven of these were direct descendants—sons (twenty-five), daughters, brothers, cousins, nephews, and kinsmen—of the previous holders of the land; to that extent there was continuity in the territorial order. But it is discontinuity which is really striking. Forfeited holdings and an unusually brisk land market provided wonderful opportunities for the entrepreneur. Many of them were Welshmen, such as Gwilym ap Gruffudd of Penrhyn or Ieuan ap Jankin in Cydweli. But few Welshmen could compete in terms of official openings or liquid assets with some of their English colleagues. Sir John Skidmore, steward of Cydweli, picked up some highly lucrative forfeited estates in his area of authority; while in Flintshire Sir Roger Leche paid over £20 for the substantial inheritance of a Welsh rebel. Burgesses were the other group who saw their opportunity and took it: John Richardson of Conway mopped up the lands of eight Welsh rebels in Flintshire, and Walter Woodburn did the same for a further eight Welshmen in Maelor Saesneg. It was not the least of the paradoxes of the Glyn Dŵr revolt that it certainly accelerated the process which brought about the collapse of the Welsh tenurial order. It was in the fifteenth century, and often out of the debris of holdings forfeited during the rebellion, that many of the landed estates which were to dominate the social and economic landscape of Wales for centuries to come were being created.[38]

Acute social observers might also have noted that there were other indications that the existing social order was disintegrating in Wales and that the revolt and its aftermath had hastened the process. Two developments in particular stood out. The first was the collapse of personal and territorial serfdom in Wales. The distinction between free and unfree (serfs) had been one of the fundamental features of the Welsh social order; indeed, it was arguably more potent in Wales than in other medieval societies precisely because freedom there was so closely

associated with lineage and nobility. It was a distinction which was increasingly undermined in the later fourteenth century, especially in the wake of the disastrous collapse of the population with the advent of plague. Yet there is little doubt that the Glyn Dŵr revolt also played its part and accelerated a process which led serfdom in Wales into terminal decline. The collapse of seignorial control and the flight of serfs during the revolt were critical. However hard government and lords might try to restore the *status quo*, the battle had clearly been lost. Bond vills remained vacant; serfs refused to perform their obligations and very often refused to succeed even to their fathers' tenements, unless they were discharged from any bond obligations and were granted the land on English terms. One cameo from the story (as yet unwritten) of the slow death of serfdom in Wales may serve for scores of others. In September 1413 the eight surviving serfs of the commote of Dogfeilyn in Dyffryn Clwyd presented a petition to Reginald Grey. Once, they observed, there had been 149 serfs in the commote, now they were the sole ones remaining. Their request was to be of free condition, in other words to be enfranchized. For this privilege they were willing to pay the lord either a lump sum or an increased rent. It was as much an ultimatum as a petition; Grey had no option but to accede to it. What is particularly interesting in the present context is that he agreed to their suggestion, accepting an increase of 3*d*. an acre, 'because their services had been cancelled on account of the war and rebellion in Wales'. Owain Glyn Dŵr had been fighting for a different kind of freedom for Wales; but the serfs of Dogfeilyn and of many other parts of Wales could credit him, however indirectly, with giving them their personal and tenurial freedom.[39]

The serfs of Dogfeilyn asked not only for personal freedom but also for English tenure. They thereby identified a second social development which was most certainly accelerated by the Glyn Dŵr revolt. The English government and lords in Wales had, ironically, been among the doughtiest upholders of Welsh tenurial practices and inheritance customs. Their commitment was, needless to say, dictated by financial profit. That was likewise the reason why they regularly vetoed attempts by the Welsh to enjoy the benefits of English inheritance law and practices. Their resistance, however, began to crumble from the 1370s as a glut of land came on the market or into the lord's hands in the wake of the dramatic population decline occasioned by the recurrent visitations of the plague. Tenants increasingly refused to accept vacant lands other than on English terms. They looked in particular for four advantages which English tenure could bestow on them: the right of impartible inheritance, thereby safeguarding the integrity of their estates and avoiding the fragmentation which could be the notorious consequence of the Welsh practice of partibility among male heirs; the right to buy, sell, and devise land freely by charter, a right likewise denied to them by Welsh law; the right to grant their wives a share of their lands

in dower; and finally, the right of succession by and through females in the event of the absence of direct male heirs, likewise not permitted under the strictly agnatic rules of Welsh law on land inheritance.

We have no evidence that the campaign for English tenure was part of Glyn Dŵr's programme, even though his own family had benefited from such practices. His sights and those of his advisers were set on a different and loftier set of targets. Yet the issue was coupled with his revolt in at least two ways. First, it was an issue which was clearly already on the agenda of Welsh social demands and had been pressed with increasing urgency in the years before the revolt. Secondly, and more importantly, the territorial shake-out occasioned by the disruption and forfeitures of Owain's revolt provided the ideal conditions in which the campaign for English tenure could make striking headway. We can turn once more to the rich evidence from the lordship of Dyffryn Clwyd to show how momentous the years immediately after Glyn Dŵr's revolt were in the reshaping of the tenurial map in Wales. The evidence is striking at the level both of statistics and individual examples. In the commote of Llanerch 118 parcels of vacant land (including many complete tenements) were leased in the years 1410–22; the figure itself is an eloquent comment on the breakup of established inheritance patterns. Only one parcel of vacant land was specifically let on Welsh terms; at least eighty-one were specifically let on English terms. In the neighbouring commote of Dogfeilyn an individual episode reflects the same transformation in miniature: in 1419 two daughters, Lleucu and Angharad, petitioned to succeed to their father's estate 'although as daughters they could not by Welsh law possess or enjoy land hereditarily'. The lord acceded to their request and allowed them to hold their lands in English tenure. It is the first such case recorded on the court rolls. The shift from Welsh to English tenure and inheritance customs happened at a very different pace in different parts of Wales; in the lowland south it had long been under way; in the fastnesses of the north-west, even for greedy estate-builders such as Gwilym ap Gruffudd of Penrhyn, it was a long time a-coming. But in general, and in north-east Wales in particular, the years immediately following the revolt of Owain Glyn Dŵr were truly formative in the redrawing of the tenurial map of Wales. The position might not be fully regularized for years to come, but one of the unintended consequences of the revolt was to clear the way for the establishment of a new territorial order in Wales.[40]

On the issues of the personal status of serfs and the shift to English tenure, the lords of Wales were clearly in major retreat in the early fifteenth century. With royal help they had eventually triumphed over Glyn Dŵr; but his revolt in many respects permanently weakened their authority. Lordship ultimately derives its justification from its powers of protection and its effective wielding of authority

over people. By almost any criterion that could be applied, the Glyn Dŵr revolt
had shown English lordship in Wales to be largely ineffective, even bankrupt. It
had failed militarily to withstand the Welsh or to seize the military initiative from
them. Its authority over its tenants had been wrenched from it unceremoniously,
creating a vacuum of power which rebel bands and local leaders quickly filled.
The fragmentation of authority that was the March of Wales proved to be the
despair of military leaders attempting to construct a coherent policy. For the first
time since the conquest of Wales, the commons in parliament in particular posed
a series of probing questions about the *raison d'être* of the archaic pattern of
governance and responsibility in Wales. The revolt did not last long enough for
answers to be required or given to those questions, but they were questions
which would have to be addressed sooner or later. Glyn Dŵr's revolt had posed
questions about the rationale of lordship in Wales which Henry VII and Henry
VIII would one day answer.

The challenge to lordship came not only from without; it was ultimately
confronted by an even more threatening challenge from within. It is now widely
recognized that throughout much of north-western Europe lordship confronted
a major crisis of authority and identity in the later Middle Ages. The structures of
regular authority over a dependent peasantry, so carefully constructed in the
twelfth and thirteenth centuries, were dramatically undermined by the collapse
in population after the Black Death and by the glut of land on the market.
Simultaneously changes in military technology and in the financing and scale of
wars were calling into question the military rationale which had underpinned
lordship in earlier days. In Wales the revolt of Owain Glyn Dŵr coincided with,
and hugely contributed towards, this crisis of lordship. Lordship had been found
wanting in power and effectiveness; thereby its credibility and authority had been
undermined. The tell-tale signs of defiance register in the documents, especially
in the decades after the end of Glyn Dŵr's revolt. In Dyffryn Clwyd fifty-seven
men were fined 'for contempt towards the officers and ministers of the lord' in
1418; a year earlier the tenants of Chirk said defiantly that they would no longer
be held responsible for communal rents and obligations, but that each would pay
what was due from his own holding, and no more; in the neighbouring lordship
of Bromfield and Yale likewise both officers and tenants went on strike, refusing
to pay outstanding arrears and debts. Defiance was becoming chronic. Lords and
officials often met defiance with counter-defiance and propped up the façade of
their authority, with greater or lesser degrees of success. But by the mid-fifteenth
century, the crisis of lordship was manifesting itself dramatically in a collapse of
seignorial revenue in many parts of Wales. That crisis was the product of many
factors, but in Wales the revolt of Owain Glyn Dŵr was one of its crucial causes
and catalysts.[41]

Most of the social and economic changes in the fabric of Wales that can be attributed, in some measure, to the revolt of Owain Glyn Dŵr were no part of its intended purpose. One change can, however, be attributed directly to the revolt and seen as its inevitable by-product, the changed relationship between the English and the Welsh, especially within Wales. As we saw in an earlier chapter, the government responded to the revolt with a series of penal statutes against the Welsh, and these were in turn amplified by local, especially borough, ordinances. Statutes and ordinances might be nine-day wonders; suspicion and mistrust had a very much longer life-span. The revolt left a legacy of bitterness which was not eradicated for generations, especially in north Wales. The penal statutes against the Welsh were in fact reissued in 1431, 1433, 1444, and 1447, often at the specific request of 'the English people of Wales'. Borough charters, such as those of Brecon, Holt, Oswestry, and Kidwelly, were reinforced with specific anti-Welsh clauses. English residents in Wales naturally distrusted the Welsh and exploited their judicial privileges to protect their position. An English burgess of Caerwys in Flintshire, for example, successfully challenged a jury empanelled in 1412 in a case against Welsh defendants on the grounds that it was composed of Welsh-men, whereas the plaintiff was an English burgess. For the same reason Reginald Grey of Dyffryn Clwyd bestowed on Simon Thelwall the privilege that he would only be tried 'by faithful Englishmen of pure blood [L. de sanguine natos] . . . and not by Welshmen'.[42]

Statutes, ordinances, and privileges could, and often did, lie dormant, as men and women rebuilt the bridges of coexistence. Yet it is of the very nature of ethnic discrimination that it can be easily whipped up into a frenzy or used whimsically to embarrass and belittle individuals. So it was in Wales in the years after the Glyn Dŵr revolt. A successful Welshman building up his territorial fortune could suddenly be stopped in his tracks by a reminder that he was 'Welsh and of Welsh condition' and that what he was doing was 'contrary to the laws of Wales'. Even an English alderman of Conway found himself hounded in 1417 for taking a Welsh wife; it was the kind of incident which explains why a prudent English widow in Caernarfon secured a licence to marry whom she wished, be he English or Welsh. Many years after the revolt and after years of distinguished service to the king or English lords in Wales, important officials found themselves attacked and removed from office because of their Welsh connections. It happened in 1433 to Sir John Skidmore, who had given a whole lifetime of distinguished govern-mental and military service to the English rulers of Wales, because of his alleged marriage, only now held against him, to Glyn Dŵr's daughter. Much at the same time whispering campaigns were initiated against Morgan ab Ieuan ap Jankyn Kemeys as deputy steward of Ogmore 'because he was a very Welshman of father and mother', and Robert Trevor, receiver of the lordship of Bromfield and

Yale, because his maternal grandfather was married to Glyn Dŵr's sister. Incidents such as these show how venomous and vindictive the atmosphere was in Wales twenty years after Glyn Dŵr's death.[43]

There was, of course, another side to the story. Welshmen served in droves in Henry V's armies in France, many of them having served their apprenticeship in Glyn Dŵr's raiding parties. Men such as Henry and Gruffudd Don or Gwilym ap Gruffudd had already showed by 1421 that few doors were closed for those Welshmen determined to make a success of their lives whatever their pasts; indeed, with the decline of effective English lordship and the opportunities offered by an accelerating land market the prospects were arguably rosier than they had ever been before. The premier posts in the governance of Wales might now be legally beyond the reach of Welshmen, but in an age when so many such posts were held by absentee sinecurists the reality of power could often be seized by local Welsh strong-men. And so it was. For those for whom legal niceties and status mattered, and who wanted an insurance against the arbitrary vindictiveness of their English neighbours, a petition to the king's council or parliament for formal letters of denizenship, making them in effect honorary Englishmen, could solve the problem. It was a route which Gwilym ap Gruffudd and his son and Gruffudd Don chose to follow.[44]

Yet the need for letters of denizenship pin-pointed the anomalous position in which Welshmen had been left by the Glyn Dŵr revolt. They were subjects of the king, yet they were not full citizens of his realm, sharing in its legal privileges and responsibilities, encompassed within its unitary tax system, or participating in its political forum. That, of course, had been the case before Glyn Dŵr launched his revolt. But the anomalous and discriminatory nature of their position was even more obvious now that a handful of privileged and well-placed Welshmen had found a loophole into the status of being honorary Englishmen through letters of denizenship. Sooner or later the question of the status of all Welshmen *vis-à-vis* the polity, laws, taxes, governance, and political processes of the realm of England would have to be addressed. It was a question which the revolt of Glyn Dŵr and the English response to it had left unanswered.

That was a question which the English government would have to answer. Glyn Dŵr's revolt left another question which could only be answered in the hearts and minds of the Welsh themselves. His had been, in many respects, the first revolt which encompassed the whole of Wales. It had not encompassed all Welshmen; but it had been fought, increasingly so, to establish an independent Wales, politically and ecclesiastically, under its own prince and archbishop. It was, or became, truly a national revolt. It drew upon historical mythologies and ideologies which stretched centuries into the past. It exploited a network of relationships, authority, and culture which was still essentially indigenously

Welsh, even if it coexisted, and had established a growing rapport, with a governmental framework which was distinctly English and answerable to the needs and policies of English kings and lords. It was a revolt which was fought against the background of the most favourable circumstances, in terms of England's domestic and foreign troubles, which the Welsh could ever hope for. Yet at the end of the day it was a comprehensive failure; indeed, it would have been remarkable had it been otherwise.

Wales's first truly national revolt was also its last. Not all contemporaries thought so, of course, least of all in the immediate aftermath of the revolt. Never was there to be a more prolific outpouring of prophetic poetry and Messianic hope in Wales than in the fifteenth century. The government's own harsh legislation and punitive financial policies kept resentment and idealistic aspiration in good heart for many years. But shrewd men and hard men surely realized that the opportunity had been—and had gone—and that the ideologies of the past were now little more than empty mantras. The fabric of Welsh society, as we have tried to show, was being changed at all levels and the revolt itself had accelerated that change. The revolt of Owain Glyn Dŵr was the last inspiring and despairing attempt to recover a world which had been forever lost, even from the dreams of most men. At the level of political loyalties and aspiration the most abiding legacy of Owain's revolt was the question: whither, indeed whether, Wales?

THE MAKING OF A HERO

We return at last to Owain Glyn Dŵr himself. This has been a book about the revolt that bears his name rather than about the man himself. This is how it had to be; and this, arguably, is how it should be. It had to be so since the sources do not exist to compose an individual portrait of the man: the best that can be done, as Sir John Edward Lloyd showed once and for all, is to piece together an account of his revolt and to catch an occasional glimpse of Owain himself. Once we accept that this is so, it is the revolt itself which deserves our attention. Furthermore, while every revolt needs a leader, and particularly so a revolt whose ultimate justification lies in the legitimist claims of such a leader, no revolt can make headway unless it commands the acquiescence or sympathy or, best of all, support of the society at which it directs its appeal. To appreciate the nature and effectiveness of that appeal requires us to penetrate, as it were, into the folds of contemporary society: such was the ambition of Part I of this book. Equally, a revolt which was so comprehensive in its impact as that of Owain Glyn Dŵr, for so many years and across the surface of the whole country, demands that we try to address what the experience of revolt meant to contemporary society: such was the theme of Part III of this volume.

Yet at the end of the day it was not the revolt itself, nor the myriad episodes of which it was composed, nor the local leaders and the guerrilla armies which sustained it for so long, which survived in popular recollection and in historiographical tradition. Rather was it the figure of Owain Glyn Dŵr himself. He established for himself both in popular consciousness and in written histories a role that no other Welshman could emulate; and he seems to have done so at a remarkably early date. Only Arthur, arguably, could compete with him; and Arthur was a very different kind of figure—mythic in the full sense of the word, timeless in his historical location and, from the twelfth century, absorbed into a much broader and European tradition. Owain Glyn Dŵr was both a historic and a mythic figure. He was a man of the recent and recoverable past who had yet secured early membership of the pantheon of timeless heroes. He was, and has remained, exclusively and proprietorially Welsh. He drew on a mythology which was ancient and British; but he, or his advisers, framed their visions in terms

which were distinctly Welsh—not the recovery of the crown of London nor the restoration of a single Britain, but the creation of an independent Wales, politically, ecclesiastically, culturally, and educationally. As such he had created an image for himself and his cause which allowed him to be converted, in the fullness of time, into a national hero. How did this process come about?

Owain's last years hardly formed a propitious basis for such a glowing future. He was personally and publicly a broken man. The revolt had brought disaster for him as head of his family. His brother Tudur, his close companion from early days, was killed at the Battle of Pwll Melyn in May 1405. At the same battle Owain's son, Gruffudd, was captured and was to spend the remainder of his life in prison in the Tower of London and at Nottingham Castle. The greatest blow of all came with the fall of Harlech early in 1409: not only did it bring the loss of his last remaining castle, but also the capture of his wife, two of his daughters, and three of his granddaughters along with all his household goods. Owain's most distinguished son-in-law, Edmund Mortimer—the man who might still have acted as a focus of disaffection against the Lancastrian dynasty—had already died in Harlech during the siege. Edmund's son Lionel—bearing the distinctive name of his great-grandfather, Lionel, duke of Clarence and son of Edward III—was already dead; Lionel's mother and two of his sisters were to die in prison in London during 1413 and were buried in St Swithin's Church. Glyn Dŵr himself had little to console him in his final years other than the memory of happier days when the poet Iolo Goch had sung the praises of his domestic contentment, his peerless wife, and his 'fair nest' of noble young children. Only one of his sons, Maredudd, kept him company in his last desperate months, as they lay, in Adam of Usk's words, 'miserably in hiding in the open country and in caves and in the thickets of the mountains'.[1]

In such desperate circumstances his spirits could only be buoyed from two directions. The optimism of prophecy, at whose wells he seems to have drunk so deeply, might have persuaded him—as it had persuaded generations of his countrymen across the centuries—that the day of deliverance would yet come. More immediately and more relevantly, he could console himself with the thought that the commitment that so many Welshmen had made to his cause, and their sullen resentment of the reimposition of English rule, might cocoon him against the final indignity of being betrayed to the English government. Indeed the government itself recognized both that Glyn Dŵr was no longer a real threat and that he was unlikely to be betrayed, because on 5 July 1415 it authorized Sir Gilbert Talbot to receive Owain and other rebels into the king's obedience if they were ready to submit. The offer was renewed on 24 February 1416, but on this occasion it was directed more specifically at Glyn Dŵr's son Maredudd, suggesting that there might be doubt whether Owain himself was still alive or at

least in a position to make a decision. It is Owain Glyn Dŵr's last appearance in the government's records. By that date he was already probably dead. It is Adam of Usk who provides the most nearly contemporary, though not necessarily accurate, account of his burial: 'he was buried at night by his followers. But his burial was detected by his opponents; so he was re-buried. But where his body lies is unknown.' The mystery surrounding his burial-place set the tone for his posthumous reputation. Owain Glyn Dŵr had embarked on a second career, that of a legendary figure.[2]

In truth the foundations for his second career had been well laid during his lifetime. The English chroniclers who reported Owain's revolt more or less contemporaneously—such as Thomas Walsingham, the monk of St Albans, the monk of Evesham who compiled *The History of the Life and Reign of Richard II*, and Adam of Usk—had already cast a mantle of mystery around him. Nor is it difficult to understand why: his David-versus-Goliath ability to withstand the might of the English Crown; his masterly elusiveness; the blind devotion of some of his followers; the extraordinary language and references of his correspondence all compounded to create an aura of mystery and even sneaking admiration around him. Here was a leader who combined the bravery of a Hector, the wizardry of a Merlin, and the elusiveness of a Scarlet Pimpernel. From such materials larger-than-life heroes are regularly constructed in each generation.

That, however, is only the beginning of the story. It is one thing to leave the memories and the materials from which a legendary hero can be constructed; it is quite another to be able to renew and re-varnish the hero in each generation so that his name and appeal survive across the centuries. Owain Glyn Dŵr belongs to this second category: he showed the same resilience and stamina in his afterlife as he had shown during his revolt. The agents of his posthumous success were popular memory on the one hand and antiquarians and historians on the other. It is only the evidence of the latter which is truly accessible to us today. From it we can see at a glance how the legend of Glyn Dŵr was cast, and recast, across the centuries.

The first generations after Glyn Dŵr's death were—or so it appears—a rather lean period in the making of the legend. Welsh poets such as Guto'r Glyn, Lewys Glyn Cothi, and Gutun Owain certainly refer to him and descent from him, and references to his prowess are no doubt buried, often unrecognizably, in the extensive corpus of prophetic or vaticinatory poetry that was composed in Wales in these years. English chronicles, more especially the popular *Brut*, transmitted the memory of his twelve-year war to future generations. But there is as yet little indication of the creation of a legend or even a stock description of Owain and of his revolt. There was probably no need as yet for legend or description: the scars

of Owain's revolt were still to be seen across the face of Wales and it required no great feat of memory to recall the author of those scars. At Llanilltud Fawr (Llantwit Major) in lowland Glamorgan a local official in 1492 felt that a reference to the devastation caused by the Welsh rebels was still a sufficiently convincing explanation of the shortfall in revenue; at Castle Martin in the lordship of Pembroke likewise, as late as 1501 it could be reported that a windmill was of no value because it had been burnt at the time of the Welsh rebellion. In a society with such conveniently elephantine memories there was no need to create a written image of Glyn Dŵr.[3]

It was in the sixteenth century that such an image was created. The advent of print on the one hand and the appearance of a remarkable group of general historians and local antiquarians on the other provided the opportunity of establishing a canonical view of the English and, to a much lesser extent, the Welsh past. Owain Glyn Dŵr had a secure, if somewhat ambivalent, place within that canon. Two rather distinct, if largely complementary, views of his revolt now became established. The first may be said to be the classical English view; it is represented, in a particularly garbled and foreshortened form, in the chronicles of Edward Hall (1548) and Richard Grafton (1563) and, much more fully and influentially, in those of Ralph Holinshed (1578, revised 1587). It was an account of the revolt focusing exclusively on a few selective incidents: the raids and burnings of Glyn Dŵr's forces, the capture of Reginald Grey and Edmund Mortimer, the alliance with the Percies, the French invasion, and the Tripartite Indenture. It became, and remained until the end of the eighteenth century, the authorized version of the revolt, and as such was endlessly repeated in all general histories of England. Its errors were likewise endlessly repeated—such as the report, already current at the time of Robert Fabyan (1516), that Reginald Grey had been compelled to marry Glyn Dŵr's daughter as part of the price for his release from captivity, or the confusion between Edmund Mortimer, captured in 1402, and his young nephew and namesake, the future earl of March. Equally the most sensational story associated with the revolt—that of the mutilation by Welsh women of the bodies of Englishmen slaughtered at the Battle of Bryn Glas (June 1402)—was given the widest possible currency and became the peg on which a great deal of moralizing condemnation was hung.

The Tudor historiographical account of the Glyn Dŵr revolt could not be substantially challenged or refined because it was fairly securely founded on such contemporary English chronicles as were then available. Welsh antiquarians of the period certainly did not question it. They might have been better placed to challenge, or at least to supplement, it had they been familiar with short accounts of the revolt in Welsh which were composed or copied in Wales in the sixteenth century but which remained in manuscript. One such was the still-untraced

narrative of the revolt composed in 1520 by David Bulkeley of Beaumaris; another was a short fifteenth-century annalistic account of the revolt copied by the poet-genealogist Gruffudd Hiraethog; a third was a brief but lively discussion of the revolt in a remarkable general history composed by the ex-soldier Elis Gruffudd. None of these accounts had an impact on the shaping of the historiographical tradition relating to Glyn Dŵr, but they are of considerable interest in showing that there was already a lively engagement with the memory of the revolt in vernacular Welsh circles in sixteenth-century Wales.[4]

Already, however, in Elizabethan Wales, Welsh antiquarians were increasingly turning in English cultural circles and writing in English. Men such as David Powel, author of the *History of Cambria, now called Wales* (1584), or Rice Merrick, alias Rhys ap Meurig (d. 1578), who wrote an unfinished volume on the antiquities of Glamorgan, or George Owen (d. 1613), the remarkable and prolific Pembrokeshire antiquary, had no reason to depart from the account of Glyn Dŵr's revolt which they read in their general histories of England. Indeed, they were often quite as outspoken in their condemnation of Glyn Dŵr as were their English contemporaries: George Owen had to admit that the chronicles proclaimed Owain to be 'a notable rebel' and 'traitor'; David Powel commented tartly that he had lived in a fool's paradise and that his rebellion had brought 'much mischief to Welshmen'. Yet both of them added a dimension to their accounts of the revolt which was totally absent from the English histories. For them the most abiding and utterly reprehensible legacy of the revolt were the penal statues issued against the Welsh in 1401–2, depriving them 'of all liberty and freedom' and barring them 'from all civil education' as George Owen put it, 'more heathenish than Christian' as David Powel said even more outspokenly. A platform had been provided from which Glyn Dŵr's career as the champion of the Welsh against English oppression could be launched.[5]

Glyn Dŵr had in fact already lost his terror for Englishmen. He had become the archetypal, hot-blooded Welshman whose bombast about his quasi-magical powers was more amusing than threatening. It is as such that he is presented by Shakespeare in his *Henry IV, Part One*. Shakespeare's Glendower is firmly grounded in Holinshed's account; but the portrait is shot through with insight, sympathy, and a human warmth altogether lacking in the one-dimensional narratives of the historians. The cut-and-thrust between the portentous and bombastic Glendower and the quick-witted and high-spirited Hotspur in Shakespeare's play is certainly not to the Welshman's advantage; but Shakespeare still conveys the impression of a Glendower who, however extraordinary his views, deserves respect for the honesty and determination with which he expounds and stands by those views. It took the genius of an Englishman to create the first credible, even attractive, characterization of the Welsh leader.

Holinshed and Shakespeare between them had established a canonical view of Glyn Dŵr which remained basically unchanged in historical writing for the better part of two centuries. When the time for a substantial revision came, the momentum was generated (as so often happens in shifts of historiographical viewpoint) from two different directions. First, new sources were made available which allowed the established account to be corrected, amplified, and substantially redrawn. Such in general and throughout Europe was the achievement of a remarkable group of scholars or *érudits* who between them transformed the foundations of historical scholarship in the century or so before 1760. In the case of the Glyn Dŵr legend the agent of transformation was Thomas Rymer, whose *Foedera* (1704–35) first made available in print a vast range of documents from the rich archives of the English government. It was an achievement which would enable the chronicle-based orthodox account of Glyn Dŵr to be challenged and amplified. Rymer provided the means for a new account to be composed; but that account would require an author, a historian, who could weld the new materials into a new account. Such was Thomas Pennant (1726–98), antiquarian, traveller, and natural scientist. It was he who, in his *Tours in Wales* (1778–81), provided a new account of Glyn Dŵr's revolt as an excursus to his observations on Llangollen. He knew the chronicle evidence but he also availed himself of the documents in Rymer's *Foedera*. What is more, he was the first historian writing in English to make use of contemporary Welsh poetry in order to provide an affectionate and attractive portrait of Glyn Dŵr in the years before the revolt; and, exact observer that he was, he was able to clear away many of the misunderstandings and errors which the conventional accounts of Glyn Dŵr had perpetuated from one generation to the next. Above all, Pennant was a warm-hearted patriot who approached Glyn Dŵr with sympathy. No longer was Glyn Dŵr a 'notable rebel' nor even the somewhat comically self- important figure of Shakespeare's imagination; he was rather 'our chieftain . . . unsubdued'. Glyn Dŵr, the truly national hero, was being born.[6]

Pennant's account, eventually published as a separate appendix to his *Tours*, quickly acquired the status of a new canonical version of Glyn Dŵr's revolt. It formed the basis of most of the very considerable number of volumes devoted to Glyn Dŵr in the nineteenth and early twentieth centuries; it was shamelessly plagiarized and was translated into Welsh for the edification of school children. Pennant laid the foundations for the new image of Glyn Dŵr; but the scholars of the nineteenth century built quickly on those foundations. As more and more record sources were made available in print, so the jejeune account based on the English chronicles was increasingly discredited. The publication of letters written during the revolt—in Henry Ellis's edition of *Original Letters illustrative of English History* (1827), *Proceedings of the Privy Council*, volumes 1 and 2 (1834), and the first

volume of *Royal and Historical Letters during the reign of Henry the Fourth* (1860)—clearly revealed the alarm that Glyn Dŵr's activities had occasioned and greatly enhanced his reputation as a military leader; while the appearance of the first printed edition of Adam of Usk's *Chronicle* in 1876 gave access to a Latin chronicle of the period of the first importance for the study of the revolt and the only such chronicle to be written by a Welshman. But, paradoxically, it was neither from England nor from Wales but from France that the greatest boost to Owain's reputation came in the nineteenth century. In 1834 the journal *Archaeologia* published (pp. 619–20 and plate lxxi) a discussion and illustration of the great and privy seals of Owain Glyn Dŵr from the French national archives; rather later scholars, working at the recently established Public Record Office, came across copies (also from the French archives) of the formal documents in which Owain announced his alliance with the French king and his blueprint for an independent Welsh state. These documents were eventually to be published by Thomas Matthews in 1910 in his *Welsh Records in Paris*. What the seals and the treaties revealed was Glyn Dŵr as an international statesman and political visionary. A new image of Glyn Dŵr was in the making.

Two other developments were crucial to the development and definition of such an image. The first was the rather belated rise in Britain in the late nineteenth century of academic historiography. If history was to establish itself as a respectable academic subject it must show that the study of the past could be conducted on scientific principles, more especially by the construction of historical accounts from a thorough reconsideration of all the published sources, records, and chronicles alike, and by research (itself a new word) in the archives. No longer would it do to rehash and touch up the narratives of Holinshed or even Pennant. In the case of Glyn Dŵr, the first two scholars who applied the critical methods of academic scholarship to his career and his revolt were Englishmen. Between 1884 and 1898 J. H. Wylie published the four forbiddingly learned volumes of his study of the reign of Henry IV, and in its course he revealed a great deal that was new about Glyn Dŵr and placed his revolt firmly in the context of the general political crisis of Henry IV's reign. At much the same time the young T. F. Tout—who had started his career as an academic historian at St David's College, Lampeter—published in the *Dictionary of National Biography* in 1890 what may be considered to be the first truly scholarly account of Glyn Dŵr and his revolt. Glyn Dŵr was being taken over by the scholars and was appearing as a much more considerable figure than at any earlier stage in his historiographical career.

Academic scholars have the power, and the duty, to rewrite the story of the past in critical terms; but it is not in their gift to create, or to demolish, heroes. The standing of men and women from the past in the esteem and collective

memory of any society depends ultimately not on scholarship but on the aspirations of that society. Wales in the late nineteenth century was a society in search for heroes to confirm its new-found confidence in itself as a people and as a nation. This was the age of *Cymru Fydd*, of Young Wales, of a society proud of its cultural identity and equipping itself with the institutional emblems of that identity—in the form of a national university, a national museum, a national library. If such a movement needed a hero from the past to validate itself, Owain Glyn Dŵr surely fitted the bill. His movement had given a glimpse of a truly independent and united Wales; his advisers had dreamt of an independent Welsh Church and two Welsh universities. As with all mythic figures, his appeal was contemporary because it was apparently timeless. It was he, not Llywelyn ap Gruffudd (d. 1282), the first and last formally acknowledged native prince of Wales, who had the makings of a national hero. A. G. Bradley devoted a volume to him in 1901 in the series on 'The Heroes of the Nation'; Cardiff, the putative capital of the new Wales, did him the honour of erecting a statue of him in the City Hall. He had been apotheosized as a, and arguably the, leading national hero of Wales.[7]

It remained only for scholarship to be brought into alignment with popular sentiment. It was Sir John Edward Lloyd who finally effected that alignment. He himself had been a prominent member of the Welsh cultural revival of the late Victorian period, and he had established the credentials of modern Welsh academic historiography when he published his monumental two-volume *History of Wales from the Earliest Times to the Edwardian Conquest* in 1911. In 1920 he chose Owain Glyn Dŵr as the subject of his Ford Lectures in English [*sic*] History at the University of Oxford; he eventually published a revised version of his lectures in 1931. Lloyd could be rhapsodical in his prose; but he was a historian of measured, even restrained, judgements. Yet when it came to Glyn Dŵr he was in no doubt about the exalted stature of his subject: he was 'a great national hero'; 'he may with propriety be called the father of modern Welsh nationalism'. Popular sentiment and scholarly judgement had coincided; the transformation of the 'notable rebel' of Tudor writers into the 'great national hero' was complete.[8]

Such in outline has been the posthumous career of Owain Glyn Dŵr in historical writing across the centuries. The remarkable resilience of his standing over such a long period prompts one to ask what constitutes the ingredients of such a historical reputation. In other words, what makes a man a historical hero? We start with a paradox. Glyn Dŵr commenced his posthumous career as a villain, an anti-hero; it was notoriety, not admiration, which launched him on that career. To Edward Hall he was 'a rebel and a sedicious seducer'; to Holinshed, 'wicked and presumptuous'; to John Hayward, 'a factious person . . . in desires

immoderate and rashly adventurous'. In Tudor times, with their obsessive fear of sedition, such condemnations are not surprising, but even in the early eighteenth century Glyn Dŵr could be dismissed as 'that impostor of a prince . . . set up to play the mimic'. Sedition might be overlooked in a Welshman—'the irregular and wild Glendower' of Shakespeare's play—but the memory of destruction could not be so easily eradicated from popular consciousness. It was the terror and sheer destruction of Owain's regime which dominated recollections of him for at least two centuries. The popular English *Brut* set the tone: 'Owain Glyn Dŵr did much harm and destroyed the king's armies and lordships throughout Wales and robbed and slew the king's people, both English and Welsh.' The Tudor antiquaries gave particularity to this reputation as they assembled their topographical descriptions of Wales: Leland listed in the 1530s the towns such as Montgomery, Hay, and Radnor which still bore the marks of Glyn Dŵr's attacks; Camden, in his *Britannia* (1586), recorded how Radnor had been 'laid in ashes' by the 'rebellious' Glyn Dŵr and how Bangor Cathedral had been burnt 'by that most profligate rebel'. The memory of the wanton destructiveness of Glyn Dŵr had become a topos which Tudor writers—such as Thomas Churchyard in *The Worthiness of Wales* (1587)—repeated as a stock theme in poetry and prose.[9]

But there was more to the villainous memory of Glyn Dŵr than mere destructiveness; there was also the vengeful terror of Owain and his followers. English disgust and fear were sustained by the story, repeated in every Tudor chronicle, of how Welsh women had obscenely mutilated the bodies of Englishmen on the field of the Battle of Bryn Glas. There were other, more localized, episodes which highlighted the savagery of Glyn Dŵr's wars. Leland recorded the story still current in Radnor in his day (the 1530s) of how Owain took sixty men who were guarding the castle 'and caused them to be beheaded on the brink of the castle yard and . . . since [that day] a certain "blood worth" grows there where the blood was shed'. In Glamorgan it was recalled how Owain had captured the castle of Peterston Super Ely and 'caused the head [of Sir Matthew Soer, its keeper] to be chopped off'. The story was reported by the local antiquary, Rice Merrick, in the 1580s, and may serve as a reminder that the memory of destructiveness and savagery of Glyn Dŵr's revolt was not confined to the English. Indeed, the most famous and vivid cameo of the long-term impact of the destructiveness was Sir John Wyn's claim that as a result of the desolation caused by Glyn Dŵr 'green grass grew on the market-place in Llanrwst . . . and the deer fed in the churchyard'. Even patriotic Welsh scholars blamed his revolt as the cause of the collapse of scholarly traditions in Wales. None was more eloquent than Bishop Richard Davies, the translator of much of the New Testament into Welsh. 'What destruction of books Wales suffered as a result of the war of Owain Glyn

Dŵr', he commented in his *Letter* to his fellow countrymen, 'may be easily understood from the townships, the bishops' houses, monasteries and churches that were burnt throughout Wales at that time.' Owain and his followers had been tarred with the same brush as the Vikings.[10]

Savagery, sedition, and destruction can bring their own rewards in terms of long-lived historical notoriety; but they are not the stuff from which the reputation of heroes are made. Even in his own lifetime some of the mystique which heroes attract had begun to be spun around the character of Glyn Dŵr. He was a military hero: in a society intoxicated on feats of arms there was no more secure passport to the portals of immortality. Owain may not have performed the kind of chivalric deeds which would have won him a place in the pages of Froissart, but there was more than enough in his career to win the sneaking admiration of his enemies. A leader who could capture Reginald Grey in an ambush, whose followers could seize Conway Castle while its garrison was at prayers, who could neutralize the might of the English war machine, and who could play hide-and-seek successfully with his English opponents for fifteen years was no mean soldier. Not a single contemporary chronicler called in doubt his military prowess: he was 'a handsome squire', 'a not ignoble squire', 'a venerable and worthy squire' (L. *armiger formosus; armiger non ignobilis; venerabilem et decentem armigerum*). Glyn Dŵr himself might not have been altogether displeased by these comments had he known them, even if he would have considered them grudging and inadequate. His poets had, after all, long since flattered his sense of military self-importance in their odes of praise to him; and had not the king of France himself commented to his ambassadors that it was well known that Owain's main delight was in arms and the equipment of war? English praise for his military prowess may initially have been rather lukewarm, but it grew in warmth across the centuries, in proportion as Wales and the Welsh ceased to be a military threat to England. To Shakespeare, Glyn Dŵr was 'valiant as a lion'; to John Hayward, writing in 1599, he was 'a man full of courage . . . very hardy in undertaking perils and no less resolute in the midst of them'. The rehabilitation of Glyn Dŵr was in full flood now that his countrymen were well behaved: in 1750 Thomas Carte paid him the ultimate compliment when he reported that 'his valour and conduct were admirable'.[11]

Glyn Dŵr's military prowess and stamina might be acknowledged; but military heroes are two a penny and their posthumous life-span is, therefore, often brief. Some more distinctive quality was necessary to secure Glyn Dŵr more firmly in historical memories. Shakespeare, as ever, identified what such a quality might be when he referred to him as 'that great magician, damn'd Glendower'. It was the exotic and the magical, the sense of some mysterious otherness, which gave Glyn Dŵr much of his distinctive mystique. Once again it was an attribute

which had fascinated contemporaries. It was the miserable failure which had attended the king's expeditions to Wales, and above all the appalling weather which had overwhelmed them, especially in 1402, which prompted the thought that Glyn Dŵr or his allies had some secret control over the forces of nature. At St Albans it was thought that the Franciscans, well-known opponents of Henry IV and by the same token well-recognized friends of Glyn Dŵr, were arranging the weather for Owain's convenience; but elsewhere the responsibility was placed more firmly at the door of Owain's own consultants in magic (L. *magi Owini*). It is not difficult to imagine how a man with such allegedly magical powers could establish himself as a legendary figure. After all, to borrow Shakespeare's memorable phrases, someone who 'can call spirits from the vasty deep' is not to be counted 'in the roll of common men'; he has the touch of immortality, or at least memorableness, about him.[12]

Prophecy and magic are close allies; so it was in Glyn Dŵr's case. Many may indeed have doubted whether he had magical powers, but that he was steeped in prophetic writings and appealed regularly to them was not open to question. Those who had known his early military career in Berwick might have recalled how he was accompanied by his personal soothsayer; during the revolt itself the news that he consulted a 'master of brut', or professional prophet, and that his most ambitious political plan, the so-called Tripartite Indenture, was suffused with the language of prophecy must have reached a wide public. What one made of that news was, of course, a different matter. It could, in Hotspur's memorable phrase in *Henry IV, Part One*, be dismissed as 'skimble-skamble stuff'. Sixteenth-century historians said as much in laboured prose: 'Such', remarked Holinshed, echoing Hall, 'is the deviation and not divination of those blind and fantastical dreams of the Welsh prophecies.' David Powel, the Welsh historian, made the same point but at least was able to locate Glyn Dŵr's obsession within its proper context in Welsh mythology:

Some others put in his head that now the time was come wherein the Britons through his means might recover again the honour and liberties of their ancestors. These things being laid before Owain by such as were very cunning in Merlin's prophecies and interpretation of the same (for there were in those days, as I fear there be now, some singular men who are deeply overseen in these mysteries . . .) brought him into a fool's paradise.[13]

Such 'skimble-skamble stuff' was ideal material for dramatic banter, and it may well be that Glyn Dŵr's memory was kept alive for English audiences as the epitome of the absurdities of such prophecies and as an easy target for Hotspur's deflating wit. But there was also a more serious side to it. The language of Merlinic prophecy and animal imagery—the moldwarp and the ant and the

dragon of Tudor histories and Shakespeare's play—may have sounded exotic and comical to English ears; but prophecy and prognostication were part of early modern culture in general and were in no way specifically or exclusively Welsh. The figure of Glyn Dŵr—half-serious, half-ridiculed—epitomized the ambivalent attitude of early modern society towards political prophecy.

Within Wales itself, ridicule was no part of this response. On the contrary, Owain Glyn Dŵr was assured of immortality because he had during his lifetime, and even more securely after his death, joined the ranks of the potential saviours of Wales. He could take his place alongside such mythic figures as Cynan and Cadwaladr and Arthur. They were men whose time had been but was yet to be; it was this very timelessness of their appeal which made them truly legendary heroes. The Welsh annals which recorded the events of Owain's revolt and which were probably compiled within ten to twenty years of its end indicated that Owain Glyn Dŵr, in the opinion of many, had already qualified for membership of this club. Recording his last appearance the annals commented: 'Very many say that he died; the prophets [W. *y brudwyr*] maintain that he did not.' The mystery surrounding the place and circumstances of his death and burial doubtless helped to confirm 'the prophets' in their opinion. Glyn Dŵr had not been betrayed, nor had he been killed. He had sidled off the stage of history at his own convenience; he could, therefore, return in the fullness of time. He had joined one of the most elusive coteries of medieval Europe, that of the Sleeping Kings. Frederick II of Germany and Baldwin IX, count of Flanders and emperor of Constantinople, were among his companions, popular political heroes who would return one day to save their peoples.[14]

Such legendary heroes survive so long as the myths which have created them retain their force. There is every reason to believe that the myths of the coming of a son of prophecy (W. *y mab darogan*) and of the ultimate realization of Merlin's prognostications were still alive in Tudor Wales. The passage quoted above from David Powel (1584) suggests as much; so likewise does the story reported by Elis Gruffudd in the 1540s of how the abbot of Valle Crucis had chided Glyn Dŵr for appearing a hundred years too early; so again, and most strikingly, does the report of how Welshmen in Queen Elizabeth's day still met on mountain-tops to relate tales 'of their wars against the kings of this realm and the English nation' and to listen to the lives of Taliesin, Myrddin (Merlin) 'and such others, the intended prophets and saints of this country'. In this atmosphere the legend of Glyn Dŵr could surely flourish and be readily assimilated into the age-old corpus of Welsh political mythology.[15]

Myths lose their appeal not through scholarly criticism but because they have outlived their usefulness to contemporary society. Owain Glyn Dŵr would survive in the social memory of the Welsh so long as he had a niche in their

collective consciousness. Once he had no such niche he would surrender his status as a legendary hero and be reduced to a mere historic figure. That was precisely in danger of happening once the historical mythology with which he was associated—that of Merlinic prophecies and the expectation of deliverance from Saxon thraldom—lost its potency. That is what seems to have happened in the seventeenth and certainly in the eighteenth century.

But Owain was rescued from the prospect of oblivion by two factors. In the late eighteenth century Wales, in common with many other societies, witnessed a wave of romantic patriotism in which a group of remarkable men sought to restore and, where necessary, create a past which manifested and confirmed the distinctive identity of Welsh culture. In this process Owain Glyn Dŵr could play a most useful role. In a country whose separate political development had been cut short by the conquest of 1282-3, his revolt afforded a solitary but invaluable glimpse of the political unity and identity which Wales might have enjoyed to match its cultural identity. Thomas Pennant saw the opportunity and the need to re-present the legend and character of Owain in a form which appealed to the new Wales. Owain became a 'hero', a word which Pennant uses, and 'our chieftain . . . unsubdued'.[16]

But the process of transformation of the legend of Owain Glyn Dŵr was not yet quite complete. It was in the nineteenth century, particularly the late nineteenth century, as we have seen, that Owain became the focus of renewed attention and reached the high-tide of his posthumous popularity. The romantic patriotism of the eighteenth century was now replaced by the much more strident and ideological nationalism of the nineteenth. The legend of Owain once more rose to the challenge, indeed magnificently so as new light was shed on his ambitions by recently published records. Who better to be the hero of Young Wales than the visionary who had dreamt of a unitary Welsh polity, an independent Church, and a national university? Who had shown better the practical possibilities of a self-ruling Wales than the leader who had summoned two Welsh parliaments? The hero had made his final reincarnation, as 'the father of modern Welsh nationalism'.

It may be truly said of Owain Glyn Dŵr that he was a man for all centuries; it is his very plasticity and multi-dimensionality which made him such a serviceable national hero. It may well also be, of course, that it is the absence of other heroes, particularly of political and specifically Welsh political heroes, which allowed him to hold centre-stage in the Welsh historical consciousness for such a long time. But there is ultimately a more important reason for the remarkable tenacity of his reputation: he had secured a place for himself in the popular historical consciousness of many different parts of Wales. Owain Glyn Dŵr was not only, indeed not primarily, a figure in the history books; he had an established place in the Welsh social memory.

*

Social memory and written history represent two very different, though sometimes not unrelated, ways of engaging with the past. They operate on different
assumptions and through very different agencies; their views of the past often
bear little relation to each other. The historiographical view of the past is
structured, linear, chronologically coherent, and causal in its explanatory patterns. While it may be partisan in its approach and choice of subject-matter, its
proclaimed intention is to provide a truthful and verifiable account of the past, at
least within the constraints of its own sources. Its authors are by definition
literate, educated, and articulate; so is their audience. What is considered to be
the appropriate subject-matter of such historians has certainly changed across the
centuries; so likewise has the identity of the groups within society who have
taken upon themselves the task of writing about the past—be they the monastic
scholars of the Middle Ages or the academic historians of today. Nevertheless,
different as are, say, Ralph Holinshed, the sixteenth-century chronicler, and Sir
John Edward Lloyd, the twentieth-century academic historian, both are united in
writing self-consciously coherent and generalized accounts of their chosen
periods of the past.

Social memory—in the sense of the common collective memory of human
groupings from the neighbourhood to the nation—operates on very different
principles. It is, in the admirable Welsh phrase for it, *cof gwlad*, the memory of the
community or *pays*. It is not structured or generalized; rather is it selective and
episodic. While narrative accounts are frequently embedded in it, it makes no
pretence to being a linear and coherent view of the past, nor does it see the need
for such a view. More often than not it is chronologically imprecise and frequently telescopes events from different periods into one incident. The pegs on which
its incidents and explanations are often hung are local places, local incidents, and
local place-names. Its purveyors are the members of the community itself,
though their memories may be jogged and improved by professional story-tellers
and remembrancers. In the era before the advent of universal education and high
rates of literacy, social memory has been pre-eminently the means whereby
society has engaged with its past. But it is a memory which is beyond the reach
of the historian of any period before the twentieth century to recover, other than
in very small fragments, and then tangentially.[17]

We may be able to recover the lineaments of Owain Glyn Dŵr's reputation in
the pages of written history from the fifteenth to the twentieth century; we have
no means of doing so in respect of the place he held, or did not hold, in the social
memory of the peoples of Wales across these centuries. Yet we have some reason
to believe that his role in the collective memories of Welsh peoples was not an
unimportant one. Those memories, it is true, may have been 'improved' and

modified by the very considerable flow of books, songs, and poetry that was published about Glyn Dŵr, especially after 1800; they certainly have been influenced by generations of school lessons about Glyn Dŵr, especially from the 1870s. But the memory of Glyn Dŵr is older than that of universal education and is often very different from that of the history books.

The social memory of Owain Glyn Dŵr, like that of many popular heroes, was often intensely localized. That does not mean that he was not seen as a national figure, but rather that his memory was kept alive through local associations. Such associations were naturally at their most potent in Glyn Dŵr's home area around Glyndyfrdwy. His 'Mount' or moated enclosure and his prison (W. *carchardy Owain Glyn Dŵr*) were certainly well known in the seventeenth and eighteenth centuries, and probably earlier; the bridle-path that crossed the Berwyn mountains towards Sycharth was, not implausibly, known as Ffordd Owain Glyn Dŵr; while the names of local meadows were garnished with explanations referring to Owain's mastery of the arts of military deceit. Much more dubiously, as the interest in Glyn Dŵr grew apace from the late eighteenth century, and also as Wales began to become aware of its tourist potential and that of Owain, so claims were advanced to associate his activities with particular buildings. Machynlleth was certainly the site of one of his two known parliaments, and the claim to have identified the building in which his assembly was held is understandable, but without historical warrant. More outrageously bogus were the claims made for Owain's link with an old mansion in Dolgellau or that the treaty with the French was concluded at Owain's residence at Plas Crug near Aberystwyth.[18]

Such transparently bogus claims may in fact tempt us to dismiss such place-name evidence and connections as utterly worthless. We would be wrong to do so. Even the late fabrications—and most of them can be shown to pre-date the early nineteenth century—indicate the esteem in which Glyn Dŵr was held and the anxiety to exploit the legends associated with his name. Furthermore, several of the place-names associated with Glyn Dŵr take us back much closer to his own time. William Camden noted in his *Britannia* (1586) that Woodbury Hill in Worcestershire was 'vulgarly called Owen Glendower's Camp', though he added shrewdly, 'which notwithstanding is probably of greater antiquity'. Likewise there is sixteenth-century evidence of the claim that Glyn Dŵr died 'upon the top of Lawtons Hope Hill in Herefordshire, as is there observed and affirmed'. If the memory of Owain was so alive in the English border counties, one may well believe that the same would be even more true in Wales. Many of the legends are only recorded at a late date; but that is no more than we would expect, especially in Wales. Several places, no doubt many of them prehistoric forts, were identified as camps occupied by Owain Glyn Dŵr: Richard Fenton on his tours of Wales in 1804–13 recorded one such at Cilycwm in north-eastern Carmarthenshire. But it

was, inevitably, caves which came to be associated with Glyn Dŵr, as refuges in his hour of need. Caves at Beddgelert (Caernarfonshire), Llangelynnin (Merionethshire), and Craig Gwrtheyrn (Carmarthenshire) were among the candidates, but many others have doubtless gone unrecorded. None of these legends and place-name associations adds anything to our knowledge of Glyn Dŵr and his revolt which can be regarded as securely authentic historical information. But they do surely warrant one conclusion: Owain Glyn Dŵr had, to a certain degree and at different periods, entered the popular historical consciousness across almost the whole of Wales and had done so in a fashion that entwined his name with that of local places and as an explanation for local place-names. In that sense he was truly a popular and a national figure.[19]

We enter much more difficult terrain when we ask what sort of a figure he was in popular consciousness. We must put aside the image of Glyn Dŵr bequeathed to us by our written sources and history books: be it the valiant warrior but 'notable rebel' of Tudor historiography, the portentous proto-wizard of Shakespeare's play, the ardent patriot of Thomas Pennant, or the embryonic nationalist of O. M. Edwards and J. E. Lloyd. Elements of these interpretations may have been part of the image of Glyn Dŵr in popular memory, but that image is likely to have been different and simpler. It would be a less cerebral image. It would be more likely to be sustained by stories which made Owain credible, appealing, and heroic to a popular audience. It would be, one imagines, a figure more like that of his son-in-law, Edmund Mortimer, whose 'wondrous deeds', so Adam of Usk tells us, 'were still commemorated on feast-days in song'.[20]

No Welsh poet or story-teller commemorated Glyn Dŵr's deeds as John Barbour did those of Robert Bruce, or at least no such compositions were committed to writing or have survived. Yet we can perhaps guess what sort of episodes such a poet or story-teller could have chosen and what sort of image he would have wished to brand into the popular memory. One such episode relates to Owain's confrontation with Hywel Sele ap Meurig of Nannau in Merionethshire. Hywel laid a plot to kill Glyn Dŵr when they met to reconcile their differences. He would indeed have killed him had not Owain been wearing armour beneath his clothes. Owain's revenge was dreadful: he burnt Hywel's house to the ground and immured Hywel in the hollow of a great oak where his body, 'a mere compost of cinders and ashes', was discovered some forty years later. The oak tree—Ceubren yr Ellyll (the Hollow Tree of the Devils) as it was known—was still being pointed out to travellers in the nineteenth century. Hywel Sele was certainly a historic figure and contemporary with Owain, but the story has all the hallmarks of a later fabrication. Yet it conveys the image that was being cultivated of Glyn Dŵr: that of the fortunate and resourceful warrior whose revenge on his enemies was terrible.[21]

It is an episode which is matched by another, not dissimilar, tale. Robert Vaughan, the great Welsh antiquarian of the seventeenth century, recorded a story—and it reached a much wider audience by being incorporated into Edmund Gibson's 1695 edition of Camden's *Britannia*—of Owain's treatment of another of his Welsh opponents, Dafydd Gam. Dafydd, so the story runs, came to Owain's parliament at Machynlleth with the express intent of killing the Welsh leader. Like Hywel Sele he was foiled in his plan, and would no doubt have suffered the same fate as Hywel had it not been for the intervention of some of Owain's close friends. Once again the story has a kernel of historical plausibility: Dafydd Gam was certainly a historic figure and an opponent of Owain; he was captured by him, but late in the revolt, in 1412. A legend had been created both to illustrate the treachery with which Owain had to cope and to demonstrate that he was more than a match for such acts of treachery.[22]

The two other episodes which may be chosen to illustrate the kind of popular image that was being created of Owain take us much closer to Owain's own time. The first is recorded in the history of the Welsh soldier-chronicler Elis Gruffudd, compiled in the 1540s. It tells how the councillors of Reginald Grey of Ruthin, who had been captured by Glyn Dŵr, tried to pay most of his ransom to the Welsh leader in false coins. The fraud was spotted by Glyn Dŵr who instantly doubled the ransom as a price for the contempt that had been shown him in assuming that, as a moneyless Welshman, he would not know the difference between false metal and gold. It is a good story, and it is a tall story. It can be dismissed as historically unfounded; but it surely also gives us a glimpse of the sort of image that men wished to create for Glyn Dŵr: that of a bluff and ready-tongued leader who might escape Houdini-like from the plots of his enemies and the armies of the king but who was too shrewd to be hoodwinked by his adversaries. The final episode is recounted in a source probably compiled only a few years after Glyn Dŵr's death; it provides us with another glimpse of the image of the man who was well on his way to becoming a hero. The Welsh annals of the revolt provide a marvellously succinct but eloquent account of Owain's response to the news that his captain, Rhys Ddu (the Black), was arranging the surrender of Aberystwyth Castle to the English. 'Rhys went to Gwynedd to ask Owain's leave . . . Owain kept Rhys with him until he had gathered his power around him, and then went with Rhys to Aberystwyth, where he threatened to cut off Rhys's head, unless he might have the castle. Whereupon the castle was given to Owain.' From such episodes are folk-tales spun and heroes created.[23]

We have, by definition, no firm historical evidence that these episodes were part of the social memory of Owain Glyn Dŵr's personality and activities; but we have good reason to believe that they take us closer to the nature of that social

memory than do the accounts of the history books from Holinshed to Sir John
Edward Lloyd. What sort of an image, therefore, do they communicate? It might
be better to indicate, first, what kind of figure Owain is not in these episodes. He
is not the legitimate descendant of the native dynasty of Powys; he is not referred
to as prince of Wales; he is not the proto-nationalist visionary nor the scheming
politician nor the would-be international statesman. Rather he is a doughty and
intrepid warrior and a proud-hearted, resourceful, and shrewd leader. It is his
bravery, his cunning, and his terrible vengeance which were remembered. There
was no need to dwell on his Welshness nor to elaborate it into nationalist
rhetoric; his memory was treasured in a society where the difference between
English and Welsh was too obvious to need to be defined and where the English
were taken for granted as the historic enemies of the Welsh. The Glyn Dŵr of
popular consciousness was a colourful, attractive, and memorable figure; he was
a hero.

Owain Glyn Dŵr was a truly national figure twice over. For those articulate
and literate people who wanted an image of the blustering, hot-blooded Welshman (as did Shakespeare), he fitted the bill admirably; for Welsh intellectuals who
pined for a national leader for their people and country he was equally well
suited, be it as 'the sole head of Wales' (W. *un pen ar Gymru*) for the poet Iolo
Goch in the fourteenth century or as 'the father of modern Welsh nationalism'
for Sir John Edward Lloyd in 1931. But he was also a hero at the popular and the
local level and across the centuries. When Daniel Defoe in the opening years of
the eighteenth century went on his tour of Wales the people of Brecon and
Radnor showed him 'several little refuges of his [Glyn Dŵr's] in the mountains,
whither he retreated'. Owain had managed to bridge the gap between the Great
and the Little Traditions in Wales; he did so even more successfully in his
posthumous career than he had done so in life. He had become a truly national
hero, however we define that concept.[24]

NOTES

INTRODUCTION

1. For the account of the outbreak of the revolt (probably to be preferred to that given in the chronicles) see the verdict given by the jury of 25 Oct. 1400 in *Select Cases in the Court of King's Bench under Richard II, Henry IV and Henry V*, ed. G. O. Sayles (Selden Society, vol. 87, 1971)), 114–7. Edeirnion and Dinmael: A. D. Carr, *J. Merionethshire Hist. Soc.*, 4 (1963–4), 187–93, 289–301; id. *T. Denbighshire Hist. Soc.*, 13 (1964), 9–21; id., *WHR* 5 (1970–1), 103–29. Note that the letters cited by Lloyd, *OG* 29, as illustrating the tumult in north-east Wales in June 1400 have been re-edited and redated to 1410–12 by J. B. Smith, *BBCS* 22 (1966–8), 250–60.

2. Identification of the persons at the gathering of 16 September: Lloyd, *OG* 31. One of those not identified by Lloyd was Ieuan ap Hywel Pickhill, a prominent landholder of Bromfield (BL Add. Ms. 10,013, fos. 30, 59ᵛ, 61ᵛ, 63ᵛ, 67ᵛ, 75ᵛ). Details of the raid on Ruthin: B. Evans, *T. Denbighshire Hist. Soc.*, 10 (1961), 239–41 and R. Ian. Jack, *WHR* 2 (1964–5), 303–22.

3. The Bala submission: KB 9/204, no. 25; submission of Glyn Dŵr's son: *CPR* 1416–22, 335; further details on collapse of revolt, below pp. 294–9.

4. Allegation that Henry IV's response was too precipitate: *PPC*, i. 134.

CHAPTER I

General Bibliographical Note

Though the journeys described in this chapter are imaginary, details of routes and stopping places are based largely on contemporary documents. The tour of north Wales is based on BL Egerton Rolls 8729 (? Nov. 1379) and 8744 (Sept.–Oct. 1386) and SC 6/1216/3 (1416–7); that of south Wales on Richard II's journeys in 1394 (Tout, *Chapters*, iii. 487, n. 1) and 1399 (*CPR* 1396–9, *CCR* 1396–9 *passim*), and on the expense accounts of a journey by Walter Brugge, receiver-general of the Mortimer estates Apr. 1389 in BL Egerton Roll 8732. For south Wales and the March William Rees's magnificent *A Map of South Wales and the Border in the Fourteenth Century* (four sheets) is indispensable. Descriptions of buildings, etc. (unless otherwise specified), are based on the splendid series of individual guides published successively by the Ministry of Works, Department of the Environment, the Welsh Office, and CADW: Welsh Historic Monuments, on the county inventories of the Royal Commission on Ancient Monuments in Wales and Monmouthshire, and on the volumes published to date in *The Buildings of Wales* series. For the towns of Wales I have relied heavily on R. A. Griffiths (ed.), *Boroughs of Medieval Wales* (Cardiff, 1978). A charming and undervalued portrait of Welsh society based on the evidence of the poetry is W. Ambrose Bebb, *Machlud yr Oesoedd Canol* (Swansea, 1951).

1. Images of Wales and the Welsh: R. R. Davies, *WHR* 12 (1984–5), 155–79; 'horrid and frightful mountains': Daniel Defoe, *A Tour Through England and Wales*, ii. 52–5; 'fierce and fickle' Welsh: D. Knowles, *Religious Orders*, ii. 205; complaints in parliament about Welsh: *Rot. Parl.*, iii. 272, 308, 474, 476; escorts and guide: SC 6/1216/3 (1417).

2. Oswestry: Llinos Smith, in R. A. Griffiths (ed.), *Boroughs*, 219–45; Arundel stock-farming: Shrewsbury Public Library 9777 (receiver of Oswestry's account 1394–5) and for full discussion Llinos Smith, Ph.D. thesis (London 1971), 144–9.

3. Arundel visits to Chirk, and glass windows: R. R. Davies, *Lordship*, 59, n. 82, 80; Llangollen: Thomas Pennant, *Tours in Wales*, i. 359.

4. Valle Crucis debts: SC 6/1215/6; slab of Madog, discovered in 1956: C. Gresham, *Medieval Stone Carving in North Wales*, 137–40; 'fine lodge': Ellis, *Letters*, 12; *PPC*, ii. 63.

5. Defoe, ii. 65; Ruthin: R. Ian Jack, in Griffiths (ed.), *Boroughs*, 245–63; Reginald Grey's presence and decrees: SC 2/221/1 m. 11ᵛ, 18ᵛ (1394–6); his father's petition about the malice of the Welsh: *Cal. Anc. Pets.*, 182–3; *Rot. Parl.*, iii. 70.

6. Denbigh: D. H. Owen in Griffiths (ed.), *Boroughs*, 165–89; Mortimer possession: *CPR* 1391–6, 375; Iolo Goch's poem: *GIG*, no. xx and Eurys Rowlands's discussion of it in *Celtic Studies: Essays in Memory of Angus Matheson*, 124–46; details on Denbigh 1390s: SC 6/1184/22 (receiver's account 1396–7).

7. John Trefor: *CPL*, iv. 29, 500; *CPR* 1396–9, 102, 105; *DNB, sub nomine*; Emden, *Biog. Reg.*, iii. 1898; Glanmor Williams, *Welsh Church*, 135 n., 160, 221–2; for the *cywydd* to his household: *GIG*, no. xvi and E. P. Roberts in *T. Denbighshire Hist. Soc.*, 23 (1974), 70–103; bridge repairs at Rhuddlan: SC 6/774/4–6; wool weighed at the staple there: SC 6/1215/5–6 (1393–5).

8. Garrisoning of Beaumaris for fear of attacks from the sea: SC 6/1215/1 (1389); thirteen Lollards imprisoned there: SC 6/1215/7 (1396).

9. Caernarfon: K. Williams-Jones, in Griffiths (ed.), *Boroughs*, 72–103; all details on the 1390s are based on the North Wales chamberlain's accounts SC 6/1215/1–9 and BL Additional Roll 26595.

10. Giraldus, *Journey through Wales*, book ii, chaps. 5–6; poem about Cricieth: *GIG*, no. ii; Tenby: R. F. Walker, in Griffiths (ed.), *Boroughs*, 289–320.

11. Unloading of cargoes at Chepstow: R. A. Griffiths, 'Medieval Severnside', in R. R. Davies *et al.* (eds.), *Welsh Society and Nationhood* (Cardiff, 1984), 86; Margaret Marshall: McFarlane, *Nobility of Later Medieval England*, 65–6. Rowena E. Archer, *Historical Research*, 60 (1987), 264–80; College of Arms, Arundel Ms. 49 (account of treasurer of household 1394–5). She did visit Wales occasionally: J. Ridgard (ed.), *Medieval Framlingham: Select Documents 1270–1524*, 93.

12. Building at Caldicot in 1380s and 1390s: DL 29/680/11005–11011; Newport: A. C. Reeves, in Griffiths (ed.), *Boroughs*, 189–201; id., *Newport Lordship 1317–1536*; T. B. Pugh (ed.), *Marcher Lordships of South Wales*, 145–153.

13. Cardiff: D. G. Walker, in Griffiths (ed.), *Boroughs*, 103–31; the Despensers: *Glam. CH*, 176–80.

14. Welsh *cywydd* on Glamorgan: *IGE*, no. l (quotations p. 145, l. 31; p. 146, l. 10); English travellers: Defoe, *Tour*, ii. 55; 'gentiles homines': Davies, *Lordship*, 414.

15. Coety Castle: Royal Commission on Ancient and Historical Monuments in Wales. *Glamorgan, III Part* 1a: *The Early Castles*, 218–58; Berkerolles: *Cartae . . . Glamorgancia*, ed. Clark, iv. 1,466–9; Coety during the revolt: below p. 246.

16. Margam: *Glam. CH*, 142, 145–6, 388 (and references); Glanmor Williams, *Welsh Church*, 155, 175–6.

17. Coal industry: 'Accounts of the receiver of the mine of coals . . .', ed. W. Rees, *S. Wales and Monmouthshire Rec. Soc.*, 1, 188–92; Swansea: W. R. B. Robinson in Griffiths (ed.), *Boroughs*, 263–89; Gower: *Glam. CH*, 253–4.

18. Castle and town of Kidwelly in 1390s: DL 29/584/9237–9 (receiver's accounts 1381–9); DL 43/15/2–3; DL29/728/11986 (valors 1388, 1391, 1395); DL 41/10/49 (ordinance regarding the town, 1401); will of one of Richard II's Cheshire followers dated at Kidwelly, 14 June 1399: P. J. Morgan, *War and Society in Medieval Cheshire*, 214.

19. Carmarthen: R. A. Griffiths in Griffiths (ed.), *Boroughs*, 131–65; repairs to bridge: SC 6/1222/6–7 (chamberlain's accounts, 1394–6); trade: E. A. Lewis in *T. Royal Hist. Soc.*, NS 17 (1903), 121–75 and *Y Cymmrodor*, 24 (1913), 86–188; tensions: *Cal. Anc. Pets.*, no. 12,729.

20. Narberth: NLW Slebech 16 (account of receiver, 1398–9); BL Egerton Roll 8718 (memorandum to Mortimer council); *CPR* 1396–9, 256.

21. Haverford: SC 6/1305/10 (ministers' accounts, 1391–3).

22. St David's: J. W. Evans and Roger Worsley, *St. David's Cathedral 1181–1981*; Henry de Gower: Glanmor Williams, *Arch. Camb.*, 130 (1981), 1–29.

23. Elizabeth Audley: *CIPM*, xviii, no. 484; her accounts are published (from NLW Bronwydd Collection) in *Baronia de Kemeys*, 93–99; Brecon: R. R. Davies, in Griffiths (ed.), *Boroughs*, 47–73; DL 29/633/10317 (local officials' accounts, 1397–8); SC 6/1157/4 (receiver's account 1398–9).

24. Bolingbroke–Gloucester settlement, 1395: DL27/170.

25. *GDG*, esp. nos. 8–10, 15, 44, 71, 99, 111; commentary: R. G. Gruffydd, *Dafydd ap Gwilym*, 19–20.

26. *GIG*, no. xiv; Iolo's career: ibid., Introduction by D. R. Johnston; for Iolo's attitude to the English: D. Johnston, *Cambridge Medieval Celtic Studies*, 12 (1986), 73–98; Iolo's odes to Edward III and Roger Mortimer: *GIG*, nos. i and xx.

27. Contemporary images of Wales: Davies, *Lordship*, 3–4.

28. Mountains: *Letters of John of Salisbury*, i. 52; Defoe, *Tour*, ii. 60; R. R. Davies, *WHR* 12 (1984–5), 157–8; forests: W. Rees, *South Wales*, 119–27; Davies, *Lordship*, 119–27; Hopedale: *Cal. Anc. Pets.*, no. 2598.

29. Dafydd ap Gwilym's nun: *GDG*, no. 99; 'Forest of the Grey Rock': *IGE*, no. lxvi; Cledwyn Fychan, *Llên Cymru*, 15 (1984–8), 289–307; the correspondence from Bryncyffo Forest: J. B. Smith in *BBCS*, 22 (1966–8), 250–60.

30. Weather: *Chronicle of Pierre de Langtoft*, ii. 177; *Register of Edward the Black Prince*, i. 148; *GDG*, esp. nos. 27, 68, 69, 117, 145; Henry IV's experience of Welsh weather: *Annales H. IV*, 343.

31. Pecham's comment: *Registrum epistolarum fratris Johannis Peckham*, ii. 476; Wales as the 'world's back-side': Sir John Vanbrugh quoted by F. Jones in *TCS* (1948), 429;

fragmentation: Davies, *Lordship*, chap. 11; 'state of mind': K. Simms, 'Guesting and Feasting in Gaelic Ireland', *J. Royal Society of Antiquaries of Ireland*, 108 (1978), 67 (Robin Frame kindly recovered this reference for me).

32. Froissart: *Chronicles*, ed. G. Brereton, 410; Gruffudd Llwyd and Sion Cent: *IGE*, nos. l, lxxxix; Philip ap Morgan: below pp. 43–4; Welsh labourers: *Rot. Parl.*, ii. 234, B. H. Putnam, (ed.), *Proceedings before Justices of the Peace Edward III–Richard III*, 410–11; Welsh troops in 1380s and 1390s: SC 6/1214/11 (chamberlain's account for North Wales, 1386); F. Devon (ed.), *Issues of the Exchequer*, 231–2; *Arch. Camb. Original Documents*, 35; pilgrims: *CIPM*, xv, no. 659; SC 2/218/9, m. 20^v; 218/11, m. 27; 219/1, m. 22^v, 26; 219/2, m. 12; 219/4, m. 13; Welsh scholars and labourers returning to Wales: *Rot. Parl.*, iii. 457.

33. Fire ordinances: R. Ian Jack, *T. Denbighshire Hist. Soc.*, 28 (1979), 5–17; Caernarfon: Keith Williams-Jones, in Griffiths (ed.), *Boroughs*, 78; Ruthin: SC 2/221/4, m. 22 (1402).

34. Carmarthen charter: Griffiths (ed.), *Boroughs*, 158; Robert Parys: ibid. 87; Richard Golding: A. D. Carr, *Medieval Anglesey*, 254; John Owen: Davies, *Lordship*, 330; loans by Carmarthen burgesses: DL 42/18, fo. 11.

35. Town walls: M. W. Beresford, *New Towns*; H. Turner, *Town Defences in England and Wales* (1970); military obligations of burgesses: Davies, *Lordship*, 323–4.

36. Importance of courts for burgesses of Cardigan: *Cal. Anc. Pets.*, no. 4886; legal knowledge and professional services of townsmen: Griffiths (ed.), *Boroughs*, 59–60, 79–80, 156–7.

37. Brecon: Davies, in Griffiths (ed.), *Boroughs*, 52–3; Caernarfon: Williams-Jones in ibid. 79; *Caernarvon Court Rolls 1361–1402*, ed. G. P. Jones and H. Owen, 113, 136–7.

38. Hope: Chester 2/73, m. 3^v (1399); Laugharne and St Clears: *C Ch R 1341–1417*, 307, 335.

39. Wrexham: B. Evans, *BBCS* 19 (1960), 42–7; id., *T. Denbighshire Hist. Soc.*, 10 (1961), 236–8; craftsmen: K. Williams-Jones, *Merioneth-lay Subsidy Roll*, pp. ci–cv.

40. Bonvilston and Wrinstone: Matthew Griffiths, *BBCS* 32 (1985), 173–202; Castlemartin: W. Rees, *South Wales*, 131, 144; Bronllys: Davies, *Lordship*, 112–13, 308; Elfael: *Calendar of Inquisitions Miscellaneous 1392–9*, no. 228.

41. Agriculture: Margaret Davies and G. R. J. Jones in Baker and Butlin (eds.), *Studies of Field Systems*; Davies, *Lordship*, 369–71 (and references); W. Rees, *South Wales*, 131–98; plough-beasts in Welsh poetry: *IGE*, no. vi, l. 19; F. Payne in *Y Llenor*, 26 (1947), 3–24.

42. Cattle trade: *BBCS* 6 (1931–3), 363–4; SC 6/1214/8 (chamberlain of North Wales's account 1382); tribute in cows in Brecon: Davies, *Lordship*, 134, 140; Gruffudd Llwyd's poem: *IGE*, no. xliv.

43. Black Death: W. Rees in *T. Royal Hist. Soc.*, 4th ser. 3 (1920), 115–35; G. J. Williams, *Traddodiad Llenyddol Morgannwg*, 29; dispersed habitat: *Registrum epistolarum fratris Johannis Peckham*, iii. 776; Davies, *Conquest*, 150.

44. Absence of money: *Cal. Anc. Corr.*, 179; starving the Welsh: Giraldus, *Description of Wales*, book ii, chap. 8; Prestwich, *Edward I*, 180, 190–1.

45. Poet's view of serfs: *GDG*, no. 39, l. 8; *IGE*, no. lxvi, l. 27.

46. Status: *GIG*, no. viii; BL Additional Ms., 10,013, o. 73^v (1366, Bromfield and Yale); kin-ties: R. R. Davies, *Conquest*, 122–7; Chester 24/240.

47. Distribution of wealth in Welsh society: Davies, *Lordship*, 392–402; K. Williams-Jones, *Merioneth Lay Subsidy Roll*, pp. lxxx–lxxxiv; Welsh 'barons': A. D. Carr in *WHR* 5 (1970–1), 103–29; Owain Glyn Dŵr: *GIG*, no. ix, l. 14.

48. *Commorthau: Cat. Mss. Wales in BM*, i. 59 (1591); fosterage: Llions Smith, *WHR* 16 (1992–3), esp. 20–8.

49. *Ynaid:* R. R. Davies, in T. M. Charles-Edwards *et al.* (eds.), *Lawyers and Laymen*, 258–74; arbitration: Llinos Smith in *English Historical Review*, 106 (1991), 835–60; *cymanfaoedd* and *dadleuoedd*: below p. 92; report on a Welsh hilltop assembly: *Cat. Mss. Wales in BM*, i. 72.

CHAPTER 2

1. Free–unfree, English–Welsh distinctions and their significance: R. R. Davies, *Lordship*, chaps. 14–18; Carr, *Anglesey*, chaps. 5–6; below pp. 65–70, 75–6.

2. Richard II's power in Wales: A Tuck, *Richard II and the English Nobility*, 192–4; R. R. Davies, 'Richard II and the Principality of Chester', in *Reign of Richard II*, ed. Du Boulay and Barron, 256–79; comparison with Edward II: J. B. Smith, *WHR* 8 (1976–7), 139–71; Welsh poets' comments: *IGE*, nos. xxxvi (p. 108, ll. 5–6); xxxvii (p. 110, l. 2); also below pp. 76–85.

3. Mortimer's career: *DNB and GEC, sub nomine*; his progress through Wales: BL Egerton Rolls 8740 (The Mortimer accounts in this collection are the single most important source for our knowledge of Earl Roger's estates); Iolo Goch's poem: *GIG*, no. xx; Mortimer's genealogy: M. E. Giffin in *Speculum*, 16 (1941), 109–20; see also below pp. 176–9.

4. Arundel's career: *DNB and GEC, sub nomine*; A. Goodman, *The Loyal Conspiracy*, chap. 6; Owain Glyn Dŵr's family connection with the Fitzalans: ibid. 34; id., *WHR* 5 (1970–1), 67–70.

5. Mortimer and Derby's progresses in Wales: BL Egerton Rolls 8740; DL 28/1/10 fos. 7ᵛ–8; gifts given on the occasion of these two progresses: SC 6/1209/2; 1157/5; surveyor's comment on Holt Castle: BL Additional Ms. 10,013 fo. 3; financial accounts: R. R. Davies, *Economic History Review*, 2nd ser., 21 (1968), 211–29.

6. Individual powers of lords: Davies, *Lordship*, chap. 7; Arundel's surveys: *Extent of Chirkland 1391–93*, ed. G. P. Jones; *The Lordship of Oswestry 1393–1607*, ed. W. J. Slack; BL Additional Ms. 10,013.

7. Earl of Arundel and the dean of St Asaph: *ANLP*, no. 30; vacuum of lordship and its consequences: R. R. Davies, in J. F. Lydon (ed.), *The English in Medieval Ireland*, 145–6.

8. Robert Eggerley: the details of his career have been assembled in Michael Rogers, 'The Welsh Marcher Lordship of Bromfield and Yale 1282–1485' (unpublished Ph.D. thesis, University of Wales, 1992), 35–6; his 1391–3 surveys see n. 6 above; Walter Brugge: for his travels see esp. BL Egerton Rolls 8732–3, 8744–5; Mortimer's testimonial *ANLP*, no. 15.

9. Skidmore: biographical detail in Griffiths, *Principality*, 139–41; J. S. Roskell, *et al.*, (eds.), *History of Parliament: The Commons 1386–1421*, iv. 391–4; service to Mortimer:

UCNW Whitney 315 (1381); Bolingbroke's regard for him: DL 28/3/4, fos. 23^v, 38^v; member of duke of Exeter's council 1399: UCNW Whitney 317.

10. Philip ap Morgan: Davies, *Lordship*, 205–6, 417. If later genealogies are correct Philip was Owain Glyn Dŵr's second cousin once removed: Bartrum, *Welsh Genealogies AD 300–1400*, sub Cydifor Hael, 14–15.

11. Recognizances from leaders of local communities: JI 1/1152, m. 5^v (Iscennen, 1401); Chester 2/75, m. 7^v, 11 (Flint, 1402); Grey's letter: Ellis, *Letters*, 3–4.

12. Terminology: Davies, *Lordship*, 76–9, 413–4; recent review of the problem in England, with full bibliographical references: C. Carpenter, *Locality and Polity*, chap. 3.

13. Sir Lawrence Berkerolles: *Cartae . . . Glamorgancia*, ed. Clark. IV. i. 116; Bryndu: Davies, *Lordship*, 420.

14. Stradlings: R. A. Griffiths, *Morgannwg*, 7 (1963), 15–47; Sir John St John: *History of Parliament 1386–1421*, iv. 280–3.

15. Robert Parys and Richard Golding: above p. 26; Thomas Rede: Griffiths, *Principality*, 113–4; John Owen: Davies, *Lordship*, 330.

16. Hywel ap Tudur: R. R. Davies, *TCS* (1968), pt. 2, 156–7, 167–8; A. D. Carr, *TCS* (1979), 141–5; Gruffudd ap Gwilym: A. D. Carr, *WHR*, 15 (1990–1), 1–20.

17. Prid: Llinos Smith, *Economic History Review*, 2nd ser., 29 (1976), 537–50 and *BBCS* 27 (1977), 263–77.

18. Military effigies: C. A. Gresham, *Medieval Stone Carving in North Wales*; Welsh military service in the fourteenth century: A. D. Carr, *WHR* 5 (1970–1), 103–29 and *TCS* (1977), 40–53; Rhys and Gwilym ap Tudur and their family: Glyn Roberts, *Aspects of Welsh History*, 179–215, 240–73; their military enterprises: E. 101/29/24 (1369); F. Devon (ed.), *Issues of the Exchequer*, 23 (1386); BL Add. Roll 26,595 (1394); *CPR* 1396–9, 400.

19. Rhydderch ab Ieuan Llwyd: Griffiths, *Principality*, 117; J. B. Smith, *BBCS* 20 (1962–4), 339–47; Llinos B. Smith, *Ceredigion*, 10 (1986), 229–52; D. Huws, *NLWJ* 22 (1981), 1–26 and *Cambridge Medieval Celtic Studies*, 21 (1991), 1–37.

20. Hopcyn ap Tomas: G. J. Williams, *Traddodiad Llenyddol Morgannwg*, 9–14, 146–8; B. F. Roberts, *BBCS* 22 (1966–8), 223–8; C. W. Lewis, *Glam. CH*, 456–9; G. Charles-Edwards, *NLWJ* 21 (1979–80), 246–56; Daniel Huws in *Cyfreithiau Hywel Dda yn ôl Llawysgrif Coleg Iesu LVII*, ed. M. Richards.

21. Observations of external observers: *Cal. Anc. Pets.*, no. 11,883; *Cal. Anc. Corr.*, 231, 233, 254; comments of native poets: *Blodeugerdd Barddas o'r Bedwaredd Ganrif ar Ddeg*, ed. Johnston, 128; *IGE*, no. l (p. 145, l. 22); goods of Flintshire gentleman: *History of Flintshire*, i. 99; wine: *GIG*, no. v, l. 23; Usk, *Chronicle*, 70; tomb of Ieuan ap Gruffudd: Gresham, *Medieval Stone Carving*, 196–8.

22. Tudur ap Goronwy and sons: *GIG*, no. v, l. 22; no. iv, ll. 79–83; kinsmen and friends: *IGE*, no. lxiv (p. 132, l. 23); liveries: *GIG*, no. vii, ll. 16–17.

23. Welsh Church in general: Glanmor Williams, *The Welsh Church*; wealth of bishoprics: ibid 271; household of bishop of St Asaph: *GIG*, no. XVI and E. P. Roberts in *Tr. Denbighshire Hist. Soc.*, 23 (1974), 70–104; Cistercian monasteries: Glanmor Williams, *Welsh Church*, 348; F. G. Cowley, *Monastic Order in South Wales*, 272.

24. The dispute over Llanrwst Church: *Cal. Anc. Pets.*, nos. 11,753, 11,852–3; *CCR* 1389–92, 295; Rhys Gethin and Hywel Coetmor: *IGE*, nos. xxxvi–xxxvii; Gresham, *Medieval Stone Carving*, 205–7.

25. John Trefor: see above, Chap. 1, n. 7.

26. Master Hywel Cyffin: Emden, *Biog. Reg., sub nomine; GIG*, no. xix; lands: NLW SA/MB 22, fos. 7ᵛ, 14; descent: Llinos Smith, 'The Lordships of Chirk and Oswestry, 1282–1415' (unpublished Ph.D. thesis, University of London, 1971), 367, 469; the funeral ode of Ithel ap Robert: *GIG*, no. xv.

27. Clerical population: Glanmor Williams, *Welsh Church*, 150; Glyn Dŵr's clerical supporters: SC 2/221/4, mm. 7ᵛ, 9; G. Roberts, *BBCS* 15 (1952), 39–61.

28. Strata Marcella: *Cal. Anc. Pets.*, no. 15,389; Margam: D. H. Williams, *Atlas of Cistercian Lands in Wales*, 11.

29. Ithel ap Bleddyn: *GIG*, no. xv, ll. 21–2; Strata Marcella: *CCR* 1330–3, 150; the Aberconwy monk: A. D. Carr, *Owen of Wales*, 42.

30. Iolo Goch's ode: *GIG*, no. xviii; for a convenient translation into English: Gwyn Jones (ed.), *Oxford Book of Welsh Verse in English*, 45–8.

31. Social and economic change in late fourteenth-century Wales: W. Rees, *South Wales*, 241–83; Davies, *Lordship*, 425–57; below pp. 74–6; revolt in Abergavenny: Usk, *Chronicle*, 63.

CHAPTER 3

1. English–Welsh relations: R. R. Davies, *TCS* (1974–5), 32–56; id. *Lordship*, 302–92 (with full references).

2. Inquiries in Flintshire: *Register of Edward the Black Prince*, iii. 179–80; Chester 38/25/3 no. 13.

3. Campaign of North Wales boroughs: E. A. Lewis, *The Medieval Boroughs of Snowdonia*, 176; Hope charter 1399: *CPR* 1396–9, 484.

4. Contravention of ordinances against appointment of Welshmen: *Register of Black Prince*, i. 159–60; iii. 137, 221, 378; *Flintshire Ministers' Accounts 1328–53*, ed. D. L. Evans, 47–8; harassment of Welsh burgesses in Ruthin: SC 2/219/1, m. 5, 32; denial of English status 1367: SC 2/219/4, m. 13.

5. Hope, 1401: Chester 38/25/3 no. 115; Hopcyn ap Tomas: B. F. Roberts, *BBCS* 22 (1966–7), 227; poem to Rhys Gethin: *IGE*, no. xxxvii, p. 109, ll. 3–4; English complaints about Welsh: *Cal. Anc. Pets.*, nos. 5,625, 12,729; *Cal. Anc. Corr.*, 231; comment of burgesses of Conway: *Cal. Anc. Pets.*, no. 9,365.

6. Parliamentary petitions: *Rot. Parl.* iii. 81, 391; *CCR* 1377–81, 365–6; anti-Welsh sentiments in towns in 1380s–90s: *CCh. R* 1341–1417, 263–4, 325, 327–8; *Cal. Anc. Pets.*, 12,729; Dyffryn Clwyd and Cydweli: SC 2/221/1, m. 19v; JI 1/1152, m. 2; 1153 mm. 11, 42; men of Englefield: Chester 25/24, m. 17 (1378/9); Narberth: BL Egerton Roll 8718.

7. Adam of Usk: Usk, *Chronicle*, 86; Principality income: SC 11/862; income from Marcher lordships: Davies, *Lordship*, 176–98; comment of the Black Prince's council: *Register of Black Prince*, i. 96–7.

8. Subsidies and aids in North Wales: SC 6/1215/6 (1394); in Brecon: SC 6/1157/4 (1397); in Cydweli: DL 29/728/11986 (1395); DL 41/9/8, m. 55 (1400).

9. Arrears lists: SC 6/1210/4 (Principality, 1395); 1112/3 (Mortimer estates, 1391); 1209/2 (Mortimer Marcher estates, 1395); DL 29/737/12071 (Lancaster estates, 1390); commission to expedite collection of revenue from Cydweli: DL 29/584/9239 (1389); earl of Arundel's financial extortions in South Wales: Griffiths, *Principality*, 272–3, 537; R. A. Griffiths, *Ceredigion*, 5 (1964–7), 166 n. 51; *Cal. Anc. Pets.*, no. 8,448 (wrongly dated); *Westminster Chronicle 1381–1394*, ed. L. C. Hector and B. F. Harvey, 382–3; communal fines in Chirkland: NLW Chirk Castle, D. 51; Denbigh: SC 6/1233/9 (list of fines, 1397).

10. Communal fines and subsidies in 1390s: SC 6/1216/6; 1222/6 (Principality); DL 29/728/11986 (Gaunt's Welsh estates); SC 6/1157/4 (earl of Derby); BL Egerton 8736, 8739; SC 6/1209/2 (Mortimer estates).

11. Revenue from Brecon and from Lancaster estates in Wales: Davies, *Lordship*, 192–3; Arundel estates in Wales: Llinos Smith, *BBCS* 28 (1978–80), 443–57; Denbigh, 1397: SC 6/1288/1; South Wales, 1400: SC 6/1222/9; yield of Welsh estates in 1390s: BL Egerton Roll 8736 (Mortimer); Shrewsbury Public Library, 9777; NLW Chirk Castle D 41–44; SC 6/1234/5 (Arundel); DL 29/728/11991, m. 5 (Brecon).

12. Aids and subsidies from royal and Lancaster estates 1400–1: SC 6/1216/1 (North Wales); SC 6/774/13 (Flint); DL 41/9/8, m. 55 (Cydweli); DL 42/16, fo. 59^v (Brecon).

13. Subsidy-raising delegation: DL 29/615/9845 (1417); report: *ANLP*, no. 111; 'unrest': *Westminster Chronicle 1381–94*, 392–3; Welsh poet's comment on taxation: *Cywyddau Dafydd ap Gwilym a'i Gyfoeswyr*, no. lxxvi, l. 31.

14. Impact of plague: W. Rees, *T. Royal Hist. Soc.*, 4th ser., 3 (1920), 115–35; id. *South Wales* 241–69; E. A. Lewis, *TCS* (1902–3), 1–75; Davies, *Lordship*, 425–56; J. B. Smith, *WHR* 3 (1966–7), 145–71; A. D. Carr, *Medieval Anglesey*, 300–12.

15. Collapse of numbers of villeins in Dyffryn Clwyd: SC 2/219/13, m. 13; seignorial attitude towards villeins; Davies, *Lordship*, 437–43; Dyffryn Clwyd evidence: SC 2/220/12, m. 33–4 (1398–9); 221/1, m. 19^v (1396); Abergavenny: Usk, *Chronicle*, 63, above p. 64

16. Defiance in Dyffryn Clwyd: SC 2/221/1 mm. 11^v, 19^v.

17. *IGE*, no. xlii, p. 125 ll. 1, 8; *Cywyddau Dafydd ap Gwilym a'i Gyfoeswyr*, no. lxxvi, l. 1.

18. The search for peace: J. J. N. Palmer, *England, France and Christendom*, 142–52, 166–79, 211–26; response of Cheshire: J. G. Bellamy, *Bull. John Rylands Library*, 47 (1965), 254–74; P. J. Morgan, *War and Society in Medieval Cheshire*, 192–8; Owain Glyn Dŵr's military career and pretensions: E 101/39/39; 40/33; *GIG*, no. ix, l. 54; below Chap. 5.

19. Richard's visits to Wales 1387: *Westminster Chronicle*, 186, 254; his visits to Flint and Holt: Chester 2/71, m. 6; 73, m 9v; R. R. Davies, in *The Reign of Richard II*, ed. Du Boulay and Barron, 272, n. 19; Henry Bolingbroke's movements in Feb. 1398: DL 28/1/10, fo. 2^v.

20. Richard's movements in May–Aug. 1399: J. W. Sherborne, *WHR* 7 (1974–5), 389–402; id., *WHR* 14 (1988–9), 217–41.

21. Welsh esquires of Richard II: *CPR 1396–9*, 281, 285, 323, 400; men of Glamorgan: Usk, *Chronicle*, 27; of Usk: ibid. 25; of Brecon: SC 6/1157/4; repairs to Lancaster castles in

Wales: DL 29/615/9840; 584/9240; 573/9063; court of Coelion cancelled: SC 2/220/12, m. 36ᵛ.

22. Cheshire rising of 1400: P. McNiven, *Bull. John Rylands Library*, 52 (1969–70), 375–96 and P. J. Morgan, *War and Society in Medieval Cheshire*, 205–7.

23. Gower: *Glam. CH*, 253: BL Egerton Roll 8769 (account of receiver-general of earl of Warwick, 1397); challenge to earl of March's title to Denbigh: G. A. Holmes, *The Estates of the Higher Nobility in Fourteenth-Century England*, 19, n. 3; Usk, *Chronicle*, 15–17.

24. Principality of Chester: R. R. Davies, in *The Reign of Richard II*, 256–79; grants to Richard's favourites: *CPR 1396–9*, 186, 196, 205, 213, 408; to Lescrope: ibid. 16, 36, 82, 196, 269, 284, 285, 322, 347, 356, 402, 408.

25. John ap Harry: Griffiths, *Principality*, 234–5; Roskell *et al.*, *History of Parliament 1386–1421*, iii. 299–301; his link with Lescrope: E 28/4, no. 88; John Skidmore: above p. 43.

26. Men of Glamorgan: Usk, *Chronicle*, 27; Aumale on the Welsh: Creton, 'Metrical History of the Deposition of King Richard the Second', ed. J. Webb, *Archaeologia*, 20 (1824), 57, 105.

27. 'Welshmen are Welshmen': quoted by J. G. Edwards, *Proceedings of the British Academy*, 32 (1950), 80–1; 'Beware of Wales': *The Libelle of Englyshe Polycye*, ed. G. Warner, 40.

28. The raid on Beaumaris: SC 6/1151/1–2 (chamberlain's accounts for North Wales): reviews of castles: *Cat. Mss. Wales in BM*, iii. 601–2; armed escort for chamberlain: SC 6/1214/11 (chamberlain's account, North Wales, 1385); garrisons: *Calendar of the Public Records Relating to Pembrokeshire*, ed. H. Owen, iii. 35–6; *Cat. Mss. Wales in BM*, iii. 345; *CPR 1374–7*, 495; SC 6/1221/16 (Carmarthen, 1385); SC 6/1215/1 (Beaumaris, 1389); the Castilian spy: *CPR 1388–92*, 9.

29. Owain Lawgoch: for all that relates to him, A. D. Carr, *Owen of Wales*; see also M. Siddons, *BBCS* 36 (1989), 161–86.

30. Commission of May 1381: *CPR 1381–5*, 17; garrisons placed in Monmouth and Three-castles, June 1381: *John of Gaunt's Register 1379–83*, i. nos. 530–4; repairs to Caernarfon Castle and guard posted there: SC 6/1214/9–1215/8 (chamberlain's accounts, North Wales); John Lawrence: Griffiths, *Principality*, 116–17; *IGE*, no. xxxix; trailbaston inquiry: *Westminster Chronicle*, 382–3; fracas in Flint County Court: Chester 25/24, m. 26; recognizance of 1398: Chester 2/71, m. 11.

31. Caerwys and Narberth: above, p. 69–70.

32. The Welsh habit of revolt: *Vita Edwardi Secundi*, ed. N. Denholm-Young, 69.

33. Defoe's comment: *Tour*, ii. 54: telescoping of heroes (including Owain Glyn Dŵr) into a single mythology: T. Roberts in *BBCS* 7 (1933–5), 231–56; prophecy in general: M. E. Griffiths, *Early Vaticination in Welsh*; Glanmor Williams, *Religion, Language and Nationality in Wales*, 71–86; *Trioedd Ynys Prydein*, ed. R. Bromwich.

34. The name of Britain: *Vita Edwardi Secundi*, 69; letter of Archbishop Hubert Walter: *Giraldus Cambrensis, Opera*, ed. J. S. Brewer, i. 120; Sir Gruffydd Llwyd: J. B. Smith, *BBCS* 26 (1975–6), 463–78; Cynan, Cadwaladr, and Arthur: *Trioedd Ynys Prydein*, 274–7, 292–3, 316–18; C. Bullock-Davies, *BBCS* 29 (1980–2), 432–40.

35. Glamorgan and Dyffryn Clwyd memories: *Cartae . . . Glamorgancia*, ed Clark, iv. no. 1,027; *Rot. Parl*. iii. 70; *Cal. Anc. Pets.*, no. 5,628; anti-English sentiment: *IGE*, xxx, p. 9, l. 6 (cf. *GIG*, pp. xxv–xxvii); Matthews, *Records*, 53.

36. *CPR 1494–1509*, 523; Mawddwy court roll in Keith Williams-Jones, *BBCS* 23 (1968–70), 342; 'dadelowes': *Flintshire Ministers' Accounts 1301–28*, ed. A. Jones, 83; report on morrow of revolt: Ellis, *Letters*, 8.

37. Strata Marcella assemblies: Glanmor Williams, *Welsh Church*, 144; Whitland: *PPC*, v. 244, 233; seditious poets: *Record of Caernarvon*, ed. H. Ellis, 131; *Rot. Parl.*, iii. 508; for prohibition of 1396 on giving money and vestments 'to those who are called in Welsh *cler*', NLW Aston Hall 5835.

38. Gruffudd Llwyd's poem: *IGE*, no. xlii.

PART II: INTRODUCTION

1. Re-dating of important documents: e.g. J. B. Smith, *BBCS* 22 (1966–8), 250–60; local studies: esp. J. E. Messham in *Flintshire Hist. Soc. Publications*, 23 (1967–8), 1–34 (Flintshire); R. A. Griffiths, *Ceredigion*, 8 (1964–7), 143–67 (Cardiganshire); W. H. Morris, *Carmarthenshire Antiquary*, 3 (1959–61), 4–16 (Cydweli); R. Ian Jack, *WHR* 2 (1964–5), 303–22 (Ruthin); use of unpublished government records: esp. R. A. Griffiths, *BBCS* 20 (1962–4), 282–92; *BBCS* 22 (1966–8), 151–68; *Bull. Institute of Historical Research*, 37 (1964), 77–100; Rhidian Griffiths, *BBCS* 32 (1985), 202–16; *BBCS* 34 (1987), 165–74; quotations from J. E. Lloyd: *OG*, preface.

2. Biography of Llywelyn ap Gruffudd: J. B. Smith, *Llywelyn ap Gruffudd, Tywysog Cymru* (1986).

3. Attack on Dyffryn Clwyd: SC 2/221/2, m. 14 v; skirmishes in Flint: Chester 3/23; for Maredudd ap Llywelyn Ddu see below, p. 139.

4. Relief of Cardiff Dec. 1404: E 101/44/5.

CHAPTER 4

1. For basic narrative and reference to the sources for the whole of this chapter, see *OG*; further details of attacks on Rhuddlan and Flint: SC 6/774/11; new Oswestry charter: BL Harleian Ms. 1981, f. 34; general pardon Mar. 1401: *CPR 1399–1401*, 451–2.

2. Garrisons at castles: *PPC* ii. 64–6; E 403/571, m. 2; executions in Dyffryn Clwyd: SC 2/221/4, m. 7v; body of Gronw ap Tudur: *CPR 1399–1401*, 359.

3. Scaling down of response at Chester and Flint: SC 6/774/11; surrender of rebels and pardons: *CPR 1399–1401*, 392, 396; measures against 'the rebels of north Wales': DL 42/15, fo. 104 (28 Feb. 1401); dispatch of spies: E 101/320/28; confiscation of Owain Glyn Dŵr's estates: *CPR 1399–1401*, 386; response in parliament: *Rot. Parl.* iii. 472–6; statutes and ordinances: *Statutes of the Realm*, ii. 124, 128–9; *CPR 1399–1401*, 469; below pp. 284–90.

4. Capture of Conway Castle: Keith Williams-Jones, *T. Caernarvonshire Hist. Soc.*, 30 (1978), 7–43; Rhys and Gwilym ap Tudur: above p. 52.

5. Dispatch of messengers to Cricieth and Harlech: E 101/320/28 (1 Apr.); correspondence between Hotspur and the king and his council: *PPC*, i, 148–53; *ANLP*, no. 27; imposition of subsidies: SC 6/1216/1; 774/13, mm. 1, 14v; 775/3; pardons to rebels of north-east Wales: *CPR 1399–1401*, 452; ordinances: *Record of Caernarvon*, ed. H. Ellis

(1838), 240, and below pp. 286–7; spies: E 101/320/28; Hotspur's letter of 3 May: *PPC*, i. 151.

6. Reports of renewed rebellion: *ANLP*, no. 228; *PPC*, i. 166; disorder in Brecon and Abergavenny: DL 42/15, fo. 105v; *CPR* 1399–1401, 518, 520; rebels in Powys, Carmarthenshire, and Kidwelly: *PPC*, i. 151–3; ii. 54–5; *CCR* 1399–1402, 389; DL 29/584/9241; Adam of Usk's evidence: Usk, *Chronicle*, 69–70; defections to rebels: *CPR* 1401–5, 8, 14, 17, 20, 22, 24; garrisons at Kidwelly and Swansea: DL 29/584/9241; SC 6/1202/16; prince of Wales's report: *ANLP*, no. 228 (this letter clearly belongs to Oct. 1401).

7. Siege and relief of Harlech: *ANLP*, no. 236 (this letter may well belong to Nov.–Dec., rather than July, 1401, since the Mortimer lands referred to in it were resumed into royal hands 7 Nov., *CFR* 1399–1405, 142); *Cal. Anc. Corr.*, 199–200; SC 6/774/13, m. 3v; E 403/571, m. 16; threat to Caernarfon and the 'battle of Tuthill': Usk, *Chronicle*, 71; E 101/320/28; Henry IV's second expedition and subsequent appointments: *OG*, 42–4; garrisons at Aberystwyth and Cardigan: *PPC*, i. 173–9; *ANLP*, no. 237.

8. Duchy of Lancaster sessions in Wales: DL 42/15, fo. 114; JI 1/1153, m. 31; commissions in south Wales: *CPR* 1401–5, 68; *ANLP*, nos. 228, 245; surrenders of men at Chester: Chester 2/75, m. 1; submission of cos. Cards. and Carms.: Usk, *Chronicle*, 71; *ANLP*, no. 245; negotiations with Glyn Dŵr: *PPC*, i. 175; *ANLP*, no. 244.

9. Raid on Ruthin and courts there: Usk, *Chronicle*, 71; SC 2/221/2, m. 11; 14, mm. 21v–22; auditors in north Wales: SC 6/774/13, m. 3v; capture of Reginald Grey and Battle of Bryn Glas: *OG*, 49–52; suggestion that Grey was betrayed by his own household: Dieulacres Chronicle, *Bull. John Rylands Library*, 14 (1930), 175.

10. Pejorative phrases about the Welsh: *PPC*, i. 134; *Eulogium Historiarum*, ed. F. S. Haydon (Rolls Series), iii. 388; mutilation of bodies by Welsh women: *Annales H. IV*, 341; dispatch of news about Bryn Glas: *PPC*, i. 185–6; SC 6/1185/4; military measures taken: E 101/43/8, 11 (Clifford and Radnor), DL 42/15, fo. 130ᵛ (Brecon), SC 6/1202/17 (Swansea).

11. Defections to Glyn Dŵr: PSO 1/1 no. 41A (Bishopscastle), Chester 2/96, m. 3 (Maelor Saesneg); Adam of Usk's report: Usk, *Chronicle*, 78; Brecon and Radnor: SC 6/1202/17; *CPR* 1401–5, 159; defection of Edmund Mortimer and his letter to his tenants: *OG*, 58–9; Ellis, *Letters*, 34–6; below pp. 179–80.

12. New military commands: Chester 2/75, m. 5 (Stafford and bishop of St Asaph); *CPR* 1401–5, 53 (Hotspur and Worcester); repairs at Kidwelly and Monmouth: DL 42/15, fos. 119v–120 (9–10 Feb. 1402); garrison at Carreg Cennen: DL 25/3477 (10 May 1402: chaplain and ten archers); DL 42/16, fo. 36 (25 June 1402; a further six archers); relief forces from Chester: SC 6/1185/4; E 101/43/9 (Denbigh).

13. New military commands and measures: *CPR* 1401–5, 139; counter-measures to relieve Harlech, Caernarfon, and Beaumaris: Rhidian Griffiths, *BBCS* 32 (1985), 202–3; SC 6/774/15; earl of Arundel's retinue in Wales: Shropshire RO, Bridgewater Accounts; Henry IV's expedition: *OG*, 54–5; SC 6/1185/4 (Llanrwst); appointment of Richard Grey: *CPR* 1401–5, 122; DL 42/15, fo. 130ᵛ.

14. Collection of revenue in North Wales: SC 6/1216/1; sessions in North and South Wales: SC 6/774/14, mm. 1v–2v; auditing accounts in Anglesey, Dec. 1402: E

101/43/9; subsidy collection in Flintshire: Chester 2/75, m. 9; details of revenue from Duchy of Lancaster estates in Wales: DL 29/729/11998; DL 28/4/2, fos. 17–17^v (Feb. 1402–Feb. 1403); DL 42/15, fo. 130^v ('war loan' from Brecon).

15. Duchy estate accounts: DL 29/729/11998; cos. Merioneth and Caerns.: SC 6/1216/1; comment of monk of Evesham: *Historia R. II*, 173–4.

16. Reports of winter activity by Welsh: *CSL*, no. 97; Chester 3/21 no. 2; deteriorating situation: SC 6/774/5 m. 3^v (Hope); Chester 2/76, m. 4 (Hope); SC 2/221/2, m. 17^v (Dyffryn Clwyd, Apr.); E 101/43/20 (Montgomery); SC 6/775/15, m. 4^v (Flint).

17. News of Harlech and Aberystwyth: *PPC*, ii. 62–3; SC 6/774/15, m. 6; Radnor and Brecon: E 101/43/11; *RLH IV*, i. 146–7; developments in the Tywi valley: *OG*, 63–8 and sources cited there.

18. Support for Hotspur in north-east Wales: J. E. Messham, *Flintshire Hist. Soc. Publications*, 23 (1967–8), 8–15; A. D. Carr *TCS* (1979), 148–9; below pp. 184–5; July 1403 as a watershed in loyalties: SC 6/774/15, mm. 3^v, 5^v; E 101/43/24, m. 5; Welsh attacks in Flintshire, Shropshire, Cheshire, and Herefordshire: Chester 30/17, m. 23; Chester 25/25, m. 1; SC 6/774/15, m. 5^v; SC 6/775/1; *CPR 1401–5*, 439.

19. Attacks of summer–autumn 1403: JI 1/1153, m. 20^v (Kidwelly); *RLH IV*, i. 152–4 (Abergavenny); ibid. 160–2; DL 29/584/9222 (second attack on Kidwelly); *CPR 1401–5*, 439 (Monmouth, Gwent, Cardiff); royal expedition: *OG*, 73–5.

20. Negotiations with Glyn Dŵr: *Cal. Anc. Corr.*, 256; Prince Hal's lieutenantship: *CPR 1401–5*, 216; E 101/404/24; E 404/18/300; Rhidian Griffiths, *BBCS* 32 (1985), 203; attack on Sycharth: *PPC*, ii. 62–3; rescue missions: E 101/404/24, fos. 12–13 (Harlech); SC 6/774/15, m. 3^v (Beaumaris).

21. Itinerary of royal expedition: E 101/404/21, fos. 32–33^v; appointment of duke of York and Lord Audley: BL Campbell Charters XXV, 13 (York); *CPR 1401–5*, 311 (Audley); garrison at Carmarthen: E 101/43/13, 21, 22.

22. Civilian control during the revolt: JI 1/1153, m. 3^v; DL 29/584/9242, below pp. 275–6 (Kidwelly); Messham, *Flintshire Hist. Soc. Pub.*, 23 (1967–8), 12–15 (Flintshire); local military commanders take over civilian rule: E 101/42/20 (Montgomery); E 101/43/11 (Radnor); *CPR 1401–5*, 122, 139; 1405–8, 107, 149 (Brecon); DL 29/584/9242 (Cydweli).

23. Attacks in early months of 1404: Ellis, *Letters*, 30–8 (Caernarfon, Harlech); *RLH IV*, ii. 15–17, 22–4 (deputy sheriff of Anglesey, Harlech); E 101/43/11 (Radnor garrison); summer attacks across Wales 1404: Messham, *Flintshire Hist. Soc. Pub.*, 23 (1967–8), 17–18; *PPC*, i. 223–5, 229; ii. 77–8; *CPR 1401–5*, 440; devastation on earl of Arundel's Shropshire estates: Shrewsbury Public Library Mss. 5319, 5788, 7276; treaties with Welsh: *PPC*, i. 236; garrisons: E 101/44/3 (Welshpool, 6 Nov. 1404–31 Jan. 1405); E 101/43/28 (Bishopscastle 23 Mar. 1404–25 Sept. 1404).

24. Capture of Kidwelly: JI 1/1153, m. 5^v; danger to Haverford: *CPR 1401–5*, 474–5; relief expeditions: Rhidian Griffiths, *BBCS* 32 (1985), 211 (Coety); E 101/44/5 (Cardiff).

25. French alliance: *OG*, 82–6; aborted French expedition, Aug. 1404: *OG*, 88; parliament: *OG*, 81–2; John Trefor: above p. 60; Lewis Byford: *OG*, 115–18.

26. Attacks on border communities: *RLH IV*, ii. 18–20; *PPC*, i. 246; the French expeditionary force: *OG*, 101–6; siege of Rhuddlan: SC 6/775/4, m. 2^v; threats in south-east: *CPR*

1405–8, 61; supplies for Coety: ibid. 163; Pembrokeshire fine with rebels: George Owen, *The Description of Penbrokshire*, ii. 482–4; the parliament at Harlech: *RLH IV*, ii. 76–9.

27. Garrisons: *PPC*, i. 251–3; *CPR* 1405–8, 5–6; Rhidian Griffiths, *BBCS* 32 (1985), 211; details of size of garrisons: E101/43/29 (Carmarthen); E 101/44/3 (Welshpool); E 101/43/35, 39 (Caernarfon: 28 Feb. 1404–16 Apr. 1407); Rhidian Griffiths, *BBCS* 34 (1987), 168–71.

28. Prince Henry's policies and problems: Rhidian Griffiths, *BBCS* 32 (1985), 202–16, esp. 210–2; *PPC*, i. 273–4; appointment as lieutenant of north Wales: *CPR* 1405–8, 5–6; garrisons: ibid; proposed royal expedition May 1405: *OG*, 98–100.

29. Victories over Welsh 1405: *OG*, 95–7; negotiations with men of Usk and Caerleon: *CPR* 1405–8, 64; Gwilym ap Gruffudd's surrender: Chester 24/245; A. D. Carr, *WHR* 15 (1990–1), 7; above pp. 51–2. (Gwilym's father); attack on Anglesey: *OG*, 99; Brecon: *CPR* 1405–8, 148; personal losses: *OG*, 96–8; John Hanmer: Chester 3/24, no. 23; SC 6/775/12, m. 2ᵛ (correcting *OG*, 98, n. 3); Pennant: T. Pennant, *Tours in Wales*, ed. J. Rhys (1883), iii. 332; 1405: K. B. McFarlane, *Lancastrian Kings and Lollard Knights* (1972), 76.

30. Financial and administrative collapse: NLW Chirk Castle D. 55 (Chirk); DL 29/729/12,003 (Monmouth area); letter to earl of Arundel's council: *ANLP*, no. 308; submission of the men of upland Brecon: DL 42/15, fo. 182ᵛ; cf. *CPR* 1401–5, 299; the Kidwelly agreement: JI 1/1152, m. 7.

31. Confirmation of alliance: Matthews, *Records*, 39 (the dating presents problems: '12 January 1405' would normally indicate 1406 by modern (post-1752) reckoning; so does the reference to the sixth year of Owain's principate, which could run Sept. 1405–Sept. 1406. Even so, Jan. 1406 is very late for the ratification of a treaty concluded in July 1404); transfer of ecclesiastical allegiance: *OG*, 119–21; below pp. 169–70; suspension of court of Coelion: SC 2/221/5, m. 16; raids into north-east Wales: Chester 25/25, mm. 1–4; Messham, *Flints. Hist. Soc. Publications*, 23 (1967–8), 22–3; garrison at Montgomery: E 101/44/14.

32. Failure of the French and Scottish threats: *OG*, 126–7; below pp. 189–96.

33. Proposed meeting of parliament at Gloucester: J. L. Kirby, *Henry IV of England* (1970), 191; appointment of prince of Wales as lieutenant: *CPR* 1405–8, 140, 156; impatience of commons: *Rot. Parl.* iii. 569 (5 Apr.), 574–6 (7 June); supplies of cash: Rhidian Griffiths, *BBCS* 32 (1985), 214.

34. Garrison at Caernarfon: E 101/43/39; the plan to recover control of Anglesey: SC 6/775/4–5; the submission at Beaumaris: Glyn Roberts, *BBCS* 15 (1952–4), 39–61; Tomos Roberts, *BBCS* 38 (1991), 129–33 (there are some anomalous features about this document); below p. 293; appointment of John Mainwaring as military commander: SC 6/1216/2, m. 6.

35. Military setbacks of 1406: *OG*, 128; death of Hywel Gwynedd: Chester 3/23, no. 9; Messham, *Flints. Hist. Soc. Publications*, 23 (1967–8), 21–4; surrenders in Flintshire: Chester 2/78, m. 5; inquiries into those who had died during the revolt: Chester 3/23; submission before Gilbert Talbot: Chester 25/25, m. 2.

36. Submission of Gower, Ystrad Tywi and Ceredigion: *OG*, 152; submission of men of north-east Wales: *CPR* 1405–8, 203 (Arundel lordships); Chester 2/78, m. 6 (Denbigh);

prince of Wales's contract of service and payment: *Historical Manuscripts Commission IV Report*, Appendix, 194; Rhidian Griffiths, *BBCS* 32 (1985), 214; escort for Gilbert Talbot: SC 6/1216/2, m. 6; siege of Aberystwyth: *OG*, 130–2; J. H. Wylie, *History of England under Henry IV*, 4 vols. (1884–98), iii. 111–14 (the fullest account).

37. The proposal for the surrender of Aberystwyth: *Rot. Parl.*, iii. 611; *CPR* 1405–8, 361–2; *The St. Albans Chronicle 1406–1420*, ed. V. H. Galbraith (1937), 22; Glyn Dŵr's response: *OG*, 153; dispatch of envoys to Paris, May 1408: Matthews, *Records*, p. xxviii; planned ambush on Chester chamberlain: Chester 24/245 (unsorted; inquisition 17 Sept. 1408); need for escorts in north Wales: SC 6/1216/2.

38. End of revolt: see below pp. 293–9; garrisons: SC 6/1216/2 (Caernarfon); Rhidian Griffiths, *BBCS* 32 (1985), 214; financial recovery as illustrated by accounts: DL 29/592/9446 (Ogmore); SC 6/924/19 (Usk); DL 29/584/9242 (Cydweli); SC 6/775/6–7 (Flint, Denbighshire); DL 29/733/12013, m. 3–4 (Brecon); SC 6/1216/2 (North Wales); fall of Aberystwyth and Harlech: *OG*, 136–7; Rhidian Griffiths, *BBCS* 32 (1985), 211.

CHAPTER 5

1. 'revolt of the Welsh': Shrewsbury Public Library, Craven Collection 7276 (account of bailiff of Ruyton, 1403); NLW Aston Hall 5319 (account of bailiff of Aston, 1404); 'sworn to Owain Glyn Dŵr'; SC 6/774/15, m. 5ᵛ; 'men of Owain': SC 2/221/2, m. 21; 221/4, m. 38v., 45v.

2. For the general approach adopted in this chapter see also R. R. Davies, in *Cof Cenedl II. Ysgrifau ar Hanes Cymru*, ed. G. H. Jenkins (1987), 3–25; Gerald of Wales's comment: *Opera*, ed. J. F. Dimock, vi. 200 (*Description of Wales*, book i, chap. 17); the poet's comment on lineage: *GIG*, no. viii, ll. 43–4.

3. Iolo Goch on Owain's lineage: *GIG*, no. viii, ll. 26–7, 46.

4. Iolo Goch: *GIG*, no. viii, ll. 7–13, 97; Owain Lawgoch: above pp. 86–7; Owain Glyn Dŵr's arms: M. Siddons, *The Development of Welsh Heraldry*, 3 vols. (1991–3), i. 285–6.

5. Styles of Owain and his ancestors: NLW Chirk Castle F. 13369 (1329); Wynnstay 105/160 (1329); Bagot 216 (1392); J. Conway Davies, *NLWJ* 3 (1943–4), 48–50.

6. Owain's estate at Glyndyfrdwy: W. H. Waters, *BBCS* 6 (1931–3), 364–6 (escheator's account for North Wales, 1309–10); also Williams-Jones (ed.), *The Merioneth Lay Subsidy Roll*, 1292–3, 75–9; his estates at Cynllaith and Sycharth: *BBCS* 6 (1931–3), 366–7, E 179/242/55 (lay subsidy roll, Chirkland 1292); *Extent of Chirkland 1391–1393*, ed. G. P. Jones, for Welsh customs in the area; Iscoed Glyn Dŵr: Griffiths, *Principality*, 304.

7. Estimates of Owain's income: *Cal. Anc. Corr.*, 118; *BBCS* 6 (1931–3), 361; Woolgar (ed.), *Household Accounts from Medieval England*, ii. 622–3 (the upper limit of 300 marks in *CPR* 1399–1401, 388 seems very unlikely); earl of Arundel's retinue 1387: E 101/40/33.

8. Gruffudd ap Gwilym: above pp. 51–2; sale of marriage of Owain's grandfather: *Cal. Anc. Pets.*, 24–5; estate officers at Glyndyfrdwy: NLW Bagot 216; Iolo Goch's poem to the *llys* at Sycharth: *GIG*, no. x and Enid P. Roberts, *T. Denbighshire Hist. Soc.*, 22 (1973), 12–47; contemporary English descriptions of Owain's residences: *PPC*, ii. 61–2;

archaeological evidence: D. B. Hague and Cynthia Warhurst, *Arch. Camb.*, 115 (1966), 108–27.

9. The entail of 1328: *CPR 1327–30*, 314; the significance of entails: K. B. McFarlane, *The Nobility of Later Medieval England*, 270–2; the explanation in *OG*, 16 is inadequate.

10. Welsh baronies: A. D. Carr, *J. Merionethshire Hist. and Rec. Soc.*, 4 (1963–4), 187–93, 289–301; id., *T. Denbighshire Hist. Soc.*, 13 (1964), 9–21; id., *WHR* 5 (1970–1), 103–30; the obligations of Welsh baronage: *CIPM*, vi. no. 256 (Owain Glyn Dŵr's great grand-father); 'king of the barons': *GIG*, no. ix, l. 14.

11. Monumental slab to Owain's great grandfather at Valle Crucis: C. A. Gresham, *Medieval Stone Carving in North Wales*, no. 122 and pp. 254–5; Castell Dinas Bran: D. J. Cathcart-King, *Arch. Camb.*, 123 (1974), 113–39; days of march and letters of march between Dyffryn Clwyd on the one hand and Glyndyfrdwy and Edeirnion on the other: SC 2/219/2, m. 39 (1365); 220/6, m. 21ᵛ. (1389); 220/12, m. 2ᵛ (1390); membership of Glyn Dŵr's initial raiding party: SC 2/221/4, mm. 7ᵛ., 9, and R. Ian Jack, *WHR* 2 (1964–5), 303–22.

12. Beer of Shrewsbury: *GIG*, no. x, l. 73; Llansilin Church: *Buildings of Wales: Clwyd*, 241; aisle-truss house in the parish: ibid 48, 245.

13. Rebels from Iscoed: *CPR 1401–5*, 17, 86.

14. Gruffudd ap Madog: *CCR 1318–23*, 290: Llinos Smith, *BBCS* 23 (1969–70), 132; Lestrange family: *GEC*, vol. 12, i, *sub nomine*; Gruffudd's offices: *Cat. Mss. Wales in BM*, iii. 751–2; *Hist Mss. Commission XIth Report*, vii, 142; NLW Plas Iolyn 421 (1331); *Rotuli Scotiae*, i. 228–9, 284, 294–5, 333. Gruffudd Fychan: NLW Aston Hall, no. 924; R. C. Purton, *T. Shropshire Archaeological Soc.*, 53 (1949–50), 99; loan to his widow: R. Ian Jack, *BBCS* 21 (1964–5), 163–6.

15. Iolo Goch's comments on Margaret: *GIG*, no. x, ll. 82, 83.

16. Poet's greeting to David Hanmer: *IGE*, no. xxxix, ll. 1–12; Marred ferch Dafydd: *CPL*, v. 44.

17. Biographical details on David Hanmer: Griffiths, *Principality*, 114–15; 'paragon of lawyers': *IGE*, no. xxxix, l. 7; his investigative commissions in Wales: SC 6/1214/5 (chamberlain's account for North Wales, 1377–8); *CPR 1381–5*, 17.

18. David Hanmer's retaining fees: *CPR 1381–5*, 148 (Charlton); Salop RO, Bridgnorth Collection, box 87 (Lestrange); DL 28/3/1, m. 6 (John of Gaunt, 1377); Staffs. RO, D 641/1/2/1 (Stafford, 1384); his membership of the councils of the earls of March and Arundel: BL Egerton Roll 8727 (1375); Salop RO, 552/A/8 (Hanmer was holding sessions at Chirk in Dec. 1386, NLW Chirk Castle D 73); notice of his death: *CPR 1385–9*, 339.

19. John Hanmer's career: *The Scrope and Grosvenor Controversy 1385–90*, ed. Nicholas (1832), i. 259; *DKR*, xxxvi. App. 218–19; Gruffudd Hanmer's career: NLW Aston Hall 5821; SC 6/1214/10–1215/8; Hanmer family settlement, 1387: *NLWJ*, iii. (1943–4), 48–50.

20. Genealogical chart: based on fifteenth–sixteenth century genealogical sources assem-bled in Bartrum, *Welsh Genealogies A.D. 300–1400*; but almost every one of the connections is verified by contemporary record. Details of family links are mainly based on the following deed collections: NLW Bachymbyd, Bettisfield, Chirk Castle,

Plas Iolyn, Puleston, Wynnstay, UCNW Bodrhyddan, Mostyn; Clwyd RO: Nerquis Hall.

21. Maredudd ap Llywelyn Ddu: Chester 3/23, m. 15; 30/17, m. 6 (estates); NLW Plas Iolyn 192 (office); John Kynaston: NLW Plas Iolyn 192; Clwyd RO, Nerquis Hall, 25.

22. Support of barons of Edeirnion: SC 2/221/4, mm. 7ᵛ, 9; A. D. Carr, *WHR* 5 (1970–1), 125–6; the royal indictments: KB 27/560 *rex*, m. 18; 567 *rex*, m. 8ᵛ.

23. Hywel Cyffin and family: Bartrum, *Welsh Genealogies, sub* Bleddyn ap Cynfyn, 7–9 (genealogy); NLW SA/MB22, fo. 7ᵛ (land); Chirk Castle D. 53 (offices); ibid. D. 73 (power of family); *ANLP*, no. 30 (dispute with Morgan Yonge); Ieuan ap Hywel Pickill: Bartrum, *Welsh Genealogies, sub* Sandde Hardd, 3 (descent); BL Add. Ms. 10,013, fos. 30, 59ᵛ, 61, 63ᵛ, 65, 67, 75 (lands and leases); NLW Peniarth 404 D, fo. 101 (1415, arrangement for descent of estates); Madog ab Ieuan ap Madog: Bartrum, *Welsh Genealogies, sub* Tudur Trefor, 24–5 (descent); BL Add. Ms. 10,013, fos. 69ᵛ, 75, 76 (lands); *Brut y Tywysogyon, Peniarth MS.* 20 version, 237; Gresham, *Medieval Stone Carving*, no. 174 (obit and effigy of grandfather); NLW Peniarth 404 D, fo. 86 (charge of homicide); UCNW Mostyn 1534 (confirmation that Madog's wife was Marged daughter of Iorwerth (Ddu)).

24. Morgan Yonge: Bartrum, *Welsh Genealogies, sub* Tudur Trefor, 12 (descent); SC 2/219/1, mm 23ᵛ–24ᵛ (evidence that he was married by 1364); Chester 38/25, m. 70; NLW Wynnstay 104/235, no. xix; SC 2/219/1, m. 23ᵛ (evidence that his wife, contrary to the genealogies, was Marred ferch Llywelyn Sais; she was grand-daughter and co-heiress of Llywelyn ap Madoc (d. 1342) of Dyffryn Clwyd, for whom R. R. Davies, *Lordship and Society*, 82, 418, 452); *DKR*, xxxix App., 523 (offices); SC 2/220/1, m. 15; 220/5, m. 7ᵛ (major leases); SC 6/1214/7; UCNW Bodrhyddan 1252 (links with David Hanmer, including collecting latter's fee in North Wales); Chester 30/17, m. 2ᵛ; Chester 25/25, m. 1; SC 2/221/9, m. 7 (defection of sons and grandsons to Glyn Dŵr); SC 2/221/9, m. 6ᵛ (pardon for his own adherence to Glyn Dŵr).

25. Evidence that Gruffudd Yonge was Morgan Yonge's illegitimate son: endorsement on NLW Wynnstay 104/235, no. xix (Morgan had conveyed all his lands in Dyffryn Clwyd to Master Gruffudd Yonge, bastard, then rector of Llanynys); Morgan seeks deanship of St Asaph for his son (? Gruffudd): *ANLP*, 77.

26. Owain's probable year of birth: *OG*, 18–19; evidence of his father's death by 1370: R. Ian Jack, *BBCS* 22 (1964–6), 163–6; Owain's legal apprenticeship: *Annales H IV*, 333 ('Hic primo juris apprenticius fuit apud Westmonasterium'); parallel example of a Lanca-shire gentleman spending four years as an apprentice at the court of common pleas: M. J. Bennett, *Bull. Institute of Historical Research*, 57 (1984), 203–8; legal education: Paul Brand, *Historical Research*, 60 (1987), 147–65.

27. Poetic tributes to Owain's military prowess: *GIG*, no. ix, ll. 35, 54; 'exemplary war-rior': *Historia R. II*, 168; views of ambassadors: *OG*, 84.

28. Sir Gregory Sais: A. D. Carr, *TCS* (1977), 40–53; P. J. Morgan, *War and Society in Medieval Cheshire*, 158–60, 166.

29. The Berwick garrison, 1384: E 101/39/39; Anglo-Scottish relations in these years: A. Grant, in *War and Border Societies in the Middle Ages*, eds. A. Tuck and A. Goodman

(1992), 30–64; bardic comment on Owain's service at Berwick: *IGE*, no. xli (Gruffudd Llwyd); *GIG*, no. ix; earl of Northumberland's presence there: *Calendar of Documents Relating to Scotland*, vol. V, *Supplementary*, nos. 4115–16, 4121.

30. Owain's service in Scotland 1385: *Scrope and Grosvenor Controversy*, i. 252–60; Arundel's retinue in the expedition: A. Goodman, *Loyal Conspiracy* (1971), 127; role of Cheshire: P. J. Morgan, *War and Society in Medieval Cheshire*, 186–7.

31. Family link with Arundel: above p. 136; Owain as squire of the earl of Arundel: *Eulogium Historiarum* III, 388.

32. The muster list of 1387: E 101/40/33.

33. Accounts of the naval battle: J. J. N. Palmer, *England, France and Christendom* (1972), 92–6; A. Goodman, *Loyal Conspiracy*, 128–9; Owain's return to north-east Wales: NLW Bagot, 216; Richard II touring in Cheshire and its environs 12 July–6 Aug.: A. Tuck, *Richard II and the English Nobility*, 227; the earl of Arundel's counter-measures: R. R. Davies, in *The Reign of Richard II*, ed. F. R. H. Du Boulay and Caroline M. Barron, 259.

34. The knighting of the three squires: E 101/40/33; David Hanmer's death: above, p. 138; Owain's enlistment in, and withdrawal from, the May 1388 expedition: E 101/41/5; A. Goodman, *WHR* 5 (1970–1), 67–70.

35. Owain's domestic contentment: *OG*, 26–7; patronage of poets: *GIG* no. ix, ll. 23–4; indult for plenary remission at death: *CPL*, v. 44; Ieuan ap Gruffudd ap Madog's effigy: Gresham, *Medieval Stone Carving*, no. 182; tempo of political change 1397–1400: above pp. 78–85.

36. Contemporary English admiration of the loyalty of the Welsh to Owain: *Historia R. II*, 170; Iolo Goch's formal portrait: *GIG* no. viii; Owain's stance during negotiations with the earl of Northumberland: *PPC*, ii. 59–60; *ANLP*, no. 244; refuses safe conduct to Skidmore's entourage: Ellis, *Letters*, 20; attending a funeral: *ANLP*, no. 210.

37. 'king of the barons': *GIG*, no. ix, l. 14; dispatch of prisoner to Owain: *RLH IV*, 16; the response to Rhys Ddu: *OG*, 153.

38. 'sole head of Wales': *GIG*, no. viii, l. 97.

CHAPTER 6

1. Evesham chronicle: *Historia R. II*, 167–8; Reginald Grey and his tenants in Scotland: SC 2/221/2, m. 3ᵛ–4; Walsingham's account: *Annales H. IV*, 333–4; border relations between Dyffryn Clwyd and Edeirnion: SC 2/219/2, m. 39ᵛ (1365); 220/6, m. 21ᵛ (1389); the reputation of the Greys: above p. 9.

2. Owain proclaimed prince of Wales 1400: Usk, *Chronicle*, 47; *Historia R. II*, 167; 'Dieulacres Chronicle', *Bull. John Rylands Library*, 14 (1930), 175; *Select Cases in the Court of King's Bench under Richard II, Henry IV and Henry V*, 114.

3. Proposals for negotiations: *PPC*, i. 175 (Nov. 1401); ii. 59–60 (late 1402); Ellis, *Letters*, 24–6; *Giles's Chronicle*, 31; *Cal. Anc. Corr.*, 256; *CSL*, no. 108 (Feb. 1403); petition of burgesses of Holt: D. Pratt, *Denbighshire Hist. Soc.*, 26 (1977), 153–5; cf. *GIG*, no. viii, ll. 7–15; Owain styles himself 'lord of Glyndyfrdwy': Matthews, *Records*, 103–4 (this letter, if genuine, is more likely to belong to 1403 than 1401. Contrast *OG*, 40–1).

4. For significance of 1403: above pp. 111–15 and below p. 273–5.

5. William Gwyn ap Rhys Llwyd: R. R. Davies, *TCS* (1968), pt. II, 158 and n. 35; Maredudd ap Llywelyn Ddu: above p. 139; *DKR*, xxxvi App., 319, 337; Chester 3/23, m. 15; 30/17, m. 6; *Oeuvre poetique de Gutun Owain*, ed Bachellery (1950–1), nos. ix, xxiii.

6. Anti-English sentiments attributed to rebels: *Eulogium Historiarum*, iii. 38 ('et bona Anglicorum undique diripiunt'); *RLH IV*, i. 142; *ANLP*, no. 230, 262.

7. Chamberlain of Chester's comment: SC 6/774/15; support of 'whole Welsh nation': *RLH IV*, i. 142, 148; motives attributed to rebels: *PPC*, ii. 60; *ANLP* no. 256 (prince of Wales); Chester 25/25, m. 1., 30/17, m. 23–23ᵛ.; R. A. Griffiths, *BBCS* 20 (1962–4), 289–90; Welsh atrocities: *Annales H. IV*, 341; anti-Welsh legislation: below pp. 281–8.

8. Owain's protestation: *PPC*, ii. 60; letters to Ireland and Scotland: Usk, *Chronicle* 72–3; his other letters quoted: Matthews, *Records*, 105, 40; anti-English sentiment: above pp. 90–2.

9. Mythology: above pp. 88–91; Great Britain: almost certainly to be contrasted with 'Britannia minor' = Brittany; English use of Brutus legend against Scots in 1401: *Anglo-Scottish Relations 1174–1328: Some Selected Documents*, ed. Stones (revised edn.), 346–55; Scottish historical mythology: Marjorie J. Dexler, in *People, Politics and Community in the Later Middle Ages*, ed. J. Rosenthal and C. F. Richmond, 60–76.

10. Crach Ffinnant: *Select Cases in the court of King's Bench, Richard II–Henry V*, 114; Lloyd, *OG*, 31, n. 5; E 101/39/39; Hopcyn ap Tomas: above p. 55; Ellis, *Letters*, 22–3 (spelling modernized); Tripartite Indenture: below 169–71.

11. Owain's descent: above pp. 129–31; grafting his lineage into the Gwynedd pedigree: *GIG*, no. viii, ll. 45–7; emphasis on Owain as successor of Owain Lawgoch: *Chronique du Religieux de Saint-Denys*, iv. 164; Welsh students in Oxford: R. A. Griffiths, *BBCS* 20 (1962–4), 291.

12. Ideas of national identity: Davies, *T. Royal Hist. Soc.*, 6th ser, 4 (1994), 1–20; statement of 1282: *Registrum epistolarum fratis Johannis Peckham*, ii. 471.

13. National phrases: Usk, *Chronicle*, 72–3; Matthews, *Records*, 23, 40–3, 105; Owain's title: Matthews, *Records*, 23, 42, but cf. 32, 41; use of God's grace as an argument by earlier Welsh princes: J. B. Smith, *Llywelyn ap Gruffudd*, 235–6.

14. Dating formula: Matthews, *Records*, 39, 54; but cf. ibid. 41 (no date); 23 (after thought); 39 (ambiguity: the letter almost certainly belongs to 1405; if so it should be dated in the fifth rather than the sixth year of Owain's principiate).

15. Owain's seals: M. Siddons, *BBCS* 29 (1980–2), 531–44 and 32 (1985), 233–40; id., *The Development of Welsh Heraldry*, i. 285–7.

16. Chancellor: Matthews, *Records*, 32; secretary: *PPC*, i. 304; *CCR* 1408–13, 148; council: *CPR* 1401–5, 155–6, 171; parliaments: Usk, *Chronicle*, 86 (the translation on p. 257 is misleading); *RLH IV*, ii. 76–9.

17. Letter to King of France: Matthews, *Records*, 52.

18. Cantref and commote: *CPR* 1321–4, 98, 136, indicate that the English government had a list of them to hand.

19. Limited Welsh representation in parliament 1322, 1327: J. B. Smith, *WHR* 3 (1966–7), 161–7; community representation in medieval society: S. Reynolds, *Kingdoms and*

Communities in Western Europe 900–1300, in Wales: J. B. Smith, *WHR* 3 (1966–7), 145–71; Davies, *Lordship and Society*, 457–66.

20. Tripartite Indenture: *Giles's Chronicle*, 39–42; Ellis, *Letters*, 27–8; discussion of value of Giles's Chronicle: Kingsford, *English Historical Literature in the Fifteenth Century*, 24–8, 155–7; M. V. Clarke, *Fourteenth-Century Studies*, 78–86.
21. Mortimer and Percy plots: below pp. 180–6.
22. Owain and prophecy: above p. 90–1; Three Realms of Britain: *Trioedd Ynys Prydain*, ed. R. Bromwich, esp. pp. cxxv–vi; River Severn as Wales's boundary: Geoffrey of Monmouth, *Historia Regum Britanniae*, ed. N. Wright, caps. 23, 68, 72, 184; Ranulf Higden, *Polychronicon* (Rolls Series), ii. 32; University of Chicago Ms. 224, fo. 12 (for this Mortimer Chronicle see below p. 178); ash trees of Meigion: *OG* 95 n.; Battle of Meigen: *Trioedd Ynys Prydein*, 151–2.
23. The Pennal Letter: Matthews, *Records*, 40–54.
24. Appointments to Welsh bishoprics in late fourteenth century: Glanmor Williams, *Welsh Church*, 114–45; appropriations: ibid. 164–9; royal chapels: J. H. Denton, *English Royal Free Chapels, 1100–1300*.
25. Proposal for university at Dublin: Rashdall, *The Universities of Europe in the Middle Ages* (1936), ii. 325–6; universities and secular rulers: Cobban, *Universities in the Middle Ages* (1990), 118.
26. Twenty five archbishops of St David's: Giraldus Cambrensis, *Opera*, vi. 102; the augmented archbishopric of St David's: ibid. iii. 229–31.

CHAPTER 7

1. Owain's response to peace initiative: *ANLP*, no. 244.
2. Turning the realm upside-down: R. A. Griffiths, *BBCS* 20 (1962–4), 288; plot to destroy king by oiling his saddle: *Select Cases in the Court of King's Bench, Richard II–Henry V*, 113.
3. Transfer of moneys to rebels in Wales: *Eulogium Historiarum*, iii. 342–3; R. A. Griffiths, *Bull. Institute of Historical Research*, 37 (1964), 77–100; Welsh students in Oxford: R. A. Griffiths, *BBCS* 20 (1962–4), 282–92; rumours in Hertfordshire: *Select Cases in the Court of King's Bench, Richard II–Henry V*, 123–4.
4. Survival of Richard II: R. Nicholson, *Scotland: The Later Middle Ages*, 222; Welsh support for Richard II: Jean Creton, 'Metrical History . . .', *Archaeologia*, 20 (1823), 69, 70, 105; Rhys and Gwilym ap Tudur: above p. 52; principality of Chester: R. R. Davies, in *The Reign of Richard II*, ed. Barron and Du Boulay; Owain's alleged comments on Henry IV and Richard II: Chester 30/17, m. 23–23ᵛ.; Ellis, *Letters*, 24–6; penance on Franciscan friars: *Eulogium Historiarum*, iii. 392–3.
5. Mortimer claim: clearly stated in *The Westminster Chronicle*, ed. B. F. Harvey, 194–5 (all the more important for being written before 1399); general discussion of the claim and the plots in support of it: T. B. Pugh, *Henry V and the Southampton Plot*, 71–87.
6. Exploitation of descent from Gwladus Ddu: Usk, *Chronicle*, 19–20, 22; Mortimer Chronicle: University of Chicago Ms. 224, f. 12ᵛ; description (not fully accurate) of this chronicle: M. E. Giffin, *NLWJ* 7 (1951–2), 316–25.

7. Iolo Goch's poem: *GIG*, no. xx; discussion: Eurys Rowlands, in *Celtic Studies: Essays in Memory of Angus Matheson*, ed. J. Carney and D. Greene; D. Johnston, *Cambridge Medieval Celtic Studies*, 12 (1986), 73–98.

8. Edmund Mortimer's endowment: *CPR 1396–9*, 256, 428; hints as to Edmund's disloyalty: *Annales H. IV*, 341; his marriage: *Historia R. II*, 175; his manifesto: Ellis, *Letters*, 24–6; grants of his land and seizure of his goods (indicating that he was considered to have defected by Oct. 1402): *CPR 1401–5*, 176, 256, 266, 267, 384, 389, 474; F. Devon, *Issues of the Exchequer*, 295.

9. Percies and Henry IV: J. M. W. Bean, *History*, 44 (1959), 212–27; Hotspur's annuity from Roger Mortimer: *CPR 1396–9*, 463; Denbigh and other Mortimer estates granted in custody to Percies: *CFR 1399–1405*, 22, 38–9.

10. Thomas Percy and his base in Wales: *GEC*, XII. ii. 838–42; Griffiths, *Principality*. 122, 125–7, 180; *CPR 1399–1401*, 110 (a consolidated but not complete list of grants made to him); Hotspur's posts and grants in north Wales and Chester: *CPR 1399–1401*, 37, 155, 158; *CFR 1399–1405*, 38–9; *CCR 1339–1402*, 437–8; Sir William Swinburne on Percy service in north Wales: Northumberland RO, ZS W1/112–115 (12 Apr. 1400–12 Aug. 1401); William Lloyd: ibid., 1/113; E. 101/43/9 (*armigerus domini*); SC 6/1185/4 (deputy steward).

11. Capture of Conway Castle: Keith Williams-Jones, *T. Caernarvonshire Hist. Soc. 39* (1978), 7–43; Hotspur's communiqués from Wales: *PPC*, i. 150–3; Welsh appointments of Percies: ibid. 173; *ANLP*, no. 237; *CPR 1401–5*, 53; Thomas Percy's military proposals and activities in Wales: *ANLP*, no. 244; SC 6/1202/17 (Swansea); 1185/4 (Denbigh).

12. Percy complaints about arrears in wages of troops: *PPC*, i. 178–9; resumption of Anglesey: ibid. *CFR 1399–1405*, 142; appointments to constableships: Rhidian Griffiths, *BBCS* 34 (1987), 142; resumption of custody of Mortimer lands: *CFR 1399–1405*, 142.

13. The differences of opinion over the Conway Castle negotiations: *CPR 1399–1401*, 470, 475; *RLH IV*, i. 69–71; Keith Williams-Jones, *T. Caernarvonshire Hist. Soc.*, 39 (1978), 13–15; the 1401 negotiations: *PPC*, i. 175; *ANLP*, nos. 238, 244 (I take all these letters as referring to the same set of negotiations. The earl of Worcester is a more likely candidate as author of *ANLP*, no. 244 than his brother, the earl of Northumberland); 1402 negotiations: *PPC*, ii. 59–60; the 1403 (?) confrontation: *Giles's Chronicle*, 30–2. (The story is also echoed in the manifesto of defiance issued by the Percies in 1403 and recorded in John Hardyng, *Chronicle*, ed. H. Ellis (1812), 351–2.) That negotiations were authorized by Henry IV is made clear by *Cal. Anc. Corr.*, 256 (for date, *CSL*, no. 108).

14. Rumours about Glyn Dŵr and estates in Percy custody: Usk, *Chronicle*, 71.

15. Evidence of passage of messengers, etc.: SC 6/1185/4 (1401–2); E 101/43/9 (1402–3); Northumberland RO, ZSW1/109–16 (Apr. 1400–July 1402); Hotspur's support in Cheshire: P. McNiven, *T. Historic Soc. Lancashire and Cheshire*, 129 (1980), 1–29 and P. J. Morgan, *War and Society in Medieval Cheshire*, 213–18; Percy preparations in Wales: E 101/43/9 (Excerpts from this account are published in Bain, *Cal. Documents re Scotland*, iv. 136. It is clearly a draft or partial account of the receiver of Denbigh for Michaelmas 1402–Michaelmas 1403. *OG*, 50, wrongly attributes it to 1402); R. A. Griffiths, *BBCS* 22 (1966–8), 155–6; increased rebel activity in Wales from mid-June:

above p. 108–9; *OG*, 63–8; possible Glyn Dŵr–Hotspur liaison: J. E. Messham, *Flintshire Hist. Soc. Publications*, 23 (1967–8), 8–15; John Kynaston: Chester 3/23, m. 5; above p. 139 for relationship to Glyn Dŵr; William Lloyd: above p. 181; *CPR* 1401–5, 391.

16. Letter reporting the flight of Lady Despenser: *CSL*, no. 936; Scrope's manifesto: *Annales H. IV*, 405; *Eulogium Historiarum*, iii. 406; *Historians of the Church of York and its Archbishops*, ed. J. Raine, ii. 304; Lewis Byford: *St Albans Chronicle 1406–1420*, ed. V. H. Galbraith, 27; *CCR* 1408–13, 82, 160; *OG*, 115–18, 134.

17. Diplomatic missions: Usk, *Chronicle*, 72–4, 106; Matthews, *Records*, 23–4, 42; R. A. Griffiths, *BBCS* 22 (1966–8), 158–9; KB9/204, m. 22; Dafydd ab Ieuan Goch: Usk, *Chronicle*, 71; letter to Irish chieftains, ibid. 73; 1405 report: *RLH IV*, ii. 78.

18. Welshmen on 1394 expedition: BL Additional Roll 26,595; E 101/402/20, fo. 39^v.; Philip ap Morgan: SC 6/1184/22; Owain's letter to the Irish: Usk, *Chronicle*, 73–4; Scrope's raid: *OG*, 99; A. D. Carr, *Medieval Anglesey*, 320–1.

19. The Welsh as a reminder to the Scots: *Chronicle of Melrose*, ed. A. O. and M. O. Anderson, 156; Walter Bower, *Scotichronicon*, ed. D. E. R. Watt and others, v. 414–15; proposals for a Welsh–Scottish alliance: J. B. Smith, *BBCS* 26 (1974–6), 463–78 and *WHR* 8 (1976–7), 139–71; Merlin's prophecy: Bower, *Scotichronicon*, viii. 110–11, 198 (important note).

20. Scottish raid on Beaumaris: SC 6/1151/2; guard at Caernarfon: SC 6/1214/10–1215/1; taking of Bardsey: *PPC*, i. 152–3.

21. Homildon Hill: A. Grant, *Independence and Nationhood*, 45; the Welsh bishops at Bass Rock: R. Nicholson, *Scotland: The Later Middle Ages*, 226–7; Welsh bishops in Scotland: Bower, *Scotichronicon*, viii. 66–7; Nicholson, *Scotland*, 254; Gruffudd Yonge: D. E. R. Watt, *Fasti Ecclesiae Scoticanae*, 268 (Yonge did not secure possession of the bishopric of Ross and was subsequently transferred to the bishopric of Hippo).

22. Lloyd, *A History of Wales* (1939), ii. 522; R. F. Treharne, *BBCS* 18 (1958–60), 60–75; Carr, *Owen of Wales*.

23. Anglo-French relations in Richard II's reign: J. J. N. Palmer, *England, France and Christendom 1377–99*; vulnerability of Wales and Castilian spies: above p. 85–6.

24. Anglo-French relations and domestic politics 1399–1415: F. Lehoux, *Jean de France, Duc de Berri. Sa vie, son action politique (1340–1416)*.

25. Attacks on Kidwelly and Caernarfon: *RLH IV*, i. 160–2; E 101/43/24, m. 3; *OG*, 77; dispatch of Welsh ambassadors to France: Matthews, *Records*, 23–4.

26. Account of Welsh ambassadors' visit: *Chronique du Religieux de Saint Denys*, iii. 164–7; the Count of La Marche's expedition: Lehoux, *Jean de France*, iii. 18, n. 2, 19, n. 2; Franco-Welsh treaty: Matthews, *Records*, 32–9.

27. Warnings of impending French invasion: *RLH IV*, ii. 282, 368; *PPC*, i. 233; La Marche's aborted voyage: *Chronique du Religieux de Saint Denys*, iii. 222–4; Lehoux, *Jean de France*, iii. 21, n. 4.

28. The Anglesey attack: *RLH IV*, ii. 15 (1405 appears to be a more plausible year than 1404); ship with wine and spices: ibid. 23.

29. The French invasion. English account: *Annales H. IV*, 415 (it is not mentioned in *Eulogium Historiarum*, iii. 405); French account: *Chronique du Religieux de Saint Denys*, iii. 322–8.

30. Pembrokeshire 'deal' with Owain: R. Fenton, *A Historical Tour Through Pembrokeshire* (1810), app , 43–4 (*OG*, 107, is in error in linking the 'deal' with an associated document in *PPC*, i. 279; the latter document belongs to Dec. 1402); reinforcements in 1406: *Annales H. IV*, 419; Welsh representatives in Paris in 1408 and 1415: Lehoux, *Jean de France*, iii. 126; Matthews, *Records*, 110.

CHAPTER 8

1. 'nobles': Matthews, *Records*, 52; Usk, *Chronicle*, 64; 'gentlemen': Ellis, *Letters*, 15; Iscennen: JI1/1152, m. 5ᵛ; Flintshire: Chester 2/76, m. 4, 8; parliamentary response: *Rot. Parl.*, iii. 509.
2. The supporters of Gwilym ap Tudur: Keith Williams-Jones, *T. Caernarvonshire Hist. Soc.*, 39 (1978), 7–43; Gwilym himself: above p. 52.
3. John Kynaston: above p. 139, Table 1; *OG*, 31; NLW Plas Iolyn, 231; Clwyd RO Nerquis Hall, 25 (official posts before 1399); J. E. Messham, *Flintshire Hist. Society*, 23 (1967–8), 10–11; *CPR* 1401–5, 253; Shrewsbury Public Library 7276 (account of Ruyton 1402–3); NLW Bettisfield 1660 (steward of Maelor Saesneg, 1414). Rhys Gethin: SC 6/1202/16. Ieuan ap Jenkin Kemeys: T. B. Pugh (ed.), *The Marcher Lordships of South Wales*, 291–2; *CPR* 1401–5, 438; Gwent RO, Llanarth D583.4; Capel Hanbury JCH 1858 (for father's posts). Rhys Ddu: Griffiths, *Principality*, 272–3; *Cal. Anc. Pets.*, 258 (but date and accompanying note are in error); *OG*, 131; Usk, *Chronicle*, 118.
4. Henry Don: estimates of value of estates: DL 43/15/2, m. 2; DL 42/16, fo. 188ᵛ.; DL 29/731/12018, m. 12, 14; military service: *Cal. Anc. Corr.*, 189, 193 (father); *John of Gaunt's Register 1372–6*, ed. S. Armitage-Smith, no. 922; *CPR* 1391–5, 483; E 101/402/20, fo. 38ᵛ–39ᵛ (Henry himself); steward of Cydweli: DL 29/584/9239; his extortions and punishments: DL 42/16, fos. 59ᵛ, 67ᵛ; DL 29/573/9063 (Carnwyllion), 9065 (Iscennen); *John of Gaunt's Register 1379–83*, eds. E. C. Lodge and R. Somerville, nos. 621, 827; *Cartularium S. Johannis Baptistae de Carmarthen*, ed. T. Phillips, no. 126; SC 6/1165/8, m. 4.
5. Attacks on Kidwelly: JI 1/1153, m. 20ᵛ; *RLH IV*, i. 138, 160; capture of ship: *CPR* 1401–5, 293; the letter from Glyn Dŵr (which no longer survives): Matthews, *Records*, 105–6 (I find it difficult to accept Lloyd's early date for this letter, *OG*, 40–1); forfeiture of lands and punishment: DL 42/16, fo. 188ᵛ; DL 42/17, fos. 17–17ᵛ; *CPR* 1413–16, 29, 44.
6. Cancellation of the fine 1445: SC 6/11168/6, m. 10 (I owe this reference to Professor R. A. Griffiths); accusations against Henry Don after the revolt: JI 1/1153, m. 16–17 (original indictments); JI 1/1152, m. 6ᵛ (enrolment of charges and verdicts); death: DL 42/17, fo. 121ᵛ.
7. Hywel ap Tudur, Rhys and Gwilym ap Tudur; Gruffudd ap Gwilym: above Chap 2; Maredudd ab Owain: Griffiths, *Principality*, 273–4; Maredudd ap Cynwrig: A. D. Carr, *Medieval Anglesey*, 211–12; *RLH IV*, ii. 13; *IGE*, 304–6.
8. Collecting *commortha* in Cydweli: JI 1/1153, m. 6, 20; Rhys Ddu's extortions: Griffiths, *Principality*, 273.
9. Gwilym ap Gruffudd ap Tudur Llwyd: Carr, *Medieval Anglesey*, 174–5, 322–3; his descent: Bartrum, *Welsh Genealogies, sub* Iarddur, 4; service of his forebears to princes of Gwynedd: D. Stephenson, *The Governance of Gwynedd*, 98–100, app. 2.

10. Rhys Ddu and Maredudd ab Owain: above n. 3 and n. 7; Reginald Grey's letter: Ellis, *Letters*, 4 (now re-dated 1410–12; J. B. Smith, *BBCS* 22 (1966–8), 250–60); view of the commons: *Rot. Parl.*, iii. 509.

11. Military careers of Owain Glyn Dŵr and his companions: above pp. 52–3; Bleddyn ap Dafydd ap Madog: A.D. Carr, *Owen of Wales*, 60–2; R. R. Davies, *TCS* (1968), 164–5; Hywel Coetmor: *IGE*, 107; C. Gresham, *Medieval Stone Carving in North Wales*, no. 187 (but the date suggested there is too late).

12. Ieuan and Robert ap Maredudd: Sir John Wynn, *History of the Gwydir Family*, ed. J. Gwynfor Jones, 19, 22; Dafydd ap Hywel Fychan: *CPR 1401–5*, 320–1; the family's role in Brecon is discussed in my unpublished Oxford D. Phil. thesis (1965), 'The Bohun and Lancaster Lordships in Wales in the Fourteenth and Early Fifteenth Centuries', 220–1, 290–2,

13. Maredudd ap Madoc: *CPR 1401–5*, 212; Hanmer and Yonge as Glyn Dŵr's kinsmen: Matthews, *Records*, 23, 25; 'kinsmen and affines' of rebel leader: Chester 24/246 ('de consanguinitate et affinitate Yokus ap Ieuan Du'); commons advocate arrest of kinsmen: *Rot. Parl.*, iii. 509, 666; the precedent of 1345: *Cal. Anc. Corr.*, 234.

14. The Tables are based on the rich deed evidence for north-east Wales in the collections of the National Library of Wales, University College of North Wales, Bangor, and Clwyd RO. They have occasionally been supplemented from the evidence of the genealogical manuscripts tabulated in Bartrum, *Welsh Genealogies A.D. 300–1400*.

15. The Church and the revolt in general: *OG*, chap. 11; Glanmor Williams, *Welsh Church*, chap. 6; Flintshire clerics: Chester 30/17, m. 2v; Anglesey clerics: Glyn Roberts, *BBCS* 15 (1952–4), 39–61.

16. Student support: *Rot. Parl.*, iii. 456–7; Ellis, *Letters*, 8–9; R. A. Griffiths, *BBCS* 20 (1962–4), 282–92; John ap Hywel of Llantarnam: Usk, *Chronicle*, 45, 103; Walter Bower, *Scotichronicon*, viii. 100–109; *OG*, 97; Franciscans of Llan-faes; *CPR 1399–1401*, 418; *Eulogium Historiarum*, iii. 388–9; G. Roberts, *BBCS* 15 (1952–4), 59; *CPR 1413–16*, 234; Hywel Edwere: R. A. Griffiths, *BBCS* 22 (1966–8), 158.

17. Byford: *OG*, 116–18; *CSL*, no. 269; Gruffudd Yonge: A. B. Emden, *A Biographical Register of the University of Oxford to 1500*, iii. 2,134–5; above p. 143.

18. John Trefor: above p. 60 and n. 25; his appointment as chamberlain of Chester: SC 6/774/10; his defection: SC 6/775/3, m. 3.

19. Contemporary observations on popular support: Usk, *Chronicle*, 69; *RLH IV*, i. 140, 142, 148; SC 6/775/1, m. 3; rebellion in Chirk: NLW Chirk Castle D55; evidence for the Lancaster lordships in Wales (Cydweli, Brecon, Ogmore, Monmouth) is based the local accounts and the central valors: DL 29/584/9240–2; 592/9446; 615/9841–2; 728/1191; 729/11993–12003; 730/12009–12015. They are fully analysed and tabulated in R. R. Davies, 'The Bohun and Lancaster Estates', D. Phil. thesis (1965), 266–7, 297–8, 322–5, 409–12.

20. Support in Bishopscastle: *CSL*, no. 119; Flintshire evidence: Chester 3/23, no. 8–3/25, no. 17 (inquisitions); Chester 25/25, m. 2 (communal fines); Anglesey: G. Roberts, *BBCS* 15 (1952–4), 39–61; A. D. Carr, *Medieval Anglesey*, 322–4; SC 6/1233/1.

21. 'Rebellion of the Welsh commons': Chester 30/17, m. 6; Sparrowhawk, Ferrour, and Perrot: *Glam. CH*, iii. 183; Chester 25/25, m. 10; *CPR 1401–5*, 219; R. K. Turvey, *WHR*

15 (1990–1), 161; Morgan ap Dafydd Fychan and John Llwyd: DL 42/15, fo. 90; R. A. Griffiths, in Griffiths (ed.), *Boroughs*, 155, n. 82; William Thorot: Chester 24/245; Philip Skidmore of Troy: Gwent R.O. Monmouth Collection 5145; DL 41/9/8, m. 38; Usk, *Chronicle*, 118; Thomas Huntley, William de la Mare, John Merlawe: *CPR* 1401–5, 328; 1405–8, 112, 219.

22. John Fairford's comment: Ellis, *Letters*, 19–20; 'sworn men of Owain': Chester 24/245; SC 6/774/15, m. 5v.; SC 2/221/4, m. 38v.; 'youngsters and rascals': Lloyd, *OG*, 151; Gruffudd ap Madog Crych: Chester 29/107, m. 17 quoted by Messham, *Flintshire Hist. Soc.*, 23 (1967–8), 17–18; Llywelyn ap Madog ap Llywelyn: SC 2/221/9, m. 1; BL Add. Chart 26, 069; William Gwyn ap Rhys Llwyd: above p. 155.

23. Gruffudd ap Gwilym: above p. 51; A. D. Carr, *WHR* 15 (1990–1), 1–20; the agreement of the communities of upland Brecon (Ystradfellte, Faenor, and Glyntawe): DL 42/15, fo. 182v.; cf. *CPR* 1401–5, 299.

24. Compulsion to join revolt: *CPR* 1408–13, 283 (Adam of Usk), 30 (men of Whittington); Chester 2/76, m. 10 (men of Flint); *CPR* 1401–5, 407; 1405–8, 366–7 (individual examples); the Denbigh man: *CPR* 1405–8, 326; contemporary views of coercion: *ANLP*, no. 227; *RLH IV*, ii. 77; the report of the keeper of Conway Castle: Ellis, *Letters*, 36–7.

25. Tudur ap Gruffudd and the dean of St Asaph: *CPR* 1399–1401, 396, 452; the three Cydweli men (Ieuan Crach ab Ieuan Moel, Gruffudd Iscoed, John ap Hywel): JI 1/1153, m. 20v.; JI 1/1152, m. 7; DL 29/584/9242; men flee to Chester: Chester 2/77, mm. 6–7; cf. Chester 30/17, m. 2 (Maredudd ap Dafydd 'who stayed in England'); David Whitmore and Ieuan ap Maredudd: *RLH IV*, ii. 76–9.

26. Casualties in Carmarthen: Ellis, *Letters*, 14; burning of houses: JI 1/1152, m. 5v.; loss of goods, E. A. Lewis, *The Medieval Boroughs of Snowdonia*, 184 (Caernarfon), 202 (John Collier); *CPR* 1401–5, 293 (Thomas Dyer).

27. Defence of Denbigh: *Cal. Anc. Pets*, no. 5218; SC 6/1185/4; Kidwelly: DL 29/584/9242; Caernarfon: K. Williams-Jones, in Griffiths (ed.), *Boroughs*, 87; E 101/43/24. Repairs to town walls: *CPR* 1401–5, 319 ('foreign English' repair town walls of Kidwelly); DL 42/15 f. 120 (king promises £10 towards repair of walls of Monmouth provided burgesses raise £50); fo. 179v (Brecon burgesses encouraged to spend 100 marks on repair of walls and gate). Thomas Rede: above p. 48; Griffiths, *Principality*, 114, 125; DL 42/16 fo. 63; DL 42/18, fo. 11. Thomas de Walton and John Sely: SC 6/1216/2, m. 8; *CPR* 1401–5, 295.

28. John Bedell: DL 29/633/10317; *CPR* 1401–5, 487; 1408–13, 307; Harvards: *CPR* 1399–1401, 49; 1401–5, 10; DL 42/15, fo. 148v; fo. 179v; DL 42/16 fo. 258v; Mortons: DL 42/15, fo. 98v; DL 42/16 fo. 188v.

29. Maredudd ab Einion of Builth: *CSL*, no. 128; parson of Hanmer and his parishioners: Chester 2/77, m. 1v (23 Nov. 1403); cf. 2/76, m. 11 (6 Sept. 1403); Bleddyn ap Madog Gryg: SC 6/778/3, m. 2v; Iorwerth ab Ithel ab Owen: Chester 25/25, m. 6; Maredudd ab Ieuan Gwyn: Chester 30/17, m. 16.

30. Ieuan and Robert ap Maredudd: Sir John Wynn, *History of the Gwydir Family*, ed. J. Gwynfor Jones, 22; Hywel Sele: Thomas Pennant, *Tours in Wales*, ed. J. Rhys, iii. 310–11; relationships: Ieuan ap Maredudd was son-in-law of Hywel Sele, and Ieuan's son and heir was married to Einion ab Ithel's daughter.

31. Thomas ap David of Brecon: DL 42/15, fo. 32v, fo. 179v; DL 42/16 fos. 116, 220v, 244; Thomas ap David of Skenfrith: DL 42/16, fo. 146; Ieuan ap David ap Richard: Griffiths (ed.), *Boroughs*, 95.

32. Maredudd ap Adda Moel: E 101/44/6; *Montgomeryshire Collections*, 10 (1877), 59–60; Rhirid de Middleton: BL Egerton Roll 8751; E 101/44/6.

33. Einion ab Ithel: DL 42/15, fo. 40v; Sir John Wynn, *History of the Gwydir Family*, 22; Hwlcyn Llwyd: *OG*, 77; Robert ap Rees: *CPR 1405–8*, 112; Rhys ap Thomas ap Dafydd: Griffiths, *Principality*, 143–5; his service in Ireland: E 101/402/20, fo. 38.

34. Early history of Dafydd Gam's family: R. R. Davies, *Lordship and Society*, 255–6; the family after 1399: *CPR 1399–1401*, 37, 45, 76.

35. Grant of confiscated lands to Dafydd Gam: *CPR 1401–5*, 11, 14; DL 42/15, fo. 148v; participation in Battle of Pwll Melyn: Walter Bower, *Scotichronicon*, viii. 97; John ap Harry: Roskell *et al.* (eds.), *History of Parliament: The Commons 1386–1421*, iii, 299–301; the legend of Dafydd Gam at Machynlleth: Thomas Pennant, *Tours*, ed. J. Rhys, iii. 322–4.

36. Annuity for Llywelyn ap Hywel: DL 42/15, fo. 159; royal pardon for same: DL 42/16, fo. 89v; capture and ransom of Dafydd Gam: see below pp 302–3.

37. Dafydd Gam at Agincourt: N. H. Nicolas, *History of the Battle of Agincourt*, 379; 'a great stickler': David Powel, *The History of Wales*, 320.

CHAPTER 9

1. Attacks on Ruthin and Conway: R. Ian Jack, *WHR* 2 (1964–5), 303–22 and K. Williams-Jones, *T. Caernarvonshire Hist. Soc.*, 30 (1978), 7–43, esp. 11; Hywel Gwynedd and Rhys Gethin: Messham, *Flintshire Hist. Soc. Publ.*, 23 (1967–8), 16–17 and *Cat. Mss. Wales in BM*. 25–6; capture of Reginald Grey and the sheriff of Anglesey: *OG*, 49 (and sources cited) and *RLH IV*, ii. 13.

2. Contemporary estimates of Glyn Dŵr's forces: Ellis, *Letters*, 16; *RLH IV*, i. 139, 155–9; *PPC*, i. 248–50; recruitment to his cause: *OG*, 151; *Historia R. II*, 73–4.

3. Military experience of Owain and his lieutenants: above pp. 52–3; co-ordination of effort with French and Scots: Ellis, *Letters*, 33; JI 1/1153, m. 20v.; Carr, *Medieval Anglesey*, 320; naval activities of David Perrot and Henry Don: *PPC*, ii. 83–4; *CPR 1401–5*, 293; Welsh rebels and the summer season: Ellis, *Letters*, 36; Thomas Walsingham's comment on Glyn Dŵr: *Annales H. IV*, 343; the Welsh poem on the River Dee: Dafydd Huw Evans, *T. Denbighshire Hist. Soc.*, 37 (1988), 5–40.

4. Welsh emblems and standards: *ANLP*, no. 226; Usk, *Chronicle*, 71; division of spoils at Carmarthen: Ellis, *Letters*, 16; John Kynaston: Shrewsbury Public Library 7276 (account of bailiff of Ruyton, 1402–3); Rhys Gethin: *Historia R. II*, 173; SC 6/1202/16; Rhys Ddu and Gwilym ap Philip: *RLH IV*, i. 138; Ellis, *Letters*, 15–16; siege of Llanymddyfri and castles of Glamorgan, etc.: *RLH IV*, i. 139; Ellis, *Letters*, 20.

5. Adam of Usk's comment: *Chronicle*, 64; raids in Flintshire and Dyffryn Clwyd: Messham in *Flintshire Hist. Soc. Publ.*, 23 (1967–8), 14–15; SC 2/221/5, m. 16; ambushes of constable of Harlech and sheriff of Anglesey: Ellis, *Letters*, 35–6; *RLH IV*, ii. 13; ransoms of high-status prisoners: *CPR 1401–5*, 155, 171, 231, 331; *CPR 1405–8*, 100, 181;

CCR 1405–9, 20, 27; F. Devon, *Issues of the Exchequer*, 335; ransoms of lesser persons: SC 2/221/5, m. 17; Chester 25/25, m. 3 (at least nine cases).

6. John Fairford's letter: *RLH IV*, i. 142; the attack on Kidwelly: ibid. i. 161; raids on Anglesey: Ellis, *Letters*, 35.

7. Treaties: Ellis, *Letters*, 16 (Dinefwr); *CPR* 1405–8, 65 (Dore Abbey); *RLH IV*, i. 155 (Herefordshire); *PPC*, i. 236 (Shropshire and Powys); SC 2/221/9, m. 3v; 221/10, m. 13 (Dyffryn Clwyd): G. Owen, *The Description of Penbrokshire*, ed. H. Owen, ii. 483–4 (Pembrokeshire); *CCR* 1409–13, 15 (March); Chester 25/25, m. 7 (Moldsdale).

8. Want of victuals: *CPR* 1401–5, 280; *PPC*, ii. 70–1; *RLH IV*, ii. 16–17 (Anglesey); economic blockade: below p. 256 and Rhidian Griffiths, *BBCS* 34 (1987), 172.

9. Siege of Caernarfon: Ellis, *Letters*, 33–6; Irish comparison: R. Frame, in J. Lydon, *The English in Medieval Ireland*, 118–41.

10. Major contributions to the military history of the revolt: Rhidian Griffiths, *BBCS* 32 (1985), 202–16; 34 (1987), 165–74, and in *Profit, Piety and Professions in later Medieval England*, ed. M. A. Hicks, 51–61. The rest of this chapter is much indebted to these studies.

11. Henry IV's expeditions: *OG*, 32–5, 42–4, 54–5, 72–5.

12. Henry IV's intentions: *CCR* 1399–1402, 587; Adam of Usk's comments on the expeditions: *Chronicle* 70–1, 78; Richard Kingston's message: *RLH IV*, i. 157–8.

13. The Brut's comment: *The Brut, or the Chronicles of England*, ed. F. W. D. Brie, ii. 363; 'the noble and wise King Edward': *Rot. Parl.*, iii. 476, cf. 457.

14. Appointment of Thomas Percy: *PPC*, i. 173.

15. Military commands 1402: *CPR* 1401–5, 53, 122, 139; DL 42/15, fo. 130v.

16. Earl of Somerset's report: *PPC*, i. 217–18; duke of York's plea: ibid. 270–4; 1403 military plans: *CPR* 1401–4, 26; E 404/18/300; subsequent military arrangements: *CPR* 1405–8, 285 (Burnell, 10 Aug.); 311 (Audley, 24 Oct.); 438 (Arundel, Burnell, and Charlton, 14 Oct.); 298 (Somerset, 29 Sept.); 311 (York, 15 Oct.).

17. Earl of Warwick's proposal: *ANLP*, no. 244 (Thomas Percy is more likely than Henry Percy to be the author of this letter. The references to Welshpool might suggest that the letter was written between 19 Oct. 1401 (when John Charlton died) and 26 Nov. 1401 (when Edward Charlton was given seisin of the lordship). The identifications of Caernarfon and Harlech are tentative since only the initial letter for each is given); earl of Worcester and the castles of Swansea and Beaumaris: SC 6/1202/17; SC 6/1185/4; earl of Arundel's letter: *PPC*, i. 246–7.

18. Prince Henry in Wales: Rhidian Griffiths in n. 10 (refs. above); T. B. Pugh, *Henry V and the Southampton Plot*, 42–3; Christopher Allmand, *Henry V*, chap. 2.

19. Biographies of major figures in next few paragraphs: *DNB*; *GEC*; Roskell *et al.* (eds.), *History of Parliament: The Commons 1386–1421*; Griffiths, *Principality*; duke of York's letters: *PPC*, i. 271–3; *ANLP*, no. 293; earl of Warwick: *PPC*, i. 230–1; *CSL* no. 168; BL Egerton Roll, 8770 (account of receiver-general of the earl, 1402–3).

20. Richard, Lord Grey of Codnor: *Rot. Parl.*, iii. 577; *CSL*, no. 453; *PPC*, i. 251–2; Gilbert Talbot: F. Devon, *Issues of the Exchequer*, 302; his career at the end of the revolt: SC 6/775/7, m. 2; SC 6/1216/2; *CPR* 1413–16, 342, 404; *CPR* 1416–22, 89.

21. Sir John Greyndour: Griffiths, *Principality*, 233–5; Roskell *et al.* (eds.), *History of Parliament*, iii. 243–6; his account at Radnor: E 101/43/11; his retinue 1403: E 101/404/24, fo. 9v.

22. The relief of Harlech: E 101/404/24, fos. 11–13v; report of the sheriff of Hereford: *RLH IV*, i. 146–7; Coety Castle: *CPR 1401–4*, 475; *CCR 1402–5*, 478–9; *Annales H. IV*, 414; *Eulogium*, 408.

23. Border garrisons: E 101/44/3, 6; Rhidian Griffiths, *BBCS* 34 (1987), 70–1; accounts of destruction in Shropshire and Herefordshire: Shrewsbury Public Library, 5319–20, 5788, 7276 (account of Arundel manors in western Shropshire); *PPC*, i. 229–32; truces: *PPC*, i. 236–7; the court at Halton: DL 30/3/42, m. 14v (I owe this reference to Philip Morgan); expeditions from Chester: SC 6/775/1, m. 4; SC 6/775/5, m. 2v; the complaint of the men of Shrewsbury: *Rot. Parl.*, iii. 618.

24. Prince of Wales' letter: Ellis, *Letters*, 11–13 (accepting Lloyd's re-dating *OG*, 61); sheriff of Hereford's letter: *PPC*, i. 235, cf. *ANLP*, no. 293; the pillaging of Glamorgan by English raiding parties: Usk, *Chronicle*, 84; *Calendar of Inquisitions Miscellaneous 1399–1422*, no. 273.

25. Contents of Harlech Castle: Chester 2/76, m. 12v; repairs at Kidwelly: DL 29/584/9241; DL 42/15, fo. 119v; DL 41/9/8, mm. 39–52; repairs at Denbigh: SC 6/1185/4; E 101/43/9; repairs at Newport: A. C. Reeves, *Newport Lordship 1317–1536*, 139.

26. Mills at Conway and Beaumaris castles: SC 6/774/15, m. 2d.; SC 6/775/3, m. 2v; Richard Grey's commission: *CPR 1401–5*, 122; DL 42/15, fo. 130v; E 403/585, m. 4; duke of York's commission: BL Campbell Charters XXV, 13; governmental powers given to castle commanders, e.g. John Greyndour at Radnor and Monmouth: E 101/43/11; DL 25/3482.

27. Discussion of castles and garrisons is based on: E 101/43/8–39; E 101/44/3–14; see also Rhidian Griffiths, *BBCS* 34 (1987), 165–73; report from Dinefwr: Ellis, *Letters*, 15; Caernarfon in 1404: Ellis, *Letters*, 33–4; E 101/43/24, 35, 39.

28. The Brecon garrison 1403–4: E 364/40, m. 4.

29. The cost of the Carmarthen garrison: E 101/43/13; the royal council's estimate of the cost of sixteen castles: *PPC*, ii. 68; the blueprint for the 1405 attack: *CPR 1405–8*, 6; *PPC*, i. 251–3.

30. Military supplies for Brecon: DL 42/15, fo. 180v; DL 28/4/3, fo. 15v; guns for Harlech: SC 6/774/14, m. 4v; the preparations for the siege of Aberystwyth: F. Devon, *Issues of the Exchequer*, 314; *PPC*, ii. 339; SC 6/1222/10; J. H. Wylie, *History of England Under Henry IV*, iii, 107

31. Siege and fall of Aberystwyth and Harlech: *OG*, 130–6; Rhidian Griffiths, *BBCS* 32 (1985), 211; SC 6/1216/2.

32. Relief troops from Bristol, Devon, and Somerset: BL Campbell Charters, XXV, 13; *CPR 1401–5*, 439; the commission for John Stevens of Bristol: *PPC*, i. 221.

33. Naval forces from Chester: SC 6/774/15, m. 1v (1403); SC 6/775/5, mm. 1v–2v (1406); the expedition of Stephen Scrope: A. D. Carr, *Medieval Anglesey*, 320–1.

34. Raids from Conway Castle on the surrounding countryside: E 101/43/24, m. 6; the capture and ransom of John Horn: *PPC*, ii. 139; provisions for Carmarthen 1404: E 101/43/37.

35. Comments of Sir Thomas Carew and the prince of Wales: *CPR* 1401–5, 280; *CCR* 1402–5, 72; earlier observations on the economic vulnerability of Wales: R. R. Davies, *Domination and Conquest* (1991), 8; prohibition on trade with the Welsh: Rhidian Griffiths, *BBCS* 34 (1987), 172; *CPR* 1399–1402, 512; *CCR* 1402–5, 179; Chester 2/76, mm. 7, 8v; 77, mm. 4, 8v, etc.; licences for specified quotas of food: Chester 2/76, mm. 10v, 12v, etc.; confiscation of goods being sent to rebels: SC 6/775/6.

36. Non-cooperation of the officers of Monmouth with Richard Grey: *PPC*, i. 279 (these petitions should be dated Dec. 1402, as the evidence of DL 41/9/8, m. 27 shows); Grey's comments on the men of Pembroke: *PPC*, i. 278; difficulties in chasing rebels across lordship boundries: *ANLP*, no. 257; Ellis, *Letters*, 3–4; attempt to co-ordinate royal expenditure in Wales: *PPC*, i. 265–6.

37. Henry IV's indebtedness: K. B. McFarlane, *Lancastrian Kings and Lollard Knights*, chap. 5; A. B. Steel, *The Receipt of the Exchequer 1377–1485*, chaps. 2–3; G. L. Harriss, *Cardinal Beaufort*, chaps. 1–2.

38. Gross annual income of the six royal shires according to 1404 valor: Rhidian Grifiths, *BBCS* 32 (1985), 205; income from Lancaster and Bohun estates in 1400: DL 29/728/11991; calculations of values of Welsh Marcher lordships: R. R. Davies, *Lordship and Society*, chap. 8; Henry IV's personal and national revenue: K. B. McFarlane, *Lancastrian Kings and Lollard Knights*, 94–5.

39. Financing of the Welsh war: on all aspects of this question I am deeply indebted to Rhidian Griffiths, *BBCS* 32 (1985), 202–15; prince to meet costs of recapture of Conway Castle: *RLH IV*, i. 72; towns to meet costs of repairs and garrisons: DL 42/15, fos. 120, 130[v], 179[v]; Commons disclaim responsibility for financing the Welsh wars: *Rot. Parl.*, iii. 610; suggestion as to how moneys to meet the expenditure should be found: *ANLP*, no. 209; *Rot. Parl.*, iii. 433, 441–2, 502, 569.

40. Adam of Usk's comment: *Chronicle*, 85–6; cost of garrisons in eight castles, 1400: *PPC*, ii. 64; Cheshire revenue diverted to Wales: A. Curry, *T. Hist. Soc. Lancashire and Cheshire*, 128 (1978), 113–38; estimate of moneys paid from royal exchequer to prince of Wales for war expenses in Wales: Rhidian Griffiths, *BBCS* 32 (1985), 213; cost of Radnor garrison 1402–5: E 101/43/11.

41. Cost of Edward I's campaigns in Wales: M. Prestwich, *Edward I*, 182, 200.

42. Prince's letter of 30 May 1403: *PPC*, ii. 62–3; royal echo of such letters: *CSL*, no. 176–7; reports of low morale among troops: *PPC*, i. 235, 270–4, 277–9; the lesson learnt by Henry V: Rhidian Griffiths, *BBCS*, 32 (1985), 213.

43. Richard Grey's commission for Radnor: *CPR* 1401–5, 483.

CHAPTER 10

1. *Levitas cervicosa:* R. R. Davies, *WHR* 12 (1984–5), 169; 'a people of mean reputation': *PPC*, i. 134; 'a good result' (*bon fin et brief*): ibid. 207; early offers of pardon: *CPR* 1399–1401, 392 (30 Nov. 1400); Northumberland RO, Swinburne (Capheaton) 1/111 (20 Dec. 1400); pardons to communities: *CPR* 1401–5, 22, 24 (Dec. 1401); negotiations with

Glyn Dŵr: above pp. 183–4; grants of confiscated rebel lands to Welshmen: *CPR* 1401–5, 14, 20, 22, etc.; Adam of Usk's comment: *Chronicle*, 61.

2. Sessions 1401–2 and revenue levels: above pp. 109–10; 'in a most submissive mood': *PPC*, i. 150–1; dismissal of justiciar; *CPR* 1399–1401, 538; income and expenditure on Duchy of Lancaster estates in Wales: DL 29/729/11998, 12000.

3. List of letters addressed to the prince of Wales, July–Sept. 1401: E 101/320/28; the letters of July 1403: Ellis, *Letters*, 14–23; *RLH IV*, i. 138–51; letters dispatched from Denbigh: SC 6/1185/4.

4. Spies: E 101/320/28 (the Traeth Mawr referred to is likely to have been the estuary near modern-day Porthmadog); SC 6/1202/17 (Gower); E 101/43/13 (Carmarthen).

5. 'No go' areas: Chester 24/245 (Glyndyfrdwy, 'Snowdon hills'); Chester 24/246 (Dolwyddelan); Chester 25/25, mm. 4ᵛ, 6ᵛ (Nantconwy; beyond Conwy); earl Marshal at Chepstow 1403–4; BL Additional Roll 16,556; Adam of Usk on Denbigh and other Mortimer lordships: *Chronicle*, 71.

6. Dyffryn Clwyd: R. Ian Jack, *WHR*, 2 (1964–5), 303–22; the letters from Bryncyffo: J. B. Smith, *BBCS* 22 (1966–8), 250–60; the court rolls of the revolt period: SC 2/221/2, 4.

7. Lease of Maesmynan: SC 2/221/5, m. 10; defendant's pleas that they were rebels: SC 2/221/5, mm. 6, 13, 16, 16ᵛ; 221/8, m. 27; 221/9, m. 3ᵛ; 221/10, m. 4ᵛ.

8. Contemporary view of holding of courts as an indicator of civilian rule: DL 42/15, f. 182; court profits; e.g. those of the commote of Coelion (Dyffryn Clwyd) in 1402–3 were only £4 13s. 4 compared with £15 10s. 6d. in 1390–1; evidence from Dyffryn Clwyd: SC 2/221/2, 4.

9. Leases of mills and churches in Cydweli: DL 42/16, fo. 26ᵛ (Dec. 1402); JI 1/1152, m. 7 (Sept. 1404); Adam of Usk's comment on Caernarfonshire and Merionethshire: *Chronicle*, 71; parliaments: above pp. 163–6; ecclesiastical administration: *OG*, 91; Henry Don: above pp. 200–1; Thomas Barneby: R. A. Griffiths, *BBCS* 22 (1966–8), 151–68.

10. The major sources for the history of Kidwelly during the period of the revolt are as follows: DL 42/15–16 (register of Duchy of Lancaster central correspondence, Henry IV); DL 29/584/9240–2 (the accounts of the receiver of Kidwelly, 1399–1400, 1400–1, 1404–7); DL 41/9/8 (a file of fifty-five writs relating to the accounts of the receiver of Kidwelly 1402–3); DL 29/729/11193–4, 11998, 12000; 730/12010, 12013, 12015 (valors of the auditors of the Duchy of Lancaster estates 1400–10); JI 1/1152–3 (assize roll of a judicial sessions held at Kidwelly 1413). Individual references will not be given below.

11. Kidwelly: D. D. Jones, *A History of Kidwelly* (1908); J. R. Kenyon, *Kidwelly Castle* (CADW Guide, 1986); W. H. Morris, *Carmarthen Antiquary*, 3 (1959), 4–16.

12. The ordinances of 6 Oct. 1401: DL 41/10/49.

13. Evidence of commercial and agricultural life in Kidwelly and its hinterland: DL 29/573/9063; NLW Muddlescombe Deeds; JI 1/1152, m. 6ᵛ.

14. Significance of Easter 1403: DL 42/15, fo. 194ᵛ; the letters: *RLH IV*, i. 138–51; Ellis, *Letters*, 14–23.

15. Repair of walls: *CPR* 1401–4, 319; John Don: ibid.; the assault of 13 Aug. 1403: JI 1/1153, m. 20; details of siege: DL 29/584/9242; *RLH IV*, i. 160–2.

16. Emergency measures and supplies for the castle: DL 29/584/9242; dispatch of cargo of arms: DL 28/4/3, fo. 15; DL 42/15, fo. 181; town court Dec. 1403: JI 1/1153, m. 3.

17. The attack of 20 Aug. 1404: JI 1/1152, m. 5^v; the rising of Aug. 1406: JI 1/1153, m. 20; garrison details: DL 29/584/9242; supplies by ship: CPR 1401–5, 486, 502.

18. Comments on damage in Kidwelly: DL 42/15, fo. 194^v; DL 42/16, fos. 89^v, 203.

19. Resumption of normal life in Kidwelly: details from DL 29/584/9242.

20. Garrison to be composed of English soldiers: DL 42/16, fo. 40; charter of 1443: DL 37/11, mm. 2^v–3.

21. John Leland: *The Itinerary in Wales*, 10, 41; Sir John Wynn: *History of the Gwydir Family*, ed. J. Gwynfor Jones, 51; government survey of 1620: quoted in A. N. Palmer and E. Owen, *A History of Ancient Tenures of Land in North Wales and the Marches*, 207.

22. Carmarthen: R. A. Griffiths, in id. (ed.), *Boroughs*, 154–5; Flintshire towns: SC 6/1191/3; Messham, *Flintshire Hist. Soc. Pubs.*, 23 (1967–8), 16; Llan-faes friary: CPR 1399–1401; 418; A. D. Carr, *Medieval Anglesey*, 318; Strata Florida: Adam of Usk, *Chronicle*, 70; *Historia R.* II, 170; CPR 1401–5, 61; PPC, ii. 146.

23. Tenants of Monmouth and Skenfrith: DL 42/16, fos. 157^v, 196^v–197; report of the officials of Bromfield and Yale: ANLP, no. 308; Thomas Dyer: CPR 1401–5, 295.

24. 'Havoc': ANLP, no. 38; Prince Henry's raid: Ellis, *Letters*, 11–12; destruction of Llanrwst by royal army: SC 6/1185/4.

25. General evidence on destructiveness of revolt: W. Rees, *South Wales and the March 1284–1415*, 273–80; the value of Glamorgan: CCR 1405–9, 367; T. B. Pugh, in *Glam. CH*, iii. 185; Shrewsbury: *Rot. Parl.*, iii. 618–19; Chester: *Historical Mss. Commission*, 8th Report, app. I, 359.

26. David Powel: *The Historie of Cambria* (1584), 391 George Owen: *The Description of Penbrokshire*, iii. 35–7.

27. 'noble and wise King Edward I': *Rot. Parl.*, iii. 476; ordinances of 1295: *Record of Caernarvon*, ed. H. Ellis, 131–2.

28. Divisions between English and Welsh: above pp. 65–70.

29. Hope charter: CPR 1396–9; 484–5; Roger ab Iorwerth: Chester 38/25, no. 3, m. 115.

30. Ethnic divisions and perception in Britain and Ireland: J. Gillingham, *J. Hist. Sociology*, 5 (1992), 392–409; R. R. Davies, *Domination and Conquest*; Robin Frame, *Colonial Ireland 1169–1369*, 105–10, 130–5; Art Cosgrove, *Late Medieval Ireland, 1370–1541*, 72–81.

31. Denizens and aliens: R. A. Griffiths, in J. G. Rowe (ed.), *Aspects of Late Medieval Government and Society* (1986) 83–105.

32. Adam of Usk's comment: *Chronicle*, 60.

33. The anti-Welsh statutes: *Statutes of the Realm*, ii. 128–9, 140–1; Ivor Bowen (ed.), *The Statutes of Wales*, 31–7; ordinances of 22 Mar. 1401: CPR 1399–1401, 469–70; prince of Wales's Chester ordinances 14 June 1401: *Record of Carnarvon*, 240 (final five clauses).

34. The petitions of the Commons: *Rot. Parl.*, iii. 457, 474, 476, 486, 502, 508–9, 528, 549, 554, 568, 615–7, 624–5, 663.

35. 'War between the English and the Welsh': SC 6/775/1; equation of Welshmen and rebels, English and loyalists: Chester 30/17, mm. 15–16; English officers to be expelled from Wales: ANLP, no. 230; destruction of English language: Chester 30/17, m. 22.

36. Edward I as mythic figure: *Rot. Parl.*, iii. 476, 509; attack on Marcher lords: ibid. 610, 624–5.

37. Legal and judicial practices in the March: R. R. Davies, *Lordship and Society*, chap. 11.

38. Hotspur's embarrassment: *PPC*, i. 149; Welshmen on garrison duty at Montgomery: E 101/44/6; 'English born' garrisons: DL 42/15, fos. 130ᵛ. 170ᵛ; DL 42/16, fo. 40; Oswestry charter: BL Harleian Ms. 1981, fo. 34.

39. Anti-Welsh measures in Chester: Chester 2/76, m. 11.

40. Charter of Welshpool: *Montgomeryshire Collections*, 7 (1874), 343–6; Kidwelly and Brecon decrees: DL 42/16, fos. 95ᵛ, 252ᵛ; Denbigh: Chester 2/78, m. 6; Gruffudd ap Llywelyn's dagger: DL 42/16, fo. 95ᵛ.

41. Commons petition: *Cal. Anc. Pets.*, 328–9.

CHAPTER 11

1. Submission by Anglesey: Glyn Roberts, *BBCS* 15 (1952–4), 39–61 and Tomos Roberts, *BBCS* 38 (1991), 129–33; surrenders to Sir Gilbert Talbot: Chester 25/25, m. 2; SC 6/1185/12; SC 6/775/7; significance of capture of Aberystwyth: *CPR* 1405–8, 362; besieging force at Harlech: F. Devon (ed.), *Issues of the Exchequer*; pardon of Maredudd ab Owain: *CPR* 1416–22, 431.

2. Pardon by Lord Charlton: *CPR* 1405–8, 376; the delay between submission and pardon in Flintshire: Chester 24/245 (unsorted); Chester 30/17, m. 1; Shrewsbury Public Library Deeds, no. 175 (Robin ap Gruffudd and his brothers, Rhys and Ednyfed, and Gruffudd ap Bleddyn ap Gwilym).

3. Negotiations at Usk and Caerleon: *CPR* 1405–8, 64–5; appointments and letting of lands in Denbigh: *CPR* 1405–8, 5, 7–8, 10; chronology of submissions: DL 29/584/9242 (Carnwyllion); Glyn Roberts, *BBCS* 15 (1952–4), 39–61 (Anglesey); Chester 25/25, m. 2 (Denbigh, Dyffryn Clwyd, Flint); *CPR* 1405–8, 203, 320, 325, 356, 365; *CPR* 1408–13, 166–7 (other regions of Wales); W. Rees, *An Historical Atlas of Wales*, plate 51.

4. Grosmont, Skenfrith, Whitecastle: DL 29/615/9842; R. R. Davies, 'The Bohun and Lancaster Lordships in Wales in the 14th and early 15th centuries' (University of Oxford, D.Phil. thesis), 322–4; revenue from North Wales: SC 6/1216/2; slowness of recovery in Newport: SC 6/924/19.

5. Military setbacks for Glyn Dŵr 1405–6: above pp. 121–4; military measures in north-west Wales 1406–7: SC 6/1216/2.

6. Surrender at Chester: Chester 2/78, 79; Chester 24/245; BL Harleian Ms. 2074, fo. 97ᵛ; Gwilym ap Gruffudd ap Gwilym: above p. 119, below pp. 314–16.

7. Hywel ap Tudur ab Ithel: above pp. 50–1; Chester 2/79, m. 4; his lands valued at £30: Chester 25/25, m. 1; conditional submission by Llywelyn ap Gruffudd Penbras: Chester 2/79, m. 3; his fine of 66s. 8d.: SC 6/775/8.

8. Government disquiet: *CCR* 1405–9, 453–4; letters of Reginald Grey and Gruffudd ap Dafydd: J. B. Smith, *BBCS* 22 (1966–8), 250–60; dating of the letters to 1411 confirmed by the fact that the earl of Arundel received an aid from the men of Chirk for his expedition that year: NLW Chirk Castle, D. 76; accusations of late negotiations with

Glyn Dŵr: Chester 25/25, m. 7 (Ithel ap Llywelyn Chwith of Moldsdale); J. B. Smith, *BBCS* 22 (1966–8), 252–3 (John Wele, steward of Oswestry); Henry Don after the revolt: JI 1/1152–3; cf. below pp. 313–14.

9. Sessions of Gilbert Talbot: SC 6/775/7–8; SC 6/1185/12 (evidence from Denbigh); of Edward, duke of York: SC 6/1222/10; on Duchy of Lancaster estates in Wales: DL 29/730/12015, m. 16.

10. Resumption of emblems of authority: SC 6/1185/12 (Denbigh): DL 29/584/9242 (Cydweli); SC 6/1216/2, m. 9 (North Wales); DL 29/730/12015, m. 16; DL 42/16, fo. 59ᵛ (Brecon).

11. Collapse of seignorial revenue: R. R. Davies, D.Phil. thesis (n. 4 above), 324–5; NLW Chirk Castle, D51, D57; SC 6/1234/9 (Chirkland); G. A. Holmes, *The Estates of the Higher Nobility in Fourteenth-Century England*, 160 (Denbigh); W. Rees, *South Wales and the March 1284–1415*, 273–80 (South Wales).

12. Recalcitrance: northern Cardiganshire: SC 6/1222/11–12; W. Rees, *South Wales and the March*, 273–4; Merionethshire: SC 6/1222/13; J. B. Smith, *BBCS* 22 (1966–8), 254, 259; *CPR 1416–22*, 294.

13. Threats of resurgence of rebel activity in Wales: *CCR 1405–9*, 453–4 (1409); Chester 2/82, m. 5 (1410); *PPC*, i. 338–9; ii. 14, 18 (naval and military measures, 1410); SC 6/1222/10, 12 (garrisons at Aberystwyth and Cardigan, 1411); *PPC*, ii. 35, 38 (men posted at Cymer and Bala, 1412); seeking information about Glyn Dŵr's plans, 1413: F. Devon (ed.), *Issues of the Exchequer*, 332; fear of Welsh involvement with Sir John Oldcastle: H. G. Richardson, *English Historical Review* 55 (1940), 432–8; J. B. Smith, *BBCS* 22 (1966–8), 254–5; precautionary measures in 1414–15: SC 6/1222/13–14; fear of Scots: Smith, *BBCS* 22, 255–9 (I assume that John Salghall's letter, ibid. 259, refers to Barmouth rather than Mawddwy).

14. Murder, kidnappings, and ransoms in north-east Wales: Chester 25/25, mm. 3–8; gang of bandits in Carmarthen: SC 6/1222/12; pledges in Dyffryn Clwyd not to support Owain 1412–14: SC 2/221/8, m. 7; 221/9, m. 13.

15. Dafydd Gam and his family: above pp. 225–7; rewards and compensation for the family: DL 42/15, fo. 139; DL 42/16, fos. 55ᵛ, 59, 62, 84; the pardon of May 1411 for Llywelyn ap Hywel: DL 42/16, fos. 89–89ᵛ.

16. The capture of Dafydd Gam: *St. Alban's Chronicle 1406–20*, ed. V. H. Galbraith, 61, 67; *CPR 1408–13*, 406; ransom and release: DL 42/16, fo. 115ᵛ; DL 42/17, fos. 80ᵛ–81.

17. Contingency clause in Flintshire deed: BL Additional Charter 73,819 (1423); expenditure on castles: SC 6/1222/10 (Carmarthen, Cardigan, Dinefwr); DL 42/16, fo. 78ᵛ; DL 42/17, fo. 75; DL 29/731/12016–8 (Monmouth); figures for Kidwelly and Carreg Cennen have been calculated from the outstanding series of Duchy of Lancaster valors for the years 1409–21: DL 29/730/12013–732/12031. The valor for 1418 (DL 29/734/12047) has been wrongly ascribed to Henry VI's reign in PRO, *Lists and Indexes* V (i). 89.

18. Examples of personal pardons: Sir John Wynn, *History of the Gwydir Family*, 20–1; Clwyd Record Office, Galltfaenan Collection, no. 1352; Shrewsbury Public Library, Deeds, no. 175; Dafydd Llwyd's pardon and the fine for it: NLW Chirk Castle, 9877;

Chester 30/17, m. 1; his lands; Chester 3/23, nos. 9, 15, 16; communal fine for men of Dyffryn Clwyd: SC 6/775/7. Fines to recover land: comment of Fitzalan officers: *ANLP*, no. 308; Carmarthenshire communal fine; SC 6/1222/12; individual fine of £20: DL 42/16, fo. 260; forfeiture of lands of rebels who died before paying their fines: Chester 3/23, no. 8 (Deicws ap Madog ap Bleddyn).

19. John Hanmer's capture and fine: Chester 3/24, no. 23 (correcting *OG*, 98, n. 3); SC 6/775/12, m. 2; 14, m. 2; Henry Don and his fine: *CPR 1413–16*, 29, 44; DL 42/17, fos. 71–71ᵛ; SC 6/1222/3; SC 6/1168/6, m. 1ᵛ (a reference which I owe to Professor Ralph Griffiths); fines for pledges of hostages of Aberystwyth: SC 6/1222/10–14.

20. Details of fines from Carmarthenshire: SC 6/1222/10–12.

21. Anglesey: Glyn Roberts, *BBCS* 15 (1952–4), 39–60; SC 6/1216/2 (which refers to fines and redemptions from Anglesey totalling £601); Flintshire: Chester 25/24, m. 2; earlier valuation of the county: SC 11/862.

22. Other recorded communal fines include the following: 500 marks from Abergavenny (*CPR 1405–8*, 365); £687 from Denbigh, £120 from Dyffryn Clwyd, £133 from Moldsdale (SC 6/775/7); £500 from Glamorgan (E 401/641 *sub* 14 June 1407); £1,000 from Caernarfonshire, £1,333 from Cardiganshire (SC 6/1216/2; 1222/10–12); fate of John Llwyd: Griffiths, *Principality*, 292; SC 6/1222/11, m. 5; extortions of Thomas Barneby: R. A. Griffiths, *BBCS* 22 (1966–8), 162; Owain ap Jankyn: SC 6/1222/12.

23. Henry V's policies in Wales in 1413. Commission to earl of Arundel (Mar.): R. A. Griffiths, *BBCS* 22 (1966–8), 152; general pardon (Apr.): *CCR 1413–19*, 67; pardon for Henry Don (May): *CPR 1413–16*, 26, 44; investigation into official misdemeanours (July): ibid. 112, 114; pardon to North Wales (Nov.): ibid. 137; purchase of cows and sheep: Griffiths, *BBCS* 22, 153.

24. Henry V's general policy on law and order, with reference to the Welsh evidence: E. Powell, *Kingship, Law and Society: Criminal Justice in the Reign of Henry V*; commissions for sessions in Wales: *CPR 1413–16*, 112–14, 179.

25. Fines and gifts on Duchy of Lancaster estates in Wales, Sept. 1413: JI 1/1152, mm. 8v–9v; DL 25/1661; DL 29/584/9243; collective fine on counties of North Wales and Flintshire: *CPR 1413–16*, 137; sessions of earl of Arundel and fines thereat: KB9/204, nos. 25–6; *CPR 1413–16*, 195, corrected in the light of figures in SC 6/1216/3.

26. Fine on counties of Cardigan and Carmarthen 1415: *Cal. Anc. Pets.*, nos. 7489, 7491; *CPR 1413–4*, 380, 405; subsidies towards Henry V's war efforts: SC 6/1216/3; 1223/1.

27. Henry V's financial policies: G. L. Harriss in id. (ed.), *Henry V: The Practice of Kingship*, 15–16, 159–79; income from North Wales, 1418: SC 6/1216/3; income collection on Duchy of Lancaster estates in Wales 1413–20: R. R. Davies, *Economic History Review*, 2nd ser., 21 (1968), 211–29; Adam of Usk's comment: *Chronicle*, 133, 320.

28. Figures on casualties: R. A. Griffiths in id. (ed.), *Boroughs* 154–5; A. D. Carr, *Medieval Anglesey*, 324; Llywelyn ap Gruffudd Fychan: Usk, *Chronicle*, 70; Griffiths, *Principality*, 360; Prince Henry executes rebels: Ellis, *Letters*, 11–13; executions of *c.* 1409: Usk, *Chronicle*, 118; Welsh annals in *OG*, 153–4; Philip Scudamore: DL 41/9/8, m. 38 (contract to defend Carreg Cennen Castle); Gwilym ap Gruffudd ap Tudur Llwyd: above p.204 SC 6/1233/1, m. 2; William Gwyn ap Rhys Llwyd: JI 1/1152, m. 5v;

imprisonment of rebels: *CPR* 1408–13, 284; SC 6/1222/10; E 403/602 *sub* 3 Oct.; *OG*, 98, 137.

29. Henry Gwyn and his son: *CPR* 1413–16, 395; John Hanmer's plight: SC 6/775/2; the fate of Rhys, Gwilym, and Maredudd ap Tudur: Glyn Roberts, *Aspects of Welsh History*, 200–4, 254–8; A. D. Carr, *Medieval Anglesey*, 204–5.

30. Rhys ap Gruffudd: Griffiths, *Principality*, 264; Rhys ap Madog Fychan: A. D. Carr, *T. Caernarvonshire Hist. Soc.*, 38 (1977), 7–32.

31. Maredudd ap Cynwrig: A. D. Carr, *Medieval Anglesey*, 211–12; family of Ieuan ap Jenkin Kemeys: T. B. Pugh (ed.), *The Marcher Lordships of South Wales 1415–1536*, 291–3; John Kynaston: NLW Plas Iolyn 192; UCNW Bodrhyddan, 1234; Maredudd ab Owain: Griffiths, *Principality*, 274.

32. Henry Don: above, pp. 200–1; value of estates: DL 42/16, fo. 188v; DL 29/731/12018, mm. 12, 14; punishment for part in revolt and subsequent pardon: DL 42/17, fos. 71–71v; *CPR* 1413–16, 24; charges against him in 1413: JI 1/1153, mm. 16–17; JI 1/1152, m. 6v. (he was found guilty on all charges except one).

33. Gruffudd Don: Griffiths, *Principality*, 201–2; *CPL*, 469; Owain Don: Griffiths, *Principality*, 322.

34. Gwilym ap Gruffudd ap Gwilym: above pp. 218–9; Glyn Roberts, *Aspects of Welsh History*, 204–14; A. D. Carr, *WHR* 15 (1990–1), 1–20; *IGE*, 310–17; *Cal. Anc. Pet.*, nos. 1,318, 1,332; UCNW Penrhyn 14 (his will).

35. Pardons issued by Edward Charlton: M. C. Jones and W. V. Lloyd, *Montgomeryshire Collections*, 4 (1871), 336–9.

36. Changes in the lordship of Ogmore: DL 42/107; R. R. Davies, in *Glam. CH*, 300–2.

37. Carnwyllion: DL 28/27/4; discussion in R. R. Davies, D.Phil. thesis (n. 4 above), 313–15

38. The post-revolt land market in Flintshire: Chester 30/17; Ieuan ap Jankin of Cydweli: DL 29/573/9063 *sub* Carnwyllion; JI 1/1153, m. 20; DL 28/27/4; Sir John Skidmore: SC 6/861/21.

39. Collapse of personal and territorial unfreedom: J. B. Smith, *WHR* 3 (1965–6), 145–71; R. R. Davies, *Lordship and Society*, 437–43; decline of serfdom in Dogfeilyn: SC 2/221/9, m. 10v; 221/10, m. 9v.

40. The shift to English tenure: R. R. Davies, *Lordship and Society*, 449–56; the Dyffryn Clwyd evidence: SC 2/221/8 (Llannerch); 221/10, m. 37 (Dogfeilyn).

41. Defiance of the lord: SC 2/221/9, m. 29v (Dyffryn Clwyd); NLW Chirk Castle, D58 (Chirkland); *CPR* 1413–16, 344 (Bromfield and Yale); collapse of seignorial revenue in Wales: R. R. Davies, *Lordship and Society*, 194.

42. Anti-Welsh measures, central and local: above pp. 281–92; challenge of the burgess of Caerwys: Chester 30/17, m. 19; privilege of Simon Thelwall: NLW Wynnstay 101/121.

43. Use of anti-Welsh sentiment: Chester 25/25, m. 17 (Flintshire); Keith Williams-Jones, *T. Caernarvonshire Hist. Soc.*, 39 (1978), 27 (English alderman of Conway); id., in Griffiths (ed.), *Boroughs*, 95 (permission for widow to marry Englishman or Welshman). Discrimination: Griffiths, *Principality*, 139–41 (Sir John Skidmore); T. B. Pugh, in *Glam. CH*, 637, n. 167 (Morgan ap Ieuan ap Jenkin Kemeys); D. Pratt, *T. Denbighshire Hist. Soc.*, 26 (1977), 153–5 (Robert Trevor).

44. Fifteenth-century developments in general: R. A. Griffiths, in *Fifteenth-Century England, 1399–1509*, ed. S. B. Chrimes and others (1972), 145–72; id. in *British Government and Administration: Studies presented to S. B. Chrimes*, ed. H. Hearder and H. R. Loyn, 69–86; Glanmor Williams, *Recovery, Reorientation and Reformation: Wales c.1415–1642*, chap. 1.

EPILOGUE

1. Owain's son, Gruffudd: *CCR 1405–9*, 213; *1409–13*, 148; F. Devon (ed.), *Issues of the Exchequer*, 305; prisoners taken at Harlech: Usk, *Chronicle*, 77; Welsh annals in *OG*, 153; death of Edmund Mortimer: Usk, *Chronicle*, 77; fate of his wife and daughters: Devon (ed.), *Issues of the Exchequer*, 321, 327; 'the fair nest of noble children': *GIG*, no. x, ll. 80–6; Maredudd and Owain: Usk, *Chronicle*, 119.

2. Offers of pardon to Glyn Dŵr: *CPR 1413–16*, 342, 404; death of Owain: J. R. S. Phillips, *BBCS* 24 (1970–2), 59–77; Adam of Usk's account of his burial: *Chronicle*, 129.

3. Poetic references to Glyn Dŵr: *Gwaith Guto'r Glyn*, no. xxiii, l. 49; *L'œuvre poétique de Gutun Owain*, nos. xv, l. 18; xvii, l. 2; xlii, l. 4; xliii, l. 8; lv, l. 29; Lewys Glyn Cothi, *Detholiad oi' Waith*, nos. 17, l. 21; 33, ll. 23; 35; prophetic poetry: M. E. Griffiths, *Early Vaticination in Welsh*; Glanmor Williams, *Religion, Language and Nationality in Wales*, chap. 3; references to impact of revolt in 1492 and 1501: DL 29/10334 (1492); *Calendar of the Public Records Relating to Pembrokeshire* iii. 191, n. 10 (1501).

4. Welsh accounts of the revolt in MSS: *OG*, 157–8 (David Bulkeley); ibid. 149–54 (the annals copied by Gruffudd Hiraethog); *Report on Mss. in the Welsh Language* (Historical Manuscripts Commission), i. 220–1 (Elis Gruffudd); cf. T. Jones, *WHR*, 1 (1960–3), 1–17.

5. Comments of George Owen: Owen, *Description of Penbrokshire*, iii. 35; David Powel: *Historie of Cambria*, 386–91.

6. 'Our chieftain . . . unsubdued': Pennant, *Tours in Wales*, iii. 358.

7. Llywelyn ap Gruffudd's posthumous reputation, or lack of it: Llinos Smith, *WHR* 12 (1984–6), 1–29; J. B. Smith, *Llywelyn ap Gruffudd* (1986), 393–421.

8. Quotations from *OG*, 4, 146.

9. Tudor chronicles on Glyn Dŵr: Edward Hall, *The Chronicle of Edward Hall*, ed. H. Ellis (1809), 31; Ralph Holinshed, *Chronicles* (1877 ed.), iii. 19; John Hayward, *The Life and Raigne of King Henrie III*, ed. J. J. Manning (1991), 169; comments on destruction caused by Glyn Dŵr: *The Brut*, ed. F. W. D. Brie, ii. 362; John Leland, *The Itinerary in Wales*, 10, 41; William Camden, *Britannia*, ed. Edmund Gibson (1695), 585, 665.

10. Owain's savagery: Leland, *Itinerary*, 41; Rice Merrick, *Morganiae Archaiographia*, ed. B. Ll. James (1983), 58; images of destruction: Sir John Wynn, *History of the Gwydir Family*, ed. J. G. Jones, 51; Richard Davies in G. H. Hughes (ed.), *Rhagymadroddion*, 24.

11. Contemporary comments on Owain's military standing: *Historia R. II*, 168; *Annales H. IV*, 333; *Giles's Chronicle*, 20; later compliments: John Hayward, *Life . . . of Henry III*, 255; Thomas Carte, *A General History of England* II (1750), 676.

12. Owain, magic and the weather: *Annales H. IV*, 343; Dieulacres Chronicle, *Bull. John Rylands Library*, 14 (1930), 176.

13. His soothsayer at Berwick: above p. 159; sixteenth-century comment on his use of prophecies: Holinshed, *Chronicles*, iii. 21; David Powel, *Historie of Cambria*, 386.

14. Comment of Welsh annals on Owain's death: *OG*, 154.

15. Elis Gruffydd: *Report on Mss. in the Welsh Language*, i. 220–1; the mountain-top boasting assemblies: *Catalogue Mss. re Wales in BM*, i. 72, cf. above p. 91.

16. The romantic movement in Wales and Owain's part in it: Prys Morgan, in E. J. Hobsbawm and T. O. Ranger (eds.), *The Invention of Tradition*, 43–100, esp. 81–2.

17. Social memory: K. V. Thomas, *The Perception of the Past in Early Modern England*; James Fentress and Chris Wickham, *Social Memory*.

18. Places associated with Glyn Dŵr: *Royal Commission on Ancient Monuments in Wales, Merionethshire Inventory*, nos. 39, 46, 58; George Borrow, *Wild Wales* (Norwich edn., 1924), i. 189–92 (mount, prison, bridle-path, meadows); Richard Haslam, *The Buildings of Wales: Powys*, 156–7; *Royal Commission, Montgomeryshire Inventory*, no. 746; *Arch. Camb.*, 2 (1847), 352 (Machynlleth, Plas Crug).

19. Owen Glendower's camp: Camden, *Britannia* (1695), 527; Lawtons Hope Hill: quoted in J. R. S. Phillips *BBCS* 24 (1970–2), 60; Cilycwm: Richard Fenton, *Tours in Wales 1804–13*, ed. J. Fisher, 343; caves: Thomas Turner, *Narrative of a Journey* (1840), 104; Pennant, *Tours*, iii. 334; John Rhys, *Celtic Folklore*, ii. 487.

20. Edmund Mortimer's wondrous deeds: Usk, *Chronicle*, 77.

21. Hywel Sele legend: Pennant, *Tours*, iii. 310–11.

22. Dafydd Gam: Camden, *Britannia* (1695), 591–2; *OG*, 147–8.

23. Reginald de Grey's ransom money: *Report on Mss. in Welsh Language*, i. 221–2; Owain and Rhys Ddu: *OG*, 153.

24. Defoe's observation: *A Tour Through England and Wales*, ii. 53–4.

BIBLIOGRAPHY

A. MANUSCRIPT SOURCES

i. Public Record Office, London

(Unless indicated otherwise all manuscript sources referred to in the book are housed in the Public Record Office)

Palatinate of Chester

Chester 2   Recognizance Rolls
Chester 3   Inquisitions Post Mortem
Chester 24   Gaol Files, Writs, etc.
Chester 25   Indictment Rolls
Chester 29   Plea Rolls (Chester)
Chester 30   Plea Rolls (Flint)
Chester 38   Miscellanea

Duchy of Lancaster

DL 25   Deeds, Series L
DL 27   Deeds, Series LS
DL 28   Accounts Various
DL 29   Ministers' Accounts
DL 30   Court Rolls
DL 41   Miscellanea
DL 42   Miscellaneous Books
DL 43   Rentals and Surveys

Exchequer

E 28   Council and Privy Seal Records
E 101   Accounts Various
E 179   Subsidy Rolls
E 403   Issue Rolls
E 404   Writs and Warrants for Issue

Judicial Records

JI 1   Justices Itinerant, Assize Rolls
KB 9   King's Bench, Ancient Indictments
KB 27   King's Bench, Plea Rolls

PSO 1   Warrants for the Privy Seal

Special Collections

SC 2   Court Rolls
SC 6   Ministers' Accounts
SC 11   Rentals and Surveys

ii. *British Library, London*

Additional Mss., Charters and Rolls
Campbell Charters
Egerton Charters and Rolls
Harleian Mss., Charters and Rolls

iii. *National Library of Wales, Aberystwyth*

The following collections: Aston Hall, Bachymbyd, Bagot, Bettisfield, Bronwydd, Chirk
   Castle, Muddlescombe, Peniarth, Plas Iolyn, Slebech, Diocese of St Asaph Records (SA)
   Wynnstay.

iv. *Other Repositories*

Clwyd Record Office: Galltfaenan, Nerquis Hall, Wynnstay
College of Arms: Arundel
Gwent Record Office: Capel Hanbury, Llanarth, Monmouth
Northumberland Record Office: Swinburne of Capheaton
Shrewsbury Public Library: Craven, Deeds
Shropshire Record Office: Bridgewater, Bridgnorth
Staffordshire Record Office: Lord Stafford
University of Wales, Bangor: Bodrhyddan, Mostyn, Whitney.

B.   PRINTED SOURCES

(Place of publication is London unless otherwise stated)

Anglo-Scottish Relations 1174–1328: Some Selected Documents, ed. E. L. G. Stones, rev. edn.
   (Oxford, 1970).
Archaeologia Cambrensis: Supplementary Volume of Original Documents (1877).
Baronia de Kemeys, ed. T. D. Lloyd (Cambrian Archaeological Soc., 1861).
BARTRUM, P. C., *Welsh Genealogies A.D. 300–1400*, 8 vols. (Cardiff, 1974).
Blodeugerdd Barddas o'r Bedwaredd Ganrif ar Ddeg, ed. D. Johnston (Llandybie, 1989).
BOWER, WALTER *Scotichronicon*, ed. D. E. R. Watt and others (Aberdeen 1987–).
Brut or The Chronicles of England, The, ed. F. W. D. Brie, 2 vols. (Early English Text Soc., 1906–8).
Brut y Tywysogyon, Peniarth Ms. 20 version, ed. Thomas Jones (Cardiff, 1952)
*Calendar of Documents relating to Scotland preserved in the Public Record Office and the British
   Library*, vol. 4, *1357–1509*, ed. J. Bain (Edinburgh, 1888); vol. 5, *1108–1516* (Supplementary),
   ed. G. G. Simpson and J. D. Galbraith (Edinburgh n.d.)
Caernarvon Court Rolls 1361–1402, ed. G. P. Jones and H. Owen (Caernarfon, 1951).

Calendar of Inquisitions Miscellaneous (1916–).

Calendar of the Public Records Relating to Pembrokeshire, ed. H. Owen, 3 vols., Cymmrodorion Record Series, no. 7 (1911–18).

Cartae et alia munimenta quae ad dominium de Glamorgancia pertinent, ed. G. T. Clark, 6 vols. (Cardiff, 1910).

Cartularium S. Johannis Baptistae de Carmarthen, ed. T. Phillips (Cheltenham, 1865).

Catalogue of Ancient Deeds, 6 vols. (1890–1915).

Chronicle of Melrose, ed. A. O. and M. O. Anderson (Edinburgh, 1936).

Chronicle of Pierre de Langtoft, ed. T. Wright, 2 vols. (Rolls Series, 1866–8).

Chronique du Religieux de Saint-Denys, ed. L. Bellaguet, 6 vols. (Paris, 1839–52).

Creton, Jean, 'Metrical History of the Deposition of King Richard the Second', ed. J. Webb, *Archaeologia*, 20 (1824), 1–441.

Cyfreithiau Hywel Dda yn ôl Llawysgrif Coleg Iesu LVII, ed. M. Richards, rev. edn. (Cardiff, 1990).

Cywyddau Dafydd ap Gwilym a'i Gyfoeswyr, ed. I. Williams and T. Roberts (Cardiff, 1935).

DEVON, F. (ed.), *Issues of the Exchequer, Henry III–Henry IV* (Record Commission, 1847).

Dieulacres Chronicle, 'Chronicle of Dieulacres Abbey, 1381–1403', ed. M. V. Clarke and V. H. Galbraith, *Bulletin of the John Rylands Library*, 14 (1930), 125–81.

Eulogium Historiarum, ed. F. S. Haydon, 3 vols. (Rolls Series, 1858–63).

Extent of Chirkland 1391–1393, ed. G. P. Jones (Liverpool, 1933).

Flintshire Ministers' Accounts 1303–28, ed. A. Jones; *1328–53*, ed. D. L. Evans (Flintshire Hist. Soc. 1913, 1929).

FROISSART, JEAN *Chronicles*, ed. G. Brereton (Harmondsworth, 1983).

GEOFFREY of MONMOUTH *Historia Regum Britanniae, I. Bern Ms.*, ed. N. Wright (Cambridge, 1984).

GIRALDUS CAMBRENSIS *Opera*, ed. J.S. Brewer *et al.*, 8 vols. (Rolls Series, 1861–91). The *Journey* and *Description of Wales* are in vol. 6.

Gwaith Guto'r Glyn, ed. I. Williams and J. Ll. Williams, 2nd edn. (Cardiff, 1961).

HARDYNG, JOHN *Chronicle, with the continuation by Grafton to 34 Henry VIII*, ed. H. Ellis (1812).

HIGDEN, RANULF *Polychronicon*, ed. C. Babington and J. R. Lumby, 9 vols. (Rolls Series, 1865–86).

Historians of the Church of York and its Archbishops, ed. J. Raine, 3 vols. (Rolls Series, 1879–94).

Historical Manuscripts Commission Reports.

John of Gaunt's Register, 1372–6, 2 vols., ed. S. Armitage-Smith; *1379–83*, 2 vols., ed. E. C. Lodge and R. Somerville (Camden Soc., 1911, 1937).

JONES, GWYN (ed.), *Oxford Book of Welsh Verse in English* (Oxford, 1977).

LELAND, JOHN *The Itinerary in Wales in or about the years 1536–9*, ed. L. Toulmin-Smith (1906).

Letters of John of Salisbury, ed. W. J. Millor *et al.*, 2 vols. (1955–79).

LEWYS GLYN COTHI *Detholiad o'i Waith*, ed. E. D. Jones (Cardiff, 1984).

Libelle of Englyshe Polycye, The, ed. G. Warner (1926).

Lordship of Oswestry 1393–1607, The, ed. W. J. Slack (Shrewsbury, 1951).

Oeuvre poetique de Gutun Owain, ed. E. Bachellery, 2 vols. (Paris, 1950–1)

OWEN, GEORGE *The Description of Penbrokshire*, ed. H. Owen, 4 vols., Cymmrodorion Record Series, no. 1 1892–1936)

PUTNAM, B. H. (ed.), *Proceedings Before Justices of the Peace Edward III–Richard III*, ed. B. H. Putnam (Ames Foundation, 1938).

Record of Caernarvon. Registrum vulgariter nuncupatum 'The Record of Caernarvon', ed. H. Ellis (Record Commission, 1838).

Register of Edward the Black Prince, 4 vols. (1930–3).

Registrum epistolarum fratris Johannis Peckham, ed. C. T. Martin, 3 vols. (Rolls Series, 1882–5).

Report on Mss. in the Welsh Language, J. Gwenogvryn Evans, 2 vols. (Historical Manuscripts Commission, 1898–1910).

RIDGARD, J. (ed.), *Medieval Framlingham: Select Documents 1270–1524*, Suffolk Rec. Soc., vol. 27 (1985).

Rotuli Scotiae, ed. D. Macpherson and others, 2 vols. (Record Commission, 1814–19)

St. Albans Chronicle 1406–1420, The, ed. V. H. Galbraith (1937).

Scrope and Grosvenor Controversy 1385–90, The, ed. N. H. Nicholas, 2 vols. (1832).

Select Cases in the Court of King's Bench under Richard II, Henry IV and Henry V, ed. G. O. Sayles, (Selden Society vol. 87, 1971)

Statutes of the Realm (Record Commission, 1810–28).

Statutes of Wales, The, ed. Ivor Bowen (1908).

Trioedd Ynys Prydein: The Welsh Triads, ed. Rachel Bromwich 2nd edn. (Cardiff, 1978).

Vita Edwardi Secundi: The Life of Edward the Second, ed. N. Denholm-Young (Oxford, 1957).

Westminster Chronicle 1381–1394, The, ed. L. C. Hector and Barbara F. Harvey (Oxford, 1982).

WOOLGAR, C. M. (ed.), *Household Accounts from Medieval England*, 2 vols. (1992).

C. SECONDARY SOURCES

ALLMAND, CHRISTOPHER *Henry V* (1992).

ARCHER, ROWENA E., 'The Estates and Finances of Margaret of Brotherton, *c.*1320–99', *Historical Research*, 60 (1997), 264–80.

BAKER, A. R. H. and BUTLIN R. A. (eds.), *Studies of Field Systems in the British Isles* (Cambridge, 1973).

BEAN, J. M. W., 'Henry IV and the Percies' *History*, 44 (1959), 212–27.

BEBB, W. AMBROSE *Machlud yr Oesoedd Canol* (Swansea, 1951).

BELLAMY, J. G., 'The Northern Rebellions in the Last Years of Richard II', *Bull. John Rylands Library*, 47 (1965), 254–74.

BENNETT, M. J., 'Provincial Gentlefolk and Legal Education in the Reign of Edward II', *Bull. Institute of Historical Research*, 57 (1984), 203–8.

BERESFORD, M. W., *New Towns of the Middle Ages* (1967).

BORROW, GEORGE *Wild Wales*, (Norwich edn., 1955).

BRAND, PAUL 'The Education of Lawyers in Britain Prior to 1400', *Historical Research*, 60 (1987), 147–65.

BULLOCK-DAVIES C., 'Exspectare Arturum: Arthur and the Messianic Hope', *BBCS* (1980–2), 432–40.

CAMDEN, WILLIAM *Britannia*, ed., with additions, by Edmund Gibson (1695).

CARPENTER, CHRISTINE *Locality and Polity: A Study of Warwickshire Landed Society, 1401–1499* (Cambridge, 1992).

CARR, A. D., 'The Barons of Edeyrnion, 1282–1485', *J. Merionethshire Hist. and Rec. Soc.*, 4 (1963–4), 187–93, 289–301.

—— 'Medieval Dinmael', *T. Denbighshire Hist. Soc.*, 13 (1964), 9–21.

—— 'Medieval Gloddaith', *T. Caernarvonshire Hist. Soc.*, 38 (1977), 7–32.

—— 'An Aristocracy in Decline: The Native Welsh Lords after the Edwardian Conquest', *WHR* 5 (1970–1), 103–29.

—— 'A Welsh Knight in the Hundred Years' War: Sir Gregory Sais', *TCS* (1977), 40–53.

—— 'The Making of the Mostyns: The Genesis of a Landed Family', *TCS* (1979), 137–59.

—— *Medieval Anglesey* (Anglesey Antiquarian Soc. 1982).

—— 'Gwilym ap Gruffydd and the Rise of the Penrhyn Estate', *WHR* 15 (1990–1), 1–21.

—— *Owen of Wales: The End of the House of Gwynedd* (Cardiff 1991).

CARTE, THOMAS *A General History of England*, vol. 2 (1750).

CATHCART KING D. J., 'Two Castles in Northern Powys: Dinas Brân and Caergwrle', *Arch. Camb.*, 123 (1974), 113–39.

CHARLES-EDWARDS G., 'The Scribes of the Red Book of Hergest', *NLWJ*, 21 (1979–80), 246–56.

CHARLES-EDWARDS T. M. *et al.*, (eds.), *Lawyers and Laymen: Studies in the History of Law presented to Dafydd Jenkins* (Cardiff, 1986).

CLARKE, M. V., *Fourteenth-Century Studies*, ed. L. S. Sutherland and M. McKisack (Oxford, 1937).

COBBAN, A. B., *Universities in the Middle Ages* (Liverpool, 1990).

COSGROVE, ART *Late Medieval Ireland 1370–1541* (Dublin, 1981).

COWLEY, F. G., *The Monastic Order in South Wales, 1066–1349* (Cardiff, 1977).

CURRY, A., 'Cheshire and the Royal Demesne 1399–1422', *T. Hist. Soc. Lancashire and Cheshire*, 128 (1978), 113–38.

DAVIES, J. CONWAY 'Some Owen Glyndŵr Documents', *NLWJ* 3 (1943–4), 48–50.

DAVIES, R. R., 'The Bohun and Lancaster Lordships in Wales in the Fourteenth and Early Fifteenth Centuries', unpublished D.Phil. thesis (University of Oxford, 1965).

—— 'Baronial Accounts, Incomes and Arrears in the Late Middle Ages', *Economic History Review*, 2nd ser., 21 (1968), 211–29.

—— 'Owain Glyn Dŵr and the Welsh Squirearchy', *TCS* (1968) pt. ii. 150–69.

—— 'Richard II and the Principality of Chester, 1397–99', in F. R. H. Du Boulay and C. M. Barron (eds.), *The Reign of Richard II: Essays in Honour of May McKisack*, (1971).

—— 'Colonial Wales', *Past and Present*, 65 (1974), 3–23.

—— 'Race Relations in Post-Conquest Wales', *TCS* (1974–5), 32–56.

——*Lordship and Society in the March of Wales 1284–1400* (Oxford, 1978).

—— 'Lordship or Colony?' in (ed.), J. F. Lydon *The English in Medieval Ireland* (Dublin, 1984), 142–61.

—— 'Buchedd a Moes y Cymry', *WHR* 12 (1984–5), 155–79.

—— *Conquest, Coexistence and Change: Wales 1063–1415* (Oxford, 1987).

DAVIES, R. R. 'Ar Drywydd Owain Glyn Dŵr', in G. H. Jenkins (ed.), *Cof Cenedl*, 2 (Llandysul, 1987), 1–26.

—— *Domination and Conquest: The Experience of Ireland, Scotland and Wales* 1100–1300 (Cambridge, 1991).

—— 'The Peoples of Britain and Ireland: Identities', *T. Royal Hist. Soc.*, 6th ser., 4 (1994), 1–20.

DEFOE, DANIEL *A Tour Through England and Wales* (1724–6) 2 vols. (Everyman edn., 1928).

DENTON, J. H., *English Royal Free Chapels, 1100–1300* (Manchester, 1970).

DEXLER, MARJORIE 'Fluid Prejudice: Scottish Origin Myths in the Later Middle Ages', in J. Rosenthal and C. F. Richmond (eds.), *People, Politics and Community* (Gloucester, 1987), 60–76.

EDWARDS, J. G., 'Edward I's Castle-Building in Wales', *Proceedings of the British Academy*, 32 (1950), 15–81.

EMDEN, A. B., *A Biographical Register of the University of Oxford to 1500*, 3 vols. (Oxford, 1955–9).

EVANS, B., 'A Grant of Privileges to Wrexham (1380)' *BBCS* 19 (1960–2), 42–7.

—— 'Owain Glyn Dŵr's Raid on Ruthin (1400)', *T. Denbighshire Hist. Soc.*, 10 (1961), 239–41.

EVANS, DAFYDD HUW 'An Incident on the Dee during the Glyn Dŵr Rebellion', *T. Denbighshire Hist. Soc.*, 37 (1988), 5–41.

EVANS, H. T., *Wales and the Wars of the Roses* (Cambridge, 1915).

EVANS, J. WYN and WORSLEY R., *St. David's Cathedral 1181–1981* (St Davids, 1981).

FENTON, RICHARD *A Historical Tour Through Pembrokeshire* (1810).

—— *Tours in Wales 1804–13*, ed. J. Fisher (Cambrian Archaeological Association, 1917).

FENTRESS, JAMES and WICKHAM CHRIS *Social Memory* (1992).

FRAME, ROBIN *Colonial Ireland, 1169–1369* (Dublin, 1981).

—— 'War and Peace in the Medieval Lordship of Ireland', in J. F. Lydon (ed.), *The English in Medieval Ireland* (Dublin, 1984), 118–42.

FYCHAN, CLEDWYN 'Llywelyn ab y Moel a'r Canolbarth', *Llên Cymru*, 15 (1987–8), 289–308.

GABRIEL, J. R., 'Wales and the Avignon Papacy', *Arch. Camb.*, 78, (1923), 70–86.

GIFFIN, M. E., 'Cadwaladr, Arthur and Brutus in the Wigmore Ms.', *Speculum*, 16 (1941), 109–20.

—— 'A Wigmore Manuscript at the University of Chicago', *NLWJ* 7 (1951–71), 316–25.

GILLINGHAM, J., 'The Beginnings of English Imperialism', *J. Hist. Sociology*, 5 (1992), 392–410.

GOODMAN, A., 'Owain Glyndŵr Before 1400', *WHR* 5 (1970–1), 67–70.

—— *The Loyal Conspiracy: The Lords Appellant under Richard II* (1971).

GRANT, ALEXANDER *Independence and Nationhood: Scotland 1306–1469* (1984).

—— 'The Otterburn War From the Scottish Point of View', in A. Tuck and A. Goodman (eds.), *War and Border Societies in the Middle Ages* (1992).

GRESHAM, C. A., *Medieval Stone Carving in North Wales, Sepulchral Slabs and Effigies of the Thirteenth and Fourteenth Centuries* (Cardiff, 1968).

GRIFFITHS, MATTHEW 'The Manor in Medieval Glamorgan: The Estates of the Ralegh Family in the Fourteenth and Fifteenth Centuries', *BBCS* 32 (1985), 173–201.

GRIFFITHS, M. E., *Early Vaticination in Welsh* (Cardiff, 1937).

GRIFFITHS, R. A., 'Some Partisans of Owain Glyndŵr at Oxford', *BBCS* 20 (1962–4), 282–92.

—— 'The Rise of the Stradlings of St. Donat's', *Morgannwg: T. Glamorgan Hist. Soc.*, 8 (1963), 15–47.

—— 'Gentlemen and Rebels in Later Medieval Cardiganshire', *Ceredigion: J. Cardiganshire Antiquarian Soc.*, 5 (1964–7), 143–67.

—— 'Some Secret Supporters of Owain Glyndŵr?', *Bull. Institute of Historical Research*, 37 (1964), 77–100.

—— 'The Glyndŵr Rebellion in North Wales Through the Eyes of an Englishman', *BBCS* 22 (1966–8), 151–68.

—— 'Wales and the Marches in the Fifteenth Century', in S. B. Chrimes and others (eds.), *Fifteenth-Century England, 1399–1509* (Manchester, 1972), 145–72.

—— 'Patronage, Politics and the Principality of Wales, 1413–61' in H. Hearder and H. R. Loyn (eds.), *British Government and Society: Studies presented to S. B. Chrimes* (Cardiff, 1974)

—— (ed.), *The Boroughs of Medieval Wales* (Cardiff, 1978).

—— 'Medieval Severnside', in R. R. Davies and others (eds.), *Welsh Society and Nationhood: Historical Essays Presented to Glanmor Williams* (Cardiff, 1984).

—— 'The English Realm and Dominions and the King's Subjects in the Later Middle Ages', in J. G. Rowe (ed.), *Aspects of Late Medieval Government and Society* (Toronto, 1986), 83–105

(Note: the above articles, with others, are now available in two volumes of Professor Griffiths's collected papers: *King and Country: England and Wales in the Fifteenth Century* (1991) and *Conquerors and Conquered in Medieval Wales* (Stroud, 1994)).

—— and THOMAS, R. S., *The Making of the Tudor Dynasty* (Stroud, 1985).

GRIFFITHS, RHIDIAN 'Prince Henry, Wales and the Royal Exchequer 1400–13', *BBCS* 32 (1985), 202–16.

—— 'Prince Henry's War: Armies, Garrisons and Supply during the Glyndŵr Rising', *BBCS* 34 (1987), 165–74.

—— 'Prince Henry and Wales, 1400–1408', in M. Hicks (ed.), *Profit, Piety and Professions in Later Medieval England* (Gloucester, 1991), 51–62.

GRUFFYDD, R. GERAINT *Dafydd ap Gwilym* (Caernarfon, 1987).

HAGUE, D. B. and WARHURST, CYNTHIA 'Excavations at Sycharth Castle, Denbighshire', *Arch. Camb.*, 115 (1966), 108–28.

HALL, EDWARD *The Chronicle of Edward Hall*, ed. H. Ellis (1809).

HARRISS, G. L. (ed.), *Henry V: The Practice of Kingship* (Oxford, 1985).

—— *Cardinal Beaufort: A Study in Lancastrian Ascendancy and Decline* (Oxford, 1988).

HASLAM, RICHARD *The Buildings of Wales: Powys* (Cardiff, 1979).

HAYWARD, JOHN *The Life and Raigne of Henry III*, ed. J. J. Manning (Camden Soc., 1991).

History of Flintshire, vol. 1, ed. C. R. Williams (Denbigh, 1961).

HOBSBAWM, E. J. and RANGER T. O., *The Invention of Tradition* (Cambridge, 1983).

HOLINSHED, RALPH *Chronicles* (1877 edn.).

HOLMES, G. A. *The Estates of the Higher Nobility in Fourteenth-Century England* (Cambridge, 1957).

HUBBARD, E., *The Buildings of Wales: Clwyd* (Cardiff, 1986).

HUGHES, GARFIELD H. (ed.), *Rhagymadroddion 1547–1659* (Cardiff, 1951).

HUWS, D. 'Llawysgrif Hendregadredd', *NLWJ* 22 (1981–2), 1–27.

—— 'Llyfr Gwyn Rhydderch', *Cambridge Medieval Celtic Studies*, 21 (1991), 1–39.

JACK, R. IAN 'New Light on the Early Days of Owain Glyn Dŵr', *BBCS* 21 (1964–6), 163–6.

—— 'Owain Glyn Dŵr and the Lordship of Ruthin', *WHR* 2 (1964–5), 303–22.

—— 'The Fire Ordinances of Ruthin, 1324', *T. Denbighshire Hist. Soc.*, 28 (1979), 5–18.

JOHNSTON, D. R., 'Iolo Goch and the English: Welsh Poetry and Politics in the Fourteenth Century', *Cambridge Medieval Celtic Studies*, 12 (1986), 73–98.

JONES, D. D., *A History of Kidwelly* (Carmarthen, 1908).

JONES, F., 'An approach to Welsh Genealogy', *TCS* (1948), 303–466.

JONES, M. C. and LLOYD W. V., 'Incidents connected with the rebellion of Owen Glendower in Powys-land', *Montgomeryshire Collections*, 4 (1871), 325–45.

JONES, T., 'A Welsh Chronicler in Tudor England', *WHR* 1 (1960–3), 1–17.

KENYON J. R., *Kidwelly Castle* (Cardiff. CADWguide, 1986).

KINGSFORD, C. L., *English Historical Literature in the Fifteenth Century* (Oxford, 1913).

KIRBY, J. L., *Henry IV of England* (1970).

KNOWLES, D., *The Religious Orders in England*, 3 vols. (Cambridge, 1948–59).

LEHOUX, F., *Jean de France, Duc de Berri. Sa vie, son action politique (1340–1416)*, 3 vols. (Paris, 1966–8).

LEWIS, E. A., 'The Decay of Tribalism in North Wales', *TCS* (1902–3), 1–75.

—— 'The Development of Industry and Commerce in Wales during the Middle Ages', *T. Royal Hist. Soc.*, 2nd ser., 17 (1903), 121–75.

—— *The Medieval Boroughs of Snowdonia* (1912).

—— 'A Contribution to the Commercial History of Medieval Wales', *Y Cymmrodor*, 24 (1913), 86–188.

LLOYD, J. E., *A History of Wales from the Earliest Times to the Edwardian Conquest*, 3rd edn. (1939).

McFARLANE K. B., *Lancastrian Kings and Lollard Knights* (Oxford, 1972).

—— *The Nobility of Later Medieval England* (Oxford, 1973).

McNIVEN P., 'The Cheshire Rising of 1400', *Bull. John Rylands Library*, 52 (1969–70), 375–96.

—— 'The Men of Cheshire and the Rebellion of 1403', *Trans. Historic Soc. Lancashire and Cheshire*, 129 (1980), 1–29.

—— 'The Scottish Policy of the Percies and the Strategy of the Rebellion of 1403', *Bull. John Rylands Library*, 62 (1980), 498–530.

MERRICK, RICE *Morganiae Archaiographia: A Book of Antiquities of Glamorganshire* (1578), ed. B. Ll. James (South Wales Rec. Soc., 1983).

MESSHAM, J. E., 'The County of Flint and the Rebellion of Owen Glyndŵr in the Records of the Earldom of Chester', *Flintshire Hist. Soc. Publications*, 23 (1967–8), 1–34.

MORGAN, P. J., *War and Society in Medieval Cheshire 1277–1403* (Chetham Soc., 1987).

MORRIS, W. H., 'Cydweli (Kidwelly) and the Glyn Dŵr Revolt', *Carmarthen Antiquary*, 3 (1959), 4–16.

NICHOLSON, R., *Scotland: The Later Middle Ages* (Edinburgh 1974).

NICOLAS, N. H., *History of the Battle of Agincourt* (1833).

PALMER, A. N, and OWEN E., *History of Ancient Tenures of Land in North Wales and the Marches*, 2nd edn. (Wrexham, 1910).

PALMER, J. J. N., *England, France and Christendom 1377–99* (1972).

PAYNE, F., 'Cwysau o Foliant Cyson', *Y Llenor*, 26 (1947), 3–24.

PENNANT, THOMAS *Tours in Wales*, ed. J. Rhys, 3 vols. (Caernarvon, 1883).

PHILLIPS, J. R. S., 'When Did Owain Glyn Dŵr Die?', *BBCS* 24 (1970–2), 59–77.

POWEL, DAVID *Historie of Cambria* (1584, repr. Amsterdam, 1969).

POWELL, EDWARD *Kingship, Law and Society: Criminal Justice in the Reign of Henry V* (Oxford, 1989).

PRATT, D., 'A Holt Petition c. 1429', *T. Denbighshire Hist. Soc.*, 26 (1977), 153–5.

PRESTWICH, M., *Edward I* (1985).

PUGH, T. B. (ed.), *The Marcher Lordships of South Wales 1415–1536: Select Documents* (Cardiff, 1963).

—— *Henry V and the Southampton Plot* (Southampton Record Series, 1988).

PURTON, R. C., 'Deeds relating to Oswestry', *T. Shropshire Archaeological Soc.*, 53 (1949–50), 94–111.

RASHDALL, H., *The Universities of Europe in the Middle Ages* new edn., ed. F. M. Powicke and A. B. Emden, 3 vols. (1936).

REES, W., 'The Black Death in Wales', *T. Royal Hist. Soc* 4th ser., 3 (1920), 115–35.

—— *South Wales and the March, 1284–1415* (1924).

—— *South Wales and the Border in the Fourteenth Century* (Ordnance Survey map, 1932).

—— 'Accounts of the receiver of the mine of coals [in the lordship of Kilvey], Michaelmas 23 Richard II to Michaelmas, Henry IV', *South Wales and Monmouthshire Rec. Soc.*, (1949), 188–92.

—— *An Historical Atlas of Wales from Early to Modern Times*, 2nd edn. (1959).

REEVES, A. C., *Newport Lordship 1317–1536* (Ann Arbor, Mich., 1979).

REYNOLDS, S., *Kingdoms and Communities in Western Europe 900–1300* (Oxford, 1984).

RHYS, J., *Celtic Folklore: Welsh and Manx* (1901).

RICHARDSON, H. G., 'John Oldcastle in Hiding, August–October 1417', *English Hist. Review*, 55 (1943), 432–8.

ROBERTS, B. F., 'Un o lawysgrifau Hopcyn ap Tomos o Ynys Dawy', *BBCS* 22 (1966–8), 223–8.

ROBERTS, ENID P., 'Tŷ Pren Glân mewn top Bryn Glas', *T. Denbighshire Hist. Soc.*, 22 (1973), 12–47.

—— 'Llys Ieuan, Esgob Llanelwy', *T. Denbighshire Hist. Soc.*, 23 (1974), 70–103.

ROBERTS, GLYN 'The Anglesey Submissions of 1406', *BBCS* 15 (1952–4), 39–61.

—— *Aspects of Welsh History* (Cardiff, 1989).

ROBERTS, T., 'Pedwar Cywydd Brud', *BBCS* 7 (1933–5), 231–46.

ROBERTS, TOMOS ' "An ancient faer Record"? Anglesey Adherents of Owain Glyndŵr', *BBCS* 38 (1991), 129–34.

ROGERS, M., 'The Welsh Marcher Lordship of Bromfield and Yale 1282–1485', unpublished Ph.D. thesis (University of Wales, 1992).

ROSKELL, J. S. et al., *A History of Parliament: The Commons 1386–1421*, 4 vols. (1992).

ROWLANDS, EURYS 'Iolo Goch', *Celtic Studies in Memory of Angus Matheson 1912–62*, ed. J. Carney and D. Greene (1968), 124–46.

Royal Commission on Ancient Monuments in Wales: Inventories of individual counties (1911–).

SHERBORNE, J. W., 'Richard II's Return to Wales', *WHR* 7 (1974–5), 389–402.

—— 'Perjury and the Lancastrian Revolution of 1399', *WHR* 14 (1988–9), 217–42.

SIDDONS, M. 'Welsh Seals in Paris', *BBCS* 29 (1980–2), 531–44.

—— 'Additions and Corrections to "Welsh Seals in Paris" ' *BBCS* 32 (1985), 233–40; 36 (1989), 185–6.

—— *The Development of Welsh Heraldry*, 3 vols. (Aberystwyth, 1991–3).

SIMMS, K., 'Guesting and Feasting in Gaelic Ireland', *J. Royal Society of Antiquaries of Ireland*, 107 (1978), 67–100.

SMITH, J. B., 'Einion Offeiriad', *BBCS* 20 (1962–4), 339–47.

—— 'Crown and Community in the Principality of North Wales in the Reign of Henry Tudor', *WHR* 3 (1966–7), 145–71.

—— 'The Last Phase of the Glyn Dŵr Rebellion', *BBCS* 22 (1966–8), 250–60.

—— 'Gruffydd Llwyd and the Celtic Alliance', *BBCS* 26 (1974–6), 463–78.

—— 'Edward II and the Allegiance of Wales', *WHR* 8 (1976–7), 139–71.

—— *Llywelyn ap Gruffydd: Tywysog Cymru* (Cardiff 1986).

SMITH, LLINOS, 'The Arundel Charters to the Lordship of Chirk in the Fourteenth Century', *BBCS* 23 (1968–70), 153–66.

—— 'The Lordships of Chirk and Oswestry, 1282–1415', unpublished Ph.D. thesis (University of London, 1971).

—— 'The Gage and the Land Market in Late Medieval Wales', *Economic History Review*, 2nd ser., 29 (1976), 537–50.

—— '*Tir Prid*: Deeds of Gage of Land in Late-Medieval Wales', *BBCS* 27 (1976–8), 263–77.

—— 'Seignorial Income in the Fourteenth Century: The Arundels in Chirk', *BBCS* 28 (1978–80), 443–58.

—— 'Llywelyn ap Gruffudd and the Welsh Historical Consciousness' *WHR* 12 (1984–6), 1–29.

—— 'Cannwyll Disbwyll a Dosbarth': Gwŷr Cyfraith Ceredigion yn yr Oesoedd Canol Diweddar', *Ceredigion*, 10 (1986), 229–53.

—— 'Disputes and Settlements in Medieval Wales: The Role of Arbitration', *English Historical Review*, 106 (1991), 835–60.

—— 'Fosterage, Adoption and God-Parenthood: Ritual and Fictive Kinship in Medieval Wales', *WHR* 16 (1992–3), 1–36.

STEEL, A. B., *The Receipt of the Exchequer 1377–1485* (Cambridge, 1954).

STEPHENSON, D., *The Governance of Gwynedd* (Cardiff, 1984).

THOMAS, K. V., *The Perception of the Past in Early Modern England* (Creighton Lecture, 1983).

TOUT, T. F., *Chapters in Medieval Administrative History*, 6 vols. (Manchester, 1923–35).

TREHARNE, R. F., 'The Franco-Welsh Treaty of Alliance in 1212', *BBCS* 18 (1958–60), 60–75.

TUCK, A., *Richard II and the English Nobility* (1973).

TURNER, HILARY *Town Defences in England and Wales AD 900–1500* (1970).

TURNER, THOMAS *Narrative of a Journey . . . from Gloucester to Aberystwyth and from Aberystwyth through North Wales, 1837* (1840).

TURVEY, R. K., 'The Marcher Shire of Pembrokeshire and the Glyndŵr Rebellion', *WHR* 15 (1990–1), 151–69.

USHER, G. A., 'Welsh Students at Oxford in the Middle Ages', *BBCS* 16 (1954–6), 193–8.

WATERS, W. H., 'Documents Relating to the Sheriff's Tourn in North Wales', *BBCS* 6 (1931–3), 354–60.

—— 'Documents relating to the office of escheator for North Wales for the year 1309–10', *BBCS* 6 (1931–3), 360–8.

WATT, D. E. R., *Fasti Ecclesiae Scoticanae Medii Aevi* (Scottish Rec. Soc., 1969).

'Welsh Pool. Materials for the History of the Parish and Borough', *Montgomeryshire Collections*, 7 (1874).

WILLIAMS, D. H., *Atlas of Cistercian Lands in Wales* (Cardiff, 1990).

WILLIAMS, GLANMOR *The Welsh Church from Conquest to Reformation*, 2nd edn. (Cardiff, 1976).

—— *Religion, Language and Nationality in Wales* (Cardiff, 1979).

—— 'Henry de Gower (?1278–1347), Bishop and Builder', *Arch. Camb.*, 130 (1981), 1–19.

—— *Recovery, Reorientation and Reformation: Wales c. 1415–1642* (Oxford, 1987).

—— *Owain Glyndŵr*, 2nd edn. (Cardiff, 1993).

WILLIAMS, G. J., *Traddodiad Llenyddol Morgannwg* (Cardiff, 1948).

WILLIAMS-JONES, K., 'A Mawddwy Court Roll, 1415–16', *BBCS* 23 (1968–70), 329–45.

—— *The Merioneth Lay Subsidy Roll 1292–3* (Cardiff 1976).

—— 'The Taking of Conwy Castle, 1401', *T. Caernarvonshire Hist. Soc.*, 39 (1978), 7–43.

WYLIE, J. H., *History of England Under Henry IV*, 4 vols. (1884–98).

WYNN, SIR JOHN, *History of the Gwydir Family*, ed. J. Gwynfor Jones (Llandysul, 1990).

INDEX

Note (*a*) Many of the entries under 'Owain Glyn Dŵr' and 'Owain Glyn Dŵr, revolt of'
constitute a broad subject index for the volume.

      (*b*) Places in Wales are identified by one of the royal counties or Marcher lordships of the
period 1284–1536 (see Map 2)

      (*c*) T1-4 refer to the numbered Genealogical Tables in the text.